Constraints in Phonological Acquisition

This outstanding volume presents a state-of-the-art overview of linguistic research into the acquisition of phonology. Bringing together well-known researchers in the field, it focuses on constraints in phonological acquisition (as opposed to rules), and offers concrete examples of the formalisation of phonological development in terms of constraint ranking.

The first two chapters situate the research in its broader context, with an introduction by the editors providing a brief general tutorial on Optimality Theory. Chapter 2 serves to highlight the history of constraints in studies of phonological development, which predates their current ascent to prominence in phonological theory. The remaining chapters address a number of partially overlapping themes: the study of child production data in terms of constraints, learnability issues, perceptual development and its relation to the development of production, and second language acquisition.

RENÉ KAGER is Associate Professor of Language Development at Utrecht University. His books include *A Metrical Theory of Stress and Destressing in Dutch* (1989), *The Prosody-Morphology Interface* (with H. van der Hulst and W. Zonneveld, Cambridge 1999) and *Optimality Theory* (Cambridge 1999).

JOE PATER is Assistant Professor at the University of Massachusetts at Amherst. He has published in a number of journals including *Phonology*, *Language Acquisition* and the *Journal of Child Language*.

WIM ZONNEVELD is Professor of Linguistics and Phonology at Utrecht University. He is the author of *A Formal Theory of Exceptions in Generative Phonology* (1978), *Klemtoon & Metrische Fonologie* (with M. Trommelen, Coutinho 1989) and *Prosody–Morphology Interface* (with R. Kager and H. van der Hulst, Cambridge 1999).

Constraints in Phonological Acquisition

Edited by
René Kager, Joe Pater, and Wim Zonneveld

CAMBRIDGE
UNIVERSITY PRESS

PUBLISHED BY THE PRESS SYNDICATE OF THE UNIVERSITY OF CAMBRIDGE
The Pitt Building, Trumpington Street, Cambridge, United Kingdom

CAMBRIDGE UNIVERSITY PRESS
The Edinburgh Building, Cambridge, CB2 2RU, UK
40 West 20th Street, New York, NY 10011–4211, USA
477 Williamstown Road, Port Melbourne, VIC 3207, Australia
Ruiz de Alarcón 13, 28014 Madrid, Spain
Dock House, The Waterfront, Cape Town 8001, South Africa

http://www.cambridge.org

First published 2004

Printed in the United Kingdom at the University Press, Cambridge

Typeface Times 10/12 pt.   *System* LATEX 2$_\varepsilon$ [TB]

A catalogue record for this book is available from the British Library

Library of Congress Cataloging in Publication data
Constraints in phonological acquisition / edited by René Kager, Joe Pater, and
Wim Zonneveld.
    p.   cm.
Includes bibliographical references and indexes.
ISBN 0-521-82963-1
1. Language acquisition.   2. Grammar, Comparative and general – Phonology.
3. Constraints (Linguistics)   I. Kagar, René.   II. Pater, Joe.   III. Zonneveld, Wim.
P118.C6727   2003
401′.93 – dc21   2003043476

ISBN 0 521 82963 1 hardback

Contents

Contributors

LISA DAVIDSON   Department of Cognitive Science, Johns Hopkins University

AMALIA GNANADESIKAN   Department of Linguistics, University of Massachusetts, Amherst

HEATHER GOAD   Department of Linguistics, McGill University

BRUCE HAYES   Department of Linguistics, University of California, Los Angeles

PETER JUSCZYK†   Department of Psychology, Johns Hopkins University

RENÉ KAGER   Utrecht Institute of Linguistics, Utrecht University

CLARA C. LEVELT   Department of General Linguistics, Leiden University

LISE MENN   Department of Linguistics, University of Colorado, Boulder

DOMINIQUE NOUVEAU   Department of French, University of Nijmegen

JOE PATER   Department of Linguistics, University of Massachusetts, Amherst

ALAN PRINCE   Department of Linguistics, Rutgers University

YVAN ROSE   Department of Linguistics, Memorial University of New foundland

SHIGEKO SHINOHARA   Centre National de la Recherche Scientifique

PAUL SMOLENSKY   Department of Cognitive Science, Johns Hopkins University

BRUCE TESAR   Department of Linguistics, Rutgers University

RUBEN VAN DE VIJVER   Institut für Linguistik, University of Potsdam

WIM ZONNEVELD   Utrecht Institute of Linguistics, Utrecht University

Abbreviations

BLS	Papers from the Annual General Meeting, Berkeley Linguistics Society
CLS	Papers from the Annual Regional Meeting, Chicago Linguistic Society
IJAL	International Journal of American Linguistics
JASA	Journal of the Acoustical Society of America
JL	Journal of Linguistics
JPh	Journal of Phonetics
Lg	Language
LI	Linguistic Inquiry
NELS	Papers from the Annual Meeting of the North East Linguistic Society
NLLT	Natural Language and Linguistic Theory
WCCFL	Proceedings of the West Coast Conference of Formal Linguistics

Preface

In current linguistics the progress made in the study of language acquisition seems to be equalled in few other areas of investigation. The goal of this collection of papers is to present an illustration of this progress, in phonology, in which – building on mid-twentieth-century revolutionary insights (Roman Jakobson, Noam Chomsky, and Morris Halle) – advances at the turn of the millennium are rapid, and exceptionally promising. The editors feel thrilled to present this volume, which contains contributions by internationally leading investigators in the field. They provide broad (but – luckily – opinionated) surveys of general issues from which also the relatively uninitiated reader may obtain an idea of the state of the art, and others give an in-depth analysis of current issues. One will find both first and second language data represented here, discussed from theoretical and empirical angles (in fact, always in combination with one another). The roots of this collection lie in a Workshop in Phonological Acquisition Research (the 'Third Biannual Utrecht Phonology Workshop') organised by the editors in June 1998 at the UiL-OTS, the Research Department for Language and Speech of Utrecht University (whose financial and organisational support we gratefully acknowledge). The volume obtained its present shape, however, principally through the addition of papers solicited by invitation, and we express our gratitude to the authors for reacting to our requests in the enthusiastic and generous way they did. Invaluable editorial assistance was provided by Brigit van der Pas, to whom we are also extremely grateful.

René Kager is Professor of Second Language Acquisition, specialising in Phonology, at the Utrecht Research Department for Language and Speech. Wim Zonneveld is Full Professor of Phonology and English Language Studies at the same institute. Joe Pater is Assistant Professor in Linguistics, specialising in Phonology and Acquisition, at the Linguistics Department of the University of Massachusetts, Amherst, Mass.

This volume is dedicated to the memory of Peter W. Jusczyk.

1 Introduction: constraints in phonological acquisition

René Kager, Joe Pater, and Wim Zonneveld

This volume presents ten studies in phonological first language acquisition, an area of research that has become one of fast-growing importance in recent years. The reason for this is not just the fruitfulness and linguistic interest of this type of study *per se*: it is also the case that the more we come to know about phonological development, by the analysis of growing numbers of data collections and increasingly sophisticated experiments, the more the field has complied with the notion that acquisition research lies at the heart of the modern study of language. One of the aims of this introduction is to illustrate and discuss these developments. In line with them, the past decade in phonology in particular has witnessed an upswell of productive interaction between empirical acquisition research and theory development. With the arrival and rise of constraint-based models, in particular Prince and Smolensky's (1993) Optimality Theory, phonological theory now provides a framework that meets the desiderata expressed more than two decades ago by Lise Menn (1980: 35–36), who is also a contributor to this volume:

(1)   . . . The child's 'tonguetiedness', that overwhelming reality which Stampe and Jakobson both tried to capture with their respective formal structures, could be handled more felicitously if one represented the heavy articulatory limitations of the child by the formal device of output constraints [. . .] The child's gradual mastery of articulation then is formalized as a relaxation of those constraints.

The rapid emergence of acquisition studies within Optimality Theory reflects the general suitability of constraints for the formalisation of developmental limitations, as well as the usefulness of constraint ranking for expressing the relaxation of these limitations. In this volume, we include several chapters that provide concrete examples of the formalisation of phonological development in terms of constraint ranking. Other chapters address fundamental issues such as learnability, the nature of the initial state, the relation between perception and production, and the contribution the experimental approach can make. They all demonstrate the successes of a constraint-based approach to these issues, but do not ignore the challenges that it faces.

In the first section of this introduction, we show how many issues and ideas that appear in this volume have important precedents in prior research. We provide a brief survey of these issues, as they have been discussed in the research tradition that links phonological theory and phonological acquisition, of which the Optimality theoretic approach is the most recent outgrowth.[1] In the second section, we provide a tutorial on the fundamentals of Optimality Theory, specifically tuned to its application to acquisition. And in the final section we give an overview of some central issues in acquisition and learnability in Optimality Theory, drawing connections between these issues and the contents of the chapters of this volume. This last section includes summaries of all of the chapters except for Lise Menn's contribution, which itself is a summary and discussion of research on phonological acquisition and its relation to Optimality Theory, from a perspective which seems to complement the one taken in this introductory chapter.

1.   The young child in generative grammar

It is not *a priori* obvious that the study of phonological theory and that of child speech should be connected in any way whatsoever. After nearly a century of prior diary studies of child utterances, and typological study of the sound systems of the world's languages, it was Roman Jakobson, in his *Child Language, Aphasia and Phonological Universals* (1941),[2] who first suggested that they were governed by the same principles: Jakobson wanted to

(2)   establish the point that adult language systems are as they are because they necessarily develop in a particular systematic way that can be studied in the form of child language. (Anderson 1985: 130)

These principles Jakobson referred to as 'laws of irreversible solidarity', but they have become known as 'implicational universals'. A typical example is this one (Jakobson 1941/1968: 51): the acquisition of fricatives presupposes the acquisition of stops in child language; and in the linguistic systems of the world the former cannot exist unless the latter exist as well. Alongside such laws,[3] Jakobson proposed principles of maximal contrast that governed the gradual emergence of phonological structures in child language, and also determined the content of many cross-linguistic implicational universals. After Jakobson, systematic research on child phonology was largely devoted to testing his claims. Its upshot appears to be that many of his principles are roughly supported (see Menn 1980, and Ingram 1989 for overviews of this stage of research), but that there is considerable unpredicted variability between children. Jakobson was not working with a very explicit ('formal') or fleshed-out phonological theory. One problem that arises is that there is no means of capturing the mapping from adult to child speech. For example, when a child lacks consonant clusters, the choice it makes between the two consonants appearing in the adult target cluster is not random, though it does vary from child to child. These mappings were brought within the purview of phonological analysis with the emergence of the much more formally oriented generative phonology.

The 'young child' appeared for the first time in the generative literature in Chomsky (1959). This is the passage where (s)he appears:

(3)   The child who learns a language has in some sense constructed [a] grammar for himself on the basis of his observation of sentences and nonsentences (i.e., corrections by the verbal community). Study of the actual observed ability of a speaker to distinguish sentences from nonsentences, detect ambiguities, etc., apparently forces us to the conclusion that this grammar is of an extremely complex and abstract character, and that the young child has succeeded in carrying out what from the formal point of view, at least, seems to be a remarkable type of theory construction. Furthermore, this task is accomplished in an astonishingly short time, to a large extent independently of intelligence, and in a comparable way by all children. [. . .]

The fact that all normal children acquire essentially comparable grammars of great complexity with remarkable rapidity suggests that human beings are somehow specially designed to do this, with data-handling or 'hypothesis-formulating' ability of unknown character and complexity.

These remarks imply a meaningful initial state or *faculté de langage* or Universal Grammar (UG), of Chomsky (1965: 5–6, 1968: 27), the study of which formulates the 'conditions that a system must meet to qualify as a potential human language, conditions that [. . .] constitute the innate organization that determines what counts as linguistic experience and what knowledge of language arises on the basis of that experience'. Universal Grammar is the innate starting point of language acquisition for each human being, and it is a Jakobsonian concept in the sense that its elements are hypothesised also to appear as 'universals' in typological language studies.

The child tries to find its way through the data maze assisted by UG, and constructs an abstract system called a grammar. This grammar is an amalgamation of persisting elements from UG (in the way envisaged by Jakobson) and acquired, language-specific components. It is the linguist's task to make sense of the structure of these grammars, and the role UG plays in their growth. The contributions discussed in this section in some way or other all take up the challenge posed by Jakobson and Chomsky. Although their topics are often intertwined, we chronologically subdivide them as follows: first Smith (1973) and Stampe (1969, 1973a, 1973b); then Braine (1976), Macken (1980), Kiparsky and Menn (1977), and Menn (1978, 1980), and finally the literature dealing with parameters starting with Chomsky (1981a, 1981b). These works raise issues of fundamental importance, arguing directly from observed properties of the acquisition process. Roughly, these issues can be subdivided into 'formal' ones, and ones of 'substance'. Among the former are formal aspects of the rule-based approach towards the phonological component; and the abstractness of the underlying forms of child speech. Among the latter are: markedness, typology and language acquisition; rules vs. processes; conspiracies and output constraints; parameters; and the perception-production dichotomy.

It is the contention of Chomsky (1965: 16, 28) that the studies of syntax, semantics, and phonology can all proceed along the lines of reasoning just described. Chomsky and Halle (1968) is the first sizeable illustration of this methodology for Generative Phonology. No secret is revealed by the assessment that this work had a very strong 'formal' bias, and that the link between form and substance was underdeveloped. At the heart of this approach were four formal devices: (i) feature representations using a UG-based set of phonological features drawn in from the pre-generative era (see Halle 1983); (ii) derivations mapping lexical representations onto surface ones by rewrite rules, formulated in a UG-based format and mutually ordered along lines also specified in UG ('linear ordering', with a number of further specifications); (iii) morpheme structure rules stating redundancies at the level of the lexicon; and (iv) an evaluation measure also located in UG, evaluating a grammar's formal complexity as a function of the number of symbols in it. This measure selected less complex grammars over more complex ones for any given body of data. Although it was intended both to contribute to an explanation of the behaviour of native speakers, including acquisitional behaviour, in actual practice it was only infrequently called upon given the complexities of the linguist's task to formulate an analysis of the empirical data under investigation at all, given the other three formal devices and their UG aspects.

A seminal acquisitional study in this framework is Smith (1973), which also presents a wealth of original data (assembled in the form of a detailed longitudinal study of the progress of the author's son Amahl between the ages of [2;3] and [3;11]). His monograph has two aims. First, to use child data to argue for the correctness of the view of the grammar as a system of ordered rules deriving an output form from an underlying form. Second, to endorse the idea that child grammars just as much as adult grammars are constrained by the universals of UG. In conformity with the priorities of the times, the principal universal discussed in Smith's study is that of rule ordering; just as rules are (linearly) ordered in an adult grammar, rules can be crucially ordered at certain acquisitional stages, they can be modified, be reordered, or disappear at later stages, until the adult grammar is reached, which contains the final stage of ordered rules. Consider Smith (1973: 158):

(4)   Chomsky [1967] suggested (p. 105) that "the rules of the grammar
        must be partially ordered," going on to claim that the principle of
        rule ordering was an a priori part of the basis which made language
        acquisition possible (Chomsky 1967, pp. 127–128). To the extent that
        one can establish the psychological validity of the realisation rules
        [of Amahl's grammar] and to the extent that the ordering relations
        established among these rules are necessary, so is Chomsky's claim
        substantiated.

Thus, the way to describe the phonological behaviour of language-acquiring
children is by means of rules, and UG says that linear ordering is an essential
property of the rule set.

Taking into account current debates, two issues in Smith's work are worth
highlighting. The first is that of 'opaque' rule interactions (which become a separate issue, for instance, once translated into Optimality Theory; see McCarthy
1999a, 2001: 163 ff.); and the second that of the nature of the underlying representations in a child grammar.

Smith (1973: 158–161) contains a long list of ordering relations among the
rules of Amahl's grammar, for a variety of successive stages of acquisition.
The most interesting ones occur at Stage 1 ([2;2]–[2;4]), when Smith started
collecting data. Included here are examples of unusual or 'marked' ordering in
the sense of Kiparsky (1968): bleeding and counterfeeding orderings, leading
to 'surface opacity'. One of these examples has grown into a celebrated one:
that of the 'chain shift' exhibited in the *puzzle/puddle* case. Observe that a
counterfeeding relation holds between the two rules of (5), coexisting from
Amahl's Stage 1 to approximately Stage 14 [2;8]:

(5)   (a) velarization of coronal stops   pedal   → bɛ[g]u
            before [l] (Rule 3)   bottle → bo[k]le
                                                kennel → ke[ŋ]el
                                                puddle → pu[g]le
        (b) neutralization of coronal   zoo   → [d]oo
            fricatives and stops (Rule 24)   bath   → b[aːt]
                                                knife   → mi[p]e
                                                puzzle → pu[d]le

The crucial pair in the data is that of *puddle* and *puzzle*, whose pronunciations
require a counterfeeding rule ordering (Kiparsky shows that such orderings are
avoided in grammars, and subject to historical change; see also Kiparsky and
Menn 1977);[4] schematically:

(6)   by (5a)   puddle → pu[g]le
        by (5b)   puzzle → pu[d]le   (→ *pu[g]le)

This chain shift also shows that the move away from a coronal in the former case cannot be due to some production inability; the striking characteristic of this case will be returned to below.

In a phonological system in which alternations based on rich morphology are (still) virtually lacking, as in early child systems, the nature of the underlying forms of the system is a potentially controversial issue. Rejecting the perhaps initially plausible view that the child's phonology acts as a self-contained system with a low degree of abstractness in which the underlying forms are very close to the output forms, Smith argues that the child's underlying forms are generally equivalent to the adult surface forms that the child takes in as his day-to-day input. This is not in his case just an *a priori* assumption or just a first approach to the problem: it is based on a range of evidence showing that the child actually operates in this manner (Smith 1973: 11). The conversions in (5a) and (5b) are not just the author's expository manipulations, but represent actual hypothesised characteristics of the child's grammar. Let us briefly review some of this evidence for such analyses (Smith 1973: 133–148).

First, Amahl must have stored the adult forms because he was able to recognise and discriminate items of the adult language which he himself could not or did not produce or discriminate in his production. Thus, he could point correctly to pictures of a *mouse* and a *mouth* 'before he was able to speak at all' and when he was 'still unable to produce the contrast between [s] and [θ]' (p. 134): both are [maut] and then [maus] at exactly the same stages. Second, in a case of so-called 'phonemic overlap', the possibility for some of his *l*-initial output words to alternate with [r-], and for other *l*-initial words not to do so, was entirely based on the adult distinction between words beginning with *r*- and *l*-, respectively (so [rait, lait] for *right*, and [lait] for *light*), implying an optional rule operating on adult-like underlying representations. Third, the development of certain items over time point to the same property of the grammar: 'before consonant+/l/ clusters appeared at all, there was neutralisation of such adult examples as *bed* and *bread* as [bεd]. Once clusters appeared these were differentiated as [bεd] and [blεd], respectively, and likewise for many comparable items' (p. 139). Fourth, Amahl, as soon as he learned a new sound or sound combination, immediately utilised it correctly 'across the board' in all the relevant words, rather than incorporating it separately and slowly into each word. This indicates 'that these sounds and sound sequences must have been stored in the brain "correctly" in order for their appearance to be so consistently right. [Thus,] once [l] appeared for /sl/ it appeared in all words containing /sl/ nearly at the same time' (p. 139). Finally, evidence for adult-like underlying forms comes from early alternations, such as those involving plural formation (p. 148). Consider the data below, resembling an alternation such as that produced by final devoicing in a language such as Dutch and German.

(7) sg. cat   → [kæt]   pl. cats   → [kæt]
     horse → [ɔːt]   horses → [ɔːtid]
     cloth → [klɔt]   cloths → [klɔtid]

In the plural, in spite of the wholesale neutralization in the singular, a distinction surfaces between adult stops and fricatives, indicating that the underlying form of these morphemes is much more adult-like than inspection of just the singulars would suggest.[5]

There is a small handful of passages in his work where Smith describes further prospects that go beyond the essentially 'formal' early-Generative Phonology Chomsky and Halle type approach that his work otherwise falls into:

(8) (a) The use of marking conventions [Chomsky and Halle 1968] in this study has been mainly conspicuous by its absence, though there are two directions in which they might be of relevance to developmental phonology [. . .]. (Smith 1973: 199)
     (b) [The realisation rules of the child phonology] clearly have much in common with the general constraints suggested in Stampe's paper (Stampe, 19[69]). (Smith 1973: 133)
     (c) Kisseberth's [1971] concept of 'functional unity' [. . .] is clearly relevant here, where there are obvious 'infantile conspiracies' – i.e., sets of rules – implementing the 'general tendencies' underlying the realisation rules discussed above . . . (Smith 1973: 204–205)

The implications of these references can be fleshed out by turning to the references mentioned in (8a–c), and to those listed earlier in this section.

In Chomsky and Halle (1968) a good grammar is one of low cost, in a formal sense. In the final chapter of their book (chapter 9), however, these authors submit that such an approach, at least as presented by them in their monograph, may have been 'overly formal', in particular in the area of the 'intrinsic content' of phonological features. They offer an outline of 'a theory of markedness', based on a proposal for extending the evaluation measure by means of 'marking conventions'. Marking conventions measure lexical representations and phonological rules in terms of their featural content, based on universal markedness. For each feature, an unmarked and a marked value are distinguished, sometimes depending on the segmental context. Two examples are given below, of a context-free and a context-sensitive convention:

(9) (a) the unmarked value for [nasal] is [−nasal]
     (b) the unmarked value for [round] is [+round], in back vowels

Lexical representations are assumed to be specified in terms of Ms and Us, which were converted into +/− feature values by the conventions. Only M-specifications contribute to the cost of a grammar. With regard to phonological rules, marking conventions can have a 'linking' function, making some rules more costly than others, hence dispreferred in grammars as well as presumably in the acquisition process. As an example, consider the rounding that often accompanies the backing of front non-round vowels: given the evaluation measure, rounding threatens to be more costly than leaving it out. If markedness convention (9b) links up to the output of a backing rule, it will supply the roundness feature, whereas blocking of the convention must be achieved by specifying the marked value in the structural change of the rule.

Smith (1973: 199–201) makes an attempt at establishing the usefulness of the marking conventions for his results. In spite of the promising beginning of this attempt quoted in (8a), his conclusion is exactly the opposite: 'it seems that with the exception of one or two isolated examples of the type cited, marking conventions are completely irrelevant', adding that '[i]n general it would seem that the present state of ignorance makes it impossible to effect any interesting correlation between acquisitional phenomena and marking conventions'. Anderson (1985: 334–342) makes a more fundamental point. In spite of the expressed aim of being less 'overly formal', Chomsky and Halle's markedness theory 'is in fact an attempt at exhaustively reducing the considerations of phonetic content that might be relevant to phonology to purely formal expression in the notation (now enhanced by its interpretation through the marking conventions). It is thus entirely consistent with the original *SPE* program of reducing all of the theory of phonological structure to a single explicit formal system including a notation and a calculus for manipulating and interpreting expressions within that notation. [. . .] The revision involved, however, was in a more complete working out of the goal of reducing phonology to a formal system rather than a replacement of that goal with some other' (pp. 333–334). He adds that 'essentially no substantial analyses of phonological phenomena have appeared subsequently in which this aspect of the theory plays a significant role. One MIT dissertation (Kean 1975) was devoted to further elaboration of the theory, but this remained (like chapter 9 of *SPE* [*The Sound Pattern of English*]) at the level of a programmatic statement rather than constituting an extended analysis of the phonology of some language(s) in the terms prescribed by the theory.'

Detailed criticism of Chomsky and Halle's markedness theory was provided by Stampe (1973a, 1973b). At first glance his distinction between (language-specific) *rules* and (universal) *processes* closely resembles the *SPE* one between rules and markedness conventions, but a closer look reveals fundamental differences. Rules 'merely govern alternations' and are more often than not 'phonetically unmotivated', his example being the English rule Velar Softening (Chomsky and Halle 1968) relating *ele*[k]*tric* and *electri*[s]*ity*: it has exceptions in the language, and the change from /k/ to [s] is a far from natural one in phonetic terms. Processes, on the other hand, 'reflect genuine limitations on what we can pronounce'. They are part of the common acquisitional starting point, i.e., of UG (a term not used in his work):

(10)   [I]n its language-innocent state, the innate phonological system ex-presses the full system of restrictions of speech: a full set of phono-logical processes, unlimited and unordered. [. . .] A phonological pro-cess merges a potential phonological opposition into that member of the opposition which least tries the restrictions of the human speech capacity. [. . .] Each new opposition the child learns to pronounce involves some revision of the innate phonological system. [. . .] The child's task in acquiring adult pronunciation is to revise all aspects of the system which separates his pronunciation from the standard. If he succeeds fully, the resultant system must be equivalent to that of the standard speakers.

In the view I'm proposing, then, the mature system retains all those aspects of the innate system which the mastery of pronunciation has left intact. (Stampe 1969: 443–447)

Language acquisition does not mean acquiring just rules (and ordering them), as in Smith's case in the Chomsky and Halle framework, but in addition to acquiring the phonetically implausible rules such as Velar Softening, the pro-cesses supplied by UG are manipulated: they can be suppressed, limited, and ordered, when they are in conflict (conflicts arise, e.g., between absolute and contextually restricted processes: obstruents are voiceless irrespective of con-text because their oral constriction impedes the airflow required by voicing, but they also prefer being voiced in a voiced environment). Stampe recognises that to a certain extent his processes resemble Jakobsonian implicational laws, but the ground covered by the latter is just a subset of that covered by the 'innate processes', namely that of 'the phonemic inventory [. . .] unaffected by contextual neutralisations' (1969: 446). The laws are static, whereas processes are active, and make predictions about representations as well as inventories; moreover, they may be *contextually conditioned*. His assessment of Chomsky and Halle's markedness theory is that it 'drastically underestimates the number of processes which are innate' and makes 'totally unsupportable claims about the nature of phonology' (1973b: 45–46).

One or two brief examples may clarify how these ideas work in practice, focusing on language acquisition. Consider Stampe's comparison of the be-haviour of coronals in Danish and Tamil (1973a: 14–16). In Danish, posttonic /t/ is pronounced as [d], which sounds just as pretonic [d]; in addition, posttonic /d/ is pronounced as [ð]. This is a counterfeeding situation similar to the one from Smith (1973) described in (8): a process of spirantisation precedes one of voicing. In Tamil, both processes have 'unrestricted' applications: /t/ is both voiced and spirantised to [ð] postvocalically. In Stampe's view, the learning going on here is just this: since the processes are part of Universal Grammar, and unrestricted application is the norm, the Danish child, in order to become an adult speaker, will have to learn the ordering of the two processes involved. That is all. The moral he draws from this example is (Stampe 1973a: 15–16):

(11)   What has not been adequately recognized in discussions of ordering is that its recognition depends on our assumption that certain phonological processes are possible and others impossible. In the Danish example the facts could be described by positing a single process which simultaneously voices postvocalic stops and, if they are already voiced, spirantizes them. In fact such an analysis would be simpler from the point of view of Danish in that the postvocalic context of both changes would be expressed just once. But from a language-universal point of view, this analysis is not satisfactory: it merely adds another process to the many we have to explain the existence of. [. . .] Furthermore, this lang[u]age-universal analysis provides us with an interesting prediction: that in no phonological system will [t] become [ð] unless [d] becomes [ð]. This follows from the assumption that the change of [t] to [ð] as in Tamil, involves two distinct processes, voicing and spirantization. If this is so, there is no way that [t] could be voiced and spirantized without [d] also being spirantized. This prediction is not overturned by any language of which I am aware.

His illustrations from language acquisition involve examples of 'one child having ordered two processes which another child has not' and, even, 'examples of a child actually performing the ordering' (Stampe 1969: 447, 1973a: 11–12, 16–17). The structure of two such cases is the following:

(12)   (a) Joan Velten (Velten 1943) pronounces *lamb* as [zab].
         This pronunciation results from three distinct processes:
         (i) delateralization: /l/ → [j] (this is common in children, cf. *lie* → [jai] by Hildegard in Leopold (1947))
         (ii) spirantization: /j/ → [ʒ] (again see Hildegard's *you* → [ʒu])
         (iii) depalatalization: /ʒ/ → [z] (as in Joan's own *wash* → [was])
         But for Hildegard /l/ remains [j], it does not become spirantized as in Joan's speech. The difference between their pronunciations lies not in the processes but in their order of application. Hildegard does not apply spirantization to the ouput of delateralization; Joan does. Thus whereas Joan cannot pronounce [j] at all, Hildegard can pronounce it if she attempts to say /l/. This apparent oddity is no stranger than the Dane's inability to say postvocalic [d] except by aiming at [t]. (Stampe 1973a: 16–17)

(b) Hildegard Leopold at 20 months said [du(ı)ʃ] 'juice', [du] 'June',
[doːi] 'Joey', beside [dʒuiʒ] 'church', [dʒudʒu] 'choo-choo', by
application of the processes (a) [dʒ] becomes [d], and (b) obstruent
voices before a vowel (compare [du] 'to, do'). But at 19 months
'choo-choo' had been [dudu] [. . .] by unordered application of the
same processes. (Stampe 1969: 447)

Stampe's ideas enjoyed considerable popularity in the 1970s; they were seen by
many as a promising variant of the then strong 'Natural Generative Phonology'
(NGP) movement,[6] and enjoyed considerable popularity among many acquisitionists (see, e.g., Edwards and Shriberg 1983). As indicated (in our (8b)), Smith
(1973) alludes to the possibility of reducing (many of) his rules to Stampe's
processes.

The wiseness of such a move, however, was seriously doubted by detractors
such as Kiparsky and Menn (1977). They argued that a careful look at first
language acquisition and its developmental properties and stages does simply
not support the main tenets of theories such as those by Jakobson and Stampe,
which they lump together as 'rather deterministic': 'In these theories, there is no
"discovery", no experimentation, no devising and testing of hypotheses. [T]he
child's speech development cannot simply be viewed as a monotonic approximation to the adult model.' Much more typical of the acquisition process is that
it proceeds as a 'problem solving' process: 'learning to talk [. . .] is a difficult
task' in which 'the child must discover ways to circumvent the difficulties'.
They see recognisable speech as *a target* which different children will attempt
to reach by a variety of means, including the 'rules' typical of child phonology
(Kiparsky and Menn 1977: 56–58):

(13)   [T]here are several ways of dealing with consonant clusters: deletion
          of all but one of the phonemes (in a stop-X or X-stop cluster, the one
          preserved is not always the stop), conflation of some of the features of
          the elements of the cluster (eg., *sm > m, fl > w*), insertion of a vowel
          to break up the cluster, metathesis (*snow > nos*), etc. [. . .]

          Different children exclude definable classes of output by different
          means. When we observe such repeated 'exclusion', we conclude that
          these classes of outputs (clusters, certain co-occurrences, the 'third
          position', etc.) represent difficulties to the child, and the various rules
          of child phonology (substitutions, deletions, etc.) as well as selective
          avoidance of some adult words, are devices the child finds for dealing
          with those difficulties. [. . .]

          The very diversity and the 'ingenuity' of these devices might indi-
          cate that early phonology should be regarded as the result of the child's
          active 'problem solving'.

They refer to Ingram (1974) for 'extensive consideration and exemplification of rules of child phonology', and add: 'Note that not all children avoid all of these difficulties; we present these as general tendencies rather than as universals.'

Clearly these remarks announce the notion of output constraint that appears in immediately adjacent work by Menn, as in the quote in (1) from Menn (1980), and the even earlier one below from Menn (1978: 162–164):

(14)   many rules are best seen in terms of the satisfaction of output con-
         straints. [. . .] These constraints are interpretable as manifestations of
         the young child's limited ability to plan and execute a complex motor
         activity.

Thus, a constraint against consonants of different places of articulation can be met by consonant harmony (as in Amahl's [gɔːk] for *talk*), but also by consonant deletion: [bu] for *boot*. A prohibition against fricatives in onsets can be met by deletion ([ɪʃ] for *fish*) or by metathesis ([nos] for *snow*).

These remarks also support Smith's original hunch in (8c), proposing the possible usefulness of Kisseberth's (1970) notion of 'conspiracy', applied to child phonology. In this latter pivotal paper, the author, having shown that in Yawelmani Yokuts rules of consonant deletion and vowel insertion all eliminate triconsonantal clusters, argued two things: first, that Yawelmani phonology appears to contain a 'conspiracy' towards a goal that can be formalised by a negative language-specific 'output constraint', namely *CCC; but second, that now the overall design of the grammar turns out to be very expensive in the sense that a much less well-balanced phonology with just an occasional deletion or insertion rule and no output constraint would be formally much cheaper. Neither Kisseberth nor Smith provide a solution to this problem, but the latter notices a parallel occurring in Amahl's phonology. According to him, an example is constituted by a series of rules in Amahl's speech eliminating consonant clusters in any position in the word:

(15)   a proposed *CC conspiracy in Amahl's speech, Smith (1973: 165–166)
         (a) tree   → [diː]   Rule 16
         (b) taxi   → [gɛgiː]   Rule 21
         (c) meant → [mɛt]   Rule 1
         (d) slip   → [lɪp]   Rule 7

Thus, a theoretical proposal by Kisseberth and an observationally based edu-cated guess by Smith converge with Kiparsky and Menn's view of an essential property of the process of first language acquisition: the usefulness of output constraints.

Up until this point the main body of this section has focused on the func-tion of UG in acquisition research, and on the way output constraints were introduced in the literature in that field. In the remainder we shall discuss two further issues. First, that of the nature of the underlying forms of a child grammar, also in relation to the perception/production dichotomy; and second, the notion of parameter as a (partial) replacement of rules. With regard to the former issue, let us reconsider Smith's contention that the underlying forms of the child's phonological component are constituted, by and large, by the adult surface forms. This view did not go unchallenged for very long. In a review of Smith's monograph, Braine (1976) suspects that the influence of perception on the underlying form must be larger than assumed by Smith. He argues in favour of what he calls a 'partial perception hypothesis', which states that (1976: 492) 'the child's perception of words contains systematic biases, and is therefore only partly accurate'. His support for this contention contains the following elements, among others: there 'is now much evidence, from discrimination testing, that children's ability to discriminate perceptually among phonemic contrasts is far from perfect . . .'. Targeting Smith's *puzzle/puddle* chain shift, he focuses on the fact that the shift away from a coronal stop does not seem to be motivated by a production difficulty because that same coronal stop is in the output of the shift away from the fricative: 'If we drop the assumption that perception inevitably recovers the adult phonemes, [these] phenomena appear in a new light. In *puddle* → pu[g]le, one wonders if A's auditory system could be ranking the flapped or glottalized intervocalics as more similar to normal adult [velars] than normal [coronals]' (1976: 494). Braine's reinterpretation of Amahl's phonological behaviour implies a model with three separate components. First, '[a]uditory encoding laws would state how the child's auditory system transcribes the acoustic input into auditory attributes'. Second, on the output side there would be realisation rules similar to Smith's. Third, the model contains 'correspondence rules that map auditory features into the articulatory features that the child controls (or partially controls). These would specify the articulatory analysis made of words in the lexical store at any point in development, and in effect associate motor commands with the auditory features.' He admits that '[u]nfortunately, the correspondence layer is unlikely to be well-defined, given the "rare mistakes of articulatory coding" exhibited by Smith's son Amahl' (and other children, too, presumably).

A multi-step procedure of a different kind but in the same perception/ production area of research was developed in work culminating in Menn (1978). Her proposal has become known as the 'two-lexicon model'. A child enters a perceived form in an input lexicon. These forms undergo reduction processes expressing the child's limited abilities; the output of these processes is stored in an output lexicon, which is completely redundancy-free. For production, a (hopefully small) set of 'production rules' or 'subroutines' convert this representation into the one entering the motor component, containing the articulatory instructions. In the case of *fish*, for instance, the perceived form (usually close to the adult surface form) is entered in the input lexicon. Reduction rules of the child phonology turn this form into one underlying production: redundancy-free [ɪ, s] is stored in the output lexicon as an unordered pair of vowel and fricative, which must be ordered by the 'production rules'; in this case this ordering process is governed by a prohibition (output constraint) against fricatives in onsets. The principal empirical observation motivating the model is that of the occasional inertia of the rule-learning process. If a new phonological rule enters the child phonology, existing pronunciations sometimes persist, as if output forms serve as independent lexical items (Menn and Matthei 1992: 213):

(16)   An example from Daniel (Menn 1971) makes this clear: fairly early on, Daniel produced 'down' and 'stone', both very frequent words, as [dæwn] and [don], respectively. Sometime later, he began to show a nasal harmony rule, producing 'beans' as [minz] and 'dance' as [næns]. For a while after this point, 'down' and 'stone' were maintained in their nonassimilated forms; then the forms [næwn] and [non] began to appear, in free variation with them. Finally, [næwn] and [non] were triumphant – [dæwn] and [don] disappeared.

It has become clear, however, that this two-lexicon design cannot be maintained in this relatively naive form. Empirical evidence has been put forward that not the purported output lexicon but simply the 'classical' input lexicon is active when the child starts to develop morphophonemic alternations. Smith's data in (6) constitute a case in point, and a similar example, originating from Stemberger (1993), is represented in Bernhardt and Stemberger (1998: 48–49) in the following manner:

(17)   At 2;10, Gwendolyn generally formed the past tense of vowel-final words by adding [d], as in adult English. There were two exceptions to this, however. First, forms that are irregular in adult speech, such as *threw*, could be produced correctly as irregulars or could be regularized (*throwed*), as is common in child language. Second, words that are consonant-final in adult speech but were vowel-final in the child's speech, such as *kiss* /kɪs/ [tʰiː], did not have *-d* added in the past tense [. . .].

     The two-lexicon approach seems to predict that all words that are vowel-final in the child's speech should be treated the same for the creation of past tense forms. Since a final /d/ is added to words like *pee*, it should also be added to words like *kiss* [tiː]. This prediction fails, suggesting that the two-lexicon approach is inadequate.

Another argument points out that the model is hard put to account for between-word phonological processes in child language, especially if the same generalisations cover both words and simple syntactic constructions in early child speech: a lexical approach seems ill-equipped to capture such cases (Menn and Matthei 1992: 223). It seems the explanation of the selective propagation of new child speech rules must lie elsewhere. In the latter paper, Menn and Matthei turn to 'connectionist' models in order to maintain 'what's good' about their approach. Menn (this volume) explains her most recent position.

Finally, in theoretical linguistics of the 1980s attempts were made to replace the view of a grammar component as a rule system by one involving a set of parameters, i.e., a set of choices specified by UG and fixed on a language-particular basis given linguistic experience in that language. Ideally in this approach the grammar becomes a collection of fixed parameter-settings. It was recognised from the very outset that not only does this view provide a framework for the study of language typology but it also has implications for the study of language learning (cf. Chomsky 1981a: 8–9, 1981b: 3–4, 1986: 52, 145–6):

(18)   It is natural to assume, then, that universal grammar consists of a system of principles with a certain degree of intricacy and deductive structure, with parameters that can be fixed in one or another way, given a relatively small amount of experience. Small changes in the values assigned to parameters in a rich system may lead to what appear to be radically different grammars, though at a deeper level, they are all cast in the same mould. [. . .]

     The ideal is to reach the point where we can literally deduce a particular human grammar by setting parameters of universal grammar in one or another of the permissible ways. The process of so-called 'language learning' can then be naturally regarded in part as a process of fixing these values; when they are fixed the 'learner' knows the language generated by the grammar that is determined by universal grammar, specified in this way. [. . .]

     The parameters must have the property that they can be fixed by quite simple evidence, because this is what is available to the child [. . .]. Once the values of the parameters are set, the whole system is operative. [W]e may think of UG as an intricately structured system, but one that is only partially 'wired up'. The system is associated with a finite set of switches, each of which has a finite number of positions (perhaps two). Experience is required to set the switches. When they are set, the system functions.

As a typological example, consider the parametric theory of syllable structure presented in Kaye (1989: 54–57). In (19), (a) gives the set of parameters and (b) some of the languages that fill the slots of the system (where '0' is no, and '1' is yes):

(19)   [I]f we take all the languages of the world, how many syllable types
must we allow for? The answer is surprising. Three parameters suffice
to define every extant syllable type. [. . .] They are:

(10)   (1) Does the rime branch?   [no/yes]
(2) Does the nucleus branch?   [no/yes]
(3) Does the onset branch?   [no/yes]   [. . .]

(13)   (a) 000   No branching rimes, nuclei or onsets: Desano
(b) 100   Branching rimes, but no branching nuclei
or onsets: Quechua
(c) 10[1]   Branching rimes and nuclei, no branching
onsets: Arabic
(d) 101   Branching rimes and onsets, no branching
nuclei: Spanish
(e) 111   Branching rimes, nuclei and onsets: English

The task of the language learning child is to fix the parameter settings. It is
usually assumed that parameters are entered in UG with a 'default setting'.
Parameter (10.1), for instance, covers the difference between open and closed
syllables, but languages actually come in two types: those with open syllables
and those with open and closed ones. The 'poverty of the stimulus' argument
applied to this case results in the default setting of NO for this parameter:
the presence of closed syllables can then be learned on the basis of positive
evidence. Among the many findings of Fikkert (1994), an elaborate study of
the acquisition of Dutch prosody in this framework, is that in this language,
which has branching rhymes, young children first omit word-final consonants
([pu:] for *poes* 'pussycat', [ka:] for *klaar* 'ready'), and start producing them
some two months later. This can be seen as the setting of this parameter away
from the default value.

Similar parameters have been proposed for the typology of word stress systems (Hayes 1980/81, Prince 1983) and the acquisition of word stress has been
studied in considerable detail in Dresher and Kaye (1990), Fikkert (1994),
and Dresher (1999), both from the acquisitional-empirical and the principled-
theoretical angle. In spite of studies such as these, it seems that the parametric
approach to acquisition has not (yet) grown to its full potential, and it seems as
if parameters are sometimes seen as a poor man's principles: fixed parameter
settings are intended to represent alternatives to rules (such as stress rules in
the Chomsky and Halle mould) but never fully replace them (see Piggott 1988),
and from the UG point of view parameters could be seen as 'failed principles',
cf. Archangeli (1997: 26):

(20)   The 'inviolable' principles of syntax have themselves proved to be
problematic in that inviolability has been purchased at the cost of

a variety of types of hedges. [S]ome principles are 'parameterized', holding in one way in one language and in another way in another language. Other principles have peculiar restrictions built-in.

2.   Linking phonological universals and acquisition through Optimality Theory

It stands to reason that a linguist working on acquisition issues does not know in advance whether her or his hypotheses had best be formulated within the rule-based framework (Chomsky 1965, Chomsky and Halle 1968), within that of Principles and Parameters Theory (Chomsky 1981a, 1981b), a combination of these (e.g., Halle and Vergnaud 1987), or something else, for instance within constraint-based Optimality Theory (Prince and Smolensky 1993). This volume argues that the last-mentioned approach, in itself and in comparison with the other frameworks, allows a very fruitful line of attack.

2.1   Optimality Theory

Studies in phonological acquisition can be said to be focused on three priorities. First, to account for universal patterns in phonological acquisition, researchers tried to establish a *substantive* theory of phonological markedness (originating with Jakobson, with incarnations in Chomsky and Halle's theory of markedness, and in Stampe's Natural Phonology). Second, especially in generative approaches, the emphasis was on developing a *formal* theory of phonology that would characterise the child's developing competence as a set of cognitive states leading up to the adult grammar, each state encoding a grammar itself (conceived as a set of linearly ordered rewrite rules in Chomsky and Halle's and Smith's views, a set of unsuppressed natural processes in combination with *ad hoc* rules in Stampe's model, with the need for output constraints being recognised by Menn and others). Finally, recent parameter-based approaches emphasised learnability as a vital issue in acquisition, recognising the need for a theory of *learnability* to explain relations between the learner's input and phonological development.

In this section we will see what Optimality Theory (OT) has to offer in these areas. After presenting an outline of OT, we shall look into the central role of markedness principles in OT. Next, we consider ways in which OT, as a formal theory of grammatical interactions, solves a number of classical problems for derivational rule-based models of phonology, focusing on the duplication problem and the conspiracy problem. This discussion leads us naturally to the notion of typological variation, and how it is captured in OT. Finally, we shall see how OT grammars are formally set up in such a way so as to be learnable. At the end of this section, we are ready to approach the issue of how OT accounts for the relation between phonological typology and phonological acquisition, which will be taken up in section 3.

2.2   An outline of Optimality Theory

Optimality Theory (Prince and Smolensky 1993, McCarthy and Prince 1993) models linguistic well-formedness by a set of conflicting constraints which state (positive or negative) absolute demands about surface forms.[7] Constraints are intrinsically in conflict, as they impose hard general structural requirements that cannot be simultaneously satisfied by any logically possible form. Conflicts between constraints are regulated in grammars by imposing a ranking – or constraint hierarchy. The hierarchy is strict, with any constraint taking priority over all lower ranked ones. Consequently, violations of constraints are allowed only to avoid violation of higher ranked ones.

As in earlier derivational theories of phonology, discussed in section 1, inputs (underlying representations) are mapped onto outputs (surface representations). But unlike derivational mappings in earlier theories, which involved a sequence or linearly ordered rules, OT mappings are single-step derivations; for a given input, the grammar selects the 'optimal' output form from an infinite set of candidate outputs, which are generated by the constraint component *Gen*. The assumption that the grammar generates and evaluates all logically possible candidate analyses for a given input is called *Freedom of Analysis*.

Each output candidate generated by *Gen* incurs different violation(s) for individual constraints. Accordingly, candidate outputs differ from one another in their 'harmonic' well-formedness, that is, the degree to which they meet a set of ranked conflicting constraints – a constraint hierarchy. The evaluation function of the grammar (*Eval*) imposes a harmonic ranking among candidates, with the most harmonic candidate at the top and the least harmonic one at the bottom. The winning ('optimal') candidate is the one that best matches the overall constraint hierarchy. Hence, violations are minimised in the optimal candidate, but violations of lower ranked constraints will be tolerated in order to satisfy higher ranking ones.

(21)   *Gen*   *Eval*

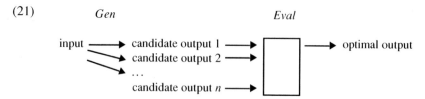

An evaluation of output candidates by a set of ranked constraints can be displayed by a 'tableau'. The tableau in (22) shows three hypothetical output candidates (a-b-c) in competition, their relative well-formedness measured by three ranked constraints (C_1-C_2-C_3). The optimal output is the one that is 'more harmonic' in all its pairwise competitions with other candidates; in each pairwise competition, the more harmonic candidate is the one that performs better on the highest-ranking constraint that distinguishes between them (McCarthy 2001: 3). The optimal candidate b beats its competitor a as it performs better on the highest-ranking constraint distinguishing between them, top-ranked C_1. The winner also outperforms candidate c as it has fewer violations of the highest-ranking constraint distinguishing between C_2.

(22)   Simple constraint interactions

	Constraint 1	Constraint 2	Constraint 3
Candidate a	*!		
☞ Candidate b		*	*
Candidate c		**!	

This tableau shows that the optimal candidate b is not the one having no or the smallest number of violation marks across columns. According to such a criterion, candidate a would have been the winner. Instead what matters is seriousness of violations, relativised to constraint ranking: Competitor a is eliminated due to its single violation of a top-ranked constraint C_1. Also, it is not the number of constraints violated by a candidate which matters, but rather the distribution of marks over cells: Candidate c loses because of its double violation of a single constraint C_2, even though it has no violations of C_3.

Many researchers assume that all constraints in grammars of natural languages are part of UG's universal inventory of constraints called *Con* (Prince and Smolensky 1993). According to this view, grammars differ exclusively in the ranking of constraints. The central assumption that typological variation is due to differences in ranking between constraints in a universal inventory has consequences for language acquisition, as it restricts the learner's search space, while establishing a direct relation between phonological typology and acquisition.

The alternative view on the status of constraints is that these emerge from articulatory and perceptual factors which are active during acquisition (Boersma 1998, Hayes 1999). This functional approach also predicts a strong relation between typology and acquisition, because universal functional factors govern the process of selection of constraints by the learner. This implies that constraints, the ingredients of typology, should not differ between languages in arbitrary ways. (See section 3.2 for discussion.)

On the standard view (originating with Prince and Smolensky 1993) constraints in *Con* fall into two broad classes, known as *markedness constraints* and *faithfulness constraints*. Interactions of these constraint types model the extent to which marked structures of certain kinds are allowed in a language.

Markedness (or 'structural') constraints express universal preferences for certain types of structure, such as syllables with (rather than without) onsets, voiceless (rather than voiced) obstruents, or oral (rather than nasal) vowels. The principal motivation for markedness constraints are Jakobsonean implicational universals: a structure S_u is unmarked (with respect to another structure S_m) if, for every language, the presence of S_m implies the presence of S_u. For example, every language allowing onsetless syllables also allows syllables with onsets, while every language allowing voiced obstruents also allows voiceless ones.

Markedness constraints are often subjected to the criterion of being 'grounded' (in the sense of Archangeli and Pulleyblank 1994) in phonetic factors (production and/or perception). As we saw, OT researchers take rather different positions on the degree to which constraints should be functionally motivated, and on the related issue of whether constraints are universal (part of UG) or emergent from functional properties.

Faithfulness constraints make a rather different type of requirement of surface forms: that they match specific properties of other forms, for example their lexical input. Their effect is to prohibit deletions, insertions, featural changes, or other changes in mappings from inputs to outputs. Faithfulness constraints are the natural antagonists of markedness constraints, since the former preserve lexical properties that the latter may ban at the surface.

Correspondence Theory (McCarthy and Prince 1995, 1999) implements faithfulness as constraints on corresponding segments in paired representations, such as input and output. For example, the constraint MAX-IO requires every segment in the input to have a correspondent in the output ('no deletion'). The constraint DEP-IO expresses a mirror-image requirement that every output segment has an input correspondent ('no insertion'), while IDENT[F]-IO requires corresponding segments to share specifications for the feature [F] ('no featural changes').

Besides input-to-output faithfulness, another type of faithfulness relation has been argued for in the literature: constraints requiring identity between an output form and another output form (*output-to-output* faithfulness). While originally motivated for reduplication (McCarthy and Prince 1995, 1999), output-to-output faithfulness has been, controversially, generalised to other domains, comprising, for example, instances of cyclic rule application proposed from early generative phonology onwards, as well as paradigm uniformity (Benua 1997, Burzio 1996, Kenstowicz 1996, Kager 1999; see Kiparsky 1999 for a different view).

In a language, the presence versus absence of marked structures of various types thus depends on the relative ranking of M(arkedness) constraints and F(aithfulness) constraints; when Markedness dominates Faithfulness (M » F), the unmarked structure surfaces, whereas the opposite ranking F » M suppresses the unmarked structure. This can be illustrated for nasality in vowels, a marked property on typological grounds: all languages have oral vowels, whereas not all languages have nasal ones. The markedness constraint militating against nasal vowels, $*V_{NAS}$ 'no nasal vowels' competes with a faithfulness constraint IDENT-IO(nas), requiring all surface vowels to preserve the specification of [nasal] of their input correspondents. Simple permutation of these constraints produces two grammars, one suppressing nasality where it is specified in the input, and another grammar which allows nasality of input vowels to surface, cf. (23).

(23)   Grammar 1: input nasality suppressed

Input: /bã/	$*V_{NAS}$	IDENT-IO(nas)
bã	*!	
☞ ba		*

Grammar 2: input nasality preserved

Input: /bã/	IDENT-IO(nas)	$*V_{NAS}$
☞ bã		*
ba	*!	

Grammar 1, which ranks the markedness constraint $*V_{NAS}$ above the faithfulness constraint IDENT-IO(nas), effectively prohibits a contrast between oral and nasal vowels. This contrast is supported in Grammar 2, which has the reverse ranking. Which features are 'contrastive', and which are 'noncontrastive', then depends on the ranking of specific markedness constraints and faithfulness constraints: F » M supports contrasts, while M » F neutralises contrasts. (To capture contextual neutralisation, as well as allophonic variation, markedness constraints must be relativised to context.)

As compared to earlier theories (in particular, standard Generative Phonology), OT directly encodes markedness into grammars, with markedness constraints constituting the substance out of which phonologies are built. Consequently, the markedness (or 'naturalness') of phonological processes and segment inventories need no longer be attributed to a grammar-external evaluation measure, as it had been in *SPE*. While deviating from classical Generative Phonology, OT is on a par with Natural Phonology (see section 1) in giving a central function to markedness principles. OT differs from Natural Generative Phonology, however, by taking hierarchically ranked constraints rather than linearly ordered (natural) processes to be the core device.

Consequently, Jakobsonean implicational universals about segment inventories can be brought within the scope of OT's grammatical explanation. The typological generalisation, for example, that all languages have oral vowels (whereas no language has only nasal vowels) is simply due to the logically possible interactions of a markedness constraint ('no nasal vowels', cf. 23) and a faithfulness constraint ('preserve input nasality'): critically, no possible ranking bans oral vowels across the board. Strong typological predictions follow from simple constraint interactions.

Unlike its ancestor theories, OT models phonological generalisations completely at the surface. The assumption that no grammatical restrictions are stated at the level of lexical representation is called *Richness of the Base* (Prince and Smolensky 1993, Smolensky 1996a, Smolensky, Davidson, and Jusczyk, chapter 10, this volume). OT thus abandons morpheme structure rules, a well-known but not uncontroversial device of *SPE*-type phonological theory whose task it is to state the generalisations holding at the level of the lexicon, where these constraints filled in unspecified (predictable) feature values (thus diminishing the cost of the lexicon; recall the evaluation measure counting symbols, mentioned in section 1). OT thus places the burden of accounting for generalisations about the phoneme inventory and phonotactics on surface constraints in a single component which also accounts for phonological alternations. This surface-oriented architecture offers a radical and principled solution to the *duplication problem*, the phenomenon that morpheme structure rules (capturing 'static phonology') are frequently redundantly duplicated by phonological rules that map lexical representations to surface representations (accounting for alternations – the 'active phonology').[8]

As an example, let us consider Dutch voicing assimilation, a set of processes (of regressive and progressive assimilation) which has the effect of eliminating obstruent clusters of mixed voicing at the surface, most notably within the domain of phonological word. That is, in phonological words no clusters such as [kd] or [bt] occur. Voicing agreement is met dynamically (e.g., in phonological alternations of the past tense suffix /-də/, which assimilates in voicing to the stem-final consonant in *maakte* /ma:k+də/ → [ma:ktə] 'made') as well as 'statically' (obstruent clusters share voicing when belonging to a single lexical item, as in *dokter* [dɔktər] 'doctor'). In classical Generative Phonology, the lack of tauto-morphemic disharmonic clusters such as hypothetical */dɔkdər/ was captured by a morpheme structure rule stating voicing agreement in obstruent clusters at the level of lexical representation. Having both a dynamic and a static version of voicing assimilation amounts to a duplication, however, missing a generalisation.

In OT, such duplication is avoided because a single constraint hierarchy captures the generalisation: the markedness constraint AGREE-VOICE 'Obstruent clusters agree in voicing' dominates the faithfulness constraint

IDENT-IO(voice) 'Output segments preserve their input voicing specification'. This accounts for the voicing alternation:

(24)   Voicing assimilation in 'dynamic' mode (alternating past tense suffix)

Input: /maːk+də/	AGREE-VOICE	IDENT-IO(voice)
[maːkdə]	*!	
☞ [maːktə]		*

Note how the same ranking accounts for the static generalisation holding for tauto-morphemic clusters (such as *dokter*). Under Richness of the Base conditions on lexical representations are not required, nor can they be stated. Regardless of whether input clusters have (dis-)harmonic voicing specifications, the grammar forces their surface correspondents to be harmonic:

(25)   Voicing assimilation in 'static' mode (tauto-morphemic context)

Input: /dɔktər/	AGREE-VOICE	IDENT-IO(voice)
[dɔkdər]	*!	*
☞ [dɔktər]		
Input: /dɔkdər/	AGREE-VOICE	IDENT-IO(voice)
[dɔkdər]	*!	*
☞ [dɔktər]		

Whereas the harmonic input /dɔktər/ is faithfully mapped onto a licit output, a hypothetical disharmonic input /dɔkdər/ cannot surface unmodified (*[dɔkdər]), and undergoes voicing assimilation.[9] In sum, voicing assimilation need not be stated twice, but acquires the status of a single grammatical generalisation, which solves the duplication problem.

The surface-oriented architecture of Optimality Theory also offers a solution for another problem for classical Generative Phonology, known as the *conspiracy problem*, noted in section 1. Kisseberth (1970) observed that within grammars different rules conspire towards a common goal: they collectively avoid a 'marked' pattern (for example, CCC clusters are broken up by epenthesis, or reduced by consonant deletion) or establish an 'unmarked' pattern (for example, syllable onsets are created by consonant epenthesis, vowel coalescence, etc.). Conspiracies are a problem for classical derivational phonology: the functional unity between conspiring rules is evident, but left without any formal expression in the grammar. Optimality Theory accounts for conspiracies since changes to inputs are always triggered by the necessity to avoid violations of a high-ranking markedness constraint; a range of resolution strategies is thus expected for principled reasons. Voicing assimilation in Dutch again serves as an example. Obstruent clusters C_1C_2 which disagree in voicing are avoided by regressive voicing assimilation (in case C_2 is a plosive, e.g., *zakdoek* [zɑɡduk] 'handkerchief'), alternatively, by progressive assimilation (in case C_2 is a fricative, e.g., *diepzee* [dipseː] 'deep sea', or C_2 belongs to an inflectional affix, e.g., *maakte* [maːktə] 'made'). These repair strategies share a common objective, that is, avoid violation of AGREE-VOICE.

If both lexical representations in (25), /dɔktər/ and /dɔkdər/, lead to the same output, which one is taken to be the correct one? Under *Lexicon Optimisation* (Prince and Smolensky 1993: 192), if a grammar maps multiple distinct lexical representations (say, L_1 and L_2) onto a single surface form S, the lexical representation is selected whose lexical-to-surface mapping is most harmonic in terms of the grammar. For the purpose of selecting lexical representations (a 'surface-to-lexical' mapping) the grammar is now used in *backward* mode. Since candidate mappings for a given surface form are all equally marked as to surface well-formedness, all candidates share the same set of violation marks on markedness constraints. Hence, selection of the optimal lexical form is solely carried out by faithfulness: the most harmonic mapping is the one which minimally violates faithfulness constraints. This is the 'identity' mapping.

(26)   Lexicon Optimisation selecting an underlying representation

Output: [dɔktər]	AGREE-VOICE	IDENT-IO(voice)
/dɔkdər/ → [dɔktər]		*!
☞ /dɔktər/ → [dɔktər]		

Lexicon Optimisation selects lexical representations which equal surface forms only in the case of non-alternating morphemes. For alternating morphemes, such as the past tense suffix [-tə]~[-də] in Dutch, the standard generative assumption of a single underlying representation of surface alternants entails that the lexical-to-surface mapping is unfaithful for at least one alternant. For alternations Lexicon Optimisation needs to be supplemented by other principles (see Tesar and Smolensky 2000: 77–83 and Hayes, chapter 5 in this volume, for some discussion of learning alternations).

The preceding discussion suggests that an OT grammar serves two duties: licensing licit outputs; and filtering out illicit ones. (See Hayes, chapter 5 this volume, for further discussion.)

First, the grammar guarantees that licit outputs are faithfully mapped from segmentally identical input forms. In such cases, the grammar functions solely as a passive filter, licensing lexical items of the language, and allowing the lexicon to be productively extended by items conforming to the language's phonological requirements. When the grammar maps an input onto an unchanged output, it performs what we may refer to as an 'identity' mapping. We may now define the notion 'possible word' in a language as an output that, *when taken as an input*, would undergo the identity mapping. Hence, to subject a form F to the 'possible word test', F is submitted as an input to the grammar. If F is mapped onto an output form F′ which is non-distinct from its input, F passes the test, showing that F is a possible word of language L.[10]

Second, the grammar functions actively as a filtering device by prohibiting illicit forms from surfacing. Note that the grammar does not filter out an illicit form by 'blocking' (prohibiting it from appearing at the surface), but rather by mapping it onto a modified licit form, a *non-identity* mapping. Submitting an illicit form F to the 'possible word' test, we feed it into the grammar as an input, which maps it onto an output F′ which is distinct from F. (In a tableau, this shows by violation marks incurred by F′ on one or more faithfulness constraints.)

There are various sources of evidence for non-identity mappings. The first, classical type of evidence comes from automatic alternations in the shapes of morphemes that depend on phonological context, such as alternations in voicing of obstruents in Dutch, triggered by the markedness constraint AGREE-VOICE.

Another type of evidence for non-identity mappings comes from *loanword adaptation*, the familiar phenomenon that words borrowed from another language are modified so as to meet an inviolate phonological requirement of the borrowing language. For example, English speakers tend to repair onset clusters which are phonotactically illicit in their language, such as /kn/, by vowel epenthesis (e.g., *Evel K*[ə]*nievel*). Loanword adaptations, because of their automatic, forced character and the broad consistency regarding choice of repair strategy (e.g., deletion, insertion, featural change of segments) applied by different speakers, give evidence for the view that it is due to an internalised grammatical system (Hyman 1970).[11]

Additional evidence for the automatic nature of non-identity mappings comes from *second language phonology*. For example, Dutch learners of English characteristically display final devoicing, neutralising contrasts such as *bit* versus *bid*. This shows the familiar effect of transfer of the first language (L1) into a second language (L2), in this case the M » F ranking for final devoicing: *VOICEDCODA » IDENT-IO(voice). More strikingly, cases are known in which L2 learners display similar mappings which apparently cannot be explained by transfer from their native language. (See discussion in Stampe 1969, Donegan and Stampe 1979, and section 4.4 below.) For example, many

Mandarin Chinese speakers learning English as their L2 go through a stage in which they display final devoicing (Broselow *et al.* 1998), just like Dutch learners of English. However, final devoicing is not observable in Mandarin as this language lacks words ending in obstruent codas. This *emergence of the unmarked* in L2 phonological acquisition follows from two assumptions about acquisition. On the basis of L1 acquisition, Smolensky (1996a, 1996b) has proposed that in UG's initial state, markedness constraints generally dominate faithfulness constraints. During acquisition, the initial state is transformed into an adult grammar by a step-wise process of constraint re-ranking, which is triggered by positive evidence in the form of input from the target language. (This process will be discussed in more detail in section 2.4.) However, Mandarin speakers never receive any positive evidence to change the initial state's M » F ranking of final devoicing, because there are no overt effects of final devoicing in their native language's input, due to a high-ranked constraint banning all coda obstruents. The observations that Mandarin L2 learners of English display final devoicing then follows straightforwardly from a second assumption, namely that of *full transfer* of the learner's L1 grammar into the initial state of the L2 grammar. The M » F ranking for final devoicing (covertly present in Mandarin) automatically transfers into the L2 learner's grammar, where it emerges as soon as the markedness constraint banning obstruent codas is demoted.

A general conclusion to be drawn from this example is that constraint rankings of the type M » F may be *covertly present* in OT grammars. Such covert rankings may be exposed (i.e., become active in non-identity mappings) when situations change minimally. Exposure may be triggered, for example, by the demotion of a higher ranking constraint that obscured the M » F ranking (as we saw in the L2 acquisition case), or by feeding the grammar with data that are not 'normally' fed into it (as in the case of loanword adaptations). This mechanism of exposure of an obscured markedness constraint is known as 'the emergence of the unmarked' (McCarthy and Prince 1994). Schematically, the M » F ranking is obscured in (27) by an 'obscuring constraint' C competing with M. Note that C may be a markedness constraint itself, or a faithfulness constraint.

(27)   M » F ranking obscured by high-ranking constraint C

	C	M	F
Candidate 1	*!		*
☞ Candidate 2		*	

The M » F ranking may become activated by a demotion of the obscuring constraint below M, as in (28):

(28)   TETU by demotion of obscuring constraint C

	M	F	C
☞ Candidate 1		*	*
Candidate 2	*!		

Alternatively, the M » F ranking may be activated by a vacuous satisfaction of C, leaving the original ranking unaffected, as in (29):

(29)   TETU by vacuous satisfaction of obscuring constraint C

	C	M	F
☞ Candidate 1			*
Candidate 2		*!	

Cases of the latter type are well known in reduplication systems (McCarthy and Prince 1995, 1999). In CV reduplication, a typologically common type, the affix copies a segmental portion from the base which equals a single open syllable (CV). For example, in Nootka (Stonham 1990), the reduplicated form či-čims-'i:ħ 'hunting bear' has a CV affix [či] which copies a substring of its base [čims'i:ħ]. This preference for unmarked syllable structure in the affix, showing the activity of NoCODA (constraint M in 29), is not a general property of Nootka, however, a language which otherwise allows for closed syllables. This property is due to domination of NoCODA by MAX-IO (constraint C in 29), which prohibits C-deletion as the general means of attaining open syllables. The CV affix in reduplication is not due to *deletion*, however. Due to the *copying* nature of reduplication, the affix lacks a proper lexical segmental representation. The syllabic shape of the Nootka affix, unchecked by MAX-IO, promptly gravitates to CV to satisfy NoCODA in an emergence of the unmarked. In this example, the role of the dominated faithfulness constraint (F in 29) is taken by MAX-BR, requiring that 'Every segment in the Base have a correspondent in the Reduplicant' (McCarthy and Prince 1995).

(30)   The emergence of the Unmarked in Nootka reduplication

Input: /RED-čims-'i:ħ/	MAX-IO	NO-CODA	MAX-BR
(a) ☞ či-čim.s'i:ħ		**	****
(b) čim.s'i:ħ-čim.s'I:ħ		***!*	
(c) či-či	*!***		

The Emergence of the Unmarked constitutes a powerful argument for OT's central assumption that grammars of natural languages consist of hierarchies of violable universal (markedness and faithfulness) constraints. The Emergence of the Unmarked (TETU) effects of this kind have been observed in a wide range of situations, and most interestingly for our purposes, in (L1 and L2) phonological acquisition; more examples will be discussed in section 3.1.

2.3   Typological variation in OT

On the (standard) assumption that constraints are universal – and in fact innate – the view of cross-linguistic variation ('typology') in OT is straightforward. If all languages build their grammars from the same substance – the full content of *Con*, UG's constraint inventory – the locus of typological variation must be in the arrangement of this substance, in the constraint rankings. Accordingly, OT's central claim about typology is that cross-linguistic differences arise by re-rankings of a set of universal constraints.

Whereas the grammars of individual languages are basically free to rank constraints of *Con* in specific hierarchies, it has been argued as early as Prince and Smolensky (1993) that UG may impose restrictions on possible hierarchies. Formally and functionally related constraints may have fixed rankings, which cannot vary cross-linguistically. For example, the assumption is often made that the markedness constraints on place of articulation are universally ranked in a sub-hierarchy with *LABIAL and *DORSAL outranking *CORONAL, which accounts for the cross-linguistically observed unmarkedness of coronals. Other constraints interact with this sub-hierarchy, producing language-specific rankings in which universal markedness relations between places of articulation are enforced in different ways.

The view that typological variation is due to constraint (re-)ranking is notably different from that taken in parametric theory (reviewed in section 1), which explains typological variation in terms of (binary) parameter values. In parametric theory, switching a parameter 'off' implies total inactivity of the requirements involved. For example, a language whose grammar sets the coda parameter to 'off' is predicted to allow codas freely. In contrast, an OT constraint which is dominated is not necessarily inactive: even in its dominated position, it may continue to exert influence on the selection of output candidates. Given the chance, a dominated markedness constraint will jump into activity, a cross-linguistically well-attested effect, and another example of the emergence of the unmarked (McCarthy and Prince 1994), as we saw in the previous section.

The *factorial typology*, a major notion of OT, allows an explicit connection between language typology and acquisition. A factorial typology of a set of constraints is defined as all the logically possible rankings of these constraints. For example, a set of three constraints, C_1, C_2, and C_3, can be ranked in six different ways:

(31)   A factorial typology of three constraints
        (a) $C_1 \gg C_2 \gg C_3$ (c) $C_2 \gg C_1 \gg C_3$ (e) $C_3 \gg C_1 \gg C_2$
        (b) $C_1 \gg C_3 \gg C_2$ (d) $C_2 \gg C_3 \gg C_1$ (f) $C_3 \gg C_2 \gg C_1$

Computing the factorial typology for a set of constraints allows testing its adequacy against typological evidence: in principle, every distinct ranking predicted by the factorial typology should match (part of) the grammar of some natural language. Factorial typologies, however, grow quickly with the size of the constraint set, for n constraints can be ranked in $n!$ different ways. Since the factorial typology for a set of the size of *Con* is huge, the task of typologically verifying all predicted grammars poses many problems. Nevertheless, if we consider smaller sets, concentrating on a single typologically variant property (for example, syllable typology or stress typology), factorial typologies usually shrink to sizes small enough to allow for full typological verification.

Consider, for example, a factorial typology of three constraints involved in patterns of obstruent voicing. In addition to the constraints NoVoicedCoda and Ident-IO(voice) that were discussed earlier, we assume a third constraint, the Voiced Obstruent Prohibition (VOP), a general markedness constraint banning voiced obstruents across the board. There are six logically possible rankings, whose characteristic patterns are indicated. Only three distinct patterns emerge:

(32)   A mini-typology of voicing
        (a) NoVoicedCoda » VOP » Ident-IO(voice)   no voiced obstruents
        (b) NoVoicedCoda » Ident-IO(voice) » VOP   final devoicing
        (c) VOP » NoVoicedCoda » Ident-IO(voice)   no voiced obstruents
        (d) VOP » Ident-IO(voice) » NoVoicedCoda   no voiced obstruents
        (e) Ident-IO(voice) » NoVoicedCoda » VOP   full voicing contrast
        (f) Ident-IO(voice) » VOP » NoVoicedCoda   full voicing contrast

All three patterns are typologically attested, in languages such as Finnish (32a), Dutch (32b), and English (32e). The full typology of obstruent voicing patterns is, of course, descriptively richer, implying that more constraints need to be assumed than those considered here (see, e.g., Lombardi 1999). Still, this example serves to illustrate a general point: since many of the rankings in factorial typologies collapse into a single pattern, the class of typologically predicted patterns is much smaller than the number of rankings.

Testing new constraints by calculating their factorial typologies (in interaction with a set of well-established constraints) is methodologically useful, if not imperative. If constraints are universal (i.e., present and ranked in every grammar), then adding a new constraint to the universal inventory may increase the predicted typology. Hence, the merits of a constraint cannot be exclusively evaluated on the basis of how well it functions in a particular grammar, but need to be projected on a larger, typological, scale. Arguably, every constraint should pass the factorial typology test: it should not overgenerate by predicting systematically unattested grammatical patterns. This establishes a second major criterion for validating a new constraint (the first being grounding). A third criterion, based on language acquisition, will be discussed in section 3.

2.4   *The learnability of Optimality theoretic grammars*

A major question is how grammars (or partial grammars, such as phonologies) can be learned on the basis of positive evidence in the learner's input. In OT, a theory of ranked constraints, any answer to this question must necessarily take into account the learnability of constraint rankings. This important issue was recognised and addressed by Tesar and Smolensky (1993, 1998, 2000). They developed a Constraint Demotion Algorithm (CDA) which ranks a set of constraints on the basis of positive input. The algorithm can deduce information about constraint ranking from surface forms which it is fed with, while an extension of the algorithm can learn to assess the correct representation of a raw surface form given in the input. The second type of algorithm which we shall discuss, the Gradual Learning Algorithm (GLA), can deal with variation in the input, and can also account for gradual well-formedness (Boersma 1997, 1998, Boersma and Hayes 2001).[12]

The idea underlying Tesar and Smolensky's CDA is that the learner can work out the target ranking of the language that (s)he is learning from inspecting patterns of constraint violations in the forms that (s)he encounters. The learner first makes the necessary assumption that all forms which (s)he hears are grammatical, hence optimal under the ranking of the target language. This assumption allows the learner to infer that any constraint violation in observed forms is forced by a high-ranking constraint. Accordingly, the violated constraint itself can be (conservatively) shifted down in the hierarchy. With each new datum encountered, the learner may be able to shift one or more constraints somewhat closer to their eventual positions in the hierarchy. In the *recursive* mode of the algorithm, the learner considers input data one by one, computing their effects on the constraint ranking immediately. Step by step, the intermediate grammar approaches the full target ranking until it finally 'converges' at a steady endpoint. In the *batch* mode, the algorithm takes in all input data in a single sweep, and processes them in a decreasing order of strictness, so that higher ranked constraints are first placed together in a stratum, before the lower ranked constraints are placed.

A simple example of the recursive mode in action clarifies the basic idea of extracting useful information from input data. Assume a learner confronted with the task of learning the distribution of voiced and unvoiced obstruents in Dutch. The generalisation that holds here is that coda obstruents are devoiced, while elsewhere (that is, in onsets), voicing is contrastive. In Dutch, the VOICED OBSTRUENT PROHIBITION (VOP) is dominated by IDENT-IO(voice) because voicing is contrastive (in onsets). The target ranking is given below:

(33)   NoVoicedCoda » Ident-IO(voice) » VOP

The following tableau shows the relevant constraint interactions in a single form:

(34)   Coda devoicing

Input: /bɛd/	NoVoicedCoda	Ident-IO(voice)	VOP
(a) bɛd	*!		**
(b) ☞ bɛt		*	*
(c) pɛd	*!	*	*
(d) pɛt		**!	

Note that in the optimal candidate (34b), the coda is devoiced, while the onset consonant is faithful to its input voicing, which shows the activity of input-to-output faithfulness.

Let us abstract away from alternations, and assume that the learner already knows the underlying representation /bɛd/. (The learning of alternations and underlying representations is discussed by Tesar and Smolensky 2000, and Hayes, chapter 5 this volume.) Under these somewhat simplified conditions, the learning task amounts to inferring the constraint ranking (33) on the basis of forms encountered in the input, such as [bɛt].

The learning process starts from an initial ranking in which all three constraints cluster together in a single stratum. The assumption of a one-stratum initial state will be reconsidered in the next section, in favour of an initial state in which markedness constraints outrank faithfulness constraints, as proposed in Smolensky (1996a, 1996b).

The learner encounters the first datum: [bɛt], which (as we assumed earlier) (s)he knows is based on the underlying representation /bɛd/. Since the observed output form [bɛt] must be *optimal* for the given input, any other candidates for the same input can be safely assumed to be less harmonic, that is, *sub-optimal*. She starts by arranging the information to be processed by the constraint ranker in the form of *mark-data pairs*, consisting of pairwise comparisons of the optimal candidate (the winner) and a sub-optimal candidate (a loser):

(35)   Mark-data pairs

sub-opt ≺ opt		loser-marks	winner-marks
b ≺ a	[bɛd] ≺ [bɛt]	{* NoVoicedCoda, *~~VOP~~* VOP}	{* ~~VOP~~,* Ident-IO(voice)}
c ≺ a	[pɛd] ≺ [bɛt]	{* NoVoicedCoda, * ~~VOP~~,* ~~Ident-IO(voice)~~}	{* ~~VOP~~,* ~~Ident-IO(voice)~~}
d ≺ a	[pɛt] ≺ [bɛt]	{* ~~Ident-IO(voice)~~, * Ident-IO(voice)}	{* VOP,* ~~Ident-IO(voice)~~}

Shared constraint violations (between a winner and a loser) are cancelled out. Consequently, the second mark-data pair ceases to be informative, as [pɛd] contains a superset of violations of [bɛt], which cannot (by definition) give any information about ranking. New mark-data pairs are drawn up, including (all and only) relevant and non-redundant information:

(36)   Mark-data pairs after marks cancellation

sub-opt ≺ opt		loser-marks	winner-marks
b ≺ a	[bɛd] ≺ [bɛt]	{* NoVoicedCoda, * VOP}	{* Ident-IO(voice)}
d ≺ a	[pɛt] ≺ [bɛt]	{* Ident-IO(voice)}	{* VOP}

This display can be (informally) interpreted as follows. We begin by interpreting the second harmonic ranking, [pɛt] ≺ [bɛt], which is the simplest case, indicating that VOP is violated in the winner [bɛt]. The only possible ground for violation could be the need to avoid a violation of another, higher ranked constraint, in this case Ident-IO(voice), which would be violated if the winner had been the loser (and conversely, the loser had been the winner). Accordingly, it must be the case that more priority is given to avoiding violation of Ident-IO(voice) than to avoidance of violation of VOP. This amounts to a ranking Ident-IO(voice) » VOP. Similarly, the first harmonic ranking, [bɛd] ≺ [bɛt], shows that Ident-IO(voice) is violated in the winner [bɛt]. In contrast to the earlier case, there are two (rather than one) constraints in loser-marks, which means that either NoVoicedCoda or VOP could have been the cause of violation of Ident-IO(voice) in the winner. To state it differently, it follows that either of the following rankings holds: NoVoicedCoda » Ident-IO(voice) or VOP » Ident-IO(voice).

We find that some information in mark-data pairs can be straightforwardly translated into a sub-ranking, while other information is ambiguous, posing a 'demotion dilemma' that requires a general resolution strategy. The CDA, by applying a procedure which we need not discuss in detail, cautiously extracts reliable information from mark-data pairs and uses this to demote constraints one by one, until the target ranking is reached.

For example, if the learner starts with the second mark-data pair in (36), working from a single-stratum initial state, (s)he can safely decide to demote VOP below IDENT-IO(voice), placing it into a new stratum.

(37)   {NOVOICEDCODA, IDENT-IO(voice)} » VOP

Continuing with the first mark-data pair, the learner is faced with a dilemma: she can demote IDENT-IO(voice) below NOVOICEDCODA, or alternatively, demote it below VOP:

(38)   (a) NOVOICEDCODA » {VOP, IDENT-IO(voice)}
         (b) NOVOICEDCODA » VOP » IDENT-IO(voice)

The correct demotion (38a) is more conservative than the one in (38b), since it does not rank VOP with respect to IDENT-IO(voice), while (38b) establishes an (incorrect) ranking between these constraints. Conservative demotion is promoted to a general strategy in the algorithm, serving the central goal of terminating the recursive demotion process. It is of use whenever the algorithm faces a dilemma about how deep to demote a constraint, that is, whenever two or more contraints occur in loser-marks (as in 36 b ≺ a). It then demotes any constraint which assigns a *winner-mark* to a stratum immediately below the *highest-ranking* constraint which assigns a *loser-mark*. The conservative demotion strategy avoids placing a demoted constraint too deep down the hierarchy, from which it could never escape except by a re-ranking of other constraints, which may produce an eternal re-ranking process, which fails to terminate.

In addition to presenting a constraint-ranking algorithm, Tesar and Smolensky (2000) address two closely related aspects of the learning process: (i) the learning of covert structural descriptions from input to the learner (including their prosodic structure); and (ii) the learning of underlying representations and morphophonological alternations. Tesar and Smolensky's theory of grammatical acquisition, as a whole, closely reflects the architecture of OT itself: maximal emphasis is put on principles such as harmonic ordering and strict domination.

Boersma (1998, 2000) and Tesar and Smolensky (1998) observed that the CDA is vulnerable to variation in the input data, a common feature of natural language. This problem is caused by the major assumption underlying the CDA that all input data are consistent with a single ranking. The CDA, when fed variable input, responds by failure to converge. For example, the recursive mode of the algorithm, when presented with inconsistent input data, never reaches a stable state, eternally going back and forth between rankings. As a solution to this problem, Boersma (1998, 2000) and Boersma and Hayes (2001) propose an alternative algorithm, the Gradual Learning Algorithm (GLA), which is designed to cope with variation in its input, and which constructs grammars reflecting input variation by variable outputs.

Before addressing the topic of learning OT grammars on the basis of noisy input data, let us address the issue of how to model variable outputs in OT.[13] The insight of Anttila (1997) is that variation can be modelled by leaving some conflicting constraints unranked. In his model, each time the grammar is deployed, it chooses an ordering of the unranked constraints at random. The result is that a single input may variably map to different outputs.[14] Boersma (1998) preserves the view of variation as variable rankings, but enriches the model by making two novel assumptions. First, the grammar ranks each constraint as a point along a *continuous scale*, with a numerical value allowing an exact measure of a constraint's distance from other constraints. When the grammar is deployed in evaluation, however, the constraints are placed in a strict domination order. Second, the order is determined by the constraints' value on the scale, together with a factor of noise, which provides an interval surrounding the mean of a *stochastic distribution*. The closer two constraints are, the more their distributions will overlap, resulting in a larger proportion of rankings in which the lower ranking constraint of the two dominates the higher ranking one.

Boersma's theory of variation provides the basis of the GLA (Boersma 1998, Boersma and Hayes 2001). This learns a grammar on the basis of variable input data, while coping with free variation and noisy inputs. The idea underlying the GLA is that the grammar changes gradually (rather than categorically) under the influence of input data. Each form fed into the learner has a small effect on the grammar, which only grows into a sizeable ranking effect when significantly amplified by many similar forms. In such cases, ranking values of responsible constraints will end up being so far apart that their distributions hardly overlap, a situation corresponding to a categorical ranking. Variable inputs, however, have effects on the grammar that go in opposite directions; in the end, the grammar reflects the distributions of variable input data by placing constraints close enough on the scale as to make their 'noisy' distributions overlap, as discussed earlier. In this way, variable input data are fruitfully processed by the learner, rather than being rejected due to 'inconsistencies'.

After this overview of the architecture of OT and the learnability of OT grammars, we now turn to the relevance of OT for phonological acquisition.

3.   Drawing connections between Optimality Theory and child phonology

In section 1, we discussed formal and substantive connections that have been drawn between child phonology and rule-based and parametric theories of phonology. Research on phonological acquisition in Optimality Theory has also brought to light both formal and substantive links between children's sound systems and cross-linguistic phonology. In this section we shall take up each of these topics in turn, focusing in particular on the contributions made by papers appearing in this volume.

3.1   *Formal connections: constraint interaction*

Optimality Theory shares with other constraint-based theories the virtue of being able to express formally the conspiratorial behaviour of phonological processes. While this sets Optimality Theory apart from a purely rule-based model, generative research on child phonology has incorporated constraints in one way or another for some time now (see, e.g., the discussion of parametric theories in section 1). Thus, the more germane comparison is between Optimality Theory and other theories that make use of constraints. In this context, the main innovation of Optimality Theory lies in the notion that constraints are minimally violable, that a constraint can be violated if and only if the satisfaction of a higher ranked constraint is at issue. This can be contrasted with the usually implicit view that an observed violation of a constraint implies its inactivity: that within a given domain or level, a constraint is either strictly inviolable or completely without force. The advantage of minimally violable constraints is that they allow for a straightforward account of non-uniform constraint application (Prince 1993), in which a constraint is only satisfied, or violated, under particular circumstances.

One type of non-uniform constraint application was discussed in section 2.2: 'the emergence of the unmarked' (McCarthy and Prince 1994). This refers to a situation in which a markedness constraint is generally violated in the language as a whole, but does have effects in a certain context. The examples McCarthy and Prince (1994) discuss are ones in which a reduplicative morpheme is subject to the effects of a markedness constraint that is violated elsewhere in the language. The other type of non-uniformity might be termed 'the emergence of the marked', in which a markedness constraint is generally satisfied, but is violated in a particular context. Both of these are readily captured through constraint ranking. A constraint can be violated only under compulsion of a higher ranked constraint. If the demands of that higher ranked constraint conflict with those of the lower ranked constraint in most, but not all, environments, then we have the emergence of the unmarked. If the demands of the higher ranked constraint only force the violation of the lower ranked constraint in a limited set of contexts, an emergence of the marked situation is produced. Neither of these situations is expected if constraints are inviolable, though they can of course be dealt with, usually by complicating the statement of the constraints in undesirable ways. Those seeking a concrete example might wish to compare the statement of NONFINALITY in Prince and Smolensky's (1993) analysis of Kelkar's Hindi with the Extrametricality Rule posited for the same data in Hayes (1995).

Starting with Prince and Smolensky (1993), phonological research has turned up a number of cases of non-uniform constraint application, and provided compelling analyses in terms of ranked constraints. Evidence of non-uniform constraint application in child language, and the accompanying analysis in terms of ranked constraints, yields an important formal parallel between phonological theory and child phonology, and a strong argument for an Optimality theoretic approach to the latter domain.

Two such cases are presented in Amalia Gnanadesikan's chapter in this volume, 'Markedness and faithfulness constraints in child phonology'. Here we shall present the simpler of the two so as to provide an explicit example of the role of ranked constraints in child phonology; we take some liberties with Gnanadesikan's analysis for the sake of expository ease. The evidence for non-uniformity comes from the activity of constraints against high sonority onsets in the forms produced by an English-learning child. In cluster reduction, we find that the sonority of the segments determines which consonant is deleted, with the higher sonority segment being lost. For example, a stop-liquid cluster will lose the liquid, rather than the stop (e.g., [piz] *please*). This can be attributed to a constraint against liquid onsets (for our purposes *L-ONS). Outside of cluster reduction, however, approximant onsets freely occur (e.g., [læb] *lab*). This would immediately raise a paradox in a theory of inviolable constraints: how could a constraint that is active in cluster reduction be violated elsewhere? In OT, the answer would be that a higher ranked constraint usually forces *L-ONS to be violated, but that this constraint does not interfere with the satisfaction of *L-ONS in cluster reduction.

One such constraint is MAX-IO, the faithfulness constraint that blocks segmental deletion by requiring every input segment to have an output correspondent (McCarthy and Prince 1999). The tableau in (39) illustrates the effect of ranking this constraint above *L-ONS when the input onset is a singleton:

(39)   Marked structure forced by constraint domination

input: /læb/	MAX-IO	*L-ONS
æb	*!	
☞ læb		*

As this tableau shows, the dominance of MAX-IO generally rules out deletion as a means to satisfy *L-ONS. Cluster reduction is different because in this context, MAX-IO must be violated, due to the dominance of a constraint against clusters, *COMPLEX. Regardless of which consonant is deleted, MAX-IO will be violated, so the decision is passed down to the lower ranked *L-ONS constraint:

(40)   Emergence of the Unmarked

input: /pliz/	*COMPLEX	MAX-IO	*L-ONS
pliz	*!		
iz		**!	
liz		*	*!
☞ piz		*	

Interestingly, Fikkert (1994: 59) documents a stage in the acquisition of Dutch in which only stops are produced, which are the least marked onsets in terms of onset sonority constraints such as those posited by Gnanadesikan:

(41)   Until 1:9.9 adult target onsets other than plosives are either realised with an initial plosive . . . or deleted by Jarmo

At this presumably prior developmental stage, constraints against sonorous onsets are fully satisfied. In terms of Optimality Theory, this would be captured by having the onset sonority constraints dominate all conflicting constraints. In terms of inviolable constraints, one could invoke a constraint, or set of constraints, against non-plosive onsets. However, such inviolable constraint(s) would be of no formal use in describing the stage discussed by Gnanadesikan, in which the constraint applies just in case one member of an onset is deleted. This developmental progression, in which a constraint is at first fully satisfied, then minimally violated, is straightforwardly expressed by Optimality Theory, and forms a second formal bridge between it and the study of phonological acquisition. For further discussion, see Barlow (1997), Pater (1997), and Barlow and Gierut (1999).

Phonological development as constraint re-ranking is discussed from a somewhat different angle by Clara Levelt and Ruben van de Vijver in their chapter 'Syllable types in cross-linguistic and developmental grammars'. Levelt and van de Vijver identify a set of markedness constraints that govern the basic structure of onsets and codas. They show that the factorial typology produced by the interaction of these constraints with a general faithfulness constraint matches the systems attested cross-linguistically. A ranking with all of the markedness constraints above the faithfulness constraint yields the least marked system, with only CV syllables. A hierarchy with faithfulness dominating all of the markedness constraints allows the full range of syllable types, that is, any expansion of the (C)(C)V(C)(C) template. For a child learning Dutch, these grammars correspond to the hypothesised initial state and the final state, respectively. Other languages have faithfulness dominating some subset of the markedness constraints, and these form possible intermediate grammars for the Dutch-learning child. Levelt and van de Vijver show that only a small number of such possible intermediate stages are attested in a corpus of data on the acquisition of Dutch. They argue that the limited range of developmental paths can be explained by considering the frequency of the various syllable types in caretaker language. The transition between developmental stages involves demotion of a markedness constraint beneath faithfulness. When there is a choice of markedness constraints to be demoted, it is made on the basis of the frequency of the syllable type that will be added to the child's repertory.

3.2   *Substantive connections: the content of constraints*

Substantive connections between cross-linguistic and developmental phonology are captured in Optimality Theory by having the same constraints apply in both domains, in a manner similar to Jakobson's Laws of Irreversible Solidarity, or Stampe's processes. Given the (standard) assumption that constraints are universal – and in fact innate – the relation between acquisition and cross-linguistic patterns ('typology') could not be accidental. Both the adult speaker's and the child's early grammar are built from the same material: UG's constraint inventory; where adult and early grammars differ, the locus of difference must be in the arrangement of the material (the constraint rankings), not in their substance. One may thus expect the typological variation between the phonologies of natural languages to be mirrored, in a general fashion, in the acquisitional variation between early and adult grammars. But not only does one expect the range of variation found in early and adult grammars to be similar; it is also predicted that for each phonological 'process' found in a child's early phonology, there is a counterpart in the phonology of some natural language.

Research in child phonology has continued to find reflections of typologically attested patterns in child sound systems, and the papers both by Gnanadesikan and Levelt and van de Vijver point out such correspondences. The pattern of sonority-based onset selection that Gnanadesikan documents in English child phonology is closely paralleled in Sanskrit reduplication, while Levelt and van de Vijver show that typologically derived syllable structure constraints characterise the stages of development that Dutch children go through. Levelt and van de Vijver do find one stage that lacks a typological correlate, but the subtlety of this restriction (against the co-occurrence of onset and coda clusters) may well explain its absence from extant linguistic descriptions.

The standard interpretation of these connections is that constraints are innate, and that acquisition consists only of constraint re-ranking, and not of constraint construction. This implicit assumption of most Optimality theoretic acquisition and learnability research is made explicit in Gnanadesikan's chapter, as well as in that of Goad and Rose (see also Kager 1999 for discussion). It is not a necessary assumption, however; one might also claim that constraints emerge in acquisition in response to articulatory and perceptual pressures (see, e.g., Bernhardt and Stemberger 1998, Boersma 1998, Hayes 1999). The universality of such phonetic and cognitive factors would then be held to explain the observed activity of similar constraints across languages, and across developing grammars. It is difficult to tease these innatist and emergentist accounts apart empirically in terms of their predictions about child language. One source of evidence in favour of an (at least partially) emergentist stance may be the occurrence of phenomena in child speech that are unattested typologically. The prototypical case is that of long-distance assimilation of primary place features between non-adjacent consonants, usually referred to as consonant harmony. Given that the pattern is unattested typologically, it would seem unlikely that it is produced by typologically derived constraints. However, Optimality theoretic analyses of consonant harmony have diverged on this issue; while Pater (1997) takes this as evidence for a child-specific articulatorily based constraint, Goad (1997) constructs an analysis using Alignment constraints that are claimed to be active cross-linguistically (see also Levelt 1995, Dinnsen, Barlow, and Morrisette 1997, Bernhardt and Stemberger 1998, and Rose 2000 on consonant harmony in Optimality Theory).

Innatist and emergentist theories appear to make different predictions about the nature of constraints. Under the emergentist view, the constraints should rather directly mirror the articulatory and perceptual factors on which they are based, while an innatist theory would expect that at least some constraints (if not all) should be purely formal in nature, with no direct phonetic motivation (see Boersma 1998 for discussion). The innatist perspective is defended in Heather Goad and Yvan Rose's chapter, 'Input elaboration, head faithfulness, and evidence for representation in the acquisition of left-edge clusters in West Germanic'. They take the sonority-based analysis of onset reduction put forth by Gnanadesikan and others as representative of a relatively phonetically based approach to the phenomenon. They point to another pattern of onset reduction attested in child speech that they term the 'head pattern', which differs from the sonority pattern in that [s]-initial clusters always lose the [s], even when the second member of the cluster is higher in sonority. They argue that an account of this pattern requires a structurally elaborated syllable structure that encodes the difference between all other obstruent-initial clusters and [s]-initial clusters: the former are left-headed branching onsets, while in the latter, [s] is analysed as an adjunct, and head status is trivially assigned to the consonant following it. Faithfulness to the head position favours the preservation of the second member of [s]-initial clusters, but the initial member of all other obstruent initial clusters. Since headedness is in this context a purely formal, rather than functional, principle, Goad and Rose take this to suggest that the substantive content of constraints, and the representations they refer to, is not just functional.

4.   Markedness » Faithfulness: implications and extensions

An overarching theme of much Optimality theoretic acquisition and learnability research, and one that connects many of the chapters in this volume, is the relative ranking of markedness and faithfulness constraints at the outset of, and through the course of, acquisition.

4.1   Data from child production and perception

To express the unmarkedness of child phonology observed by Jakobson and subsequent researchers, it is often maintained that acquisition starts with markedness constraints ranked above faithfulness constraints. This ranking results in output structures that conform to the demands of the markedness constraints, and are thus simple. As faithfulness constraints come to dominate markedness constraints, structures gradually increase in complexity.

Several of the chapters in this volume present data from child production that provide evidence of structures that are unmarked relative to the adult target language, and put forth analyses in which markedness constraints outrank faithfulness constraints, rankings that are reversed in the target language. The chapters by Gnanadesikan, Goad and Rose, and Levelt and van de Vijver all focus on syllable structure, and, in particular, the reductions in complexity of children's syllable structure relative to that of adults (see also Barlow 1997, Ohala 1996, 1999). Other research has examined similar reductions in complexity at higher levels of prosody, evidenced in particular by truncation (Demuth 1995, 1996, 1997, 2000, Pater and Paradis 1996, Kehoe and Stoel-Gammon 1997, Kehoe 1999, Pater 1997, Curtin 2001, 2002, Ota 1999). There has also been some debate on whether early child productions are in fact correctly characterised by a Markedness » Faithfulness ranking; see Bernhardt and Stemberger (1998) and Velleman and Vihman (2000).

Two of the chapters in this volume discuss evidence for Markedness » Faithfulness ranking in experiments on infant speech perception. In the contribution by Lisa Davidson, Peter Jusczyk, and Paul Smolensky, 'The initial and final states: theoretical implications and experimental explorations of Richness of the Base', an experimental paradigm is introduced that is aimed to assess directly the predictions of this initial ranking. Infants from 4.5 to 20 months of age were presented triples of syllables of the form 'A B AB' in which 'AB' was either a faithful concatenation of A and B, or one in which a markedness-reducing sound change had occurred. Under the hypothesis that infants prefer stimuli which conform to their grammar, and that infants interpret the triples as analogous to /A + B/ → [AB], the prediction of Markedness » Faithfulness is that sound-change stimuli should be preferred over faithful but marked stimuli.

This was confirmed by the Headturn Preference Procedure for children at 4.5, 10, and 20 months, although no significant difference was found at 15 months.

Joe Pater's chapter 'Bridging the gap between receptive and productive development with minimally violable constraints' draws on previously published studies of infant speech perception to make the case that receptive acquisition follows a course similar to that of productive development: initial stages permit only unmarked structures; more complex structures emerge later. To account for these parallels, Pater develops a model in which markedness constraints apply in perception as well as in production. Since receptive development does typically precede the development of production, it is necessary to allow for differences in the complexity of structures permitted at a single time. Pater's proposal is that faithfulness constraints can be indexed to perception or production, thus allowing for a situation in which perceptual representations are of greater complexity than those created for production.

4.2   The initial state: an argument from learnability

Learnability considerations provide an argument for the ranking of markedness constraints above faithfulness constraints at the outset of acquisition. This argument was first made in Smolensky (1996a), who attributes the basic insight to Alan Prince (personal communication); it is further elaborated on in the chapter by Davidson, Jusczyk, and Smolensky in this volume, as well as in the contributions by Hayes, and Prince and Tesar, which will be discussed in section 4.3. Before proceeding with an outline of this argument, we should note that, while widely accepted, it is not universally so. In the somewhat different approach to learnability advocated by Hale and Reiss (1998), an initial state with Faithfulness » Markedness is in fact held to be necessary.

Suppose that a language lacks a particular structure, such as syllable codas. An account of this gap in terms of Optimality Theory requires that a markedness constraint militating against that structure dominate a faithfulness constraint that would prefer its preservation; for the restriction against codas, NOCODA must dominate a faithfulness constraint like DEP ('no epenthesis'). As discussed in section 2.2, this ranking would need to hold even in a language without overt alternations, since in contrast with earlier generative theories of phonology, Optimality Theory countenances no restrictions on the form of inputs, under the principle of Richness of the Base (Prince and Smolensky 1993).

The learnability issue arises in just this case of languages that do not have alternations, since they provide no positive evidence of the need for the markedness constraints to outrank the faithfulness constraint. A learner with DEP » NOCODA would correctly parse the codaless strings of the ambient language, since no constraint would prefer adding a coda. Assuming that learning is error-driven (Tesar and Smolensky 1998), this ranking would be a trap, and the learner would not be guaranteed to converge on the correct NoCoda » Dep hierarchy. This can be seen as an instance of the Subset problem discussed in Principles and Parameters theories (e.g., Berwick 1985); the language produced by M » F (e.g., NoCoda » Dep; with only V rimes) is a subset of the language produced by F » M (e.g., Dep » NoCoda; V and VC rimes). Since all of the data of the subset language are consistent with the superset language, positive evidence alone will not move the learner out of the superset state.

The solution to this problem suggested by researchers such as Demuth (1995), Gnanadesikan (1995, this volume), Levelt (1995), and Smolensky (1996a, 1996b) is to posit an initial state in which all of the markedness constraints outrank the faithfulness constraints. Positive evidence will be available for any Faithfulness » Markedness rankings that are inconsistent with this initial state.

4.3   *Persistence of Markedness » Faithfulness: learnability issues*

Bruce Hayes's chapter, 'Phonological acquisition in Optimality Theory: the early stages', and Alan Prince and Bruce Tesar's 'Learning phonotactic distributions' both independently argue that an initial ranking does not go far enough, and claim that a bias for low-ranked faithfulness constraints must persist past the initial state, and be incorporated into the learning algorithm itself. While the fundamental insight of the chapters is a shared one, their implementations and extensions of it are quite different, which makes their inclusion in a single volume particularly opportune.

Prince and Tesar introduce an explicit measure of the degree to which a hierarchy possesses M » F structure, and investigate the consequences of trying to maximise this measure by low placement of F in suitably biased versions of the Recursive Constraint Demotion Algorithm (Tesar 1995, Tesar and Smolensky 1998). The key issue is deciding which F to demote when there is more than one F constraint to choose from. They suggest that the main desideratum is the 'freeing up' of further M constraints for ranking, though they also show that such decisions have further consequences downstream for the resultant hierarchy that may motivate a certain kind of 'look ahead' in the decision-making process. Prince and Tesar also consider issues arising in the context of constraints that are in a 'special/general' relationship (see Prince and Smolensky 1993 on Panini's Theorem). They suggest that this consideration yields learning-theoretic motivation for resolving the Positional Markedness versus Positional Faithfulness controversy (Beckman 1998, Zoll 1998) and for deeper scrutiny of faithfulness theory as a whole.

Bruce Hayes also develops a version of Tesar and Smolensky's (1998) Constraint Demotion Algorithm that incorporates a bias towards low-ranked faithfulness. He illustrates his algorithm's effectiveness by having it learn the phonotactic pattern of a simplified language modelled on Korean. Based on literature from infant speech perception, Hayes suggests that infants accomplish much of this phonotactic learning in the first year of life. The later learning of morphological alternations is guided by an additional default ranking: in contrast to input–output faithfulness, output–output faithfulness constraints start out in a dominant position in the hierarchy (see also McCarthy 1999b). Hayes finds empirical evidence from production data showing that children do in fact sometimes assume a higher rank of output-output faithfulness than is necessary in the language.

4.4   Persistence of Markedness » Faithfulness: production data

Whether the bias towards low-ranked Faithfulness is inherited from an initial ranking or explicitly maintained throughout learning, the Markedness » Faithfulness ranking is predicted to persist through subsequent developmental stages, and into the adult grammar, when there is no evidence to force a re-ranking. Evidence of this ranking cannot be obtained through simple inspection of the forms of a language. For example, to show that a speaker of a language without codas in fact encodes a restriction against codas in the phonological grammar, one cannot simply point to the fact that the language lacks syllable-final consonants. Instead, to show the productivity of such a restriction, one might invoke data from loanword adaptations or from the production of nonce words with codas. The Markedness » Faithfulness schema also makes predictions beyond the productivity of static restrictions, since it may be that a language provides no evidence at all for the ranking of some constraints. In our language without codas, inspection of overt forms would reveal nothing about the ranking of a markedness constraint against voiced coda obstruents (NoVoicedCoda) relative to the faithfulness constraint demanding preservation of underlying voice Ident (voice). Data bearing on just this situation are presented by Broselow et al. (1998). They show that when Mandarin learners of English start to acquire codas, they do go through a stage in which they devoice the codas, as the M » F ranking of NoVoicedCoda » Ident (voice) would predict (see section 2.2). In Natural Phonology, innate processes are similarly held to persevere into the mature system when they are not contradicted in the language being learned. In support of this position, Stampe (1969) and Nathan (1984) point to several other cases of the emergence of innate processes in second language phonology that are parallel to Broselow et al.'s L2 English example. In this volume, instances of persistent Markedness » Faithfulness ranking are provided in data from child productions, loanword adaptation, and second language acquisition.

In chapter 11, 'Child word stress competence: an experimental approach', Wim Zonneveld and Dominique Nouveau report on an experiment conducted to establish whether Dutch 3- and 4-year-olds have mastery of the Dutch stress system. Based on elicited production data of real and nonsense words, they find that the answer to this question seems to be an affirmative one, and also that a developmental pattern can be detected from one age group to the next. The chapter goes on to show, however, that some subtle patterns in these experimentally collected data are not captured by any existing standard analysis, whether formulated in rules, parameters, or constraints. It is indicated that, by hindsight, these patterns occur in the adult system too, and an analysis is proposed with two properties: irregularity is treated with the aid of deviating hierarchies; and in some of these hierarchies constraints become visible only because they are active in subpatterns first discovered in the child language experiment. In particular, Zonneveld and Nouveau uncover evidence in their experiment for an undominated *CLASH constraint, whose activity is generally masked by other constraints.

Shigeko Shinohara's chapter, 'Emergence of Universal Grammar in foreign word adaptations', presents a study of the adaptation of French loanwords by Japanese speakers. Shinohara discusses patterns of segmental change and insertion as well as accent placement. Some of the phenomena point to the activity of constraints that govern the phonology of the language as a whole, but others, such as avoidance of stressed epenthetic vowels, and stem–syllable alignment, implicate constraints that are uniquely active in the loanword phonology. Since these constraints do have considerable cross-linguistic justification, Shinohara takes them to be part of the constraint set supplied by Universal Grammar. For the most part, their activity in loanword adaptation can be understood as the emergence of latent M » F rankings, but some ranking among the markedness constraints is also required. These rankings of markedness constraints, Shinohara suggests, are potentially universal, and derivable from phonetic scales (see Prince and Smolensky 1993: ch. 5).

Davidson, Jusczyk, and Smolensky present an experimental paradigm that is designed to induce speakers to subject non-native inputs to their English grammars, to quantitatively assess the M » F-based prediction that non-English clusters would be repaired to meet the requirements of English syllable structure. In the condition that best approximated this prediction, non-English clusters divided into several groups which could be ordered according to their probability of repair. They show that appropriate interaction of constraints independently needed to bar non-English clusters can account for the relative markedness of different non-English clusters, suggesting a final English ranking that makes such distinctions, without apparent motivation in the English data in which none of these clusters appears. They go on to suggest possible analyses of how such a ranking might arise, and point out the importance of such 'hidden rankings' in the final state for pursuing the hypothesis that the initial state for second language acquisition is the final state for first language acquisition.

5.   Conclusion

In this introduction, we have emphasised the theme of formal and substantive connections between phonological theory and child phonology. Across theories, a basic formal connection is made by positing mappings between underlying and surface representations in child phonology, analogous (but not necessarily equivalent) to such mappings in phonological theory. In rule-based theories this connection is strengthened by arguing that the rules that perform the mappings in both domains are similar in terms of their formal makeup, as well as in how they interact with one another, specifically, through ordering (Stampe 1969, 1973a, 1973b, Smith 1973). Similarly in OT, constraints are argued to interact through ranking in child language as well as in mature grammars. Substantive connections between child and adult phonology were made in rule-based phonology by positing a set of processes that apply in both domains (Stampe 1969, 1973a, 1973b), and in constraint-based phonology, by having constraints that apply to child and adult grammars. Many of the same issues that confronted earlier attempts to connect child phonology and phonological theory continue to apply today; this is particularly obvious from a reading of Lise Menn's contribution to this volume, 'Saving the baby: making sure that old data survive new theories'. At the same time, however, we should not underestimate the progress that has been made on several fronts. Along with the continued discovery of basic formal and substantive parallels between child and adult phonology, recent research has succeeded in providing explicit proposals about difficult issues such as the learnability of phonology, variation, similarities and differences in comprehension and production, and the genesis of constraints. The rapid progress that is being made, combined with the wide range of issues that remain to be explored, makes the intersection between phonological theory and phonological acquisition such an exciting area for ongoing research.

NOTES

1. Those wishing to expand their knowledge of its subject-matter beyond what is discussed in this section, and/or to familiarise themselves with the view of others on similar material and issues, may wish to consult a number of other texts: out of some handfuls we recommend Ingram (1989), Ferguson, Menn, and Stoel-Gammon (1992), Fletcher and MacWhinney (1995), Vihman (1996), Jusczyk (1997), Bernhardt and Stemberger (1998), and Tesar and Smolensky (1998, 2000).
2. First published in German in Uppsala, Sweden, when Jakobson was in Norway as a World War Two refugee; this version was reprinted in 1962 in *Selected Writings I*. An English translation, from which we quote here, appeared in 1968.
3. The expected value of the opposition is often called the 'unmarked' one, the unexpected value the 'marked' one (in this example: stop is unmarked, fricative is marked).

4. Kaye (1974) argues that some cases of opaque rule interaction may be interpreted as functionally motivated in that they contribute to the recoverability (in a technical, non-learning sense) of underlying representations, namely if the opaque derivation produces a segment that occurs nowhere else in the language, as when [ŋ] is the unique product of assimilation > velar deletion. Notice, however, that this is not a case of counterfeeding. For further discussion, see McCarthy (1999a: section 3.1).

5. Smith does not literally claim that underlying forms of the child grammar will by definition be *always identical* to the adult form: empirical evidence may suggest otherwise. Consider the rule of Consonant Harmony, whereby a coronal consonant becomes velar under the influence of a velar later in the word; [gɛgiː] for *taxi*, [gɔːk] for *talk*. The rule also neutralised *take* and *cake*, for instance. When the rule disappeared, in 'hundred or more examples' (p. 144) the completely regular coronal appeared, as expected; as a single exception, the verb *take* remained [geik], later [kʰeik]. What apparently had happened was that Amahl assumed the underlying form of this verb to be /keik/, only turning to a different assumption, leading to the correct output, in the face of consistent positive evidence.

Recently, and more fundamentally, Macken (1995) distinguishes between three acquisitional rule types (related to perception, articulation, and generalisation) that each have their own functional and developmental characteristics. Her model allows for underlying representations which are the same as surface representations in cases of perception-based neutralisation, which is typically eliminated slowly and word by word. Interestingly, Macken (1980) eliminated Smith's velarisation rule (= 5a) in this latter manner.

6. See, e.g., Anderson (1985: 342 ff.) for a discussion and an assessment; some of NGP's leading ideas have resurfaced in a much different form in OT.

7. For general introductions to OT, we refer to Archangeli and Langendoen (1997), Kager (1999), and McCarthy (2001).

8. The duplication problem was recognised as early as *SPE* (Chomsky and Halle 1968: 382): 'Thus certain regularities are observed within lexical items as well as across boundaries – the rule governing voicing in obstruent sequences in Russian, for example – and to avoid duplication of such rules in the grammar it is necessary to regard them not as redundancy rules but as phonological rules that also happen to apply internally to a lexical item.' This solution to the duplication problem, to order morpheme structure rules among the other phonological rules, was shown to be insufficiently general by Kenstowicz and Kisseberth (1979), for the reason that it cannot handle cases in which a phonological rule is blocked from applying because its output would violate a static condition on the lexicon. After discussing examples from Russian and Tonkawa, Kenstowicz and Kisseberth (1979: 433) conclude: 'In both cases a constraint on UR affects the application of a phonological rule – by adjusting the output of the rule in one case and by preventing application of the rule in the other. An ordering solution works for the former but not the latter. Thus, the ordering solution cannot be accepted as a totally general solution to the duplication problem. It would seem that once a way is found to express the conspirational relation between MSRs and the application of phonological rules in examples such as the Tonkawa one, the duplication involved in examples such as Russian should fall out as a special subcase.' This sketches in essence the approach taken in OT: surface phonological constraints account for generalisations on lexical items, and also

function to trigger and block phonological changes with respect to the input – that is, alternations.

9. There is one case which is not covered by a possible word test based on identity mapping. Chain shifts (see Kirchner 1996 for an OT analysis) are mappings in which an input /A/ is mapped onto [B], while input /B/ maps onto [C]. If 'B' undergoes the test, it will change, and hence fail the test; however, [B] is also the legitimate output of the mapping /A/ ⇒ [B]).

10. The fact that Dutch phonology has an alternative way of repairing the input /kd/ (by regressive voicing assimilation) into [ɡd] is beside the point: both mappings involve a ranking indicated in (25).

11. In the OT literature, loanword adaptations have been argued to bear on various issues, such as the universality of markedness constraints, as opposed to the language-specific nature of rewrite rules. References include Yip (1993), Itô and Mester (1995), Paradis (1996), Paradis and LaCharité (1997), Gussenhoven and Jacobs (2000), LaCharité and Paradis (2000), and the contributions in this volume by Shinohara, and Davidson, Jusczyk, and Smolensky.

12. For another approach to the issue of the learnability of OT grammars, see Pulleyblank and Turkel (1998, 2000).

13. See also Demuth (1997), Curtin (2002), Curtin and Zuraw (forthcoming), and Pater and Werle (2001) on the use of these models to deal with variation in acquisition.

14. See Reynolds (1994) for a slightly different view of variation in OT.

References

Anderson, S. R. (1985). *Phonology in the Twentieth Century. Theories of Rules and Theories of Representations.* The University of Chicago Press.

Anttila, Arto (1997). *Variation in Finnish Phonology and Morphology.* Ph.D. dissertation, Stanford University.

Archangeli, D. (1997). Optimality Theory: an introduction to linguistics in the 1990s. In D. Archangeli and D. T. Langendoen (eds.) *Optimality Theory: an Overview.* Malden, Mass.: Blackwell Publ. 1–32.

Archangeli, D. and D. T. Langendoen (eds.) (1997). *Optimality Theory: an Overview.* Oxford: Basil Blackwell.

Archangeli, D. and D. Pulleyblank (1994). *Grounded Phonology.* Cambridge, Mass.: MIT Press.

Barlow, J. (1997). *A Constraint-Based Account of Syllable Onsets: Evidence from Developing Systems.* Ph.D. dissertation, Indiana University.

Barlow, J. and J. Gierut (1999). Optimality Theory in phonological acquisition. *Journal of Speech, Language, and Hearing Research* **42**. 1482–1498.

Beckman, J. (1998). *Positional Faithfulness.* Ph.D. dissertation, University of Massachusetts.

Benua, L. (1997). *Transderivational Identity: Phonological Relations Between Words.* Ph.D. dissertation, University of Massachusetts. [ROA-259] http://roa. rutgers.edu

Bernhardt, B. H. and J. P. Stemberger (1998). *Handbook of Phonological Development.* San Diego: Academic Press.

Berwick, R. (1985). *The Acquisition of Syntactic Knowledge*. Cambridge, Mass.: MIT Press.

Boersma, P. (1997). How we learn variation, optionality, and probability. *Proceedings of the Institute of Phonetic Sciences* **21**. Amsterdam. 43–58. [Also ROA 221, http://roa.rutgers.edu]

(1998). *Functional Phonology: Formalizing the Interactions between Articulatory and Perceptual Drives*. Ph.D. dissertation, University of Amsterdam, The Hague: Holland Academic Graphics.

(2000). Learning a grammar in Functional Phonology. In J. Dekkers, F. van der Leeuw and J. van de Weijer (eds.) *Optimality Theory: Syntax, Phonology, and Acquisition*. Oxford University Press. 465–523.

Boersma, P. and B. Hayes (2001). Empirical tests of the Gradual Learning Algorithm. *Linguistic Inquiry* **32**. 45–86.

Braine, M. D. S. (1976). Review of Smith (1973). *Lg* **52**. 489–498.

Broselow, E., S.-I. Chen, and C. Wang (1998). The Emergence of the Unmarked in second language phonology. *Studies in Second Language Acquisition* **20**. 261–280.

Burzio, L. (1996). Surface constraints versus Underlying Representation. In J. Durand and B. Laks (eds.) *Current Trends in Phonology: Models and Methods*. CNRS, Paris X, and University of Salford. University of Salford Publications.

Chomsky, N. (1959). A review of B. F. Skinner's *Verbal Behavior*. *Lg* **35**. 26–58.

(1965). *Aspects of the Theory of Syntax*. Cambridge, Mass.: MIT Press.

(1968). *Language and Mind* (1st edn), page reference to the 1973 enlarged edition. New York: Harcourt, Brace, and Jovanovich.

(1967). Some general properties of phonological rules. *Lg* **43**. 102–128.

(1981a). *Lectures on Government and Binding*. Dordrecht: Foris.

(1981b). On the representation of form and function. *The Linguistic Review* **1**. 3–40.

(1986). *Knowledge of Language: Its Nature, Origin and Use*. New York: Praeger.

Chomsky, N. and M. Halle (1968). *The Sound Pattern of English*. New York: Harper & Row.

Curtin, S. (2001). Children's early representations: evidence from production and perception. In the *Proceedings of the Holland Institute of Linguistics* (HILP 5), Potsdam, Germany.

(2002). *Representational Richness in Phonological Development*. Ph.D. dissertation, University of Southern California.

Curtin, S. and K. Zuraw (forthcoming). Explaining constraint demotion in a developing system. In the *Proceedings of Boston University Conference on Language Development*, Boston, Mass.

Demuth, K. (1995). Markedness and the development of prosodic structure. *NELS* **25**. 13–25. [Also ROA 50, http://roa.rutgers.edu]

(1996). Alignment, stress, and parsing in early phonological words. In B. Bernhardt, J. Gilbert and D. Ingram (eds.) *Proceedings of the UBC International Conference on Phonological Acquisition*. Somerville, Mass.: Cascadilla Press.

(1997). Multiple optimal outputs in acquisition. In B. Moren and V. Miglio (eds.) *University of Maryland Working Papers in Linguistics*. College Park: University of Maryland Department of Linguistics.

(2000). Prosodic constraints on morphological development. In J. Weissenborn and B. Höhle (eds.) *Approaches to Bootstrapping: Phonological, Syntactic and*

Neurophysiological Aspects of Early Language Acquisition, Vol. 2. Amsterdam: John Benjamins.

Dinnsen, D. A., J. A. Barlow, and M. L. Morrisette (1997). Long-distance place assimilation with an interacting error pattern in phonological acquisition. *Clinical Linguistics and Phonetics* **11**. 319–338.

Donegan, P. J. and D. Stampe (1979). The study of Natural Phonology. In D. A. Dinnsen (ed.) *Current Approaches to Phonological Theory.* Bloomington: Indiana University Press. 126–173.

Dresher, B. E. (1999). Charting the learning path: cues to parameter setting. *LI* **29**. 27–67.

Dresher, B. E. and J. Kaye (1990). A computational learning model for metrical phonology. *Cognition* **34**. 137–195.

Edwards, M. L. and L. Shriberg (1983). *Phonology: Applications in Communication Disorders.* San Diego, Calif.: College-Hill Press.

Ferguson, C. A., L. Menn, and C. Stoel-Gammon (eds.) (1992). *Phonological Development: Models, Research, Implications.* Parkton, Md.: York Press.

Fikkert, P. (1994). *On the Acquisition of Prosodic Structure.* The Hague: HAG.

Fletcher, P. and B. MacWhinney (eds.) (1995). *The Handbook of Child Language.* Cambridge, Mass.: Blackwell.

Goad, H. (1997). Consonant harmony in child language: an optimality-theoretic account. In S. J. Hannahs and M. Young-Scholten (eds.) *Focus on Phonological Acquisition.* Amsterdam: John Benjamins. 113–142.

Hale, M. and C. Reiss (1998). Formal and empirical arguments concerning phonological acquisition. *LI* **31**. 157–169.

Halle, M. (1983). On the origins of the distinctive features. In M. Halle (ed.) *Roman Jakobson: What He Taught Us. International Journal of Slavic Linguistics and Poetics, Vol. XXVII: Supplement.* Columbus, OH: Slavica Publ. 77–86.

Halle, M. and J.-R. Vergnaud (1987). *An Essay on Stress.* Cambridge, Mass.: MIT Press.

Hayes, B. (1980/81). *A Metrical Theory of Stress Rules.* Ph.D. dissertation, MIT, Cambridge, Mass. Revised version distributed by Indiana University Linguistics Club, Bloomington, Ind.

—— (1995). *Metrical Stress Theory: Principles and Case Studies.* Chicago: University of Chicago Press.

—— (1999). Phonetically-driven phonology: the role of Optimality Theory and inductive grounding. In M. Darnell, E. Moravscik, M. Noonan, F. Newmeyer and K. Wheatly (eds.) *Functionalism and Formalism in Linguistics, Vol. I: General Papers.* Amsterdam: John Benjamins. 243–285.

Hyman, L. (1970). The role of borrowing in the justification of phonological grammars. *Studies in African Linguistics* **1**. 1–48.

Ingram, D. (1974). Phonological rules in young children. *Journal of Child Language* **1**. 49–64.

—— (1989). *First Language Acquisition. Method, Description, and Explanation.* Cambridge: Cambridge University Press.

Itô, J. and R. A. Mester (1995). The core-periphery structure of the lexicon and constraints on reranking. In J. Beckman, L. Walsh Dickey and S. Urbanczyk (eds.) *Papers in Optimality Theory.* [University of Massachusetts Occasional Papers in

Linguistics 18.] Amherst, Mass.: Graduate Linguistic Student Association. 181–210.

Jacobs, H. and C. Gussenhoven (2000). Loan phonology: perception, salience, the lexicon and Optimality Theory. In J. Dekkers, F. van der Leeuw and J. van de Weijer (eds.) *Optimality Theory: Phonology, Syntax, and Acquisition.* Oxford University Press. 193–210.

Jakobson, R. (1941/1968). *Kindersprache, Aphasie und allgemeine Lautgesetze.* Uppsala Universitets Aarskrift. Translated by R. Keiler as *Child Language, Aphasia and Phonological Universals.* The Hague: Mouton.

Jusczyk, P. W. (1997). *The Discovery of Spoken Language.* Cambridge, Mass.: MIT Press.

Kager, R. (1999). *Optimality Theory.* Cambridge: Cambridge University Press.

Kaye, J. (1974). Opacity and recoverability in phonology. *Canadian Journal of Linguistics* **19**. 134–149.

(1989). *Phonology: a Cognitive View.* Hillsdale, New Jersey: Lawrence Erlbaum Assoc.

Kean, M. L. (1975). *The Theory of Markedness in Generative Grammar.* Ph.D. dissertation, MIT, Cambridge, Mass.

Kehoe, M. (1999). Truncation without shape constraints: the latter stages of phonological acquisition. *Language Acquisition* **8**:1. 23–67.

Kehoe, M. and C. Stoel-Gammon (1997). The acquisition of prosodic structure: an investigation of current accounts of children's prosodic development. *Lg* **73**. 113–144.

Kenstowicz, M. (1996). Base-identity and uniform exponence: alternatives to cyclicity. In J. Durand and B. Laks (eds.) *Current Trends in Phonology: Models and Methods.* CNRS, Paris X, and University of Salford. University of Salford Publications. 363–393. [ROA-103]

Kenstowicz, M. and C. Kisseberth (1979). *Generative Phonology: Description and Theory.* New York: Academic Press.

Kiparsky, P. (1968). Linguistic universals and linguistic change. In E. Bach and R. T. Harms (eds.) *Universals in Linguistic Theory.* New York: Holt, Rinehart and Winston. 171–204.

(1999). Paradigm effects and opacity. MS., Stanford University.

Kiparsky, P. and L. Menn (1977). On the acquisition of phonology. In J. Macnamara (ed.) *Language Learning and Thought.* New York: Academic Press.

Kirchner, R. (1996). Synchronic chain shifts in Optimality Theory. *LI* **27**. 341–350.

Kisseberth, C. W. (1970). On the functional unity of phonological rules. *LI* **1**. 291–306.

LaCharité, D. and C. Paradis (2000). Derivational residue: hidden rules in Optimality Theory. In J. Dekkers, F. van der Leeuw and J. van de Weijer (eds.) *Optimality Theory: Syntax, Phonology, and Acquisition.* Oxford: Oxford University Press. 211–233.

Levelt, C. (1995). Unfaithful kids: Place of Articulation patterns in early vocabularies. Colloquium presented at the University of Maryland.

Lombardi, L. (1999). Positional faithfulness and voicing assimilation in Optimality Theory. *NLLT* **17**. 267–302.

McCarthy, J. J. (1999a). Sympathy and phonological opacity. *Phonology* **16**. 331–399.

(1999b). Morpheme Structure Constraints and Paradigm Occultation. MS., University of Massachusetts at Amherst. *CLS* **32**.

(2001). *A Thematic Guide to Optimality Theory*. Cambridge: Cambridge University Press.

McCarthy, J. and A. Prince (1993). Prosodic Morphology I: constraint interaction and satisfaction. MS., University of Massachusetts, Amherst and Rutgers University. [To appear, Cambridge, Mass.: MIT Press. Technical report 3, Rutgers University Center for Cognitive Science.]

(1994). The emergence of the unmarked: Optimality in prosodic morphology. In M. Gonzàlez (ed.) *NELS* **24**. 333–379.

(1995). Faithfulness and reduplicative identity. In J. Beckman, L. Walsh Dickey and S. Urbanczyk (eds.) *Papers in Optimality Theory*. [University of Massachusetts Occasional Papers in Linguistics 18.] Amherst, Mass.: Graduate Linguistic Student Association. 249–384.

(1999). Faithfulness and identity in prosodic morphology. In R. Kager, H. van der Hulst and W. Zonneveld (eds.) *The Prosody–Morphology Interface*. Cambridge: Cambridge University Press. 218–309.

Macken, M. A. (1980). The child's lexical representation. *JL* **16**. 1–17.

(1995). Phonological acquisition. In J. A. Goldsmith (ed.) *The Handbook of Phonological Theory*. Cambridge, Mass.: Blackwell. 671–696.

Menn, L. (1971). Phonotactic rules in beginning speech. *Lingua* **26**. 225–241.

(1978). Phonological units in beginning speech. In A. Bell and J. B. Hooper (eds.) *Syllables and Segments*. Amsterdam: North-Holland. 157–171.

(1980). Phonological theory and child phonology. In G. H. Yeni-Komshian, J. F. Kavanagh, and C. A. Ferguson (eds.) *Child Phonology. Vol. 1: Production*. New York: Academic Press. 23–42.

Menn, L. and E. Matthei (1992). The 'Two-Lexicon' account of child phonology: looking back, looking ahead. In C. A. Ferguson, L. Menn and C. Stoel-Gammon (eds.) *Phonological Development: Models, Research, Implications*. Timonium, Md.: York Press. 211–248.

Nathan, G. S. (1984). Natural Phonology and interference in second language acquisition. In G. S. Nathan and M. E. Winters (eds.) *The Uses of Phonology: Proceedings of the First Conference on the Uses of Phonology* (Southern Illinois University Occasional Papers in Linguistics 12). Carbondale: Department of Linguistics, Southern Illinois University. 103–113.

Ohala, D. (1996). *Cluster Reduction and Constraints in Acquisition*. Ph.D. dissertation, University of Arizona.

(1999). The influence of sonority on children's cluster reductions. *Journal of Communication Disorders* **32**. 397–422.

Ota, M. (1999). *Phonological Theory and the Acquisition of Prosodic Structure: Evidence from Child Japanese*. Ph.D. dissertation, Georgetown University.

Paradis, C. (1996). The inadequacy of filters and faithfulness in loanword adaptation. In J. Durand and B. Laks (eds.) *Current Trends in Phonology: Models and Methods*. University of Salford Publications. 509–534.

Paradis, C. and D. LaCharité (1997). Preservation and minimality in loanword adaptation. *JL* **33**. 379–430.

Pater, J. (1997). Minimal violation and phonological development. *Language Acquisition* **6**. 201–253.

Pater, J. and J. Paradis (1996). Truncation without templates in child phonology. In A. Stringfellow, D. Cahana-Amitay, E. Hughes and A. Zukowski (eds.) *Proceedings of the 20th Annual Boston University Conference on Language Development.* Somerville, Mass.: Cascadilla Press.

Pater, J. and A. Werle (2001). Typology and variation in child consonant harmony. In C. Féry, A. Dubach Green and Ruben van de Vijver (eds.) *Proceedings of HILP5.* University of Potsdam. 119–139.

Piggott, G. L. (1988). The parameters of nasalization. MS., McGill University.

Prince, A. S. (1983). Relating to the Grid. *LI* **14**. 19–100.

Prince, A. and P. Smolensky (1993). Optimality Theory: constraint interaction in generative grammar. MS., Rutgers University, New Brunswick and University of Colorado, Boulder. [Technical report 2, Rutgers University Center for Cognitive Science. To appear, Cambridge, Mass.: MIT Press.]

Pulleyblank, D. and W. J. Turkel (1998). The logical problem of language acquisition in Optimality Theory. In P. Barbosa, D. Fox, P. Hagstrom, M. McGinnis and D. Pesetsky (eds.) *Is the Best Good Enough? Optimality and Competition in Syntax.* Cambridge, Mass.: MIT Press and MITWPL. 399–420.

(2000). Learning phonology: genetic algorithms and Yoruba tongue root harmony. In J. Dekkers, F. van der Leeuw and J. van de Weijer (eds.) *Optimality Theory: Phonology, Syntax and Acquisition.* Oxford: Oxford University Press. 554–591.

Reynolds, W. T. (1994). *Variation and Phonological Theory.* Ph.D. dissertation, University of Pennsylvania.

Rose, Y. (2000). *Headedness and Prosodic Licensing in the L1 Acquisition of Phonology.* Ph.D. dissertation, McGill University.

Smith, N. V. (1973). *The Acquisition of Phonology: a Case Study.* Cambridge: Cambridge University Press.

Smolensky, P. (1996a). *The Initial State and 'Richness of the Base' in Optimality Theory.* Technical Report JHU-CogSci-96-4, Cognitive Science Department, Johns Hopkins University. [ROA 154, http://ruccs.rutgers.edu/roa.html]

(1996b). On the comprehension/production dilemma in child language. *LI* **27**. 720–731. [ROA 118, http://ruccs.rutgers.edu/roa.html]

Stampe, D. (1969). The acquisition of phonetic representation. In R. I. Binnick *et al.* (eds.) *CLS* **5**. 443–454.

(1973a). *A Dissertation on Natural Phonology.* Ph.D. dissertation, University of Chicago.

(1973b). On chapter nine. In M. J. Kenstowicz and C. W. Kisseberth (eds.) *Issues in Phonological Theory.* The Hague: Mouton. 44–52.

Stemberger, J. P. (1993). Rule ordering in child phonology. In M. Eid and G. Iverson (eds.) *Principles and Prediction: the Analysis of Natural Language.* Amsterdam: Benjamins. 305–326.

Stonham, John (1990). *Current Issues in Morphological Theory.* Ph.D. dissertation, Stanford University.

Tesar, Bruce (1995). Computational Optimality Theory. Ph.D. dissertation, University of Colorado at Boulder.

Tesar, Bruce and Paul Smolensky (1993). The Learnability of Optimality Theory: an Algorithm and Some Basic Complexity Results. Technical Report cu-cs-678-93, Department of Computer Science, University of Colorado at Boulder. Rod-2.

(1998). Learnability in Optimality Theory. *LI* **29**. 229–268.

(2000). *Learnability in Optimality Theory.* Cambridge, Mass.: MIT Press.

Velleman, S. L. and M. M. Vihman (2000). The optimal initial state. Paper read at the Annual Meeting of the Linguistic Society of America, Chicago, January.

Vihman, M. M. (1996). *Phonological Development: the Origins of Language in the Child*. Cambridge, Mass.: Blackwell.

Yip, M. (1993). Cantonese loanword phonology and optimality theory. *Journal of East Asian Linguistics* **2**. 262–291.

Zoll, C. (1998). Positional asymmetries and licensing. MS., Cambridge, Mass.: MIT.

2   Saving the baby: making sure that old data survive new theories*

Lise Menn

1.   Introduction

At the peak of the influence of Generative Phonology, Charles Ferguson and Carol Farwell of the Stanford Child Phonology Project published a troubling observation (Ferguson and Farwell 1975), based on longitudinal data: they showed that the construct of 'phoneme' did not (indeed, does not) do justice to the patterns of variation in some young children's production of speech sounds (see also Menyuk *et al.* 1986). But data which, like these, do not fit any recognisable theory are like a strange tool that comes without instructions, or an unfamiliar spice for which one has no recipe. They stay in a box, untouched. Perhaps they are retrieved from storage when some use for them comes along; but more likely, they are only noticed lurking there after something similar has been rediscovered somewhere else, at a time and place where the odd item can at last be assimilated (cf. the rediscovery of Mendelian heredity).

Once we do have a new beautiful theory that can handle data which were previously intractable, we tend to go on a binge: we try to show that it can do almost everything. That is good – we have to check out its power. But we also tend to shove all the data that do not fit the new theory into that storage box, whether or not they were well handled by a previous approach.

What every field needs, I think, is an inventory – a kind of second-order data base. What old unassimilated results are in the storage box? What's been shoved back in there recently? Let's bring them out and highlight them as exhilarating challenges, like David Hilbert's famous list of unsolved problems of mathematics, or the Guinness list of world records. Reality is richer and more complex than any of its approximations; for the scientist, as well as for the developing child, glee at what we have just learned to do soon has to be replaced by a new round of efforts to approximate the complex reality-out-there.

It is, of course, not the case that a theory needs to explain all the phenomena related to its domain. I think that a number of the properties of early phonology which I shall describe are probably not data that Optimality Theory (OT; Prince and Smolensky 1993) should try to account for – for example, the problem that I started out with, of speech sounds that fail to be phonemes in any normal sense, because they are conditioned by the lexical items they appear in rather than by any phonological property of those items. (This behaviour is rare but not unknown for adult language – consider the huge range of phonetic variation of the word *no* vs. the smaller range of variation of the word *know* in its normal uses vs. the different set of variations in the filler phrase *y'know*.) But by bringing my inventory to the attention of current OT theorists, I hope to encourage metatheoretical reflection: what is OT about, what can and can't it account for, and why can it account for some things but not others? In other words, what is the proper domain of OT, and what should people be using other tools to account for?

This chapter presents an overview of the history of the study of constraints in child phonology, and then a start at a Historical Annotated Inventory of Things We Know About Child Phonology. I shall pay attention both to the necessity for a constraint-based theory like OT, and to the types of data that I think currently pose challenges to this powerful new paradigm. As I am not active in this rapidly developing area, I am sure that some of the problems I raise will have been dealt with – perhaps in several ways – since the publication of the OT papers I have been able to study. But what I have been requested to do is to provide a historical perspective on OT as a theory of phonological development for this volume, and as a member of the second generation of research in child phonology (principally, in the US, the students of Charles Ferguson and Paula Menyuk), I have been around long enough to do that. Again, I am not an OT expert; if the theory has already been enriched so that it can deal with some of the issues I raise, so much the better for OT!

2. A short history: fifty years of trying to handle output constraints in phonology and child phonology

Some readers may not be aware that constraint-based approaches have a considerable history in phonology before Smolensky and Prince (Prince and Smolensky 1993) created a tractable formalism to express them, and thus finally made them acceptable to mainstream theorists. The existence of language-specific constraints on word forms has been clear for a long time. In the mid-1950s, Robert Stockwell coined the term *phonotactics*, which he used at an unpublished Georgetown Roundtable meeting to describe such phenomena as constraints on permissible consonant clusters (Stockwell, email, 6 October 2000). Phoneme-sequence constraints as potential language universals were surveyed by Alan Bell (1971) in his dissertation under Joseph Greenberg; and a number of phoneticians in the 1970s and 1980s investigated acoustic and articulatory reasons for the existence of such constraints (for recent treatments of this topic, see Kawasaki-Fukumori 1992, Ohala and Kawasaki-Fukumori 1997).

The big problem in dealing with phonotactic constraints was, as I have indicated, not the notion or the motivation, but the formalism. The rewrite rules of generative grammar became available to phonology with the publication of Halle (1959), and swept over the linguistic world much as OT has done. However, while rewrite rules can capture roughly the same regularities as output constraints, their focus on input-and-change makes the constraints themselves hard to see. Jakobson (1941/1968), the first linguistic theorist to take child language seriously, did not attempt to deal with constraints beyond the level of phoneme inventory; however, his student Lawrence Jones published an approach to a generative phonotactics of English called 'English phonotactic structure and first-language acquisition' (the invocation of language acquisition in the title was purely speculative). Jones's approach was to capture the structure of English words by generating them from a 'Word' node using rewrite rules, just as generative syntax captured sentence structure by rules starting from an 'S' node (Jones 1967). I happened to hear Jones lecture on this work at about that time, while I was analysing the 'Daniel' acquisition diary data, and I was tremendously excited. With his help, I cast my data in his formalism, thereby producing the rule-jungle called 'Phonotactic rules in beginning speech' (Menn, 1971).

However, Jones's formalism was a methodological dead end, because it was an intuition-killer. First, it was just as difficult to get a sense of what the output constraints were like as it is with any other rewrite rule formalism; the output constraints still are formal epiphenomena. Second, word-generation rules are also no help in showing the relation between underlying morphemes and output phonemes, which is the other thing we want to know about. Capturing that relation requires morpheme-based rules, such as the rewrite rules of classical generative phonology.

Nevertheless, Jones's approach did call attention to the importance of constraints on the output form of the word. With its help, one could capture the overall difference between the child's word and its adult model like this: the child's output word-grammar contains much less information than the adult form, in that there are fewer choices among phonemes, fewer phonemes per word, and fewer admissible sequences of phonemes. The child form has less to specify, less to remember, fewer articulatory movements to control.

This was a move towards explanation in less grand terms than Jakobson's – a common-sense (or, if you prefer, empiricist) reaction to 'Laws of Irreversible Solidarity'. (It also reflected my caution as a pre-doctoral researcher who was working with a one-child data set.) No innate knowledge or pattern was invoked; constraints were seen as the outcome of a limited ability to process articulatory instructions. The information-theoretic formulation also avoided appealing to 'ease of articulation' explanations, because after all, we had no independent evidence that what the child said was 'easier' than the adult model (indeed, we still have none). On the contrary, what we needed to ask was: what kind of creature is the child such that *guck* may be easier than *duck*? And why do some children prefer *dut*, others *da*, etc.? This is the task that I think the field is still about.

Meanwhile, David Ingram (1974), working with Charles Ferguson, developed a much more tractable approach to child phonology, dealing with the constraints in terms of Stanley's morpheme structure conditions (1967). After his example, child phonologists used rules only to derive child forms from adult ones. (For more details, see Vihman 1996: chapter 2.) And the field soon had an important caution about constraints to bear in mind: the fact that not all of a child's rules at a given time can be accounted for by constraints that are synchronically valid. Some of the rules are needed to capture held-over patterns of dealing with adult sounds that were established earlier in the child's development. A famous case is the *puzzle-puddle-pickle* story from Smith (1973), reanalysed brilliantly by Macken (1980); in Pater's OT bibliography (2000) an unpublished paper by Dinnsen *et al.* (2000) is cited that now attempts to deal with this phenomenon in OT.

Rules that are not motivated by synchronic constraints thus pose an important challenge to all constraint-based approaches. Indeed, the constant changes in a developing phonology create problems that even a typical rule-based approach cannot handle without much *ad-hoc* machinery. Smith, Macken (*op. cit.*) and many others followed mainstream Generative Phonology in assuming a single underlying form; for child phonology, this was taken to be approximately equal to the adult surface phonemic form. The rules then performed an on-line mapping from adult to child form. Such a model is able to capture the regularities of mappings from adult surface form to child's produced form, but it is unable to capture output constraints – also, it cannot account for phonological idioms and other lags in updating the mapping. It is also unable to handle 'cross-talk' between forms (rule interaction), as is true for any generative model.

To handle phonological idioms and other rule-updating lags, I developed a 'two-lexicon' model, articulating it with help from Paul Kiparsky (Menn 1976, Kiparsky and Menn 1977). Such models assume a stored input representation which is close to the adult surface form, plus an output representation which is derived from the input form, but also stored. (The term 'two lexicons' is slightly misleading, since only a single semantic representation is postulated.) The stored output form is accessed on-line, and updated from the input form irregularly. The two-lexicon model yielded some improvement: in addition to capturing the regularities of mappings from adult surface form to child's produced form and lags in updating the mapping, it provided a conceptual framework for the child's eventual construction of abstract underlying forms. However, it was still unable to capture output constraints, 'cross-talk', competition between alternative rule-governed forms for the same word, or the operation of output constraints across word boundaries (Menn and Matthei 1992).

Meanwhile, in adult phonology, the problem of constraints remained a steady, if almost subterranean, rumble. Within a few years of the publication of *The Sound Pattern of English* (Chomsky and Halle 1968), Kisseberth (1970) was calling attention to the fact many rules were 'motivated', rather than arbitrary – that is, that generative rules typically formed 'conspiracies' to get rid of consonant clusters, final consonants, or other sequences of phonemes which would violate a language's phonotactic constraints. Therefore, leaving constraints as formal epiphenomena clearly failed to capture a basic fact about language. However, there was at the time no way to fine-tune the operation of output constraints well enough actually to replace generative rules, nor any thought of doing so.

During the same period, David Stampe (1969) was trying to account for the intuitively obvious difference between 'natural' phonological rules – those that could be seen as reflexes of the 'natural' way the articulatory system works (flapping, final devoicing) when speakers are not being careful – and 'non-natural' ones – those whose original naturalness, if any, has been obscured by subsequent changes in the conditioning factors. Stampe (1969) claimed that natural rules were innate and unlearned, while other rules had to be learned during the course of language acquisition. His account thus attempted to link natural fast-speech rules and other shallow rules of Generative Phonology to the markedness constraints that operate shortly after the onset of speech (for a critique, see Kiparsky and Menn 1977). This view of the acquisition of phonology as the suppression or re-ordering of innate natural processes (see also Edwards and Shriberg 1983) is logically equivalent to some – perhaps much – of what is now considered to be the re-ordering of markedness and faithfulness constraints (cf. Pater 1997).

As a deterministic theory, Stampe's approach shares a key weakness with all others of that type, including those of Jakobson, of Dresher and Van der Hulst (1995), and of Rice and Avery (1995): it simply cannot handle U-shaped curves. Daniel, for example, did not show nasal harmony until after he had learned to say several words which violated it (Menn 1971, 1983). How could a child in a deterministic theory start out able to say 'down' without nasal harmony, and then regress to the point of being constrained to say [næwn]? And, of course, Stampe could not handle child phonology rules that did not resemble fast-speech processes, such as consonant harmony.

By 1980, output constraints in child phonology had been observed by several researchers. Reviewing theories of the acquisition of phonology, Menn (1980) noted:

Child speech, from the possibly prephonemic early stage and on through perhaps the first nine months of speaking, is subject to severe output constraints, stronger than anything found in adult phonology . . . Rewrite-rule notation can handle such phenomena (Langendoen 1968), but only by brute force (Clements 1976), not perspicuously . . . This is the area in which generative phonology was seriously deficient with respect to British (Firthian) prosodic phonology, and where Waterson's 1971 prosodic approach to child phonology yielded important insights: For example, that the child might be seeking out whole-word patterns in the adult language that were similar to whole-word patterns that the child had learned to produce. (p. 31)

. . . the child's 'tonguetiedness', that overwhelming reality which Stampe and Jakobson both tried to capture with their respective formal structures, could be handled more felicitously if one represented the heavy articulatory limitations of the child by the formal device of output constraints . . . The child's gradual mastery of articulation then is formalized as a relaxation of those constraints . . . (pp. 35–36)

As we have noted, child-phonology constraints include some that apply to various adult languages (prohibition of consonant clusters, widespread but not universal prohibition of syllable-final consonants, severe restrictions on word-final consonants, weak forms of vowel harmony), but they also include some that apply to adults rarely (nasal harmony, i.e., prohibition of nasal and non-nasal consonants within the word). Some are not present in adult language at all: consonant place harmony, that is, prohibition of consonants having different places of articulation within a word; discontinuous vowel sequence constraints; and consonant sequence templates. An attested discontinuous vowel sequence constraint is 'first vowel of a disyllable higher than second vowel' (Vihman 1981); a well-known consonant template is 'first consonant labial, second consonant dental' (Macken 1979); and another is CVjVC (Priestly 1977). These notably apply to whole words in ways that dramatically reduce the number of within-word choices a speaker can make. Presumably, adult languages cannot afford such constraints because they impose extremely severe restrictions on the number of possible words in the lexicon (unless they grow to enormous lengths).

An elaboration of the constraint problem (Menn 1983) addressed a more general audience who could still not be presumed to find the data familiar:

. . . it will help to develop some terms for dealing with sets of rules which appear to serve some common function. Suppose none of the forms produced by a child contain consonant clusters, or that none have final stops, or that none have disharmonic [consonant] sequences. A statement that a particular sound-pattern does not appear in a corpus and is not expected to appear if we get a larger sample is a statement of an output constraint. Adult languages have output constraints as well; consonant clusters are absent from many languages, and every language has restrictions on how many and what kind of consonants form a pronounceable cluster (Bell 1971). Vowel harmony, present in quite a number of languages, is also describable as an output constraint.

> Following Kisseberth (1970), when we have a set of rules that all contribute to elim-
> inating sound patterns which would violate a particular output constraint, we say that
> those rules form a conspiracy . . .
> Conspiracies of rules are not the only devices that children use to maintain output
> constraints, however. Selection strategies may also contribute – children may avoid adult
> words which violate a constraint . . . (Menn 1983: 16–17)

However, I find a formal account unsatisfying unless it can be interpreted
psycholinguistically. So I continued:

> . . . it is time to take a critical look at the notion [of output constraint] itself. So far,
> all we have is description, not explanation. But once we organize the data in this way,
> a plausible explanation of the data leaps out at us: this child is modifying unfamiliar
> sound patterns to make them like the ones he has already mastered. *And that means the
> child has to learn sound patterns, not just sounds.* Again, output constraints are only
> descriptive devices; what they describe are those sound patterns a child has mastered
> vs. those he has not. That is why words which do not fit the constraints are almost all
> avoided or modified. That is the central thesis of this chapter . . . (p. 19)

One might think that this was merely a way of avoiding commitment to
the construct of output constraint, since it was not yet widely accepted and
it belonged to no phonological theory then articulated. But there were some
properties of the data that the construct could not handle, and which are still
problematic today. One is the idiosyncratic individuality of some of the constraints which seem to develop from favourite babble patterns (Vihman 1996).
Another is the fact, already noted, that some of them may not be present at the
onset of speech. This delayed onset of presumably innate behaviours was also
a problem for Stampe's notion of innate natural processes. And so I added:

> . . . one cannot explain lexical exceptions [to rules] or overgeneralizations within a theory
> [which holds] that the acquisition of phonology is purely a matter of overcoming output
> constraints, as I might have tempted you to think . . . Such a theory would be subject to
> exactly the same inadequacies as Jakobson's in these cases . . . if we want a functional,
> explanatory theory . . . , we need a theory which is more complicated. (pp. 28–29)

To be more explicit: there are standard hard problems for theories that operate
only with across-the-board changes – whether these are conceptualised as the
acquisition of phonemic contrasts, the suppression of natural processes, or the
re-ordering of constraints. One of these is accounting for lexical exceptions to
general rules/constraints, like progressive phonological idioms (special cases
of words that violate otherwise general constraints) and regressive overgeneralisation (words that escape a constraint and then later become subject to it). How
can a constraint be innate if it neither applies from the beginning nor marks a
maturational advance?

A related hard problem is how to handle fossils (regressive phonological
idioms), that is, forms that do not 'update', but instead maintain an older

mapping from the adult form to the child form, even though new forms are being made with a newer mapping. For example, a child whose newer vocabulary shows that she has learned to overcome consonant harmony may still use harmonised forms for older words – that is, the words that she began to use before she was able to violate that constraint. Again, this was the problem that stimulated the development of a 'two-lexicon' model; either the output forms or the mapping rules that derive them must be stored.

So much for history; for those who wish to look further into the substantial older literature on child phonology, I suggest starting with the handbook chapters by Gerken (1994) or Menn and Stoel-Gammon (1995), and then for a more comprehensive look at pre-OT work, Yeni-Komshian *et al.* (1980), Ferguson *et al.* (1992), and Vihman (1996), and going back to the primary sources cited therein. For emergence of prosody in production, see Snow and Stoel-Gammon (1994) and papers by Gerken and colleagues (e.g., Gerken and McIntosh 1993, Gerken 1994). For more recent work in connectionist modelling approaches to OT, see Stemberger and Bernhardt (1999); for other computational modelling approaches, see Lindblom (1992), Plaut and Kello (1999), Gupta and Dell (1999), and Markey (1994). A review emphasising both constraints and autosegmental analysis is Bernhardt and Stemberger (1998).

3.   How does OT meet the challenges of classic acquisition data?

I shall now turn to OT, continuing to focus on the development of segmental production. As for perception, OT-relevant recent results may be summarised by noting that the children who are beginning to produce words have already learned most of the prosody, phonetic inventory, and phonotactic constraints of the ambient language(s) as auditory targets (Jusczyk 1997, Hayes this volume). Furthermore, by the time intelligible speech begins, children have begun to modify their babble towards the probability of those sounds in the ambient language (see Vihman *et al.* 1985, Vihman 1996, Velleman and Vihman 2000); so even at the time they are producing their very first words, children cannot be said to be in an 'initial state' with respect to acquiring phonology.

I take the agenda of OT to be the description of the forms speakers produce in terms of the ranking of constraints that an output form should satisfy if possible, accounting for cross-linguistic, dialectal (and possibly lower?) levels of variability in terms of differences in constraint rankings. The adult state of knowledge is taken to develop from the child's initial state by re-ranking constraints, since this is the only available formal device, at least within the initial versions of the theory. There are disagreements about the source of the constraints – crudely, innate Universal Grammar vs. articulatory/acoustic/psycho-linguistic factors. When the adult language maintains rules that cannot be handled by the output constraints that are in force synchronically (e.g., velar softening and a number of other non-productive rules in English), these constraints cannot express the fact that these regularities still give redundancy to the lexicon – but that problem for OT extends beyond the scope of early acquisition, and therefore of this chapter.

4.   An Annotated Inventory: some things we know about the early development of phonology, based on longitudinal production studies

In this Annotated Inventory, items which I think directly support a constraint-based approach are marked with ✓; those which pose significant challenges to the OT approaches (that I am aware of) are marked with *. Again, there may be developments by various OT authors which already deal felicitously with the phenomena that I list. In some instances, I have in fact been informed that this is the case, but I am not yet in a position to judge for myself the adequacy of the author's treatment, and so I leave that to the reader.

4.1   Regularity/incompleteness of regularity/*mushiness

Most young children display regular context-dependent mappings from adult surface form to child's produced form. Others operate, for at least part of their output, by Template Matching (see next item) rather than using regular input-output mappings. *However, some children are much 'mushier' in their holistic approximations to adult productions; these phenomena are rarely written about because they are hard to describe in any theory (Peters 1977). Boersma and Pater, in editorial comments on a draft of this chapter, indicate that recent OT elaborations involving unranked constraints, continuous constraint ranking with noisy evaluation, and other devices can deal with variable patterns (they cite, e.g., Boersma and Hayes 1999, Boersma and Levelt 2000, Anttila 1997, and Ito and Mester 1997). These accounts could be tested against the data in the Peters paper.

4.2   ✓ Template Matching

Some young children create output forms adhering to phonotactic constraints by selecting phonemes from the target word (Macken 1978, 1992, Priestly 1977) in ways that cannot be captured by ordinary generative rules. For the particular Spanish-speaking child of Macken (1978, also presented in Macken 1992: 265), roughly: 'If a target word (CV)CVC(V) contains a labial and an alveolar, make the labial the first consonant and the alveolar the second consonant; discard all other consonants.' Her forms included *zapato* > [patda], *Fernando* > [wanno], *manzano* > [mana], *pelota* > [patda], *sopa* > [pwaeta], *elefante* > [batte]

(fricatives became stops if attempted). *Note again that constraints like this are not found in adult languages; this may be a problem for OT.

4.3   ✓ Relation of mapping rules and constraints

Mapping rules mostly seem to exist to guarantee that the output satisfies statable constraints, such as consonant cluster restrictions.

*However, some rules seem to exist to preserve phonemic contrasts (not identities); these have nothing to do with current output constraints on the child's language (Macken 1980, 1992, Smith 1973), although they may have been motivated by constraints that the child has since overcome. For example, Ingram's Jennika (1975), at a time when she had no low-vowel contrast, pre-served the contrast between *hot* and *hat* by rendering *hot* as [at] and *hat* as [ak]. Boersma (editorial comments) indicates that adding contrast preservation con-straints can handle this. And determining the solutions that an individual child will come up with are probably the kind of thing that OT should not be expected to handle. After all, we do not expect a diachronic theory to specify truly 'wild' developments such as determining which morphemes will be recruited into a suppletive paradigm.

4.4   *Delayed emergence of constraints

Enough has been said about this already, and it is closely related to the next item.

4.5   *Regression: U-shaped developmental curves

Most changes over time bring the child's pronunciation closer to the adult model, but there are U-shaped curves: in addition to early accurate *down* becoming /næwn/ after Daniel invented his nasal harmony rule, there are progres-sive phonological idioms which fail to accord with general current patterns (Moskowitz 1970, re-analysing data from Leopold 1939–1949). To model this with OT requires some interesting fiddling with constraint re-ordering, although it is not impossible.

4.6   *Lags in updating/inertia of the system

Progressive and regressive phonological idioms persist for varying periods of time (Moskowitz 1970); new mappings show up on new words, and spread slowly to older words. Boersma suggests handling this with separate OT gram-mars for perception and production, but I think there will be a problem with the fact that some items lag and some do not. Some relevant data are reviewed in Menn and Matthei (1992).

4.7   ✓ *Lexical variations in form*

There can be free variation between alternative forms for the same word (*boat* =
/bowt/, /dowp/); this problem for the two-lexicon model could be handled by
OT with equally ranked constraints (Menn and Matthei 1992). *Possibly more
difficult to handle is contextually conditioned alternation. Sometimes the choice
among output forms can depend on the adjacent word in a phrase (Donahue
1986, Matthei 1989); Pater (editorial comments) suggests that alternation can
be handled by OT if constraints apply to the word in context.

4.8   ✓ *Articulatory/acoustic naturalness*

Consonant cluster simplification, various 'natural processes' such as final devoicing, and omission of unstressed syllables are well-known in both L1 and
L2.

4.9   ✓ ? *Existence of non-natural rules/constraints*

Templates can require sequences of places of articulation, such as the labial-
vowel-dental-vowel pattern cited above (Macken 1978). This phenomenon, as
well as the use of 'dummy' syllables, appears to need explanation in terms of
reducing the amount of information that must be individually specified for the
word. OT could simply stipulate specific templates.

*This does, however, become a problem if all constraints must be innate –
the same problem that we face with items 4, 5, and 12.

4.10   ✓ *Existence of whole-word constraints*

These include consonant harmony, vowel harmony, and also templates. Harmony rules can be seen as a special case of limitation on the amount of information that the child is able to maintain in an output word; the most general
formulation is that only one position of articulation may be specified per word.
This general constraint may also be realised by deletion of one of the consonants, or by replacing one of them with an /h/ or a glottal stop as a 'dummy'
consonant.

Levelt (1994) shows that consonant harmony in her Dutch data can be accounted for by rules affecting only contiguous segments, as the children's consonants in harmonised CVC forms could be predicted by the intervening vowel.
However, this is not the case in English (see table 2.1, also Pater 1997). This
difference between the languages might be due to the fact that vowel roundness
is redundant with front/back position in English, whereas roundness must be
specified independently of backness in Dutch. Dutch-speaking children who

Table 2.1. *Word patterns showing consonant harmony independent of vowel features in Daniel (Menn 1971)*

	Labial harmony			Alveolar harmony		Velar harmony		
	front V	*central V*	*back V*	*front V*	*back V*	*front V*	*central V*	*back V*
high	bip 'jeep'		muf 'move'	dit 'meat'	dut 'boot'	gɪg 'pig'		gʊk 'book'
mid		bʌb 'tub'	bop 'boat'		dot 'boat'		gʌŋ 'tongue'	gɔg 'dog'
low	bæf 'bath'	bap 'stop'		næwn 'down' næt 'snap'		gæk 'cracker'		

have mastered these features as independent specifications on vowels might well spread them to adjacent consonants. (Testing this proposed explanation would be a nice topic for cross-linguistic comparison.)

4.11 ✓ *Least-effort (jaw-only) articulatory control*

Some researchers have found extensive correlation between early consonants and the adjacent vowel (MacNeilage and Davis 1990), which can be explained by the tongue riding passively on the jaw; others have not found this, or find it weakly (Oller and Steffens 1994). Presumably, the phenomenon is real but variable across children. Like consonant harmony, this is an example of a constraint that is present in early child language, but is too vocabulary-limiting to appear (except perhaps as a statistical tendency) in adult language. The fact that these constraints do not exist in adult language is not a problem if OT can allow a constraint to be so deeply submerged that it has no effect on adult language or on L2. Pater (editorial comments) points out that McCarthy and Prince (1994) predict that even low-ranked constraints can have effects in particular phonological environments.

4.12 * *'Cross-talk' between forms*

Similar words appear to exert mutual influence on each other during an early period of rule-formation. Examples from longitudinal work (Menn 1976/1979: Jacob) showed the vowels of *tea, key, table,* and *tape* influencing each other, resulting eventually in a rule /ei/ > [ij]; later, *bus, bike, eyes, ice* somehow interacted so that *bus* became /bajs/, *bang* became [bajŋ], and *mess* became [majs] (Menn and Matthei 1992: 228–231).

4.13 ? *Gradual acquisition of contrasts*

Feature contrasts are not acquired across-the-board; for example, Jacob (Menn 1976/1979) had at one point the following output phonemic inventory:

    b
t   d
k

Pater (editorial comments) suggests that this would be tractable, given appropriate feature co-occurrence constraints.

4.14 *Continuity with babble and individual differences*

The phonological patterns of late babble are very similar to those of early words within a given child, as compared with the greater differences across children, except for children who are conspicuously late talkers (Stoel-Gammon 1989; Vihman *et al.* 1994, Vihman 1996). This should not be a problem for OT if ranking of constraints can be carried out during babble – that is, before the child has specific words as output targets.

4.15   *? Probability envelopes

Variations across children are common, but, as in many other natural patterns, the variations are not equiprobable. Some patterns, some rules, and/or some constraints are more probable, and others are less probable. Boersma (editorial comment) suggests that 'if the ranking of faithfulness constraints is based on the amount of perceptual confusion, and the ranking of structural constraints is based on the amount of articulatory effort, these constraints will be ranked around cross-linguistic averages, leading to statistical tendencies'. This sounds like a promising approach.

4.16   ? Development of abstract underlying forms

Phonology exists largely to explain allomorphy, and the standard approach since Chomsky and Halle (1968) has been to do so by postulating for each morpheme, wherever possible, an abstract single underlying form from which the surface shape is derived. Therefore the input to constraints in the adult is an abstract string of morphemes specified at some sort of phonemic level. But children must discover that different surface forms are allomorphs of the same morpheme (Kiparsky and Menn 1977); indeed, beginning speakers are still trying to segment what they hear into morphemes and words (Peters 1983, 1985). The 'input to the constraints' for the child must therefore be a phonemicisation of the collection of adult outputs, not an abstract morpheme or even a particular concrete representative of a set of allomorphs. Somehow, this input must become more abstract as the child discovers the allomorphic patterns of the ambient language, but it is not clear within OT how this psychological shift happens. Boersma (editorial comment) indicates that several scholars have been working on this problem.

5.   Conclusion: description and explanation

Summarising the * and ✓ annotations of the Inventory section above, the strengths of OT, unsurprisingly, seem to be in dealing with children's phonotactic constraints as evidenced by templates and harmony, and in being able to handle both natural and unnatural rules. Major challenges are posed by mushy and non-phonemicised early outputs, by rules that are no longer constraint-based, by U-shaped developmental curves, by lags in updating the adult–child mappings, and by rule cross-talk. Possibly more tractable are the issues of constraints that operate across word boundaries, the need to explain the probability envelope of variation across individuals, and the need to differentiate 'input' in the sense of 'the adult form the child is trying to approximate' from 'input' in the sense of 'abstract strings of concatenated morphemes to be parsed'.

However, if OT does not claim to be a Theory of Everything, there is no reason why it should be expected to meet *all* these challenges. The solutions to many of them probably lie outside the scope of OT. I do not think that it is likely that any single unified theory will be able to handle all the phenomena of the acquisition of phonology; expecting this would be an impossible standard for OT or any of its competitors. Furthermore, there is no reason to believe that concepts developed to handle only adult phenomena will be adequate for describing acquisition; the unskilled speaker is not just a miniature of the skilled speaker. The stance taken by Ferguson and Farwell (1975: 437) is no less valid today: 'Our approach is to try to understand children's phonological development in itself in order to improve our phonological theory, even if this requires new constructs for the latter.'

Instead of a single unified theory, I suggest that several good partial theories (or models or accounts) are needed, each handling various aspects of the phenomena of our Inventory. Each of these theories/models/accounts should be psychologically responsible; by this, I mean that they should be mappable into psycho-linguistic concepts, for at some level the psycho-linguistic constructs of auditory similarity, articulatory control, memory, maintenance of distinction, generalisation, and information flow are the primitives of phonological explanation. Below these, in turn, lie the mechanics of neural computation, sensory response, and muscle innervation; it must be at this level that the probabilities of finding the various types of constraints and mappings are determined.

It may be that some facts about phonology are indeed not explainable in such psychological terms, but to concede this until one is forced to do so is a counsel of despair. Calling a rule 'natural' or a constraint 'innate' is like calling a hurricane 'an act of God'; having said so, one knows no more than before about how to predict it or to understand its causes. We can do better than that.

Acknowledgements

*I am grateful to my students George Figgs, Holly Krech, Matthew Maraist, and Hiromi Sumiya for their thoughtful discussion of many issues raised above; to Shelley Velleman and Marilyn Vihman for sharing the manuscript of their Linguistic Society of America (LSA) paper; to Shelley Velleman and LouAnn Gerken for comments on an early draft of this paper; to Bruce Hayes for making a draft of his chapter for this volume available on the web; and to Bill Bright, as always, for editorial advice throughout.

In later revisions, I am happy to acknowledge the extensive and helpful comments of Marilyn Vihman, Joe Pater, and Paul Boersma.

References

Anttila, A. (1997). Deriving variation from grammar. In F. Hinskens, R. van Hout and L. Wetzels (eds.) *Variation, Change and Phonological Theory*. Amsterdam: Benjamins.

Bell, A. (1971). Some patterns of occurrence and formation of syllable structures. In *Working Papers on Linguistic Universals* **6**. 23–137. Stanford University Linguistics Department.

Bernhardt, B. H. and J. P. Stemberger (1998). *Handbook of Phonological Development*. San Diego: Academic Press.

Boersma, P. and B. Hayes (1999). Empirical tests of the gradual learning algorithm. [ROA 348, http://roa.rutgers.edu] Published version, (2001) *LI* **32**. 45–86.

Boersma, P. and C. Levelt (2000). Gradual constraint-ranking learning algorithm predicts acquisition order. *Proceedings of Child Language Research Forum* **30**. 229–237. Stanford University.

Chomsky, N. and M. Halle (1968). *The Sound Pattern of English*. New York: Harper and Row.

Clements, G. N. (1976). Vowel harmony in non-linear generative phonology. MS., Linguistics Department, Harvard University.

Dinnsen, D. A., K. M. O'Connor, and J. A. Gierut (2000). An optimality-theoretic solution to the *puzzle-puddle-pickle* problem. MS., Indiana University.

Donahue, M. (1986). Phonological constraints on the emergence of two-word utterances. *Journal of Child Language* **13**. 209–218.

Dresher, B. E. and H. van der Hulst (1995). Global determinacy and learnability in phonology. In J. Archibald (ed.) *Phonological Acquisition and Phonological Theory*. Hillsdale, N.J.: Erlbaum. 1–22.

Edwards, M. L. and L. Shriberg (1983). *Phonology: Applications in Communicative Disorders*. San Diego: College-Hill Press.

Ferguson, C. A. and C. B. Farwell (1975). Words and sounds in early language acquisition. *Lg* **51**. 419–439.

Ferguson, C. A., L. Menn, and C. Stoel-Gammon (eds.) (1992). *Phonological Development: Models, Research, Implications*. Timonium, Md.: York Press.

Gerken, L. (1994). Child phonology: past research, present questions, future directions. In M. A. Gernsbacher (ed.) *Handbook of Psycholinguistics*. San Diego: Academic Press. 781–820.

Gerken, L. and B. J. McIntosh (1993). The interplay of function morphemes and prosody in early language. *Developmental Psychology* **29**. 448–457.

Gupta, P. and G. S. Dell (1999). The emergence of language from serial order and procedural memory. In B. MacWhinney (ed.) *The Emergence of Language*. Hillsdale, N.J.: Erlbaum. 447–482.

Halle, M. (1959). *The Sound Pattern of Russian*. The Hague: Mouton.

Hayes, B. (1999). Phonological acquisition in Optimality Theory: the early stages. This volume.

Ingram, D. (1974). Phonological rules in young children. *Journal of Child Language* **1**. 49–64.

(1975). Surface contrast in children's speech. *Journal of Child Language* **2**. 287–292.

Itô, J. and A. Mester (1997). Correspondence and compositionality: the *ga-gyo* variation in Japanese phonology. In I. Roca (ed.) *Derivations and Constraints in Phonology*. Oxford: Clarendon Press.

Jakobson, R. (1941). *Kindersprache, Aphasie und allgemeine Lautgesetze*. Uppsala. [Trans. by A. R. Keiler as *Child Language, Aphasia and Phonological Universals*. The Hague: Mouton, 1968.]

Jones, L. G. (1967). English phonotactic structure and first-language acquisition. *Lingua* **19**. 1–59.

Jusczyk, P. (1997). *The Discovery of Spoken Language*. Cambridge, Mass.: MIT Press.

Kawasaki-Fukumori, H. (1992). An acoustical basis for universal phonotactic constraints. *Language and Speech* **35**. 73–86.

Kiparsky, P. and L. Menn (1977). On the acquisition of phonology. In J. Macnamara (ed.) *Language Learning and Thought*. New York: Academic Press. 47–78. [Reprinted in G. Ioup and S. H. Weinberger (eds.) (1987) *Interlanguage Phonology: The Acquisition of a Second Language Sound System*. Cambridge, Mass.: Newbury House. 23–52.]

Kisseberth, C. W. (1970). The functional unity of phonological rules. *LI* **1**. 291–306.

Langendoen, D. T. (1968). *The London School of Linguistics*. Cambridge, Mass.: MIT Press.

Leopold, W. F. (1939–49). *Speech Development of a Bilingual Child*. 4 vols. Evanston, Ill.: Northwestern University Press.

Levelt, C. C. (1994). *On the Acquisition of Place*. Ph.D. Dissertation, Leiden University.

Lindblom, B. (1992). Phonological units as adaptive emergents of lexical development. In C. A. Ferguson *et al.* (eds.) (1992). 131–163.

Macken, M. A. (1978). Permitted complexity in phonological development: one child's acquisition of Spanish consonants. *Lingua* **44**. 219–253.

(1979). Developmental reorganization of phonology: a hierarchy of basic units of acquisition. *Lingua* **49**. 11–49.

(1980). The child's lexical representation: the 'puzzle-puddle-pickle' evidence. *JL* **16**. 1–17.

(1992). Where's phonology? In C. A. Ferguson *et al.* (eds.) (1992). 249–269.

MacNeilage, P. F. and B. Davis (1990). Acquisition of speech production: frames, then content. In M. Jeannerod (ed.) *Attention and Performance XIII*. Hillsdale, N.J.: Erlbaum.

Markey, K. L. (1994). *The Sensorimotor Foundations of Phonology: a Computational Model of Early Childhood Articulatory and Phonetic Development*. Ph.D. dissertation, University of Colorado.

Matthei, E. (1989). Crossing boundaries: more evidence for phonological constraints on early multi-word utterances. *Journal of Child Language* **16**. 41–54.

McCarthy, J. and A. Prince (1994). The emergence of the unmarked: optimality in prosodic morphology. In M. Gonzalez (ed.) *NELS* **24**. 333–379. Amherst, Mass.: Graduate Linguistic Student Association.

Menn, L. (1971). Phonotactic rules in beginning speech. *Lingua* **26**. 225–241.

(1976). *Pattern, Control, and Contrast in Beginning Speech: a Case Study in the Development of Word Form and Word Function*. Ph.D. dissertation, University of Illinois, Urbana. [Distributed by Indiana University Linguistic Club, Bloomington, 1979. Available from University Microfilms.]

(1980). Child phonology and phonological theory. In G. Yeni-Komshian *et al.* (eds.) (1980). 23–42.

(1983). Development of articulatory, phonetic, and phonological capabilities. In B. Butterworth (ed.) *Language Production* **2**. London: Academic Press. 3–50.

Menn, L. and C. Stoel-Gammon (1995). Phonological development. In P. Fletcher and B. MacWhinney (eds.) *A Handbook of Child Language*. Oxford: Blackwell. 335–359.

Menn, L. and E. Matthei (1992). The 'two-lexicon' model of child phonology: looking back, looking ahead. In C. A. Ferguson *et al.* (eds.) (1992). 211–247.

Menyuk, P., L. Menn, and R. Silber (1986). Early strategies for the perception and production of words and sounds. In P. Fletcher and M. Garman (eds.) *Language Acquisition* **2**. Cambridge: Cambridge University Press. 198–222.

Moskowitz, A. (1970). The two-year-old stage in the acquisition of phonology. *Lg* **46**. 426–441.

Ohala, J. J. and H. Kawasaki-Fukumori (1997). Alternatives to the sonority hierarchy for explaining the shape of morphemes. In S. Eliasson and E. Håkon Jahr (eds.) *Studies for Einar Haugen*. Berlin: Mouton de Gruyter. 343–365.

Oller, D. K. and M. L. Steffens (1994). Syllables and segments in infant vocalizations and young child speech. In M. Yavas (ed.) *First and Second Language Phonology*. San Diego: Singular Publishing Group. 45–62.

Pater, J. (1997). Minimal violation and phonological development. *Language Acquisition* **6**. 201–253.

(2000). OT acquisition bibliography. Archived on Linguist List, accessible via CHILDES (Child Language Data Exchange). http://listserv.linguistlist.org/cgi-bin/wa?A2=ind0006B&L=info-childes&P=R74

Peters, A. M. (1977). Language learning strategies. *Lg* **53**. 560–573.

(1983). *The Units of Language Acquisition*. Cambridge: Cambridge University Press.

(1985). Language segmentation: operating principles for the analysis and perception of language. In D. I. Slobin (ed.) *The Crosslinguistic Study of Language Acquisition* **2**. Hillsdale, N.J.: Erlbaum. 1029–1067.

Plaut, D. C. and C. T. Kello (1999). The emergence of phonology from the interplay of speech comprehension and production: a distributed connectionist approach. In B. MacWhinney (ed.) *The Emergence of Language*. Hillsdale, N.J.: Erlbaum. 381–416.

Priestly, T. M. S. (1977). One idiosyncratic strategy in the acquisition of phonology. *Journal of Child Language* **4**. 45–66.

Prince, A. and P. Smolensky (1993). Optimality Theory: constraint interactions in generative grammar. MS., New Brunswick, N.J.: Rutgers University; Boulder, Col.: University of Colorado. To appear as Linguistic Inquiry Monograph, MIT Press, Cambridge, Mass.

Rice, K. and P. Avery (1995). Variability in a deterministic model of language acquisition: a theory of segmental elaboration. In J. Archibald (ed.) *Phonological Acquisition and Phonological Theory*. Hillsdale, N.J.: Erlbaum. 23–42.

Smith, N. V. (1973). *The Acquisition of Phonology: a Case Study*. Cambridge: Cambridge University Press.

Snow, D. and C. Stoel-Gammon (1994). Intonation and final lengthening in early child language. In M. Yavas (ed.) *First and Second Language Phonology*. San Diego: Singular Publishing Group. 81–106.

Stampe, D. (1969). The acquisition of phonemic representation. *CLS* **5**. 433–444.

Stanley, R. (1967). Redundancy rules in phonology. *Lg* **43**. 393–435.

Stemberger, J. and B. H. Bernhardt (1999). The emergence of faithfulness. In B. MacWhinney (ed.) *The Emergence of Language*. Hillsdale, N.J.: Erlbaum. 417–446.

Stoel-Gammon, C. (1989) Prespeech and early speech development of two late talkers. *First Language* **9**. 207–224.

Velleman, S. L. and M. M. Vihman (2000). The optimal initial state. Paper read at the Annual Meeting of the Linguistic Society of America, Chicago, January.

Vihman, M. M. (1981). Phonology and the development of the lexicon: evidence from children's errors. *Journal of Child Language* **8**. 239–264.

    (1996). *Phonological Development*. Oxford: Blackwell.

Vihman, M. M., M. A. Macken, R. Miller, H. Simmons, and J. Miller (1985). From babbling to speech: a reassessment of the continuity issue. *Lg* **61**. 395–443.

Vihman, M. M., S. L. Velleman, and L. McCune (1994). How abstract is child phonology? Toward an integration of linguistic and psychological approaches. In M. Yavas (ed.) *First and Second Language Phonology*. San Diego: Singular Publishing Group. 9–44.

Waterson, N. (1971). A tentative developmental model of phonological representation. In T. Myers, J. Laver, and J. Anderson (eds.) *The Cognitive Representation of Speech*. Amsterdam: North-Holland. Reprinted in N. Waterson (ed.) *Prosodic Phonology: The Theory and its Application to Language Acquisition and Speech Processing*. Newcastle: Grevatt and Grevatt, 1987.

Yeni-Komshian, G., J. Kavanagh, and C. A. Ferguson (eds.) (1980). *Child Phonology. Vol. 1: Production; Vol. 2: Perception*. New York: Academic Press.

3   Markedness and faithfulness constraints in child phonology*

Amalia Gnanadesikan

1.   Introduction

This chapter argues that constraint-based Optimality Theory (Prince and Smolensky 1993) provides a framework which allows for the development of a unified model of child and adult phonology and the relation between the two. In Optimality Theory (OT) an adult phonology consists of a set of ranked constraints. The ranking, but not the constraints, differs from language to language. The constraints are universal. If phonological constraints are universal, they should be innate.[1] I claim that these innate constraints are operative in child phonology. The constraints used in adult language should therefore be adequate to account for child phonology data as well, without attributing to the child, as in previous theories, more representational levels or more rules than adults have. This chapter shows that this is indeed the case.

The initial state of the phonology, I propose, is one in which constraints against phonological markedness outrank the faithfulness constraints, which demand that the surface form (output) is identical to the underlying form (input, in OT terminology).[2] The result is that in the initial stages of acquisition the outputs are unmarked. The process of acquisition is one of promoting the faithfulness constraints to approximate more and more closely the adult grammar, and produce more and more marked forms.[3] The path of acquisition will vary from child to child, as different children promote the various faithfulness constraints in different orders.

In adult languages certain faithfulness constraints outrank certain markedness constraints. This is required by the need to have enough contrasts to support a large lexicon. By interspersing the markedness and faithfulness constraints in a ranked hierarchy, every adult language balances markedness and unmarkedness. Each language will differ from others in its ranking of particular constraints, and so each language will express markedness and unmarkedness in different ways. The child, who begins with dominant markedness constraints – and hence unmarked outputs – has the task of achieving the particular ranking of unmarkedness and faithfulness found in her target language.

The markedness constraints do not simply disappear when they come to be dominated by faithfulness constraints. When the requirements of a dominant faithfulness constraint conflict with those of the dominated markedness constraint, the effects of the markedness constraint will naturally be obscured. There are cases where the dominating faithfulness constraint is irrelevant, however. In such cases the effects of the markedness constraint will be clearly seen. Examples of this phenomenon, known as the *Emergence of the Unmarked* (McCarthy and Prince 1994), provide strong evidence that adult phonology is best described by the ranking of a set of universal constraints, as proposed by OT. This chapter discusses certain examples of the emergence of the unmarked in child language. These cases do not receive adequate explanation in traditional rule-based theories. The success of OT in accounting for such cases demonstrates that the ranking of constraints in OT provides the correct model of both child and adult phonology.

I restrict my attention in this chapter to a single child phonology. This allows focus on a single grammar, and hence a consistent constraint ranking. The particular child phonology I shall consider in this chapter is that of Gitanjali (G), my daughter, a 2-year-old raised in a monolingual Standard American English environment. The characteristics of her phonology discussed below have been consistent for a period of several months, roughly 2;3 to 2;9, indicating that they are properties of a semi-steady state grammar. The properties of G's phonology are consistent with those reported elsewhere for the normal acquisition of English (see, for example, Edwards and Shriberg 1983, Grunwell 1981, Ingram 1989a, 1989b, and Stoel-Gammon and Dunn 1985).

I shall give evidence that G's inputs (underlying forms) are in general segmentally accurate, that is, the inputs are adult-like.[4] The difference between G's phonology and that of the target English lies in the fact that G still ranks certain markedness constraints above certain faithfulness constraints. It does not lie in having different segments in the inputs, different rules or constraints, or a different model of grammar.

G's grammar produces syllables which have at most one consonant in onset position. Her inputs, however, have up to three consonants in onset. In limiting onsets to one segment G's grammar displays less markedness than the target English. The unmarked structure of G's onsets is the result of ranking the markedness constraint *COMPLEX (the constraint forbidding complex onsets) above faithfulness. Although G's onsets are always maximally unmarked in segment number, they vary in markedness with respect to the sonority of the onset. When G's input has only one consonant available for onset it will be used regardless of how marked an onset it makes. When G's input provides a choice of onset consonants, however, her grammar selects as onset the one which is least sonorous and thus the least marked syllable onset. This selection of one onset consonant demonstrates Emergence of the Unmarked: low-ranking constraints on sonority have the power to select the least marked onset when there is underlyingly more than one onset consonant. The sonority constraints are too low ranked to have an effect on marked underlyingly single onsets. The Obligatory Contour Principle (OCP) also emerges to influence the selection of the onset consonant in some cases, but it does not rank highly enough to do so in all cases.

The onset consonants I discuss in this chapter are specifically word-initial or stressed-syllable-initial. Section 3 introduces G's reduction of onset clusters, showing how *COMPLEX outranks faithfulness. Constraints on sonority select the least marked onset. Section 3 assumes that G has segmentally accurate (that is, adult-like) inputs. Section 4 demonstrates, based on the evidence of a dummy syllable, that G's inputs are indeed segmentally accurate. It discusses cases of onset selection in the presence of the dummy syllable, where the potential onset consonants are not underlyingly in a single cluster. Section 5 considers the behaviour of labial clusters where the output onset consonant is not the same as any of the input consonants. The labial cluster data are used to show that G's preferred method of satisfying *COMPLEX is through coalescence. This section puts together the effects of sonority, *COMPLEX, faithfulness constraints on features, and faithfulness constraints on segments. Section 6 looks at the exceptions to the pattern of labial coalescence in section 5 and shows that these supposed exceptions provide a clear example of the Emergence of the Unmarked in the interaction between the OCP and the faithfulness constraints. The OCP is dominated and thus disabled in certain cases, but emerges to play a crucial role in others.

Before beginning the analysis of G's onsets, I present in section 2 a brief outline of Optimality Theory and the view of faithfulness presupposed in the rest of this chapter.

2.   Optimality Theory and Correspondence

In Optimality Theory (Prince and Smolensky 1993) the heart of the phonology consists of a hierarchy of ranked constraints. For any given lexical input a universal function, Gen, supplies an exhaustive list of potential outputs. The hierarchy of constraints selects the candidate output which best satisfies the constraints. This winning candidate is the true phonological output.

Constraint rankings and their effects on selecting outputs are conventionally represented in tableaux. The following tableau gives a schematised example of output selection by ranked constraints.

(1)

	Constraint A	Constraint B
candidate$_1$	*!	
☞ candidate$_2$		*

In tableau (1) Constraint A dominates Constraint B (abbreviated Constraint A »
Constraint B). This means that for any two candidates with otherwise identical constraint violations, one which violates Constraint A will be discarded
in favour of one which satisfies Constraint A and violates Constraint B instead. Constraint violations are shown with stars, and the constraint violation which eliminates a candidate from further consideration is marked with
an exclamation point. Thus in tableau (1) the violation of Constraint A by
candidate₁ eliminates it as a potential output. Although it violates Constraint
B, candidate₂ best satisfies the simplified constraint hierarchy in (1). It is
therefore the candidate which is selected as output. This is shown by the
pointing hand to the left of candidate₂. Since candidate₁ is eliminated by the
highest constraint, the satisfaction or violation of Constraint B is *irrelevant*.
Candidate₂ is optimal regardless of the presence or absence of stars under
Constraint B, since all competition was eliminated by Constraint A. The irrel-
evance of Constraint B violations is emphasised by shading the boxes under
Constraint B.

There are two basic types of constraints which are relevant to this chapter.
One is the markedness constraints, which militate against marked structures.
The other type comprises the faithfulness constraints, which demand identity
between input and output. The particular model of faithfulness I adopt here is
the Correspondence Theory of McCarthy and Prince (1995a), which expands
on the notion of faithfulness developed by Prince and Smolensky (1991, 1993).

In Correspondence, the segments of two phonological representations (here
input and output, but also base and reduplicant in reduplicative morphology) are
seen as being related by a mapping from one to the other. Where the mapping
does not describe identity between input and output (or base and reduplicant),
violations occur.

For concreteness, consider two families of constraints on correspondence,
MAX and IDENT[F]. MAX (specifically MAX-IO, which evaluates the mapping from input to output) requires that each segment in the input have a correspondent in the output. In other words, deletion is disallowed by this constraint,
since deletion would result in a segment in the input that corresponds to no
segment in the output. MAX-IO replaces the PARSE of the Parse/Fill model of
faithfulness in Prince and Smolensky (1991, 1993).

IDENT[F] is a family of constraints which demand identity between a segment's value for some feature [F] and the value of that feature in the segment's correspondent. Thus IDENT[F]-IO requires that if an input segment
possesses the feature value [αF] the output correspondent of that segment
must also possess the value [αF]. IDENT[F] replaces the PARSE-FEATURE
constraints of Parse/Fill versions of faithfulness, but is not identical in its
effects. IDENT[F] can only be violated by a segment which has an output
correspondent. If the segment is deleted, MAX is violated, but IDENT[F]
is not.

For a hypothetical input /skat/ and candidate output *ska*, the output incurs one violation of MAX-IO, but no IDENT[F] violations. The candidate output *ska?* does not incur a MAX violation if the final glottal stop is derived from the input *t*. It does, however, violate IDENT[Coronal], as the [Coronal] feature of the input *t* is not present on its correspondent *?*. The correspondence between segments which are not featurally identical can be made explicit by coindexing, as in input $s_1k_2a_3t_4$ and output $s_1k_2a_3?_4$.

3.   Selection of an unmarked onset: *COMPLEX and sonority

In G's language syllables may begin with at most one consonant. Underlyingly complex onsets must therefore be reduced to a single segment. Examples of such reduction are shown in (2). The examples in (2a) all violate faithfulness to the input in order to have well-formed onsets. The examples in (2b) and (2c) show that the non-realisation of liquids is not due to a production flaw, although some liquids are realised as glides.

(2)   (a) clean   [kin]   (b) room   [wum]   (c) you   [yu]
            please [piz]   roof   [wuf]   yellow   [yælo]
            blue   [bu]   lab   [læb]   yeah   [yæ]
            draw   [dɔ]   listen [lɪsən]   woah   [wo]
            friend [fɛn]

Vowel-initial output occurs too: 'icecream' [ayskim], 'I' [ay], 'elephant' [ɛfənət].

Prince and Smolensky (1993) provisionally propose the constraint *COMPLEX to rule out more than a single consonant in onset position. This markedness constraint rules out all complex onsets in G's language, that is, *COMPLEX is unviolated in G's language.[5] In order to satisfy *COMPLEX, the output forms in (2a) are unfaithful to the input, and as such violate one of the faithfulness constraints on correspondence between input and output. For the time being I shall identify this constraint as FAITH. Considered in isolation the data in (2a) would lead to the conclusion that the FAITH constraint is MAX-IO, the constraint (described in section 2 above) which demands that all the segments in the input have a correspondent element in the output. As section 5 will show, however, further details lead to the conclusion that the violated constraint is not MAX.

The tableau in (3) illustrates how the ranking of *COMPLEX above FAITH forces violation of FAITH. Any attempt to retain both onset segments of 'please' in the output will violate the higher ranked *COMPLEX, so such a candidate is ruled out. The winning candidate satisfies *COMPLEX by losing one consonant. In the case of underlying /piz/ 'peas', however, losing a consonant results in a gratuitous FAITH violation. The winning candidate respects FAITH, and so the onset *p* is retained in the output.

(3)

	*COMPLEX	FAITH
please: pliz → pliz	*!	
☞ pliz → piz		*
peas: ☞ piz → piz		
piz → iz		*!

The situation is more complex than tableau (3) indicates, however. Since
*COMPLEX requires simply that the onset contain maximally one segment,
either the *p* or the *l* could have been deleted in 'please'. Although the first
consonant is the surviving one in the examples in (2a), the examples in (4)
show that this is not always the case.

(4)   (a) sky   [gay]   skin   [gɪn]
           spill   [bɪw]   spoon   [bun]
           straw   [dɔ]   star   [dɑ]

      (b) snow   [so]   snookie   [sʊki]
           slip   [sɪp]   sleep   [sip]

In the examples in (4a), the initial *s* is lost. This is not true of all initial *s*s,
however, as (4b) shows. When the *s* is less sonorous than the following consonant (nasal or liquid) it is retained in the output. If the *s* is more sonorous
than the following consonant (plosive), it is deleted. Similarly, it is the more
sonorous consonant in (2a) that is deleted. Thus it is only the least sonorous of
a string of onset consonants that is present in G's output. This means that G
produces syllables that optimise syllable shape not only with respect to segment
number (restricting to one onset consonant), but also with respect to sonority
requirements. The optimal syllable begins with an onset of low sonority and is
followed by a vowel.

    G's reduction of multiple onset consonants to a single onset consonant in
the mapping between input and output is analogous to the reduction of onset
clusters in the mapping between base and reduplicant in Sanskrit. In Sanskrit
reduplication a single-onset syllable is prefixed to the verb stem. The segments
of the prefixal syllable are determined by the stem. With minor changes such as
deaspiration, the least sonorous onset consonant of the stem begins the prefix
and is followed by the vowel. Examples of perfect reduplication are shown
in (5a), while (5b), (5c), and (5d) show forms in the aorist, intensive, and
desiderative, respectively (from Whitney 1889, who does not supply glosses).

Markedness and faithfulness

In the examples in the left column the first consonant is least sonorous and thus appears in the reduplicant. In the right column it is the second consonant that is least sonorous and shows up in the reduplicant.

(5)   (a) perfect

           pa - **pr**ach   **ta** - st^{h}a:
           ši - **šr**i   **cu** - šcut
           sa - **sn**a: **pu** - sp^{h}uṭ
           su - **sr**u
           ši - **šl**iṣ

        (b) aorist

           a - **ti** - **tr**asam   a - **pi** - **spr**šam
           a - **si** - **sy**adam

        (c) intensive

           ša: - **šv**as   **kani** - ṣkand ∼ **cani** - ṣkand
           ve - **vl**i:
           po - **pr**ut^h

        (d) desiderative

           šu - **šr**u:ṣa   **ti** - **st**i:rṣa

As the examples in (5) show, the onset reduction occurs in all cases of reduplication in Sanskrit. Onset reduction is thus not a special rule of some mood or tense but rather a general property of Sanskrit reduplicants. In Correspondence Theory, the reduplicant is related to the base by a mapping analogous to the mapping between the output and the input. Sanskrit reduplicants obey *COMPLEX at the cost of violating faithfulness to the base, while in G's language the outputs obey *COMPLEX at the cost of violating faithfulness to the input.

The difference between Sanskrit reduplication and G's treatment of onset clusters in (2) and (4) is that in the Sanskrit case the optimised syllable of the prefixed reduplicant stands in relation to the more complex verb stem base, while in G's speech the output unmarked syllable stands in relation to the more complex input form. G's grammar ranks *COMPLEX above FAITH-IO, the constraint requiring faithfulness of the output segments to the input segments. This was shown in tableau (3). In Sanskrit FAITH-IO outranks *COMPLEX, since underlying /st^{h}a:/ surfaces as st^{h}a: and not *t^{h}a: or *sa:. FAITH-BR, the constraint requiring faithfulness of the reduplicant to the base, is dominated by *COMPLEX, with the result that the reduplicant may not have the base's complex onset.[6]

Sanskrit reduplication is a typical case of the Emergence of the Unmarked discussed in McCarthy and Prince (1994) (compare Steriade's 1988 discussion of unmarkedness in Sanskrit reduplicants). In non-reduplicative environments

Sanskrit yields no evidence for the existence of the constraint *COMPLEX. (See *prach*, (5a).) The grammar of Sanskrit does possess *COMPLEX, however, because in reduplicative environments it is clearly active (*pa-prach*, (5a)). The limiting of the effects of *COMPLEX to reduplicative contexts can be described by the ranking of *COMPLEX below FAITH-IO but above FAITH-BR: FAITH-IO » *COMPLEX » FAITH-BR.

Such cases of the Emergence of the Unmarked support the claim of OT that constraints are universal. Even though *COMPLEX appears inactive in Sanskrit bases, the reduplicants show that it is indeed active in Sanskrit in spite of being dominated by constraints such as FAITH-IO. The ranking of *COMPLEX in Sanskrit shows that a dominated constraint is still present in a grammar. The natural extension of the Sanskrit case is a language in which *COMPLEX is ranked yet lower, and so is never active. Based on this reasoning OT assumes that all constraints which are not active in a particular language are still present in the constraint hierarchy of that language. They are rendered inactive by the operation of the constraints which dominate them. Thus English possesses the constraint *COMPLEX, but it is obscured by the faithfulness constraints.

If constraints are universal, they should be innate. Therefore G's grammar possesses *COMPLEX in spite of the fact that she has never heard evidence for such a constraint in her target language. *COMPLEX is active in her language because the faithfulness constraints have not yet been promoted enough to obscure it. The difference between G's language and English is thus not the presence of the *COMPLEX constraint. The difference is that G ranks the markedness constraint *COMPLEX above FAITH-IO and English ranks FAITH-IO above *COMPLEX. To acquire the English phonology in this respect G will need to promote FAITH-IO above *COMPLEX. The relevant constraint rankings of Sanskrit, G's English, and adult English are shown in (6). (The ranking of FAITH-BR in English and G's speech is indeterminable, since these languages do not employ reduplication.)

(6)   (a) Sanskrit: FAITH-IO » *COMPLEX » FAITH-BR   (pa-prach)
        (b) G: *COMPLEX » FAITH-IO   (clean [kin])
        (c) English: FAITH-IO » *COMPLEX   (clean [klin])

The constraint rankings in (6) account for the reduction of complex onsets to single segments in G's words and in Sanskrit reduplicants. What is not yet accounted for is the choice of which segment survives in the output or reduplicant. In selecting the onset, G and Sanskrit display unmarkedness. The least marked syllable onset is the least sonorous one. An optimal onset consists of a voiceless stop. A voiced stop is the next best, and so on down the universal Sonority Hierarchy in (7).[7]

(7)   voiceless stop   e.g.,   p, t, k
         voiced stop   b, d, g
         voiceless fricative   f, s, x
         voiced fricative   v, z, ɣ
         nasal stops   n, m, ŋ
         liquids   l, r
         high vowels/glides   i/y u/w
         mid vowels   e, o
         low vowels   a

In a word such as /sbun/ 'spoon',[8] the *s*, as a fricative, is more sonorous than
the stop *b*. The stop is thus the best available onset, so the *s* is deleted and the *b*
remains in the output *bun*. In a word like /sno/ 'snow', the *s* is less sonorous than
the nasal *n*, so the *s* is retained in the output *so*. In a word like /pliz/ 'please',
the stop *p* is less sonorous than the *l*, so it is the surviving output onset in
piz.

The selection of the one least sonorous (and therefore least marked) onset
is a form of Emergent Unmarkedness. In simple onsets, marked segments can
occur freely. In Sanskrit reduplication and in G's speech syllables may begin
with consonants of high sonority, including glides. When the base (in Sanskrit)
or the input (in G's language) has a single onset consonant, that consonant
surfaces in the reduplicant or output even when it is very sonorous. Marked
onsets are thus allowed in G's language and in Sanskrit reduplication. The
effect of sonority emerges only when there is a choice of consonants. In such
cases G and Sanskrit both select the least sonorous consonant as onset, thus
optimising the shape of the syllable.

Gnanadesikan (1995) proposes that the preference for low sonority in onsets
derives from the related preference for high sonority in moraic (non-onset) positions. If a segment is excluded from onset position on the grounds of sonority,
it is because the segment is better parsed as moraic. The preference for sonorous
segments to be moraic can be captured by the family of constraints shown in
(8) where μ/Y stands for 'each Y must be parsed as a mora'.[9] For example, an *i*
which is not assigned a mora in the output violates μ/i. An *m* which is assigned
a mora satisfies μ/m, but is irrelevant to μ/i.

(8)   μ/a » μ/e,o » μ/i,u » μ/r,l » μ/m,n » μ/v,z » μ/f,s » μ/b,d » μ/p,t

The sub-hierarchy of constraints in (8) ensures that segments of a given sonority will be assigned moras preferentially over segments of lower sonority.[10] Thus
l, for instance, will be assigned a mora preferentially over a segment such as
s. As a result, it is worse to assign *l* to a non-moraic onset position than it is
to assign *s* to an onset. That some segment must be assigned to onset position

is assured by the constraint ONSET, which demands that every syllable have an onset.[11] This is demonstrated in tableau (9) for examples from G's speech (only the relevant part of the μ/Y subhierarchy is shown). The effect of *COM-PLEX (shown above in tableau (3)) is assumed, so only candidates without complex onsets are considered. All the candidates shown violate FAITH-IO in addition to the violations shown in (9), but the ranking of FAITH-IO with respect to the sub-hierarchy of constraints in (9) cannot be determined on the basis of the data presented thus far. The crucial point is that given the undominated ranking of *COMPLEX, FAITH-IO must be violated in complex onset cases, and the sonority constraints take advantage of this forced violation to minimise μ/Y sonority violations.

(9)

		ONSET	μ/r,l	μ/m,n	μ/v,z	μ/s,f	μ/b, d,g
sky:	sgay → say					*!	
☞	sgay → gay						*
	sgay → ay	*!					
snow: ☞	sno → so					*	
	sno → no			*!			
	sno → o	*!					
sleep: ☞	slip → sip					*	
	slip → lip		*!				
	slip → ip	*!					
draw: ☞	drɔ → dɔ						*
	drɔ → rɔ[12]		*!				
	drɔ → ɔ	*!					

This section has demonstrated the power of OT to capture both child and adult phonology. OT provides a set of universal constraints which are operative in both children and adults. Comparison of G's phonology with that of Sanskrit shows that G is using the same constraints as those present in adult language. This was shown by the similar action of *COMPLEX and the sonority constraints in Sanskrit and in G's language.

Comparison of English and G's language demonstrates the innateness of the phonological constraints. G uses the constraint *COMPLEX in spite of the fact that English, her target language, provides her with no evidence for its existence. English contains a high percentage of words with complex onsets, so that G would not postulate *COMPLEX as a property of her target language. G does use *COMPLEX, however, and ranks it highly enough that it is never violated in her language. By the ranking of *COMPLEX over FAITH-IO (as shown in tableau (3)) English 'straw', 'please', and 'friend' become *dɔ, piz, fɛn.*

In Sanskrit *COMPLEX is ranked less highly. It is dominated by FAITH-IO but it outranks FAITH-BR. The result is that the effects of *COMPLEX emerge in reduplicants but not in bases, yielding reduplicant-base forms such as *ta-st^{h}a*. Sanskrit, G, and English provide a paradigm of rankings of the universal constraint *COMPLEX with respect to faithfulness constraints. In G's language *COMPLEX is undominated and hence unviolated. In Sanskrit *COMPLEX is dominated but still active where the dominating constraint (here FAITH-IO) is irrelevant, demonstrating Emergence of the Unmarked. In English *COMPLEX is dominated and never active.[13]

G's ranking of *COMPLEX over FAITH-IO in the face of the opposite ranking in English is in keeping with the proposal made in section 1 that initially markedness constraints outrank faithfulness constraints. To acquire the English ranking she will have to promote FAITH-IO above *COMPLEX. The sonority constraints are at this point already dominated by faithfulness constraints, since very sonorous consonants can be onsets. When there is a choice of onset segments, though, the effects of sonority emerge, selecting *s* in *so* 'snow', but *d* in *dɔ* 'draw' (as shown in tableau (9)).

4.   Dummy syllable, onset selection, and the nature of the input

The previous section assumed that G's inputs are segmentally like those of adults, that is they contain the phonemes of the forms she hears around her. The sonority constraints and *COMPLEX were used to derive her less marked outputs from the more complex inputs. The assumption of generally accurate inputs is not universally accepted in child phonology (see, for example, Ingram 1976 *et seq.*, discussed in section 7 below). The unmarked outputs of child language could theoretically be derived from unmarked inputs, obviating the need for output constraints in child phonology. This section discusses the phenomenon of the 'dummy syllable' in order to provide an argument that G's inputs are indeed segmentally accurate, that is, adult-like. The outputs, however, are subject to interacting constraints. This strengthens the claim that the difference between child language and adult language lies in different constraint rankings, as predicted by OT.

One of the most obfuscating elements of G's language is her use of a dummy syllable *fi-*, used for word-initial unstressed syllables. Examples are shown in (10).

(10)   umbrella   [fi-bɛyə]   container   [fi-tenə]
        mosquito   [fi-giɾo]   spaghetti   [fi-gɛɾi]
        Christina   [fi-dinə]   Rebecca   [fi-bɛkə]
        adviser   [fi-vayzə]   rewind   [fi-wayn]

As the forms in (10) demonstrate, the *fi-* syllable appears in a pretonic initial syllable, regardless of that syllable's phonological content in the adult language.[14] The segments of the initial unstressed syllable are deleted, but a syllable still appears there (it receives secondary stress). This implies that G's inputs contain syllable structure. By using *fi-*, G's output is faithful to the input at the syllable level, since the output has the same number of syllables as the input. At the segmental level, however, G's *fi-* outputs are wildly unfaithful to the input.[15] If G's inputs did not contain syllable structure there would be no syllables to be faithful to, and there would be no reason to insert *fi-*. G's grammatical inputs reflect the syllabified adults' outputs.[16]

We are now in a position to make the crucial argument of this section: it can be determined that, despite the *fi-*induced disparity between G's forms and the adult forms, G still retains the segments of the first syllable in her underlying form. The evidence for this comes from the interaction of *fi-* with the sonority constraints on the onset of the stressed syllable (the first syllable that is segmentally related to the adult form). In a word like 'koala', realised by G as *fi-kala*, straightforward *fi-* insertion would lead one to expect an output of *fi-ala or *fi-wala. To have no onset, as in *fi-ala, violates ONSET, while to have a glide onset, as in *fi-wala, induces a high-ranking µ/glide violation. To remedy this, G uses the onset consonant which has been removed from the first syllable to make room for *fi-*, resulting in *fi-kala*. This shows that G, in her underlying representations, retains the consonants she perceives in adult output, even when she does not pronounce them (e.g., 'container' *fi-tenə*, (10)). When markedness constraints (ONSET) require them, she still has the consonants available.

In producing *fi-kala* G violates the faithfulness constraint I-CONTIG, which demands that the segments of the input which stand in correspondence to segments of the output form a contiguous string.[17] The mapping from input to output forms is shown in (11), where 'koala' is compared with 'Rebecca'. Bold-face lines show segmental correspondence between input and output. Note that these are not association lines, but simply the equivalent of coindexing between input and output corresponding segments. Dotted lines show correspondence between input and output syllables. Light lines show the association of segments with syllables.

(11)

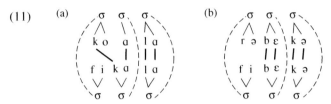

In (11) both outputs violate FAITH, but (11a) also violates I-CONTIG, since the segments of the input which participate in the correspondence from input to output do not form a contiguous string. The transfer of a better onset to the second syllable in defiance of the contiguity constraint occurs in cases where the adult syllable is onsetless or begins with a glide or liquid. It does not occur if the adult syllable begins with a nasal or an obstruent. Compare (12a) with (12b).

(12)   (a) balloon   [fi-bun]   (b) tomorrow   [fi-mɑwo]
            police   [fi-pis]   potato   [fi-tero]
            below   [fi-bo]   Simone   [fi-mon]
            barrette   [fi-bɛt]
            koala   [fi-kɑlɑ]

Onset replacement occurs in cases where the input stressed syllable has a glide or liquid onset, but not if that onset is any less sonorous.[18] Unlike in the onset reduction discussed in section 3 the *fi-* related onset replacement does not occur in all cases where the unstressed syllable has a less sonorous onset than the stressed syllable. This is demonstrated in forms such as 'Simone'. As section 3 showed, contiguous *s*-nasal clusters lose the nasal in favour of the fricative *s*. As a result 'snow' is pronounced *so*. In the non-contiguous *fi-* cases a nasal remains and is not replaced by a fricative. 'Simone' is *fi-mon* not **fi-son*. The data in (12) thus show that although sonority constraints are at work in both the contiguous cluster cases of section 3 and the non-contiguous *fi-* cases, the faithfulness constraint which interacts with the sonority constraints must be different in the two types. I-CONTIG is therefore separate, and separately ranked from the FAITH of section 3.[19] Violation of I-CONTIG is forced by μ/glide (12a), but not by the lower-ranked μ/Y constraints (12b). μ/liquid may also dominate I-CONTIG. It is difficult to tell, since all onset *r*s are pronounced as *w*s and many (but not all) onset *l*s are *y*s. In what follows, μ/glide should be considered to include μ/liquid. FAITH-IO, on the other hand, is dominated by *COMPLEX and unrankable with respect to the μ/Y sub-hierarchy.

Tableau (13) illustrates the action of sonority requirements and I-CONTIG in the presence of *fi*-insertion. For the purposes of this tableau, all candidates are assumed to have *fi*-, and the mechanism responsible for the *fi*- is not included here.

(13)

		ONSET	μ/glide	I-CONTIG	μ/nasal	μ/fricative	μ/stop
balloon: ☞	fi-bun			*			*
	fi-yun		*!				
Rebecca: ☞	fi-bɛkə			*			*
	fi-wɛkə		*!				
koala: ☞	fi-kɑlɑ			*			*
	fi-ɑlɑ	*!					
	fi-wɑlɑ		*!				

In spite of the fact that G's use of *fi*- leads to significant divergence from the segments of the adult unstressed syllable, the interaction between *fi*- and the sonority requirements on the following onset shows that G's inputs coincide segmentally with the adult forms. When required by ONSET or μ/glide, the onset of the syllable replaced by *fi*- shows up on the next syllable, demonstrating that the replaced segments are still present and available for use by the phonology. Furthermore, the presence of the dummy syllable *fi*- shows that her inputs are prosodically accurate even when her outputs are segmentally divergent. Although the segmental content of the *fi*- syllable is idiosyncratic, the constraints with which it interacts are not. The constraints that select G's output, namely the μ/Y constraints and I-CONTIG, are precisely those which have been independently proposed as universally existing in adult grammar.

Just as in the case of Sanskrit, G's use of *fi*- is analogous to a phenomenon found in adult natural languages. More specifically, it resembles melodic overwriting such as that commonly seen in echo word formation (McCarthy and Prince 1986, 1990, 1995b, Steriade 1988, Yip 1992). Echo words are formed by reduplication with a fixed melody replacing part of the base melody in the reduplicative morpheme. This is shown in (14) for echo words in Kolami (from McCarthy and Prince 1986, citing Emeneau 1955).

(14)   pal   pal-gil   'tooth'
       kota   kota -gita   'bring it!'
       iir   iir - giir   'water'
       maasur   maasur-giisur   'men'
       saa   saa - gii   'go, cont. ger.'

In Kolami, the melodic overwriting replaces the first consonant (if any) and the first vowel (long or short) of the base. Coda consonants after the first vowel remain faithful to the base. In G's language she overwrites a whole syllable whether open or closed. Thus both the *chris* in 'Christina' and the *re* of 'Rebecca' are replaced by *fi-*. The difference between adult language overwriting and G's overwriting is that in G's overwriting a whole syllable is replaced, while in adult overwriting only segments are replaced. Kolami therefore has *pal-gil*, replacing the first two segments, but leaving the coda *l* of the base to show up after the overwriting *gi*. G, on the other hand, has forms such as *fi-tenə* 'container', which replaces the *con* syllable with the codaless *fi-*, rather than **fi-ntenə*, which leaves the coda. If G's inputs possess prosodic structure and if adult inputs do not (see again note 16), this difference is not surprising. In G's language the initial unstressed syllable is required to stand in correspondence to a syllable whose segments are *fi-*. If adults do not have syllables in their inputs they cannot overwrite whole syllables (as G does with *fi-*), but only segments.[20]

5.   Identifying FAITH: interaction of labials with *COMPLEX

Section 3 described how G's grammar selects one of a series of onset consonants as output onset, yielding unmarked syllable shape. At that time the constraint violated by cluster reduction was referred to simply as FAITH-IO. This section takes up the question of the identity of FAITH. The relevant data come from onsets which contain labial or labialised consonants. In certain labial clusters the output onset consonant is not identical to any of the input consonants. Examples are shown in (15).[21]

(15)   tree   [pi]   drink   [bɪk]
       cry   [pay]   grape   [bep]
       quite   [payt]   squeeze   [biz]
       string   [bɪn]   twinkle   [pɪkəw]
       sweater   [fɛɾə]   smell   [fɛw]
       between   [fi-pin]

In each case in (15) the last consonant in the adult onset is labial (in the case of *w*) or labialised (in the case of *r*).[22] G's output consonant is also labial. (See Allerton (1976), and Chin and Dinnsen (1992) for similar patterns of cluster simplification where [labial] dominates.) In voicing, stricture, and nasality, however, it matches the least sonorous onset consonant, the one which the facts in section 3 would lead us to expect in the output. The consonants in (15) coalesce, with the sonority of one consonant showing up with the place of another. The correspondence between input and output for 'tree' is shown in (16). The indices show that both the *t* and the *r^w* in the input are mapped to the *p* of the output. The affected features are shown for each segment.[23]

(16)

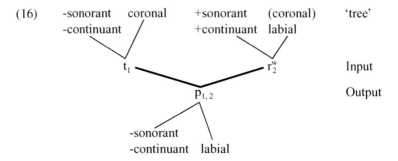

In *pi* 'tree', the *p* corresponds to both the /t/ and the /r^w/ of the input, since it bears features of each.[24] By coalescing the segments G can avoid deleting either one of the segments while still obeying the high-ranking *COMPLEX. Such a view of coalescence as a strategy to preserve the input segments is in contrast with a spreading and deletion model of coalescence (such as Chin and Dinnsen 1992) where one of the consonants in the cluster is deleted. Since one of the segments is lost anyway, the motivation for the spreading of features is arbitrary.

In OT coalescence makes sense as a way of remaining faithful to the input segments even in the face of *COMPLEX. Coalescence is not a cost-free procedure, however. In coalescing these segments G violates NO-COALESCENCE (NO-COAL), the faithfulness constraint that requires an output segment to correspond to only one input segment.[25] The violation of NO-COAL in reducing onset clusters demonstrates that NO-COAL is lower ranked than *COMPLEX.

There is good evidence that these labial cases do represent a coalescence and not an error in perception. That is, the coalescence occurs in the mapping between a segmentally accurate input and G's output. It is not the case that she hears the consonant cluster as a single labial consonant and therefore has a single labial in her input onset. The evidence for grammatical coalescence comes from forms where labial coalescence occurs in the non-contiguous consonants of *fi*- words. This is shown in (17).

(17)

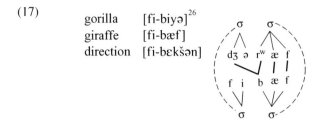

gorilla   [fi-biyə][26]
giraffe   [fi-bæf]
direction   [fi-bɛkšən]

In (17) the input onset of the stressed syllable is labial, but it is a glide in G's language. The facts in the previous section suggest that it should be replaced by the onset of the first syllable. As in the contiguous cluster examples in (15), coalescence occurs instead of outright replacement. The onset of the first syllable and the onset of the second syllable coalesce, yielding an output onset with the sonority of the first input onset and the labial place of the second.

In these cases of long-distance coalescence, G could not perceive the two consonants as one, as the adults pronounce them in separate syllables. G clearly recognises the two syllables as distinct, since she replaces one of them with *fi-*. Thus it is not the case that the distinction between the two consonants is not being perceived. While words like *pi* ('tree') could conceivably stem from misperception or some other mechanism that produces apparent coalescence ready-made at the input, the long-distance coalescence facts demand a more accurate input, suggesting that words like *pi* ('tree') have accurate inputs too.[27] The coalescence in labial clusters is best analysed as a grammatical process, which occurs in the mapping between input and output, rather than a perceptual error or other process that would provide G with inputs that were already coalesced.

The labial cases provide evidence that the preferred way of avoiding a *COMPLEX violation is through coalescence (violating NO-COAL) rather than outright deletion (violating MAX-IO). If deletion were the optimal way of avoiding *COMPLEX violations, labial glides in input clusters would simply disappear in the output. This implies that for G it is better to coalesce segments, violating NO-COAL, than it is to delete them and violate MAX. In terms of G's constraint ranking, MAX dominates NO-COAL. By this ranking 'tree' is *pi*, not *ti, as shown in tableau (18) (as elsewhere, the effects of undominated *COMPLEX are assumed).

(18)

	MAX	NO-COAL
tree: ☞ $t_1 r^w{}_2 i_3 \rightarrow p_{12} i_3$		*
$t_1 r^w{}_2 i_3 \rightarrow t_1 i_3$	*!	

Note that MAX is not violated in the winning candidate since each input segment has an output correspondent, as indicated by the indices (see McCarthy and Prince 1995a, 1999).

The ranking of MAX over NO-COAL would suggest that coalescence is always better than deletion and so this is always the option that G pursues. In a case such as *kin* 'clean', however, the *l* apparently has no correspondent in the output. It appears as though deletion has taken place, not coalescence. In other words, it seems that NO-COAL is not violated but MAX is. The answer to this apparent paradox is in the definition of correspondence of segments. In the example below in (19), Gen, which freely generates candidates for evaluation by the constraint hierarchy, generates both the form in (19a) and that in (19b) as potential outputs of 'clean'.

(19)   (a) 'clean' $k_1 l_2 i_3 n_4$ (I)   (b) $k_1 l_2 i_3 n_4$ (I)

                      $k_1 i_3 n_4$ (O) $k_{12} i_3 n_4$ (O)

In (19a) *Gen* deletes the /l/ of the input, incurring a MAX violation.[28] In (19b) Gen maps both the input /k/ and the /l/ onto the output *k*. The output *k* is thus the correspondent of both the underlying /k/ and the /l/, as emphasised by the indices. No segment has been deleted, since all input segments have an output correspondent. Therefore the candidate in (19b) violates NO-COAL but not MAX. The output (19b) also violates a number of IDENT[F] constraints, the class of constraints discussed in section 2 which control featural faithfulness. In fact none of the *l*'s features shows up on its output correspondent, and the coalescence is vacuous.

Such flagrant violation of the IDENT[F] constraints is driven mainly by the sonority constraints mentioned earlier. The μ/Y sub-hierarchy will pick out the manner features of the least sonorous input segment to show up on the coalesced output segment. This leaves the place features as the only way features of the more sonorous input consonant could show up on the coalesced output consonant. In the case of the labial or labialised consonants, the labial surfaces, as in the examples in (15) above. As forms such as *bin* 'green' testify, IDENT[labial] is higher ranked than IDENT[dorsal].[29] This is shown in tableau (20).

(20)

	IDENT[labial]	IDENT[dorsal]
green: ☞ $g_1 r^w_2 i_3 n_4 \rightarrow b_{12} i_3 n_4$		*
$g_1 r^w_2 i_3 n_4 \rightarrow g_{12} i_3 n_4$	*!	

Forms such as *pi* 'tree' demonstrate that IDENT[labial] outranks IDENT[coronal] as well. This is shown in (21).

(21)

	IDENT[labial]	IDENT[coronal]
tree: ☞ $t_1 r^w_2 i_3 \rightarrow p_{12} i_3$		*
$t_1 r^w_2 i_3 \rightarrow t_{12} i_3$	*!	

The rankings in (20) and (21) assure that [labial] will show up when it is part of a coalesced sequence. The relative ranking of IDENT[dorsal] and IDENT[coronal] is demonstrated by forms such as *kin* 'clean'. IDENT[dorsal] is higher ranked than IDENT[coronal], since the [dorsal] of /k/ rather than the [coronal] of /l/ surfaces. Tableau (22) illustrates this ranking.

(22)

	IDENT[dorsal]	IDENT[coronal]
clean: ☞ $k_1 l_2 i_3 n_4 \rightarrow k_{12} i_3 n_4$		*
$k_1 l_2 i_3 n_4 \rightarrow t_{12} i_3 n_4$	*!	

To summarise the above tableaux, IDENT[labial] outranks IDENT[dorsal], which outranks IDENT[coronal].[30] Tableau (23) shows how the IDENT[Place] constraints interact with the sonority constraints, No-COAL, and MAX. For reasons of space, the operation of *COMPLEX is assumed, and only the μ/Y constraints relevant to the given examples are shown. Constraints which are separated by a dotted line cannot be ranked with respect to each other based on the available data. Again, since G produces most glides as liquids and no distinction is made between μ/glide and μ/liquid, they are shown in the output candidates as glides.

As tableau (23) shows, No-COAL is actually the FAITH of section 3. The behaviour of labial clusters indicates that clusters undergo coalescence to satisfy *COMPLEX. Although many of the cases look like outright deletion, these are actually cases of vacuous coalescence, where the sonority and IDENT[Place] constraints select all of one segment's features to show up in the output but none of another's.

(23)

	IDENT [lab]	μ/glide	MAX	IDENT [dors]	μ/b,d,g	μ/p,t,k	IDENT [cor]	No-COAL
tree: ☞ $t_1 r^w_2 i_3 \rightarrow p_{12} i_3$						*	*	*
$t_1 r^w_2 i_3 \rightarrow t_{12} i_3$	*!					*		*
$t_1 r^w_2 i_3 \rightarrow t_1 i_3$			*!			*		
$t_1 r^w_2 i_3 \rightarrow w_{12} i_3$		*!					*	*
$t_1 r^w_2 i_3 \rightarrow y_{12} i_3$	*(!)	*(!)						*

	IDENT [lab]	μ/glide	MAX	IDENT [dors]	μ/b,d,g	μ/p,t,k	IDENT [cor]	NO-COAL
clean:								
☞ $k_1l_2i_3n_4 \rightarrow k_{12}i_3n_4$						*	*	*
$k_1l_2i_3n_4 \rightarrow t_{12}i_3n_4$				*!		*		*
$k_1l_2i_3n_4 \rightarrow k_1i_3n_4$			*!			*	*	
$k_1l_2i_3n_4 \rightarrow y_{12}i_3n_4$		*!		*				*
green:								
$g_1r^w{}_2i_3n_4 \rightarrow g_{12}i_3n_4$	*!				*			*
☞ $g_1r^w{}_2i_3n_4 \rightarrow b_{12}i_3n_4$				*	*			*
$g_1r^w{}_2i_3n_4 \rightarrow g_1i_3n_4$			*!		*			
$g_1r^w{}_2i_3n_4 \rightarrow w_{12}i_3n_4$		*!						*

G's pattern of coalescence is very similar to that found in Navajo (Lamontagne and Rice 1995a, 1995b). In Navajo, a /d/ prefix coalesces with the onset of the stem, as shown in (24) (Lamontagne and Rice, citing Kari 1973).[31]

(24)   /na + ii + **d** + xaał / → neigaał
        /ʔi + ii + **d** + kááh/ → ʔiikááh

By Lamontagne and Rice's account the first example is one of coalescence, with the manner of the *d* showing up with the place of the *x*, while in the second example the *d* deletes. Under the conception of coalescence developed in this section, however, both can be seen as coalescence, although in the second example it is vacuous. In both G's language and in Navajo the manner features of the least sonorous consonants are selected, while a non-coronal place ousts a coronal place. The parallel between G's speech and Navajo is as expected given the universality of the Sonority Hierarchy (and thus of the ranking of constraints based upon it). Further, the selection of non-coronal over coronal place in both languages is as expected given the proposal by Kiparsky (1994) that faithfulness to non-coronals universally outranks faithfulness to coronals.

This section has shown that G reduces complex onsets through coalescence, with sonority and featural faithfulness constraints determining which features end up on the output segment. Her pattern of coalescence is highly similar to that of Navajo, providing another example to support the position that child and adult languages use the same set of constraints. Cases of long-distance coalescence in *fi*- forms yielded further evidence that G's input is segmentally accurate and that the coalescence occurs in the mapping from input to output. As a phonological process coalescence is properly captured as the coindexation of two (or more) input segments with one output segment, governed by the interaction of ranked output constraints, such as the μ/Y constraints, the IDENT[Place] constraints, and No-COAL.

6.   Labials and the OCP: the emergence of the unmarked

The constraints in tableau (23) do not describe all the properties of labial clusters in G's language. As this section shows, the Obligatory Contour Principle (OCP) plays a role in determining the output shape of certain labial clusters, providing an excellent case of the Emergence of the Unmarked in child language. Cases such as this demonstrate that child phonology, like adult phonology, is best described by a system of ranked constraints.

Labialising coalescence of the onset consonants does not occur if the following vowel is rounded (and thus itself labial), as the following forms attest.

(25)   draw   [dɔ]   grow   [ɡo]
        straw   [dɔ]   stroller [doyə]

In most cases, the labialisation is also blocked if the next consonant is labial, as in the examples in (26). The forms marked '•' were acquired after the time discussed in this chapter, but while G still used the same treatment for labial clusters. I include them since they provide an excellent minimal contrast.

(26)   grandma   [ɡæmɑ]
        • grandparent   [ɡæmpæwət] vs. • granddaughter [bændɔtə]
          drop   [dɑp]
          icecream   [ayskim]
          trouble   [tʌbu]
          but cf. grape   [bep], crumb [pʌm]

The blocking of labialisation is due to the ranking of the OCP in the constraint hierarchy, as described below. The OCP serves to prohibit adjacent instances of particular features. In the present case it proscribes adjacent instances of the feature Labial. OCP effects on labials are common in adult languages (Selkirk 1993), although it is more frequently effective between two consonants than between consonants and vowels. An example similar to G's use of the OCP on adjacent labials occurs in Cantonese. In Cantonese the OCP prevents sequences of rounded vowel plus labial consonant, labial consonant plus front rounded vowel, and labial consonant plus vowel plus labial consonant (Yip 1988, citing data from Hashimoto 1972, and Light 1977). In G's case the OCP is evidently evaluated both between consonant and following vowel, and from consonant to consonant, but not from vowel to following consonant.[32] The consonant-to-consonant evaluation is weaker than the consonant-to-vowel evaluation, leading to pairs such as *tʌbu* 'trouble' versus *bep* 'grape'.[33]

The OCP in G's language is powerful enough to prevent the derivation of adjacent labials, but not powerful enough to prevent the surfacing of segments which are underlyingly labial. This is a clear instance of the Emergence of the Unmarked. The OCP is dominated, so it cannot insist on well-formed sequences in cases of underlying labials. Thus 'room' is *wum* (2b), 'blue' is *bu* (2a), and 'spoon' is *bun* (4a), displaying the marked labial–labial sequences and demonstrating domination of the OCP. In the case of derived labials, however, the OCP emerges to rule out the ill-formed labial–labial sequences. The result is that 'draw' is *dɔ*, not **bɔ*, showing emergent unmarkedness due to the action of the OCP. The particular constraint ranking which allows the OCP to operate in some environments and not others is developed below.

The reason that the OCP cannot select **du* over *bu* for 'blue' through coalescence of the labial *b* and the coronal *l* is the high ranking of the IDENT[labial] constraint. IDENT[labial] requires the correspondent of an input segment which bears the feature [labial] also to bear the feature [labial]. Therefore a [coronal] place cannot be chosen over [labial] in coalescence. Furthermore, in words with a single onset (and hence no coalescence) [labial] cannot simply be deleted (and replaced by, say, [coronal]). IDENT[labial] outranks the OCP, as illustrated in tableau (27).

(27)

	IDENT[labial]	OCP
blue: ☞ $b_1 l_2 u_3 \rightarrow b_{12} u_3$		*
$b_1 l_2 u_3 \rightarrow d_{12} u_3$	*!	
room: ☞ $w_1 u_2 m_3 \rightarrow w_1 u_2 m_3$		*
$w_1 u_2 m_3 \rightarrow y_1 u_2 m_3$	*!	

IDENT[labial] thus has the power to force the correspondents of *b* and *w* to be labial in spite of the OCP.

In cases such as *gɔ* 'grow', coalescence is blocked. Tableau (27) has demonstrated that if a labial segment undergoes coalescence the output must be labial regardless of the OCP. So if the *g* and the *rʷ* in 'grow' coalesced the output would have to be **bɔ*. Since this does not occur the *g* and the *rʷ* must not be coalescing. If the *rʷ* deletes instead of coalescing with the *g*, IDENT[labial] is rendered irrelevant, since there is no output correspondent of *rʷ* for the [labial] to show up on.[34] Put differently, IDENT[labial] cannot be violated by a segment that is deleted. If there is a segment that can safely be deleted, the high-ranking IDENT[labial] can be bypassed. If the entire labial segment is deleted, the OCP is also satisfied. Deletion is therefore the best option in this case because it satisfies the OCP and IDENT[labial], although it violates MAX instead. This demonstrates that the OCP dominates MAX, as shown in tableau (28) (which considers only forms which do not violate IDENT[labial], based on the ranking in (27)).

(28)

	OCP	MAX
grow: ☞ $g_1r^w{}_2o_3 \rightarrow g_1o_3$		*
$g_1r^w{}_2o_3 \rightarrow b_{12}o_3$	*!	

If labials can delete to avoid violating the OCP, one would expect the *b* to delete in *bu* 'blue', yielding **lu* (or **yu*). It turns out that true consonants may not delete, although glides (and liquids) can.[35] Compare the forms in (25) and (26), where /r^w/ deletes, with that in (29a), where the labial consonant coalesces.[36]

(29)   (a) blue   [bu]   small   [fɔw]
             balloon   [fi-bun]   smoke   [fok]
         (b)

	IDENT[labial]	OCP	MAX
blue: $b_1l_2u_3 \rightarrow b_{12}u_3$		*!	*
$b_1l_2u_3 \rightarrow d_{12}u_3$	*!		
✖ $b_1l_2u_3 \rightarrow l_2u_3$			*

Tableau (29b) shows that, given the current constraint ranking, the incorrect candidate **lu* (with deletion of the input labial /b/) is the winner. The constraint MAX in tableau (28) must therefore be parameterised to include glides (and liquids) but not true consonants. I shall call this constraint MAX(GL). It demands that all glides and liquids present in the input must be present in the output. The forms in (29) obey the constraint MAX(CONS), the analogous constraint for true consonants. MAX(CONS) is ranked above the OCP, since true consonants cannot be deleted under pressure from the OCP. This is shown in tableau (30).

(30)

	IDENT [labial]	MAX (CONS)	OCP	MAX (GLIDE)
blue:				
☞ $b_1l_2u_3 \rightarrow b_{12}u_3$			*	
$b_1l_2u_3 \rightarrow d_{12}u_3$	*!			
$b_1l_2u_3 \rightarrow l_2u_3$		*!		
smoke:				
☞ $s_1m_2o_3k_4 \rightarrow f_{12}o_3k_4$			*	
$s_1m_2o_3k_4 \rightarrow s_1o_3k_4$		*!		

Cases such as *fi-bun* 'balloon', where a labial-round vowel sequence is derived to avoid a glide onset show that μ/glide must also outrank the OCP. This is shown in (31).

(31)

	μ/glide	OCP
balloon:		
☞ $b_1ə_2l_3u_4n_5 \rightarrow fi\text{-}y_3u_4n_5$	*!	
$b_1ə_2l_3u_4n_5 \rightarrow fi\text{-}b_{13}u_4n_5$		*

As the cases of coalescence before front vowels (discussed in section 5) showed, coalescence is the preferred way of satisfying *COMPLEX. As forms like *go* 'grow' attest, however, deletion of glides/liquids occurs when necessary to satisfy the highly ranked OCP. Deletion occurs in cases where the labial consonant is a glide/liquid (as in 'grow'), but it does not occur in cases where the labial is a stop (as in 'blue'). Because of the more highly ranked MAX(CONS), the *b* (unlike the *r'''* in 'grow') cannot be deleted to satisfy the OCP.

The diagrams in (32) illustrate the segmental correspondence of various labial clusters.

(32)   (a) 'green'   (b) 'grow'   (c) 'blue'

As the correspondence lines show, *bin* 'green' is a straightforward case of coalescence which preserves underlying labial place and the manner features of the least sonorous consonant, as discussed in section 5. *Go* 'grow' shows deletion under pressure from the OCP, as in tableau (28). In *bu* 'blue', the labial cannot be deleted because it is a true consonant (as shown in tableau (30)). Instead we have coalescence, with IDENT[labial] ensuring that the labial shows up in spite of the OCP (as in (27)).

The rankings responsible for the forms in (32) are summarised in tableau (33). Once again, only candidates satisfying *COMPLEX are considered, as *COMPLEX is never violated.

(33)

	IDENT [lab]	MAX (CONS)	OCP	MAX (GL)	NO-COAL
green: ☞ $g_1 r^w_2 i_3 n_4 \rightarrow b_{12} i_3 n_4$					*
$g_1 r^w_2 i_3 n_4 \rightarrow g_{12} i_3 n_4$	*!				*
$g_1 r^w_2 i_3 n_4 \rightarrow g_1 i_3 n_4$				*!	
grow: $g_1 r^w_2 o_3 \rightarrow b_{12} o_3$			*!		*
$g_1 r^w_2 o_3 \rightarrow g_{12} o_3$	*!				*
☞ $g_1 r^w_2 o_3 \rightarrow g_1 o_3$				*	
blue: ☞ $b_1 l_2 u_3 \rightarrow b_{12} u_3$			*		*
$b_1 l_2 u_3 \rightarrow d_{12} u_3$	*!				*
$b_1 l_2 u_3 \rightarrow y_{12} u_3$	*!				*
$b_1 l_2 u_3 \rightarrow y_2 u_3$		*!			
$b_1 l_2 u_3 \rightarrow b_1 u_3$			*	*!	

The non-coalescing cases such as *go* 'grow' provide yet more evidence for segmentally accurate inputs. Although 'green' and 'bean' are homophonous for G – both are *bin* – *gr* and *b* must be separate at underlying representation, since the OCP distinguishes between them. If the following vowel is rounded, the OCP forces a labial glide to be deleted instead of coalescing. Thus 'grow' is *go*, not **bo*. Due to the high-ranking of IDENT[labial], however, an underlying *b* surfaces, so 'boat' is *bot*. G must therefore distinguish between underlying *gr* and *b*. It cannot be maintained that the difference between 'green' (which coalesces) and 'grow' (which deletes r^w) lies in perception and that the labial vowel obscures G's perception of the r^w. The same lack of labialisation is often observed when the consonant after the vowel, but not the vowel itself, is labial. In a word like 'grandma', which G pronounces *gæma*, the coalescence of *g* and r^w is blocked by the presence of *m* in the next syllable. *gæma* and *gæmpæwət* 'granddparent' contrast clearly with *bændɔtə* 'grandaughter' where there is no labial consonant after the *æ* and so coalescence does occur. Although blocking of coalescence does not always occur across vowels, it occurs quite frequently. In 'grandma', the labial r^w and the labial *m* are separated by an unrounded vowel that is stressed and therefore perceptually salient. Such cases of the OCP operating across a stressed unrounded vowel show that it is very unlikely that the two labial articulations could be heard as one. The effect of the OCP on such forms is therefore strong support for the view that G's *input forms* are segmentally accurate, and that G's divergence from the adult forms is due to a difference in constraint ranking. Specifically, G ranks the OCP constraint on markedness above the faithfulness constraint MAX(GL).

As the ranking of constraints in tableau (33) shows, the OCP is not a simple surface-true constraint. Rather it is a violable constraint that has its place in a whole hierarchy of constraints. Because it is dominated by the faithfulness constraints IDENT[labial] and MAX(CONS), the OCP is frequently violated. This is the case in forms such as *bu* 'blue', **du*. Where IDENT[labial] is irrelevant, the effect of the OCP emerges. It then plays a crucial role in selecting the output, as in *go* 'grow', **bo*.

7.   Comparison with other models

The action of the OCP in G's language is a perfect example of the Emergence of the Unmarked. Optimality Theory captures such behaviour by making the OCP one of a hierarchy of ranked, violable constraints. Models of phonology which rely on either unranked constraints or the serial application of rules fail to derive the Emergence of the Unmarked. Constraint-based models which do not employ ranking have no way of explaining why the OCP is only obeyed where it does not conflict with certain other constraints. By ranking the constraints, OT can represent which constraints must be obeyed at the expense of which other constraints.

Rule-based derivational models also fail to derive the Emergence of the Unmarked. The simple, unmarked forms must be derived as the result of complex and arbitrary rules which can make no reference to the general constraints motivating the appearance of the unmarked forms. An attempt to describe the effects of the OCP in G's language as the result of simple, general rules would have to include a dissimilation rule which deleted the feature [labial] on an onset when it occurred adjacent to a labial vowel (or a vowel followed by a labial consonant). A default rule would presumably supply segments with the default place [coronal] where necessary. The coalescence of labial onsets would also be the result of a rule. No matter which order [labial] dissimilation and coalescence are applied in, the wrong result obtains. The two orders of application are shown in (34).

(34)　(a)

	green	grow	room	small
Input	gr^win	gr^wo	r^wum	smɔl
Delete Labial (+ default [cor])	gr^win	go	yum	sɔl
Coalesce	bin	go	yum	sɔl
Output	bin	go	*yum	*sɔl

　　(b)

	green	grow	room	small
Input	gr^win	gr^wo	r^wum	smɔl
Coalesce	bin	bo	r^wum	fɔl
Delete Labial (+ default [cor])	bin	do	yum	sɔl
Output	bin	*do	*yum	*sɔl

In (34a) 'grow' undergoes dissimilation (Delete Labial) before coalescence so that labial coalescence correctly does not apply. The dissimilation wrongly targets the onset of 'room', however, yielding *yum. In 'small' the dissimilation also misapplies, bleeding the coalescence rule to produce *sɔl. In (34b) the opposite order does even worse. Coalescence wrongly applies to 'grow' and the r^w in 'room' is still wrongly a target of dissimilation. Coalescence applies properly to 'small', but then the dissimilation also applies, yielding *sɔl. One could remove the r^w in 'room' from the list of targets by restricting dissimilation to derived environments. Only forms which were affected by coalescence would be subject to dissimilation. This would protect the r^w in 'room'. The appeal to the derived environment, however, crucially relies on the ordering of coalescence (which provides the derived environment) *before* dissimilation. This is the order of (34b). Even if 'room' were properly given as *wum* in (34b) the ordering still fails on the derivation of 'grow' and 'small', predicting *do and *sɔl rather than *go* and *fɔl*.

The only way to make the derivation model in (34) work is to restrict the labial deletion rule in the (34a) ordering to *glides/liquids that occur as the second consonant in an onset* before a rounded vowel or unrounded vowel plus labial consonant. This is a very restricted and arbitrary rule to derive from the general motive of the OCP which looks only for successive labials. Why a child would posit such a rule is left unexplained.

OT, on the other hand, succeeds in describing the complex behaviour of the OCP through the interaction of constraints which are in themselves simple and independently motivated. It captures the emergence of the unmarked in the action of the OCP because it represents the OCP not as the motivation for an idiosyncratic ordered rule or as a surface-true constraint but as one constraint among many which will be violated when it is dominated by the appropriate constraint. The dominating constraints ensure that the OCP in this case emerges only in a very restricted environment. The OCP effects in G's language show that child phonology, like adult phonology, is best described by a hierarchy of ranked, violable constraints as provided by Optimality Theory.

8.   Conclusion

This chapter has demonstrated that Optimality Theory succeeds in describing child phonology by ascribing to the child's grammar the same constraints and ranking properties as are required for adult languages. In particular, section 3 showed how G's treatment of onsets is driven by the same constraints as onset simplification in Sanskrit reduplication, while section 5 showed that G's pattern of coalescence is like that in Navajo.

An OT model of child phonology neatly accounts for the fact that the child frequently derives outputs which diverge quite strongly from the adult forms. The divergence stems from a difference in constraint rankings between the child language and the target language. It need not lie in a difference in input forms, as this child's inputs have been shown to be segmentally accurate. The evidence for this came from the facts of onset replacement in *fi*- words, described in section 4.

The fact that the child language displays less markedness than the adult language is due to the initial state of the grammar, in which the marked-ness constraints are ranked above the faithfulness constraints, as proposed in section 1. As the phonology develops, the faithfulness constraints move upward as required to approximate the adult language. At the stage of the data in this chapter, G still ranked the markedness constraints *COMPLEX, μ/glide, and the OCP above the faithfulness constraints MAX, NO-COAL and I-CONTIG. *COMPLEX was at this point still undominated by any faithfulness constraints.

As children begin to promote the faithfulness constraints, their phonology is predicted to display cases of the Emergence of the Unmarked. This was shown to be the case for G's ranking of the OCP in section 6. In some cases the OCP played a crucial role in selecting the output, while in others it was rendered powerless by the demands of the constraints which dominate it. G's treatment of labial clusters could not be captured using a system of unranked constraints, while a rule-based derivation was arbitrary in its connection to the OCP. Only

OT, which imposes a ranking on a set of violable constraints, could account for the OCP's behaviour in G's language.

This chapter has shown that the application of OT to acquisition allows both child and adult language to be analysed using the same model of phonology, and using the same constraints. This unity of approach has in general not been achieved in other models of child phonology. For comparison, consider three alternative models of child phonology. Smith (1973) considers the child's system of phonology a mapping from an adult-like underlying form to the child's surface form. Working in a rule-based framework inspired by *SPE* (Chomsky and Halle, 1968), he ascribes to the child a long series of 'realisation rules' deriving the child's output forms from the adult-like underlying forms. By using such rules Smith attempts to describe child language in the model used for adult language. Using this model has the unsatisfactory result that the child has more phonological rules than the adults do. The child is seen as having formulated a large number of rules for which he has never received any evidence. Also, as Smith (1973: 176 ff.) and Ingram (1976, 1989a) point out, many of these rules have the same purpose. For example, 7 of 23 rules have the function of eliminating consonant clusters.

Ingram (1976, 1989a, 1989b) avoids the proliferation of formally unrelated rules by ascribing to the child an extra phonological level. In his model the three levels of child phonology are perception, organisation, and production. Constraints may operate at each level. Perceptual constraints, such as the inability to perceive coda consonants, may be translated into organisational rules or production rules after the child becomes able to perceive codas. For instance, if a child is at first unable to perceive codas she may hypothesise that all words consist of CV syllables. She will then map new words onto this CV pattern at the organisation level even after she has begun to perceive codas. Once the child can process and produce coda consonants at all phonological levels, the rule is suppressed.

Stampe (1973) uses a two-level model like Smith, with adult-like inputs, but the outputs are derived by a set of innate natural processes which serve to reduce markedness. In the earliest stage of acquisition the processes operate freely whenever their conditions are met. As the phonology develops, these processes are ordered (and re-ordered), limited in application, or suppressed as needed to approximate more and more closely the adult grammar. Thus a child with only CV syllables would derive them from adult CVC syllables by a natural process deleting coda consonants. If the child's target language has codas the natural process which deletes them is eventually suppressed.

Ingram's model is one in which constraints or rules operate on both the input (organisation) and the output (production). Smith's is one in which a long series of ordered rules operate directly on the input to derive the output. Stampe's model provides universal rules, but still relies on serial derivation of the output from the input. All three give the child more tasks and hence a larger processing load than the adult has. Smith gives the child more rules, Ingram gives her an extra level, and Stampe and Ingram both ascribe to the child processes that are later suppressed. Stampe's model is closest to that provided by OT in that it proposes innate processes. The difference is that it relies on ordering, not ranking, as OT does. Such ordered derivations will fail at a natural description of the Emergence of the Unmarked, as noted in section 6.

By contrast, Optimality Theory does not give the child an extra processing load. The child does not have more rules or more levels than the adult. In the OT framework the phonology is one of output constraints which are universal, and hence shared by children and adults. The output candidates evaluated by children and adults are the same, but children select different winning candidates than do adults. Re-ranking of the constraints provides the means by which the phonology develops. Certain rankings of the constraints will cause the child's language to exhibit Emergence of the Unmarked. Such cases provide strong evidence that child phonology is best modelled by a hierarchy of constraints as in OT.

NOTES

* This is a revised version of a 1995 University of Massachusetts, Amherst paper. I should like to thank Gitanjali for cheerfully providing the data for this paper and occasionally allowing me time to work on it. I am also grateful to John McCarthy, Linda Lombardi, Joe Pater, Lisa Selkirk, and Shelley Velleman (and three anonymous referees for this volume) for much needed suggestions and criticisms. Remaining errors are my own. This work was supported in part by NSF grant SBR–9420424.
1. [Editors' note] For different views, see Boersma (1998) and Hayes (1999).
2. A similar proposal, namely that constraints requiring unmarked prosodic forms initially outrank constraints requiring faithfulness to input segments, is made by Demuth (1995).
3. [Editors' note] Acquisition as the demotion of markedness constraints rather than the promotion of faithfulness constraints is discussed in detail by Tesar and Smolensky (1998, 2000).
4. Like other children (Macken 1980) G uses a few forms which can only be explained by assuming 'incorrect' inputs, i.e., inputs with different segments than the adults have. Presumably these forms originate in misperceptions. Such words are very few in G's speech, however. The vast majority of G's words can be systematically derived with the assumption of 'correct' inputs.
5. [Editors' note] See Goad and Rose's contribution to this volume, and references cited there, for more elaborate remarks on the behaviour of initial clusters.
6. In Sanskrit FAITH-IO and FAITH-BR are, respectively, the MAX-IO and MAX-BR of McCarthy and Prince (1995a). I use the more general FAITH to facilitate comparison with G's language.
7. For the use of sonority to optimise syllable shapes in OT, see Prince and Smolensky (1993). For other references establishing the sonority hierarchy, see Sievers (1881), Jespersen (1904), de Saussure (1916), Zwicky (1972), Hankamer and Aissen (1974), Hooper (1976), Steriade (1982), and Selkirk (1984) among others.

8. Since G produces s+stop clusters as a simple voiced stop, I assume that she has assigned the neutralised voiceless unaspirate of this position to the voiced (unaspirated) phoneme. This is not uncommon, although children vary as to whether they treat these unaspirated stops as voiced or voiceless (Bond and Wilson 1980).

9. The constraint family in (8) is closely related to Prince and Smolensky's (1993) *MARGIN hierarchy which prohibits segments from being parsed as syllable margins (forcing them to be parsed as nuclei). The difference between the *MARGIN hierarchy and the μ/Y hierarchy is that by the use of moraic versus nonmoraic positions (instead of nuclear versus margin positions) the μ/Y hierarchy accounts for the fact (discussed by Zec 1988) that codas are of high sonority relative to onsets.

10. Given the universal nature of the Sonority Hierarchy, the ranking of the constraints in (8) should also be universal.

11. Recall that G's speech has vowel-initial words ('I' [ay]), which suggests that segmental faithfulness dominates ONSET. Not resolved here is what prohibits the whole μ/Y hierarchy from outranking ONSET and thus producing a language with no onsets at all. The same open question exists in Prince and Smolensky's (1993) presentation of syllabification, since theoretically their whole *MARGIN/λ hierarchy (which prohibits segments from being parsed as margins) could outrank ONSET, yielding a language with only nuclear segments.

12. Recall that input /r/ would be realised as [w] in onsets in G's speech, cf. (2b).

13. [Editors' note] A referee notes that *COMPLEX appears to be active in English hypocoristics (cf. Sandy from *Sandra*).

14. G's use of *fi-* is very similar to A's (Smith 1973) use of the syllable *ri-* in practically the same environment (A's was initial unstressed syllables whose vowel was *i* or *ə*. It is hard to tell whether the vowel quality is important or not, since virtually all unstressed vowels can be reduced to *ə*). Like A, G shows some variation, so that G's 'piano' has been pronounced as both *pinæno* and *fi-næno*. In G's case it is my impression that the occasional non-use of *fi-* is most likely to occur in words which begin with labial consonants. I assume this is because G can pronounce an underlying labial consonant with as little violence as possible to the set *fi-* form. It is worth speculating on why these two children, but apparently no others in the acquisition literature, used this type of pretonic dummy syllable. My hunch is that, while the strategy may be quite rare, it is probably more common than the literature suggests. G used *fi-* for almost a year, but it might be that a child with nonlinguist parents would experience such a lack of parental comprehension in the face of a dummy syllable that she would be highly motivated to switch to almost any other grammar that she was developmentally ready for. Dummy syllables might therefore occur in a number of children, but usually be rapidly suppressed.

15. At an earlier stage the initial unstressed syllables were deleted, as is typical in child language (Kehoe and Stoel-Gammon 1997, Pater 1997, and references cited there). The dummy syllable stage represents an intermediate stage where faithfulness to the *syllable* has been promoted, but faithfulness to the *segments* has not.

16. [Editors' note] The issue of syllable structure in adult lexical representations has not been settled; see Inkelas (1995) and references cited there.

17. See McCarthy and Prince (1995a) for the motivation of this constraint in adult languages, the evidence for which includes the preservation in languages such as Diyari (Austin 1981) of word-internal codas but not word-final ones in the face of a prohibition on syllable codas.

104 *Amalia Gnanadesikan*

18. A potential obstacle to this interpretation is that *h* is left in words such as *fi-hayn* 'behind', and *h* is arguably more sonorous than liquids (Gnanadesikan, 1995, 1997) since it patterns with the more sonorous glides in processes such as nasal harmony. Although G's liquids were realised as glides (and so were safely more sonorous than *h*) at the time of the transcriptions shown here, later pronunciations have onset *l*s which are pronounced as lateral. Notice also that, although *h* patterns as very sonorous in harmony processes, it behaves as nonsonorous in syllabification, avoiding moraic positions and preferring onsets.

19. Forms discussed in section 3, such as *piz* from /pliz/ 'please', seem to violate I-CONTIG as well, since the /l/ is absent in the output. As section 5 will show, however, most of G's onset reductions are actually effected through coalescence, which is vacuous in a word like 'please'. As a result, the forms in section 3 (in which the coalescing segments of the input onset cluster are themselves contiguous) do not violate I-CONTIG. The *fi-* forms do violate I-CONTIG, however, since the coalescing consonants are separated by a vowel.

20. An analysis of the mechanism that produces the *fi-* is tangential to the present treatment of G's onsets. I would suggest, however, that the *fi-* can be analysed as resulting from the conflict of faithfulness constraints (here faithfulness to syllables) with markedness constraints of the alignment family proposed by McCarthy and Prince (1993). An alignment constraint requiring the stem of a word to coincide at the left edge with the tonic syllable would have the result that underlying stem material in an unstressed initial syllable is deleted. (This would also account for the earlier stage in which unstressed initial syllables were merely absent.) Faithfulness to the syllable (but not the segments) has been promoted by the *fi-* stage, and can be satisfied by prefixation. An analysis of *fi-* as a prefix could account for its nondefault shape and its secondary stress, which sets it off somewhat from the following stem (something I have tried to represent by the hyphen between *fi* and the following segments). It is my suspicion that the segmental content of the prefix *fi-* came from 'VNA', the name of G's day-care centre, which G pronounced as *fi-ɛn*. Other types of melodic overwriting, such as in Kolami, may be due to a conflict between alignment constraints on a prefix and alignment constraints on the stem segments.

21. [Editors' note] The apparent discrepancy between forms like *tree* [pi] in (15) and *draw* [dɔ] in (2) will be explained in section 6.

22. G pronounces English *r* and *w* both as [w], cf. (2). I leave aside the question of whether this substitution is in the input or the output. To stress the labiality of *r*, I henceforth render *r* as *rʷ* in G's input. In her output, of course, it is *w*.

23. [Editors' note] For a fusion analysis of coalescence in correspondence theory, see McCarthy and Prince (1995) and Pater (1999: 315).

24. [Editors' note] The output [tʷ] (labialised t) will have to be eliminated by some independent markedness constraint.

25. NO-COAL is part of the LINEARITY constraint of McCarthy and Prince (1995a) which serves to prohibit both coalescence and metathesis. McCarthy and Prince suggest that the two functions might need to be separated, and I have done so in this chapter because G's grammar treats coalescence and metathesis separately. Specifically, µ/glide could force NO-COAL violations (in the *fi-* cases) when it could no longer force metathesis. The constraints forbidding coalescence and metathesis must be different and separately ranked to produce different ranges of application. NO-COAL is like Lamontagne and Rice's (1995a,b) *Multiple Correspondence,

except that NO-COAL refers only to segments. It is violated by segment coalescence, but not featural assimilation. This is in accord with the spirit of the McCarthy and Prince (1995a) model which distinguishes the constraints on faithfulness to segments from the constraints on faithfulness to features.

26. [Editors' note] As noted before, in some cases onset /l/ is represented by a glide [y]. This typically occurs in the onsets of unstressed syllables, although not systematically so, cf. *koa*[l]*a* versus *gori*[y]*a*. (Amalia Gnanadesikan, personal communication.)

27. The fact that 'koala' becomes *fi-kala* and not *fi-pala* suggests that G regards its stressed syllable as onsetless, rather than having a labial glide onset.

28. The output in (19a) also incurs an I-CONTIG violation. In developing the ranking argument for MAX and NO-COAL in this section it is difficult to separate the effects of MAX and I-CONTIG. It is possible to separate the effects of I-CONTIG and NO-COAL enough to show that MAX does dominate NO-COAL, since in the *fi-* cases of noncontiguous onsets (where an I-CONTIG violation is unavoidable) coalescence, not deletion, is still the preferred operation (as in *fi-bæf* 'giraffe'). It is more difficult to rank MAX and I-CONTIG with respect to each other and establish the precise ranking of MAX alone. For simplicity I concentrate on MAX in this section.

29. As McCarthy and Prince (1995a) use it, IDENT[F] refers to either value (+ or −), or in privative terms presence or absence of a feature: input and output values must be the same. As Pater (1999) notes, however, the *loss* of a feature (or switch from + to −) cannot always be ranked the same as the *gain* of a feature (or switch from − to +). He uses IDENT I→O [F] to rule out loss of a feature and IDENT O→I[F] to rule out the gain of a feature. Here we are concerned with IDENT I→O[Place], i.e., the set of constraints which demand the retention of underlying Place values.

30. The high ranking of IDENT[lab] in G's language is confirmed by the fact that in her consonant harmony days labials did not undergo harmony, although dorsals and coronals did. Gnanadesikan (1997) suggests that the place features may actually be scalar in at least some respects, in which case the ranking IDENT[labial] » IDENT[dorsal] » IDENT[coronal] would be universal. The universal ranking of faithfulness to labials and dorsals over coronals (but not labials over dorsals) was proposed by Kiparsky (1994).

31. Where Navajo can form a complex segment by coalescence, it does, yielding *d* + *l* → *dl*, etc. In such cases Navajo does not require a choice of which features to retain in the output. Since G does not allow such segments, these are irrelevant for the comparison here.

32. I leave open the question of whether the OCP is parameterised, thus yielding different contexts of evaluation, or whether it is not parameterised but has its application affected by other constraints which are independently rankable in different languages.

33. This is the kind of weakening with distance that Pierrehumbert (1993) discusses. Pierrehumbert notes that in Arabic verbal roots adjacent consonants show very strong OCP place effects while nonadjacent consonants show weakened but persistent OCP effects. In her model, the OCP is not categorical but gradient, affected by similarity of manner features and proximity of the segments evaluated. An important difference between Arabic and G's English-based language is that in Arabic successive

consonants are adjacent at the morphological level, while in G's language they are not.

34. This illustrates a consequence of adopting McCarthy and Prince's (1995a) distinction between the IDENT[feature] constraints and MAX. IDENT[feature] is only violable by a segment that actually appears in the output. Therefore the same segment cannot violate both MAX and IDENT[feature]. This is in contrast with views of faithfulness which use PARSE-SEGMENT and PARSE-FEATURE, both of which are violated when an underlying segment fails to be parsed in the output.

35. Glides in glide-initial words such as *wum* 'room' cannot delete because of the constraint ONSET, discussed in section 3, which requires syllables to have an onset.

36. The behaviour of the small sample of words such as *fok* 'smoke', with $s + m +$ rounded vowel, points to a further aspect of G's coalescence. The f of *fok* ('smoke') combines the place of the m with the manner features of the s. The manner features do not 'mix and match' in the coalescence (e.g., **pok*, with a stop from the m that is voiceless like the s), but rather all the manner features of the least sonorous consonant remain. This suggests some feature-geometric clumping of the manner features that does not include the place features. The same clumping is also presumably responsible for examples such as *ɡay* ('sky'), where the underlying form is presumably /sɡay/. The voicelessness of the s does not transfer to the neutralised stop G has assigned to the voiced phoneme *ɡ*.

References

Allerton, D. J. (1976). Early phonotactic development: some observations on a child's acquisition of initial consonant clusters. *Journal of Child Language* **3**. 429–433.

Austin, P. (1981). *A Grammar of Diyari, South Australia*. Cambridge: Cambridge University Press.

Boersma, P. (1998). *Functional Phonology. Formalizing the Interactions between Articulatory and Perceptual Drives*. The Hague: Holland Academic Graphics.

Bond, Z. S. and H. F. Wilson (1980). /s/ plus stop clusters in children's speech. *Phonetica* **37**. 149–158.

Chin, S. B. and D. A. Dinnsen (1992). Consonant clusters in disordered speech: constraints and correspondence patterns. *Journal of Child Language* **4**. 417–432.

Chomsky, N. and M. Halle (1968). *The Sound Pattern of English*. New York: Harper and Row.

Demuth, K. (1995). Markedness and the development of prosodic structure. In J. N. Beckman (ed.) *Proceedings of NELS* **25**. GLSA, University of Massachusetts, Amherst.

Edwards, M. L. and L. D. Shriberg (1983). *Phonology: Applications in Communications Disorders*. San Diego: College-Hill Press.

Emeneau, M. B. (1955). *Kolami: a Dravidian Language*. University of California Publications in Linguistics, Vol. 12. Berkeley: University of California Press.

Gnanadesikan, A. E. (1995). Deriving the Sonority Hierarchy from ternary scales. Paper presented at the 1995 Annual Meeting of the Linguistic Society of America.

(1997). *Phonology with Ternary Scales*. Ph.D. dissertation, University of Massachusetts, Amherst.

Goad, H. and Y. Rose (this volume). Input elaboration, head faithfulness, and evidence for representation in the acquisition of left-edge clusters in West Germanic.

Grunwell, P. (1981). *Clinical Phonology*. London: Croom Helm.

Hankamer, J. and J. Aissen (1974). The sonority hierarchy. In A. Bruck, R. A. Fox, and M. W. La Galy (eds.) *Papers from the Parasession on Natural Phonology. CLS*. 131–145.

Hashimoto, O.-K. Y. (1972). *Phonology of Cantonese*. Cambridge: Cambridge University Press.

Hayes, B. (1999). Phonetically-driven phonology: the role of Optimality Theory and inductive grounding. In M. Darnell, E. Moravscik, M. Noonan, F. Newmeyer, and K. Wheatly (eds.) *Functionalism and Formalism in Linguistics, Vol. I: General Papers*. Amsterdam: John Benjamins. 243–285.

Hooper, J. B. (1976). *An Introduction to Natural Generative Phonology*. New York: Academic Press.

Ingram, D. (1976). Phonological analysis of a child. *Glossa* **10**. 3–27.

(1989a). *First Language Acquisition: Method, Description, Explanation*. Cambridge: Cambridge University Press.

(1989b). *Phonological Disability in Children*. London: Cole and Whurr (2nd edn).

Inkelas, S. (1995). The consequences of optimization for underspecification. In J. Beckman (ed.) *Proceedings of the NELS* **25**. 287–302.

Jespersen, O. (1904). *Lerhbuch der Phonetik*. Leipzig: Teubner.

Kari, J. (1973). *Navajo Verb Prefix Phonology*. Ph.D. dissertation, University of New Mexico (published 1976, Garland Press).

Kehoe, M. M. and C. Stoel-Gammon (1997). The acquisition of prosodic structure: an investigation of current accounts of children's prosodic development. *Lg* **73**. 113–144.

Kiparsky, P. (1994). Remarks on markedness. Paper presented at TREND 2.

Lamontagne, G. and K. Rice (1995a). Navajo coalescence, deletion and faithfulness. Paper presented at the 1995 Annual Meeting of the Linguistic Society of America.

(1995b). A Correspondence account of coalescence. In J. N. Beckman, L. Walsh Dickey, and S. Urbanczyk (eds.) *Papers in Optimality Theory*. University of Massachusetts Occasional Papers in Linguistics 18. Amherst: GLSA. 211–223.

Light, T. (1977). The Cantonese final: an exercise in indigenous analysis. *Journal of Chinese Linguistics* **5**. 75–102.

Macken, M. A. (1980). The child's lexical representation: the 'puzzle-puddle-pickle' evidence. *JL* **16**. 1–17.

McCarthy, J. and A. Prince (1986). Prosodic morphology. MS., University of Massachusetts, Amherst and Brandeis University.

(1990). Foot and word in prosodic morphology: the Arabic broken plural. *NLLT* **8**. 209–283.

(1994). The emergence of the unmarked: optimality in prosodic morphology. In M. Gonzàlez (ed.) *Proceedings of the NELS* **24**. 333–379. Amherst: GLSA.

(1995a). Faithfulness and reduplicative identity. In J. N. Beckman, L. Walsh Dickey, and S. Urbanczyk (eds.) *Papers in Optimality Theory*. University of Massachusetts Occasional Papers in Linguistics 18. Amherst: GLSA. 249–384.

(1995b). Prosodic morphology. In J. Goldsmith (ed.) *The Handbook of Phonological Theory*. Cambridge, Mass.: Blackwell.

(1999). Faithfulness and identity in prosodic morphology. In R. Kager, H. van der Hulst, and W. Zonneveld (eds.) *The Prosody–Morphology Interface*. Cambridge: Cambridge University Press. 218–309.

Pater, J. (1997). Minimal violation and phonological development. *Language Acquisition* **6**. 201–253.

(1999). Austronesian nasal substitution and other NÇ effects. In R. Kager, H. van der Hulst, and W. Zonneveld (eds.) *The Prosody–Morphology Interface*. Cambridge: Cambridge University Press. 310–343.

Pierrehumbert, J. (1993). Dissimilarity in the Arabic verbal roots. In A. Schafer (ed.) *Proceedings of the NELS* **23**. 367–381. Amherst: GLSA.

Prince, A. and P. Smolensky (1991). Notes on Connectionism and Harmony Theory in Linguistics. Technical report CU-CS-533–91, Department of Computer Science, University of Colorado, Boulder.

(1993). Optimality Theory: constraint interaction in Generative Grammar. MS., Rutgers University and University of Colorado, Boulder.

De Saussure, F. (1916). *Cours de linguistique générale*. Lausanne and Paris: Payot.

Selkirk, E. O. (1984). On the major class features and syllable theory. In M. Aronoff and R. T. Oehrle (eds.) *Language Sound Structure: Studies in Phonology Dedicated to Morris Halle by his Teacher and Students*. Cambridge, Mass.: MIT Press. 107–113.

(1993). [Labial] relations. MS., University of Massachusetts.

Sievers, E. (1881). *Grundzüge der Phonetik*. Leipzig: Breitkopf und Härtel.

Smith, N. V. (1973). *The Acquisition of Phonology: a Case Study*. Cambridge: Cambridge University Press.

Stampe, D. (1973). *How I Spent my Summer Vacation: a Dissertation on Natural Phonology*. Ph.D. dissertation, University of Chicago.

Steriade, D. (1982). *Greek Prosodies and the Nature of Syllabification*. Ph.D. dissertation, MIT, Cambridge, Mass.

(1988). Reduplication and syllable transfer in Sanskrit and elsewhere. *Phonology* **5**. 73–155.

Stoel-Gammon, C. and C. Dunn (1985). *Normal and Disordered Phonology in Children*. Baltimore: University Park Press.

Tesar, B. and P. Smolensky (1998). Learnability in Optimality Theory. *LI* **29**. 229–268.

(2000). *Learnability in Optimality Theory*. MIT Press.

Whitney, W. D. (1889). *Sanskrit Grammar, Including Both the Classical Language and the Older Dialects, of Veda and Brahmana*. Cambridge, Mass.: Harvard University Press (2nd edn).

Yip, M. (1988). The Obligatory Contour Principle and phonological rules: a loss of identity. *LI* **19**. 65–100.

(1992). Reduplication with fixed melodic material. In K. Broderick (ed.) *Proceedings of the NELS* **22**. Amherst: GLSA.

Zec, D. (1988). *Sonority Constraints on Prosodic Structure*. Ph.D. dissertation, Stanford University.

Zwicky, A. (1972). Note on a phonological hierarchy in English. In R. P. Stockwell and R. K. S. Macauley (eds.) *Linguistic Change and Generative Theory*. Bloomington: Indiana University Press. 275–301.

4 Input elaboration, head faithfulness, and evidence for representation in the acquisition of left-edge clusters in West Germanic

Heather Goad and Yvan Rose

1. Preliminaries*

Several recent investigations of the development of left-edge clusters in West Germanic languages have demonstrated that the relative sonority of adjacent consonants plays a key role in children's reduction patterns (e.g., Fikkert 1994, Gilbers and Den Ouden 1994, Chin 1996, Barlow 1997, Bernhardt and Stemberger 1998, Gierut 1999, Ohala 1999, Gnanadesikan this volume). These authors have argued that, for a number of children, at the stage in development when only one member of a left-edge cluster is produced, it is the least sonorous segment that survives, regardless of where this segment appears in the target string or the structural position that it occupies (head, dependent, or appendix). To illustrate briefly, while the more sonorous /S/[1] is lost in favour of the stop in /S/+stop clusters, /S/ is retained in /S/+sonorant clusters; similarly, the least sonorous stop survives in both /S/+stop and stop+sonorant clusters, in spite of the fact that it occurs in different positions in the two strings. To account for reduction patterns such as these, a structural difference between /S/-initial and stop-initial clusters need not be assumed. This would seem to fare well in view of much of the recent constraint-based literature which de-emphasises the role of prosodic constituency in favour of phonetically based explanations of phonological phenomena (see, e.g., Hamilton 1996, Wright 1996, Kochetov 1999, Steriade 1999, Côté 2000).

In this chapter, we focus on a second set of reduction patterns for left-edge clusters, one which is not addressed in most of the sonority-based literature on cluster reduction in child language (L1): these patterns reveal a preference for structural heads to survive. For example, while the stop is retained in clusters of the shape /S/+stop and stop+sonorant, it is the sonorant that survives in /S/+sonorant clusters. The only sources that we have found where explicit reference is made to the retention of heads are Spencer (1986), who re-analyses Amahl's data (from Smith 1973) within the context of non-linear phonology, and Gilbers and Den Ouden (1994), who nonetheless appear to reject a head-based approach at the end of their paper in favour of one based on sonority.

Not surprisingly, reference to heads is also absent from the L1 literature which predates the development of non-linear phonology, when the syllable was not widely accepted as a formal constituent (following Chomsky and Halle 1968). For example, although Amahl's grammar shows a preference for the maintenance of heads, Smith (1973) appeals to sonority in his discussion of cluster reduction.[2]

In order to provide a unified account for both patterns of cluster reduction, we adopt the position that the theory of syllable structure must encode a formal difference between /S/-initial clusters and obstruent-initial clusters more generally,[3] where /S/ is represented as an appendix, as was standardly assumed in the literature on non-linear phonology (see below). We shall demonstrate further that constraints must make explicit reference to heads of syllable constituents; specifically, the constraint MAXHEAD(ONSET) will play a crucial role in our analysis.

This approach entails that (adult) inputs are fully prosodified. However, full prosodification requires knowledge of the structures that are permitted in the target language. Accordingly, we propose that children's inputs are initially prosodified for simplex onsets and rhymes/nuclei, that is, for heads of sub-syllabic constituents only (cf. Dresher and Van der Hulst 1998). While there is often a correlation between the head of a left-edge cluster and low sonority, we demonstrate that heads cannot be determined solely on the basis of relative prominence; distributional evidence must be factored in and understanding this evidence requires knowledge that is relatively sophisticated. We propose that children initially make decisions about headedness on the basis of sonority until the distributional facts are understood. We argue that it is for this reason that two patterns of cluster reduction are observed in the acquisition data, what we will henceforth call the *sonority pattern* and the *head pattern*.

The chapter is organised as follows. In section 2, we introduce the two patterns of cluster reduction under investigation. The data on which we focus are drawn from children learning three West Germanic languages: English, German, and Dutch. We turn in section 3 to our assumptions about acquisition in the context of Optimality Theory (OT), the framework in which our analysis is couched. Our central point will be to demonstrate that the acquisition of an OT grammar involves two components: (i) the elaboration of inputs; and (ii) constraint re-ranking. Our focus will primarily be on the former, specifically on the development of prosodic structure. In section 4, we turn to an investigation of sub-syllabic structure in West Germanic. We motivate representations for various cluster types and go through the evidence that children require in order to achieve target-like syllabification of these clusters. As will be seen in section 5, for clusters whose structural head corresponds to the least sonorous segment, a single pattern of cluster reduction is observed in the acquisition data. However, when the head does not correspond to what is least sonorous in the adult grammar, namely in /S/+sonorant clusters, patterns of variation are observed across children; indeed, we shall argue that the distinction between the sonority and head patterns arises from this mismatch between relative prominence (low sonority) and structural headedness. We demonstrate in section 5.1 that the head pattern can be accounted for if target-like inputs are posited, that is, highly articulated representations where obstruent-initial clusters are organised as branching onsets while /S/-initial clusters involve appendix licensing. The sonority pattern, by contrast, arises from less articulated inputs; only heads of sub-syllabic constituents are specified, where heads are defined by low sonority alone. In section 5.2, we provide the necessary constraints for the analysis. As will be seen, one of these constraints, MAXHEAD, requires that inputs be fully prosodified. In order to establish the viability of this approach beyond accounting for children's cluster reduction, we briefly demonstrate in section 5.3 that this approach makes the right predictions when confronted with data from adult grammars as well, in particular, from one dialect of Brazilian Portuguese. Section 5.4 shows that, for both patterns of cluster reduction, undominated structural well-formedness constraints yield outputs with simplex onsets and rhymes/nuclei only, the unmarked syllable shape provided by Universal Grammar (hereafter UG). In section 6, we turn to the syllabification of /Sr/ clusters which, of the three languages under investigation, are only tolerated in German (see note 10 on Dutch and English). Following from section 4 where we argue that the representation of /r/ makes /Sr/ clusters marked as appendix-initial structures, we demonstrate in section 6 that Annalena, the German-speaking child from whom our data are drawn, initially analyses them as branching onsets. For completeness, in section 7, we attempt a strictly linear analysis of the head pattern, that is, one which does not exploit syllable-internal constituency but, instead, stems from the observation that (strident) fricatives emerge late in acquisition. We demonstrate that such an approach cannot lead to a satisfactory analysis when confronted with data from children like Amahl. A brief conclusion is provided in section 8.

2.   Patterns of cluster reduction

As mentioned in the introduction, at the point when left-edge clusters are produced as a single segment, several scholars have remarked that the segment which survives is determined by relative prominence: the least sonorous consonant is retained, as can be seen from the first column in (1).[4] This represents the sonority pattern of cluster reduction. Children who unambiguously display this pattern are listed in the second column by language.[5] Age ranges are given in parenthesis (note that Subject 25 is language-delayed). The age ranges provided in (1), as well as those in (3), are conservative; they represent the period of time for which a given child displayed all three of the substitution patterns listed in the first column. A subset of these patterns was attested before the dates provided and, for some children, after these dates as well. Note, finally, that concerning the Dutch children, because few forms are provided by Fikkert (1994) for a given child at any particular point in time, it is difficult to get a clear sense of the beginning and end points for the stages described in (1) and (3). The classification of children into patterns and the age ranges provided are therefore drawn from the tables that Fikkert provides in Appendix D (pp. 318–329).

(1)   Sonority pattern:

Substitution patterns:	Children:		Sources:
obs+son → obs	Dutch:	Noortje (2;5.23-2;11.0)	Fikkert (1994)
S+obs → obs		Robin (1;10.9-2;0.20)	Fikkert (1994)
S+son → S		Tirza (2;0.18-2;1.17)	Fikkert (1994)
	English:	Gitanjali (2;3-2;9)	Gnanadesikan (this volume)
		Subject 25 (4;10)	Chin (1996), Barlow (1997)

Representative data from Gitanjali and Robin are provided in (2). (All forms are transcribed as in the original sources.) Empty cells represent gaps for the particular cluster or segment type in a given language.[6] As can be seen, the least sonorous segment is preserved for each cluster type, regardless of its position in the target string.[7] For Gitanjali, the [p]-initial outputs for 'twinkle' and 'quite' and the [f]-initial outputs for 'smoke' and 'sweater' arise through coalescence (see Gnanadesikan this volume); as features from the least sonorous consonants survive, these forms are consistent with the sonority pattern as well. Coalescence also seems to be responsible for Robin's [f]-initial output for *[zʋ]aaien*. The consonants that survive from Robin's clusters in *ver[st]opt* and *[sl]apen*, [p] and [f], appear to be due to consonant harmony; importantly, in both cases, the non-harmonised counterparts, [t] and [s], correspond to the least sonorous member of the cluster.

(2)   Sonority pattern data:

		Gitanjali		Robin		
		Output	Gloss	Output	Orthog/Target	Gloss
obs+son	pl-bl	[piz]	'please'	[puːnt]	[pl]ons	'splash'
	kl-gl	[kin]	'clean'	(no data)		
	fl-vl	(no data)		[ˈfiːχˈdɑχ]	[vl]iegtuig	'aeroplane'
	χl			[ˈkaˌkaːn]	[χl]ijbaan	'slide'
	pr-br	[fibɛyʌ]	'umbrella'	[bɑt]	[br]and	'fire'

	tr-dr	[dɒ]	'draw'	['tɪkə]	[dr]inken	'to drink'
	kr-gr	[go]	'grow'	['miːkə'foːn]	mi[kr]ofoon	'microphone'
	fr-vr	[fɛn]	'friend'	[fɑχ]	[vr]acht	'load'
	θr	(no data)				
	ʃr	(no data)				
	χr			[suːnt]	[χr]ond	'ground'
	kn			['kɪpɔ]	[kn]uppel	'club'
	tw-dw	[pɪkəw]	'twinkle'	(no data)		
	kw	[payt]	'quite'	(no data)		
S+obs	Sp	[bun]	'spoon'	['pɪlə'tiːk]	[sp]eel-o-theek	'playground'
	St	[daː]	'star'	[puːft]	ver[st]opt	'hidden'
	Sk	[gay]	'sky'			
	Sχ			[zoː]	[sχ]ool	'school'
S+son	Sl	[sip]	'sleep'	['faːpə]	[sl]apen	'to sleep'
	Sm	[fok]	'smoke'	(no data)		
	Sn	[so]	'snow'	['suːpiː]	[sn]oepje	'sweet'
	Sw	[fɛDʌ]	'sweater'	['faːjə]	[zʊ]aaien	'to sway'

Previous studies have shown that the sonority pattern of cluster reduction can be analysed without drawing a formal distinction between obstruent-initial and /S/-initial clusters; indeed, no syllable-internal constituency need be assumed at all (e.g., Barlow 1997, Bernhardt and Stemberger 1998, Gnanadesikan this volume). However, there is a second pattern of cluster reduction, what we refer to as the head pattern, which seems to require reference to syllable-internal structure: it is the head of the onset constituent that survives, as can be observed in (3).[8] Heads are underlined.

(3)   Head Pattern:

Substitution patterns:	Children:		Sources:
obs+son → obs	Dutch:	Tom (1;6.11-1;6.25)	Fikkert (1994)
S+obs → obs		Robin (2;1.9-2;3.24)	Fikkert (1994)
S+son → son		Catootje (2;0.6)	Fikkert (1994)
	English:	Joan (1;10-2;1)	Velten (1943)
		Amahl (2;2-2;6)	Smith (1973)
	German:	Annalena (1;4-1;9)	Elsen (1991)
		Naomi (1;4.26-1;7.27)	Grijzenhout and Joppen-Hellwig (2002)

The table in (4) provides representative data from Amahl and Annalena.[9] This pattern is characterised by reduction of a cluster to the head of the target structure, which does not necessarily correspond to the least sonorous segment of the string. We can observe in (4a) that for left-headed clusters, it is the initial obstruent that survives. In (4b) and (4c), by contrast, the constituent head is the second member of the cluster, and it is this consonant that survives, regardless of its relative sonority. While Amahl's [w]-initial outputs for 'flag' and 'friend' in (4a) may appear to interrupt the pattern, [w] is his substitute for /f/, not for /l,r/; in non-harmonising contexts, /l,r/ are realised as liquids at this stage in development (cf. Goad 1997). Note as well that in 'three' and 'Shreddies', [d] is Amahl's substitute for both /θ/ and /ʃ/ in initial position.

For completeness, we have included the /S/+rhotic data in (4d), as this cluster is licit in German.[10] However, the acquisition of /Sr/ is complicated, which is why it is listed separately from the other S+sonorant clusters and why the head of the cluster has not been underlined. On the basis of what was observed in (4c), we would have expected /r/ to be retained in (4d). Counter to expectation, though, it is /S/ that survives. /S/ is realised by Annalena most often as [θ,ð] at this stage in development; /r/, on the other hand, surfaces as [ʁ] or [x], aside from a few cases of [ʔ,h] and [g], the latter due to consonant harmony. We delay further discussion of /Sr/ until sections 4.3 and 6.

(4)   Head pattern data:

		Amahl		Annalena		
		Output	Gloss	Output	Orthog/Target	Gloss
(a) <u>obs</u>+son	pl-bl	[beːt]	'plate'	[bʊmə]	[bl]ume	'flower'
	kl-gl	[gɔk]	'clock'	[kāˡn]	[kl]ein	'small'
	fl	[wæg]	'flag'	[fɪkə]	[fl]iege	'fly'
	pr-br	[bɛd]	'bread'	[baʊxst]	[br]auchen	'to need'
	tr-dr	[dei]	'tray'	[daʊbɛ]	[tr]aube	'grape'
	kr-gr	[gɔt]	'cross'	[gɪf]	[gr]iff	'grip'
	fr	[wɛnd]	'friend'	[vɔxθ]	[fr]osch	'frog'
	θr	[diː]	'three'			
	ʃr	[dɛdiː]	'Shreddies'			
	kn			[kʊ]	[kn]ie	'knee'
	tw-dw	[daif]	'twice'			
	kw	[giːm]	'queen'	[gāk]	[kv]ark	'quark'
(b) S+<u>obs</u>	Sp	[baidə]	'spider'	[pɪgəl]	[ʃp]iegel	'mirror'
	St	[dif]	'stiff'	[daɪnə]	[ʃt]ein	'stone'
	Sk	[gip]	'skipping'			

(c) S+<u>son</u>	Sl	[lʌg]	'slug'	[lɑ̄fə]	[ʃl]afen	'to sleep'
	Sm	[mɔ:]	'small'	[mɪšən]	[ʃm]eißen	'to throw'
	Sn	[ni:d]	'sneezed'	[nɛl]	[ʃn]ell	'quick'
	Sw	[wiŋ]	'swing'	[vaɪn]	[ʃv]ein	'pig'
(d) S+rhotic	Sr			[θɪb̥ə]	[ʃr]eiben	'to write'

Similarities and differences between the head and sonority patterns can be seen most clearly from the summary table provided in (5).

(5)   Sonority pattern versus head pattern:

	Sonority pattern:	Head pattern:
(a) obstruent+sonorant	obstruent	obstruent
(b) S+obstruent	obstruent	obstruent
(c) S+sonorant	S	sonorant

The two patterns diverge for /S/-initial clusters that rise in sonority (5c). This is precisely where there is a mismatch between the head of the cluster and the segment that is least sonorous. This mismatch precludes any comprehensive analysis of the head pattern which relies on constraints that refer to relative sonority.

We shall provide a unified account for both the head and sonority patterns in section 5, one which focuses on the retention of heads in both cases. We must first discuss our assumptions about acquisition (section 3) and provide the structures that we adopt for obstruent-initial and /S/-initial clusters in the target grammars (section 4).

3.   Acquisition of an Optimality theoretic grammar

3.1   General assumptions

As mentioned in the introduction, we adopt the framework of Optimality Theory (OT) (Prince and Smolensky 1993), with the more recently developed view that faithfulness constraints are defined under Correspondence Theory (McCarthy and Prince 1995). Within OT, the linguistic competence of a speaker comprises a universal set of hierarchically ranked and thus violable constraints. Different constraint rankings yield different grammars; therefore, variation observed across languages, or across stages in the acquisition of a single language, is accounted for by alternative rankings of this finite set.

When applied to acquisition, the basic premises of OT are compatible with Pinker's (1984) continuity assumption: child and adult languages are not formally different in the sense that early grammars, at every stage in their development, reflect possible adult grammars. Thus, we contend that all systematic alternations observed in child data must be analysed using constraints that are independently motivated in adult grammars, and further, we adopt the strong position that all constraints are innate (Gnanadesikan this volume). Consequently, (i) children's grammars contain no more than adult grammars, that is, there are no child-specific constraints (for a different view, see Pater 1997); and (ii) they contain no less than adult grammars, that is, there is no emergence of constraints or of the primitives, structures, and operations that they refer to (Goad 2001).

To a great extent, children's early grammars differ from adult languages in predictable ways. Perhaps the most obvious of these is that children's early outputs are prosodically unmarked. For example, there is an initial preference for CV syllables, yielded primarily by segmental deletion. As patterns such as these are systematically observed across children, they must reflect early grammatical organisation. In the OT literature on acquisition, this is typically expressed in terms of preferred constraint rankings where markedness constraints initially outrank faithfulness constraints (Demuth 1995, Smolensky 1996, Gnanadesikan this volume, *inter alia*; cf. Hale and Reiss 1998). This view formally expresses the observations of Jakobson (1941/68) and Stampe (1969), that early grammars reflect what is cross-linguistically unmarked. A crucial part of the acquisition process therefore involves re-ranking of constraints, on the basis of positive evidence (Chomsky 1981), in order to allow for the production of more marked structures when these are found in the target language.

3.2   Full specification of inputs

Most of the OT literature on acquisition has focused on the child's ranking at a particular stage in development or on re-ranking across stages over time. Less attention has been devoted to the shapes of early inputs. At the segmental level, it is typically assumed, following Smith (1973), that children's inputs are in essential respects identical to adult outputs (modulo perceptual problems; see Macken 1980). In its strongest interpretation, this means that children's inputs are not underspecified, nor are they in any way impoverished. In the OT literature, the discussion in Hale and Reiss (1998) is particularly clear in this respect. They state that 'children have access to the full set of universal features in constructing URs and that they store URs fully and accurately specified, according to what they hear in the target language' (p. 660). Indeed, if Lexicon Optimisation guides acquisition from the outset (Prince and Smolensky 1993), learners are forced to this: they are reconciled to one input–output pairing, that where faithfulness is maximally respected, except in the face of alternations.[11] In short, children's segmental inputs must be fully specified.

At the level of prosodic structure, the literature is less explicit (but see Pater this volume). However, if constraints express faithfulness to prosodic heads (e.g., Alderete 1995, Itô *et al.* 1996, McCarthy 1997, Pater 2000), then inputs must be fully prosodified. We provide empirical evidence in favour of this view from Brazilian Portuguese in section 5.3. As far as the learner is concerned, once faithfulness constraints take prosodic constituents as arguments, then Lexicon Optimisation must guide the learner to select appropriate inputs at all levels of representation, both segmental and prosodic (*contra* Inkelas 1994). Accordingly, children's inputs must be fully prosodified. However, as mentioned earlier, since adult-like prosodification requires an understanding of the structures that are tolerated in the target language, children's inputs can only be prosodified to the extent that they reflect the knowledge that learners have at a particular stage in development. Throughout the course of acquisition, then, inputs become more elaborate as the structural relations that hold across segments in the target language come to be understood.[12]

In short, our central point is that the acquisition of an OT grammar involves two components: (i) the elaboration of inputs; and (ii) constraint re-ranking. And while most research has focused on the latter, we focus primarily on the former. Indeed, our account of the two patterns of cluster reduction will be built around the elaboration of inputs. Our analysis will rely on the following premises: (i) syllables are highly articulated structures (*contra* Kahn 1976, and what is explicit or implied in the phonetically motivated constraint-based approaches of Hamilton 1996, Wright 1996, Kochetov 1999, Steriade 1999, Côté 2000, and others); (ii) obstruent-initial clusters are left-headed branching onsets, while /S/-initial clusters begin with an appendix; and (iii) the appendix-initial structure holds for /S/-initial clusters that rise in sonority, not only for those with flat or falling sonority (*contra* Giegerich 1992, Hall 1992, Fikkert 1994, and others). In the following section, we discuss these premises in greater depth.

4. Representations

As already mentioned, an analysis of the sonority pattern can be provided without reference to syllable-internal structure: what survives can be determined solely by a prohibition on consonant sequencing and by a family of constraints that reflect relative prominence in the acoustic signal. By contrast, it appears that the head pattern cannot be so analysed: obstruent-initial clusters must be distinguished from /S/-initial clusters on structural grounds.

Outside of acquisition, the clearest evidence of the need for two types of structures can be found by observing that the presence or absence of obstruent-initial clusters in a language is independent of the presence or absence of /S/-initial clusters. A comparison of (6a) and (6b) reveals that Spanish, for example, contains only the former structure, while Acoma (Miller 1965) allows only for the latter.

(6)   Four-way typology:

Languages	Obstruent-initial	/S/-initial
(a) Spanish	yes	no
(b) Acoma	no	yes
(c) Maori, Japanese	no	no
(d) German, Dutch, English	yes	yes

In section 2, we observed that early child language resembles languages like Maori and Japanese (6c) in the sense that there are no left-edge clusters present in output representations. Nevertheless, in the three West Germanic languages under investigation (6d), there is ample evidence available that left-edge clusters are tolerated. The child's task is to determine what the appropriate representations are for these clusters.

As can be seen from (7), in the unmarked case, we consider obstruent+liquid clusters to be branching onsets (7a) and /S/-initial clusters to involve a left-edge appendix (7b). These representations are consistent with much of the literature on West Germanic. In particular, the special status assigned to /S/ in at least some /S/-initial clusters has typically been captured by positing that this segment is an appendix or is extrametrical (see, e.g., Vennemann 1982, Wiese 1988, Hall 1992 on German; Trommelen 1984, Van der Hulst 1984, Kager and Zonneveld 1985/86, Fikkert 1994 on Dutch; Steriade 1982, Levin 1985, Giegerich 1992, Kenstowicz 1994 on English).[13]

As we accept the standard view that segments are organised into prosodic constituents, we also consider all constituents to be headed. The notion of headedness refers to an asymmetrical relation that holds between adjacent elements within or across constituents. Heads have a primacy not accorded to non-heads: (i) they display distributional freedom in the sense that heads can license more melodic content than non-heads; and (ii) non-heads – whether internal or external to the relevant constituent – are dependent for their very existence on the presence of a head. The vertical line linking the skeletal position to O(nset) in (7) indicates that we consider branching onsets to be universally left-headed (following, e.g., Kaye, Lowenstamm, and Vergnaud 1990). In the case of two-member appendix-initial clusters, head status is trivially assigned to the only segment in the onset constituent, that is, to the rightmost member of the cluster. Following from this, we distinguish two types of non-heads: dependents which are constituent-internal; and appendices which are linked to some higher prosodic constituent, in the unmarked case, to the prosodic word (PWd), as we discuss below.

(7)   Unmarked syllabification options for left-edge clusters:

        a Branching onset: b Appendix+onset:

The notion head of onset will play a significant role in our account of L1 cluster reduction. Outside of this context, in section 5.3, we shall provide supporting evidence for this notion from cluster reduction in southeastern Brazilian Portuguese, as well as in German (hypocoristics) and Québec French.

In some languages, syllabification options other than those in (7) will be required. For example, as concerns the structure in (7a), Kaye (1985) has argued that, in Vata, obstruent+liquid strings are syllabified with the liquid in the nucleus. Concerning appendixal /S/, two options are required for West Germanic. While German respects the unmarked option in (7b), Dutch and English require /S/ to be linked to the syllable node in /S/+obstruent clusters. In German, /ʃ/+C clusters occur stem-initially (e.g., *be-stehen* [bə.ʃteː.hən] 'insist'), but they do not occur morpheme-internally (see, e.g., Hall 1992). /ʃ/ must therefore link to the PWd. In Dutch and English, by contrast, /s/+C clusters have a wider distribution. Van der Hulst (1984) uses examples such as *ek.ster* 'magpie' to argue against analyses along the lines of (7b) for Dutch and in favour of one where /s/ is a 'syllable prefix' (*contra* Trommelen 1984, Fikkert 1994: 51). Similar arguments are made by Zonneveld (1993) and Booij (1995), as well as by Levin (1985) for English. We elaborate on the problem for English as follows. There are many words like *con.sta.ble* where the rhyme preceding /s/ is binary branching. Given that, with limited exceptions, ternary-branching rhymes are not permitted in English (see esp. Harris 1994), /s/ must be analysed as an appendix to the following syllable.

Clearly, word-internal data are required to determine whether the syllable or PWd is the appropriate host for /S/. If /S/ were linked to the syllable in the unmarked case, the German-speaking child would require indirect negative evidence to arrive at the alternative analysis in (7b). We propose, therefore, that association to the PWd is the unmarked case. Positive evidence will then be available for learners to determine that the syllable is the correct host in Dutch and English.

While the typology in (6) demonstrates the need for two different representations for left-edge clusters, (7a) and (7b), it does not address the question of where to draw the line between cluster type. As UG requires branching onsets to rise in sonority, there is little dispute about the correct representations for obstruent+liquid and /S/+stop clusters (but see note 13).[14] Accordingly, once the child attempts to build structures other than singleton onsets at the left edge, representations for these two cluster types should pose little difficulty: obstruent+liquid clusters fit the ideal profile for a branching onset (Clements 1990), (7a); and a sonority fall or plateau is observed in /S/+obstruent clusters, so the child will realise that /S/ cannot be part of the onset and must instead occupy an appendix position, (7b). In the latter case, the child's analysis will be consistent with the observation that left-edge appendices are limited to /S/ in the unmarked case.[15] Additional positive evidence for the postulation of these two types of structures is readily available through the child observing that three-member clusters at the left edge are (virtually) always /S/-initial. If UG permits onset constituents to be at most binary, as is standardly assumed, sequences of the shape /S/+stop+liquid must involve a combination of the structures in (7a) and (7b).

One of the greatest difficulties for the linguist lies in determining the appropriate representation for /S/-initial clusters that rise in sonority. In section 4.2 below, we shall provide a number of arguments to demonstrate that, at least in West Germanic, all /S/-initial clusters are syllabified with left-edge appendices. Importantly, then, there is no direct correlation between headedness and some phonetic property (low sonority or low air flow); instead, distributional facts must be taken into consideration. In section 5.1, we shall propose that it is for this reason that these clusters also pose the greatest challenge for the learner. However, based on the data from Amahl and Annalena provided earlier in (4c), where /S/+sonorant → sonorant in the head pattern, we hope that the sceptical reader who equates rising sonority with branching onset status can accept that this is the analysis that these two children have arrived at.

4.1   *Place specifications in coronals*

Before we can compare alternative representations for rising sonority /S/-initial clusters, we must briefly consider liquid-final clusters, as one constraint – that which rules out place identity within a branching onset – must be introduced first. This, in turn, will lead to a discussion of the representations that we adopt for coronals.

As can be seen from (8a.i), in all three languages under consideration, stops can freely combine with liquids in branching onsets with one exception: /t/ cannot combine with /l/. (We limit the discussion to voiceless obstruent heads.)

(8)   Liquid-final clusters:

		English			Dutch			German		
a Branching onsets	i Stop+liquid	pl	*tl	kl	pl	*tl	kl	pl	*tl	kl
		pr	tr	kr	pr	tr	kr	pr	tr	kr
	ii Fric+liquid	fl	*θl	*ʃl	fl		χl	fl		
		fr	θr	ʃr	fr		χr	fr		
b Appendix-initial	/S/+liquid	sl			sl			ʃl		
		*sr			*sr			ʃr		

The absence of */tl/ is typically attributed to a constraint that forbids the two members of a branching onset from agreeing in place, what we have called *PLACEIDENT in (9). The constraint holds for all places of articulation; thus, alongside */tl/, */pw/ is illicit in English, as is */pʊ/ in Dutch and */pv/ in German.

(9)   *PLACEIDENT:
        Adjacent consonants within an onset constituent cannot be specified
        for the same articulator

The restriction on place identity in onsets is widely attested across languages, strongly suggesting that it is the UG unmarked option. Accordingly, the child needs no evidence to rule out clusters of this shape.[16]

Turning to (8a.ii), the ungrammatical branching onsets with fricative heads in the English column provide us with more information on how *PLACEIDENT works. On the one hand, exact identity is not enough to rule out a cluster: dental /θ/ cannot combine with alveolar /l/. At the same time, palato-alveolar /ʃ/ and post-alveolar /r/ are not close enough to be ruled out. In order to reconcile these facts, we adopt Lebel's (1998) proposal that *PLACEIDENT targets the level of the articulator node, and not the level of the feature that a given articulator dominates. If all coronals – with the exception of /r/ – are specified for a Coronal node, the correct results will obtain. See (10).[17] Importantly, we assume that the representation in (10b) holds, independently of whether /r/ is articulated as coronal or dorsal. Indeed, in two of the languages under investigation, Dutch and German, both coronal and dorsal variants are attested (see, e.g., Booij 1995 on Dutch, Hall 1992 and Wiese 1996 on German).

(10)   Place specifications for coronals and /r/:

a   /t-d, θ-ð, s-z, ʃ-ʒ, l, n/   b   /r/
       Root   Root
        |
      Place
        |
     Coronal
        |
       (α)

Before we elaborate on the motivation for /r/ as placeless, let us compare
(8a.ii) and (8b) in the context of (9) and (10). /S/+liquid clusters are included in
(8) for comparison, but they are not organised as branching onsets (see section
4.2 for evidence). Undoubtedly, some confusion may arise in a comparison
of English and German. In English, /S/ is always realised as /s/, and so /ʃr/
is not appendix-initial but is, instead, organised as a branching onset, (8a.ii).
Indeed, branching-onset status of /ʃ/-initial clusters is what accounts for the
ill-formedness of */ʃl/ in this language, as both segments bear a Coronal node,
(10a). In German, by contrast, where /S/ is realised as /ʃ/, both /ʃl/ and /ʃr/ are
appendix-initial; the constraint in (9) is thus irrelevant to their well-formedness.
The cross-language comparison is further complicated by the fact that, while
appendix-initial /ʃr/ is attested in German, the corresponding cluster, */sr/, is
illicit in English, as well as in Dutch (see note 10); we shall come back to this
in section 4.3.

We return now to furnish additional support for (10b). The representation
provided reveals that we consider /r/ to be permanently unspecified for place
(see also Rice 1992: 76); it is thus the sonorant counterpart to /ʔ/. Such a
representation is motivated by the fact that /r/ behaves asymmetrically in the
phonologies of several languages. For example, it is the only consonant that
cannot undergo (partial) gemination in Japanese (Mester and Itô 1989: 275),
the only non-labial consonant that cannot host palatalisation in Muher (S. Rose
1997), and it behaves asymmetrically in the L1 consonant harmony patterns
observed in Québec French (Y. Rose 2000). In the underspecification literature of the 1980s and 1990s, facts such as these were commonly captured
through /r/ being minimally placeless and possibly featureless in a number of
languages. Importantly, the asymmetric behaviour that /r/ displays is observed
independently of how it is articulated, as expected from the representation
in (10b).

One can conclude from the discussion thus far that we draw a formal distinction between phonological representation and phonetic interpretation, standard
in the 1980s and early 1990s, but counter to a commonly observed trend in the
OT literature. Motivating this distinction is far beyond the scope of the present
chapter. We merely demonstrate the advantages of treating /r/ as articulatorless in the languages under present discussion. The most obvious advantage of

adopting the representation in (10b) is that it enables us to account for the place facts observed in (8a): coronal-initial branching onsets which contain /r/ as their dependent will not violate *PLACEIDENT in (9). Beyond this, however, the representation in (10b) will also factor into our analysis of the asymmetries in the inventories of /S/-initial clusters provided in (8b) above; in particular, it will play a central role in our explanations for: (i) why /sl/ is licit in English and Dutch while */sr/ is not (section 4.3); and (ii) why Annalena incorrectly analyses German /ʃr/ as branching onset (section 6).

4.2   Rising sonority /S/-initial clusters

Now that we have provided some background on the properties that characterise branching onsets, we are in a position to compare alternative analyses for rising sonority /S/-initial clusters. We adopt the position of Trommelen (1984), Van der Hulst (1984), and Kager and Zonneveld (1985/86) that all /S/-initial clusters (at least in West Germanic) contain appendices. In the literature, however, this point of view is often not accepted. Indeed, a number of scholars have proposed that /S/+sonorant clusters are instead organised as branching onsets (see, e.g., Giegerich 1992 on English, Hall 1992 on German, Fikkert 1994 on Dutch). The most common argument in favour of this alternative is that, in contrast to /S/+obstruent clusters, these sequences abide by the requirement that branching onsets rise in sonority. In spite of their rising sonority, we shall provide three arguments in favour of the appendix-initial analysis for /S/+sonorant clusters: the syllabification of /S/-initial clusters in intervocalic position in Dutch; the absence of place identity effects in /S/+coronal clusters; and the lack of place restrictions on nasals in /SN/ clusters.[18]

We begin with intervocalic /S/-initial clusters in Dutch. Trommelen (1984) and Kager and Zonneveld (1985/86) have noted that /S/+obstruent clusters are syllabified as heterosyllabic in this position, e.g., *pás.ta* 'paste', *és.ki.mo* 'eskimo', in contrast to branching onsets, e.g., *lé:.pra*, **lép.ra* 'leprosy', *zé:.bra*, **zéb.ra* 'zebra'. Notably, /s/+sonorant clusters pattern with /s/+obstruent clusters in this respect, e.g., *prís.ma* 'prism', *ós.lo* 'Oslo'. This strongly suggests that all /s/-initial clusters are analysed in the same fashion, differently from how branching onsets are syllabified.

Turning to the second argument, we have seen that *PLACEIDENT in (9) rules out strings of segments which bear the same articulator node within the onset constituent. Let us look at /S/-initial clusters that are followed by coronals in this context. As it is generally accepted that /S/+obstruent clusters are represented as appendix+onset structures, /st/ clusters should not be subject to (9). This is indeed the case: /st/ is well-formed in English and Dutch, as is /ʃt/ in German. However, the absence of place-identity effects is also observed with /S/+sonorant clusters: /sl/ and /sn/ are licit in English and Dutch, as are /ʃl/

and /ʃn/ in German. If these clusters were organised as branching onsets, they would violate *PLACEIDENT in (9). This would seem to be strong evidence that they are instead syllabified with initial appendices. Perhaps, however, place identity is only apparent in these cases; if /S/ were analysed as placeless, then /Sl, Sn/ clusters would not violate the constraint in (9) and rising sonority clusters could be represented as branching onsets. While this approach would provide us with an explanation for why, under the branching onset analysis, /Sl/ and /Sn/ are licit, it will not enable us to account for the absence of /Sr/ in English and Dutch. As a branching onset, this cluster should be well-formed and yet, it is not, a fact which we return to in section 4.3. We thus reject the placeless /S/ option as spurious and contend that /S/+coronal strings are licit because, as appendix-initial, they are not subject to *PLACEIDENT in (9).

We consider finally the evidence from /S/+nasal strings. Across languages, nasal dependents in branching onsets are restricted to /n/, if not universally, then at least in the vast majority of languages that permit such clusters (see Humbert 1997 for related discussion). Indeed, this restriction holds of languages with large inventories of CN clusters like Greek, as well as in languages like Dutch and German. If /S/+nasal clusters were organised as branching onsets, we could not account for the fact that /Sm/ is well-formed in the languages under present investigation. If, by contrast, /S/+nasal clusters are analysed with initial appendices, we expect to find no restrictions on the place of the nasal, parallel to what is observed for /S/+stop clusters. This is true: /sm/-/sn/ and /sp/-/St/ are well-formed in English and Dutch, as are /ʃm/-/ʃn/ and /ʃp/-/ʃt/ in German.

In section 5.1, we shall demonstrate how the last two of these arguments – the lack of place identity effects and of place constraints on the nasal in /SN/ clusters – have important consequences for the child's building of input representations for rising-sonority /S/-initial clusters.

4.3   Licensing and /S/+rhotic clusters

In this final subsection on representations, we turn to /S/+rhotic clusters. We must motivate the syllabification of /Sr/ clusters in German, and provide an explanation for their absence from Dutch and English. Recall that /Sr/ is realised as /ʃr/ in German. Although /sr/ is illicit in English, /ʃr/ is a well-formed branching onset in this language. We thus end up with two possible analyses for the string /ʃ/+/r/, as can be seen from a comparison of (11a) and (11b). We shall detail the arguments for these two structures below.

(11)   Sibilant+rhotic clusters:

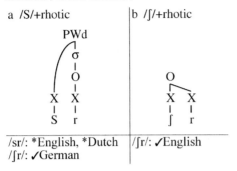

	a /S/+rhotic	b /ʃ/+rhotic
/sr/: *English, *Dutch		/ʃr/: ✓English
/ʃr/: ✓German		

We begin by returning to place identity in branching onsets. In section 4.1, we proposed that /r/ is articulatorless, which accounts for why it can freely combine with coronals in branching onsets, whereas /l/ cannot (English: ✓/θr/, ✓/ʃr/; */θl/, */ʃl/). At the same time, however, we mentioned that the well-formedness of /Sl/ and /Sn/ – in spite of place identity – does not necessarily rule out the analysis that these clusters form branching onsets: /S/ could be placeless and these clusters could thereby escape the *PLACEIDENT constraint in (9). This analysis, however, offers no explanation for the ill-formedness of */sr/ in Dutch and English. If /Sr/ were a branching onset, we should have no explanation for it being illicit in these two languages. /S/, then, must be an appendix, as we have suggested holds for all /S/-initial clusters in the unmarked case.

We are now faced with the task of explaining why the appendix+onset representation is not permitted for /Sr/ in Dutch and English. We propose that the ill-formedness has to do with properties of the head, /r/. In the spirit of Harris (1997: 363–364), we suggest that, in the unmarked case, in order to license a non-head position, a head must have certain strength, where strength is defined in terms of its featural content; specifically, in order to support an appendix or coda, the head of the following onset must bear a Place node.

To exemplify, NC coda+onset clusters which share place are well-formed in most languages, as the onset licenses the place specification (cf. Itô 1986), e.g., [Vm.pV] in (12a).[19] By contrast, /ʔ/ in onset position has no articulator to support a preceding coda, and thus, [VN.ʔV] is most often illicit, even when the coda is itself placeless, (12b). Indeed, when /ʔ/ is syllabified as an onset, it is typically restricted to word-initial and intervocalic position. The representation in (12c) demonstrates how this proposal is extended to account for the ill-formedness of */sr/ in English and Dutch. The appendix+onset construction involves a non-head being supported by a placeless head, parallel to the configuration in (12b). Like /ʔ/, /r/ is a well-formed onset when it is word-initial or intervocalic (and also, a dependent in an onset cluster); as it is articulatorless, however, it cannot license a preceding appendix in the unmarked case.

(12)   Licensing of non-head:

a Coda+strong onset   b Coda+weak onset   c Appendix+weak onset

To capture this restriction on appendix licensing, we propose the constraint in (13). This constraint is part of a family of constraints which reflects the melodic restrictions that heads must satisfy in order to support non-heads.

(13)   APPENDIXLICENSING(ONSETHEAD/PLACE):

An onset head must bear a Place node in order to license an appendix.

While (13) is dominant in a number of languages, like Dutch and English, it is violated in German, as indicated in (11a). To be certain of this, however, we must ensure that /ʃr/ is truly appendix-initial in German. This sequence could instead have the branching onset structure assigned to English /ʃr/ in (11b). Evidence in favour of the appendix-initial structure comes from the fact that German /ʃr/ displays exactly the same distributional restrictions as do all other appendix-initial clusters in the language; in contrast to branching onsets, it does not occur morpheme-internally (cf. section 4).

We have arrived at a predicament where both the branching onset and appendix-initial analyses for /Sr/ are marked. The former is disfavoured on grounds that initial /S/ is optimally syllabified as an appendix. The latter is also disfavoured, as /r/ should ideally not support an appendix. Languages which respect markedness should therefore not tolerate clusters of this shape at all, as is the case in Dutch and English (*/sr/). The German-speaking child, on the other hand, must determine what the appropriate analysis is for the /ʃr/ strings encountered in this language. In section 6, we shall see that Annalena, who follows the head pattern of cluster reduction (cf. (4)), incorrectly treats /ʃr/ as a branching onset: it is /ʃ/ that survives. More generally, we expect to observe variation across German children who follow the head pattern as concerns their treatment of /ʃr/ clusters.

4.4   Consequences for acquisition

In sum, apart from /ʃr/ in German, the representations required for obstruent+liquid and /S/-initial clusters in West Germanic correspond to what UG provides as unmarked.[20] Thus, children should not have too much difficulty building appropriate input representations for such clusters in these languages. It may be the case that cluster reduction prevails for some time, due to high-ranking structural well-formedness constraints; however, the patterns of cluster reduction should reveal that the appropriate input representations have been assigned, namely that it is the head of the cluster that survives. As we shall see, this holds true for children who follow the head pattern of cluster reduction. For those who follow the sonority pattern, however, things are not as straightforward. Recall from section 2 that, in this pattern, /S/, the non-head, survives in rising sonority /S/-initial clusters. This could indicate that these children have syllabified both members of the cluster in the input, but incorrectly; that is, that they have posited a marked (branching onset) syllabification for /S/+sonorant clusters. We do not accept this view, as indirect negative evidence would be required for the learner to arrive at an analysis where these clusters are syllabified as appendix-initial (cf. Fikkert 1994: 119–120). We proposed earlier that all /S/-initial clusters are appendix-initial in the unmarked case, and if this is indeed true, no indirect negative evidence should ever be required: the first full syllabification analysis entertained by the child should be appendix-initial. If this is so, it must be the case that in the sonority pattern of cluster reduction, inputs are not exhaustively prosodified, that is, that they are impoverished relative to the adult's inputs. This is the position which we adopt, as will be elaborated on in the next section.

5.   Analysis of cluster reduction

5.1   Building inputs

Recall from section 3 that we consider adult inputs to be fully prosodified. In order for learners to achieve adult-like inputs, they must have some knowledge of the structures that are permitted in the target language, as well as of the relationships that hold across different syllabic projections. For example, syllabification of the branching onset /pl/ in (14a) requires (i) an understanding of headedness, which is assigned to the obstruent (this much comes for free; see below); and (ii) knowledge that complexity is tolerated within the onset constituent, where the liquid constitutes the dependent member of this constituent.[21] In comparison, understanding of the rising sonority /S/-initial cluster in (14b) requires knowledge (i) that a different headedness relationship is involved (it is the liquid which is assigned as the onset head); consequently,

(ii) that there is no branching within the onset constituent, which is universally left-headed (see (7)); and (iii) that the initial /S/ is linked directly to higher
prosodic structure (to the PWd, in the unmarked case, as discussed in section 4).
(14c) requires knowledge similar to that involved in the analysis of (14b); however, in all cases other than Dutch /sχ/ which we leave aside, head status is
assigned to the least sonorous segment in the string and, thus, comes for free,
as in (14a).

(14)   Adult inputs:

a Branching onset   b Rising sonority /S/-initial   c Falling sonority /S/-initial

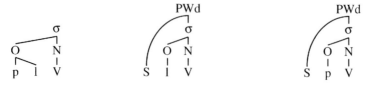

We propose that these elaborate input structures are not mastered at the
earliest stage in acquisition. Indeed, they cannot be, as not all languages allow for branching constituents and appendices. Children's inputs are initially
prosodified for simplex onsets and rhymes/nuclei only, as in (15). That is, as
far as prosodic structure is concerned, inputs only contain CV (core) syllables.
Any non-prosodified segmental material that is perceived by the child remains
unassociated. As all constituents must be headed, the segments syllabified as
singleton onsets and nuclei from each of the strings in (15) are by definition the
heads of their respective constituents.

What mechanism, though, does the child use to select heads? Without any
knowledge of the relations that hold across strings of segments, the head of the
onset and the head of the rhyme/nucleus can only be defined on the basis of
relative prominence, low sonority (or low airflow) in the former case and high
sonority in the latter, in the spirit of Jakobson's (1941/68) Principle of Maximal
Contrast. In the strings in (15), which represent the first stage in development
(stage 1), the least sonorous consonant will be assigned head status by default.
This strategy leads to selection of the correct onset head in (15a) and (15c),
as in these cases, there is a correlation between the head of a left-edge cluster
and low prominence. However, the incorrect head is selected in rising sonority
/S/-initial clusters, (15b).

(15)   Inputs for sonority pattern child (stage 1):

a Branching onset   b Rising sonority /S/-initial   c Falling sonority /S/-initial

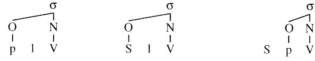

The result is the input specifications for the sonority pattern. Indeed, we propose that the source for the two patterns of cluster reduction is the mismatch between the head of the onset and relative prominence in rising sonority /S/-initial clusters. Correct selection of the head requires an understanding of the distributional (positive) evidence available in the ambient language. The child will be forced to take account of this evidence as s/he attempts to prosodify the remaining segments in the cluster, on the way to achieving adult-like inputs. Accordingly, through the course of acquisition, inputs become more elaborately structured, reflecting this new understanding. The inputs in (16) for the head pattern correspond to this stage in acquisition, which we label stage 2.

(16)   Inputs for head pattern child (stage 2):

a Branching onset   b Rising sonority /S/-initial   c Falling sonority /S/-initial

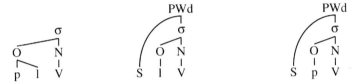

Our analysis of the sonority pattern assumes that there is a stage in development before there is any understanding of syllable-internal complexity beyond the UG-given simplex onsets and rhymes/nuclei. By definition, then, the sonority pattern must precede the head pattern, as is the case for Robin (see section 2: sonority pattern 1;10.9-2;0.20; head pattern 2;1.9-2;3.24).[22] However, it need not be the case that all children exhibit both patterns of cluster reduction in their outputs. On the one hand, head-pattern children may have come to understand the relations that hold across strings of consonants by the time they attempt to produce words with target clusters, thereby displaying no evidence of having gone through the sonority stage. Prior to this, they may have only selected words for production which do not contain (/S/+sonorant) clusters; this so-called selection and avoidance strategy is common in early acquisition (e.g., Ferguson and Farwell 1975, Schwartz and Leonard 1982, Stoel-Gammon and Cooper 1984). On the other hand, sonority-pattern children may skip the head stage of cluster reduction, as their building of target-like input structures may coincide with the demotion of the markedness constraints which had previously prevented the realisation of clusters in their outputs. The latter scenario is perhaps most commonly attested, thereby accounting for the fact that many scholars have remarked on the role that sonority plays in cluster reduction (see section 1 for references).

For children who exhibit both the sonority and head patterns of cluster reduction, the development from stage 1 to stage 2 will presumably be gradual, unlike what is reflected in the transition from (15) to (16). It is likely that the child will find it easiest to build the target-like input for a branching onset, as (i) the head corresponds to the least sonorous segment and thus is correct from the outset; and (ii) all that is required to prosodify the dependent is to establish an additional link to the onset constituent. However, as long as the markedness constraints which preclude clusters from appearing in outputs are dominant, any stage intermediate between stages 1 and 2 for obstruent-initial and /S/+stop clusters will be impossible to observe in the child's outputs. An empirical difference will only be observable for rising sonority /S/-initial clusters.

Concerning the latter, a common stage intermediate between stages 1 and 2 appears to be that where target-like inputs are built for /S/+nasal clusters, but where stage 1 inputs persist for /S/+lateral clusters. With markedness constraints ranked high, this yields the head pattern of cluster reduction for /SN/ clusters, /SN/ → /N/, but the sonority pattern for /Sl/ clusters, /Sl/ → /S/. Recall in this context that the Dutch children in Fikkert's study who follow the head pattern (Tom, Robin, Catootje) unexpectedly treat /sl/ in the same manner as fricative-initial clusters. This is probably also true of English-speaking Joan (see note 8).[23] These children thus display reductions as follows: /s/+nasal → nasal, but /sl/ → /s/ parallel to /fl/ → /f/. We believe that these children, in contrast to Amahl and Annalena, are in a stage intermediate between the head and sonority patterns: they have adult-like (stage 2) inputs for /SN/ clusters, but stage 1 inputs for /Sl/ clusters. Below, we elaborate on why we consider their /Sl/ clusters to behave unexpectedly from the point of view of the head pattern.

As discussed in section 4.2, both /Sl/ and /SN/ are ill-formed as branching onsets, and some children, those who follow the head pattern in its entirety, clearly attend to the various types of evidence available for this at once. Other children, those who fall into the intermediate pattern, seem to have latched onto the fact that there are significant differences between laterals and nasals as concerns their distribution in clusters. On the one hand, the lack of place constraints on the nasal in /SN/ clusters provides clear evidence for the child to come to an early understanding of clusters of this shape. Specifically, in spite of the rising sonority, labial place on /m/ signals that /Sm/ could never be a branching onset. Thus, once the child attempts to incorporate the nasal into his/her stage 1 input syllabification, labial place forces a re-analysis of this segment as head. This results in the appendix-initial input representation at stage 2 for /Sm/ and, by extension, for /Sn/ as well.

Building adult-like input representations for /Sl/ clusters, on the other hand, is less straightforward, because /l/, unlike /m/, is an optimal onset dependent. Thus, when the child attempts to incorporate /l/ into his/her stage 1 input forms, s/he may first try to syllabify /Sl/ as a branching onset. The place identity facts, however, are not consistent with this analysis. There is thus a conflict as concerns the syllabification of /l/ that may delay some children's incorporation of this segment into their input syllabification, resulting in the maintenance of the impoverished stage 1 structure for /Sl/ for some time after /SN/ clusters have been appropriately prosodified (as per stage 2). This, in essence, is a type of selection and avoidance. What, though, ultimately compels these children to move beyond their stage 1 forms and to posit the appropriate input representation for /Sl/? We suggest that it must take place on grounds of parsimony, that is, to resolve the fact that /Sl/ is an outlier as concerns the full prosodification of inputs.

Henceforth, we shall ignore the different treatment of /Sl/ and /SN/, and shall consider the learners as falling into two groups only, as we had earlier: head-pattern children and sonority-pattern children, where those children who fall into the intermediate stage are grouped with those who follow the head pattern in its entirety.

In the following two sections, we turn to the constraints required to capture cluster reduction. We then demonstrate in section 5.4 that, in comparing the sonority- and head-pattern children, even though their input representations differ in terms of how elaborately structured they are, the same set of marked-ness constraints yields only CV syllables on the surface for both groups. In comparing the head-pattern children with adults, we maintain that, although these children have target-like inputs, their grammar differs from the end-state grammar in terms of the relative ranking of markedness constraints and seg-mental faithfulness.

5.2   Constraints

To reflect the structural differences that are observed between branching onsets and appendix-initial clusters, two markedness constraints are required, those in (17).

(17)   Markedness constraints:
    (a) *COMPLEX(α)
        Sub-syllabic constituents cannot branch
        $\alpha \in \{$Onset, Rhyme, Nucleus$\}$
    (b) *APPENDIX-LEFT/(RIGHT)
        A consonant at the left/(right) edge must be immediately dominated by Onset/(Rhyme)

*COMPLEX, initially proposed by Prince and Smolensky (1993), rules out branching within a constituent. We assume, as do others, that *COMPLEX is a family of constraints that takes syllable-internal constituents as its arguments. We limit these constituents to onset, rhyme, and nucleus.[24] Since our focus is on left-edge clusters, we are concerned only with *COMPLEX(ONSET), but we shall use the label *COMPLEX for convenience. *APPENDIX-LEFT/(RIGHT) requires a consonant to be directly dominated by the constituent that would normally organise it: by the onset at the left edge, and by the rhyme at the right edge (see Sherer 1994 for a different formulation of this constraint). *APP-LEFT is violated when a segment is linked directly to the PWd (or syllable node), as in the case of /S/ in left-edge clusters.

For children who follow either the sonority or head pattern of cluster reduction, *COMPLEX and *APP-LEFT must both be undominated. These two constraints cannot be collapsed. First, we observed in (6) that the presence or absence of branching onsets is independent of the presence or absence of appendix+onset clusters: in Spanish (6a), *APP-LEFT must be undominated while *COMPLEX is lowly ranked; in Acoma (6b), *COMPLEX is undominated and *APP-LEFT lowly ranked. Second, in the acquisition literature on West Germanic, it has often been observed that branching onsets and appendix+onset clusters do not emerge at the same point in development (e.g., Smith 1973, Fikkert 1994, Barlow 1997, 1999).

Satisfaction of the constraints in (17) comes at the expense of violating segmental faithfulness. Faithfulness constraints favour a good match between any two pairs of strings that stand in a dependency or correspondence relation. Correspondence is defined in (18) (from McCarthy and Prince 1995: 262). For our purposes, S_1 is the input, and S_2, the output.

(18)   Correspondence:
        Given two strings S_1 and S_2, correspondence is a relation $\Re$ from the elements of S_1 to those of S_2. Elements $\alpha \in S_1$ and $\beta \in S_2$ are referred to as correspondents of one another when $\alpha \Re \beta$.

As children rarely epenthesise into consonant clusters, we shall only be concerned with the faithfulness constraint that forbids deletion, MAX-IO, as defined in (19). This constraint must be lowly ranked in children's early grammars, as satisfaction of *COMPLEX and *APP-LEFT comes at the expense of segmental deletion.

(19)   Segmental faithfulness:
        MAX-IO: Every segment of the input has a correspondent in the output

A second faithfulness constraint is required, MAXHEAD-IO, as defined in (20). This constraint ensures that segments prosodified in the head of a constituent are preserved as such in the output. While MAXHEAD is technically a faithfulness constraint, it has a markedness element to it as well, as it makes reference to heads which, we have already mentioned, have a primacy not accorded to non-heads.

(20)   Head faithfulness:
         MAXHEAD(PCat)-IO: Every segment prosodified in the head of some prosodic category in the input has a correspondent in the head of that prosodic category in the output
         PCat ∈ {Onset, Nucleus, Rhyme, σ, Foot . . .}

A number of questions emerge from the formulation of this constraint, concerning the arguments that it takes, the way that headedness is expressed in inputs, and the role that this constraint plays outside of child language. We shall address each of these in turn in the next section.

5.3   More on MAXHEAD

Constraints that express faithfulness to prosodic heads have been proposed throughout the OT literature, in particular, those that express faithfulness to heads of feet (see, e.g., Alderete 1995, Itô *et al.* 1996, McCarthy 1997, Pater 2000).[25] In the spirit of Alderete (1995), we have proposed a generalised head faithfulness constraint, one that takes a number of prosodic categories as arguments. As we assume that the sub-syllabic constituents of the syllable are onset, rhyme, and nucleus, these constituents fall into the class of categories that can be exploited by (20). The category that may appear suspect is onset. We shall see in section 5.4 that MAXHEAD(ONSET) plays a crucial role in our analysis of L1 cluster reduction. A question that immediately arises is whether there is any evidence for MAXHEAD(ONSET) outside of acquisition. We shall briefly demonstrate below that it plays a role in the distribution of branching onsets in a dialect of Brazilian Portuguese. More generally, the analysis of Brazilian Portuguese provides empirical support in favour of the position that adult inputs must be fully prosodified, thereby confirming the need for a generalised head faithfulness constraint like (20).

In southeastern Brazilian Portuguese, branching onsets are tolerated only in stressed syllables. Input clusters are otherwise reduced, as can be seen from the data in (21) (from Harris 1997: 363).

(21)   Branching onsets in southeastern Brazilian Portuguese:

a	prátu	'plate'
	patʃíɲu, *pratʃíɲu	'small plate'
b	lívu, *lívru	'book'
	livrétu	'small book'

Harris (1997) points out that branching onsets are restricted to prosodically strong positions in other languages as well. For instance, in German hypocoristics, such structures are not permitted in unstressed syllables, e.g., *Gabriella* → *Gábi*, *Gábri (see Itô and Mester 1997). Further, in most languages, branching onsets are not tolerated before phonetically empty nuclei (with the notable exception of continental French, e.g., *sablØ* 'sand' (Charette 1991)); most dialects of Québec French are like this and alternations are observed in this context, e.g., *sabØ*, *sablØ 'sand' vs. *sabl-e* 'to sand' (see Nikièma 1999 for a recent structurally based account). Finally, Y. Rose (2000) has shown that the Brazilian Portuguese pattern is found in the L1 acquisition of Québec French. Importantly, in all of these cases, it is the head of the onset which survives cluster reduction.

Let us turn now to demonstrate how MAXHEAD interacts with *COMPLEX to arrive at the pattern observed in Brazilian Portuguese. The tableau in (22) reveals that two MAXHEAD constraints are required, MAXHEAD(FOOT) and MAXHEAD(ONS), both of which must be ranked above *COMPLEX. (Parentheses mark the edges of feet, and periods, the edges of syllables.)

(22)   Southeastern Brazilian Portuguese:

		MAXHD(FT)	MAXHD(ONS)	*COMPLEX	MAX
a li(vré.tu)	☞ i. li(vré.tu)			*	
	ii. li(vé.tu)	*!			*
b (lí.vru)	i. (lí.vru)			*!	
	☞ ii. (lí.vu)				*
	iii. (lí.ru)		*!		*

Dominant MAXHEAD(FT) ensures that all segments contained in the head of the foot, [vré], will be realised on the surface. Thus, in (22a), the optimal candidate is (i), in spite of the violation incurred for *COMPLEX. In (22b), the input branching onset is not located in head position. Thus, MAXHEAD(FT) is not relevant, and the cluster is reduced to satisfy *COMPLEX, as in candidates (ii) and (iii). MAXHEAD(ONS) factors into the selection between these two candidates. The former is selected as optimal, as the consonant that survives, [v], is the head of the onset cluster in the input.

Importantly, all segments prosodified within the head of the foot, the syllable underlined in li(vré.tu), must surface in order to completely satisfy MAXHEAD(FT), as defined in (20). This requires that inputs be fully prosodified. If only syllable peaks were prosodified in inputs, MAXHEAD(FT) could not select between (22a.i) and (22a.ii), as the vowel from the input stressed syllable is present in both candidate outputs.

A consequence of full syllabification is that heads of constituents must be structurally defined, rather than based on relative prominence. This is particularly important as concerns onsets; although in the case of feet, the head syllable is the most salient, recall from earlier discussion that in left-edge clusters, there is no correlation between relative prominence and headedness. This, in fact, is central to our explanation of the two patterns of cluster reduction observed in early grammars.

5.4   Tableaux

In the following sections, we illustrate how highly ranked MAXHEAD(ONS) yields the desired outputs for both the head and sonority patterns of cluster reduction. Recall from earlier discussion that the difference between these patterns can only be observed in /S/+sonorant clusters. In input branching onsets and /S/+obstruent clusters, the distinction is obscured by the fact that the head of the cluster is also the segment that has the lowest sonority. In this section, we shall exemplify how the constraints presented in section 5.2, in combination with the input representations proposed in section 5.1, yield the correct results for the patterns observed. We shall focus on branching onsets and on rising sonority /S/-initial clusters only.

5.4.1   Branching onsets   For children who follow either pattern of cluster reduction, the ranking of constraints is the same: the markedness constraints *COMPLEX and *APP-LEFT dominate, thereby ensuring that no clusters are realised on the surface, at the expense of violating MAX. The highly ranked MAXHEAD will determine which consonant from the input survives. (As our focus is now on onsets, we abbreviate MAXHEAD(ONS) as MAXHEAD for convenience.)

As discussed earlier, children who follow the sonority pattern equate headedness with low sonority. Headedness is thus correctly assigned to the stop in (23), in spite of the fact that input obstruent+liquid clusters contain no knowledge of branching structure.

(23)   Stage 1: sonority pattern:

Input: σ [O→p,l N→V]	*COMPLEX	*APP-LEFT	MAXHEAD	MAX
a. σ [O→(p,l) N→V]	*!			
☞ b. σ [O→p N→V]				*
c. σ [O→l N→V]			*!	*

For children who follow the head pattern, by contrast, inputs are adult-like and headedness is thus structurally determined, as can be seen from the input in (24).

(24)   Stage 2: head pattern:

Input: σ [O→(p,l) N→V]	*COMPLEX	*APP-LEFT	MAXHEAD	MAX
a. σ [O→(p,l) N→V]	*!			
☞ b. σ [O→p N→V]				*
c. σ [O→l N→V]			*!	*

In the list of candidates in (23) and (24), those which preserve the input cluster, (23a) and (24a), fail on the markedness constraint *COMPLEX.[26] The decision between the remaining two candidates rests with MAXHEAD. While the inputs for children who follow the sonority versus head patterns differ, in both cases, the head of the cluster is the obstruent. Thus, MAXHEAD selects candidate (b) in both (23) and (24). In candidate (c), the input head has been deleted in favour of the liquid.

In the interest of space, we shall not provide a tableau for the adult grammar. As mentioned earlier, the adult inputs are the same as those for the head-pattern child. The two grammars differ in terms of their ranking. In the adult grammar, the faithfulness constraints dominate the markedness constraints under discussion with the result that the candidate with the branching onset, (24a), is selected as optimal.

5.4.2 */S/+sonorant clusters* While the same output is selected for both head- and sonority-pattern children in obstruent+liquid and /S/+obstruent clusters, this is not the case in /S/+sonorant clusters, as the structurally determined head does not correspond to the segment that is least sonorous. Although the correct head in clusters of this shape is the second consonant, children who abide by the sonority pattern wrongly assign head status to /S/, as depicted in the input representation in (25).

(25)   Stage 1: sonority pattern:

Input: σ O⏐S N⏐l V	*COMPLEX	*APP-LEFT	MAXHEAD	MAX
a. PWd σ O⏐S N⏐l V		*!	*	
☞ b. σ O⏐S N⏐V				*
c. σ O⏐l N⏐V			*!	*

The input structure in (26), by contrast, reveals that children who follow the head pattern have correctly assigned head status to the sonorant, on the basis of the patterns of distribution to which they have been exposed. It is this difference in headship in inputs that yields the two patterns of cluster reduction observed on the surface.

The first candidate in each of (25) and (26) violates the undominated *APP-LEFT.[27] Interestingly, (25a), which is the correct adult output, also violates MAXHEAD. This would not be the case in the adult grammar, as inputs for clusters of this shape have head status assigned to the liquid. (25b) and (25c) are the remaining contenders for the sonority pattern. As the latter fatally violates MAXHEAD, the form with liquid deletion is selected as optimal. The same reasoning applies to the remaining two candidates for the head pattern in (26), with one crucial difference: children who follow this pattern correctly assign head status to the sonorant. Thus, MAXHEAD preserves this segment over /S/, as in (26c).

(26)   Stage 2: head pattern:

Input: PWd → σ → (O N) / S l , V	*COMPLEX	*APP-LEFT	MAXHEAD	MAX
a. PWd → σ → (O N) / S l , V		*!		
b. σ → (O N) / S V , —			*!	*
c. ☞ σ → (O N) / l V , —				*

In the adult grammar, inputs are identical to those posited by children who follow the head pattern, as discussed earlier. Since both faithfulness constraints dominate *APP-LEFT, (26a) would be selected as optimal.

Our analysis of the head and sonority patterns has appealed to highly articulated representations as well as to constraints that directly reference these representations. It has not relied on a difference in constraint ranking across the two stages. While our account of the sonority pattern, stage 1, was built on the relationship between sonority and headedness, this was only true as concerns the elaboration of inputs. We did not invoke a family of sonority-based constraints for the selection of outputs, because these constraints appear to play no role in the head pattern. In the next section, we briefly consider an alternative analysis, one where the differences observed between the two patterns of cluster reduction arise because of differences in ranking between sonority-based constraints and MAXHEAD. We shall argue that such an analysis must be rejected.

5.5   Is constraint re-ranking an alternative?

We have put the burden of explanation for the two patterns of cluster reduction on the elaboration of inputs, rather than on constraint re-ranking. Under our approach, both groups of children preserve constituent heads in their outputs. The difference between the two groups rests with children's (mis)understanding of what constitutes the head in a given cluster type. An approach which instead relies on constraint ranking would entail that, at stage 1, sonority pattern children have constituent heads correctly assigned, but that they are not faithful to heads when considerations of sonority take precedence, that is, in rising sonority /S/-initial clusters. Let us call this ranking LOWSONORITY >> MAXHEAD for convenience (cf. section 7.2 where LOWSONORITY is spelled out as Prince and Smolensky's (1993) *M(ARGIN)/λ). At stage 2, head preservation would become more central, reflected in a grammar where sonority-based constraints rank below MAXHEAD (ranking MAXHEAD >> LOWSONORITY). We reject this approach for three reasons.

First, while the ranking at stage 1 is consistent with what most scholars accept to be the initial ranking provided by UG, Markedness >> Faithfulness (e.g., Demuth 1995, Smolensky 1996, Gnanadesikan this volume), there is no evidence in the language to which children are exposed that would lead to the new ranking at stage 2: while heads are faithfully produced in adult outputs, so are non-heads. Thus, there is no evidence to trigger, and nothing to be gained by, the re-ranking observed at stage 2. The only positive evidence that will lead to a re-ranking is the fact that clusters are tolerated, demonstrating that the relevant markedness constraints must be dominated in the target grammar.

Second, at this early stage in our investigation, we regard as somewhat dubious any explanation of cluster reduction that does not rely on faithfulness to heads, given that all linguistic constituents are headed, that heads have a primacy not accorded to non-heads, and following from this, that non-heads are dependent for their very existence on the presence of a head (see earlier section 4).

Finally, as far as we have observed, the only widely attested pattern of cluster reduction that appears not to rely on head preservation is the sonority pattern.[28] Other possible patterns seem to be rare at best, for instance, the contiguity pattern where the consonant which survives is the one contiguous with the input vowel: obstruent+sonorant → sonorant, /S/+stop → stop, /S/+sonorant → sonorant. Indeed, our investigations have turned up only two children whose grammars follow this pattern (see also Bernhardt and Stemberger 1998: 388–389). One is Subject 12, a language-delayed learner of English (from Chin and Dinnsen 1992); the other is María, a normally developing learner of Spanish (Lleó and Prinz 1996).[29] The rarity of children whose cluster reduction patterns respect contiguity is consistent with the analysis provided earlier in section 5. As we proposed a head-based analysis of the sonority pattern, we reiterate our point that heads have a primacy not granted to non-heads.

Before concluding our discussion of cluster reduction, one pattern remains to be analysed: Annalena's treatment of /S/+rhotic clusters. We turn to this topic next.

6.   /S/+rhotic clusters in the head pattern: Annalena's grammar

The analysis that we have provided for rising sonority /S/-initial clusters in the head pattern cannot account for Annalena's treatment of /ʃr/ clusters in German. Recall from (4) that while in /ʃ/+lateral, nasal, glide clusters, it is the sonorant that survives cluster reduction, in /ʃ/+rhotic clusters, it is /ʃ/ that survives. The table in (27) reflects the analysis: although Annalena has the correct appendix-initial structure for /ʃl/, /ʃN/, and /ʃv/, she has assigned branching onset status to /ʃr/.

(27)   Analyses for /S/+sonorant clusters:

	Target German	Annelena
a. /ʃl/ /ʃN/ /ʃv/	Appendix-initial Appendix-initial Appendix-initial	Appendix-initial Appendix-initial Appendix-initial
b. /ʃr/	Appendix-initial	Branching onset

Beyond the reduction patterns, additional support for the branching onset analysis of Annalena's /ʃr/ comes from examining the point at which she acquires the various cluster types. The table in (28) reveals that /ʃr/ clusters emerge as target-like at the same point as do obstruent+/r/ (Cr) clusters. The remaining /ʃ/-initial clusters (/ʃ/+stop, /ʃ/+nasal, /ʃl/, /ʃv/) are not acquired until much later.[30]

(28)   Annalena's order of acquisition:

C1	Cr	ʃr	ʃC (except ʃr)
1;11.15–2.0	1;09–1;10	1;09–1;10	2;02.15–2;04

In section 4.3, we attributed the markedness of the appendix-initial structure for /ʃr/ to properties of the head. Specifically, we proposed that an onset head must bear a Place node in order to license an appendix, APPLIC(ONSHD/PL) in (13). While (13) is undominated in English and Dutch, it is violated in adult German, as indicated earlier in (11a) and again in (27b). We can appeal to the marked status of the appendix-initial structure for /ʃr/ to explain why Annalena does not analyse this cluster in this fashion. However, this will not explain why she treats /ʃr/ as a branching onset, as the branching onset analysis of this cluster is also marked (see section 4.3 and note 27 on S = APP).

The fact that both parses for German /ʃr/ are marked may have led us to expect that Annalena would avoid clusters of this shape altogether, as do adult Dutch and English (*/sr/). This, however, is not the case (although it is for German-speaking Naomi (Janet Grijzenhout, personal communication)). As to why Annalena opts for the branching onset analysis over the appendix-initial analysis, we cannot be sure. Nevertheless, we speculate that it is tied to the fact that German /S/ appears as /ʃ/ and not as /s/. Recall from (11) that in English, where /s/ appears as /s/, /ʃr/ clusters are tolerated as branching onsets. Given that UG permits two analyses for the string /ʃr/, it is possible that Annalena has analysed the /ʃ/ of German /ʃr/ like English /ʃ/, and thus differently from the /ʃ/ of other /S/-initial clusters in the language. In the absence of evidence to the contrary, we shall assume that this analysis is correct.

The tableaux in (29) and (30) contrast Annalena's treatment of /ʃr/ and /ʃl/, respectively. As compared to the tableaux provided earlier in (23)–(26), we have added the constraint APPLIC(ONSHD/PL) which is directly relevant to the assessment of /Sr/ clusters. In the case of the input branching onset in (29), the faithful candidate, (a), violates *COMPLEX. Candidate (b) violates a number of markedness constraints, notably APPLIC(ONSHD/PL), because the head of the cluster, /r/, cannot support an appendix. In adult German, this constraint must be lowly ranked to permit /ʃr/ to be well-formed as an appendix-initial cluster. Among the two remaining candidates, (c) is selected as optimal in Annalena's grammar, as it does not incur a violation of MAXHEAD.

(29)   Annalena's grammar for /ʃr/:

Input: σ (O N, ʃ r V)	APPLIC (ONSHD/PL)	*COMPLEX	*APP-LEFT	MAXHEAD	MAX
a σ (O N, ʃ r V)		*!			
b PWd σ (O N, ʃ r V)	*!		*	*	
☞ c σ (O N, ʃ V)					*
d σ (O N, r V)				*!	*

Turning to (30), in this case, Annalena has the correct adult input. APPLIC (ONSHD/PL) is not violated by candidate (a) because the head of the cluster, /l/, bears a Place node (cf. (10a)). Nevertheless, dominant *APP-LEFT prevents this form from surfacing in favour of candidate (d), the only other form where MAXHEAD is respected.

(30)   Annalena's grammar for /ʃl/:

Input: PWd	AppLic (OnsHd/Pl)	*Complex	*App-Left	MaxHead	Max
a (PWd → σ → O N / ʃ l V)			*!		
b (σ → O N / ʃ l V)		*!		*	
c (σ → O N / ʃ V)				*!	*
☞ **d** (σ → O N / l V)					*

The final question we must address concerning /ʃr/ is how the German-speaking child like Annalena ultimately arrives at the correct analysis for clusters of this shape. She cannot appeal to the absence of morpheme-internal /ʃr/ (cf. section 4), as this would require access to indirect negative evidence. The adult analysis can only be arrived at through tidying up the grammar; that is, it must be driven by the learner's desire to treat all /ʃ/-initial clusters in the same fashion on grounds of parsimony. This does not require indirect negative evidence, but it does require that the child undertake cross-form comparison with the other /S/-initial clusters in the language. We leave further investigation of this issue to future research.

7.   Is reference to heads truly necessary?

Our analysis of cluster reduction has provided an important role for highly articulated prosodic representations and for constraints that make explicit reference to heads of syllable constituents, in particular MAXHEAD(ONSET). At the same time, we mentioned in the introduction that a recent trend observed in the constraint-based literature involves a move away from prosodic constituency in favour of phonetically motivated explanations of phonological phenomena. The sonority pattern of cluster reduction would seem to offer support for the latter approach, as this pattern can be accounted for purely on phonetic grounds: no reference to sub-syllabic structure is required, as the consonant that survives can be determined solely by a set of constraints which assess the sonority value of syllable margins (see Barlow 1997, Gnanadesikan this volume). While, on the face of it, a structural approach to the head pattern would seem to be required, we have not yet demonstrated that a strictly linear analysis cannot work. In the following sections, we shall argue that such an approach does not lead to satisfactory results for Amahl's grammar.

7.1   Constraints against fricatives

The approach that we shall consider stems from the observation that (strident) fricatives emerge late in acquisition. Grijzenhout and Joppen-Hellwig (2002) point out that, at early stages in development, many children avoid fricatives at the left edge, whereas nasals and stops are favoured in this position. They capture these observations through the constraint Word([-cont]. Grijzenhout and Joppen-Hellwig focus primarily on German-speaking Naomi, a child we have listed in (3) as following the head pattern from 1;4.26-1;7.27. For us, Naomi falls into the head pattern on the basis of the following reductions: obstruent+liquid → stop, /ʃ/+stop → stop, and /ʃ/+nasal → nasal (recall from note 8 that she does not attempt /ʃl/). Grijzenhout and Joppen-Hellwig take a different approach; they attribute Naomi's cluster reduction patterns to her general dislike for fricatives, that is, to highly ranked Word([-cont].

A similar analysis is provided for English-speaking Child 24 by Barlow and Gierut (1999) at age 5;0 (this child is language-delayed). They propose that a constraint against /s/, *S, is undominated in Child 24's grammar, thereby ensuring that this segment never surfaces, whether in singleton onsets or in clusters, e.g., 'sun' → [ʌn], 'swim' → [wɪm]. Barlow and Gierut further demonstrate that, at the next stage in development, age 5;3, singleton /s/ shows up as target-like, but /s/+C clusters still undergo /s/ deletion, an effect which is achieved through the ranking they provide in (31). (*COMPLEX is responsible for reduction of all types of clusters in their account.)

(31)   Child 24 at age 5;3:

		MAX	*S	*COMPLEX	ONSET
a /sʌn/	☞ i. [sʌn]		*		
	ii. [ʌn]	*			*!
b /swɪm/	i. [swɪm]		*	*!	
	ii. [sɪm]	*	*!		
	☞ iii. [wɪm]	*			

From the limited data provided in Barlow and Gierut, Child 24 appears to follow the head pattern at age 5;3.[31] Importantly, then, (31) demonstrates that we cannot reject an analysis of the head pattern which appeals to high-ranking *S, rather than to MAXHEAD(ONS), merely by observing a child who deletes /s/ only in clusters. We must therefore consider other evidence to tease apart the two approaches. In the next section, we demonstrate that evidence is available from Amahl's grammar to support the MAXHEAD approach.

7.2   Amahl's grammar

In the following lines, we address whether *S can capture the cluster re-ductions observed in Amahl's outputs. Amahl has no fricatives at all in his productions until late in development; thus, on the face of it, it might seem that an appeal to the more general *FRIC would be able to capture his patterns of cluster reduction. In (3), we listed Amahl as following the head pattern from 2;2–2;6. At this point, all of his coronal fricatives are re-alised as stops, and all sub-coronal contrasts are neutralised: in initial posi-tion, coronal obstruents surface as [d], and somewhat later in development, as [t].

If Amahl's treatment of /s/-initial clusters were due to his general avoid-ance of (coronal) fricatives, we would expect to find that /θr/ and /ʃr/ pat-tern with /sl/ and /sw/ as concerns reduction. Specifically, /θr/ and /ʃr/ should surface as [r], alongside /sl/ → [l] and /sw/ → [w]. This, however, is not the case. While we admit that there is some variation in the data, the prevailing pattern is that the obstruent is retained in the case of /θr/ and /ʃr/, while the approximant is retained in /sl/ and /sw/. As we have analysed the former as branching onsets and the latter as appendix-initial clusters, in both situations, it is the head of the cluster that is retained. The patterns observed can be seen most clearly in (32) (heads are underlined).[32]

(32)   Summary of Amahl's cluster development (2;2–2;8.13):

Target Cluster		Preservation of head			Preservation of non-head		
		Output	N	%	Output	N	%
a Branching	/θr/	[d, t]	(8)	67	[r, l]	(4)	33
onset	/ʃr/	[d]	(2)	67	[ʁ]	(1)	33
b Appendix-	/sl/	[l]	(24)	80	[d]	(6)	20
initial	/sw/	[w]	(13)	100	[d]	(0)	0

If the absence of fricatives alone were driving Amahl's cluster reductions, we should expect all of the clusters in (32) to be treated in the same fashion. This is clearly not the case. Nevertheless, we cannot hastily conclude that reference to onset heads is necessary. We must first look at the interaction of *FRIC with other high-ranking constraints. Since we cannot exploit the fact that the clusters in (32b) begin with /s/ while those in (32a) do not (given that all coronal fricatives are realised as [d] on the surface), we must instead consider the quality of the second consonant. Since the sonority value of this consonant – rhotic versus lateral or glide – divides the patterns in (32) into two, the logical place to begin is with the interaction of *FRIC with sonority-based constraints.

Concerning the latter, Prince and Smolensky (1993) have proposed a fixed ranking of constraints which assess syllable margin well-formedness, following the schema *M(ARGIN)/λ. To ensure that the margin constraints treat Amahl's /ʃr/ differently from his /sl/, we must appeal to a sonority difference between liquids, something which has been independently motivated by Kahn (1976) for English and by Hall (1992) for German. Building on this, we arrive at the partial ranking . . . *M/RHOT >> *M/LAT . . . The tableau in (33) shows that if IDENT(cont), the constraint responsible for stop–fricative alternations (McCarthy and Prince 1995), is ranked between *M/RHOT and *M/LAT, the correct results obtain for target /θr/, /ʃr/, and /sl/.

(33)   Coronal fricative + liquid clusters:

		*FRIC	*M/RHOT	IDENT (cont)	*M/LAT
a /θr/	i. θ	*!			
	☞ ii. d			*	
	iii. r		*!		
b /ʃr/	i. ʃ	*!			
	☞ ii. d			*	
	iii. r		*!		
c /sl/	i. s	*!			
	ii. d			*!	
	☞ iii. l				*

However, a problem immediately arises when we attempt to extend the analysis to target /sw/. With the addition of *M/GLIDE to the hierarchy, we incorrectly predict that /sw/ should surface as [d], instead of [w], as demonstrated in (34).

(34)   Coronal fricative + glide clusters:

		*FRIC	*M/GLIDE	*M/RHOT	IDENT (cont)	*M/LAT
a /sw/	i. s	*!				
	☹ ii. d				*	
	iii. w		*!			

What appears to be needed is a constraint, like *FRIC, that can be ranked independently of the margin constraints, *RHOT. If *RHOT were the constraint to dominate IDENT(cont) in place of *M/RHOT, it could be ranked higher than the offensive *M/GLIDE, and the correct results would obtain. See (35).

(35)   Introducing *RHOT:

		*FRIC	*RHOT	IDENT (cont)	*M/GLIDE	*M/RHOT	*M/LAT
a /θr/	i. θ	*!					
	☞ ii. ḍ				*		
	iii. r		*!			*	
b /ʃr/	i. ʃ	*!					
	☞ ii. ḍ				*		
	iii. r		*!			*	
c /sl/	i. s	*!					
	ii. ḍ			*!			
	☞ iii. l						*
d /sw/	i. s	*!					
	ii. ḍ			*!			
	☞ iii. w				*		

We have arrived at an analysis of Amahl's outputs that is descriptively adequate, but one which we reject nonetheless on grounds that it lacks explanatory adequacy. Prince and Smolensky's *M(ARGIN)/λ is designed to express sonority constraints on the shape of (left-edge) margins and, as such, the ranking is non-commutable: *M/GLIDE >> *M/RHOT >> *M/LAT >> *M/NASAL >> *M/FRIC. An analysis of cluster reduction that appeals to high-ranking *FRIC and *RHOT circumvents this fixed ranking by exploiting their rankable equivalents. Our approach, by contrast, appeals to cross-linguistically supported facts about left-edge clusters to account for Amahl's treatment of /s/-initial clusters on the one hand versus fricative-initial clusters on the other. The segment that survives cluster reduction is not tied to the shape of Amahl's inventory of singleton consonants, but instead, arises from the structural relationships that these segments enter into.

8.   Conclusion

In this chapter, we have discussed two patterns of reduction for left-edge clusters that are observed in the acquisition of West Germanic languages. These patterns, which we called the sonority and head patterns, differ in their treatment of rising sonority /S/-initial clusters: in the sonority pattern, the least sonorous consonant is retained in output forms (e.g., /Sl/ → [S]); in the head pattern, it is the sonorant that survives (e.g., /Sl/ → [l]), that is, the consonant that is the head of the onset in the target form.

We argued that the two patterns of cluster reduction are representative of distinct stages in development that differ in the degree to which inputs are elaborated, rather than differing in constraint ranking. We proposed that the head pattern, stage 2 in development, can best be accounted for if highly structured target-like inputs are posited, while the sonority pattern, stage 1, arises from inputs that are less articulated: only heads of sub-syllabic constituents are specified. At stage 1, there is no knowledge of the structural relations that hold across strings of consonants, and thus, the head of the onset can only be defined on the basis of relative prominence. This led to incorrect head selection for rising sonority /S/-initial clusters, clusters where the head in the target grammar is unexpectedly the segment of highest sonority.

Correct understanding of the head of a cluster requires that children take account of the distributional evidence available in the ambient language. In order to determine the type of evidence that is available, we systematically examined the distributional facts for the three languages under investigation. These facts support the view that all /S/-initial clusters, regardless of their sonority profile, are represented with a left-edge appendix. We argued that the sonority pattern child will be forced to take account of this evidence as s/he attempts to prosodify all of the segments in a cluster, on the way to achieving target-like inputs.

We demonstrated that a single ranking can be motivated for both patterns of cluster reduction if a constraint requiring faithfulness to the head of the onset constituent, MaxHead(Ons), is highly ranked. The markedness constraints *Complex and *App-Left must be undominated, thereby ensuring that no clusters are realised on the surface. As we argued that the inputs for the two groups of children differ in terms of headedness, MaxHead(Ons) will appropriately select the consonant that survives from the input cluster.

Finally, our analysis has relied on the premiss that children's inputs are built up through the course of acquisition until they reach the target stage when inputs are fully prosodified. While we provided some evidence from Brazilian Portuguese for fully prosodified inputs in adult grammars, the implications of such a proposal have not been thoroughly explored. We leave this to future research.

NOTES

* Earlier versions of this paper were presented at the 1st North American Phonology Conference and at the 26th Annual Boston University Conference on Language Development. We should like to thank the audiences for questions and comments. We should also like to thank Angela Carpenter, Della Chambless, Suzanne Curtin,

Janet Grijzenhout, John Matthews, Joe Pater, and Wim Zonneveld for comments that greatly improved the chapter. This research was supported by grants from FCAR and SFB (to H. Goad), from SSHRC (to G. L. Piggott and H. Goad), as well as by a SSHRC postdoctoral fellowship (to Y. Rose). The authors can be reached at: heather.goad@mcgill.ca and yrose@mun.ca.

1. We use the symbol /S/ as a cover for segments which will be analysed as left-edge appendices below. For the most part, /S/ corresponds to /s/ in English and Dutch and to /ʃ/ in German, the three languages under investigation. Further details are provided in sections 2 and 4.

2. Smith states that /s/+sonorant clusters are exceptions to the pattern that the least sonorous member is retained, as /s/ is always deleted 'despite its inherent prominence' (p. 166). In discussing the same type of data, Ingram (1989: 32) states that 'deletion of the marked member' is the strategy most commonly observed in children's cluster reductions, but no definition of markedness is provided.

3. Henceforth, we use the term obstruent to refer to all obstruents with the exception of /S/.

4. The label /S/+obstruent in (1) is used throughout the chapter instead of /S/+stop, as Dutch permits /sχ/ (see further section 4.2). (All three languages also contain /sf/, but it is restricted to a handful of low-frequency loans.)

5. While Fikkert (1994) mentions the important role played by sonority in cluster reduction, only three of the nine children for whom she provides summaries in her Appendix D (see below in the text) are listed in (1), as these are the only subjects whose outputs unambiguously support the sonority pattern. As we shall see shortly, the crucial difference between the sonority and head patterns rests with the treatment of /S/+sonorant clusters. However, all of the Dutch children in Fikkert's study treat /sl/ and /zʋ/ in the same manner as fricative–initial clusters. (The same probably holds true of English-speaking Joan for /sl/; see note 8.) Thus, the only potential difference between the sonority and head patterns rests with the treatment of /S/+nasal clusters. Fikkert points out (p. 92) that clusters of this shape are rarely attempted by Dutch children. (A similar observation is made by Lohuis-Weber and Zonneveld 1996: note 20.) Indeed, two of her subjects (Jarmo, Elke) never attempt clusters of this shape and some avoid /S/+nasal until too late in development; thus, we cannot tell from their outputs which reduction pattern was favoured. In section 5.1, we shall provide an explanation for the treatment of /sl/ as fricative-initial.

6. Regarding the gap for /Sk/, Dutch – as well as German – has a number of /sk/-initial loans (German no longer has /ʃk/-initial words). Some of these loans are high frequency and will no doubt be present in the early input to which children are exposed. However, we have no information on their acquisition in either language, and so they will not be considered further.

7. This assumes that fricatives are more sonorous than stops, a proposal which is supported on phonetic grounds but which has been challenged on phonological grounds (see, e.g., Hall 1992 and Wiese 1996 on German). As will be seen in section 5.1, the phonetic difference between the sonority value of stops and fricatives also plays a role in our analysis of the construction of inputs by children who follow the sonority pattern.

8. As alluded to in note 5, for Joan, definitive evidence for the head pattern is found in /s/+nasal reductions only. (/sw/ undergoes fusion to [f], which is compatible with both patterns of cluster reduction.) When /sl/ is attempted at 2;1, it is realised as [s],

not as [l]. However, target /l/ is realised as [z] at this stage; thus, we cannot be entirely sure about whether output [s] from /sl/ is preservation of /s/ or whether it arises from fusion of /s/ and /l/. For Naomi, evidence for the head pattern is also limited to /ʃ/+nasal; she does not attempt /ʃl/ (Janet Grijzenhout, personal communication).

9. [b̥, d̥, g̊] represent voiceless unaspirated lenis stops in Amahl's outputs (Smith 1973: 37). Overdots in Annalena's forms indicate that a consonant is ambisyllabic (Elsen 1991: 10).

10. This implies that /Sr/ is illicit in Dutch and English. As concerns Dutch, /sχr/ is realised as [sr] by many speakers (see Waals 1999: 23 for acoustic evidence). If this reflects a re-analysis of /sχr/, then /Sr/ clusters may be present in this language as well. However, unlike with German, we have no information on the acquisition of [sr] in Dutch. We shall henceforth consider this cluster to be ill-formed in Dutch, although nothing rests on this. As concerns English, [ʃr] is not /S/-initial but is, instead, analysed as a branching onset, as can be seen from its location in (2) and (4). See sections 4.1 and 4.3 for further discussion.

11. This is in spite of Richness of the Base, which contends that all inputs are possible, as the burden of selecting the correct output rests solely with constraint ranking (Prince and Smolensky 1993). We agree with Hale and Reiss (1998) that Richness of the Base is concerned with OT as a computational system, and not with real language learners.

12. This is opposite to the view espoused by Gnanadesikan (this volume). She proposes that the child's inputs are specified for syllable structure, although she does not accept that this holds true of the target grammar. The child first builds inputs on the basis of adult outputs, that is, from forms which are fully prosodified. Throughout the course of acquisition, these representations must be pruned back.

13. Two alternative options for /S/ at the left edge are as follows: (i) /S/+stop clusters form single (complex) segments (e.g., Fudge 1969, Ewen 1982, Selkirk 1982, Van de Weijer 1996, Wiese 1996); and (ii) /S/ is the coda of an empty-headed syllable (Kaye 1992). We shall not address these options further.

14. The representation in (7a) has been provided as the unmarked structure for obstruent+liquid clusters only. Nasal- and glide-final clusters are not included, in spite of the fact that we listed /kn/ and /CW/ alongside what are indisputably branching onsets in section 2. In the case of /kn/, this was because Dutch and German children who follow the head pattern of cluster reduction retain the stop, not the nasal, consistent with the branching onset analysis. Further, Fikkert (1994) points out that all of the Dutch children go through a stage where /kn/ clusters are produced as [kl]. The same observation holds for German-speaking Annalena (Elsen 1991). However, the issues that arise in the syllabification of /kn/ are complicated; we refer the interested reader to Trommelen (1984) and Kager and Zonneveld (1985/86), who treat Dutch /kn/ as appendix-initial (see also Van der Hulst 1984), and to Hall (1992), Booij (1995), and Wiese (1996), who treat /kn/ as a branching onset. In the case of /CW/, these clusters are branching onsets in the languages under consideration. However, the possibility that this reflects the unmarked representation for clusters of this shape has been challenged by Y. Rose (1999). Further, early French learners treat obstruent+liquid clusters differently from obstruent+glide, casting doubt on the branching onset structure as the unmarked analysis for obstruent+glide (see Y. Rose 2000). In the interest of space, we do not consider /kn/ and /CW/ clusters further.

15. Beyond the fact that the coronality of /S/ makes it unmarked on the place dimension, this restriction on the quality of appendices appears to be due to the fact that the stridency of /S/ makes it audible in all contexts, even when adjacent to a stop.
16. Somewhat surprisingly, children do produce clusters of this type, e.g., Amahl's [tlæmp] 'tramp'. Goad (1996) has argued that, in such cases, the constraint in (9) has not been violated, as Coronal has not yet been projected for [l], evidence for which comes from the behaviour of liquids in consonant harmony. Fikkert (1994: 120–122) provides similar examples from the acquisition of Dutch, e.g., Jarmo's [tlɛi] 'train'.
17. The representations in (10) reveal that we assume feature geometry. Although this is the case, it is not essential to the point being made. All that is required is for the segments in (10a) to bear Coronal; exactly how this is formally expressed is somewhat tangential.
18. Other arguments are available which, in the interest of space, we do not provide; on English, for example, see Kaye (1992), which includes discussion of the psycholinguistic evidence obtained by Treiman, Gross, and Glavin (1992). Additional arguments appeal to gaps in the expected inventory of clusters; if rising-sonority /S/-initial clusters were branching onsets, the child would have to use indirect negative evidence to come to the conclusion that this analysis is unavailable for certain combinations of segments, counter to expectation.
19. Throughout the rest of the chapter, segments abbreviate skeletal positions as well as featural content.
20. This is somewhat of a simplification. In contrast to German, recall that English and Dutch are marked in requiring the appendix in /S/-initial clusters to link to the syllable node, rather than to the PWd (see section 4). Henceforth, we will ignore this difference.
21. In the interest of space, rhyme nodes have been omitted from all structures.
22. One of Fikkert's (1994) subjects, Eva, appears to contradict this claim. From Fikkert's Appendix D (p. 326), we observe that Eva's /SN/ clusters initially follow the head pattern, and later, the sonority pattern. Two things make us reluctant to conclude that Eva's data are problematic. First, recall from note 5 that Fikkert remarks that /SN/ clusters are rarely attempted by Dutch-speaking children. We suspect that this is true of Eva, as only one example for each pattern is provided by Fikkert (head pattern: /snœyt/ → [nœys] 'snout' (1;6.1); sonority pattern: /snuːpiː/ → [zuːpiː] 'Snoopy' (1;9.8)). It is therefore difficult to get a sense of how representative these forms are of Eva's overall profile. Second, the output provided for the sonority pattern surfaces with an initial [z] which could be due to fusion of /s/ and /n/. If this were the case, then [zuːpiː] would be compatible not only with the sonority pattern, but with the head pattern of cluster reduction as well.
23. Joe Pater (personal communication) informed us that this holds of English-speaking Trevor as well.
24. As was evident from our structures in (12a, 12b), we do not accept the coda as a formal constituent (see esp. Kaye 1990); coda consonants are instead linked directly to the rhyme. This is in part because we do not accept the existence of branching codas, as would be expected if the coda were a licit argument of *COMPLEX. Instead, we adopt the view that final clusters which fall in sonority are heterosyllabic, with the second consonant syllabified as the onset of an empty-headed syllable (on the

latter, see, e.g., Giegerich 1985, Kaye 1990, Piggott 1991, Rice 1992, Zonneveld 1993, Harris 1994; see Goad and Brannen 2003 on L1).

25. These proposals, including the one in (20), make different empirical claims which will not be addressed here. The reader is referred to the original sources for further details.

26. We have not provided candidates where [p] is syllabified as an initial appendix. Such candidates will violate *App-Left, MaxHead, and other constraints which assess the segmental content of left-edge appendices.

27. The branching onset candidate has not been provided for input /Sl/. This candidate will violate a constraint such as S=App which requires that /S/ be optimally syllabified as an appendix. In the case of left-edge clusters, S=App will interact with other constraints on syllabification, in particular Onset, to ensure that /S/ is only syllabified as an appendix when followed by another consonant.

28. Here, we are concerned with children whose reduction patterns can be described by reference to prosodic structure, linear position, or sonority. Beyond sonority, we do not consider patterns which may be defined on the basis of the featural content of the segments involved. For the latter, we draw the reader's attention to Jongstra (2000).

29. Of the four Spanish learners investigated by Lleó and Prinz, one other child, Juan, produced a relatively high number of outputs consistent with the contiguity pattern, 54 percent (cf. María's 84 percent). (Note that the percentages provided by the authors collapse C+liquid and C+glide clusters, even though glides are syllabified in the nucleus in the adult grammar.) Finally, recall from (6a) that Spanish does not tolerate /s/+C clusters at the left edge and, thus, the data include obstruent-initial targets only.

30. Concerning Annalena's relatively late acquisition of obstruent+/l/ (Cl) clusters, it is worth pointing out that Van der Torre (2001) has provided cross-linguistic evidence in favour of obstruent+/l/ branching onsets as more marked than obstruent+/r/. Prior to 1;11.15, Annalena goes through a brief period of metathesis, ClV -> CVl. Concerning 2;02.15 as the point of acquisition of ʃC, there are a few cases of target-like productions of these clusters before this time, starting at about 1;11; however, systematic productions are not attested until 2;02.15.

31. The data provided in Barlow (1997) on Child 24's other clusters (obstruent+liquid, /s/+stop, /s/+nasal) reveal that this is not the case, but this is tangential to the point being made here.

32. The output segments in (32) abstract away from consonant harmony which applies in some of the data; however, one can always reconstruct what the target segments are in such forms.

References

Alderete, J. (1995). Faithfulness to prosodic heads. Paper presented at The Derivational Residue in Phonology Conference, Tilburg University.

Barlow, J. (1997). *A Constraint-based Account of Syllable Onsets: Evidence from Developing Systems*. Ph.D. dissertation, Indiana University.

(1999). An argument for adjuncts: evidence from a phonologically disordered system. In A. Greenhill, H. Littlefield, and C. Tano (eds.) *Proceedings of the 23rd*

Annual Boston University Conference on Language Development. Somerville, Mass.: Cascadilla Press. 44–55.

Barlow, J. and J. Gierut (1999). Optimality Theory in phonological acquisition. *Journal of Speech, Language, and Hearing Research* **42**. 1482–1498.

Bernhardt, B. H. and J. P. Stemberger (1998). *Handbook of Phonological Development from the Perspective of Constraint-Based Nonlinear Phonology*. San Diego: Academic Press.

Booij, G. (1995). *The Phonology of Dutch*. Oxford: Clarendon Press.

Charette, M. (1991). *Conditions on Phonological Government*. Cambridge: Cambridge University Press.

Chin, S. B. (1996). The role of the Sonority Hierarchy in delayed phonological systems. In T. W. Powell (ed.) *Pathologies of Speech and Language: Contributions of Clinical Phonetics and Linguistics*. New Orleans: International Clinical Phonetics and Linguistics Association. 109–117.

Chin, S. B. and D. A. Dinnsen (1992). Consonant clusters in disordered speech: constraints and correspondence patterns. *Journal of Child Language* **19**. 259–285.

Chomsky, N. (1981). *Lectures on Government and Binding*. Dordrecht: Foris.

Chomsky, N. and M. Halle (1968). *The Sound Pattern of English*. New York: Harper & Row.

Clements, G. N. (1990). The role of the sonority cycle in core syllabification. In J. Kingston and M. E. Beckman (eds.) *Papers in Laboratory Phonology I: Between the Grammar and Physics of Speech*. Cambridge: Cambridge University Press. 283–333.

Côté, M.-H. (2000). *Consonant Cluster Phonotactics: a Perceptual Approach*. Ph.D. dissertation, MIT.

Demuth, K. (1995). Markedness and the development of prosodic structure. *NELS* **25**. 13–25.

Dresher, B. E. and H. van der Hulst (1998). Head-dependent asymmetries in phonology: complexity and visibility. *Phonology* **15**. 317–352.

Elsen, H. (1991). *Erstspracherwerb: der Erwerb des Deutschen Lautsystems*. Wiesbaden: Deutscher Universitäts-Verlag.

Ewen, C. (1982). The internal structure of complex segments. In Van der Hulst & Smith (1982: part 2). 27–67.

Ferguson, C. A. and C. B. Farwell (1975). Words and sounds in early language acquisition. *Lg* **51**. 419–439.

Fikkert, P. (1994). *On the Acquisition of Prosodic Structure*. Ph.D. dissertation, Leiden University/HIL. The Hague: Holland Academic Graphics.

Fudge, E. (1969). Syllables. *JL* **5**. 193–320.

Giegerich, H. (1985). *Metrical Phonology and Phonological Structure*. Cambridge: Cambridge University Press.

(1992). *English Phonology*. Cambridge: Cambridge University Press.

Gierut, J. (1999). Syllable onsets: clusters and adjuncts in acquisition. *Journal of Speech Language and Hearing Research* **42**. 708–726.

Gilbers, D. and D.-B. den Ouden (1994). Compensatory lengthening and cluster reduction in first language acquisition: a comparison of different analyses. In A. de Boer, H. de Hoop, and H. de Swart (eds.) *Language and Cognition 4: Yearbook 1994 of the Research Group for Theoretical and Experimental Linguistics*. University of Groningen. 69–82.

Gnanadesikan, A. E. (this volume). Markedness and faithfulness constraints in child phonology.

Goad, H. (1996). Consonant harmony in child language: evidence against coronal underspecification. In B. Bernhardt, J. Gilbert, and D. Ingram (eds.) *Proceedings of the UBC International Conference on Phonological Acquisition*. Somerville, Mass.: Cascadilla Press. 187–200.

(1997). Consonant harmony in child language: an optimality-theoretic account. In S. J. Hannahs and M. Young-Scholten (eds.) *Focus on Phonological Acquisition*. Amsterdam: John Benjamins. 113–142.

(2001). Assimilation phenomena and initial constraint ranking in early grammars. In H.-J. A. Do, L. Dominguez, and A. Johansen (eds.) *Proceedings of the 25th Annual Boston University Conference on Language Development*. Somerville, Mass.: Cascadilla Press. 307–318.

Goad, H. and K. Brannen (2003). Phonetic evidence for phonological structure in syllabification. In J. Van de Weijer, V. Van Heuven, and H. van der Hulst (eds.) *The Phonological Spectrum*. Vol 2. Amsterdam: John Benjamins. 3–30.

Grijzenhout, J. and S. Joppen-Hellwig (2002). The lack of onsets in German child phonology. In I. Lasser (ed.) *The Process of Language Acquisition*. Frankfurt/Berlin: Peter Lang Verlag. 319–339.

Hale, M. and C. Reiss (1998). Formal and empirical arguments concerning phonological acquisition. *LI* **29**. 656–683.

Hall, T. A. (1992). *Syllable Structure and Syllable-Related Processes in German*. Tübingen: Max Niemeyer Verlag.

Hamilton, P. (1996). *Phonetic Constraints and Markedness in the Phonotactics of Australian Aboriginal Languages*. Ph.D. dissertation, University of Toronto.

Harris, J. (1994). *English Sound Structure*. Oxford: Blackwell.

(1997). Licensing inheritance: an integrated theory of neutralisation. *Phonology* **14**. 315–370.

Hulst, H. van der (1984). *Syllable Structure and Stress in Dutch*. Dordrecht: Foris.

Hulst, H. van der and N. Smith (eds.) (1982). *The Structure of Phonological Representations*. 2 parts. Dordrecht: Foris.

Humbert, H. (1997). On the asymmetrical nature of nasal obstruent relations. *NELS* **27**. 219–233.

Ingram, D. (1989). *Phonological Disability in Children*. 2nd edn. London: Cole & Whurr.

Inkelas, S. (1994). The consequences of optimization for underspecification. MS., University of California, Berkeley.

Itô, J. (1986). *Syllable Theory in Prosodic Phonology*. Ph.D. dissertation, University of Massachusetts, Amherst. Published 1988, New York: Garland.

Itô, J. and R. A. Mester (1997). Sympathy Theory and German truncations. MS., University of California, Santa Cruz.

Itô, J., Y. Kitagawa, and R. A. Mester (1996). Prosodic faithfulness and correspondence: evidence from a Japanese argot. MS., University of California, Santa Cruz.

Jakobson, R. (1941). *Child Language, Aphasia and Phonological Universals*. The Hague: Mouton. Translated 1968, A. R. Keiler.

Jongstra, W. (2000). Variability in the acquisition of word-initial consonant clusters. MS., University of Toronto.

Kager, R. and W. Zonneveld (1985/86). Schwa, syllables, and extrametricality in Dutch. *The Linguistic Review* **5**. 197–221.

Kahn, D. (1976). *Syllable-based Generalizations in English Phonology*. Ph.D. dissertation, MIT. Published 1980, New York: Garland.

Kaye, J. (1985). On the syllable structure of certain West African languages. In D. Goyvaerts (ed.) *African Linguistics: Essays in Memory of M. W. K. Semikenke*. Amsterdam: John Benjamins. 285–308.

(1990). 'Coda' licensing. *Phonology* **7**. 301–330.

(1992). Do you believe in magic? The story of s+C sequences. *SOAS Working Papers in Linguistics* **2**. 293–313.

Kaye, J., J. Lowenstamm, and J.-R. Vergnaud (1990). Constituent structure and government in phonology. *Phonology* **7**. 193–231.

Kenstowicz, M. (1994). *Phonology in Generative Grammar*. Oxford: Blackwell.

Kochetov, A. (1999). Constraints on distribution of palatalized stops: evidence for licensing by cue. *NELS* **29**. 167–181.

Lebel, É. (1998). On first language acquisition of word-initial English clusters: a case study. M.A. thesis, McGill University.

Levin, J. (1985). *A Metrical Theory of Syllabicity*. Ph.D. dissertation, MIT.

Lleó, C. and M. Prinz (1996). Consonant clusters in child phonology and the directionality of syllable structure assignment. *Journal of Child Language* **23**. 31–56.

Lohuis-Weber, H. and W. Zonneveld (1996). Phonological acquisition and Dutch word prosody. *Language Acquisition* **5**. 245–283.

Macken, M. (1980). The child's lexical representation: the 'puzzle-puddle-pickle' evidence. *JL* **16**. 1–17.

McCarthy, J. J. (1997). Faithfulness in prosodic morphology and phonology: Rotuman revisited. MS., University of Massachusetts, Amherst.

McCarthy, J. J. and A. S. Prince (1995). Faithfulness and reduplicative identity. *University of Massachusetts Occasional Papers* **18**. 249–384.

Mester, R. A. and J. Itô (1989). Feature predictability and underspecification: palatal prosody and Japanese mimetics. *Lg* **64**. 258–293.

Miller, W. R. (1965). *Acoma Grammar and Texts*. Berkeley and Los Angeles: University of California Press.

Nikièma, E. (1999). Government-licensing and consonant cluster simplification in Quebec French. *Canadian Journal of Linguistics* **44**. 327–357.

Ohala, D. (1999). The influence of sonority on children's cluster reductions. *Journal of Communication Disorders* **32**. 397–422.

Pater, J. (1997). Minimal violation and phonological development. *Language Acquisition* **6**. 201–53.

(2000). Non-uniformity in English secondary stress: the role of ranked and lexically specific constraints. *Phonology* **17**. 237–274.

(this volume). Bridging the gap between receptive and productive development with minimally violable constraints.

Piggott, G. L. (1991). Apocope and the licensing of empty-headed syllables. *The Linguistic Review* **8**. 287–318.

Pinker, S. (1984). *Language Learnability and Language Development*. Cambridge, Mass.: Harvard University Press.

Prince, A. S. and P. Smolensky (1993). Optimality Theory: constraint interaction in generative grammar. MS., Rutgers University and University of Colorado.

Rice, K. (1992). On deriving sonority: a structural account of sonority relationships. *Phonology* **9**. 61–99.

Rose, S. (1997). *Theoretical Issues in Comparative Ethio-Semitic Phonology and Morphology*. Ph.D. dissertation, McGill University.

Rose, Y. (1999). A structural account of Root node deletion in loanword phonology. *Canadian Journal of Linguistics* **44**. 359–404.

(2000). *Headedness and Prosodic Licensing in the L1 Acquisition of Phonology*. Ph.D. dissertation, McGill University.

Schwartz, R. G. and L. B. Leonard (1982). Do children pick and choose? An examination of phonological selection and avoidance. *Journal of Child Language* **9**. 319–336.

Selkirk, E. O. (1982). The syllable. In Van der Hulst and Smith (1982: part 2). 337–383.

Sherer, T. (1994). *Prosodic Phonotactics*. Ph.D. dissertation, University of Massachusetts, Amherst.

Smith, N. V. (1973). *The Acquisition of Phonology: a Case Study*. Cambridge: Cambridge University Press.

Smolensky, P. (1996). The comprehension/production dilemma in child language. *LI* **27**. 720–731.

Spencer, A. (1986). Towards a theory of phonological development. *Lingua* **68**. 3–38.

Stampe, D. (1969). The acquisition of phonetic representation. *CLS* **5**. 433–444.

Steriade, D. (1982). *Greek Prosodies and the Nature of Syllabification*. Ph.D. dissertation, MIT.

(1999). Phonetics in phonology: the case of laryngeal neutralization. In M. K. Gordon (ed.) *UCLA Working Papers in Linguistics: Papers in Phonology* **3**: 25–246.

Stoel-Gammon, C. and J. A. Cooper (1984). Patterns of early lexical and phonological development. *Journal of Child Language* **11**. 247–271.

Torre, E. J. van der (2001). Asymmetries within obstruent-liquid clusters. Paper presented at the Montréal-Ottawa-Toronto Phonology Workshop, University of Ottawa.

Treiman, R., J. Gross, and A. Glavin (1992). The syllabification of /s/ clusters in English. *Journal of Phonetics* **20**. 383–402.

Trommelen, M. (1984). *The Syllable in Dutch: with Special Reference to Diminutive Formation*. Dordrecht: Foris Publications.

Velten, H. V. (1943). The growth of phonemic and lexical patterns in infant language. *Lg* **19**. 281–292.

Vennemann, T. (1982). Zur Silbenstruktur der deutschen Standardsprache. In T. Vennemann (ed.) *Silben, Segmente, Akzente*. Tübingen: Max Niemeyer Verlag. 261–305.

Waals, J. (1999). *An Experimental View of the Dutch Syllable*. Ph.D. dissertation, Utrecht University/HIL. Published 1999, The Hague: Holland Academic Graphics.

Weijer, J. van de (1996). *Segmental Structure and Complex Segments*. Tübingen: Max Niemeyer Verlag.

Wiese, R. (1988). *Silbische und Lexikalische Phonologie: Studien zum Chinesischen und Deutschen*. Tübingen: Max Niemeyer Verlag.

(1996). *The Phonology of German*. Oxford: Clarendon Press.

Wright, R. A. (1996). *Consonant Clusters and Cue Preservation in Tsou*. Ph.D. dissertation, University of California, Los Angeles.

Zonneveld, W. (1993). Schwa, superheavies, stress and syllables in Dutch. *The Linguistic Review* **10**. 61–100.

5   Phonological acquisition in Optimality Theory: the early stages*

Bruce Hayes

1.   Introduction

The study of phonological acquisition at the very earliest stages is making no-table progress. Virtuosic experimental work accessing the linguistic knowledge of infants has yielded extraordinary findings demonstrating the precocity of some aspects of acquisition. Moreover, phonologists now possess an important resource, Optimality Theory (OT) (Prince and Smolensky 1993), which per-mits theorising to relate more closely to the findings of experimental work. The purpose of this chapter is to outline one way in which these experimental and theoretical research lines can be brought closer together. The central idea is that current phonological theory can, without essential distortion, be assigned an architecture that conforms closely to the process of acquisition as it is observed in children. I conclude with a speculative, though reasonably comprehensive, picture of how phonological acquisition might proceed.

2.   Empirical focus

To avoid confusion, I will try to make clear that my view of what 'phonological acquisition' involves may be broader than the reader is predisposed to expect.

When we study how very young children learn language, we can follow two paths. One is to examine what children say; the other is to develop methods that can determine what children understand or perceive. The reason these two methods are so different is that (by universal consensus of researchers) acqui-sition is always more advanced in the domain of perception than production: children often cannot utter things that they are able to perceive and understand.

A fairly standard view of children's productions (e.g., Smith 1973) is that the internalised representations that guide children are fairly accurate,[1] and that the child carries out her own personal phonological mapping (Kiparsky and Menn 1977) which reduces the complex forms she has internalised to something that can be more easily executed within her limited articulatory capacities. The study of this mapping is a major research area. For literature review, see Gerken (1994: 792–799), and for some recent contributions Levelt (1994), Fikkert (1994),

Pater (1997), Bernhardt and Stemberger (1998), Boersma (2000), and various chapters in this volume.[2]

But it is also important to consider acquisition from another point of view, focusing on the child's *internalised conception of the adult language*. As just noted, this will often be richer and more intricate than can be detected from the child's own speech. Indeed, the limiting case is the existence (see below) of language-particular phonological knowledge in children who cannot say anything at all. The focus of this chapter is the child's conception of the adult language, a research topic which can perhaps be fairly described as neglected by phonologists.

To clarify what is meant here, consider the classic example of *blick* [blɪk] vs. **bnick* [bnɪk] (Chomsky and Halle 1965). Speakers of English immediately recognise that *blick* is non-existent but possible, whereas *bnick* is both non-existent and ill-formed; it *could not* be a word of English. This is a purely passive form of linguistic knowledge, and could in principle be learned by an infant before she ever was able to talk. As we shall see shortly, there is experimental evidence that this is more or less exactly what happens.

I advocate, then, a clear separation between the child's phonological analysis of the ambient language vs. her personal production phonology. This view can be opposed, for example, to that of Smolensky (1996a), who takes the (*a priori*, rather appealing) view that the child's grammars for production and perception are the same. I will argue that this cannot be right: children whose production rankings generate very primitive outputs – or none at all – nevertheless can pass the 'blick' test. They could not do this unless they had also internalised an adult-like constraint ranking, separate from their production grammar.[3]

3.   Some results from the acquisition literature

To start, I will present a quick summary of results from the experimental literature on the early stages of phonological acquisition; see Gerken (1994) for more detail on most of the material treated here. All of these results are likely to be modified by current or future research, but I think a useful general trend can be identified.

Before presenting these results, it is worth first mentioning that they were made possible by the development of a high level of expertise in designing experiments that can obtain evidence about what infants know. Here is a very brief review. At birth, infants can provide information about what interests them in their surroundings when they vary the rate of sucking on an electronically monitored pacifier. Older babies can turn their heads in the direction they choose, and the duration of their head turns can be used to establish their degree of interest in linguistic material presented to them – most crucially, *relative* differences of interest in different linguistic material. Methods have been developed to ensure that the observations (e.g., 'How long did this head turn last?') are unbiased and do not reflect wishful thinking on the part of the observer. In addition, experimentalists rely on the testimony of many babies, and do careful statistical significance testing before any claims are made on the basis of the results.

3.1   Abilities present at birth: inherent auditory boundaries

Eimas *et al.* (1971) raised the intriguing possibility that there might exist innate 'feature detectors'. Neonates apparently best perceive distinctions along the acoustic Voice Onset Time continuum that match those characteristically used in human languages. This remarkable result was later rendered perhaps somewhat less exciting when similar perceptual abilities were located in non-linguistic species, in particular chinchillas (Kuhl and Miller 1975, 1978) and macaques (Kuhl and Padden 1982, 1983). These later results forced a more modest interpretation of the Eimas *et al.* findings, of a rather functionalist character (Kuhl and Miller 1975, Keating 1984): human languages tend to place their phoneme boundaries at locations where they are readily distinguished by the mammalian auditory apparatus.

3.2   Language-specific knowledge at 6 months: perceptual magnets

Six-month-old infants apparently know few if any words. Thus, whatever language learning they are doing must take place in the absence of a lexicon – plainly, a major handicap! Nevertheless, the work of Kuhl (1991, 1995) shows that 6-month-olds have already made a certain sort of progress towards attaining the ambient phonological system, which plausibly serves them well during the following months, as they acquire the ability to recognise words.

Kuhl's work demonstrates what she calls a 'perceptual magnet' effect: when 6-month-olds listen to various acoustic continua (such as synthesised vowels varying in F2), they discriminate tokens relatively poorly when token pairs lie close to the phonetic norms for the ambient language's categories; and relatively well when the token pairs lie midway between phonetic norms. This result is somewhat like the familiar pattern of categorical perception (e.g., Fodor, Bever, and Garrett 1974), but in a more sophisticated, gradientised form. Kuhl's term 'perceptual magnet' refers to the phonetic category centre, which acts like a magnet in causing closely neighbouring tokens to sound more like it than they really are.

Kuhl's findings were later submitted to theoretical modelling in the work of Guenther and Gjaja (1996). Guenther and Gjaja deployed a neural net model that directly 'learned' the set of perceptual magnets found in the input data, relying *solely on facts about token distributions*. That is, if the input set of formant frequencies has a cluster that centres loosely on the phonetic target for (say) [i], the Guenther/Gjaja model would learn a perceptual magnet in this location. The model mimics the behaviour of humans with respect to perceptual magnets in a number of different ways.

As Kuhl (1995) has pointed out, a very appealing aspect of the 'perceptual magnet' concept is that it represents a form of information that can be learned before any words are known. In any phonemic system, the phonetic tokens of actual speech are distributed unevenly. By paying attention to these asymmetries, and by processing them (perhaps in the way Guenther and Gjaja suggest), the child can acquire what I will here call *distributional protocategories*. These protocategories are not themselves phonemes, but as Kuhl points out, they could in principle serve as discrete building-blocks for the later construction of a true phonological system. Thus, for example, some distributional protocategories may turn out to be only strongly differentiated allophones of the same phoneme. These are only later united into a single category during the next phase of learning, when the child discovers that the protocategories have a predictable phonological distribution. The means by which this might be done are explored below.

3.3   The revolution at 8–10 months

By about 8 months, research suggests, babies start to understand words. This coincides, probably not accidentally, with an extraordinary growth of phonological ability, documented in two research traditions.

(1) Studies by Werker and Tees (1984) and Werker and Lalonde (1988) have shown that at this age, babies start to resemble adult speakers in having difficulty in discriminating phonetically similar pairs that do not form a phonemic opposition in their language. What is a loss in phonetic ability is, of course, a gain in phonological ability: the infant is learning to focus her attention on precisely those distinctions which are useful, in the sense that they can distinguish words from one another. This effect has been demonstrated by Werker and her colleagues for retroflex/alveolar contrasts in Hindi and for uvular/velar contrasts in Nthlakampx.[4]

(2) At more or less the same time, infants start to acquire knowledge of the legal segments and sequences of their language (cf. [blɪk] vs. *[bnɪk], above). This is shown in work by Jusczyk, Friederici, Wessels, Svenkerud, and Jusczyk (1993), Friederici and Wessels (1993), and Jusczyk, Luce, and Charles-Luce (1994). In carefully monitored experimental situations, 8- to 10-month-old infants come to react differently to legal phoneme sequences in their native language than to illegal or near-illegal ones.[5]

Both phenomena suggests that the ages of 8–10 months are the birth of true phonology; the infant at this stage takes the distributional protocategories obtained in earlier infancy and processes them to form a first-pass phonological system. It is worth pondering, I think, what might be done to characterise in a formal phonological theory what a 10-month-old has already learned.

4.   Phonological knowledge

To clarify this task, it will help to review received wisdom about what kinds of phonological knowledge adult speakers possess. Note that we are speaking here only of *unconscious* knowledge, deduced by the analyst from linguistic behaviour and from experimental evidence. Overt, metalinguistic knowledge is ignored here throughout.

There are basically three kinds of phonological knowledge. For each, I will review how such knowledge is currently described formally in Optimality Theory (Prince and Smolensky 1993), the approach to phonology adopted here.[6]

4.1   Contrast

To start, phonological knowledge includes knowledge of the system of contrasts: the speaker of French tacitly knows that [b] and [p], which differ minimally in voicing, contrast in French; that is, they can distinguish words such as [bu] 'end' vs. [pu] 'louse'. Korean also possesses [b] and [p], but the speaker of Korean tacitly knows that they are contextually predictable variants. Specifically, as shown by Jun (1996), [b] is the allophone of /p/ occurring between voiced sounds when non-initial in the Accentual Phrase.

In Optimality Theory, knowledge of contrasts and their distribution is reflected in the language-specific rankings (prioritisations) of conflicting constraints. For example, in French the faithfulness constraint of the IDENT family that governs voicing outranks various markedness constraints that govern the default distribution of voicing. This permits representations that differ in voicing to arise in the output of the grammar. In Korean, the opposite ranking holds, with Markedness over Faithfulness; thus *even if* Korean had underlying forms that differed in voicing, the grammar would alter their voicing to the phonological defaults; thus no contrast could ever occur in actual speech.[7]

In some cases, the situation is more complex than what was just described: the ranking of constraints is such that a contrast is allowed only in particular contexts. Thus, French generally allows for a voicing distinction in stops, but there is a high-ranking markedness constraint that requires voicing agreement in obstruent clusters. This constraint outranks Faithfulness for stop voicing, so that the contrast is suspended in certain contexts. For instance, there is no voicing contrast after an initial [s]; there are pairs like [bu] vs. [pu], but no pairs like [speˈsjal] ('spéciale') vs. *[speˈsjal].

It will be important to bear in mind that in mainstream Optimality Theory, constraint ranking is the *only* way that knowledge of contrast is grammatically encoded: there is no such thing as a (theoretically primitive) 'phoneme inventory' or other restrictions on underlying forms. The experience of analysts applying Optimality Theory to diverse languages shows that such theoretical entities would perform functions that are already carried out adequately by constraint ranking, and they are accordingly dispensed with. This point is made by Smolensky (1996b).

4.2 Legal structures

The second aspect of phonological knowledge is the *set of legal structures*: specifically, the legal sequencing of phonemes, as well as the structures involved in suprasegmental phenomena such as syllables, stress, and tone. The case of legal [blɪk] vs. illegal *[bnɪk] noted above is an example. To designate this sort of knowledge, I will use the somewhat archaic term *phonotactics*: a speaker who knows the phonotactics of a language knows its legal sequences and structures.

In Optimality Theory, the phonotactics of a language is, just like the system of contrasts, defined exclusively by constraint ranking. In particular, the legal sequences are those for which the faithfulness constraints that protect them outrank the markedness constraints that forbid them. As with contrast, theorists have found no reason to invoke any mechanisms other than constraint ranking in defining the phonotactics.

4.3 Alternation

The third and remaining kind of phonological knowledge is knowledge of the *pattern of alternation*: the differing realisations of the same morpheme in various phonological contexts. To give a commonplace example, the plural ending of English alternates: in neutral contexts it is realised as [z], as in *cans* [kænz]; but it is realised as [s] when it follows a voiceless consonant: *caps* [kæps].

The [s] realisation is related to the phonotactics in an important way: English does not tolerate final sequences like [pz], in which a voiced obstruent follows a voiceless one. For example, there are monomorphemic words like *lapse* [læps], but no words like *[læpz].

Optimality Theory treats most alternations as the selection of an output candidate that deviates from the underlying form in order to conform to a phonotactic pattern. In this way, it establishes an especially close relationship between phonotactics and alternation. Thus, for underlying /kæp+z/, the winning candidate is [kæps], in which the underlying value of [voice] for /z/ is altered in order to obey the markedness constraint that forbids final heterovoiced obstruent clusters. We shall return to the connection between phonotactics and alternation below.

4.4   Interpreting the acquisition literature

Turning now to the acquisition results reviewed earlier, I adopt the following interpretations of them within Optimality Theory.

System of contrasts: the evidence gathered by Werker and her colleagues indicates, at least tentatively, that by the time infants are 8–10 months old, they have gained considerable knowledge of the correct ranking of IDENT constraints with respect to the relevant markedness constraints, which in Optimality Theory establishes what is phonemic.

Phonotactics: the work of Jusczyk and others suggests that by the time infants are 8–10 months old, they have considerable knowledge of the constraint rankings (often markedness constraints vs. MAX and DEP) that determine the legal phonotactic patterns of their language.

Pattern of alternation: ??? I leave question marks for this case, because my literature search has yielded little evidence for just when infants/young children command patterns of alternation. In fact, I believe much interesting work could be done in this area. The next section outlines some findings that seem relevant.

5.   The acquisition timetable for morphology and alternation

Learning alternations demands that one has first learned morphology. It makes no sense to say that a morpheme alternates if the learner has not yet learned to detect that morpheme as a component substring of the words she knows. If we have good evidence that a child does not know a morpheme, then we can infer that she does not know its pattern of alternation.

It is often feasible to show that a child does not command a particular morpheme. For example, Smith (1973: 17) was able to show that his son Amahl did not command plurals by the following observation: '[At 2;2] Amahl had no contrast anywhere between singular and plural, e.g., [wut] and [wiːt] were in free variation for both *foot* and *feet*.' Given this, we can hardly suppose that Amahl had made sense of the alternation pattern ([z]/[s]/[əz]) of the English plural suffix; and indeed, there is evidence (Smith 1973: 17) that Amahl wrongly construed the data as involving an optional process of phonological /z/ deletion.

Note that the age of 2 years and 2 months arrives a very long time (as children's lives go) after 10 months. It is thus likely, I think, that Amahl went through a long period in which he tacitly knew that English words cannot end in heterovoiced obstruent sequences, but was in no position to make use of this knowledge to help him with the plural allomorphy seen in *dogs* [dɔgz] and *cats* [kæts].

Some morphology seems to be learned considerably later than this. An extreme case is the non-concatenative morphology of Modern Hebrew, which is rendered particularly difficult by historical changes that rendered the system opaque in various areas. According to Berman's (1985) study, children learning Modern Hebrew fail to achieve productive command over some parts of the non-concatenative morphology before they reach 4–5 years of age.

Berko's (1958) famous 'Wug'-testing study, in which children were asked to inflect novel stems like *wug*, also provides support for the view that morphophonemic acquisition happens relatively late. Specifically, quite a few of Berko's subjects, particularly the 4-year-olds, did rather badly on their Wug tests. It seems clear that many of them did not possess full, active command over the patterns of alternation in English inflectional suffixes. Much the same holds true for the children described in a similar study by Baker and Derwing (1982), as well as studies reviewed by Derwing and Baker (1986, 330–331).

The earliest evidence I have seen for command of morphology is correct usage of the Turkish accusative suffix [-a] ~ [-e] at 15 months, documented by Aksu-Koç and Slobin (1985). In principle, knowledge might come earlier, since all evidence I have seen in the literature involves active production by the child rather than experimental tests of perceptual knowledge.

To sum up this somewhat inconclusive picture: we earlier asked what is the *relative timing* of the acquisition of the three general areas of phonological knowledge – contrasts, phonotactics, and alternation. For the first two, it appears that acquisition is precocious, with much progress made by the age of 10 months. For the third, the data are skimpy, and there seems to be quite a bit of variation between morphological processes. Certainly, we can say that there are at least *some* morphological processes which are acquired long after the system of contrasts and phonotactics is firmly in place, and it seems a reasonable guess that in general, the learning of patterns of alternation lags behind the learning of the contrast and phonotactic systems.

A moment's thought indicates why this is a plausible conclusion: for the child to learn a morphological process, she must presumably learn an actual *paradigm* that manifests it (e.g., for English plurals, a set of singular–plural pairs). But the learning of contrasts and phonotactics can get started when the child merely possesses a more-or-less random inventory of words and short phrases.[8] We thus should expect the learning of alternations to be delayed.

6.   The appropriateness of Optimality Theory

I will now argue that current Optimality theoretic approaches are particularly well adapted to modelling the course of acquisition as it is laid out above.

Optimality Theory has been widely adopted by phonologists in part because it solves (or certainly appears to solve) the long-standing problem of *conspiracies*. Early theories of phonology were heavily focused on accounting for alternation, with large banks of phonological rules arranged to derive the allomorphs of the morphemes. It was noticed by Kisseberth (1970) and subsequent work

that this alternation-driven approach characteristically missed crucial generalisations about phonologies, generalisations that were statable as constraints.
These include bans on consonant clusters, adjacent stresses, onsetless syllables,
and so on. The rules posited in the phonology of the 1960s–1980s were said
to 'conspire' to achieve these surface generalisations; but the generalisations
themselves never appeared in the actual analysis. Two decades of research following Kisseberth's article addressed, but never fully solved, the 'conspiracy
problem'.

In OT, the treatment of alternation is subordinated to the general characterisation of phonotactics in the language. OT delegates the problem of deriving
output forms to an entirely general procedure, and dispenses with rules. Under
this approach, the conspiracy problem disappears, since the rules that formerly
'conspired' are absent, and the target of the conspiracy is itself the core of the
analysis.[9]

This theoretical architecture is strongly reminiscent, I think, of the acquisitional sequence laid out in sections 3 and 5 above. In OT, knowledge of contrast
and phonotactics is logically prior to knowledge of alternations; and in the acquisition sequence, knowledge of contrast and phonotactics are (at least usually)
acquired before knowledge of alternations.

More important, I believe that prior knowledge of phonotactics would actually *facilitate* the acquisition of alternation. The reason is that most alternation
is directly driven by the need for morphologically derived sequences to conform
to the phonotactics – that is, most alternation is conspiratorial.

To follow up on an earlier example: the English plural suffix is [z] in neutral
environments (e.g., *cans* [kænz]) but [əz] after sibilants (*edges* [ɛdʒəz]) and
[s] after voiceless sounds other than sibilants: *caps* [kæps]. The allomorphs
[əz] and [s] can be traced directly to patterns of English phonotactics, patterns
that can be learned prior to any morphological knowledge. Specifically, English
words cannot end in sibilant sequences (hence *[ɛdʒz]), nor can they end in a
sequence of the type *voiceless obstruent + voiced obstruent* (*[kæpz]). These
phonotactic constraints hold true in general, and not just of plurals; English
has no words of any sort that end in *[dʒz] or *[tz]. It is easy to imagine that
knowledge of these phonotactic principles, acquired early on, would aid the
child in recognising that [əz] and [s] are allomorphic variants of [z].

We can put this slightly more generally if we adopt some terminology from
the older rule-based theory. A rule has a *structural description* (the configuration that must be present for a rule to apply) and a *structural change* (the change
the rule carries out). In these terms, a child who has already achieved a good
notion of the phonotactics of her language need not, in general, locate structural
descriptions to cover cases of regular phonological alternation. These structural
descriptions are already implicit in the child's internalised knowledge of phonotactics. All that is necessary is to locate the crucial structural change. More
precisely, within Optimality Theory, the learner must locate the faithfulness

constraint that must be ranked lower in order for underlying forms to be altered to fit the phonotactics. By way of contrast, earlier rule-based approaches require the learner to find both structural description and change for every alternation, with no help from phonotactic knowledge.

The 'Wug'-testing study of Berko (1958) suggests that children actually do make practical use of their phonotactic knowledge in learning alternations. Among the various errors Berko's young subjects made, errors that violate English phonotactics, such as *[wʌgs] or *[gʌtʃs] (Berko, pp. 162–163) were quite rare. This observation was confirmed in more detail in the later work of Baker and Derwing (1982). In the view adopted here, the children's greater reliability in this area results from their having already learned the phonological constraints that ban the illegal sequences.

Summing up, it would appear that the OT answer to the conspiracy problem is more than just a gain in analytical generality; it is the basis of a plausible acquisition strategy.

7.   Learning phonotactics in Optimality Theory

Let us assume, then, that it is appropriate to tailor phonological theory to match acquisition order, letting the prior acquisition of phonotactics aid in the later acquisition of alternations. What I want to focus on at this point is the core issue of this chapter: how might we model the stage occurring at 10 months, where the child's knowledge is solely or mostly phonotactic knowledge?

There is now a research tradition within which this question can be explicitly addressed. Its goal is to develop algorithms that, given input data and constraint inventories, can locate appropriate constraint rankings, and thus 'learn' phonological systems. Research in this tradition began with Tesar and Smolensky (1993) and includes later work such as Tesar (1995a, 1995b, 1999), Tesar and Smolensky (1996, 1998, 2000), Boersma (1997), Pulleyblank and Turkel (2000), and Boersma and Hayes (2001).

Constraint ranking algorithms have characteristically attempted to learn whole grammars at a time. But further progress might be possible by taking incremental steps, paralleling those taken by real children. In the present case, the goal is to develop what I will call a *pure phonotactic learner*, defined as follows:

(1)   A *pure phonotactic learner* is an algorithm that, given (only) a set of words that are well-formed in a language, creates a grammar that distinguishes well-formed from ill-formed phonological sequences.

Following a commonplace notion in learnability, this definition stipulates that a pure phonotactic learner must make no use of negative evidence. That is, while it can be given a long and variegated sequence of examples showing what is well-formed, it can never be overtly told what is ill-formed. This seems to be a realistic requirement in the present case.[10]

The rankings obtained by a pure phonotactic learner can be tested in the following way: we feed *hypothetical* underlying forms, including illegal ones, to a grammar that respects the rankings that have been learned. If the rankings are correct, the grammar will act as a filter: it will alter any illegal form to something similar which is legal, but it will allow legal forms to persist unaltered. This idea is based on the discussion in Prince and Smolensky (1993: 175).[11]

An intriguing aspect of pure phonotactic learning is that, as far as I can tell, the notion of underlying representation would play no significant role. Specifically, if we consider the two primary purposes to which underlying forms have been put, neither is applicable.

First, in earlier theories of phonology, underlying representations were deemed necessary in order to depict the inventory of contrasting phonological units. As noted above, the shift to OT renders such a function unnecessary; this was shown by Smolensky (1993) and Kirchner (1997). Both authors show that, in OT, the notion of possible contrast is fully encoded in the system of constraint rankings, and that reference to underlying forms is not needed to characterise contrast.

Second, underlying forms are posited as a means of establishing a unifying basis for the set of allomorphs of a morpheme: the allomorphs resemble one another, and diverge in systematic fashion, because each is derived from a unique underlying representation. This second assumption is likewise not needed in pure phonotactic learning: our (somewhat idealised) view is that we are dealing with a stage at which the child has identified individual words but not yet parsed them into morphemes. In such a system, there are no alternations, so there is no need for underlying forms to account for them.[12]

With both functions of underlying forms dispensed with in the present context, we can suppose that underlying representations are the same as surface representations;[13] this follows the principle of Lexicon Optimisation of Prince and Smolensky (1993). In principle, this should help: acquisition can proceed, at least for the moment, without the need to explore the vast set of possible underlying representations corresponding to each surface form.

7.1   *Constraint ranking in Tesar and Smolensky's model*

In trying to design a pure phonotactic learner, I took as my starting-point the Constraint Demotion algorithm of Tesar and Smolensky (1993, 1996, 1998, 2000). When applied to conventional data sets (involving alternation), Constraint Demotion arrives quite efficiently at suitable constraint rankings. Constraint Demotion serves here as the base algorithm, to be augmented to form a pure phonotactic learner. The expository tasks at hand are first to review Constraint Demotion, then to show that, without modification, it is not suited to the task of pure phonotactic learning. The version of Constraint Demotion I will review here is the simplest one, namely the 'batch' version described in Tesar and Smolensky (1993).[14]

Constraint Demotion is provided with: (1) a set of paired underlying and surface representations; (2) an appropriate set of ill-formed rival outputs for each underlying form, assumed to be provided by the GEN function; (3) an appropriate set of markedness and faithfulness constraints; and (4) violation data: the number of times each winning or rival candidate violates each constraint. From this, it finds a ranking (should one exist) that generates the correct output for each underlying form.

A term from Prince and Tesar (this volume) that is useful in understanding Constraint Demotion is *prefers a loser*: a constraint prefers a loser if an ill-formed rival candidate violates it fewer times than the correct form does. The leading idea of Constraint Demotion is to demote those constraints that prefer losers to a position just low enough in the hierarchy so that, in the candidate-winnowing process that determines the outputs of an OT grammar, winners will never lose out to rivals.

The batch version of Constraint Demotion is summarised as follows:

(2)   **Constraint Demotion**
        I. Find all constraints that don't prefer any losers. Place them in a 'stratum', a set of constraints assumed to occur together at the top of the ranking hierarchy.
       II. Where a rival candidate violates a constraint in a newly-established stratum more times than the winner does, it may be considered to be 'explained': the winnowing procedure of OT is guaranteed at this point never to select the rival in preference to the winner. As soon as a rival candidate is explained in this sense, it must be removed from the learning data set, as nothing more can be inferred from it.
      III. Of the constraints that have not yet been placed in a stratum, find those which prefer no losers in the remaining data. Place them in the next stratum of constraints.
       IV. Cull out explained rivals again, as in II.
        V. Repeat steps III and IV ad libitum, until all the constraints have been assigned to a stratum.

The result (when ranking is successful) is the placement of every constraint in a stratum. As Tesar and Smolensky show (in a formal proof), any ranking of the constraints that respects the stratal hierarchy (so that any constraint in a higher stratum is ranked above any constraint in a lower stratum) will derive only winning candidates.

Sometimes, step III of the algorithm yields no constraints at all; all the remaining constraints prefer losers. In such cases, it turns out, there *is no ranking* of the constraints that will generate only winners. Thus, Constraint Demotion has the ability to detect failed constraint sets.[15] A constraint set also fails if it is insufficiently rich, assigning identical violations to a winner and rival.

The Constraint Demotion algorithm is, in my opinion, an excellent contribution, which opens many avenues to the study of phonological learning. However, it is not suited to the task of pure phonotactic learning, as I shall demonstrate.

The next few sections of the chapter are laid out as follows. In sections 7.2 and 7.3, I present a simple data example, 'Pseudo-Korean', to be used as an illustration for the ranking algorithms. Section 7.4 applies Constraint Demotion to Pseudo-Korean, and shows how it is unable to learn its phonotactics. Sections 7.5–7.7 lay out my own algorithm, and section 7.8 shows how it learns the Pseudo-Korean pattern.

7.2   'Pseudo-Korean': basic pattern and constraints

Imagine a language in which stops contrast for aspiration; thus /p t k/ and /pʰ vʰ kʰ/ form separate phonemic series and are attested in minimal pairs, such as [tal] 'moon' vs. [tʰal] 'mask'. Assume further that, while /pʰ tʰ kʰ/ show no significant allophonic variation, /p t k/ are voiced to [b d g] when intervocalic: thus [ke] 'dog' but [i **ge**] 'this dog'. The voicing pattern is allophonic; thus [bdg] occur only as the voiced allophones of /p t k/, and never in other positions. Lastly, assume that in final and preconsonantal position, aspiration is neutralised, so that the only legal stops are the voiceless unaspirated [p t k]. Thus while [tʃipʰi] 'straw-nom.' and [tʃibi] 'house-nom.' show the phonemic contrast between /pʰ/ and the [b]-allophone of /p/, this contrast is neutralised to plain [p] in final position, so that unsuffixed [tʃip] is in fact ambiguous between 'straw' and 'house'.

This phonological arrangement is essentially what we see in Korean, which is the source of the examples just given. Such arrangements are cross-linguistically quite characteristic. A number of languages voice their unaspirated stops intervocalically (Keating, Linker, and Huffman 1983), and it is common for languages to suspend contrasts for laryngeal features in positions other than prevocalic (Lombardi 1995, Steriade 1997). I will call the hypothetical example language 'Pseudo-Korean', since all the phenomena of Pseudo-Korean occur in Korean, but Pseudo-Korean has only a small subset of the Korean phenomena.

A suitable set of constraints and rankings for analysing Pseudo-Korean in Optimality Theory is given below.

7.2.1   Markedness constraints

(3)   *[−SONORANT, +VOICE]

The default, normal state of obstruents is voiceless, for aerodynamic reasons laid out in Ohala (1983) and Westbury and Keating (1986). The constraint above encodes this phonetic tendency as a grammatical principle.

(4)

    *[+VOICE][−VOICE][+VOICE]   (abbreviation: *[+v][−v][+v])

This constraint bans voiceless segments surrounded by voiced ones. The teleology of the constraint is presumably articulatory: forms that obey this constraint need not execute the laryngeal gestures needed to turn off voicing in a circumvoiced environment. For evidence bearing on this point from an aerodynamic model, see Westbury and Keating (1986).

With these two constraints in hand, we may consider their role in Pseudo-Korean. As will be seen, the faithfulness constraints for voicing are ranked so low as to make no difference in Pseudo-Korean; therefore voicing is allophonic. The distribution of voicing is thus determined by the ranking of the markedness constraints. In particular, *[+v][−v][+v] must dominate *[−SON, +VOICE], so that obstruents will be voiced in voiced surroundings:

(5)

/ada/	*[+v][−v][+v]	*[−SON, +VOICE]
☞ [ada]		*
*[ata]	*!	

Under the opposite ranking, obstruents will be voiceless everywhere; Keating *et al.* (1983) note that this is the pattern found in Hawaiian and various other languages.

(6)   *[+SPREAD GLOTTIS]   (abbr. *ASPIRATION or *ASP)

This constraint, too, has an articulatory teleology: aspiration involves a glottal abduction gesture of considerable magnitude.

(7)   *[+VOICE, +SPREAD GLOTTIS]   (abbr. *Dʰ)

Voicing and aspiration are inherently not very compatible, and indeed most languages lack voiced aspirates. Note that *Dʰ bans a subset (a particularly difficult subset) of the cases banned by *ASPIRATION.

In pseudo-Korean, *Dʰ must be ranked above *[+v][−v][+v]; otherwise, aspirated stops would be voiced intervocalically.

(8)

/atʰa/	*Dʰ	*[+v][−v][+v]
☞ [atʰa]		*
*[adʰa]	*!	

Hence we have the three-way ranking $*\text{D}^h >> *[+v][-v][+v] >> *[-\text{SON}, +\text{VOICE}]$.

7.2.2   *Faithfulness constraints*   The constraint in (9):

(9)   IDENT([SPREAD GLOTTIS]) / __ V   (Abbr.: IDENT(ASP) / __ V)

is a 'positional faithfulness' constraint, of the type explored by Beckman (1998) and others. It is violated when a segment occurring prevocalically in a candidate surface form corresponds to an underlying segment with which it disagrees in the feature [spread glottis]; that is, aspiration. The constraint is 'positional' because it relies on a phonological context.[16]

The rationale for the particular context invoked, prevocalic, has been explicated by Steriade (1997), who offers an explanation for the fact that aspiration and other laryngeal contrasts gravitate cross-linguistically to prevocalic position. In Steriade's view, this has an acoustic explanation: vowels[17] provide a clear 'backdrop' against which aspiration and other laryngeal phenomena can be perceived; and languages characteristically limit their phonemic contrasts to locations where perceptibility is maximised.

I also assume a general, context-free Faithfulness constraint for aspiration:

(10)   IDENT([SPREAD GLOTTIS])   (Abbr.: IDENT(ASP))

The type of aspiration pattern a language will allow depends on the ranking of *ASPIRATION in the hierarchy: if *ASPIRATION is on top, then aspiration will be missing entirely (as in French); if *ASPIRATION is outranked by IDENT(ASP) (and perhaps, also redundantly by IDENT(ASP) / __V), aspiration will be contrastive in all positions, as in Hindi. Pseudo-Korean reflects the ranking IDENT(ASP) / __ V >> *ASP >> IDENT(ASP), which permits aspiration prevocalically ((11)) but not in other positions ((12), where an illegal input */at^h/ loses out to a legal winner [at]).

(11)

/t^{h}a/	ID (ASP)/ _V	*ASP
☞ [t^{h}a]		*
*[ta]	*!	

(12)

*/at^h/	*ASP	ID (ASP)
☞ [at]		*
*[at^h]	*!	

A more subtle ranking argument concerns the possibility of *[ada] as the winning candidate for underlying /atʰa/. *[ada] satisfies both *Dʰ and *[+v][−v][+v], at the expense of IDENT(VOICE) / ＿ V. In order for [atʰa] to win out over [ada], IDENT(ASP) / ＿ V must be ranked above *[+v][−v][+v].

(13)

/atʰa/	*Dʰ	ID (ASP) / ＿V	[+v][−v][+v]
☞ [atʰa]			*
*[ada]		*!	
*[adʰa]	*!		

The following Faithfulness constraints for voicing:

(14)   IDENT(VOICE) /＿ V

(15)   IDENT(VOICE)

work just like the analogous constraints for aspiration. However, in Pseudo-Korean, where voicing is allophonic, both are at the bottom of the grammar, where they have no influence. The ranking *[+v][−v][+v] >> *[−SON, +VOICE] >> {IDENT(VOICE) / ＿V, IDENT(VOICE)} forces a distribution where unaspirated stops are voiced in intervoiced position, and voiceless elsewhere. The following tableaux illustrate this; they show how underlying forms containing stops with the wrong voicing would lose out to well-formed alternatives:

(16)

/da/	*[+v][−v][+v]	*[−SON, +VOICE]	ID(VOICE)/ ＿V	ID(VOICE)
☞ [ta]			*	*
*[da]		*!		

(17)

/ata/	*[+v][−v][+v]	*[−SON, +VOICE]	ID(VOICE)/ ＿V	ID(VOICE)
☞ [ada]		*	*	*
*[ata]	*!			

7.2.3   Target ranking   The following diagram summarises all rankings required to derive the Pseudo-Korean pattern.

(18)

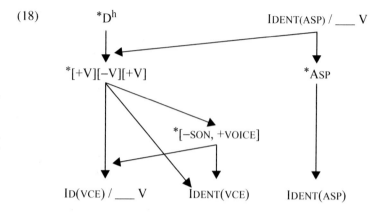

An adequate ranking algorithm must learn *at least* these rankings. It may also without harm posit additional ranking relationships, so long as they do not conflict with those of (18).

7.3   Pseudo-Korean: candidates

To provide a reasonable test for ranking algorithms, I developed a large set of Pseudo-Korean forms, with rival candidates for each. The rivals included all possible combinations of voicing and aspiration in all positions. A representative subset is given in (19):

(19)

Input	Winning Output	Rivals
/ta/	[ta]	*[tʰa], *[da], *[dʰa]
/tʰa/	[tʰa]	*[ta], *[da], *[dʰa]
/ada/	[ada]	*[ata], *[atʰa], *[adʰa]
/atʰa/	[atʰa]	*[ata], *[ada], *[adʰa]
/at/	[at]	*[ad], *[atʰ], *[adʰ]
/tada/	[tada]	*[tata], *[tatʰa], *[tadʰa], *[dada], *[tʰada], *[dʰada]
/tatʰa/	[tatʰa]	*[tata], *[tada], *[tadʰa], *[datʰa], *[dʰatʰa], *[tʰatʰa]
/tʰada/	[tʰada]	*[tʰatʰa], *[tʰata], *[tʰadʰa], *[tada], *[dada], *[dʰada]
/tʰatʰa/	[tʰatʰa]	*[tʰata], *[tʰada], *[tʰadʰa], *[tatʰa], *[datʰa], *[dʰatʰa], *[tata], *[tada]
/tat/	[tat]	*[tatʰ], *[tad], *[tadʰ], *[tʰat], *[dat], *[dʰat]
/tʰat/	[tʰat]	*[tʰad], *[tʰatʰ], *[tʰadʰ], *[tat], *[dat], *[dʰat]

Following the assumption made above in section 7, I consistently made the underlying form the same as the winning candidate. Note that all the forms in the simulation were *legal surface forms* of Pseudo-Korean; thus, the training set provided only positive evidence.

7.4   Application of Constraint Demotion to Pseudo-Korean

I will first show how, and why, Tesar and Smolensky's Constraint Demotion algorithm is not suited to pure phonotactic learning. If we apply the Constraint Demotion to the Pseudo-Korean data, it will install in the top stratum the following five constraints, which never prefer losers:

(20)   **Stratum 1**
   IDENT(ASPIRATION)
   IDENT(VOICE)
   IDENT(ASPIRATION) / __V
   IDENT(VOICE) / __V
   *Dʰ

*Dʰ reflects a patently true regularity of Pseudo-Korean, and the four Faithfulness constraints are never violated, as a result of the positive-data-only learning situation.

   With all these constraints in place, all of the learning data are explained, and the remaining, loser-preferring constraints end up in the second stratum:

(21)   **Stratum 2**
   *[+v][−v][+v]
   *[−SON/+VOICE]
   *ASPIRATION

The result is a perfectly good grammar for the data that fed it, in the sense that it generates the correct outcome for every input form. But it is not a good grammar for Pseudo-Korean, because it fails to describe Pseudo-Korean phonotactics. To illustrate this, we can feed to this grammar a set of underlying forms that are illegal in Pseudo-Korean, and check to see what emerges as the winner. Omitting the tableaux, I will simply list here some representative cases that emerge from this procedure:

(22)

Input	Output	Input	Output
/da/	*[da]	/ad/	*[ad]
/dʰa/	*[dʰa] or *[tʰa] or *[da]	/atʰ/	*[atʰ]
/ata/	*[ata]	/adʰ/	*[adʰ] or [atʰ] or *[ad]
/adʰa/	*[adʰa] or *[atʰa] or [ada]		

The crucial point is that a large number of illegal forms is generated. It can be noted in passing that there is also a good deal of free variation: it matters how *Dʰ is ranked with respect to the faithfulness constraints; but Constraint Demotion is unable to establish this ranking.

The basis of the bad outcomes is not hard to see: since all the faithfulness constraints are at the top of the hierarchy, it is always possible to generate an output that is identical (or at least, very similar) to an illegal input. Moreover, this is an *inevitable* result, given the nature of Constraint Demotion as applied to learning data of the type considered here.

Recall now what we wanted our grammar to do: given a legal input, it should simply reproduce it as an output; and given an illegal input, it should alter it to form a legal output. It is evident that the ranking learned by Constraint Demotion succeeds in the first task, but not the second.

7.5   *Adapting constraint demotion to pure-phonotactic learning*

We begin by invoking a fundamental idea of recent theoretical acquisition work in Optimality Theory (Gnanadesikan this volume, Smolensky 1996b, and much other work): faithfulness constraints should be assigned a default location at the bottom of the constraint hierarchy. From the viewpoint of this chapter, this proposal is actually two proposals.

First, in the production grammars that children use to generate their own outputs, the gradual approximation by the child's own output to adult speech reflects a gradual rise of the faithfulness constraints upward from the bottom of the hierarchy.

Second, and more relevant here, default low-faithfulness ranking can be applied to the learner's internalised conception of the adult language. Here, the need to favour rankings with low Faithfulness arises for a different reason: the problem of learning in the absence of negative evidence. To learn that (say) *[ad] is ill-formed, Pseudo-Korean infants must use a conservative strategy, plausibly along the lines 'if you haven't heard it, or something like it, then it's not possible'. As Smolensky (1996b) showed, this has a direct formal implementation in Optimality Theory: we must locate a constraint ranking that places Faithfulness as low as possible.

Note that by using general phonological constraints, we can in principle solve a major problem. We do not want the finished grammar to admit only those words that it has heard before; rather, we want the grammar to *project* beyond this minimum to allow similar forms. Thus (to take up a familiar example again) English speakers accept *blick* [blɪk] as well-formed because the real words they learned in childhood (such as *blink* and *kick*) led them to adopt a constraint ranking in which *blick* emerges as a legal form. It is the phonological generality of the constraint inventory that makes this possible.

Turning to the question of an actual algorithm: what we want is an algorithm that will produce a ranking that (a) correctly derives all attested forms; and (b) places the faithfulness constraints as low as possible, in some sense yet to be defined precisely.

7.6   An approach that won't work: initial rankings

The simplest approach, which emerges directly from the discussion above, is to let Constraint Demotion start not with a 'blank slate', with all constraints considered equally, but rather with an *a priori* initial ranking in which all markedness constraints outrank all faithfulness constraints. In this approach, there would be a Stratum 1, containing all of the markedness constraints, and a Stratum 2, containing all of the faithfulness constraints.

It appears that this approach is unworkable, as we can see by applying it to Pseudo-Korean. When it first encounters the data, Constraint Demotion will find that only *D^h prefers no losers and may thus remain in Stratum 1. The remaining three markedness constraints of Pseudo-Korean prefer losers:

(23)   (a) *[+v][−v][+v] prefers loser *[ada] to winner [atʰa].
        (b) *[−SON/+VOICE] prefers loser *[ata] to winner [ada].
        (c) *ASPIRATION prefers loser *[ta] to winner [tʰa].

Thus, they must be demoted to a lower stratum: either Stratum 2, or a newly formed Stratum 3, depending on the details of the algorithm. If the demoted constraints move only to Stratum 2, then on the next round they will *still* prefer losers, and thus will move on down to Stratum 3. At the same time, all the faithfulness constraints remain in Stratum 2, because they never prefer a loser. The result is again a grammar with all faithfulness constraints ranked high, resulting in massive overgeneration.

The upshot is a point made by Prince and Tesar (this volume): a ranking algorithm is unlikely to succeed simply by using a starting-point that favours Markedness over Faithfulness; rather, the bias must be enforced throughout the ranking process.

7.7   A new algorithm: Low Faithfulness Constraint Demotion[18]

As a tentative solution to the problem of pure phonotactic learning, I propose a Low Faithfulness Constraint Demotion algorithm. This algorithm is identical to the batch version of classical Constraint Demotion, with the following crucial exception. Whenever a new stratum is to be created, the criteria that a constraint must pass to be eligible to be installed in the new stratum are made more stringent in various ways. Among other things, this implements the consistent bias for Markedness just described.

In Low Faithfulness Constraint Demotion, the principles for ranking are prioritised; higher priority principles get first say in which constraints are or are not eligible for installation in the new stratum. The exclusion of constraints from the next stratum is formally reminiscent of the exclusion of candidates in OT derivations. The full set of principles, in priority order, are given below; ranking principles will be designated typographically with bold-face italics.

7.7.1   *Avoid Preference for Losers*

Avoid Preference for Losers   This principle is taken from classical Constraint Demotion. It forbids the admission to the current stratum of constraints that prefer a losing to a winning candidate. It plainly must be an 'undominated' ranking principle, since if one admits such a constraint to the current stratum, the finished grammar will itself prefer losers and generate incorrect outputs.

7.7.2   *Favour Markedness*

Favour Markedness   Suppose that, after we have culled out the constraints that prefer losers, we are left with both faithfulness and markedness constraints. In such cases, Low Faithfulness Constraint Demotion installs only the markedness constraints in the new stratum. The faithfulness constraints must await a later opportunity to be ranked, often the next stratum down. Only when the eligible set consists entirely of faithfulness constraints may faithfulness constraints be considered for ranking.

Here is the rationale: often a rival candidate can be ruled out either because it violates a markedness constraint, or because it is unfaithful. In such cases, we want the markedness constraint to do the job, because if we let faithfulness do it, it is likely to lead to overgeneration in the finished grammar.

7.7.3   *Favour Activeness*

Favour Activeness   We consider next the principles that must be invoked when the pool of rankable constraints contains only faithfulness constraints, so that *Favour Markedness* is unable to decide.

Consider that it is quite common for a constraint not to prefer any losers – but not to prefer any winners either. Such constraints are, in the terminology of Prince and Tesar (this volume), *inactive*. It plainly does no good to rank inactive constraints high, and may well do harm in terms of overgeneration for data yet unencountered. Therefore, Low Faithfulness Constraint Demotion excludes such constraints from the set allowed to join the next stratum.

An exception is necessary: if the set of eligible candidates contains only inactive faithfulness constraints, they must all be assigned to the next stratum anyway, to permit the algorithm to terminate. This step usually turns out to be the last stage of ranking: it dumps the inactive faithfulness constraints into the bottom stratum, where they will do no harm in overgenerating.[19]

7.7.4   *Favour Specificity*

Favour Specificity   Often, two faithfulness constraints fall into a specific-general relation; for example, IDENT(ASP) / __ V is a more specific version of IDENT(ASP). Suppose we have two such constraints, both found in the pool of constraints still eligible to be ranked after we have invoked

Avoid Preference for Losers, *Favour Markedness*, and *Favour Activeness*. In such cases, the principle *Favour Specificity* requires that the general constraint must be excluded from the next stratum; only the specific constraint remains eligible.

The rationale for *Favour Specificity* is again conservatism: there is no point in using a general constraint to rule out a rival candidate if a specific one will suffice. Ranking the specific constraint alone often permits the possibility of ranking its general partner deep in the grammar, below markedness constraints not yet ranked, so overgeneration is avoided. In contrast, if one admits the general constraint to the current stratum right away, one gives up on this possibility from the start.

In most cases, it is straightforward to assess specificity: a constraint that properly includes another in its structural description (Koutsoudas, Sanders, and Noll 1974) is the more specific of the two and will normally have a subset of the other's violations (it will never have a superset, which is most crucial). Thus the additional material '/ __ V' in IDENT(ASP) / __V identifies it as a more specific version of IDENT(ASP). For further discussion of specificity, see appendix A.

7.7.5 Favour Autonomy If the algorithm has gotten this far, it has culled the set of rankable constraints down to a set of active faithfulness constraints, none of which is a more general version of some more specific constraint. If this set consists of just one member, it can be selected as the sole constraint of the current stratum, and we can move on. But what if more than one faithfulness constraint is still eligible? It would certainly be rash to install all of the eligible constraints, because it is quite possible that we can ward off overgeneration by installing just some of them.

My proposal is that there should a criterion of *autonomy*. As an approximation, we can say that for an eligible faithfulness constraint F_i to be installed in the current stratum, it should exclude at least one rival R autonomously, acting without help from any other constraint C. By 'help', I mean that C, working alone, would likewise exclude R (in other words, R violates C more than the winner). This is the core idea, and I will try to justify it below.

Before doing so, I must add some details. First, we must consider the possibility that there might not be any constraints that exclude a rival without help. In such cases, I propose that we should loosen the criterion, seeking constraints that exclude some rival with the help of just one other constraint, or (failing that) just two, and so on. In other words, autonomy is relative, not absolute. Eventually, the criterion of relative autonomy will select a constraint or set of constraints that can be installed in the new stratum.

The other detail concerns what constraints may be considered as eligible 'helpers' in assessing autonomy, filling the role of C. We shall see below that markedness constraints must be considered, even if at the stage in question they prefer losers.[20] I also conjecture, for concreteness's sake, that Faithfulness constraints excluded by **Favour Specificity** should not be included, though I do not yet know of any evidence to bear on this question.

With these modifications in place, I state **Favour Autonomy** formally in (24c), following two preliminary definitions:

(24)   (a) Defn.: *helper*
             Let F be a yet-unranked faithfulness constraint, and R be some
             rival candidate such that F prefers the winner to R. Let C be a
             yet-unranked constraint not excluded by **Favour Specificity**. If C
             also prefers the winner to R, then C is a *helper* of F.

         (b) Defn.: *minimum number of helpers*
             Let F be a yet-unranked faithfulness constraint, and $\{R_1, R_2, \ldots$
             $R_n\}$ be the set of all rival candidates R_i such that F prefers the
             winner to R_i. Let $\{h_1, h_2, \ldots h_n\}$ be the number of helpers of F
             for each of $\{R_1, R_2, \ldots R_n\}$ respectively. The minimum number
             of helpers of F is the lowest value in $\{h_1, h_2, \ldots h_n\}$.

         (c) **Favour Autonomy**
             Of the constraints that satisfy all higher priority ranking principles
             (see 7.7.1–7.7.4), install on the current stratum the constraint or
             constraints whose minimum number of helpers is the lowest.

I now turn to why **Favour Autonomy** is a plausible ranking principle. In brief, what it does is *force the algorithm to use data that are maximally informative*. When we are dealing with a rival candidate in which the number of helpers for each constraint is high, it means that there are many possible explanations for why the rival is excluded. Such cases tell us little. In contrast, when a faithfulness constraint excludes a rival on its own, it is usually a very simple case, with implications that are clear. Intermediate cases, with few but more than zero helpers, have an intermediate evidentiary value, and for this reason Low Faithfulness Constraint Demotion is set up gradiently, to go with the best cases available.

As an illustration, let us compare two cases. When Low Faithfulness Constraint Demotion is run on Pseudo-Korean (full details below in section 7.8), it reaches a stage where it must select among the pair {IDENT(ASP) / __V, IDENT(VOICE) / __V} for which should join the new stratum. If we leave out constraints already ranked and constraints excluded by **Favour Specificity**, the constraint violations for the winner–rival pair [ada] ∼ *[ata] look like this:

(25)

/ada/	ID (ASP) / _V	*[+v][−v][+v]	*ASP	*[−SON/+VCE]	ID (VCE) / _V
☞ [ada]				*	
*[ata]		*			*

From this pattern, it is evident that if we let ID (VCE) / _V join the next stratum, *[ata] will be ruled out. But ID (VCE) / _V has a helper, namely *[+v][−v][+v], so perhaps it is really *[+v][−v][+v] (yet unrankable) that is ultimately responsible for ruling out *[ata]. We cannot know at this stage. As it turns out in the end, it would be rash to pick IDENT(VOICE) / _V, because in the correct grammar ((18) above), it emerges that *[+v][−v][+v] must outrank IDENT (VOICE) / _V to avoid overgeneration.

By way of comparison, (26) shows the violation pattern for winner [tʰa] vs. rival *[ta], at the same stage of learning:

(26)

/tʰa/	ID (ASP)/_V	*[+v][−v][+v]	*ASP	*[−SON/+VCE]	ID (VCE)/ _V
☞ [tʰa]			*		
*[ta]	*				

Here, IDENT (ASP) / _V rules out *[ta] alone, with no help from any other eligible constraint. Its autonomy constitutes plain evidence that IDENT(ASP) / _V needs to be ranked high. *Favour Autonomy* thus selects it for the stratum under construction, which, as it turns out, permits the rest of the grammar to be constructed straightforwardly (see section 7.8).

Summing up: *Favour Autonomy*, by seeking the examples where a constraint acts with the fewest possible helpers, singles out the cases where a constraint is most clearly shown to require a high ranking. By only allowing maximally autonomous faithfulness constraints to be installed, we can limit installation to cases that are most likely to be truly necessary, letting the less autonomous constraints sink further down to a point where they will not lead to overgeneration.

Favor Autonomy, being relatively defined, will always place at least one constraint in the current stratum. Thus, when invoked, it is the last criterion used in stratum formation. Once the stratum is created, Low Faithfulness Constraint Demotion continues just like classical Constraint Demotion: rival forms explained by the constraints of the new stratum are culled from the learning set, and the next stratum down is created by invoking the criterion hierarchy again, beginning with *Avoid Preference for Losers*.

7.7.6   Terminating the algorithm   Low Faithfulness Constraint Demotion
terminates under conditions identical to those of classical Constraint Demotion.
Specifically, when the constraint inventory is adequate (can be ranked to prefer
all and only winners), both algorithms terminate in success when all constraints
have been assigned to a stratum and all rival candidates have been ruled out.
Both terminate in failure when *Avoid Preference for Losers* is unable to locate
constraints that favour no losers.

7.8   *Pseudo-Korean and Low Faithfulness Constraint Demotion*

To illustrate how Low Faithfulness Constraint Demotion works, I will now
apply it to the Pseudo-Korean problem, for which the candidate set was given
in (19). For convenience, the full constraint inventory is repeated below:

(27)   (a) **Markedness**   (b) **Faithfulness**
         D^h   IDENT(ASPIRATION) / __ V
         *[+v][−v][+v]   IDENT(ASPIRATION)
         *[−SON/+VOICE]   IDENT(VOICE) / __ V
         *ASPIRATION   IDENT(VOICE)

The strata of the grammar are formed as follows:

Stratum 1: As it would in classical Constraint Demotion, *Avoid Preference for Losers* excludes the markedness constraints *[+v][−v][+v],
*[−SON/+VOICE], and *ASPIRATION. The losers that these constraints
prefer were given in (23).

The remaining five constraints are *D^h* plus the four faithfulness constraints.
Favour Markedness selects *D^h*, which forms the top stratum alone. All rival
candidates containing [d^h] are pruned from the learning set.

Stratum 2: We first evaluate *Avoid Preference for Losers*. *[+v]
[−v][+v], *[−SON/+VOICE], and *ASPIRATION continue to prefer losers
and still cannot be ranked. *Favour Markedness* cannot be satisfied, so we must
consider the faithfulness constraints. All of them pass *Favour Activeness*, as
shown in (28):

(28)   IDENT(ASP) / __ V   prefers winner   [t^ha]   over rival   *[ta]
         IDENT(ASP)   prefers winner   [t^ha]   over rival   *[ta]
         IDENT(VOICE) / __ V   prefers winner   [ada]   over rival   *[ata]
         IDENT(VOICE)   prefers winner   [ada]   over rival   *[ata]

Control thus passes to *Favour Specificity*, which excludes IDENT (ASPIRA-
TION) and IDENT(VOICE).

With two constraints left in the running (IDENT(ASP)/__V and IDENT
(VCE) / __V), control passes to *Favour Autonomy*. The assessment of

autonomy for these constraints was already illustrated in (25) and (26), which show the fewest-helper cases for each. Since IDENT(ASP) / __V is the more autonomous (zero helpers to one), it is selected as the sole member of Stratum 2. The rival candidates that it explains, such as *[ta] for /tʰa/, are excluded from the learning set.

Stratum 3: We first evaluate *Avoid Preference for Losers*: *[−SON/ +VOICE] still prefers *[ata] for underlying /ada/, and so must remain un-ranked. But two other markedness constraints now prefer no losers among the remaining data. One such constraint is *[+v][−v][+v]. Earlier it preferred *[ada] for /atʰa/, but that form is now explained by IDENT(ASP) / __V. There-fore, *Avoid Preference for Losers* permits *[+v][−v][+v] to join the new stratum. Likewise, *ASP no longer prefers losers (*[ta] for /tʰa/ is now ruled out by IDENT(ASP) / __V), so it too may join the third stratum. The remain-ing constraints are faithfulness constraints, and they are shut out by *Favour Markedness*.

Once *[+v][−v][+v] is placed in Stratum 3, then *[ata] for /ada/ is ex-plained and excluded from the learning set. This vindicates the earlier decision ((25)) not to place ID(VCE) / __ V in Stratum 2.

Stratum 4: *Avoid Preference for Losers*: *[−SON/+VOICE] no longer prefers a loser, since *[ata] for [ada] is now ruled out by *[+v][−v][+v]. Thus *[−SON/+VOICE] may now be ranked in the fourth stratum. Since *[−SON/+VOICE] is a markedness constraint, *Favour Markedness* contin-ues to shut out the remaining faithfulness constraints.

Stratum 5: By this stage, all the rival candidates are excluded by some ranked constraint. The remaining three constraints (ID(ASP), ID(VCE) / __V, and ID(VCE)) prefer no losers, so are passed first to the jurisdiction of *Favour Markedness*, then to *Favour Activeness*. The latter, noticing that none of these constraints is active, invokes its special termination provision and dumps them all into the bottom stratum. The procedure that checks for termination (section 7.7.6) notices that all constraints are ranked and that all rival candi-dates are ruled out, so it records success.

Summing up, the ranking obtained by Low Faithfulness Constraint Demotion for Pseudo-Korean is as follows:

(29)   **Stratum 1**   **Stratum 4**
         *Dʰ   *[−SON/+VOICE]
       Stratum 2   **Stratum 5**
         IDENT(ASPIRATION) / __V   IDENT(ASPIRATION)
       Stratum 3   IDENT(VOICE)
         *[+v][−v][+v]   IDENT(VOICE) / __V
         *ASPIRATION

Comparing this with (18), it can be seen that all of the crucial rankings are reflected in the stratal assignments. The distinction of Strata 1 and 2 (imposed by **Favour Markedness**) does not reflect a crucial ranking, but no harmful consequences result from ranking *D^{h} over IDENT(ASPIRATION) / __ V .[21]

By inspection, the grammar of (29) reveals what is phonemic in Pseudo-Korean stops: aspiration in prevocalic position. This is because IDENT(ASP) / __V is the only faithfulness constraint that doesn't reside at the bottom of the grammar. Voicing is allophonic, and aspiration in non-prevocalic position is likewise predictable.

As a check on the finished grammar, we can test to see if it overgenerates. To do this, I fed the grammar the larger set of inputs which had earlier shown that regular Constraint Demotion overgenerates. From these inputs, the new grammar derived the following outputs:

(30)

Well-formed inputs		**Ill-formed inputs**	
input	output	input	output
/ta/	[ta]	/da/	[ta]
/ada/	[ada]	/d^{h}a/	[t^{h}a]
/t^{h}a/	[t^{h}a]	/ata/	[ada]
/at^{h}a/	[at^{h}a]	/ad^{h}a/	[at^{h}a]
/at/	[at]	/ad/	[at]
/tada/	[tada]	/at^{h}/	[at]
/tat^{h}a/	[tat^{h}a]	/ad^{h}/	[at]
/t^{h}ada/	[t^{h}ada]		
/t^{h}at^{h}a/	[t^{h}at^{h}a]		
/tat/	[tat]		
/t^{h}at/	[t^{h}at]		

Specifically, all well-formed inputs are retained, and all ill-formed inputs are 'fixed'; that is, converted by the grammar into a well-formed output.[22] Thus, Low Faithfulness Constraint Demotion succeeded in learning a ranking that defines Pseudo-Korean phonotactics, based on only positive evidence.

I have tried out Low Faithfulness Constraint Demotion on a number of data files similar in scope to Pseudo-Korean.[23] In these data files, it succeeds in producing 'tight' grammars, which generate only forms that match (or are less marked than)[24] those given to it in the input.

7.9   Caveats

To recapitulate: infants are apparently able to learn a great deal about the phonology of the ambient language – specifically, the phonotactics – in the absence of negative evidence. Moreover, they most likely accomplish this learning with little or no information about morphology and alternations, hence without knowledge of underlying forms. I have developed a ranking algorithm, Low Faithfulness Constraint Demotion, with the goal of modelling this stage of phonological acquisition, and have found that, at least in a number of representative cases, the algorithm accomplishes its intended purpose.

This said, I wish to mention three limitations of Low Faithfulness Constraint Demotion.

7.9.1 Gradient well-formedness The algorithm cannot deal with the fact that judgements of phonotactic well-formedness are gradient (Algeo 1978); for example, a form like ?[dwɛf] seems neither perfectly right nor completely ill-formed. Moreover, such patterns appear to be learned by infants. An example is the unusual status of final stress in English polysyllabic words, e.g., *ballóon*. Jusczyk, Cutler, and Redanz (1993) give evidence that this pattern is learned by infants at the same time they are learning the exceptionless patterns.

There *is* an algorithm that has proved capable of treating gradient well-formedness, namely the Gradual Learning Algorithm of Boersma (1997), applied to gradient well-formedness in Boersma and Hayes (2001). I have not yet succeeded in incorporating a suitable downward bias for Faithfulness into this algorithm.

7.9.2 A priori knowledge I find it a source of discontent that Low Faithfulness Constraint Demotion, like regular Constraint Demotion, relies so heavily on *a priori* knowledge: specifically, a universal inventory of constraints and a universal feature system. It would count as a considerable advance, I think, if it could be shown that these analytical elements are themselves learnable. For some discussion along these lines, see Boersma (1998, 2000).

The close reliance of Low Faithfulness Constraint Demotion on an adequate constraint inventory is highlighted by the following fact: if 'irrational' markedness constraints are included in the constraint set, the algorithm can fail. I have found that, for Pseudo-Korean, the algorithm fails to learn the correct ranking if one adds in a constraint (both typologically and phonetically unmotivated) that bans *un*aspirated stops. The reason is that *NOT ASPIRATED counts as a helper for IDENT(ASP) / __ V in ruling out /tʰa/ → *[ta], which in turn robs the algorithm of its ability to recognise the special effectiveness of IDENT (ASP)/ __ V.

It follows that, whatever system learns the constraints must learn only sensible ones; it will not do to throw a great pile of arbitrary constraints into the algorithm's lap and hope that it will weed out the foolish ones by ranking them low. For a proposed method for discovering only sensible constraints, see Hayes (1999a).

7.9.3   Effectiveness   Low Faithfulness Constraint Demotion, unlike classical Constraint Demotion, is not backed by a mathematical proof establishing the conditions under which it will find an effective grammar.[25]

In the face of these caveats, I would say that the main point of this section is simply to establish the plausibility of an Optimality theoretic approach to pure phonotactic learning, making no use of negative evidence.

8.   The learning of alternations

What happens in the phonology as the child comes to parse words into their component morphemes and starts to notice alternations? Learning patterns of phonological alternation (i.e., morphophonemics) is probably a harder problem than phonotactics; some efforts in this direction are given by Tesar and Smolensky (2000), Zuraw (2000), and Albright and Hayes (1998).

One major issue in morphophonemics concerns the kinds of representations that are invoked to explain alternation. A classical approach is to assign every morpheme a unique *underlying form*, which abstracts away from the variety of surface realisations in a way that permits every surface allomorph to be derived by the phonology. The underlying form unifies the paradigm, because all the inflected forms are derived from it. Under this approach, the way to learn morphophonemics is to locate an underlying form for each morpheme, and adjust (perhaps by reapplying the same algorithm) the rankings of Faithfulness that were learned for phonotactics so that they cover alternations as well.

More recently, research has suggested (see, for example, Benua 1997, Kenstowicz 1998, Burzio 1998, Hayes 1999b, Kager 1999a, Steriade 2000) that underlying representations alone do not suffice to unify the paradigm: there is reason to think that the mutual resemblance of the surface realisations of a morpheme are due (either in addition, or perhaps entirely) to Optimality theoretic constraints. The new constraint type posited is 'output-to-output correspondence' constraints. These formally resemble faithfulness constraints, but they require that a surface form not deviate in some phonologically defined property from the surface form of its morphological base, rather than from its underlying representation. Plainly, under this view a major task in the learning of phonological alternations is the ranking of the output-to-output correspondence constraints.

With this background, I turn to two particular problems in morphophonemic learning.

8.1   The multiple-repair problem

To start, it is worth re-emphasising a point made above: because phonology is conspiratorial, knowing the phonotactics in advance is a powerful tool to use in learning morphophonemics. For example, Albright and Hayes's (1998) rule-based morphophonemic learning algorithm relies crucially on pre-existing knowledge of the phonotactics. Thus, in English past tenses, the algorithm experiments by taking the [-d] suffix it learned from verbs like *planned* or *hugged*, and attaching it to stems like *sip* or *need*, yielding *[sɪpd] and *[nidd]. Knowledge of phonotactics (the algorithm is told in advance that no words can end in *[pd] or *[dd]) permits the algorithm to discover phonological rules of voicing assimilation (/sip+d/ → [sɪpt]) and schwa epenthesis (/nid+d/ → [nidəd]). This in turn permits the unification of the structural change for past tense formation, as simply /X/ → /Xd/.

Within Optimality Theory, a particular difficulty for the transition from phonotactic to morphophonemic learning is that a phonotactically illegal form can be 'fixed' in various different ways. For example, a final /tʰ/ in Pseudo-Korean could be fixed by deaspirating it, by deleting it, or by appending a final vowel. Low Faithfulness Constraint Demotion, however, seizes on just one way (note 22). Whatever turns out to be the right algorithm for morphophonemic learning in OT must be able to rearrange the ranking of the faithfulness constraints during the transition from the phonotactics-only grammar to the more mature grammar. In particular, the faithfulness constraints that are violated in accommodating underlying forms to the phonotactics must be ranked lower than those that are not – even if this was not the ranking that pure-phonotactic learning had earlier settled on.

8.2   A trim-back problem: grammatically conditioned allophones

Another interesting problem in the study of morphophonemic learning is posed by the existence of 'grammatically conditioned allophones': sounds whose distribution is predictable, but only if one knows the grammatical structure of the words in question.

Such allophones arise in part from what classical generative phonology called 'boundary phenomena': instances where a stem + affix combination receives a different treatment than the same sequence occurring within a morpheme. For instance, in some English dialects *bonus* ['bõũnəs], with nasalised [õũ], fails to form a perfect rhyme with *slowness* ['slouʊnəs], with oral [ou]. In traditional terms, nasalisation is said to be 'blocked across a suffix boundary'. A similar case, worked out in Optimality theoretic terms in Hayes (2000), is the non-rhyming pair some English speakers have for *holy* ['holi] vs. *slowly* ['slouli]: *slowly* avoids the monophthongal [o] characteristic of pre-/l/ position in stems, and thus shows blockage of monophthongisation across the suffix boundary. Further cases are cited by Kiparsky (1988: 367).

Another case of grammatically conditioned allophones is found with the dialectal English forms *writer* ['rʌɪɾɚ] and *rider* ['raɪɾɚ]. These are well known from the early rule-ordering analysis of Chomsky (1964): in Chomsky's account, /raɪt+ɚ/ becomes intermediate [rʌɪt+ɚ] by raising before voiceless consonants, then [rʌɪɾɚ] by Flapping of pre-atonic intervocalic /t/. The result is a surface minimal pair.

Infants, who often lack the morphological knowledge needed to identify grammatically conditioned allophones, are liable to mistake them for cases of outright phonemic contrast.[26] Assuming (correctly, I think) that such sounds do not have phonemic status for adults, we thus have an important question: how can the older child, who has come to know the relevant morphology, do the backtracking needed to achieve a full understanding of the system?

I believe there is a straightforward way to do this, based on output-to-output correspondence constraints.

8.2.1   The ranking of output-to-output correspondence   I will borrow from McCarthy (1998) the idea that output-to-output correspondence constraints are ranked high *a priori* by children acquiring language. McCarthy bases his claim on considerations of learnability: high ranking of output-to-output correspondence is needed to learn the absence of certain patterns of phonological alternation. Another source of evidence on this point comes from observations of children during the course of acquisition: children are able to innovate sequences that are illegal in the target language, in the interest of maintaining output-to-output correspondence. This was observed by Kazazis (1969) in the speech of Marina, a 4-year-old learning Modern Greek. Marina innovated the sequence *[xe] (velar consonant before front vowel), which is illegal in the target language. She did this in the course of regularising the verbal paradigm: thus [ˈexete] 'you-pl. have' (adult [ˈeçete]), on the model of [ˈexo] 'I have'.

The example is interesting from the viewpoint of the *a priori* assumptions brought by the child to acquisition. Marina presumably had never heard an adult say [xe], and had every reason to think that the constraint banning it should be ranked at the top of the hierarchy. Yet she ranked an output-to-output correspondence constraint (the one regulating the [x]/[ç] distinction) even higher, to establish a non-alternating paradigm. A reasonable guess, then, is that output-to-output correspondence constraints have a default ranking at the top of the hierarchy, and that they are demoted only as the child processes the evidence that justifies their demotion.[27]

An example similar to the Marina case, involving American English Flapping (*[ˈsɪtɪŋ] for [ˈsɪɾɪŋ], on the model of [sɪt]), is given by Bernhardt and Stemberger (1998: 641).

8.2.2   Output-to-output constraints facilitate backtracking   Let us now return to grammatically conditioned allophones and the backtracking problem. One important point about grammatically conditioned allophones is that they seem quite generally to be amenable to analyses making use of output-to-output correspondence. For example, the oral vowel of *slowness* ['slouↄnəs] is plausibly attributed to a correspondence effect with its base form *slow* ['slou], where orality is phonologically expected. Likewise the diphthongal vowel quality of /ou/ of *slowly* [slouli] can be treated as a correspondence effect from the same base. The pair *writer* ['rʌɪɾɚ] vs. *rider* ['raɪɾɚ], though treated very differently in traditional phonology, likewise emerges as a correspondence effect: *writer* inherits its raised diphthong from the base form *write* ['rʌɪt], where it is justified by a phonetically grounded markedness constraint that forces raising.

Output-to-output correspondence provides a plausible strategy by which the child could backtrack, undoing earlier errors on grammatically conditioned allophones. The two elements of the strategy are as follows. First, as just proposed, output-to-output correspondence must be ranked *a priori* high. Second, the faithfulness constraints must be forced to continue to 'justify themselves' throughout later childhood, by continuing to rule out ill-formed rival candidates. Otherwise, they are allowed to sink back down in the ranking.

Here is how the scheme would work. As soon as the child learns that (say) *lowly* is derived from *low* ['lou], she will expect its pronunciation to be ['louli] *irrespective of the ranking of the relevant faithfulness constraints*. This is because the output-to-output correspondence constraint governing diphthongal [ou] quality is *a priori* undominated. At this point, *lowly* can no longer serve as an input datum to justify a high ranking for the faithfulness constraints that support the putative [o]/[ou] distinction. After the other relevant forms are also morphologically analysed, then the entire burden of accounting for the [o]/[ou] distinction is assumed by output-to-output correspondence, and the erstwhile dominant faithfulness constraints may safely sink to the bottom of the grammar. The result is that [o]/[ou] ceases to be a phonemic distinction.

Naturally, where there *is* phonological alternation, the learning process must demote the output-to-output correspondence constraints that would block it. Thus, for example, when the child comes to know that *sitting* ['sɪɾɪŋ] is the correct present participle for *sit* [sɪt], she must demote the constraints IDENT-OO(VOICE) and IDENT-OO (SONORANT), which preserve the distinction of [t] vs. [ɾ], from their originally undominated position.[28]

8.2.3 *A stage of vulnerability*

If the view taken here is correct, then children often go through a stage of innocent delusion: they wrongly believe that certain phones which are lawfully distributed according to a grammatical environment are separate phonemes. The effects of this errorful stage can be seen, I think, in cases where the erroneous belief is accidentally cemented in place by the effects of dialect borrowing.

Consider the varieties of American English noted above in which *writer* ['rʌɪɾɚ] and *rider* ['raɪɾɚ] form a minimal pair. As just mentioned, they can be analysed in OT with markedness constraints that require the appearance of the raised diphthong [ʌɪ] before voiceless consonants (accounting for ['rʌɪt]), along with a higher ranked output-to-output correspondence constraint requiring the vowel quality of bases to be carried over to their morphological derivatives. But to the infant who does not yet understand the morphology, ['rʌɪɾɚ] vs. ['raɪɾɚ] looks just like a minimal pair.

Further light on the *writer/rider* phenomenon was shed by Vance (1987), who made a careful study of the idiolects of three native speakers. Vance elicited hundreds of relevant words from his consultants, and made a striking discovery. For these speakers, [ʌɪ] and [aɪ] are *phonemes*, with a fair number of straightforward, monomorphemic minimal and near-minimal pairs. There was much variation among the three consultants, but at least one of Vance's speakers provided each of the following cases:

(31)   *idle*   ['ʌɪɾəl]   *idol*   ['aɪɾəl]
        tire   ['tʌɪɹ]   *dire*   ['daɪɹ]
        bicycle   ['bʌɪsəkəl]   *bison*   ['baɪsən]
        miter   ['mʌɪɾɚ]   *colitis*   [kə'aɪɾəs]

It is plausible to imagine that the newly phonemic status of [ʌɪ] and [aɪ] for these speakers had its origin in the failure to do the crucial backtracking. For backtracking to be successful, [ʌɪ] must be discovered to be a grammatically conditioned allophone. Instead, it was kept as a phoneme.

Why did this happen? A reasonable guess can be based on the extreme geographic mobility of American English speakers: ['rʌɪɾɚ]/['raɪɾɚ] speakers are constantly migrating to ['raɪɾɚ]/['raɪɾɚ] dialect regions, and vice versa. The ['raɪɾɚ]/['raɪɾɚ] speakers of course have no [ʌɪ], and say *bison* ['baɪsən], *colitis* [kə'aɪɾəs], and so on. If a young learner of the ['rʌɪɾɚ]/['raɪɾɚ] dialect encountered such speakers during the crucial period of vulnerability, it might indeed prove fatal to the delicate restructuring process described above, whereby what the child thought were phonemes are restructured as grammatically conditioned allophones. Note in particular that the crucial 'contaminating' words would likely be encountered from different speakers more or less at random. This fits in well with the rather chaotic situation of lexical and interspeaker variation that Vance found.

It can be added that children whose primary learning source comes from the ['raɪɾɚ]/['raɪɾɚ] dialect are *not* analogously susceptible when they are exposed to migratory ['rʌɪɾɚ]/['raɪɾɚ] speakers. For these children, [ʌɪ] and [aɪ] are never distinct phonological categories – indeed, they probably never even make it to the status of distributional protocategories (section 3.2). When such children hear outsiders say ['rʌɪɾɚ] and ['raɪɾɚ], they will most likely simply fail to register the difference, which is of course the normal way that listeners hear phonetically similar sounds that are not phonemic for them. Indeed, my impression is that, unlike ['rʌɪ rɚ]/['raɪ rɚ] speakers, adult ['raɪ rɚ]/['raɪ rɚ] speakers find the [ʌɪ]/[aɪ] distinction to be rather difficult to hear.

Summing up: the overall view taken here that the acquisition of contrast and phonotactics precedes the acquisition of morphophonemics is supported by the vulnerability of young children to dialect contamination. Since the order of acquisition forces them to assume that what ought to be grammatically conditioned allophones are simply phonemes, exposure to forms from other dialects readily upsets the former system, turning the former allophones into phonemes in the restructured system.

9.   Synoptic view of phonological acquisition

To conclude, we can now assemble the discussion above into a view of phonological acquisition as a whole, which uses Optimality Theory to model the learning process. It is worth pointing out that this scheme involves three types of default ranking.

(1) **Starting-point**. Phonological learning is facilitated by good language design: through processes that are not well understood, languages come to place their phoneme boundaries at locations that render distinct phonemes readily discriminable, by matching phoneme boundaries with inherent auditory boundaries (Eimas *et al.* 1971 and subsequent work).

(2) **Distributional protocategories**. By the age of 6 months, infants have used knowledge of the statistical distribution of tokens to establish language-specific distributional protocategories, which form the currency of computation for later phonological acquisition (Kuhl 1995, Guenther and Gjaja 1996).

(3) **Acquisition of 'pure phonotactics'**. At 8–10 months, infants make very rapid progress in learning the pattern of contrast and phonotactics in their language. They do this largely in ignorance of morphology, and thus (following current OT assumptions) in a model in which underlying and surface representations are the same.

In the view presented here, learning at this phase takes place through the ranking of faithfulness constraints against markedness constraints, using positive evidence only. It is assumed (given how effectively they perform the task) that infants must be using some very efficient algorithm, for which Low Faithfulness Constraint Demotion (section 7.7) is intended as a first approximation. What is crucial about this algorithm is that it is designed to place the faithfulness constraints as low as possible, following Smolensky (1996b).

(4) **Learning production**. Shortly thereafter, children start to try to say words. Since their articulatory capacities at this stage are limited, they use a powerful existing cognitive capacity – phonology – to make at least some output possible. Specifically, they form a production phonology that maps adult surface forms onto their own, simpler, output representations. Through the first years

of childhood, this personal phonology gradually recedes to vacuity, as children acquire the physical ability to render accurate surface forms.

Faithfulness also starts out low in this production grammar. This low ranking corresponds to the initial state of the infant, namely an inability to say anything at all.

(5) **Morphology and alternation**. At the same time (roughly 1–5 years), the child comes to be able to factor words into morphemes, to understand the principles of the ambient language's morphology, to apprehend phonological alternations, and to develop an internalised grammar to predict them (say, in deriving novel forms). Here, the mechanisms used are not at all clear. But there are two plainly useful tools that the child brings to the task. First, her relatively full knowledge of phonotactics is surely useful, since so much phonological alternation exists simply to bring concatenated sequences of morphemes into conformity with phonotactic principles (i.e., phonology is conspiratorial). Second, it appears that output-to-output correspondence constraints are given an *a priori* high ranking. This ranking gives the child a straightforward means of identifying grammatically conditioned allophones (section 8.2.2). Once these are identified and suitably attributed to high-ranking output-to-output correspondence constraints, the faithfulness constraints that were wrongly promoted too high in infancy are allowed to recede towards their preferred low positions. This yields the final, correct phonemic system.

Appendix A: Discussion of Prince and Tesar's paper[29]

Shortly after completing the first version of this chapter (Hayes 1999c) I was pleased to learn that Alan Prince and Bruce Tesar had been working simultaneously (Prince and Tesar 1999) on lines very similar to ideas in my own paper, in particular those in sections 6 and 7 above. They likewise lay out pure phonotactic learning as a useful goal for learnability theory, and propose their own ranking algorithm, which they call Biased Constraint Demotion. Just as I suggest here, their algorithm ranks constraints based on an identity mapping in which each surface form is taken to be its own underlying form. Their algorithm also makes use of the principles that I refer to here as *Avoid Preference for Losers*, *Favour Markedness*, and *Favour Activeness*. They eschew – deliberately (Prince and Tesar 1999: 19, this volume) – the principle of *Favour Specificity*, and instead of *Favour Autonomy* they adopt principles that have the goal of 'freeing up' markedness constraints; that is, faithfulness constraints are selected for ranking with the goal of allowing markedness constraints to be placed in the immediately following strata.

Since the two algorithms have the same purpose, I became curious to compare them. To this end, I tested both on three data simulations:[30] (1) the Pseudo-Korean problem laid out above; (2) the *azba* case invented by Prince and Tesar

(1999: 20–22, this volume) and presented by them as a problem for Biased Constraint Demotion; and (3) a simulation of the legal vowel sequences of Turkish: rounding may occur on noninitial vowels only when they are high and preceded by a rounded vowel in the previous syllable. Since detailed discussion of these simulations would exceed the space available here, I refer the interested reader instead to a Web page from which full descriptions of the simulations can be downloaded (http://www.linguistics.ucla.edu/people/hayes/acquisition). The result of all three simulations was that Low Faithfulness Constraint Demotion learned the correct (i.e., non-overgenerating) grammar, and Biased Constraint Demotion failed to learn this grammar; that is, learned a less-restrictive ranking.

This difference is less than meets the eye, however, because Low Faithfulness Constraint Demotion makes use of a ranking principle that Prince and Tesar deliberately avoid, namely *Favour Specificity* (section 7.7.4). *Favour Specificity* could easily be incorporated into Biased Constraint Demotion. In fact, I have experimented with doing this, and I find that when Biased Constraint Demotion is thus modified, it learns all three simulations correctly.

My simulations suggest a diagnosis of the problem that is faced by Biased Constraint Demotion when *Favour Specificity* is not included: general faithfulness constraints, because they are general, tend to free up more markedness constraints down the line. This problem was also noticed by Prince and Tesar (1999: note 9, this volume).

Given that both algorithms benefit from *Favour Specificity*, it is worth considering Prince and Tesar's objections to it. The crucial point (see their discussion of the "*paːto*' language; 1999: 19–20, this volume) is that we cannot always read special-to-general relations off the structural descriptions of the constraints themselves (i.e., a superset structural description singles out a subset of forms). In some cases, the special–general relation is established only when we consider the action of higher ranked constraints. Thus, in the "*paːto*' language, where all initial syllables, and a number of other syllables as well, are stressed, the environment 'in initial syllables' is special relative to the general environment 'in stressed syllables'. *Favour Specificity* cannot be applied here, given that the contingent special–general pattern is not yet known.

The answer to this problem, I suggest, may lie in having the learning algorithm work harder. Contingent subset relations among faithfulness constraints are, I believe, learnable from the input data even where the constraint ranking is yet unknown, using computations whose scope would be extensive but hardly astronomical. In particular, if an algorithm kept track of the comparative applicability of the faithfulness constraint environments to the available learning data, it would emerge clearly after only a few thousand words that the structural description 'initial syllable' in the "*paːto*' language never targets material not also targeted by the structural description 'stressed syllable'.[31]

I have also noticed what may be a positive attribute of Biased Constraint Demotion as amplified with ***Favour Specificity***. I noted earlier (section 7.9.2) that Low Faithfulness Constraint Demotion can be fooled by including an 'irrational' constraint *NOT ASPIRATED. This is not so for the augmented version of Biased Constraint Demotion. Thus, whereas Low Faithfulness Constraint Demotion is dependent on the pre-existence of a 'rational' set of markedness constraints, specificity-amplified Biased Constraint Demotion perhaps may not be. Simulation histories for this comparison are given at the same Web page noted above.

In general, I would judge that any evaluation of algorithms for pure phonotactic learning must currently be considered tentative: given the history of linguistic theory in general, we can safely predict that no algorithm is likely to survive in the long term without modification. What is likely to produce the fastest progress, I think, is the accumulation of empirically realistic examples that test the capacities of ranking algorithms in a serious way.

Appendix B: Where do rival candidates come from?

An Optimality theoretic grammar is an abstract formal object that selects for each input a winning candidate provided by the GEN function. The GEN function provides for each input a potentially infinite[32] number of output candidates, each one lined up with the elements of the input form in all possible ways. The freedom provided to GEN implies that the explanatory force of any OT analysis derives entirely from the constraint set.

At a level closer to implementation (e.g., as part of a processing model), this abstract conception is supplemented with additional mechanisms that guarantee that the winning candidate will be located correctly and efficiently. In one view, developed by Ellison (1994), Eisner (1997), and Albro (1997), GEN is modelled by a finite-state machine, and all operations using GEN are recast as operations on this grammar. The finite-state machine permits an infinite set to be modelled with finite means. Other approaches that also circumvent the infinite include work of Tesar (1995a, 1995b, 1999) and Walther (1996).

A more specific question for the present context is how to find the rival candidates that will lead to effective phonotactic learning. To solve this problem, Tesar and Smolensky (1996, 1998, 2000) and Prince and Tesar (this volume) propose that learning is *error-driven:* rival candidates are provided by running the grammar as learned so far and examining its errors. Another approach, however, would be to inspect fully the nearby regions of 'phonotactic space', examining all candidates which are phonologically similar to the winner (differing from it by just one or two feature values or segment insertions/deletions).

In the simulations reported here, I used the latter approach, trying to make sure that my search went far enough to be sure that all the necessary candidates were found. As a check, however, I reran all the simulations with smaller learning data sets, in which every rival candidate could arise as an error from a partial grammar. Every simulation came out identically.

It remains an issue for the long term whether the use of rival candidates that are not in the error-driven set aids – or perhaps hinders – phonotactic learning.

Appendix C: Batch vs serial processing

Ranking algorithms can process their data either *serially* (examine one datum at a time, and modify the grammar on the basis of this examination) or in *batch mode* (act at all times on the basis of knowledge of all the data). Tesar and Smolensky's original presentation of Constraint Demotion (1993) gives both batch and serial versions of the algorithm.

Low Faithfulness Constraint Demotion, in contrast, is necessarily a batch-mode algorithm. This follows from the definition of 'minimum number of helpers' in (24b), which requires that all the rival candidates be inspected at once. Therefore, it presupposes that the child learning the phonotactics of her language can assemble a representative sample of data and retain the sample in memory for processing. This data sample might be the child's lexicon, or perhaps is simply a set of stored utterances that the learner (who is, perhaps, only 8 months old) is not yet able fully to interpret; cf. Jusczyk and Aslin (1995: 19–20).

The batch processing mechanism of Low Faithfulness Constraint Demotion therefore presupposes that infants and children have capacious memory for phonological forms, an assumption that is plausible, I think, in light of the research literature.[33]

NOTES

* For advice that helped to improve this chapter I would like to thank Adam Albright, Sun-Ah Jun, René Kager, Patricia Keating, Alan Prince, Charles Reiss, Donca Steriade, Bruce Tesar, Bernard Tranel, Colin Wilson, and audience members at Utrecht, San Diego, Berkeley, and Johns Hopkins. All are absolved from any remaining shortcomings. Prince and Tesar (1999/this volume) was composed simultaneously with, but independently from, the present chapter. The authors present a proposal about phonotactic learning that is quite similar to what is proposed here. In clarifying and focusing the original version of this paper (Hayes 1999c) for the present volume I have benefited considerably from reading Prince and Tesar's work. For a comparison of the ranking algorithms proposed in the two papers, see Appendix A.
1. With important exceptions; see for instance Macken (1980), the literature review in Vihman (1996: ch. 7), and Pater (this volume). What is crucial here is only that perception has a wide lead over production.
2. Hale and Reiss (1998) likewise propose that the child's output mapping is separate from her phonological system *per se*. However, they go further in claiming that the child's mapping is utterly haphazard, indeed the result of the child's 'body' rather than her 'mind'. I cannot agree with this view, which strikes me as an extraordinary denigration of research in child phonology. To respond to two specific contentions:

(1) The free variation and near-neutralisations seen in the child's output (Hale and Reiss 1998: 669) are common in adult phonology, too. Whatever is developed as a suitable account of these phenomena (and progress is being made) is likely to yield insight into children's phonology as well.

(2) Claimed differences between children's constraints and adults' (see Hale and Reiss 1998 (18a)) can be understood once we see constraints (or at least, many of them) as grammaticised principles that address phonetic problems. Since children employ different articulatory strategies (such as favouring jaw movement over articulator movement), they develop different (but overall, rather similar) constraint inventories.

3. Separating the child's internalised conception of the adult grammar from her production grammar also helps to clarify various patterns in the child phonology literature. For instance, before age 4;3 Gwendolyn Stemberger produced /niːd+d/ as [niːdəd] 'needed', but /hʌg+d/ as [hʌdd] 'hugged' (Bernhardt and Stemberger 1998: 651). This mapping makes sense if /niːd+d/ → [niːdəd] was part of Gwendolyn's conception of adult phonology, but /hʌg+d/ → [hʌdd] was part of her production mapping from adult outputs to Gwendolyn-outputs. A similar example appears in Dinnsen *et al.* (2000).

4. Best *et al.* (1988) have shown that English-learning infants do not have difficulty in discriminating a click contrast of Zulu. This is probably unsurprising, given that adult monolinguals can also discriminate contrasts that are not phonemic for them when the phonetic cues are extremely salient. A further relevant factor is that English has no existing phonemes that could be confused with clicks and would distort their perception.

5. Examples from Jusczyk *et al.* (1993): Dutch *[rtum], English ?[jiːdʒ]. Many of the sequences used in Jusczyk *et al.*'s experiment violate formalisable phonotactic restrictions that are exceptionless in English; the others are sufficiently rare that they could in principle be describable as ill-formed, from the point of view of the restricted data available to the infant.

6. For reasons of space, I cannot provide a summary of Optimality Theory (OT), now the common currency of a great deal of phonological research. A clear and thoughtful introduction is provided in the textbook of Kager (1999b). Another helpful account, oriented to acquisition issues, is included in Bernhardt and Stemberger (1998).

7. And, in fact, it is plausible to suppose that Korean learners would never uselessly internalise underlying representations with contrastive voicing, since the distinction could never be realised.

8. Evidence for rather impressive ability among infants to extract and remember words and phrases from the speech stream is presented in Jusczyk and Aslin (1995), Jusczyk and Hohne (1997), and Gomez and Gerken (1999).

9. The production phonologies of toddlers, mapping adult surface forms to simplified child outputs, are also conspiratorial, as has been pointed out forcefully by Menn (1983). This is a major rationale for current efforts to use Optimality Theory to model these production phonologies.

10. Phonological alternations provide a weak form of negative evidence: the fact that the [-z] suffix of *cans* [kænz] shows up altered to [-s] in *caps* [kæps] is a clue that final *[pz] is not legal in English. It is for this reason that constraint ranking is often an easier problem for alternation data than for purely phonotactic data. Given

that alternations can provide negative evidence, it is relevant that the learning of alternations appears to happen relatively late (section 5); and also that in many languages only a fraction of the phonotactic principles are supported by evidence from alternations.

11. The reader should not scoff at the idea of a grammar being required to rule out hypothetical illegal forms. To the contrary, I think such ability is quite crucial. The real-life connection is speech perception: given the characteristic unclarity and ambiguity of the acoustic input, it is very likely that the human speech perception apparatus considers large numbers of possibilities for what it is hearing. To the extent that some of these possibilities are phonotactically impossible, they can be ruled out even before the hard work of searching the lexicon for a good match is undertaken.

12. Plainly, there is a potential debt to pay here when we consider languages that have elaborate systems of alternation at the phrasal level; for example, Kivunjo Chaga (McHugh 1986) or Toba Batak (Hayes 1986). Here, one strategy that might work well would be for the child to focus on one-word utterances, where the effects of phrasal phonology would be at a minimum. Another possibility is for the child to internalise a supply of short phrases, and learn their phonotactics without necessarily parsing them.

13. I am grateful to Daniel Albro for suggesting this as a basis for pure phonotactic learning.

14. In work not described here, I have examined the more sophisticated Error Driven Constraint Demotion variant of the algorithm, obtaining essentially the same results as are described below for the batch version.

15. Or, in some cases, to correct assumptions made earlier about 'hidden structure' in the input data; Tesar and Smolensky (2000).

16. There is a current open research issue in OT: whether contextual information properly belongs within the markedness constraints or the faithfulness constraints. For useful argumentation on this point, see Zoll (1998). The account here places contexts primarily in the faithfulness constraints; I have also tried a parallel simulation using the opposite strategy, and obtained very similar results.

17. More accurately: sonorants, but for Pseudo-Korean I will stick with vowels for brevity.

18. The algorithm given here is the same as the one in the earlier Web-posted version of this article (Hayes 1999c). However, the presentation has been substantially re-shaped, taking a lesson from the presentation of similar material in Prince and Tesar (this volume). In addition to increasing clarity, the changes should also facilitate comparison of the two algorithms.

19. When the constraint set is inadequate (cannot derive the winners under any ranking), the dumping of the inactive faithfulness constraints into a default stratum will be the penultimate phase. In the final phase, the algorithm learns that it has only loser-preferring markedness constraints to work with, and is unable to form any further strata. It thus terminates without yielding a working grammar (cf. section 7.1, 7.7.6).

20. Markedness constraints already assigned to a stratum can never be helpers in any event: the rivals they explain have been culled from the learning set.

21. This is because the completed grammar maps underlying /dʰa/ to [tʰa], so that both *Dʰ and IDENT(ASPIRATION) / __ V are satisfied.

22. The reader may have noted that the 'fixes' imposed by the grammar conform to the behaviour of alternating forms in real Korean. This outcome is accidental. A larger Pseudo-Korean simulation, not reported here, included candidates with deletion and insertion, and indeed uncovered grammars in which illegal forms were repaired by vowel epenthesis and consonant deletion, rather than by alteration of laryngeal feature values. For further discussion, see section 8.1.

23. Specifically: a file with the legal vowel sequences of (the native vocabulary of) Turkish, a file embodying the *azba* problem of Prince and Tesar (1999/this volume), and a family of files containing schematic 'CV' languages of the familiar type, banning codas, requiring onsets, banning hiatus, and so on. See Appendix A for further discussion.

24. Thus, for instance, when given a (rather unrealistic) input set consisting solely of [CV.V], the algorithm arrived at the view that [CV.CV] is also well-formed. This is because, given the constraints that were used, there was no ranking available that would permit [CV.V] but rule out [CV.CV]. This fits in with a general prediction made by Optimality Theory, not just Low Faithfulness Constraint Demotion: in any language, a hypothetical form that incurs a subset of the Markedness violations of any actual form should be well-formed.

25. Moreover, for purposes of such a proof, one would have to state precisely what is meant by 'effective' in the context of pure phonotactic learning. One possible definition is the subset definition adopted by Prince and Tesar (this volume): a ranking R is the most effective if there is no other ranking R' that covers the input data and permits only a subset of the forms permitted by R. However, in the long run I think our main interest should lie in an empirical criterion: a phonotactic learning algorithm should make it possible to mimic precisely the well-formedness intuitions of human speakers.

26. The reader who doubts this might further consider the effects of forms that are not morphologically transparent. A child exposed to the children's book character 'Lowly ['louli] Worm' will not necessarily be aware that most worms live underground (Lowly doesn't); and will take *Lowly* to form a near-minimal pair with, e.g., *roly-poly* ['roli 'poli]. Lack of morphological knowledge is particularly likely for infants, who probably learn phonology in part on the basis of stored phonological strings whose meaning is unknown to them (for evidence, see Appendix C).

27. Note that innovation of grammatically conditioned allophones probably arises historically from the same effects seen synchronically in Marina. Had Marina been able to transmit her innovation to the speech community as a whole, then Modern Greek would have come to have [x] and [ç] as grammatically conditioned allophones.

28. An issue not addressed in the text is which of the child's two emerging grammars contains output-to-output correspondence constraints – is it her own production phonology, or her conception of the adult system? If the discussion above is right, they must occur at least in the internalised adult system, though perhaps they occur in the production system as well. The crucial empirical issue, not yet investigated to my knowledge, is this: do children like Marina and Gwendolyn recognise that forms like *['exete] or *['sɪtɪŋ] would be aberrant coming from adults?

29. This appendix has benefited greatly from advice I have received from Colin Wilson; he is absolved, however, of responsibility for errors. For Wilson's own new proposals in this area, see Wilson (2001).

30. Testing was greatly facilitated by software code for Biased Constraint Demotion provided by Bruce Tesar as a contribution to the 'OTSoft' constraint ranking software package (http://www.linguistics.ucla.edu/people/hayes/otsoft).

31. Method: form an *n* by *n* chart, where *n* is the number of contexts employed in faithfulness constraints, and enter a mark in row *i* and column *j* whenever structural material in some word is included in context *i* but not context *j*. After sufficient data have been processed, any blank cell in row *p*, column *q*, together with a marked cell in row *q*, column *p*, indicates that context *p* is in a special-to-general relationship with context *q*. It can be further noted that paired blank cells in row *p*, column *q* and row *q*, column *p* reveal contexts that – in the target language – turn out to be *identical*. This information would also be very helpful to Low Faithfulness Constraint Demotion. Accidentally duplicate constraints would be likely to distort the crucial measure 'number of helpers' on which *Favour Autonomy* depends. An environment-tabulation procedure of the type just described could be used to ward off this problem.

32. Infinite candidate sets arise as the result of epenthesis; thus for underlying /sta/, GEN could in principle provide [əsta], [əəsta], [əəəsta], etc.

33. Jusczyk and Hohne (1997) show that 8-month-old infants recall words they heard in tape-recorded stories when tested in a laboratory two weeks later. Since only a small sampling of the words in the stories was tested, the number memorised by the infants must be far larger. Gomez and Gerken (1998) supplement this result by demonstrating the great speed and facility with which infants can internalise potential words: 12-month-olds, on very brief exposure, can rapidly assimilate and remember a set of novel nonsense words, well enough to use them in determining the grammatical principles governing the legal strings of an invented language.

References

Aksu-Koç, A. A. and D. I. Slobin (1985). The acquisition of Turkish. In D. Slobin (ed.) *The Crosslinguistic Study of Language Acquisition, Vol. 1: the Data*. Hillsdale, N.J.: Lawrence Erlbaum Associates.

Albright, A. and B. Hayes (1998). An automated learner for phonology and morphology. MS., Department of Linguistics, UCLA.
[http://www.linguistics.ucla.edu/people/hayes/learning]

Albro, D. (1997). Evaluation, implementation, and extension of Primitive Optimality Theory. M.A. thesis, UCLA.
[http://www.linguistics.ucla.edu/people/grads/albro/papers.html]

Algeo, J. (1978). What consonant clusters are possible? *Word* **29**. 206–224.

Baker, W. J. and B. L. Derwing (1982). Response coincidence analysis as evidence for language acquisition strategies. *Applied Psycholinguistics* **3**. 193–221.

Beckman, J. (1998). *Positional Faithfulness*. Ph.D. dissertation, University of Massachusetts. [ROA 234, http://roa.rutgers.edu]

Benua, L. (1997). *Transderivational Identity: Phonological Relations Between Words*. Ph.D. dissertation, University of Massachusetts.
[ROA 259, http://roa.rutgers.edu]

Berko, J. (1958). The child's learning of English morphology. *Word* **14**. 150–177.

Berman, R. A. (1985). The acquisition of Hebrew. In D. Slobin (ed.) *The Crosslinguistic*

Study of Language Acquisition, Vol. 1: the Data. Hillsdale, N.J.: Lawrence Erlbaum Associates.

Bernhardt, B. H. and J. P. Stemberger (1998). *Handbook of Phonological Development from the Perspective of Constraint-Based Nonlinear Phonology.* San Diego: Academic Press.

Best, C. T., G. W. McRoberts, and N. M. Sithole (1988). Examination of the perceptual re-organization for speech contrasts: Zulu click discrimination by English-speaking adults and infants. *Journal of Experimental Psychology: Human Perception and Performance* **14**. 345–360.

Boersma, P. (1997). How we learn variation, optionality, and probability. *Proceedings of the Institute of Phonetic Sciences of the University of Amsterdam* **21**. 43–58.

(1998). *Functional Phonology.* The Hague: Holland Academic Graphics.

(2000). Learning a grammar in Functional Phonology. In Dekkers *et al.* (2000). 465–523.

Boersma, P. and B. Hayes (2001). Empirical tests of the Gradual Learning Algorithm. *LI* **32**. 45–86.

Burzio, L. (1998). Multiple correspondence. *Lingua* **103**. 79–109.

Chomsky, N. (1964). Current issues in linguistic theory. In J. A. Fodor and J. J. Katz (eds.) *The Structure of Language.* Englewood Cliffs, N.J.: Prentice-Hall.

Chomsky, N. and M. Halle (1965). Some controversial questions in phonological theory. *JL* **1**. 97–138.

Dekkers, J., F. van der Leeuw, and J. van de Weijer (eds.) (2000). *Optimality Theory: Phonology, Syntax, and Acquisition.* Oxford: Oxford University Press.

Derwing, B. L. and W. J. Baker (1986). Assessing morphological development. In P. Fletcher and M. Garman (eds.) *Language Acquisition: Studies in First Language Development.* Cambridge: Cambridge University Press.

Dinnsen, D. A., L. W. McGarrity, K. O'Connor, and K. Swanson (2000). On the role of sympathy in acquisition. *Language Acquisition* **8**. 321–361.

Eimas, P. D., E. R. Siqueland, P. Jusczyk, and J. Vigorito (1971). Speech perception in infants. *Science* **171**. 303–306.

Eisner, J. (1997). Efficient generation in primitive Optimality Theory. In *Proceedings of the 35th Annual Meeting of the Association for Computational Linguistics*, Madrid. [ROA 259, http://roa.rutgers.edu]

Ellison, M. (1994). Phonological derivation in Optimality Theory. In *COLING*, Vol. 2. 1007–1013, Kyoto. [ROA 75, http://roa.rutgers.edu]

Fikkert, P. (1994). *On the Acquisition of Prosodic Structure.* Leiden and Amsterdam: Holland Institute of Generative Linguistics.

Fodor, J. A., T. G. Bever, and M. F. Garrett (1974). *The Psychology of Language.* New York: McGraw Hill.

Friederici, A. D. and J. E. Wessels (1993). Phonotactic knowledge of word boundaries and its use in infant speech perception. *Perception and Psychophysics* **54**. 287–295.

Gerken, L. (1994). Child phonology: past research, present questions, future directions. In M.A. Gernsbacher (ed.) *Handbook of Psycholinguistics.* San Diego: Academic Press.

Gomez, R. L. and L. Gerken (1999). Artificial grammar learning by 1-year-olds leads to specific and abstract knowledge. *Cognition* **70**. 109–135.

Guenther, F. H. and M. N. Gjaja (1996). The perceptual magnet effect as an emergent property of neural map formation. *JASA* **100**. 1111–1121.

Hale, M. and C. Reiss (1998). Formal and empirical arguments concerning phonological acquisition. *LI* **29**. 656–683.

Hayes, B. (1986). Assimilation as spreading in Toba Batak. *LI* **17**. 467–499.

—— (1999a). Phonetically-driven phonology: the role of Optimality Theory and Inductive Grounding. In M. Darnell, E. Moravscik, M. Noonan, F. Newmeyer, and K. Wheatly (eds.) *Functionalism and Formalism in Linguistics, Vol. 1: General Papers*. Amsterdam: John Benjamins. 243–285.

—— (1999b). Phonological restructuring in Yidiɲ and its theoretical consequences. In B. Hermans and M. Oostendorp (eds.) (1999). *The Derivational Residue in Phonological Optimality Theory*. Amsterdam: John Benjamins. 175–205.

—— (1999c). Phonological acquisition in Optimality Theory: the early stages. [ROA 327, http://roa.rutgers.edu]

—— (2000). Gradient well-formedness in Optimality Theory. In Dekkers *et al.* (2000). 88–120.

Jun, S.-A. (1996). *The Phonetics and Phonology of Korean Prosody: Intonational Phonology and Prosodic Structure*. New York: Garland.

Jusczyk, P. W. and R. N. Aslin (1995). Infants' detection of sound patterns of words in fluent speech. *Cognitive Psychology* **29**. 1–23.

Jusczyk, P. W., A. Cutler, and N. J. Redanz (1993). Infants' preference for the predominant stress patterns of English words. *Child Development* **64**. 675–687.

Jusczyk, P. W., A. D. Friederici, J. M. I. Wessels, V. Y. Svenkerud, and A. Jusczyk (1993). Infants' sensitivity to the sound patterns of native language words. *Journal of Memory and Language* **32**. 402–420.

Jusczyk, P. W. and E. A. Hohne (1997). Infants' memory for spoken words. *Science* **277**. 1984–1986.

Jusczyk, P. W., P. A. Luce, and J. Charles-Luce (1994). Infants' sensitivity to phonotactic patterns in the native language. *Journal of Memory and Language* **33**. 630–645.

Kager, R. (1999a). Surface opacity of metrical structure in Optimality Theory. In B. Hermans and M. Oostendorp (eds.) *The Derivational Residue in Phonological Optimality Theory*. Amsterdam: John Benjamins. 207–245.

—— (1999b). *Optimality Theory*. Cambridge: Cambridge University Press.

Kazazis, K. (1969). Possible evidence for (near-)underlying forms in the speech of a child. *CLS* **5**. 382–388.

Keating, P. A. (1984). Phonetic and phonological representation of stop consonant voicing. *Lg* **60**. 286–319.

Keating, P., W. Linker, and M. Huffman (1983). Patterns in allophone distribution for voiced and voiceless stops. *Journal of Phonetics* **11**. 277–290.

Kenstowicz, M. (1998). Uniform Exponence: exemplification and extension. [ROA 218, http://roa.rutgers.edu]

Kiparsky, P. (1988). Phonological change. In F. J. Newmeyer (ed.) *Linguistics: the Cambridge Survey, Vol. 1: Linguistic Theory: Foundations*. Cambridge: Cambridge University Press. 363–415.

Kiparsky, P. and L. Menn (1977). On the acquisition of phonology. In J. Macnamara (ed.) *Language Learning and Thought*. New York: Academic Press.

Kirchner, R. (1997). Contrastiveness and Faithfulness. *Phonology* **14**. 83–113.

Kisseberth, C. (1970). On the functional unity of phonological rules. *LI* **1**. 291–306.

Koutsoudas, A., G. Sanders, and C. Noll (1974). The application of phonological rules. *Lg* **50**. 1–28.

Kuhl, P. K. (1991). Human adults and human infants show a 'perceptual magnet effect' for the prototypes of speech categories, monkeys do not. *Perception and Psychophysics* **50**. 90–107.

(1995). Mechanisms of developmental change in speech and language. *Proceedings of the International Congress of Phonetic Sciences, Stockholm*, Vol. 2. 132–139.

Kuhl, P. K. and J. D. Miller (1975). Speech perception by the chinchilla: voiced–voiceless distinction in alveolar plosive consonants. *Science* **190**. 69–72.

(1978). Speech perception by the chinchilla: identification functions for synthetic VOT stimuli. *JASA* **63**. 905–917.

Kuhl, P. K. and D. M. Padden (1982). Enhanced discriminability at the phonetic boundaries for the voicing feature in macaques. *Perception and Psychophysics* **32**. 542–550.

(1983). Enhanced discriminability at the phonetic boundaries for the place feature in macaques. *JASA* **73**. 1003–1010.

Levelt, C. C. (1994). *On the Acquisition of Place*. Leiden and Amsterdam: Holland Institute of Generative Linguistics.

Lombardi, L. (1995). Laryngeal neutralization and syllable well-formedness. *NLLT* **13**. 39–74.

Macken, M. (1980). The child's lexical representation: the *puzzle-puddle-pickle* evidence. *JL* **16**. 1–17.

McCarthy, J. (1998). Morpheme structure constraints and paradigm occultation. *CLS* **34**, *Vol. 2: The Panels*.

McHugh, B. (1986). Cyclicity in phrasal phonology: evidence from Chaga. *WCCFL* **5**. 154–164.

Menn, L. (1983). Development of articulatory, phonetics, and phonological capabilities. In B. Butterworth (ed.) *Language Production, Vol. 1*. London: Academic Press. 3–47.

Ohala, J. J. (1983). The origin of sound patterns in vocal tract constraints. In P. F. MacNeilage (ed.) *The Production of Speech*. New York: Springer. 189–216.

Pater, J. (1997). Minimal violation and phonological development. *Language Acquisition* **6**: 3. 201–253.

(this volume). Bridging the gap between receptive and productive development with minimally violable constraints.

Prince, A. and P. Smolensky (1993). Optimality Theory: constraint interaction in generative grammar. MS., available from http://ruccs.rutgers.edu/publicationsreports.html.

Prince, A. and B. Tesar (1999). Learning phonotactic distributions. [ROA 353, http://roa.rutgers.edu]

Pulleyblank, D. and W. J. Turkel (2000). Learning phonology: genetic algorithms and Yoruba tongue root harmony. In Dekkers *et al.* (2000). 554–591.

Smith, N. (1973). *The Acquisition of Phonology*. Cambridge: Cambridge University Press.

Smolensky, P. (1993). Harmony, markedness, and phonological activity. [ROA 87, http://roa.rutgers.edu]

(1996a). On the comprehension/production dilemma in child language. *LI* **27**. 720–731.

(1996b). The initial state and 'Richness of the Base' in Optimality Theory. [ROA 154, http://roa.rutgers.edu]

Steriade, D. (1997). Phonetics in phonology: the case of laryngeal neutralization. http://www.linguistics.ucla.edu/people/steriade/papers/phoneticsinphology.pdf.

(2000). Paradigm Uniformity and the phonetics-phonology boundary. In J. Pierrehumbert and M. Broe (eds.) *Acquisition and the Lexicon: Papers in Laboratory Phonology V*. Cambridge: Cambridge University Press. 313–334.

Tesar, B. (1995a). *Computational Optimality Theory*. Ph.D. dissertation, University of Colorado. [ROA 90, http://roa.rutgers.edu]

(1995b). Computing optimal forms in Optimality Theory: basic syllabification. [ROA 52, http://roa.rutgers.edu]

(1999). Robust interpretive parsing in metrical stress theory. *WCCFL* **7**. 625–639. [ROA 262, http://ruccs.rutgers.edu/roa.html]

Tesar, B. and P. Smolensky (1993). The learnability of Optimality Theory: an algorithm and some basic complexity results. [ROA 2, http://roa.rutgers.edu]

(1996). Learnability in Optimality Theory. [ROA 156, http://roa.rutgers.edu]

(1998). Learnability in Optimality Theory. *LI* **29**. 229–268.

(2000). *Learnability in Optimality Theory*. Cambridge, Mass.: MIT Press.

Vance, T. (1987). 'Canadian Raising' in some dialects of the Northern United States. *American Speech* **62**. 195–210.

Vihman, M. (1996). *Phonological Development: the Origins of Language in the Child*, Oxford: Blackwell.

Walther, M. (1996). OT SIMPLE – a construction kit approach to Optimality Theory implementation. [ROA 152, http://roa.rutgers.edu]

Werker, J. F. and C. E. Lalonde (1988). Cross-language speech perception: initial capabilities and development change. *Developmental Psychology* **24**. 672–683.

Werker, J. F. and R. C. Tees (1984). Cross-language speech perception: evidence for perceptual reorganization during the first year of life. *Infant Behavior and Development* **7**. 49–63.

Westbury, J. R. and P. Keating (1986). On the naturalness of stop consonant voicing. *JL* **22**. 145–166.

Wilson, C. (2001). Learning phonotactic distributions with targeted constraints. Paper presented at the 6th Southwest Workshop on Optimality Theory, Department of Linguistics, University of Southern California.

Zoll, C. (1998). Positional asymmetries and licensing. MS., MIT. [ROA 282, http://roa.rutgers.edu]

Zuraw, K. (2000). *Patterned Exceptions in Phonology*. Ph.D. dissertation, UCLA. [http://www.linguistics.ucla.edu/people/zuraw/dnld pprs/diss.pdf]

6 Syllable types in cross-linguistic and developmental grammars*

Clara C. Levelt and Ruben van de Vijver

1. Introduction

In this chapter we consider syllable types in acquisition, language typology, and also in a third dimension, namely production frequency in the language surrounding the language learner.

In Optimality Theory (OT) (Prince and Smolensky 1993) both language acquisition and language typology can be accommodated. The basic assumption is that constraints are universal, but that the rankings of these constraints are language particular. For language typology the idea is that different rankings reflect different (possible) languages. For acquisition the idea is that the learner needs to acquire the language-specific ranking of his mother tongue. The assumption here, like in most other work on acquisition to date (Gnanadesikan this volume, Hayes this volume, Davidson *et al.* this volume, Prince and Tesar this volume), is that structural constraints initially outrank faithfulness constraints. The grammar in this state prefers structurally unmarked outputs to faithful ones. By promoting faithfulness constraints in the ranking, or by demoting structural constraints, the outputs can become more marked and more faithful to their inputs.[1]

What is the expected relation between language typology and language acquisition? Concentrating here on syllable types, languages can be structurally marked or unmarked with respect to the structural constraints that refer to syllable type: ONSET, NO-CODA, *COMPLEX-ONSET, and *COMPLEX-CODA. A language is structurally unmarked with respect to a structural constraint when such a constraint dominates faithfulness constraints, and it is marked when such a constraint is dominated by faithfulness constraints. For language acquisition the assumption is that the child's output is initially structurally totally unmarked. All structural constraints dominate all faithfulness constraints. If this initial state of the grammar is equal to the final state grammar of the language to be learned, no further developmental steps need to take place. However, if the language to be learned is marked in one or more ways, the learner needs to acquire the appropriate grammar. The assumption is that this is done by promoting faithfulness constraints to positions that outrank specific structural constraints. This will lead to outputs that can be marked with respect to the outranked structural constraint. When the language to be learned is marked in several respects, it can be hypothesised that the learner acquires these marked aspects of the grammar gradually. That is, there could be a learning path where the learner, in going from the initial state of the grammar, $G_{initial}$, to the final state of the grammar, G_{final}, passes through several intermediate grammars. To combine language acquisition with language typology, the expectation is that the intermediate grammars of the language learner are also final state grammars of languages of the world. Vice versa, it is expected that since languages can be marked in different respects, there are different possible learning paths the learner of a very marked language can take to reach the final state. For example, as we shall see below, there are languages that can violate NO-CODA but not ONSET, like Thargari; and there are languages that can violate ONSET but not NO-CODA, like Cayuvava. A learner who has to acquire a language that can violate both NO-CODA and ONSET, like Mokilese, can either get to the G_{final} of that language through an intermediate Thargari stage, or through an intermediate Cayuvava stage. In its strongest form the hypothesis is thus that there is a 1:1 relation between grammars of languages in the world and intermediate grammars in language acquisition.

In order to check these assumptions, we have combined data on cross-linguistic variation in syllable types (Blevins 1995) with data on the acquisition of syllable types (Levelt *et al.* 2000). In the remainder of this chapter we shall first present the OT grammars of languages of the world, to which we refer, slightly off the mark, as 'cross-linguistic grammars', that were deduced from data in Blevins. Then we shall proceed to the developmental grammars discussed in Levelt *et al.* (2000), and the two sets of grammars will be lined up. The similarities and differences will be discussed, and, finally, a solution for the particular nature of the learning path for Dutch children is presented in terms of syllable type frequencies in the input.

2. Cross-linguistic grammars for syllable type

Blevins (1995) presents twelve different syllable type inventories. These are listed in (1):

(1)   Syllable Type Inventories (from Blevins (1995))

Language	example	Language	example
Hua	CV	Klamath	CV(C)(C)
Thargari	CV(C)	Mokilese	(C)V(C)
Cayuvava	(C)V	Totonac	C(C)V(C)(C)
Arabela	C(C)V	Finnish	(C)V(C)(C)
Sedang	C(C)V(C)	Spanish	(C)(C)V(C)
Mazateco	(C)(C)V	Dutch	(C)(C)V(C)(C)

As can be seen in (1), languages allow syllable types with different degrees of complexity. The language Hua has only one syllable type, namely CV, while Dutch, like English, on the other end, allows a whole set of more complex syllable types. The one syllable type that all languages have in common is CV, and this type is regarded to be totally unmarked. In terms of markedness it can thus be said that Hua is structurally the most unmarked language with respect to syllable type, while Dutch is the most marked one.

In OT there are two main types of constraints. On the one hand, there are structural constraints that demand outputs to be structurally unmarked; while on the other hand, there are faithfulness constraints that demand outputs to be faithful to their inputs, whether these are structurally marked or not. The ranking of structural constraints *vis-à-vis* faithfulness constraints in a grammar determines the structural markedness allowed in a language. When all structural constraints outrank all faithfulness constraints the language is structurally totally unmarked; and when all faithfulness constraints outrank all structural constraints the language allows outputs that are structurally marked in any possible way. When faithfulness constraints are ranked among structural constraints, the language allows for a certain degree of complexity in output forms. The structural constraints that are relevant here are in (2):

(2)   Structural constraints
        ONSET   A syllable should have an onset
        NO-CODA   A syllable should not have a coda
        *COMPLEX-ONSET   A syllable should not have a complex onset
        *COMPLEX-CODA   A syllable should not have a complex coda

The constraints ONSET and NO-CODA are well known from the literature. The more general constraint *COMPLEX is split up into one constraint referring to onsets and one referring to codas (see Kager 1999 for a similar move). This is necessary to differentiate between languages that allow complex onsets but no complex codas and vice versa, and also to differentiate language learners who acquire complex onsets first from those who acquire complex codas first.

In (3), then, are the different rankings of the structural constraints from (2) *vis-à-vis* a general faithfulness constraint FAITH, that characterise the typologically different languages in (1). This is called a factorial typology. Since we are not interested here in the ways an output can be unfaithful, but only in the ways in which an output syllable can be marked, a single faithfulness constraint FAITH is used here as an expository simplification. Also, the rankings of the structural constraints among each other are not relevant here because they do not conflict with one another.

(3)   Factorial typology

(a) Unmarked

| *Hua* | ONSET | NO-CODA | *COMPLEX-O | *COMPLEX-C | >>FAITH |

(b) Marked I

Cayuvava	NO-CODA	*COMPLEX-O	*COMPLEX-C	>>FAITH>>	ONSET
Thargari	ONSET	*COMPLEX-O	*COMPLEX-C	>>FAITH>>	NO-CODA
Arabela	ONSET	NO-CODA	*COMPLEX-C	>>FAITH>>	*COMPLEX-O

(c) Marked II

Sedang	ONSET	*COMPLEX-C	>>FAITH>>	NO-CODA	*COMPLEX-O
Mazateco	NO-CODA	*COMPLEX-C	>>FAITH>>	ONSET	*COMPLEX-O
Mokilese	*COMPLEX-O	*COMPLEX-C	>>FAITH>>	ONSET	NO-CODA
Klamath	ONSET	*COMPLEX-O	>>FAITH>>	NO-CODA	*COMPLEX-C

(d) Marked III

Totonac	ONSET	>>FAITH>>	NO-CODA	*COMPLEX-C	*COMPLEX-O
Spanish	*COMPLEX-C	>>FAITH>>	ONSET	NO-CODA	*COMPLEX-O
Finnish	*COMPLEX-O	>>FAITH>>	ONSET	NO-CODA	*COMPLEX-C

(e) Marked IV

| *Dutch* | FAITH>> | ONSET | NO-CODA | *COMPLEX-O | *COMPLEX-C |

So long as NO-CODA dominates FAITH, the ranking between FAITH and *COMPLEX-C is irrelevant. Therefore the logically possible rankings where NO-CODA dominates FAITH, and FAITH in turn dominates *COMPLEX-C are not considered. All other possible rankings are attested in the world's languages, as given in Blevins (1995), and there are apparently no other languages that require different constraints and/or rankings in order to characterise their syllable type inventories. The rankings are grouped according to the degree of complexity that is allowed in outputs. In (a) is the *Unmarked* ranking for Hua; in (b) are *Marked I* rankings, that lead to syllable outputs that can be structurally marked in maximally one way; in (c) are *Marked II* rankings that allow well-formed syllables to be marked in two different ways; in (d) are *Marked III* rankings that allow well-formed syllables to be marked in three different ways; and in (e) are *Marked IV* rankings that allow well-formed syllables to be marked in four different ways.

3.   Factorial typology and learning paths

Assuming that the initial grammar in acquisition, G_i, leads to language output that is structurally maximally unmarked, and assuming that the final-state grammar, G_f, is either equal to G_i or a grammar that allows structurally more marked outputs, the learning path from G_i to the final-state grammar G_f is expected to link grammars that allow increasingly marked outputs. From the factorial typology in (3) above we can deduce twelve different paths that link the grammar from *Unmarked* languages, through those of *Marked I*, *Marked II*, and *Marked III* languages respectively, to the grammar of the most marked

Marked IV languages. These are depicted in (4). In all of these linkings, FAITH gradually moves up in the constraint ranking from the lowest position in the ranking to the highest position by promoting over one structural constraint at a time. The linkings of the grammars from *Unmarked* to *Marked IV* languages are hypothesised to be the learning paths that a language learner could take, going from unmarked G_i to a most marked G_f. For ease of exposition, in (4) languages and a typical example of the added syllable types are mentioned instead of grammars.

(4)   Learning paths deduced from the factorial typology

G_i	G_2	G_3	G_4	G_f
			Totonac (CCV)	Dutch (V)
		Klamath (CVCC)		
			Finnish (V)	Dutch (CCV)
			Spanish (V)	Dutch (CVCC)
	Thargari (CVC)	Sedang (CCV)		
			Totonac (CVCC)	Dutch (V)
			Spanish (CCV)	Dutch (CVCC)
		Mokilese (V)		
			Finnish (CVCC)	Dutch (CCV)
		Mazateco (CCV)	Spanish (CVC)	Dutch (CVCC)
Hua (CV)	Cayuvava (V)			
			Spanish (CCV)	Dutch (CVCC)
		Mokilese (CVC)		
			Finnish (CVCC)	Dutch (CCV)
		Mazateco (V)	Spanish (CVC)	Dutch (CVCC)
	Arabela (CCV)			
			Spanish (V)	Dutch (CVCC)
		Sedang (CVC)		
			Totonac (CVCC)	Dutch (V)

The Dutch children of our study appear to follow only a small subset of the possible learning paths that go from an unmarked initial stage to a final marked stage. These paths are marked by the shaded boxes in (4). In the next section we shall discuss how these stages have been established. In section 5, the relation between cross-linguistic grammars and acquisition stages will be discussed, and in section 6 the specific learning paths taken by Dutch children will be explained through an interaction of the adult grammar and frequency.

4.   Language acquisition

In Levelt *et al.* (2000) the development of syllable types in longitudinal data of twelve children acquiring Dutch as their first language was examined. For a period of one year these children were recorded every other week. The children's ages ranged between 0;11 and 1;11 at the start of the data-collecting period. Approximately 20,000 spontaneous utterances formed the input to a syllabification algorithm developed by Schiller (Schiller *et al.* 1996). See Schiller *et al.* (1996) or Levelt *et al.* (2000) for details on this algorithm. The resulting syllable type data from primary stressed positions were then submitted to a Guttman scale, at four different points in time: namely, first recording, first three recordings, first six recordings, and all recordings. With a Guttman scale, a shared order – of development in this case – can be established, and it can be seen to what extent a particular order is followed by individual subjects. It turned out that there was a shared developmental order, with two variants. This order is shown in (5):[2]

(5)   Developmental order for the acquisition of syllable types
                    A: > (5) CVCC, VCC> (6) CCV, CCVC
(1) CV > (2) CVC > (3) V > (4) VC   >(7) CCVCC
                    B: > (5) CCV, CCVC > (6) CVCC, VCC

The structures CV, CVC, V, and VC were acquired in this order by all the children. One group of children (A, N=9) then went on to acquire CVCC, VCC, and CCV, CCVC, while another group (B, N=3) acquired the same structures in a different order, namely CCV, CCVC and CVCC, VCC. The last syllable type for both groups to be acquired was CCVCC.

From these data a learning path through grammatical stages was deduced, from a G_i allowing only a structurally most unmarked output, via intermediate grammars, to a G_f similar to the grammar of Dutch. In these grammars, the structural constraints from (2) above featured, next to a general faithfulness constraint FAITH. We shall come back to the exact nature of these developmental grammars below.

5.   Cross-linguistic grammars versus developmental grammars

Given the linked cross-linguistic grammars in (4) and the developmental stages in (5), it is shown in (6) how these line up:

(6)   Comparison between cross-linguistic grammars and developmental stages

Acquisition	Corresponding language	Non-corresponding G_n alternative
G_i	Hua	
G_2	Thargari	Cayuvava, Arabela
G_3	?	
G_4	Mokilese	Sedang, Klamath
G_{5A}	Finnish	Spanish
G_{5B}	Spanish	Finnish
G_6	?	
G_f	Dutch	

As can be seen in (6), the hypothesis formulated above, namely that there is a 1:1 relation between developmental grammars and cross-linguistic grammars, appears to be too strong in two ways.

First, the process of the acquisition of syllable types appears to require more grammars than the established cross-linguistic grammars: from the data in Blevins it appears that no cross-linguistic grammar exists that corresponds to the developmental grammars G_3 and G_6.

The developmental grammar G_3 allows CV, CVC, and V syllables, but no syllables of the type VC, and no syllables with complex onsets or codas. The problem here is how specifically VC syllables can be disallowed. Since both CVC and V are allowed, both the structural constraints ONSET and NO-CODA must be dominated by FAITH. However, such a grammar would also allow VC syllables.

A similar problem arises for G_6. This developmental grammar allows, apart from CV, CVC, V, and VC syllables, syllables with complex onsets and syllables with complex codas. However, syllables with both complex onsets and complex codas, CCVCC, are not allowed. In order for CCVC and CVCC to be allowed, FAITH must dominate both *COMPLEX-ONSET and *COMPLEX-CODA. This grammar, however, would also allow CCVCC syllables.

Both situations can be captured grammar-wise by invoking Local Conjunction (Smolensky 1993, Kirchner 1996, Ito and Mester 1998). Here two (or more) constraints are conjoined to form a derived constraint, which is violated just in case all the conjoined constraints are violated by an output candidate.[3] This was done in Levelt *et al.* (2000). In order to capture the situation in the third developmental stage, in the grammar a conjoined constraint ONSET&NO-CODA dominated FAITH, while FAITH dominated both ONSET and NO-CODA. Output candidates of the type VC would violate this conjoined constraint, unlike V and CVC. For the situation in the sixth developmental stage, a conjoined constraint *COMPLEX-ONSET&*COMPLEX-CODA was invoked, which dominated FAITH while FAITH in turn dominated both *COMPLEX-ONSET and *COMPLEX-CODA. This grammar disallowed CCVCC syllables, while allowing both CVCC and CCVC.

Several questions concerning this solution remain to be answered. First of all, do we need to take every developmental stage deduced from the Guttman scale seriously, i.e., as reflecting a specific developmental grammar? If we do, then the second question is whether cross-linguistically a grammar exists which unexpectedly makes use of either of the proposed conjoined constraints. Indeed, such an unexpected language is attested.[4] Apparently, the syllable inventory of Central Sentani (Hartzler 1976) has three basic syllable types: CV, V, CVC. Crucially, it lacks VC, arguing for the presence of the conjoined constraint ONSET & NOCODA in the grammar. This finding inspires confidence in the conjoined constraint *COMPLEX-ONSET & *COMPLEX-CODA.

In (7), then, the sequence of developmental grammars, from G_i to G_f, is presented. Like in (3) above, we are concerned only with the dominance relations of structural constraints versus faithfulness, not with the rankings of structural constraints among each other. No ranking is indicated here. The conjoined constraints in (7) are *COMPLO&C for *COMPLEX-ONSET and *COMPLEX-CODA, and ONS&NC for ONSET & NO-CODA.

(7) Developmental grammars for syllable type

G_i	*ComplO&C	*Complex-C	*Complex-O	Ons&NC	Onset	No-Coda	>>Faith
G_2	*ComplO&C	*Complex-C	*Complex-O	Ons&NC	Onset	>>Faith>>	No-Coda
G_3	*ComplO&C	*Complex-C	*Complex-O	Ons&NC	>>Faith>>	Onset	No-Coda
G_4	*ComplO&C	*Complex-C	*Complex-O	>>Faith>>	Ons&NC	Onset	No-Coda
G_{5A}	*ComplO&C	*Complex-O	>>Faith>>	*Complex-C	Ons&NC	Onset	No-Coda
G_{5B}	*ComplO&C	*Complex-C	>>Faith>>	*Complex-O	Ons&NC	Onset	No-Coda
G_6	*ComplO&C	>>Faith>>	*Complex-C	*Complex-O	Ons&NC	Onset	No-Coda
G_f	Faith>>	*ComplO&C	*Complex-C	*Complex-O	Ons&NC	Onset	No-Coda

Let us now turn to the second problem for the hypothesis that there is a 1:1 relation between developmental grammars and cross-linguistic grammars: there is less variation in development than expected. If we neglect G_3 and G_6 for a moment, of the twelve possible learning paths that link G_i to G_f only two are taken by the Dutch language learners (the shaded boxes in (4)). The developmental grammar G_2, for example, corresponds to the grammar of Thargari (CV, CVC), not to the grammars of either Cayuvava (CV, V) or Arabela (CV, CCV), which are equally possible. In going from G_i to G_2, FAITH could have promoted over *COMPLEX-ONSET, resulting in the grammar for Arabela, or over ONSET, resulting in the grammar for Cayuvava. The learners of Dutch, however, promote FAITH over NO-CODA. The only variation is for G_5. The learners of Group A (N=9) acquire complex codas before they acquire complex onsets, and their grammar at that point is equal to the grammar for Finnish, which allows complex codas but not complex onsets. The learners of Group B (N=3) acquire complex onsets first, and their grammar at this point corresponds to the grammar for Spanish, which allows complex onsets, but not complex codas. One explanation for the lack of variation is that we do not have enough acquisition data yet. Awaiting a larger study, an alternative explanation is explored below.

6.   Guides through the learning paths

It is thought that the structure of a grammar, combined with the assumptions that (1) in the initial state of the grammar structural constraints dominate faithfulness; and (2) that development consists of promotions of faithfulness in the hierarchy, determines which developmental steps can be taken. The twelve learning paths relating G_i to G_f are determined in this way. However, the idea is that when the grammar provides the learner with a choice, other factors will push the learner in a certain direction.

We shall follow the learning path of Dutch learners in (4),[5] and see what could force the choice for a specific learning path over other possible learning paths.

6.1 G_i to G_2: Hua to Thargari

In this developmental step, FAITH can be promoted over NO-CODA (Thargari), ONSET (Cayuvava) or *COMPLEX-ONSET (Arabela). In addition to CV, Thargari would allow CVC, Cayuvava would allow V and Arabela would allow CCV.

The question here is why the learners at this stage prefer CVC syllables to both V and CCV syllables. For CCV, the answer could simply lie in the fact that the sounds needed for the production of complex onsets, especially liquids, are not acquired at this point (Fikkert 1994). The CCV option is therefore not a very likely one.

The learner's choice for CVC syllables instead of V syllables could be due to the special role of codas in Dutch. Lax vowels in Dutch can only appear in closed syllables (cf. Van der Hulst 1984, Kager 1989, Fikkert 1994, Van Oostendorp 1995 and Booij 1995, to give a non-exhaustive list). This generalisation is based on three observations. First, words cannot end in lax vowels (/tɑksi/, but not /tɑksɪ/). Second, lax vowels cannot appear in hiatus (/piano/

but not/piano/). Finally, lax vowels can be followed by at most two non-coronal consonants (/ramp/), while tense vowels can be followed by at most one non-coronal consonant (/ram/ but not /ramp/). These observations can be explained if it is assumed that lax vowels only appear in closed syllables and that syllables can have at most one extra non-coronal consonant following the coda. In other words, syllables with lax vowels are *obligatorily* closed. In contrast to this, there is no process in Dutch that requires syllables to be *onsetless*. The picture that emerges is that CVC syllables are more salient than onsetless syllables. This phonological saliency could draw the attention of learners, and could lead to the acquisition of CVC before V.

One problem with this phonological explanation is that the distinction between lax and tense vowels is acquired relatively late in the acquisition process (Fikkert 1994). As a consequence, the distinction between tense and lax vowels is not yet acquired at the stage in which the children master the closed syllable. It is not clear, then, whether children at this stage would recognise the significance of codas, and therefore of CVC syllables, in Dutch. However, CVC syllables could also attract the attention of the learner by their frequency of appearance in speech input to the learner.

In order to check this hypothesis, we looked at actual child-directed speech. The corpus of syllable types in child-directed speech that was used here (J. C. van de Weijer, personal communication (1997)) contained 112,926 syllables.[6]

The syllable type CVC has a frequency of 32.1 percent (N = 36,196) in the speech corpus, and is the most frequent syllable by far after CV (44.8 percent, N = 50,603). Moreover, it is far more frequent than both V (3.8 percent, N = 4,345) and CCV (1.4 percent, N = 1,564), and the choice for a G_2 that would allow for CVC syllables could thus very well be based on frequency information.

6.2 G_2 to G_3: Thargari to Mokilese

FAITH can now be promoted over ONSET (Mokilese), *COMPLEX-CODA (Klamath) or *COMPLEX-ONSET (Sedang). In addition to CV and CVC, Mokilese would allow V and VC, Klamath CVCC, Sedang CCV and CCVC.

The choice here for onsetless syllables instead of a syllable with a complex margin could have the phonological explanation offered before: the sounds needed to produce clusters of consonants are still problematic. For this explanation to be tested, the data on the acquisition of certain sounds and the data on the acquisition of syllable types need to be compared.

Another explanation is again provided by frequency information. The frequency of the new syllable types that would be allowed by a grammar that has

FAITH promoted over ONSET, V and VC, is 15.8 percent (N = 17,883). The frequency of new syllables types that would be allowed by a grammar that has FAITH promoted over *COMPLEX-CODA, CVCC, is 3.2 percent (N = 3,669). Finally, if FAITH were to be promoted over *COMPLEX-ONSET, the types CCV and CCVC would be allowed. These types together have a frequency of 3.4 percent (N = 3,804). The onsetless syllables V and VC, with a frequency of 15.8 percent, are more frequent than either the type CVCC (3.2 percent) or the types with complex onsets CCV and CCVC (3.4 percent). In order to allow for the most frequent set of syllables, the onsetless syllables, FAITH is promoted over ONSET.

6.3 G_3 to G_4: Mokilese to Finnish (A) or Mokilese to Spanish (B)

FAITH can now be promoted over either *COMPLEX-ONSET (Spanish) or *COMPLEX-CODA (Finnish). In addition to CV, CVC, V, and VC, Spanish would allow CCV and CCVC; Finnish would allow CVCC and VCC.

At this point variation is found. Some learners take the direction of Spanish (N = 3), while others take the direction of Finnish (N = 9). The frequency of the syllable types that would be added to the inventory by promoting FAITH over *COMPLEX-O, CCV and CCVC, is 3.4 percent (N = 3,804), while the frequency of the types CVCC and VCC, that would be allowed by promoting FAITH over *COMPLEX-C, is 3.7 percent (N = 4,146). This difference is small, but it is still significant (Fisher Exact test, $p < 0.001$).[7] It is thus necessary to become more specific about the possible effect of input frequency on acquisition. Apparently, learners need a certain threshold to notice a frequency difference. So let us follow the learning path again, taking into account the ratios of the different syllable type inputs (standard-error analysis).[8] The idea is that the learner has to hear some syllable type X not just more often but considerably more often than some other syllable type Y in order for a grammar change to take place in the direction of syllable type X, rather than in the direction of syllable type Y.

(8)

G_i: *COMPLEX-C, *COMPLEX-O, ONSET, NO-CODA >> FAITH

G_2 options	result	Input frequency
1: >>FAITH >> NO-CODA	Thargari. Adds CVC	CVC: 36,196
2: >>FAITH >> ONSET	Cayuvava. Adds V	V: 4,345
3: >>FAITH > >*COMPLEX-O	Arabela. Adds CCV	CCV: 1,564
Option 1 is taken		

The CVC/V ratio is 8.33 (95 percent confidence interval: 8.08 to 8.58), the CVC/CCV ratio is 23.14 (95 percent confidence interval: 21.98 to 24.29).

(9)

G_2: *COMPLEX-C, *COMPLEX-O, ONSET >> FAITH >> NO-CODA

G_3 options	result	Input frequency
1: >> FAITH >> ONSET, . . .	Mokilese. Adds V and VC	V + VC: 17,883
2: >> FAITH >> *COMPLEX-O, . . .	Sedang. Adds CCV and CCVC	CCV + CCVC: 3,804
3: >> FAITH >> *COMPLEX-C, . . .	Klamath. Adds CVCC	CVCC: 3,669
Option 1 is taken		

The ratio V+VC/CCVC+CCV is 4.70 (95 percent confidence interval: 4.54 to 4.86), the ratio V+VC/CVCC is 4.87 (95 percent confidence interval: 4.71 to 5.04).

(10)

G_3: *COMPLEX-C, *COMPLEX-O, >> FAITH >> ONSET NO-CODA

G_4 options	result	Input frequency
1: >> FAITH >>*COMPLEX-O, . . .	Spanish. Adds CCV and CCVC	CCV + CCVC: 3804
2: >>FAITH >> *COMPLEX-C, . . .	Finnish. Adds CVCC and VCC	CVCC + VCC: 4146
Some learners take option 1, other learners take option 2		

The ratio CCV+CCVC/CVCC+VCC is 1.09 (95 percent confidence interval: 1.04 to 1.14). What we have, then, is four large ratios, ranging from 4.77 to 23.14, and one small ratio, 1.08. We thus hypothesise that a ratio of at least 4.77 is large enough to ensure that the frequency effect prevails over other factors that could influence acquisition. That is, the frequency differences cause the acquisition of codas before onsetless syllables, and the acquisition of onsetless syllables before complex onsets. We find that these learning orders unambiguously apply to all twelve subjects. By contrast, we hypothesise that the CVCC+VCC/CCVC+CCV ratio of about 1.08 is so close to 1 that other factors may mask the small frequency difference. In this case, we find that the twelve subjects vary in their order of learning complex onsets and complex codas. However, the majority (9) learn complex codas first, which is in accordance with the CVCC+VCC/CCVC+CCV ratio, which we found to be reliably greater than 1.04 (p = 0.025).

On the whole, then, the frequency of syllable types in (Dutch) speech appears to be a good candidate for a learner's guide through the possible learning paths. Large frequency ratios (>4.77) can certainly be detected by the learner, and we hypothesise that these push the learner along the learning path. It is also clear that a ratio that is close to 1, like in the case of complex onsets and complex codas, is probably not noticed by the learner and is therefore unable to force an unambiguous decision.

The role of input frequencies in language acquisition has, of course, been considered before (see, e.g., Hoff-Ginsberg 1992, Jusczyk *et al.* 1994, Schwartz and Terrell 1983). To the best of our knowledge, however, it has until now neither been used to account for phonological development in production nor has it been considered in the way outlined here.

7.   Conclusion

Syllable types have been considered from three different angles in this chapter: acquisition; typology; and production frequency. In line with OT literature on language acquisition, it is assumed that acquisition is a process in which faithfulness dominates more and more structural constraints. Second, the syllable types of a number of languages have been considered and, in line with one of the central claims of OT, it was concluded that differences between languages are represented as a difference in the ranking of constraints. This served as the basis for the hypothesis that every stage in the acquisition of a language should correspond to a cross-linguistic grammar.

This correspondence has been found for all but two stages in the acquisition of Dutch syllable types. It could be that the relevant non-corresponding stages, requiring reference to conjoined constraints, are acquisition-specific. However, the conjoined constraint ONSET and NOCODA appears to be necessary in the analysis of the syllable in Central Sentani (Hartzler 1976), too. As far as we can see, then, there is no principled reason why *COMPLEX-ONSET & *COMPLEX-CODA should not be active in some, as yet unknown, language. The hypothesis that every stage in the acquisition of a language corresponds to a cross-linguistic grammar is thus, at least with respect to syllable type, largely borne out.

The other part of our hypothesis implied that every cross-linguistically determined grammar could form an intermediate developmental grammar in the learning path from unmarked G_i to the G_f of a very marked language. It turned out, however, that learners of Dutch followed a specific learning path, from numerous possible paths.

This lack of variation is attributed to factors that guide the learner through the possibilities. The frequency of syllable types in the speech input to the learner appears to determine which learning path is followed. If the child has a choice between various paths, the path of the noticeably most frequent syllable type is chosen. If there is no noticeable difference between the frequencies of syllable types that correspond to different possible paths, variation is expected and attested. Future research should determine what the exact threshold is for a difference to be noticeable and effective. Based on our findings regarding the effect of frequencies in the speech input on the learning path, many new hypotheses can be formed. For instance, it follows that learners of languages with similar syllable types but with different speech input frequencies should show different learning paths. Combining acquisitional data with typological data in the way outlined here thus appears to provide a good method for research, leading to interesting hypotheses and findings in both fields.

NOTES

* This chapter was presented at the Third Biannual Utrecht Phonology Workshop, 11–12 June 1998, Utrecht, The Netherlands, organised by René Kager and Wim Zonneveld. We thank Paul Boersma, Nine Elenbaas, Vincent van Heuven, Joe Pater, Shigeko Shinohara, and Joost van de Weijer for their helpful comments and their contributions to this chapter. Financial support to Clara Levelt was provided by the Netherlands Organisation of Scientific Research (NWO).

1. The input is assumed to be similar to the adult surface form. That is, we assume that the child perceives the adult form quite accurately (Jusczyk 1997) and that this perceived form is taken to be the underlying form. If necessary, knowledge of morphological alternations, acquired at a later stage, will lead to changes in the input forms.

2. The developmental order here has been slightly simplified compared to the order given in Levelt, Schiller, and Levelt. In their article, syllable types with complex onsets and those with complex codas are analysed as being acquired in two steps: CVCC before VCC and CCV before CCVC.

3. As an alternative to conjoined constraints, Shigeko Shinohara suggests high-ranked constraints against more than one deviation from the canonical syllable types. We leave this suggestion open for future consideration.

4. Thanks to Nine Elenbaas for providing us with this example.

5. For now we disregard the developmental stages that require reference to conjoined constraints. G3 and G4 from (6) are thus collapsed, as are G6 and Gf.

6. We are grateful to Joost van de Weijer for generously sharing his data with us. For details on the speech input database and an analysis of the caretaker's speech, see Van de Weijer (1999).

7. The data base of child-directed speech that was available to us contains data from one caretaker only. It could thus be that the frequencies of these syllable types are balanced slightly differently for different speakers, to the advantage of complex clusters in the speech of one speaker, but to the advantage of complex onsets in another speaker. However, in the Dutch data base CELEX, which is based on printed texts, the frequency for CCV plus CCVC is 6.15 percent, the frequency for CVCC plus VCC is 6.53 percent, thus showing the same slightly higher frequency for syllable types with complex codas.

8. Special thanks to Paul Boersma for his help with the statistics.

References

Blevins, J. (1995). The syllable in phonological theory. In J. Goldsmith (ed.) *The Handbook of Phonological Theory*. Oxford: Blackwell.

Booij, G. (1995). *The Phonology of Dutch*. Oxford: Clarendon Press.

Davidson, L., P. Jusczyk, and P. Smolensky (this volume). The initial and final states: theoretical implications and experimental explorations of Richness of the Base.

218   *Clara C. Levelt and Ruben van de Vijver*

Fikkert, P. (1994). *On the Acquisition of Prosodic Structure*. Ph.D. dissertation, Leiden University, HIL Dissertation Series 6.

Gnanadesikan, A. (this volume). Markedness and faithfulness constraints in child phonology.

Hartzler, M. (1976). Central Sentani phonology. *Irian* **5**. 66–81.

Hayes, B. (this volume). Phonological acquisition in Optimality Theory: the early stages.

Hoff-Ginsberg, E. (1992). How should frequency in input be measured? *First Language* **12**: **3**. 233–244.

Hulst, H. van der (1984). *Syllable Structure and Stress in Dutch*. Dordrecht: Foris.

Itô, J. and A. Mester (1998). Markedness and word structure: OCP effects in Japanese. MS., UC Santa Cruz. [ROA 255, http://roa.rutgers.edu]

Jusczyk, P. (1997). *The Discovery of Spoken Language*. Cambridge, Mass.: MIT Press.

Jusczyk, P., P. Luce, and J. Charles-Luce (1994). Infants' sensitivity to phonotactic patterns in the native language. *Journal of Memory and Language* **33**. 630–645.

Kager, R. (1989). *A Metrical Theory of Stress and Destressing in English and Dutch*. Dordrecht: Foris.

(1999). *Optimality Theory*. Cambridge University Press.

Kirchner, R. (1996). Synchronic chain shifts in Optimality Theory. *LI* **27**. 341–350.

Levelt, C., N. Schiller, and W. Levelt (2000). The acquisition of syllable types. *Language Acquisition* **8**: **3**. 237–264.

Oostendorp, M. van (1995). *Vowel Quality and Phonological Projection*. Ph.D. dissertation, University of Tilburg.

Prince, A. and P. Smolensky (1993). Optimality Theory. RuCCS-TR-2, Rutgers Center for Cognitive Science. To appear, MIT Press.

Prince, A. and B. Tesar (this volume). Learning phonotactic distributions.

Schiller, N., A. Meyer, H. Baayen, and W. Levelt (1996). A comparison of lexeme and speech syllables in Dutch. *Journal of Quantitative Linguistics* **3**. 8–28.

Schwartz, R. and B. Terrell (1983). The role of input frequency in lexical acquisition. *Journal of Child Language* **10**: **1**. 57–64.

Smolensky, P. (1993). Harmony, markedness, and phonological activity. Paper presented at the Rutgers Optimality Workshop-1, Rutgers University, New Brunswick.

Weijer, J. van de (1999). *Language Input for Word Discovery*. Ph.D. dissertation, Nijmegen University, The Netherlands.

7 Bridging the gap between receptive and productive development with minimally violable constraints*

Joe Pater

1. Introduction

It is a commonplace observation that there are gaps between perception and production in child phonology; that children often appear to have receptively acquired a segmental or prosodic contrast that is neutralised in production (see section 2 below for a review of some evidence). The developmental lag of productive behind receptive ability raises a fundamental question: does perception or production reflect the state of phonological competence in the child's emerging linguistic system? The answer given in this chapter is that the child's knowledge of phonology is displayed in both domains, and that linguistic competence can be sufficiently variegated to handle gaps between their development.

Studies of phonological acquisition usually take children's productions as the data to be accounted for by phonological analysis, and studies of child phonology in Optimality Theory (OT) usually follow this tradition (see the Introduction to this volume for references to this literature; cf. Hale and Reiss 1998, Hayes this volume). However, there do exist data on the development of perception that appear to demand a phonological treatment. The experimental tasks used in recent research in infant speech perception tap not only phonetic discrimination but also the ability to store contrasts in memory, and to link these phonetic contrasts with meaning distinctions. This research suggests that the representations accessed in these tasks develop gradually, in ways quite parallel to the later growth in complexity of the structures employed in production. The theoretical challenge that arises is to account for the parallels in development across these domains, while at the same time allowing for synchronic differences in whether structures have been acquired productively and receptively.

Optimality Theory is well suited to meet this challenge because its constraints are minimally violable. The activity of a constraint is not an *all or nothing* affair; rather, a constraint is violated only to meet the demands of a higher ranked constraint. I assume that the role of the phonological grammar in perception is to regulate the complexity, or markedness, of representations that are constructed, and/or accessed, on the basis of the acoustic signal. This is done by having markedness constraints evaluate candidate lexical representations for the perceived surface string (though cf. section 4.2 for an alternative approach). Parallels in development across perception and production occur because the same markedness constraints apply in both domains.

A gap between receptive and productive competence arises when the perceptual representations are more marked than the representations evinced in production. I propose to capture this by invoking perception specific faithfulness constraints. When such a constraint ranks above the relevant markedness constraint, complexity of perceptual representation along the dimension regulated by these constraints is permitted. In production, however, the perception faithfulness constraint does not apply, so that the markedness constraint will be obeyed, and the unmarked structure will emerge.

In what follows, I first discuss evidence of segmental and prosodic phonological development in infant speech perception (section 2), and then account for this perceptual development, and its relation to the later development of production, in terms of the proposed model (section 3). Section 4 compares this proposal with three other ways of accounting for perception/production differences in terms of properties of the phonological grammar: the Optimality theoretic precedent to the present model in Smolensky (1996), a 'mixed model' that contains some attributes of the Smolensky (1996) proposal and some of the one presented in section 3, and finally, the dual-lexicon model proposed in the acquisition literature reviewed in Menn and Matthei (1992).

2.   The development of receptive competence

Gaps between perception and production are *almost* a logically necessary aspect of the acquisition process. Linguistic input must, of course, be perceived and given structure before that structure can then be applied in producing new utterances (except for unmarked structures that are available in the initial state). However, such gaps might not exist if grammatical development is in fact monolithic, that is, if the receptive acquisition of a structure entails that it can be immediately employed in production. And even given empirical evidence of perception/production gaps, one might explain them away by claiming that restrictions on receptive and productive ability are entirely separate, so that only one, or the other, is controlled by the grammar.

The aim of this section is to provide some arguments from the study of phonological acquisition against these positions. We shall see that early receptive phonology is subject to restrictions strikingly similar to those governing later production, which argues against treating them as products of entirely separate linguistic subsystems. We shall also see that restrictions on the complexity of the structures employed in perception are overcome well before the parallel restrictions are overcome in production, thus showing that grammatical development is not monolithic across these domains.

Before proceeding any further, an important point of definition must be addressed: what counts as evidence of phonological acquisition in the domain of perception? Given infants' precocious ability categorically to discriminate between almost any of the segmental contrasts of the world's languages (Eimas, Siqueland, Jusczyk, and Vigorito 1971, *et seq.*; see Jusczyk 1997 for an overview), one might conclude that there is precious little to study in terms of perceptual phonological acquisition. But as among others Barton (1980), Werker (1995), Brown and Matthews (1997), and Jusczyk (1997) point out, the tasks employed in these early infant speech perception studies do not require the subjects to use the contrasts either in forming a sound/meaning pairing, or in differentiating sound patterns stored in memory. Both of these characteristics seem to be implicated in a standard definition of what it means for an individual (or a language) to have a phonological contrast. Here, I assume that either storage in memory or pairing with meaning brings a perceived contrast into the realm of the phonological. In section 3.2, I discuss how the proposed model can deal with differences between what can be stored in memory, and what can be paired with meaning.

Of course, tasks that tap the ability of 6–18-month-old infants to use language in these ways are difficult to develop and implement, especially given infants' limited ability and/or inclination to produce meaningful speech, or even to respond to it gesturally. However, Jusczyk (1997) and Werker (1995), as well as Werker and Stager (2000), review an impressive body of recent research that has overcome many of these methodological hurdles. Here I shall discuss just a few of these studies. Section 2.1 addresses the development of segmental structure, while section 2.2 focuses on prosodic development.

2.1   *Segmental constraints in early perception*

A number of studies have investigated the development of what Barton (1980) calls 'phonemic' perception, that is, the ability to pair a segmental phonetic contrast with a meaning difference. Experiments of this type usually require the subjects to choose between two objects forming a minimal pair (e.g., between a ball and a doll). The first of these experiments was conducted in the 1940s by Schvachkin (1948/1973), who proposed that the ability to distinguish various contrasts emerges in a relatively fixed sequence. Barton (1976, 1980) provides an excellent review of research in this tradition (see also now Brown and Matthews 1997, as well as Hallé and Boysson-Bardies 1996 for a somewhat different approach). Barton makes the important point that task demands may well cause an underestimation of children's abilities lexically to represent contrasts. He further emphasises the potential for word frequency to act as a confound in the determination of sequences of acquisition. Therefore, claims about the age at which particular contrasts emerge, as well as about precise developmental sequences, have to be viewed with some caution. However, these studies do converge in suggesting that phonemic perception may well develop gradually, and that the ability to perceive a contrast does not entail the ability to use it to distinguish minimal pairs.

The experiments reported in Stager and Werker (1997) and Werker and Stager (2000) provide a particularly compelling demonstration that pairing sound with meaning can lead to a decrease in sensitivity to phonetic detail. They employ a version of the habituation/dishabituation procedure developed by Werker, Cohen, Lloyd, Casasola, and Stager (1998). Infants are presented with a novel brightly coloured moving object on a video screen, while simultaneously hearing a novel syllable being spoken by a recorded female voice over a loudspeaker. Nonce sound/meaning pairings are used to control for possible effects of familiarity. Each trial lasts 14 seconds, and includes 7 repetitions of the syllable. Trials are repeated until habituation, which is reached when the mean looking time across two sequential trials falls below 65 percent of the mean of the first four trials. Following habituation, the first test trial presents the moving object paired with a different syllable, which is then followed by another trial in which the pairing reverts to the same as in the habituation phase. The order of these two test trials is counterbalanced across subjects. Mean looking time is compared between the trials in which the sound/meaning pairing is switched from the habituation phase, and those in which it is the same. If infants notice the change in the aural stimulus, looking time should be longer in the switch trials than in the same trials.

Results from this procedure with 14-month-olds are presented in (1). When the syllables differ only in the place of articulation of the initial consonant (i.e., [bɪ] vs. [dɪ]), looking time in the same and switch trials does not differ significantly (experiment 1); the error bars indicate Standard Error. When the syllables differ more greatly ([lɪf] vs. [nim]), looking time in the switch trials is significantly higher (experiment 2). To control for the possibility that the infants simply did not perceive the consonantal place distinction in experiment 1, a further experiment was run in which the moving object on the video monitor was replaced by a chequer-board pattern. Since an unbounded display of this type is not likely to be perceived as a nameable object at this stage of development, this removes meaning from the task, and turns it into a pure test of perception. In this case, the infants did respond to a switch in the aural stimulus, as shown by the significantly higher looking time in switch than same trials in experiment 3 (overall lower looking time in this experiment is likely due to the difference in visual displays).

(1)   Results from Stager and Werker (1997)

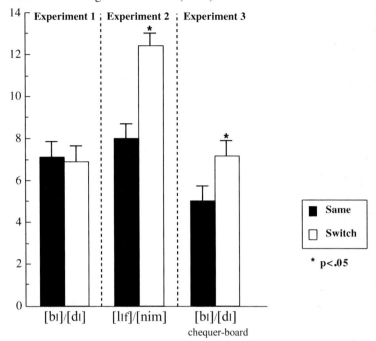

This experiment provides an elegant demonstration that infants can perceive a contrast (experiment 3), yet still be unable to pair it with meaning (experiment 1). Furthermore, by employing looking time as the dependent variable, task complexity is minimised, especially in comparison with the paradigm initiated by Schvachkin (1948/1973). For other experimental methodologies that use looking time as a measure of 'phonemic' discrimination, see Swingley *et al.* (1999), Swingley and Fernald (2000), Hoskins and Golinkoff (2000), as well as Werker *et al.* (2000) for discussion of the differences between the outcomes of the looking time studies.

   Cast in terms of linguistic constructs, this pattern of results leads to the conclusion that at this stage of development, the consonantal place distinction is not encoded in lexical representations, though it is present in phonetic representations. I use a 'C' to denote a representation that does not distinguish between labial and coronal place of articulation, since there is no evidence for exactly how this consonant should be represented (it could be labial, coronal, or lack place specification entirely).

(2)   Phonetic/Surface Representations: [bɪ]   [dɪ]
           Lexical/Underlying Representations: /Cɪ/   /Cɪ/

Experiment 3 shows that at some level of representation, 14-month-olds do encode the place distinction, since they are capable of perceiving it. Here this level is taken to be the Phonetic/Surface level. In experiment 1, however, when sound is paired with meaning, 14-month-olds ignore the place difference. This leads to the conclusion that in lexical representations in which sound is linked with meaning the place distinction is absent. In experiment 2, the syllables are distinguished along some dimension other than consonantal place which is presumably encoded in lexical representations at this stage; this experiment does not allow us to determine which of the many differences between [lɪf] and [nɪm] are lexically encoded.

An alternative account of these results might be that [bɪ] and [dɪ] fail to be given lexical representation because they violate English phonotactics: lexical words in English are minimally bimoraic (i.e., *[bɪ] vs [biy] and [bɪt]). Evidence against this alternative comes from a follow-up study conducted by Pater *et al.* (1998) (see also Pater *et al.* 2001). Using the same methodology as Stager and Werker (1997), they examined whether 14-month-olds would notice a switch in voicing from [bɪn] to [pɪn], as well as a combined place and voice switch [dɪn] vs [pɪn], when the presentation of the sounds was paired with the moving colourful object. They found that the infants showed no evidence of noticing the switch, which indicates that the sub-minimal status of the [bɪ]/[dɪ] pair in Stager and Werker (1997) was not at issue. These results also suggest that the voice distinction, along with place, is typically absent from lexical representations at 14 months of age.

One might accept these results as indicating a developmental difference between what is perceived and what is lexically encoded, and question whether there is in fact any later difference between what is lexically encoded and what is produced. For segmental contrast, there is a significant body of evidence, both anecdotal and experimental, that lexical encoding of contrast does precede production (see section 2.2 on prosody). Anecdotally, there are reports that when children reduce many segmental distinctions, they respond appropriately to minimal pairs containing such distinctions (see, e.g., Smith 1973, Menn and Matthei 1992). These anecdotal reports are confirmed by several experimental studies, including Edwards (1974), Barton (1976), Strange and Broen (1980), and Velleman (1988). While assessing perception and production of a contrast in children of this age encounters a number of methodological hurdles, the weight of the evidence supports the genuineness of the comprehension/production gap. In fact, as the survey in Vihman (1996: 56) emphasises, the main research question in this area is not whether perception precedes production, but whether some neutralisations of adult contrasts in children's production are in fact due to misperception. This research seems to indicate that for some perceptually difficult contrasts (e.g., [θ]/[f]) this is the case, but that for most contrasts, accurate lexical representations do exist for distinctions that are lost in production. And when the difficult-to-perceive contrasts are acquired, they are also accurately represented lexically before being produced (Velleman 1988: 233).

Though many details remain to be filled in through further experimentation, the picture that emerges from the extant research is that the lexical representations that children initially construct are reduced in segmental complexity compared to what they can perceive. And at a later stage, when these lexical representations are enriched, production representations remain to be elaborated. What remains to be determined is the extent to which the restrictions on the segmental complexity of early lexical representations exactly mirror the ones that apply to early productions. In the development of prosody, however, there does exist evidence for the activity of quite similar restrictions on complexity across perception and production.

2.2   *Prosodic constraints in early comprehension*

In production, children learning English, as well as the prosodically similar Dutch, often go through a stage in which words are limited in size to a single initially stressed disyllable, that is, a trochaic foot (Smith 1973, Ingram 1974, Allen and Hawkins 1978, Echols and Newport 1992, Fee 1992, Fikkert 1994, Gerken 1994, Wijnen *et al.* 1994, Demuth 1995, Pater 1997). This stage is illustrated in the following data from Trevor (Compton and Streeter 1977, Pater 1997), in which initially stressed disyllables are produced intact, while finally stressed disyllables lose their stressless initial syllable (Trevor was learning American English, which has retained gallic final stress in *garage*):

(3)   (a) [gaːbɛdʒ]   garbage (1;10.5)   [wæːdɪt]   rabbit (1;9.2)
        (b) [gaːdʒ]   garage (1;10.5)   [wæːf]   giraffe (1;9.1)

In terms of prosodic phonology, the operative restriction on word size is one that allows words to consist only of a single trochaic foot. This restriction is obeyed by the structures in (4a) and (4b), which correspond to Trevor's productions of the words in (3a) and (3b), respectively. Accurate production of the targets in (3b) would require either the creation of an iambic (right-headed) foot (4c), or the adjunction of the initial syllable to the Word level (4d), either of which would exceed the 'Word=Trochaic Foot' limitation.

(4)   (a) W   (b) W   (c) W   (d) W
            | | | /\
            F   F   F   /F
           |\ | Λ   /|
          'σ σ   'σ   σ 'σ   σ 'σ

Jusczyk (1997: 186) notes a striking similarity between such restrictions on early child productions and ones that make their mark on early perception, as evidenced in two studies. Jusczyk *et al.* (1999; cited as in preparation in Jusczyk 1997) used a version of Headturn Preference Procedure to examine children's early word recognition capabilities (see also Smolensky *et al.* this volume for explanation of this methodology). In the experiments I shall discuss here, the subjects are first familiarised with a pair of disyllabic words produced in isolation, with either trochaic or iambic stress (e.g., *kingdom* and *hamlet* or *guitar* and *device*). They then listen to four passages of connected speech, two of which contain six instances of the familiarised words, with the other two passages lacking the familiarised words, but containing six instances of a non-familiarised word of the same prosodic shape. The dependent variable is the infants' orientation time towards the speaker from which the passage is played; orientation time is compared between the sentences containing the familiarised words and those that do not.

Jusczyk *et al.* (1999) tested two groups of subjects: 7.5-month-olds and 10-month-olds. The younger subjects (5a) listened longer to passages containing the familiarised words when the targets were trochaic. However, infants at this age showed no preference for passages containing familiarised words when the targets were iambic. The older group (5b) did listen longer to the familiarised words when they were iambic.

(5)   Results from Jusczyk *et al.* 1999

(a) 7.5 months	*Familiarised*	*Unfamiliar*	*Significant Difference?*
Trochees	*7.92 s (SD 2.77)*	*6.80 s (SD 2.71)*	**Yes** *(t(23) = 2.67, p < .02)*
Iambs	*7.19 s (SD 2.08)*	*7.55 s (SD 2.30)*	**No** *(t(23) = −1.19, p < .25)*
(b) 10 months	*Familiarised*	*Unfamiliar*	*Significant Difference?*
Iambs	*7.48 s (SD 2.18)*	*6.17 s (SD 2.17)*	**Yes** *(t(23) = 4.19, p < .0005)*

The results of this study suggest that trochees are receptively acquired before iambs. Further evidence for this comes from another study using the Headturn Preference Procedure, in which Jusczyk *et al.* (1993) show that 9-month-old English infants listen longer to lists of initially stressed disyllables than to lists containing finally stressed disyllables.

Here we have a considerable age gap between the reductions in complexity evidenced in perception (about 7.5–9 months of age) and those seen in production (around 18–24 months). Although Echols and Newport (1992) do propose that truncations in production are due to the initial syllable being missed in perception, considerable evidence supports the position that children do lexically encode the initial unstressed syllable (Fikkert 1994, Gerken 1994, Paradis, Petitclerc and Genesee 1996, Jusczyk 1997: 186). We can conclude, then, that there is a genuine comprehension/production gap when children are producing truncated words.

The challenge therefore, is to capture the parallels between receptive and productive development (initially simplified representations growing in complexity), while allowing for differences (relatively rich receptive representations at the same time as reduced production). In what follows, I show that minimally violable constraints allow the construction of a model that does precisely that. Since we have relatively clear evidence of perception/production parallels in the constraints governing in prosodic complexity, the present proposal will be illustrated using that example.

3.   Minimal violation across perception and production

3.1   *The proposal*

For simplicity's sake, I shall here employ a single markedness constraint as the driving force behind truncation: WORDSIZE. I do emphasise, though, that the effects of this constraint can be reduced to the interaction of more basic prosodic requirements; see Pater (1997) for discussion. The admittedly stipulative WORDSIZE constraint is given in (6).

(6)   WORDSIZE
        A word is made up of a single trochee

In Pater (1997), truncation results from the satisfaction of this (set of) constraint(s), at the expense of Faithfulness, that is, of preservation of lexical structure. The violated faithfulness constraint is MAX (McCarthy and Prince 1999):

(7)   MAX
        Every segment of the input has a correspondent in the output.

The effect of ranking WORDSIZE above MAX is shown in (8):

(8)   WORDSIZE ≫ MAX: *Production*

L: gərádʒ	WORDSIZE	MAX
☞ S_1 [[gádʒ]$_{Ft}$]$_{PrWd}$		**
S_2 [gə[rádʒ]$_{Ft}$]$_{PrWd}$	*!	

This tableau evaluates two candidate output surface forms, S_1 and S_2, for the input lexical form L. Bracketing represents prosodic structure; the structure of S_1 corresponds to (4b), and S_2 to (4d). The failed candidate S_2, with an initial syllable outside of foot structure corresponds to the adult prosodification (Kager 1989, Pater 2000). It violates two of the stipulations of the WORDSIZE constraint, and is thus marked with a violation. Candidate S_1 violates none of the structural conditions encoded in WORDSIZE, though it does violate MAX twice due to the loss of two Input segments (the [g] is preserved rather than the [r] because of independent sonority-based constraints; see Pater 1997). It would be possible to satisfy WORDSIZE and MAX by placing stress on the initial syllable (e.g., gárədʒ), but this would violate other constraints not under consideration here (i.e., stress faithfulness; Pater 1997). With a ranking of WORDSIZE above MAX the truncated candidate is optimal; in the adult grammar the ranking would be reversed, and the parsing of S₂ would be chosen.

I assume that the role of the phonological grammar in the development of receptive competence is to regulate the structure, and therefore the complexity, of the representation(s) used in perception. This can be seen as an integral part of the learning process: by subjecting incoming data to phonological analysis, the grammar is not only placing limits on the complexity of lexical representations but is also being itself shaped to conform with the regularities of the language. In this view, the grammar intervenes between the incoming data and the stored representation(s), as well as taking its usual place between the stored representation(s) and the concatenated utterance. A diagram of this scenario is presented in (9):

(9) | Perceived form | Stored form | Produced form |
        |---|---|---|

        gərádʒ → Grammar → gərádʒ → Grammar → gərádʒ

In the scenario in (9), the phonetic form of the word *garage* passes through the grammar twice, once in perception, and once in production, and each time is given a perfectly faithful representation.[1] However, with the ranking WORDSIZE ≫ MAX, this would not occur in production, as the initial syllable would be lost. And under the most straightforward interpretation of this scenario, the perception mapping would also yield a reduced output. Such an interpretation interprets the diagram in (9) literally and takes the perceived form as the input to the grammar, and the lexical form as the output. In tableaux for this mapping, I label the input as S to indicate its status as a (perceived) surface form, and the output as L, a stored (lexical) form. With WORDSIZE ≫ MAX, structures are also reduced on their way to lexical representation.

(10)   WORDSIZE ≫ MAX: *Perception*

S: gərádʒ	WORDSIZE	MAX
☞ L₁ [[gádʒ]Ft]PrWd		**
L₂ [gə[rádʒ]Ft]PrWd	*!	

The tableaux in (8) and (10) are identical, except for the labelling in (10) of the input as the surface form, and of the candidate outputs as lexical forms. I make the standard assumption that structural constraints, like WORDSIZE, apply to output forms. The innovation here is that in perception, the surface form is the input to the grammar, and the lexical form the output; this leads to lexical forms being subject to structural constraints in this mapping. The ranking WORDSIZE ≫ MAX thus yields reduced structures in comprehension, corresponding to a stage in receptive development consistent with the evidence that Jusczyk (1997) discusses for English learning infants at the age of 7.5–9 months as outlined in section 2.[2]

It is worth noting that in this account, lexical representations end up being endowed with prosodic structure, since prosodification will be required by the same constraints that force segments to be parsed in surface structure, including those encapsulated in the WORDSIZE constraint. In the generative tradition, predictable stress would typically be absent in the lexicon (cf. Burzio 1996). However, in Optimality Theory, predictability is not accounted for by omitting structure from the lexicon and inserting it in the proper environments by rule. Rather, phonotactic generalisations emerge from the interaction of output markedness constraints and faithfulness constraints (see Prince and Smolensky 1993 on Richness of the Base and Lexicon Optimisation). For example, stress is predictable in a given language because lexically specified stress in any other position would be filtered out by dominant markedness constraints (much like iambs are filtered out by the grammar being considered here). Therefore, there is no general imperative to remove predictable information from the lexicon.

The next stage of development that we need to account for is one in which the WORDSIZE limit is overcome in perception, but not in production. This situation, in which a constraint is obeyed in one domain, but not in another, is paralleled in phonological typology in a class of phenomena that Prince (1993) refers to as instances of *nonuniformity* of constraint application. Nonuniformity encompasses cases of the 'Emergence of the Unmarked' (McCarthy and Prince 1994), in which a markedness constraint is generally violated in a language, but its effects are seen in a particular domain, as well as what we might refer to as the 'Emergence of the Marked', where a markedness constraint is violated only in a particular environment (see, e.g., McCarthy and Prince 1993 on ONSET in Axininca Campa, or McCarthy 2000 on NOCODA in Rotuman).

Nonuniformity is handled straightforwardly in Optimality Theory: a constraint applies nonuniformly because it conflicts with a higher ranked constraint in some environments. Usually, the constraint that stops a markedness constraint from applying uniformly is a faithfulness constraint that applies only in a subset of the environments targeted by the markedness constraint. For example, in McCarthy and Prince's (1994, 1999) analysis of reduplication, markedness constraints apply to both reduplicants and their bases, as well as all other forms in the language. Faithfulness constraints, however, are specified as to whether they apply to the Input–Output mapping, thus targeting bases and other non-reduplicated strings, or to the Base/Reduplicant mapping, in which case they control the extent to which reduplicants resemble their bases. Structural limitations that apply only to reduplicants are derived by having a markedness constraint dominate Base/Reduplicant Faithfulness, but not Input Output Faithfulness:

(11)   Ranking schema for the emergence of the unmarked in reduplication
        FAITH(I-O) ≫ MARKEDNESS ≫ FAITH(B-R)

For example, in Diyari (McCarthy and Prince 1994), the constraints encapsulated in our WORDSIZE dominate Base/Reduplicant faithfulness, forcing a one-foot maximum on the reduplicated string, but are in turn dominated by Input/Output Faithfulness, allowing bases and other lexical words to exceed the one foot limit. Generalising beyond reduplication, nonuniformity is often produced by the following ranking (where FAITH(D_1) and FAITH(D_2) are faithfulness constraints indexed to different domains, and MARKEDNESS is a well-formedness constraint):

(12)   Typical ranking schema for Nonuniformity
        FAITH(D_1) ≫ MARKEDNESS ≫ FAITH(D_2)

Besides reduplication, some of the other domains targeted by special faithfulness constraints include paradigmatic relations (e.g., Benua 1995, 1997, Burzio 1996, Kenstowicz 1996, McCarthy 1998), specific morpheme classes (McCarthy and Prince 1994b, Urbanczyk 1996, Beckman 1998, Struijke 1998) and specific sets of lexemes (Itô and Mester 1999, Pater 2000).

To handle discrepancies between the amount of complexity permitted of structures accessed in perception and production, I propose that faithfulness constraints can be specified to apply either to the Lexical-to-Surface mapping of production – FAITH(LS), or to the Surface-to-Lexical mapping of perception – FAITH(SL). When the Input to the grammar is a Lexical form, FAITH(LS) constraints are relevant, and when the Input to the grammar is a Surface form, FAITH(SL) is at issue. Thus, we now have two versions of MAX, given in (13):

(13)   MAX(LS)
        If the input is a lexical form, every segment of the input has a corre-
        spondent in the output
        MAX(SL)
        If the input is a surface form, every segment of the input has a corre-
        spondent in the output

When initial unstressed syllables begin to be represented in comprehension, this indicates the promotion of MAX(SL) above WORDSIZE. With MAX(LS) resting beneath WORDSIZE, we get the following ranking, which instantiates the nonuniformity schema:

(14)   MAX(SL) ≫ WORDSIZE ≫ MAX(LS)

The following tableau shows the effect of this ranking in perception

(15)   MAX(SL) ≫ WORDSIZE ≫ MAX(LS): *perception*

S: gərádʒ	MAX(SL)	WORDSIZE	MAX(LS)
L₁ [[gádʒ]_{Ft}]_{PrWd}	** !		
☞ L₂ [gə[rádʒ]_{Ft}]_{PrWd}		*	

The initial unstressed syllable is represented in the lexical form, in violation of WORDSIZE, due to the dominance of MAX(SL). In the production mapping, however, MAX(SL) does not apply, and we get truncation as the optimal result:

(16)   MAX(SL) ≫ WORDSIZE ≫ MAX(LS): *production*

L: [gʌ́[rádʒ]_{Ft}]_{PrWd}	MAX(SL)	WORDSIZE	MAX(LS)
☞ S₁ [[gádʒ]_{Ft}]_{PrWd}			**
S₂ [gʌ́[rádʒ]_{Ft}]_{PrWd}		*!	

The pair of tableaux in (15) and (16) represent the stage of development in which children lexically represent initial unstressed syllables, but fail to produce them. The WORDSIZE constraint is violated in comprehension to satisfy higher MAX(SL), but continues to force truncation in production where MAX(SL) fails to apply. The comprehension/production gap is thus dealt with as an instance of minimal constraint violation.

The adult state would be characterised by the re-ranking of MAX(LS) above WORDSIZE, as illustrated by (17):

(17)   MAX(SL), MAX(LS) ≫ WORDSIZE: *adult production*

L: [gə[rádʒ]_{Ft}]_{PrWd}	MAX(SL)	MAX(LS)	WORDSIZE
S₁ [[gádʒ]_{Ft}]_{PrWd}		**!	
☞ S₂ [gə[rádʒ]_{Ft}]_{PrWd}			*

This, of course, abstracts from the rich interactions in the adult grammar between faithfulness and the structural constraints encapsulated in WORDSIZE (Pater 2000).

Summing up, we have seen that the effects of the WORDSIZE constraint change over the course of development due to its ranking with respect to the posited faithfulness constraints:

(18)

Stage 1 – Fully satisfied WORDSIZE: **WORDSIZE** ≫ MAX(SL), MAX(LS)
Stage 2 – Minimally violated WORDSIZE: MAX(SL) ≫ **WORDSIZE** ≫ MAX(LS)
Stage 3 – 'Inactive' WORDSIZE: MAX(SL), MAX(LS) ≫ **WORDSIZE**

In stage 1, the structural constraint is satisfied in both perception and production, due to its dominance over both faithfulness constraints. In stage 2, it is violated only when it conflicts with the requirement of perceived surface structures to be represented lexically, but not in production. And finally, in the last stage, it is violated both in perception and production (though its component constraints do continue to play an active role in the grammar). This account captures the parallels between the restrictions imposed on early perception and on early production by attributing them to a single set of markedness constraints. Differences between the state of development of receptive and productive competence are dealt with in terms of differential rankings of the respective faithfulness constraints with respect to the markedness constraints.

From a learnability perspective, one might ask why the grammar does not immediately converge on the final state (cf. Hale and Reiss 1998). After all, the learner at stage 1 does have evidence that initial unstressed syllables are permitted in the language, and given an algorithm like Error-Driven Constraint Demotion (Tesar and Smolensky 1998), the WORDSIZE constraint should be demoted immediately so that the grammar produces an output matching the adult form. This suggests, I believe, that real-life acquirers of language either require, or wait for, a certain weight of evidence before adjusting rankings (see Boersma's 1998 Gradual Constraint Demotion algorithm for another approach).

3.2   Further articulating the model

In this section, I shall suggest how this model can be further articulated to handle data that are at this point problematic. Using the same Headturn Preference Procedure as in the studies by Jusczyk and colleagues described above, Jusczyk and Aslin (1995) showed that 7.5-month-olds familiarised with words like *cup* and *dog* would listen significantly longer to passages containing those words than to passages containing the minimally different *tup* and *bawg*. This result stands in contrast to the evidence from Stager and Werker (1997) that infants at 14 months of age do not lexically represent consonantal place of articulation differences, as well the results of Hallé and Boysson-Bardies (1996).

Jusczyk and Aslin (1995) are careful to point out that though their results do show that the infants are capable of representing relatively fine phonological detail in memory, they do not show that the infants are capable of linking these minimal phonological distinctions to meaning differences. The apparent contradiction between the results of Jusczyk and Aslin (1995) and Stager and Werker (1997) can be resolved if we acknowledge the existence of two levels of representation. The level of lexical representation links phonological form to meaning, and structures at this level are accessed in the methodology employed by Werker and colleagues. The surface phonological representation, however, is meaning-free, and this is the level accessed by the methodology used by Jusczyk and colleagues.

Under this view, we would need separate faithfulness constraints for the mapping from perceived acoustic representation to the surface representation (FAITH(AS)), as well as the constraints mapping from surface to lexical representation (FAITH(SL)). A ranking of FAITH(AS) ≫ MARKEDNESS ≫ FAITH(SL) would produce richer surface representations than lexical ones, consistent with the divergence between the Jusczyk and Aslin (1995) and Stager and Werker (1997) results. The posited levels of representations, along with the relevant faithfulness constraints, are illustrated in (19).

(19)

Acoustic Representation	Present at birth; non-language-specific
⇓ FAITH(AS) ⇓	
Surface Representation	Language-specific; established at 6–9 months
⇓ FAITH(SL) ⇓	
Lexical Representation	Established at 11–18 months
⇓ FAITH(LS) ⇓	
Surface Representation	Established at 18–24 months

Each of these levels of representation is elaborated sequentially through development, and the extant literature on segmental perception and production provides a relatively clear outline of this process (see Werker and Pegg 1992, Jusczyk 1997 for relevant discussion). The acoustic representation is assumed to be relatively richly specified even in the infant's earliest exposure to language; this representation is the one tapped by experiments showing infants' ability to discriminate almost any contrast from among the world's languages (see Jusczyk 1997 on the controversy about whether this level of representation is language-specific or not). The surface representation is elaborated once the relevant FAITH(AS) constraints are promoted above the relevant MARKEDNESS constraints after some amount of exposure to the language being learned (20b); this corresponds to the language-specific perception that emerges between 6 and 9 months. Learning of sound/meaning pairings between around 11–18 months would force the elaboration of lexical representations and the consequent ranking of FAITH(SL) above markedness constraints (20c). Appearance of contrasts in production of meaningful words in the period between about 18 and 24 months would entail the ranking of FAITH(LS) above markedness (20d).[3]

(20) (a) MARKEDNESS ≫ FAITH(AS), FAITH(SL), FAITH(LS)
      (b) FAITH(AS) ≫ MARKEDNESS ≫ FAITH(SL), FAITH(LS)
      (c) FAITH(AS), FAITH(SL) ≫ MARKEDNESS ≫ FAITH(LS)
      (d) FAITH(AS), FAITH(SL), FAITH(LS) ≫ MARKEDNESS

Here, one might ask whether there is any reason acquisition should follow this particular path. Why could not FAITH(LS) be ranked above MARKEDNESS before FAITH(AS) and FAITH(SL), yielding productive competence ahead of receptive? The answer, I believe, lies in the nature of the triggering evidence: in order for the structures that would trigger re-ranking of a FAITH(LS) constraint over MARKEDNESS to exist in the lexical forms, the analogous FAITH(SL) constraint must already dominate MARKEDNESS.

4.   Comparison with other approaches

4.1   Smolensky (1996)

The present proposal borrows much from the one in Smolensky (1996) (see also Ohala 1996 for a similar, independently developed approach). There too, a single Optimality theoretic grammar is invoked in both production and comprehension, and is involved in the latter in evaluating candidate lexical forms for a fixed surface form. However, in Smolensky's proposal, the choice between candidate lexical forms is made solely on the basis of compliance to faithfulness, rather than because of differences in markedness violations. This is because the choice of lexical form is irrelevant to the assessment of markedness violations.

Taking the case of truncation discussed in the previous section, I provide in (21) examples of competing candidates in the production and comprehension mappings, and an indication of which is optimal under the WORDSIZE ≫ FAITH ranking.

(21) WORDSIZE ≫ FAITH
      Candidates competing in production:
          (a) L: /gərádʒ/   S: [gərádʒ]   Structure: [gə[rádʒ]_Ft]_PrWd
      ☞ (b) L: /gərádʒ/   S: [gádʒ]   Structure: [g<ər>ádʒ]_Ft]_PrWd
      Candidates competing in comprehension:
          (c) L: /gádʒ/   S: [gərádʒ]   Structure: [gə[rádʒ]_Ft]_PrWd
      ⇒ (d) L: /gərádʒ/   S: [gərádʒ]   Structure: [gə[rádʒ]_Ft]_PrWd

In production, the WORDSIZE violation in (21a) is fatal, because of the existence of candidate (21b), which satisfies WORDSIZE at the expense of faithfulness violations, here indicated in the structure in terms of unparsed segments enclosed in '< >' (Smolensky 1996 assumes the Parse/Fill version of Faithfulness of Prince and Smolensky 1993). In comprehension, candidates sharing the surface form [gərádʒ] compete, and a mapping like (21b) is therefore not in the candidate set. Since any candidate with the surface form [gərádʒ] will necessarily violate WORDSIZE, the decision falls down to the faithfulness constraints. Here a constraint against insertion between lexical and surface form would choose (21d) over (21c); inserted segments are italicised.[4] Markedness constraints might choose between possible structural interpretations of a surface string (using this case as an example, they would choose between leaving the initial syllable outside of foot structure and creating an iambic foot; i.e., between 21c and 21d). However, the mapping between the underlying and surface form will always be purely faithful, as dictated by the faithfulness constraints.

This model of establishing lexical representations does successfully capture a situation in which comprehension is advanced relative to production, as it is intended to. However, because only faithfulness determines the choice of lexical forms in the comprehension mapping, it is incapable of dealing with a situation in which phonological comprehension is anything less than perfect. As a result, the development of comprehension must be taken to be purely extra-grammatical. Not only is this implausible but it would entail much duplication of analytic effort and machinery, in so far as early comprehension and early production, and grammars in general, are subject to similar restrictions, as the evidence reviewed in section 2 of this chapter suggests they are.[5]

4.2   A mixed model

In the basic model of the development of receptive competence proposed in section 3.1 above, markedness constraints influence comprehension because the lexical form is taken to be the output that they assess; it denies the standard equivalence between 'lexical form' and 'input', and between 'surface form' and 'output'. It is possible, however, to recast the proposal in such a way as to restore that equivalence, and in so doing, create a model that incorporates some aspects of the proposal in the present chapter and some of the one in Smolensky (1996). The key is in recognising, as in section 3.2, that the perceived string is not simply equivalent to a phonological surface string; rather, the phonological surface string must be derived from the acoustic-phonetic representation. This could be done by taking the acoustic–phonetic string as input to the grammar, as suggested in section 3.2. However, let us instead follow the standard assumption that grammatical inputs are strictly equivalent to lexical forms. The following, then, would be potential grammatical mappings for the perceived acoustic–phonetic string [gərádʒ]. Note that we are dropping Smolensky's (1996) premiss that the surface strings must faithfully represent the phonetic form:

(22)   Acoustic–phonetic   Surface   Lexical
        (a) gərádʒ   [gádʒ]ꜰₜ]ₚᵣWd   /gádʒ/
        (b) gərádʒ   [gə[rádʒ]ꜰₜ]ₚᵣWd   /gərádʒ/

Markedness constraints would prefer (22a); this would be the correct outcome for the earliest stages of acquisition, in which comprehension representations are simplified. To make (22b) optimal, it must be the case that there are constraints that conflict with markedness besides ordinary lexical–surface faithfulness, which are fully satisfied in both (22a) and (22b). Here we need to allow at least a limited grammatical status to acoustic–phonetic representations, as the targets of FAITH(AS) constraints. Such constraints are in a sense analogous to Output–Output constraints (see, e.g., McCarthy and Prince 1995, 1999, Benua 1997) in demanding identity between the surface form and some non-input form. The rankings that generate the three stages of development would be identical to those proposed in section 3.1, with the exception of the substitution of FAITH(AS) for FAITH(SL); faithfulness between lexical and surface forms is now governed by a single set of constraints. Generalising over markedness and faithfulness constraints, the schema for the stages of acquisition would be as follows:

(23)   Stage 1: MARKEDNESS ≫ FAITH(AS), FAITH(LS)
        Stage 2: FAITH(AS) ≫ MARKEDNESS ≫ FAITH(LS)
        Stage 3: FAITH(AS), FAITH(LS) ≫ MARKEDNESS

Stage 1 is the schema for reduced representations in comprehension and production, stage 2 for faithful comprehension and reduced production, and stage 3 for faithful comprehension and production. In (24) I provide a tableau for perception at stage 1, using the structural constraint WORDSIZE, along with general 'FAITH' constraints that are violated by any change to the segmental makeup of a string:

(24)   WORDSIZE ≫ FAITH(AS), FAITH(LS): *perception*

Acoustic–phonetic form: gərádʒ	WORDSIZE	FAITH (AS)	FAITH (LS)
☞ (a) L: /gádʒ/ ~ S: [[gádʒ]ꜰₜ]ₚᵣWd		*	
(b) L: /gərádʒ/ ~ S: [gə[rádʒ]ꜰₜ]ₚᵣWd	*!		
(c) L: /gádʒ/ ~ S: [gə[rádʒ]ꜰₜ]ₚᵣWd	*!		*

At the earliest stage of acquisition, words are limited to a single trochaic foot, in comprehension as well as production. Here this limitation is enforced by having the structural constraints apply to the surface phonological form constructed on the basis of the perceived acoustic–phonetic representation.

Following McCarthy and Prince (1999), I take the candidates supplied by Gen to be input~output pairs (= lexical~surface). Given by the perceptual system is the form gərádʒ. Because of the ranking of FAITH(AS) beneath WORDSIZE, the reduced structure (24a) is preferred over the faithful representations of the acoustic–phonetic string in (24b) and (24c). Note that candidate (24c) is harmonically bounded by (24b); no ranking of these constraints will ever make it optimal. This points to the fact that this model cannot produce lexical representations that are simplified relative to surface ones; the consequences of this will be taken up below. For now, the important point is that this model does allow for initially impoverished comprehension, and subsequent development, unlike the proposal in Smolensky (1996).

The subsequent development is captured by the re-ranking of FAITH(AS) above WORDSIZE; with FAITH(LS) remaining beneath the markedness constraint, we produce the comprehension/production gap:

(25)   FAITH (AS) ≫ WORDSIZE ≫ FAITH (LS): *perception*

Acoustic–phonetic form: gərádʒ	FAITH (AS)	WORDSIZE	FAITH (LS)
(a) L: /gádʒ/ ~ S: [[gádʒ]ₚₜ]ₚᵣwd	*!		
☞ (b) L: /gərádʒ/ ~ S: [gə[rádʒ]ₚₜ]ₚᵣwd		*	

In comprehension, the marked prosodic structure is now created, as in (24b), in order to satisfy the higher ranked FAITH(AS). In production, though, the continued dominance of WORDSIZE over FAITH(LS) leads to the emergence of the unmarked structure:

(26)   FAITH(AS) ≫ WORDSIZE ≫ FAITH(LS): *production*

L = /gərádʒ/	FAITH (AS)	WORDSIZE	FAITH (LS)
(a) L: /gərádʒ/ ~ S: [gə[rádʒ]ₚₜ]ₚᵣwd		*!	
☞ (b) L: /gərádʒ/ ~ S: [[gádʒ]ₚₜ]ₚᵣwd			*

In production, the lexical form is given, and the candidate set is thus restricted to mappings that contain it. Candidate (26b) is chosen due to its satisfaction of WORDSIZE; here it satisfies FAITH(AS) vacuously, since working memory contains no trace of the adult pronunciation. Interestingly, this suggests an approach to the greater pronunciation accuracy often observed in imitation: if the adult acoustic–phonetic representation were still in memory, FAITH(AS) would target the surface forms in production, and would favour faithful pronunciations.

This alternative model retains the key element of the proposal presented earlier in this chapter: structural constraints influence the outcome of comprehension. In deriving the structure of lexical forms from surface forms without the influence of markedness, and in treating the 'input~output' mapping as equivalent to a 'lexical~surface' mapping it is consistent with Smolensky

(1996), and more generally, with standard assumptions in Optimality Theory. However, a possible shortcoming of this compromise proposal comes from the immunity of lexical forms to markedness constraints. Because of this, it is impossible to articulate this model so as to allow for lexical representations that are impoverished relative to surface ones (cf. section 3.2). The choice between this approach, and the one suggested in sections 3.1 and 3.2, seems to hinge on whether restrictions on the complexity of lexical representations are truly phonologically determined, which can only be ascertained through further empirical research (see Pater *et al.* 2001 for some discussion).

4.3   The dual-lexicon model

The present proposal might appear to be simply an Optimality theoretic recasting of the dual-lexicon model (see, e.g., Menn and Matthei 1992). Where that model posits separate representations for production and perception, and different constraints on what is permitted at each level, here we have separate faithfulness constraints for each domain.

There are some important differences, however. First of all, the present model is constrained by having a single set of markedness constraints operating across both domains. There are two advantages to this. The obvious one is that in allowing levels to differ only in ranking of faithfulness constraints, limits are placed on the extent to which they can diverge (see Benua 1997, and Itô and Mester 1999 for related discussion). However, a more important difference in the present context is that knowledge gained from receptive ranking of markedness constraints is directly transferred to production. For example, when a child learning Dutch or English receptively learns that feet are left-headed trochees rather than right-headed iambs, a constraint favouring the former type of foot would be ranked over one favouring the latter. This ranking of markedness constraints would not have to be relearned in the production grammar (see Fikkert 1994 for evidence of productive imposition of trochaic form).

In addition, this approach avoids a fatal flaw in the dual-lexicon model, pointed out by Menn and Matthei (1992: 223). They note that there is evidence of processes that apply both within and across words (Donahue 1986, Stemberger 1988, Matthei 1989). In the dual-lexicon model, the stored output representation is the target of production constraints, which leads to an inability to deal with between-word processes.

(27)   we must assume that the same constraints are operating both within and across words. We might, as Matthei (1989) proposed, move the output constraints from the output lexicon to somewhere else – but where? And if we do that, how do we specify the way that those constraints will interact with the lexicon to create the child's output representations?

In terms of Optimality Theory, the answers to these questions are now obvious: output constraints are in the grammar, and they interact with the lexicon through the mediation of faithfulness constraints.

5.   Conclusions

This proposal follows Smolensky (1996) in using Optimality Theory to model developing receptive and productive phonology with a single grammar. Where it differs is in that the grammar constrains early comprehension as well as early production, instead of simply mapping perceived surface forms to identical lexical forms and thus making receptive phonology flawless from the outset of acquisition.

While it might seem obvious that comprehension does in fact develop, current evidence from developmental speech perception further suggests that receptive competence unfolds in a manner parallel to the later development of productive competence, with similar initial unmarked segmental and prosodic structures in the two domains.

These parallels can be captured by having a single set of structural constraints that applies to both the produced surface form as well as the receptively created and accessed lexical form. With these constraints ranked over faithfulness constraints, the initial state of the grammar admits only structurally unmarked representations. Receptive competence develops by the promotion of comprehension specific faithfulness constraints above the structural constraints, as well as the establishment of rankings between the structural constraints. Productive competence is allowed to lag behind, however, by the lower rank of the production specific faithfulness constraints, whose later promotion is indicated by the evidence that relatively complete lexical representations underlie simplified productions.

From the perspective of phonological acquisition, one might question whether receptive development is in fact subject to all and only the constraints that are later seen in production. Indeed, a strong version of this proposal would hold exactly that, and it is worth maintaining that position in the absence of evidence to the contrary. It is likely that some structural constraints are comprehension or production specific, but at this point, the extent to which receptive and productive development converge on the same constraints remains an empirical question. This question seems independently interesting, since in attempting to answer it, we shall likely forge a deeper understanding of what the shared grammatical core is between domains, as well as where they diverge.

Beyond the domain of first language acquisition there is also a growing body of evidence that shows that phonotactic restrictions play a role in adult speech perception (Dupoux *et al.* 1999, Moreton 1999, 2000). This can be taken as additional support for the central thesis of this chapter: that in perception, markedness constraints do intervene between the raw acoustic signal and the lexical representation.

NOTES

* Portions of this chapter were presented at *From Speech Perception to Word Learning: A Workshop*, at the University of British Columbia, as well as in colloquia at Utrecht University, the Max Planck Institute for Psycholinguistics, Nijmegen, University of Groningen, SUNY Stonybrook, and the University of Massachusetts, Amherst. Special thanks to Janet Werker for inviting me to speak on these issues at the workshop, and for much helpful subsequent discussion, as well as to Paul Smolensky for extensive comments on an earlier version of this chapter. Conversations with Ellen Broselow, Angela Carpenter, Suzanne Curtin, Della Chambless, Anne Cutler, Lyn Frazier, Bruce Hayes, Peter Jusczyk, René Kager, John Kingston, Clara Levelt, John McCarthy, Steve Parker, Doug Pulleyblank, Chris Stager, and Wim Zonneveld also helped to clarify my thoughts on the topic. This research was supported by SSHRC postdoctoral fellowship 756-96-0521 1 and SSHRC research grant 410-98-1595, for which I am grateful.

1. One might instead posit a more indirect link between performance and grammar, as suggested by the linking hypotheses of Smolensky *et al.* (this volume). There do not seem to be any obvious barriers to implementing the present proposal in such terms; one would simply need a means for the rank of faithfulness constraints to vary depending on the use to which the grammar is being put.

2. Interestingly, for one account of Jusczyk *et al.*'s (1999) findings to go through, we must assume that the onset is at least sometimes borrowed from the initial syllable. Recall that when the 7.5-month-olds are trained on *guitar*, they do not listen longer to *guitar* passages. We might assume that in familiarisation, a lexical form is created which is then matched against the passage. If the infants stored [tɑr], then this would match perfectly with the stressed portion of *guitar.* And indeed, when 7.5-month-olds are trained on *tar*, they *do* listen longer to *guitar* passages. If, however, [gɑr] is the lexicalised form, then it does not match the stressed syllable of *guitar* (due perhaps to FAITH-based preference for dorsal over coronal). I should emphasise, however, that my strategy in this chapter is not to provide such a direct account of the experimental evidence. Rather, I make the minimal inference from these experiments that trochaic forms are acquired before iambic ones, and then I provide a grammatical account of the stage of development at which only trochees are present.

3. In so far as babbling is taken to interact with the grammar, one might hypothesise that constraints mapping perceived surface representations to produced surface representations would be at issue.

4. Under a Parse/Fill theory, this candidate could not even be generated, since inserted segments are empty syllabic nodes, rather than featurally specified phones (unless phonetic interpretation happened to supply a [ə] and [r] as the default vowel and consonant, respectively). This would be another difficulty in producing reductions in structure in lexical structures under the account presented in Smolensky (1996).

5. Similar difficulties also face the alternative to Smolensky's model presented in Hale and Reiss (1998), where an initial ranking of Faithfulness over Markedness is posited

to yield initially rich lexical representations. In this proposal though, not only is it impossible to portray the development of receptive competence but the development of production is also explicitly claimed to be extra-grammatical. One is therefore led to wonder what empirical domain in acquisition would be considered under the provenance of grammar; while Hale and Reiss suggest that perceptual experiments might be used to tap phonological competence, it is not clear whether any of those reviewed in the present chapter would be considered suitable.

References

Allen, G. and S. Hawkins (1978). The development of phonological rhythm. In A. Bell and J. Hooper (eds.) *Syllables and Segments*. New York: Elsevier-North-Holland.

Barton, D. (1976). *The Role of Perception in the Acquisition of Phonology*. Ph.D. dissertation, Stanford University. Distributed 1978, Indiana University Linguistics Club. (1980). Phonemic perception in children. In Yeni-Komshian *et al.* (eds.). 97–116.

Beckman, J. (1998). *Positional Faithfulness*. Ph.D. dissertation, University of Massachusetts, Amherst.

Benua, L. (1995). Identity effects in morphological truncation. *University of Massachusetts Occasional Papers in Linguistics 18: Papers in Optimality Theory*. Amherst, Graduate Linguistic Studies Association (GLSA), University of Massachusetts.

(1997). *Transderivational Identity: Phonological Relations between words*. Ph.D. dissertation, University of Massachusetts, Amherst.

Brown, C. and J. Matthews (1997). The role of feature geometry in the development of phonemic contrasts. In S. J. Hannahs and M. Young-Scholten (eds.) *Focus on Phonological Acquisition*. Philadelphia: Benjamins.

Boersma, P. (1998). *Functional Phonology*. Ph.D. dissertation, University of Amsterdam.

Burzio, L. (1996). Surface constraints versus underlying representation. In J. Durand and B. Laks (eds.) *Current Trends in Phonology: Models and Methods*. Manchester: European Studies Research Institute, University of Salford.

Compton, A. J. and M. Streeter (1977). Child phonology: data collection and preliminary analyses. In *Papers and Reports on Child Language Development* 7. Palo Alto, Calif.: Stanford University.

Demuth, K. (1995). Markedness and the development of prosodic structure. In *NELS* **25**. Amherst: GLSA, University of Massachusetts.

Donahue, M. (1986). Phonological constraints on the emergence of two-word utterances. *Journal of Child Language* **13**. 209–218.

Drachman, G. (1976). Child language and language change: a conjecture and some refutations. In J. Fisiak (ed.) *Recent Developments in Historical Phonology*. The Hague: Mouton.

Dupoux, E., K. Kakehi, Y. Hirose, C. Pallier, and J. Mehler (1999). Epenthetic vowels in Japanese: a perceptual illusion? *Journal of Experimental Psychology: Human Perception and Performance* **25**. 1568–1578.

Echols, C. and E. Newport (1992). The role of stress and position in determining first words. *Language Acquisition* **2**. 189–220.

Edwards, M. L. (1974). Perception and production in child phonology: the testing of four hypotheses. *Journal of Child Language* **1**. 205–219.

Eimas, P., E. Siqueland, P. Jusczyk, and J. Vigorito (1971). Speech perception in infants. *Science* **171**. 303–306.

Fee, J. (1992). Exploring the minimal word in early phonological acquisition. In C. Dyck, J. Ghomeshi, and T. Wilson (eds.) *Proceedings of the 1992 Annual Conference of the Canadian Linguistics Association*.

Fikkert, P. (1994) *On the Acquisition of Prosodic Structure*. Ph.D. dissertation, Holland Institute of Generative Linguistics, Leiden University.

Gerken, L. (1994). A metrical template account of children's weak syllable omissions from multisyllabic words. *Journal of Child Language* **21**. 564–584.

Hale, M. and C. Reiss (1998). Formal and empirical arguments concerning phonological acquisition. *LI* **29**. 656–683.

Hallé, P. and B. de Boysson-Bardies (1996). The format of representation of recognised words in infants' early receptive lexicon. *Infant Behavior and Development* **19**. 463–481.

Hayes, B. (this volume). Phonological acquisition in Optimality Theory: the early stages.

Hoskins, S. and R. Golinkoff (2000). Novel minimal pair discrimination in 31–35-month-olds. MS., University of Delaware.

Ingram, D. (1974). Phonological rules in young children. *Journal of Child Language* **1**. 49–64.

Itô, J., Y. Kitagawa, and A. Mester (1996). Prosodic faithfulness and Correspondence: evidence from a Japanese Argot. *Journal of East Asian Linguistics* **5**.

Itô, J. and A. Mester (1999). The phonological lexicon. In N. Tsujimura (ed.) *The Handbook of Japanese Linguistics*. Oxford: Blackwell.

Jusczyk, P. (1997). *The Discovery of Spoken Language*. Cambridge, Mass.: MIT Press.

Jusczyk. P. and R. Aslin (1995). Infants' detection of sound patterns of words in fluent speech. *Cognitive Psychology* **29**. 1–23.

Jusczyk, P., A. Cutler, and N. Redanz (1993). Preference for the predominant stress pattern of English words. *Child Development* **64**. 675–687.

Jusczyk, P., D. Houston, and M. Newsome (1999). The beginnings of word segmentation in English-learning infants. *Cognitive Psychology* **39**. 159–207.

Kager, R. (1989). *A Metrical Theory of Stress and Destressing in English and Dutch*. Dordrecht: Foris.

Kenstowicz, M. (1996). Base-identity and uniform exponence: alternatives to cyclicity. In J. Durand and B. Laks (eds.) *Current Trends in Phonology: Models and Methods*. Manchester: European Studies Research Institute, University of Salford.

Matthei, E. (1989). Crossing boundaries: more evidence for phonological constraints on multi-word utterances. *Journal of Child Language* **16**. 41–54.

McCarthy, J. (1998). Morpheme structure constraints and paradigm occultation. *Proceedings of CLS 32*. Chicago: Chicago Linguistics Society.

(2000). The prosody of phase in Rotuman. *NLLT* **18**. 147–197.

McCarthy, J. and A. Prince (1993). Prosodic morphology I: constraint interaction and satisfaction. MS., University of Massachusetts, Amherst, and Rutgers University, New Brunswick, N.J. [Forthcoming, MIT Press]

(1994). The emergence of the unmarked: optimality in prosodic morphology. *NELS* **25**. Amherst: GLSA, University of Massachusetts.

(1999). Faithfulness and identity in prosodic morphology. In R. Kager, H. van der Hulst, and W. Zonneveld (eds.) *The Prosody Morphology Interface*. Cambridge: Cambridge University Press. 218–309.

Menn, L. and E. Matthei (1992). The 'two-lexicon' approach to child phonology: looking back, looking ahead. In C. A. Ferguson, L. Menn, and C. Stoel-Gammon (eds.) *Phonological Development: Models, Research, Implications*. Timonium, Md.: York Press.

Moreton, E. (1999). Evidence for phonotactic grammar in speech perception. *Proceedings of the 14th International Congress of Phonetic Sciences*. San Francisco.

(2000). *Phonological Grammar in Speech Perception*. Ph.D. dissertation, University of Massachusetts.

Ohala, D. (1996). *Cluster Reduction and Constraints in Acquisition*. Ph.D dissertation, University of Arizona.

Paradis, J., S. Petitclerc, and F. Genesee (1996). Word truncation in early child language: perception or production? MS., McGill University.

Pater, J. (1997). Minimal violation and phonological development. *Language Acquisition* **6: 3**. 201–253.

(2000). Nonuniformity in English stress: the role of ranked and lexically specific constraints. *Phonology* **17**. 237–274.

Pater, J. and J. Paradis (1996). Truncation without templates in child phonology. In *Proceedings of the 20th annual Boston University Conference on Language Development*. Somerville, Mass.: Cascadilla Press.

Pater, J., C. Stager, and J. Werker (1998). Additive effects of phonetic distinctions in word learning. In *Proceedings: 16th International Congress on Acoustics and 135th Meeting Acoustical Society of America*. 2049–2050.

(2001). The lexical acquisition of phonological contrasts. MS., University of Massachusetts, Amherst, and University of British Columbia.

Prince, A. (1993). Minimal violation. Handout of talk presented at ROW-1, Rutgers University, New Brunswick, N.J.

Prince, A. and P. Smolensky (1993). Optimality Theory: constraint interaction in generative grammar. MS., Rutgers University and University of Colorado, Boulder. [Forthcoming, MIT Press]

Shvachkin, N. Kh. (1973). The development of phonemic speech perception in early childhood. In C. A. Ferguson and D. I. Slobin (eds.) *Studies of Child Language Development*. New York: Holt, Rinehart and Winston.

Smith, N. (1973). *The Acquisition of Phonology: a Case Study*. Cambridge: Cambridge University Press.

Smolensky, P. (1996). On the comprehension/production dilemma in child language. *LI* **27**. 720–731.

Smolensky, P., L. Davidson, and P. Jusczyk (this volume). The initial and final states: theoretical implications and experimental explorations of Richness of the Base.

Stager, C. and J. Werker (1997). Infants listen for more phonetic detail in speech perception than in word-learning tasks. *Nature* **388**. 381–382.

Stemberger, J. (1988). Between word processes in child phonology. *Journal of Child Language* **15**. 39–61.

Steriade, D. (1995). Positional neutralization. MS., University of California, Los Angeles.

Strange, W. and P. A. Broen (1980). Perception and production of approximant consonants by 3-year-olds: a first study. In Yeni-Komshian *et al.* (eds.). 117–154.

Struijke, C. (1998). Reduplicant and output TETU in Kwakwala: a new model of correspondence. *Papers in Phonology, University of Maryland Working Papers in
Linguistics* **7**. 150–178.

Swingley, D. and R. Aslin (2000). Spoken word recognition and lexical representation
in very young children. *Cognition* **72**. 147–166.

Swingley, D., J. Pinto, and A. Fernald (1999). Continuous processing in word recognition
at 24 months. *Cognition* **71**. 73–108.

Tesar, B. and P. Smolensky (1998). The learnability of Optimality Theory. *LI* **29**. 229–
268.

Urbanczyk, S. (1996). *Patterns of Reduplication in Lushootseed.* Ph.D. dissertation,
Amherst: University of Massachusetts.

Werker, J. (1995). Age-related changes in cross-language speech perception: standing at
the crossroads. In W. Strange (ed.) *Speech Perception and Linguistics Experience:
Issues in Cross-Language Research.* Timonium: York Press.

Werker, J. and C. Stager (2000). Developmental changes in infant speech perception and
early word learning: is there a link? In J. Pierrehumbert and M. Broe (eds.) *Papers
in Laboratory Phonology V: Acquisition and the Lexicon.* Cambridge: Cambridge
University Press.

Werker, J., L. Cohen, V. Lloyd, M. Casasola, and C. Stager (1998). Acquisition of
word-object associations by 14-month old infants. *Developmental Psychology* **34**.
1289–1309.

Werker, J., K. Corcoran, C. Fennell, and C. Stager (2000). Infants' ability to learn
phonetically similar words: effects of age and vocabulary size. MS., University of
British Columbia.

Wijnen, F., E. Krikhaar, and E. den Os (1994). The nonrealization of unstressed elements in children's utterances: evidence for a rhythmic constraint. *Journal of Child
Language* **21**. 59–83.

Yeni-Komshian, G., J. Kavanagh, and C. Ferguson (eds.) (1980). *Child Phonology,
Vol. 2: Perception.* New York: Academic Press.

8   Learning phonotactic distributions*

Alan Prince and Bruce Tesar

1.   The problem

All languages have distributional regularities: patterns which restrict what sounds can appear where, including nowhere, as determined by local syntagmatic factors independent of any particular morphemic alternations. Early Generative Phonology tended to slight the study of distributional relations in favour of morphophonemics, perhaps because word-relatedness phonology was thought to be more productive of theoretical depth, reliably leading the analyst beyond the merely observable. But over the last few decades it has become clear that much morphophonemics can be understood as accommodation to phonotactic requirements, e.g., Kisseberth (1970), Sommerstein (1974), Kiparsky (1980), Goldsmith (1993), etc. A German-like voice-neutralising alternation system resolves rapidly when the phonotactics of obstruent voicing is recognised. And even as celebrated a problem in abstractness and opacity as Yawelmani Yokuts vocalic phonology turns on a surface-visible asymmetry in height-contrasts between long and short vowels.[1]

Distributions require nontrivial learning: the data do not explicitly indicate the nature, or even the presence, of distributional regularities, and every distributional statement goes beyond what can be observed as fact, the 'positive evidence'. From seeing X in this or that environment the learner must somehow conclude 'X can *only* appear under these conditions and *never* anywhere else' – when such a conclusion is warranted.

A familiar learning hazard is immediately encountered. Multiple grammars can be consistent with the same data, grammars which are empirically distinct in that they make different predictions about other forms not represented in the data. If learning is based upon only positive evidence, then the simple *consistency* of a grammatical hypothesis with all the observed data will not guarantee that the hypothesis is correct, even when adequate data are provided. This problem is typically characterised in terms of relationships among grammars. If one grammar generates all the observable forms licensed by another grammar along with yet other forms, then it is tricky to tell them apart, though crucial to do so. All positive data that support the less-inclusive grammar also support the broader grammar. More precisely, no fact consistent with narrower grammar can ever be *inconsistent* with the predictions of its more-inclusive competitor, even though the broader grammar also allows forms not generable – ruled out (negative evidence!) – by the less-inclusive grammar. This is the *Subset Problem*, familiar from the work of Angluin (1980) and Baker (1979). If a learner mistakenly adopts the superset grammar when the subset grammar is correct, no possible positive evidence can contradict the learner's adopted but incorrect hypothesis. The misstep of choosing a superset grammar makes the subset grammar unreachable (from positive evidence). By contrast, if on the basis of the same ambiguous evidence the subset grammar is chosen, positive evidence – observable forms licensed by one grammar but not the other – will exist to move the learner along when the superset grammar is the actual target.

As an abstract example of the problem, consider two languages: $A = \{a^n, n \geq 1\}$ which consists of every string of *a*s and $AB = \{a^n b^m, n \geq 1, m \geq 0\}$, which consists of any strings of *a*s possibly followed by a string of *b*s. A is a proper subset of AB. Suppose that the target language for learning is A. If, upon encountering data from the target language (strings of *a*s), the learner should guess that the language is AB, then there will be no positive evidence contradicting this hypothesis, and the learner is stuck in error. Now consider the situation in which the target of learning is AB. If the learner happens to encounter data consisting only of strings of *a*s, and guesses A, an error has also been made. But here positive evidence exists which contradicts this hypothesis – namely strings containing *b*s – and when any such are encountered, the grammar A can be rejected as inconsistent with observation.

To see the relevance to phonotactic learning, consider the case of complementary distribution. Imagine a language in which *s* and *š* both appear: what is the learner to conclude if the first encounter with *š* occurs in a word like *šite*? Suppose that as in Nupe and (Yamato) Japanese and many other languages, *š* can in fact only occur before *i*. The overhasty generaliser who decides that *š* occurs freely can never be liberated from this notion, because every further *š*-word that comes in is entirely consistent with it. The negative fact that *š* fails to occur before *a, e, o, u* simply does not register on the positive-minded learner. If the learner had opted for a narrower grammar – say one in which *š* is derivable by palatalisation of *s* – not only would the irrecoverable overgeneralisation have been avoided, but there would be no difficulty in correcting the hypothesis, should the target language turn out upon further sampling to be more like English: observation of words like *šem* and *šam* would refute the subset grammar.

Within the tradition of language learnability work, the standard response to the subset problem is the *Subset Principle* of Berwick (1982): whenever more than one language is consistent with the data, and there is a subset relation between the languages, always select the grammar for the subset language.

Table 1. *Hypothetical parametric system: the subset/superset implications of P1 depend upon the settings of P2 and P3 (Note: a-f are observable forms, not entire structural descriptions)*

P1	P2	P3	Language	Subset relations
−	−	−	$\{a,b,c,d\}$	*Neither subset of other*
+	−	−	$\{a,b,e,f\}$	
−	+	−	$\{a,b\}$	$-P1 \subseteq +P1$
+	+	−	$\{a,b,e\}$	
−	−	+	$\{a,c,d\}$	$+P1 \subseteq -P1$
+	−	+	$\{a,d\}$	

That way, a grammar is not selected which *overgenerates*, that is, generates forms which are illicit when the target language is the subset language.

It might seem that the subset principle is the last word to be had on the issue: include the step in any learning algorithm, and the subset problem will be avoided. However, implementation is far from trivial. Empirical linguistic reality forces linguistic theories to permit large numbers of possible grammars, and this makes it impractical to equip a learner with an exhaustive lookup-table indicating subset relations between the languages generated by each and every pair of grammars. Given the combinatorial structure of modern linguistic theories, such a table would threaten to eclipse in size the linguistic system giving rise to the grammars. Linguistic theory aims to ease the learning problem, not to magnify it into something that requires a huge paralinguistic life-support system.

A reasonable response would be to try to compute subset relations on the basis of the individual analytical atoms of linguistic systems. For instance, different settings of a particular parameter might result in languages with subset relations. This approach has been commonly assumed when the subset principle is discussed in the context of the Principles and Parameters framework (see, e.g., Jacubowitz 1984, Wexler and Manzini 1987). But it does not provide a complete and principled solution. Clark (1992), using what he calls 'shifted languages', shows that a learner can obey the subset principle on a parameter-by-parameter basis, yet may still end up (incorrectly) in a superset language, when subset relations depend on correlated parameter settings. Even more radically, when the elements of a linguistic theory *interact*, in violation of the *Independence Principle* of Wexler and Manzini (1987), the possible subset (and non-subset) relationships between different settings of one parameter may depend crucially upon how other parameters of the system are set.

Consider the following schematic example. Suppose a subsystem in the Principles and Parameters framework has three binary parameters, as illustrated in table 1. The subset/superset relations of languages distinguished by the settings of P1 depend upon how the other parameters, P2 and P3, are set.

Observe the relationship between the languages defined for the opposing values of P1. When, as in the first pair of rows, the other parameters are set $-$P2 /$-$P3, the $-$P1 and $+$P1 languages have no subset relations. When, as in the middle pair of rows, the other parameters are set $+$P2/$-$P3, the language with $-$P1 is a subset of the language with $+$P1. Finally, when the setting is $-$P2/$+$P3, the language with $-$P1 is now a *superset* of the $+$P1 language. The learner cannot assume in advance that a particular value for parameter P1 is *the* subset value.[2] Positing interaction is an almost inevitable consequence of the drive for generality in theories of linguistic form, and in section 6 below, we point to a realistic analogue within Optimality Theory (OT).

The Subset Principle, then, is really more of a *goal* than a computational means for achieving that goal. It is a property possessed by a satisfactory theory of learning-from-positive evidence: not a mechanism within the theory, but a desired consequence of its mechanisms. *Given a set of data and a set of grammars which are consistent with that data, the learning device functions to pick the grammar generating the language which is a subset of the languages generated by the other consistent grammars, when the subset/superset relation exists.* There is no guarantee as to the computational ease of determining which of the grammars is the subset; indeed difficult theorem-proving may be required.

The Subset Principle can be seen as an instance of the general occamite analytical strategy: an inquirer should always select the 'most restrictive' hypothesis consistent with the data. But the term 'restrictive' has a number of different applications in the grammatical context, and it is worth while to sort out the one that is relevant here. Under certain interpretations, it applies *only* to candidate theories of Universal Grammar (UG) and not at all to individual grammars. In one such sense, perhaps the primary sense of the term, a grammatical *theory* is 'restrictive' to the degree that it provides few grammars consistent with determinative data (cf. the concept of VC-dimension in formal learning theory, as in Vapnik and Chervonenkis 1971); a 'restrictive' theory eases the learning task by limiting ambiguity in the interpretation of the data. In another sense, also applied at the same level, a theory of grammar is sometimes said to be 'restrictive' if it allows for a relatively limited typology of distinct grammars. A theory of UG that predicts only the basic word orders {SOV, SVO} is sometimes said to be more restrictive than one that predicts, say, {SOV, SVO, VSO}. This second sense is independent of the first and need have no relevance to learnability, so long as the evidence for each of the options is readily available and unambiguous. In contrast to these, the sense that interests us applies to individual grammars within a *fixed* theory of grammar: if grammar G1 generates a language which is a subset of the language of grammar G2, then we will say that G1 is 'more restrictive' than G2. Yet further uses of 'restrictive' at this level of analysis are occasionally found, as the term comes to be associated with any property presumed desirable that involves having less of something. But criteria of relative grammatical desirability where no subset relationship exists – for example, having fewer rules – have been considered to be of limited concern for language learnability. Competing grammar-hypotheses that do not lead to subset languages can be distinguished by data: each generated language has forms not found in the other, which can appear as positive evidence.

The subset issue appears in full force in the learning of distributional regularities. Indeed, the descriptive language used to depict phonotactics usually takes the form of stating what *cannot* occur in the language, even though the data available as evidence depict only those things which *can* occur. For the learning of phonotactic distributions, then, the goal is always to select the most restrictive grammar consistent with the data. The computational challenge is efficiently to determine, for any given set of data, which grammar is the most restrictive. Since psychological realism demands efficient computability, solving this problem is crucial to the generative enterprise.

2.   The target grammar

Under OT, the restrictiveness of a grammar depends upon the relative ranking of the constraints: given several alternative grammars that are equivalent over the observed data, we need to be able to choose the ranking that projects the most limited language. The possible interactions among constraints can be quite complex, but a first cut can be made by observing the interactions between markedness constraints and faithfulness constraints in the core theory. Markedness constraints, violated by structures in the output, can function to prevent such structures from appearing in grammatical forms. Faithfulness constraints, on the other hand, are violated by input–output disparities, and can be ranked so as to require that input structures be retained even when they are marked or entail the presence of other marked structure. Broadly speaking, increased domination of markedness constraints over faithfulness constraints will lead to a reduced language consisting of relatively unmarked forms. This suggests that subset/superset configurations among observable language data can be managed by attention to markedness/faithfulness relationships within the grammar.

Important steps in this direction have been taken by theorists of child acquisition of phonology such as Gnanadesikan (this volume), Levelt (1995), Demuth (1995), Smolensky (1996a), and Bernhardt and Stemberger (1997), who have shown how the limited early repertory, and progress away from it, can be understood in terms of an initial stage where all markedness constraints dominate all faithfulness constraints (M»F, for short).[3] Sherer (1994), van Oostendorp (1995), Smolensky (1996b), and Hayes (this volume) have also observed the relation between markedness dominance and the subset principle. It is important, however, to keep the subset issue notionally distinct from issues in the analysis of early acquisition patterns. The proposals we shall entertain are not intended to provide a direct account for child language data, although we expect that they ought to bear on the problem in various ways. Speech relates to grammar as behaviour to knowledge, with all the attendant complexities of interpretation.

To see the differences between markedness and faithfulness explanations for the same ambiguous data, let us reconsider the complementary distribution problem mentioned above. Suppose a language allows *š* only before *i*, and bans *s* from that environment. When presented with a form . . . *ši* . . . , why doesn't the learner simply conclude that the segment *š* is generally and freely admitted in the language? UG must provide a constraint that is effectively antagonistic to *š*, call it M(*š), and a constraint with the effect of banning the sequence *si*, M(*si).[4] Restricting discussion to the faithfulness constraint F(ant) demanding the preservation of *anteriority*, we have two distinct accounts of the observed datum:

> (a) **F(ant)** » {M(*š), M(*si)}   • the Faithfulness explanation.
> (b) **M(*si)** » **M(*š)** » F(ant)   • the Markedness explanation.

The first, via dominant Faithfulness, admits *all š*. The second enforces the M»F structure and admits *š* only in *ši*, eliminating it elsewhere: this is the most restrictive way to admit some *š* under the assumptions we have made about the constraint system. The M»F solution obtains a *ši*→*ši* map by specifying a ranking *entirely within* the M bloc.

Several properties of the account are worth noting.

• In = Out. No special assumptions about distinctions between underlying and surface form are required, and consequently no techniques for hypothesising, testing, or constraining underlying forms need be called on. The learner encounters a datum and tries to get the grammar to reproduce it exactly, taking input and output to be identical.[5] This involves active learning, because the M » F condition generally encourages *non*identity between input and output.

• Richness of the Base. Because the learner manipulates constraints on the elements of structure rather than simply listing encountered forms, the grammar that is learned will have consequences beyond the motivating data. In the case at hand, the learner must also have grasped M(*š) » M(*s), for those constraints M(*s) that penalise *s*. This ranking could come from whatever cognitive mechanisms lead to universal Markedness hierarchies; or it could come from direct observation of the distribution of *s* in the language. For example, given the occurrence of . . . *sa* . . . , the mapping /sa/→*sa* will be posited, and under the M » F regime, this requires M(*š) » M(*s); the reverse ranking would need Faithfulness to preserve *s*. Consequently, when the learner opts for the markedness solution to the appearance of . . . *ši* . . . , a grammar banning **si* is automatically obtained; crucially, there is no contemplation of the unobserved /si/ as a *possible input*. The distinction between *s* and *š* has been contextually neutralised in the effort to reproduce observed . . . *ši* . . . against the background supposition that *š* should not exist. By configuring a grammar to perform the identity map under M » F bias, the learner will end up with a grammar that deals with all possible inputs (*Richness of the Base*), without having to review each of them.

• Durability of M » F structure. Learning takes place over time as more data accumulate. The choice between Faithfulness and Markedness solutions recurs at each stage of the process. It is not enough to set up an initial state in which M » F; rather, this must be enforced throughout learning, at each step. This point figures in Itô and Mester (1999b) and is also explicitly recognised by Hayes (this volume). Further justification is provided in section 4.4 below.

The basic strategy, then, is to seek the most restrictive grammar that maps each observationally validated form *to itself*. This grammar will give us $G(d_i) = d_i$ for every datum d_i – the d_i are the 'fixed points' of the mapping – and should give us as few other output forms as possible, given arbitrary input. Although we seek restrictiveness, we do not attempt directly to monitor the contents of the output language, i.e., to compute the entirety of $G(U)$, where U is the set of universally possible inputs. In essence, we have set ourselves a different but related goal: to find a grammar that *minimises* the number of fixed points in the mapping from input to output. Each faithfulness constraint demands that some piece of linguistic structure be fixed in the grammatical mapping, and faithfulness constraints combine to force fixed-point mappings of whole composite forms. By keeping the faithfulness constraints at bay, we shall in general discourage fixed-point mappings in favour of descent to the lowest Markedness state possible. The goal of fixed point minimisation is not abstractly identical to language-based restrictiveness – they are the same only when the generated language is exactly the set of fixed points – but they appear to be quite close under standard assumptions about the nature of markedness and faithfulness constraints.[6]

Minimisation of fixed points is, again, not something to be directly computed. We need a measure that can be applied to the grammar itself, without reviewing its behaviour over the set of possible inputs. The idea, of course, as in the literature cited above, is that markedness constraints should be ranked 'as high as possible' and faithfulness constraints 'as low as possible'. We can move in the direction of greater precision by specifying that the faithfulness constraints should be dominated by as many markedness constraints as possible. This is precise enough to generate a numeric metric on constraint hierarchies, which we shall call the *r-measure*.

(1)   **R-measure**. The r-measure for a constraint hierarchy is determined by adding, for each faithfulness constraint in the hierarchy, the number of markedness constraints that dominate that faithfulness constraint.

The measure is coarse, and it does not aim to reckon just the crucial M/F interactions; but the larger the r-measure, the more restrictive the grammar ought to be, in the usual case. Even so, the r-measure is not the end-all, be-all characterisation of restrictiveness. It says nothing of the possible restrictiveness consequences of different rankings among the markedness constraints or among the faithfulness constraints. Below we shall see that the intra-Markedness issue is solved automatically by the class of learning algorithms we deal with; the intra-Faithfulness problems are distinctly thornier and will be the focus of much of our discussion.

It is also not obvious (and perhaps not even likely) that for every data set there is a unique hierarchy with the largest r-measure.[7] But the r-measure is a promising place to start. Given this metric, we can offer a concrete, computable goal: any learning algorithm should return a grammar that, among all those consistent with the given data, has the largest r-measure.

A conflict avoided: high vs. low. Before asking how to achieve this goal, it is worth noting a couple of the r-measure's properties. First, the most restrictive possible grammar, by this measure, will have all of the faithfulness constraints dominated by all of the markedness constraints, with an r-measure that is the product of the number of faithfulness constraints and the number of markedness constraints. Thus, for a given OT system, the maximum possible r-measure is that product.

Second, selecting the hierarchy with the largest r-measure is consistent with the spirit of ranking each of the markedness constraints 'as high as possible', i.e., with respect to all other constraints, both Markedness and Faithfulness. This distinguishes the r-measure from another possible measure: that of adding together, for each faithfulness constraint, the number of constraint *strata* above it – call it the *s-measure*. (A stratum is a collection of constraints undifferentiated in rank, produced by the learning algorithms we employ.) Consider the stratified hierarchy in (2): the r-measure is $2 + 3 = 5$, while the s-measure is $1 + 3 = 4$.

(2) $\{M_1\ M_2\} \gg \{F_1\} \gg \{M_3\} \gg \{F_2\}$ $r = 5, s = 4$

Now consider the stratified hierarchy in (3), which is just like (2) save that the top stratum has been split, creating a dominance relationship between M_1 and M_2.

(3) $\{M_1\} \gg \{M_2\} \gg \{F_1\} \gg \{M_3\} \gg \{F_2\}$ $r = 5, s = 6$

Adding this new intra-Markedness relationship does not directly change the relationship between any of the faithfulness constraints and any of the markedness constraints. Correspondingly, the r-measure of (3) is 5, the same as for (2). However, the s-measure of (3) is 6, larger than the s-measure for (2). Maximising the s-measure will have the effect of demoting markedness constraints in ways not directly motivated by the data. By maximising the r-measure instead, learning can be biased towards having faithfulness constraints low in the ranking without directly impacting the relative ranking of the markedness constraints. This turns out to be a good thing because, as discussed below, it permits the continued use, when ranking the markedness constraints, of the principle of Constraint Demotion (CD), which mandates that constraints be ranked as high as possible. Using the r-measure instead of the s-measure to characterise 'as low as possible' for faithfulness constraints avoids a possible conflict between such low-ranking and the goal of ranking markedness constraints maximally high.

3.   The learning situation

For the purposes of this chapter, we assume a learner not (yet) interested in unifying underlying forms for morphemes. Such a learner is responsive only to syntagmatic factors, and may simply treat prosodic words as morphologically opaque entities. If some surface morphological segmentation has been achieved, the learner could also detect distributions sensitive to whatever categories can be posited as present in observed forms; similarly for the analysis of prosodic structure. We further assume that the learner always adopts, as the underlying form, precisely the surface analysis of the overt form that has been heard, i.e., whatever analysis the learner is currently capable of. The correct mapping will always be an identity mapping for the structures in the surface form; these must be fixed points for the grammar. This does not mean that the correct mapping is identity over all inputs; in the vast majority of cases there are other inputs not observed or contemplated that are mapped unfaithfully to lower markedness outputs. All overt forms actually observed as positive data must be generable by the grammar, and their corresponding underlying forms must, we assume, be mapped faithfully.

These assumptions are not adopted solely to keep the problem simple. Ecologically, it is reasonable to start the learning process with observations that can be made without extensive comparative analysis of words and their meanings; hence the overlap in assumptions with empirical work on early phonological acquisition in children, such as Gnanadesikan (this volume), Levelt (1995), Demuth (1995), and others. Linguistically, it is clear from studies, such as those by Kisseberth (1970), Sommerstein (1974), and by now many others, that phonotactic knowledge is of significant benefit when the task of learning the morphophonology is taken up.

Distributional evidence has some inherent limitations: from data with only CV syllables, one cannot distinguish whether epenthesis or deletion is responsible for dealing with problematic inputs. In general, if UG allows a range of solutions to a markedness constraint, distributional evidence will only assure the learner that at least one of them is in use, without specifying which one. The more tightly the range is specified, either by UG or by other informative constraint interactions, the more the learner will grasp. But even in the case of ambiguity, the analysis of distributional data will give excellent evidence about relations within the markedness subcomponent of the grammar, and very good evidence as well about the niches in the hierarchy where faithfulness constraints fit. The stage investigated here will typically not fix the complete constraint hierarchy for the entire phonology of the language, but it will aim to provide a crucial infrastructure that limits the range of options that the learner must consider. According to this programme of explanation, the increasingly sophisticated learner will have the luxury of revising the constraint hierarchy developed through phonotactic learning as knowledge of morphophonemic relations develops, using further techniques for hypothesising and testing nontrivial underlying forms, ultimately arriving at the correct adult grammar.

Having taken via the r-measure a global stance on the restrictiveness of grammars, the challenge we face is to devise an efficient and local step-by-step algorithm that produces grammars in accord with it. The transition between global goal and local implementation is not entirely trivial, as we shall see.

Our point of departure is an existing procedure for constructing a constraint hierarchy from data: Recursive Constraint Demotion (RCD). RCD generates a grammar consistent with a set of *mark-data pairs*. A mark-data pair (mdp) is an elementary ranking argument: a competition between two candidates from the same input, one of them optimal, the other not, along with the information about their constraint-violation profiles. The member of the pair that is (desired to be) optimal will be termed *the winner*; the other, suboptimal competitor will be *the loser*. The important action takes place comparatively: the raw quantitative violation data must be analysed to determine, for each constraint, which member of each pair does better on that constraint, or whether the constraint is neutral between them; mere violation is, of course, meaningless by itself. (This step is known as *mark cancellation*.) We need a technical term to describe the basic comparative relationship that emerges after mark cancellation: let us say that a constraint *prefers* one candidate to another when the first candidate has fewer violations than the second. Note that a candidate can satisfy a constraint completely, yet still not be 'preferred'; it all depends on how its mdp competitor fares.

A single mark-data pair contains information about how the constraints must be ranked so that the desired winner actually wins. At least one of the

constraints preferring the winner must dominate *all* of the constraints preferring the loser. This, rephrased, is the Cancellation/Domination Lemma of Prince
and Smolensky (1993: 148). We know from Cancellation/Domination that the
loser-preferring constraints must *all* be subordinated in the ranking, and subordinated to constraints that prefer the associated winners. Turning this around,
we see that the complementary set of constraints – those that *do not prefer any
losers* among the mark-data pair list, those that only prefer winners when they
prefer anything – can all be ranked at the top. The algorithm develops from this
observation.

RCD applies to a constraint set coupled with a list of elementary ranking
arguments (mdps, possibly arising from different inputs), and recursively as-
sembles a constraint hierarchy consistent with the information in the mdp-list.
RCD does not aim to construct all possible totally ordered rankings consistent
with an mdp-list. The goal of RCD is to produce a single *stratified hierarchy*,
where the strata consist of non-conflicting constraints. Various total orderings
can be produced by ranking the constraints within the strata, retaining the domination order between strata. The stratified hierarchy produced by RCD has
a unique property: each constraint is placed in the highest stratum that it can
possibly occupy.

The goal of grammar-building is to organise the constraints so that all known
ranking arguments are simultaneously satisfied. If any such constraint hierarchies exist, the stratified hierarchy produced by RCD algorithm will be among
them.

RCD starts by collecting all the constraints that prefer only winners when
they prefer anything (they *prefer no losers*). These are placed at the top of the
hierarchy, forming a stratum of non-conflicting winner-preferring and winner-
loser-neutral constraints. The learner then dismisses from further consideration
all those mark-data pairs $W_i \sim L_i$ on which some constraint just ranked *prefers*
winner W_i to loser L_i. This move discards those competitors that lose on some
constraint in this stratum, and leaves behind those mark-data pairs where both
members have done equally well. In this way, the list of mark-data pairs shrinks
just as the list of constraints to be ranked is shrinking.

The learner then faces exactly the same problem again – ranking a set of constraints so as to be consistent with a list of ranking arguments, but with fewer
constraints and fewer mark-data pairs. This is a canonical recursive situation,
and RCD simply repeats its ranking-and-elimination procedure on the depleted
collection of mark-data pairs and constraints. The second stratum of the hierarchy is now filled with those constraints that prefer only winners among the
mark-data pairs left over from the first round. If the ranking arguments in the
mark-data pairs list are mutually consistent, the RCD process will repeat until
all mark-data pairs have been dismissed, and all constraints have been placed
in the hierarchy. A grammar will have been found.

Should the data be inconsistent, a point will be reached where none of the remaining constraints prefers only winners – each yet-to-be-ranked constraint will prefer at least one loser on the remaining mark-data pairs list. These constraints cannot be ranked, and it follows that no grammar exists for the original mark-data pairs list over the constraint set. Our focus here will be on finding grammars for consistent data, but we note that detection of inconsistency via RCD can play an important role whenever generation and pruning of tentative, fallible interpretations of data are required, as shown in Tesar (1997, 1998).

Here is a brief example that illustrates the use of RCD. The mark-data pairs list is presented in the form of a comparative tableau (Prince 2000, 2001a,b), the appropriate representation for ranking arguments. Competing members of a mark-data pair are shown as 'x ~ y', where 'x' is the desired optimum or winner, and 'y' is a competitor and desired loser. As always, we say that a constraint *prefers* candidate x to candidate y if x has fewer violations of the constraint than y does; and vice versa. If a constraint prefers one candidate of the pair to the other, then a token that indexes the preferred candidate is placed in the appropriate cell: 'W' if it prefers the winner, 'L' if it prefers the loser. If a constraint prefers neither candidate (because both violate it equally), the cell is left blank. A constraint hierarchy (arrayed left-to-right in domination order, as usual) is successful over a mark-data pairs list if the first non-blank cell encountered in each row, going left to right, contains W. This indicates that the highest ranking constraint that distinguishes the members of the pair prefers the winner. In terms of the comparative representation, then, the action of RCD is to take a tableau of Ws and Ls and find an arrangement of the columns in which all Ls are preceded by at least one W. Let us perform RCD.

MDP: Winner ~ Loser	C1	C2	C3
(a) W1 ~ L1	W	L	
(b) W2 ~ L2	L	W	W

Of the three constraints, C3 alone *prefers only winners* (prefers no losers). The first round of RCD will therefore place C3 in the top stratum. This eliminates mark-data pairs (b) by virtue of the 'W' awarded by C3, leaving the following:

MDP: winner ~ loser	C1	C2
(a) W1 ~ L1	W	L

Now C1 *prefers only winners* (and more, albeit rather trivially: lacking neutral cells, it prefers *all* winners). C1 goes into the second stratum and eliminates mark-data pair (a), exhausting the mark-data pairs list and relegating C2 to the lowest stratum.

Notice that C1 did not at first *prefer-only-winners*, prior to the elimination of mark-data pair (b), because C1 prefers L2. Thus, we can say that C1 was *freed up for ranking* when C3 entered the first stratum. The resulting hierarchy, C3 » C1 » C2, leaves the tableau looking like this:

MDP: winner ~ loser	C3	C1	C2
(a) W1 ~ L1		W	L
(b) W2 ~ L2	W	L	W

As promised, each row begins with a 'W' that settles the competition in favour of the winner.

A full presentation of RCD, along with a formal analysis of its basic properties, can be found in Tesar (1995), and Tesar and Smolensky (2000); for an informal account, see Prince (2000). Samek-Lodovici and Prince (1999) explores the relationship between harmonic bounding and RCD, and provides an order-theoretic perspective on both. Prince (2001b) further explores the relationship between RCD and the logic of ranking arguments.

RCD applies not to raw data but to mark-data pairs: observable winners paired with unobserved and ungrammatical forms (losers). The learner must therefore be equipped to construct an appropriate mark-data pairs list from observed data, algorithmically supplying the losing competitors. Two criteria must be satisfied by any competitor-generating mechanism. First, the generated loser must in fact be ungrammatical as an output for the given input. Second, the comparison thus constructed should be *informative*: of all the multitudes of ungrammatical outputs, the one chosen to compete should lead to the imposition of new ranking relations through RCD; otherwise there is no point to computing the comparison.

The method of error-driven learning discussed in Tesar and Smolensky (2000) satisfies both criteria. Suppose a hypothesised grammar at some stage of learning produces an *error*, an incorrect mapping from input to output. Rectifying the error requires re-ranking so that the desired candidate fares better on the constraint hierarchy than the currently obtained but spurious optimum. RCD will accomplish this if the new mark-data pair ⟨*desired winner*⟩ ~ ⟨*currently obtained winner*⟩ is added to the mark-data pair list. The grammar itself, through its errors, thus supplies the meaningful competitors that are needed to improve its performance.[8] Other methods of finding useful competitors can be imagined – for example, conducting some kind of search of the 'nearby' phonological or grammatical space – but we will adhere to the error-driven method in the interests of focus, well-definition, and gaining a more precise understanding of its strengths and weaknesses.

It is important to note that intermediate grammar hypotheses, based on partial data, will often have strata containing constraints that turn out to conflict when more mark-data pairs are considered. By consequence, such grammars will tend to produce multiple outputs for each input, due to undecided conflicts, in cases where the final grammar would produce only one. Following Tesar and Smolensky (2000), we regard each output that is distinct from the observed datum as an error to be corrected. We abstract away from issues of variation, then, and work under the idealisation that each input corresponds to only one legitimate output.

The course of learning is assumed to proceed over time as in the Multi-Recursive Constraint Demotion (MRCD) of Tesar (1998). Rather than manipulating a grammar-hypothesis *per se* by switching rankings around, the learner develops and retains a permanent data base of mark-data pairs. A grammar hypothesis can be generated easily from the current data base by the application of RCD. From this point of view, the contribution of the phonotactic/identity-map learning stage is precisely the accumulation of a valuable mark-data pair data base. MRCD allows RCD to be utilised with 'online' learning, that is, with progressive augmentation of the learner's data base. The learner uses the current grammar to apply error-driven learning to each form as it is observed. When an error occurs on a form, the learner constructs a new mark-data pairs and adds it to the list (which was initially empty). A new constraint hierarchy is then generated by applying RCD to the entire accumulated mark-data pairs list, and the learner is ready to assess the next piece of data when it arrives. In this way, the learner responds to incoming data one form at a time, constructing and storing mark-data pairs only when necessary.

4.   Postponing the placement of faithfulness constraints

4.1   *Biasing RCD*

While any given set of mark-data pairs is typically consistent with quite a number of stratified hierarchies, RCD returns the unique stratified hierarchy in which each constraint is ranked as high as it will go. Unmodified, the algorithm will give exactly the opposite of what we want for faithfulness constraints. In the complementary distribution case, for example, the presence of . . . *ši* . . . in the data is entirely compatible with top-ranking of F(ant), and so up it goes. Indeed, this ranking is compatible with the *absence* of . . . *ši* . . . from the data, and the absence of *š* generally. Under simple RCD, all constraints – and hence all faithfulness constraints – will reside at the top until there is evidence to contrary.

No such evidence will ever arise for faithfulness constraints when the identity map is optimal. Faithfulness will be demoted only when non-identity mappings are desired; that is, when input and output differ crucially, a situation that for us requires knowledge of morphophonemic alternations. A strictly RCD-based learner cannot grasp distributions from positive evidence alone.

RCD must therefore be reconfigured so as to impose high-ranking *except for faithfulness constraints*. The modified algorithm should place a faithfulness constraint into a hierarchy only when absolutely required. If successful, this strategy will yield a hierarchy with a maximal r-measure. Let us call the new algorithm – or rather *class of algorithms*, since a number of variants are possible – Biased Constraint Demotion (BCD): the ranking procedure will be biased against faithfulness and in favour of markedness constraints as candidates for membership in the stratum under construction.

On each recursive pass, RCD places into the next stratum those constraints that prefer only winners among the mark-data pairs list. Our basic principle takes the form of the following modification to RCD, given in (4):

(4) **Faithfulness Delay**. On each pass, among those constraints suitable for membership in the next stratum, if possible place only *markedness constraints*. Only place faithfulness constraints if no markedness constraints are available to be placed in the hierarchy.

In this way, the placement of faithfulness constraints into the hierarchy is delayed until there are no markedness constraints that can do the job. If all the mark-data pairs are consistent with a hierarchy having the entire set of faithfulness constraints at the bottom, that is what will be returned.

However, the data may require at least one faithfulness constraint to dominate some markedness constraint. This will happen only when all of the constraints available for placement into the next stratum are faithfulness constraints. At this point, the algorithm must place at least one faithfulness constraint into the next stratum in order to continue.

What is not obvious is what, precisely, to do at this point. At least one faithfulness constraint must be ranked, but which one?

4.2 *Don't place inactive faithfulness constraints*

All unranked faithfulness constraints will be available for ranking at each step of BCD. The identity map satisfies every criterion of Faithfulness, and no faithfulness constraint can ever *prefer a loser* under such circumstances. All faithfulness constraints prefer only winners from the outset, and any F constraint not already ranked will be in a state of permanent readiness.

With markedness constraints, the situation is quite different; they have no affinity for the identity map or any other and are as likely to prefer losers as winners. Assuming that no markedness constraints are rankable at some stage, the crucial question is this: which faithfulness constraints *need* to be ranked? From the point of view of unbiased RCD, any F constraint at all will do. But if F constraints are to be ranked as low as possible, in accord with the r-measure, the answer must be: just those faithfulness constraints whose ranking will free up markedness constraints for ranking in the next round.

'Freeing up' comes about in general when a just-ranked constraint dismisses a mark-data pair in which the loser is preferred by certain constraints. With this mark-data pair gone, such once-problematic constraints may now fall into the prefers-only-winners category, and therefore be rankable. The following tableau illustrates this property:

MDP: Winner ~ Loser	M1	M2	F1	F2
(a) W1 ~ L1	W	L		
(b) W2 ~ L2	L	W	W	

At this stage, neither M1 nor M2 can be ranked – both prefer some loser (marked by L in the cell). If we rank F2, we accomplish nothing, since the set of mark-data pairs remains the same. If we rank F1, however, the problematic mark-data pair (b) will be eliminated, taking with it the L-mark that holds M1 in check. With mark-data pair (b) gone, M1 is 'freed up' and may be ranked next.

As a first step towards identifying the best F constraints to rank, we can set aside a constraint-type that is definitely **not necessary** to rank: the F that prefers no winners, being neutral over the mark-data pairs at hand. Any such constraint, when ranked, will never eliminate any mark-data pairs and cannot free up markedness constraints. This gives us our second principle:

(5)   **Avoid the Inactive**. When placing faithfulness constraints into the hierarchy, if possible only place those that *prefer some winner*.[9] If the only available faithfulness constraints *prefer no remaining winners*, then place all of them into the hierarchy.

Observe that the second clause only applies when the bottom-most stratum is being constructed. Following the principle will ensure that completely inactive faithfulness constraints always end up at the very bottom of the hierarchy. (Completely inactive markedness constraints will, of course, end up at the top.) With this much of a selection-criterion at hand, we can give a version of the Biased Constraint Demotion algorithm. This is not the final version of our proposal, but it expresses the ideas presented thus far. We write it out as generic pseudocode, with italicised comments on the side.

4.2.1   Version 1 of the BCD ranking algorithm
Repeat the procedure until all constraints have been ranked.

Given: a list of mark-data pairs, and a set of constraints distinguished as
Markedness/Faithfulness:

	[*Comment*:
Identify the constraints NoL that prefer	[*Collect the rankable*
no losers (*prefer only winners*)	[*constraints*;
If at least one of NoL is a markedness	[*Place only M constraints*
constraint place only the markedness	[*whenever possible*;
constraints of NoL in the next stratum	
else	[*but if* NoL *consists*
if at least one of NoL *prefers* a winner	[*entirely of F*,
place [only those members of NoL	[*place only active F;*
that prefer a winner] in the	
next stratum	
else	[*but if no F in* NoL *are*
place all of NoL in the next stratum	[*active, from bottom-*
end-if	[*most stratum from* NoL.
end-if	

Remove all mark-data pairs where the winner is
preferred by one of the just-ranked constraints.

4.2.2   The logic of the algorithm (version 1)   The initial *If*-clause ensures
that faithfulness constraints are not ranked when markedness constraints are
available. Markedness constraints will continue to be ranked as high as possible,
because they are placed into the ranking as *soon* as they prefer-only-winners
among the current mark-data pairs list. Faithfulness constraints are placed into
the hierarchy when they are the only ones available for ranking. In such a
circumstance, all remaining markedness constraints must be dominated by at
least one of the rankable faithfulness constraints.

   The bracketed, bolded section of the algorithm contains the conditions determining which among the available faithfulness constraints will be ranked; it
is this section that we must scrutinise and sharpen. Currently, it places a necessary condition, one that will persist, but needs further elaboration. Looking
only at the isolated behaviour of individual F constraints, it picks up the weak-
est form of activity. All that is asked for is that an F constraint *prefers* some
winner; the behaviour of other constraints on the relevant mark-data pairs is not
considered.

   Remark. Because discussion in the literature often concentrates only on M/F
conflict, it is important to recall that for a markedness constraint M1 to be

rendered inactive, it is not always necessary that it be dominated by every faith-fulness constraint whose violation could satisfy M1. Suppose that a (suboptimal) form satisfying M1 via the violation of faithfulness constraint F1 necessarily also violates another *markedness* constraint M2. It would be adequate if M2 were to dominate M1, which in turn dominates F1. This would also be prefer-able due to the lower ranking of F1. (In the complementary distribution case mentioned above, M1 = *š, M2 = *si; the failure of *ši→si* is guaranteed not by F(ant) but by M2.) This is the kind of competition between markedness and faithfulness explanations which the algorithm will handle correctly.

4.3   Locating the competition

Optimality Theory (OT) does not run on positive evidence alone: each ele-mentary ranking argument turns on the contrast between an optimal form and another form presumed to be *suboptimal* – ungrammatical, in a word, as the output for the given input. The desired optima come from observation, but se-lecting their failing competitors asserts a kind of negative evidence. Where do they come from?

Above we sketched the notion of error-driven learning (as in Tesar 1997), by means of which the grammar itself is used as the source of informative contrasts, those which compel modification of the current hierarchy. Let us consider how this applies in the phonotactic learning context. Given a stratified hierarchy current at some stage of learning, one can compute the optima that it predicts as output for some input. When an observationally supported *output* form is used as *input*, the current grammar may produce unwanted output from it. It may fail to reproduce the input in the output, or it may produce other forms as co-optima, because the strata contain constraint-ties that have not yet been worked out. On the assumption that there is a unique output for each input, all such non-matching forms are guaranteed to be suboptimal, and they can be used as fodder for ranking arguments (mark-data pairs). They are errors, useful because they can be identified and corrected.

Because the identity map is the sought-for optimum, the losing competitors produced by this method do not earn their erroneous superiority being more faithful, and must instead be *less marked*, in terms of the current stratified hierar-chy. Expanding the mark-data pairs list to include these implied suboptima leads to a new grammar when BCD is applied, either through new rankings within the markedness group, or through high-ranking of a faithfulness constraint, if necessary.

Negative evidence acquired in this fashion does not provide the learner with the tools to resolve the subset problem. The driving assumption – that each input gives rise to one output – is no help at all. Having spotted *ši* in the environment, the learner can be sure that /ši/ must come out only as *ši*, not as *si* or *ša*. But no evidentiary hint is offered as to what an input like /ša/ should lead to, when *ša* has never been observed. The information gained from errors is not evidence about what is missing from the overt, observable language. This is the key question, and the one that cannot be asked: is *š* free or restricted in distribution? Is *ša* in the language *or not*? In the absence of positive evidence to the contrary, BCD aims to resolve such questions in favour of the restrictive pole of the disjunction.

4.4   The initial state: one among many

Linguistic theorists and language acquisitionists alike often focus on the *initial state* as having special properties. Under BCD, the initial state is not arbitrary, nor does it require special stipulation. Assume a state of complete ignorance in the learner; apply the algorithm to an *empty* list of mark-data pairs. All of the markedness constraints are placed into the hierarchy first, followed by the faithfulness constraints. The initial hierarchy is useful in the present context because it provides a starting-point for error-driven learning.

This hierarchy is the familiar M»F configuration: it is the same initial state that has been proposed by Smolensky (1996a,b) and others cited above. Smolensky proposes that the learner starts with this initial hierarchy, and constraint demotion subsequently mixes the faithfulness and markedness constraints, with the expectation that markedness constraints would only be demoted below faithfulness constraints to the extent necessary. (Independent of constraint demotion, Itô and Mester (1999a) propose a principle of 'ranking conservatism' that aims to have the effect of maximally preserving initial-state ranking relations.) The present proposal is another, stronger version of the same theme: instead of confining the asymmetry between Markedness and Faithfulness to the initial state, we posit a constant Markedness-favouring force throughout learning. Under the new proposal, at any given time, the subordination of markedness to faithfulness constraints will always aim to be the minimum necessary to accommodate the data. The initial state is but one consequence of this constant force.

The two approaches are not equivalent. Consideration of their differences shows that M»F cannot just be an *initial state*, subject to minimal perturbation by any version of CD that fails to take direct account of the M/F distinction. As new data arrive, on the Smolensky and Itô and Mester views, learning involves a revision of the currently maintained hierarchy or hierarchies, and under standard 'on-line' CD theory, any such revision can upset the general M»F relation quite massively.

Imagine the two initial strata:

$$\{M_1, M_2, \ldots, M_n\} \gg \{F_1, F_2, \ldots, F_k\}.$$
$$|\leftarrow \quad M \quad \rightarrow| \quad |\leftarrow \quad F \quad \rightarrow|$$

Suppose a datum comes in which requires $F_1 \gg M_1$. Standard 'on-line' CD, operating on the current hierarchy, demotes M_1 to the highest possible stratum, a new one in this case, retaining as much as possible of the current hierarchy:

$$\{M_2, \ldots, M_n\} \gg \{\mathbf{F_1}, F_2, \ldots, F_k\} \gg \{\mathbf{M_1}\}$$

The measure r diminishes by k, the number of F constraints that M_1 no longer dominates, which is in fact the entire list of faithfulness constraints! CD has grossly upset the M»F relation, with potentially great and unwanted consequences for the violation of M_1. Standard CD is conservative of the hierarchy's stratum structure, but allows very significant shifts in domination relations. Under BCD, the resulting hierarchy would have more strata, but minimal dominance of F over M:

$$\{M_2, \ldots, M_n\} \gg \{F_1\} \gg \{M_1\} \gg \{F_2, \ldots, F_k\}$$

Here r descends by just 1, and F_1 dominates only the single M constraint that the data compels it to. Recall that BCD does not directly transform one ranking into another, but re-derives an entire hierarchy from the enhanced list of mark-data pairs.

Itô and Mester's notion of ranking conservatism seeks to regulate transition from one state of the grammar to the next by avoiding, to the extent possible, the imposition of new rankings that contradict those already established. This leads to a preference for within-stratum refinement, which establishes rankings where none had existed before, as opposed to reversing dominance relations that are currently present. The expectation, then, is that the initial two stratum M»F structure will be carried forward as an M»F preference, via conservatism, into the hierarchies that descend from it. The idea is plausible and attractive, but it encounters at least two serious difficulties. First, the dynamics of ranking change under this proposal can be rather complex, due to the effects of transitivity, and the original relations (and stratum-internal non-relations) can get lost after a few steps, so that it is no longer possible to distinguish correctly on the basis of conservatism between markedness and faithfulness solutions, when both are possible. Second, it runs into a problem diagnosed by Broihier (1995) for a modification of the CD algorithm that incorporates a kind of ranking conservatism. It turns out that a conservative strategy can stumble badly over the rankings it preserves from previous states, in ways that depend pathologically on the sequencing of the data. In the worst case, the strategy will interpret consistent data as if it were inconsistent, leading to a non-terminating loop of demotion and re-demotion of the same pair of constraints. (Details of these problems are presented in Appendix 1.) Until such issues are resolved, we feel compelled to maintain the hypothesis that the M»F bias is an intrinsic, persistent property of the learning algorithm.

Other articulations can be added to the initial state, e.g., Markedness scales enforced through fixed domination relationships, etc. As with the M » F bias, any such additional fixed relationships must be actively enforced throughout learning. Ongoing respect for fixed constraint relationships is not an additional burden created by the RCD-based approach; any theory of learning constraint rankings must achieve it. Under the approach proposed here, based on RCD, all such relationships must be continuously active, and the initial state follows as a consequence.

5.   Freeing up markedness constraints

5.1   The problem

The overarching goal in placing F constraints is to free up markedness constraints for ranking in such a way as to maximise the r-measure: typically, this will mean freeing up the maximal number of markedness constraints, and freeing them up as soon as possible. A markedness constraint is fully rankable when it reaches the prefers-winners-only state, a purely constraint-internal matter. The F constraints, by contrast, are in that state from the start, and it is their interaction with other constraints that determines when they should be ranked. F constraints should go into the hierarchy only when no markedness constraints are rankable; but when several F constraints are available, the correct choice among them need not be straightforward. Here we review the kind of situations that can arise and develop a strategy that leads to a sharpened version of the BCD algorithm.

Role of Conflict. Consider first the configuration portrayed below. No M constraints are rankable.

MDP: Winner ~ Loser	F1	F2	M1
(a) W1 ~ L1	W		L
(b) W2 ~ L2		W	

Should we rank F1, F2, or both? Observe that F2 is quite useless, even though it prefers a winner and is therefore active in the sense used above. By contrast, F1 *conflicts* with M1 and *must* be ranked above it. (Constraint conflict means that 'W' and 'L' both occur in the same row.) Even better, when F1 is ranked, it frees up M1. Because F2 conflicts with nothing, it makes no difference at all where it is ranked. By the r-measure, it should be ranked at the bottom. This would also be true if M1 preferred the winner for mark-data pairs (b). The first moral, then, is that F constraints should be ranked only if they *conflict* with other constraints.

The present approach already achieves this result without the need for further intervention. In cases of *non*-conflict where F is active, the loser is harmonically bounded by the winner. (Harmonic bounding by the winner in comparative tableaux is signalled by the occurrence of a tableau row containing only Ws and possibly blanks.) The error-driven competitor-selection mechanism will not find harmonically bounded losers, because they never appear as winners for any provisional hierarchy. Consequently, no such competitions will arise under the error-driven regime, and no special clauses will be required to interpret them. In addition, error-driving aside, it should be noted that some logically possible patterns may simply not occur: winner/loser pairs distinguished by Faithfulness but not by Markedness (as in mark-data pair (b) above).

Freeing up. Conflict is a necessary precondition for freeing up, because every removal of an L-containing row involves conflict resolution. But it is not sufficient. *All* Ls in a constraint column must go, if the (M) constraint is to become rankable. In general, there may be many paths to freedom. Let us examine two fundamental complications: gang-effects, and cascading consequences.

F-Gangs. It can easily be the case that no single F constraint working by itself can free up a markedness constraint, yet a set of them can combine to do so. Here is an illustration:

MDP: Winner ~ Loser	F1	F2	F3	M1
(a) W1 ~ L1	W		W	L
(b) W2 ~ L2		W		L
(c) W3 ~ L3	W			L

M1 will be freed up if both F1 and F2 are ranked. F3 can also be thrown into the mix, but it merely duplicates the work already done. For maximal r-measure, F3 should not be ranked at this point. (Note that this also means that a procedure of randomly ranking active F constraints one-at-a-time is sure to be r-wise defective.) The algorithm must not only be able to identify effective sets of F constraints, it must be able to adjudicate between different such 'gangs' in order to determine which is most efficient.

There are two dimensions of efficiency to be measured: the size of the F-gang, and the size of the set of M constraints that it frees up (on which more immediately below). These two measures can trade off under special circumstances. Although the general expectation in ranking F is surely that fewer is better, it is possible to construct cases in which a greater initial investment in F yields a better r-measure in the relative ranking of M and F overall.[10] Pursuing this potential trade-off with full vigour is computationally unattractive, and therefore offensive to mental realism. Until there is evidence that it is meaningful or even likely to occur with realistic F and M constraints, we prefer to develop a version of BCD that simply favours smaller F-gangs. This leads to the following principle:

(6)   **Smallest effective F sets.** When placing faithfulness constraints into the hierarchy, place the *smallest set* of F constraints that *frees up some markedness constraint.*

This strategy leaves open the action to be taken when more than one F-gang is of minimal size. To see what hangs on the choice between them, we turn to our second focus, the cascade of distant consequences that can flow from an F-ranking decision.

M-Cascades. Placing an F constraint may not only free up *some* markedness constraint – it may free up a markedness constraint that itself frees up yet more markedness constraints. Setting loose such a cascade can result in higher ranking of M and lower ranking of F than would otherwise occur.

Suppose that at a certain stage there are two F constraints freeing up distinct markedness constraints. Consider the following situation:

When should F1 and F2 be ranked?

MDP: Winner ~ Loser	F1	F2	M1	M2
(a) W1 ~ L	W		L	
(b) W2 ~ L2		W	W	L

Neither M constraint can be placed at this point, since each prefers at least one loser (cells marked L). We must look to the F constraints. Both F1 and F2 are equally suitable by the freeing-up criterion, and each forms a smallest set of rankable F. If F2 is ranked first, the following hierarchy results:

(7)   F2 » M2 » F1 » M1   r = 1

If F1 is ranked first, though, the mark-data pair (a) is eliminated, and with (a) gone, the constraint M1 suddenly becomes available for ranking. Ranking M1 next then frees up M2 for ranking, and F2 drops to the bottom. The result is hierarchy (8):

(8)   F1 » M1 » M2 » F2   r = 2

These considerations indicate that the r-measure can respond to effects that are not immediately visible in the next round of ranking, but are consequences of that next round, or consequences of consequences, and so on. Here again a tactical issue arises: to pursue the global r-measure unrelentingly would probably require, in the worst case, sorting through something close to all possible rankings. It is doubtful that there is much pay-off in this mad pursuit. We conjecture that it will suffice for linguistic purposes to consider only the M-freeing consequences up to the next point where an F constraint must be ranked, i.e., until the cascade of M constraints arising from F-placement runs out. This leads to our last principle:

(9)   **Richest Markedness Cascade.** When placing faithfulness constraints into the hierarchy, if more than one F-set *freeing up some markedness constraint* is of smallest size, then place the F-set that yields the largest set of M constraints in contiguous subsequent strata, i.e., until another F constraint must be ranked. If there is more than one of these, pick one at random.

As with the smallest-F-set criterion, it is possible with a sufficient number of suitably interacting M and F constraints to craft a case where going for a smaller immediate M-cascade is offset by gains further on.[11] More investigation is needed to see what role, if any, this might play in linguistic systems, and whether such distinctions actually lead to discernible differences in substantive restrictiveness. If, as we suspect, they do not, then the suggested criterion may be more than just a reasonable heuristic compromise between the r-measure and computational efficiency. On the other hand, if distinctions of richness between immediate cascades fail to lead to discernible differences in restrictiveness of the resulting grammars, then it might even be preferable to forgo the effort of computing them as well.

5.2   BCD revised

Implementing the principles developed above requires further articulation of the F-placement clause given in the preliminary version of the algorithm. We need to install a subroutine that seeks the smallest effective set of F constraints – the smallest set that collectively frees up some markedness constraint – and in case of ties on size, looks for the one that releases the biggest markedness cascade.

The subroutine we propose starts out by looking for single effective F constraints and, if this fails, advances to looking for two-member sets, and so on. Although the combinatorics are unpleasant in the worst case, experience to date suggests that the routine will never have to look very far. If the result of the sizing subroutine is unique, it is turned over to the main routine for ranking. If non-unique, it is turned over to a further subroutine that pursues the markedness cascade released by each contender, looking ahead, as it were, via calls to the main BCD routine. The most successful F-set is returned to the main routine for ranking; ties for success are decided randomly.

We note that the algorithm could be pushed in the direction of greater complexity by being restructured to chase down ever more distant consequences of ranking decisions. It could also be scaled back, if its level of sensitivity to the ultimate M»F structure turns out to be excessive when the limitations of realistic constraints are taken into account. At present, it stands as a reasonable, if in part conjectural, compromise between the global demands of the r-measure and the need for local computability.

5.2.1   The full BCD algorithm

Given: a list of mark-data pairs, a set of constraints distinguished as markedness/faithfulness

Main Routine
BCD( ):
Repeat (until all constraints have been ranked)
    Set NoL to be the constraints not yet ranked that prefer no losers
    If at least one of NoL is a markedness constraint
        Set RankNext to be the set of markedness constraints in NoL
    Else
        If at least one of NoL prefers a winner
            Set RankNext to be the constraint set returned by
            Find-minimal-faith-subset (NoL)
        Else
            Set RankNext to be all the constraints of NoL
        End-if
    End-if
    Place RankNext in the next stratum
    Delete all mark-data pairs where the winner is preferred by a constraint
    in RankNext
End-Repeat

Faithfulness Constraint Set Selection
Find-minimal-faith-subset(NoL):
Set ActiveFaith to be those members of NoL that prefer a winner in one
of the remaining md-pairs
Set FSetSize to start at 0
Repeat (until a constraint set freeing a markedness constraint is found)
    Increase FSetSize by one
    Generate all subsets of ActiveFaith that are of size FSetSize
    For each such subset FaithSet-x
        If FaithSet-x frees up a markedness constraint,
            add it to FreeingFaithSets
    End-for

End-Repeat
If `FreeingFaithSets` contains only one faithfulness constraint set
    Set `BestFaithSet` to be the constraint set in `FreeingFaith`
    `Sets`
Else
    Set `BestFaithSet` to the constraint set returned by **Select-best-faith-set**(`FreeingFaithSets`)
End-if
Return(`BestFaithSet`)

Choosing Between Same-sized Minimal Faithfulness Constraint Subsets
Select-best-faith-set(`FreeingFaithSets`):
For each set `FaithSet-y` in `FreeingFaithSets`
    Place `FaithSet-y` in the next stratum of the constraint hierarchy
    under construction
    Continue BCD forward until another faithfulness constraint must be
    placed in the hierarchy
    Set `Value-y` to the number of markedness constraints ranked after the
    placement of `FaithSet-y`
End-for
Set `BestFaithSet` to the member `FaithSet-y` of `Freeing-FaithSets` with the largest `Value-y`
If there is a tie for the largest Value-y, pick one of them at random
Return(`BestFaithSet`)

5.3   Alternative criteria for selecting faithfulness constraints

In BCD, the selection of what faithfulness constraints to rank at a given point during learning is driven primarily by the freeing up of markedness constraints. This is a consequence of the use of the r-measure to characterise restrictiveness: BCD strives to optimise the r-measure, which values the ranking of M constraints above F constraints, and the algorithmic decisions are determined largely by that imperative.

Hayes (1999: section 7.6.3, this volume) proposes a different basis for the selection of faithfulness constraints, and in fact the major differences between our proposal and Hayes's reside in the approach to faithfulness selection. Rather than trying to enforce the M»F bias within the F selection routine, Hayes's Low Faithfulness CD algorithm aims to identify which faithfulness constraints are least likely to be *redundant* with other constraints. Consider the situation in which a certain faithfulness constraint F_k can account for a mark-data pair, and no other constraint can. So long as the loser of the pair is not harmonically bounded, i.e., so long as there is at least one L in its tableau row, then the constraint F_k cannot be relegated to the bottom of the hierarchy: it must dominate at least one other constraint. Hayes proposes that because such constraints are clearly needed to explain at least some data, they are good candidates to place into the ranking. The general '(data-)effectiveness' of a faithfulness constraint is characterised in terms of its ability to eliminate some mark-data pair which could be eliminated by *as few* other constraints as possible. (The ability to eliminate a pair that no other constraints can eliminate indicates the maximum possible degree of data-effectiveness.) The Low Faithfulness CD algorithm, when called upon to choose among faithfulness constraints to be ranked, selects (all of) those that have a maximum effectiveness measure. The hope is that greater restrictiveness will be achieved by postponing the ranking of less-effective F constraints.

The difference between the two proposals can be cast (roughly) as a difference in focus on the problem of F selection. BCD focuses on relationships between constraints in the hierarchy under construction, aiming directly to maximise the collective domination of M over F. Low Faithfulness CD focuses on the relationship between constraints and data, working within individual mark-data pairs, seeking to deal with each pair according to a criterion of constraint efficiency. A complete evaluation of the consequences of pursuing these disparate foci is, of course, quite nontrivial, and will doubtless be the subject of future investigation.

6.   Special/general relationships: F vs. M

Faithfulness constraints may stand in a kind of special/general relationship, called 'stringency' in Prince (1997): one may be more stringent in its requirements than the other, in that violation of the one (the special case) entails violation of the other, but not vice versa. Canonical examples are provided by the positional faithfulness constraints of Beckman (1998): since F:IDENT/ONS(φ) is violable only when the bearer of feature φ appears in onset position, the constraint F:IDENT(φ) is more general and more stringent, being violable everywhere. Gnanadesikan (1997) notes the same relationship among her scale-based faithfulness constraints.[12]

As demonstrated in Smith (1999) and Hayes (this volume), special/general relationships among F constraints can cause significant difficulty for distributional learning. The general F constraint will always be available to do any work that its specialised cognate can. But if the learner mistakenly high-ranks the general version, no positive evidence can contradict the error. To see this, let us review a Lombardi (1999)-style treatment of voicing. The relevant constraints are F:IDENT(voi), F:IDENT/ONS(voi), and M:*+voi, where by 'voi' is meant the feature of *obstruent* voicing. Working from distributional evidence only, consider the observation that *da* occurs in the language. What should the learner deduce?

/da/ →	F:IDENT/ONS(voi)	F:IDENT(voi)	M:*+voi
(a) da ∼ ta	W	W	L

This is the canonical situation in which some F must be ranked, since the only available M prefers the loser. The tableau puts both F constraints on an equal footing, and BCD would pick randomly between them. But the choice is consequential. If the general constraint is placed, then no amount of *rat* and *tat* will inspire the positive-only German learner to imagine that *rad* and *tad* are forbidden. But if the special constraint is placed, the German learner is secure, and the English learner can be disabused of over-restrictiveness by subsequent encounters with positive data.

A plausible move at this point would be to add an injunction to the F-selection clause of BCD, along the lines of Hayes (1999: 19, this volume) and Smith (1999), giving priority of place to the special constraint (or to the most special, in case of a more extended hierarchy of stringency). We are reluctant to take this step, because it does not solve the general problem. There are at least two areas of shortfall, both arising from the effects of constraint interaction. Both illustrate that the relation of stringency is by no means limited to what can be computed pairwise on the constraints of CON. First, two constraints that have only partial overlap in their domain of application can, under the right circumstances, end up in a special-to-general relationship. Second, the special/general relation-that is relevant to restrictiveness can hold between constraints that seem quite independent of each other. Let us review each in turn.

Derived subset relations. The first effect is akin to the one reviewed above in section 1 for parameter-setting theories, where dependencies among the parameters can reverse or moot subset relations. Two constraints which do not stand as special to general *everywhere* can end up in this relation within a hierarchy where higher ranking constraints reshape the candidate set in the right way. Because the set of candidates shrinks as evaluation proceeds down the hierarchy, the general Venn diagram for overlap between domains of relevance of two constraints can lose one of its 'ears' at a certain point, converting overlap into mere subsetting.

Consider two such generally overlapping constraints: F:IDENT/$\sigma_1(\varphi)$, which demands identity when the φ-bearer is in the first syllable, and F:IDENT/$\sigma'(\varphi)$, which demands identity when the φ-bearer lies in a *stressed* syllable. Neither environment is a subset of the other over the universal set of forms, but if there are higher ranked constraints that ensure stress on initial syllables as well as other stresses elsewhere in the word, then suddenly any violation of

F:IDENT/$\sigma_1(\varphi)$ is also interpretable as a violation of F:IDENT/$\sigma'(\varphi)$, though not vice versa. Contrapositively put, Faithfulness in σ' implies Faithfulness in σ_1, but it is possible to be narrowly faithful in σ_1 without being faithful in all σ'. In short, the σ_1 constraint has become a special case of the σ' constraint, contingently. Suppose φ is vowel-length, and the relevant markedness constraint is M:*V:, banning long vowels generally. Upon observation of a word like *pá: to*, we have a situation like this:

/pá:to/	M:InitialStress	F:IDENT/ $\sigma_1(\varphi)$	F:IDENT/ $\sigma'(\varphi)$	M:*V+
pá:to ~ páto		W	W	L

The learner who picks the stressed-based condition will have made an irrecoverable overgeneralisation error if the target language only allows long vowels in the first syllable. (As always, if the learner chooses σ_1 incorrectly, when the target language allows long vowels in all stressed syllables, or freely distributed without regard to stress, then positive evidence will be forthcoming to force correction.)

The direction of implication will be reversed in a language which allows at most one stressed syllable, always initial, so long as words with *no* stressed syllables also occur. Here Faithfulness in σ_1 implies Faithfulness in σ', but not vice versa. (As for the plausibility of this case, we note that although stress is usually required in all content words, in languages where stress behaves more like pitch accent, stressless words may indeed occur; see, e.g., the discussion of Seneca in Chafe (1977: 178–180) and Michelson (1988: 112–113).)

This result effectively rules out a solution to the general problem that is based on direct comparison of the internal syntactic structures of constraints, in the manner of Koutsoudas, Sanders, and Noll (1974) or Kiparsky (1982). The constraint-defining expression simply does not contain the required information, which is contextually determined by the operation of individual constraint hierarchies on individual candidate sets. We tend to regard this tactic as distinctly implausible anyway, since it requires a meta-knowledge of the structure of formal expressions which is otherwise quite irrelevant to the working of the theory. Nor is it plausible to imagine that the learner is somehow equipped to characterise surviving sets of candidates in such a way that subset relations could be computed. Here again, an appeal would have to be made to a kind of meta-knowledge which the ordinary functioning of the theory quite happily does without, and which will be in general quite difficult to obtain.

Third party effects. To see how independent-seeming constraints may be tied together by the action of a third constraint, let us examine a constructed voicing-agreement pattern of a type that can be legitimately abstracted from present theoretical and empirical understanding of such systems. It is similar to that of Ancient Greek and, as Bruce Hayes reminds us, also resembles the aspects of Russian used by Halle (1959) in his celebrated anti-phoneme argument.

Suppose a language has a contrast between voiced and voiceless stops, which we shall write as *p* and *b*, but no contrast among the fricatives, with voiceless *s* as the default and *z* arising only by regressive assimilation in clusters. Let us assume simple syllable structure, no clusters of stops, and agreement of voicing in clusters. We then have the following distribution of forms in the output:

| pa | ap | sa | *za | apsa | aspa |
| ba | ab | as | *az | *abza | azba |

What we are aiming for is a grammar in which the mappings *asba, azba* → *azba* provide (by regressive voicing) the *only* source of *z*, while *z, s* → *s* prevails everywhere else. The key datum is *azba*, which has multiple interpretations. It can be non-restrictively interpreted as evidencing general Faithfulness to *b*, implying that *abza* ought to be admitted, since clusters must agree in voicing. Even worse, the existence of *azba* might be to taken to evidence general Faithfulness to *z*, implying *za* and *az* in addition to *abza*. We actually want *azba* to be interpreted in terms of special onset-sensitive Faithfulness to the voicing of *b*: this admits *azba* but no other instances of output *z*.

Even at this coarse level of description, the problem is already clear: the datum *azba* admits of three distinct Faithfulness explanations, each with different restrictiveness consequences: how do we choose the *most* restrictive placement of these F? As we shall see, the r-measure-driven BCD conflicts with the special-over-general criterion, which itself has nothing to say about the choice between faithfulness to b-voicing and faithfulness to z-voicing.

For concreteness, let us assume the following constraints, which are like those in Lombardi (1999):

M:AGREE(voi)	Adjacent obstruents agree in voicing.
M:*b	No b (voiced stops).
M:*z	No z (voiced fricatives).
F:STOP-VOI/ONS	Preserve stop-voicing when output correspondent is in Onset.
F:STOP-VOI	Preserve stop voicing.
F:FR-VOI/ONS	Preserve fricative voicing when output correspondent is in Onset.
F:FR-VOI	Preserve fricative voicing.

The error-driven method of selecting suboptimal candidates for comparison, which collects false optima from the immediately prior grammar (here, the initial M»F stage), will find competitors for *ba* (*pa* is less marked no matter what the ranking of the M constraints is), *ab* (*ap* is less marked) and *azba* (*aspa* is less marked). This yields the following tableau:

W ~ L	M:Agree	M:*b	M:*z	F:stp-voi/O	F:stp-voi	F:fr-voi/O	F:fr-voi
ba ~ pa		L		W	W		
ab ~ ap		L			W		
azba ~ aspa		L	L	W	W		W

Recall that the left-hand member of each pair x ~ y is not only the desired winner, but also an exact match with its assumed input.

BCD puts the constraint M:Agree at the top, as shown, but after that, no other M constraint is immediately rankable. Each remaining active F frees up an M constraint; which should be chosen?

• BCD as currently formulated unambiguously chooses the *general* F:stop-voi, because it frees up both remaining M constraints. The other two F constraints free up only one M constraint.

• The doctrine of preferring special to general favours the placement of F:stop-voi/Ons over placing its general cognate, regardless of the diminished freeing-up capacity of the special constraint. But this doctrine *makes no distinction* between F:stop-voi/Ons and F:fr-voi, which are not members of the same stringency family.

Each choice determines a distinct grammar with different predictions about what additional forms are admitted (see Appendix 3 for details). High-ranking of F:stop-voi leads to this:

(10) General F:stop-voi high. **r=10**
   {M:Agree}»{**F:stop-Voi**}»{M:*b, M:*z}»{F:stop-voi/O, F:fr-voi/O, F:fr-voi}

   ▶ This grammar predicts /**absa**/ → **abz**a, introducing *z* in a non-observed context.

High-ranking of the special version of the stop-voicing Faithfulness leads to this:

(11) Special F:stop-voi/Ons high. **r=9**
   {M:Agree}»{**F:stop-voi/O**}»{M:*z}»{F:stp-voi}»{M:*b}»{F:fr-voi/O, F:fr-voi}

   ▶ This grammar introduces no further *z* than are observed: /**abz**a, absa/ → a**ps**a.

High-ranking of fricative-voicing Faithfulness leads to this:

(12)   F:FR-VOI high. **r=9**
{M:AGREE}»{**F:FR-VOI**}»{M:*z}»{F:STP-VOI}»{M:*b}»
{F:FR-VOI/O, F:STP-VOI/O}

▶ This grammar preserves all /z/, and therefore predicts the widest range of non-observed forms through new identity maps: /abza/ → abza, /za/ → za, /az/ → az.

It is worth noting that BCD has successfully found the hierarchy with the optimal r-measure. It is the r-measure's characterisation of restrictiveness that has failed.

Stepping back from the details, we see that the path to greatest restrictiveness will be obtained by ranking those F constraints with, roughly speaking, *fewest additional consequences*. In the case of an F:α vs. F:α/Ons pair, it is clear that the restricted version will have this property. But here we face an additional choice, from outside a single stringency family. F:STOP-VOI/ONS is by no means a special case of F:FR-VOI, and indeed one might naively imagine them to be completely independent – what should *az* have to do with *ba*? In isolation, nothing: yet they are connected by the force of M:AGREE in *azba*.

It is tempting to imagine that the notion of *fewest additional consequences* might be reducible to some computable characteristic of performance over the mark-data pair list. In the case of the special/general stringency pair operative here, observe that the special F constraint deploys fewer Ws than the general version. This is precisely because the special constraint is relevant to fewer structural positions and will be vacuously satisfied in regions of candidate space where the general version assesses violations. Since in the current learning context the optimal form satisfies all faithfulness constraints, it either ties or beats the suboptimum on each of them. One might then attempt to capitalise on this observable property, and add a bias to the algorithm favoring an M-freeing F constraint that assesses fewest Ws over the mark-data pair list.[13] (A similar effect would be obtained if the algorithm monitored and favoured vacuous satisfaction.) But the data that are available to the learner under error-driven learning will not always include the relevant comparisons.[14] In the case at hand, it is the dangerously general F:FR-VOI that is observably the most parsimonious of Ws, using just one while successfully freeing up M:*z.

It appears that the algorithm should choose the F constraint that is relevant to the narrowest range of structural positions. By this, any F/P for some position P should be favoured over any F, given the choice, even if they constrain different elements. But in general this property need not be obviously marked in the constraint formulation itself. Between F/P$_1$ and F/P$_2$ the choice will be more subtle, as we saw in our first example, and subject to conditioning by other constraints.

We must leave the issue unresolved, save for the certainty that managing the special/general relationship cannot be reduced to statements about the formulations of constraints in CON as they are presently understood. A natural further question arises immediately: what of the special/general relations among *markedness* constraints? Somewhat surprisingly, perhaps, it turns out that absolutely nothing need be done about these. The RCD method of ranking as high as possible handles these relations automatically and correctly. The learner can be completely oblivious to them.

To see this, let us reconstruct the German-like situation along markedness lines, following Itô and Mester (1997). In addition to a single monolithic F:IDENT(voi), we need the following constraints:

(13)   M:*+voi   Obstruents must not be voiced.

(14)   M:*+voi/Coda   *Coda* obstruents must not be voiced.

Suppose now that the learner must deal with the form *da*.

/da/ →	M:*+voi/Coda	F:IDENT(voi)	M:*+voi
(a) da ∼ ta		W	L

BCD applied here will yield the following hierarchy:

> M:*+voi/Coda » F:IDENT(voi) » M:*+voi

Codas are predicted to be voiceless, but outside of codas, the voiced–voiceless contrast is preserved.

With M constraints ranked as high as possible, both special and general remain in force at the top until forms are observed that violate them (positive evidence). Under the Markedness account, the special constraint directly forbids what is to be forbidden. (By contrast, the Faithfulness approach derives the forbidden as the complement of what must be preserved.) The learner will be motivated to *demote* a special constraint like M:*+voi/Coda only by a form that violates it, one that actually contains a voiced obstruent coda, like *ad*. (The Faithfulness account reaches its crux as soon as it encounters *da*, with a voiced obstruent in the onset.) Absent such forms, the learner stays with the most restrictive grammar. The affinity for restrictiveness falls directly out of the core constraint demotion idea.

In a world without positional Faithfulness, some of the pressure on BCD to decide among F constraints would go away; in particular, all special/general issues associated with positional specification would evaporate. We do not presume to adjudicate the issue here, but it is worth noting that complete elimination of the special/general problem would require developments in the theory of Faithfulness that would handle the kinds of emergent relationships illustrated above. It is at least intriguing that relationships of arbitrary complexity between markedness constraints are always handled with ease by constraint demotion. This provides strong learning-theoretic motivation for attention to the character of the faithfulness system. Short of complete elimination of positional Faithfulness, one might nevertheless hope to minimise the problem by minimising dependence on positional Faithfulness in favour of positional Markedness, as in Zoll (1998).

Another case of constraints with complicating relationships has been discussed by McCarthy (1998), that of output-output Faithfulness. He argues that the default in learning must be to favour hierarchies in which output–output faithfulness constraints, like markedness constraints, dominate ordinary faithfulness constraints. In the present context, output–output faithfulness constraints receive no special recognition, and require no extra apparatus; they are treated just like markedness constraints, and ranked as high as possible by the learner. The bias exerted by BCD is reserved for input–output faithfulness constraints. The default learner behaviour of ranking constraints as high as possible treats output–output faithfulness constraints properly. The justification for this derives from the fact that the learner has access, in the form of positive data, to the base output form: whenever OOF is violated, there will be positive evidence, in the visible lack of base/derived-form identity, that will indicate the need for domination of OOF. The analogous structure in input–output faithfulness, the input, is precisely what the learner does *not* have direct access to. (On this, see also Hayes, this volume, who envisions an important role for these in recovery from mistaken conclusions drawn from distributional learning.)

7.   'As low as possible': the disjunction threat

The chief problem addressed in this chapter – choosing which minimal set of faithfulness constraints to place next into the developing hierarchy – is symptomatic of a fundamental danger lurking in the effort to rank constraints *as low as possible*. The formal problem addressed by the original Constraint Demotion principle had to do with the intrinsic computational difficulties involved in working out which constraints *must* dominate which others, described by Tesar and Smolensky (1998). Consider the scheme given in (15), which describes the information contained in a mark-data pair. Here, W1, W2, . . . , are constraints preferring the winner of the pair, while L1, L2, . . . , are constraints preferring the loser. By the Cancellation/Domination Lemma, it must be the case that if the winner is to beat the loser, the full hierarchy must meet the following condition:

(15)   (W1 **or** W2 **or** W3 **or** . . .) » (L **and** L2 **and** L3 **and** . . .)

For a given mark-data pair, **at least one** constraint preferring the winner (W1 **or** W2 **or** W3 **or** . . .) must dominate **all** of the constraints preferring the loser (L1 **and** L2 **and** L3 **and** . . .). The formula condenses a potentially very large number of distinct hypotheses: one for each non-empty subset of Ws. And this statement gives the hypothesis set for just one mark-data pair. Multiplying them all out is sure to produce an impressive tangle of ranking arguments. Constraint demotion avoids the problem of 'detangling the disjunction' of the constraints favouring the winner, by instead focusing on demoting the constraints in the *con*junction, those preferring the loser. When rendered into an algorithm, the effect of focusing on the conjunction is to leave constraints as high as possible, because constraints are only demoted when necessary, and then only as far down as necessary. A correct hierarchy is guaranteed to emerge, even though the algorithm has never attempted to determine precisely which constraints *must dominate* which others, satisfying itself with finding out instead which constraints *can* dominate others.

But when we attempt to determine which faithfulness constraints to rank next, we are precisely trying to 'detangle the disjunction', by picking from among the (faithfulness) constraints preferring the winner(s). Attempting to select from among the faithfulness constraints preferring winners steers a course straight into the formal problem that constraint demotion avoids. This does not inspire great confidence in the existence of an *efficient* fully general solution to the formal problem.

Fortunately, a fully general solution is probably not required: the choice is only made from among faithfulness constraints, and only under certain circumstances. Recall the simple example of indeterminacy: F1 must dominate M1, and F2 must dominate M2, with no dependencies indicated by the mark-data pairs between (F1 and F2) or between (M1 and M2). If there are in fact no dependencies at all (indicated by the mark-data pairs or not) between (F1 and F2), (M1 and M2), (F1 and M2), or (F2 and M1), then the choice will not matter. The same grammar should result from either of the hierarchies in (16) and (17).

(16)   F1 » M1 » F2 » M2

(17)   F2 » M2 » F1 » M1

Indeed, ranking (18) should also give the same grammar, although it would fare worse on the r-measure than the other two.

(18)   {F1, F2} » {M1, M2}

In such a circumstance, there really would be no harm in randomly picking one of {F1, F2} to rank first. So, the fact that there is no obvious basis for a choice does not automatically mean that there is 'wrong choice' with attendant overgeneration.

More generally, how much the learner needs to care about such choices will depend upon the structure of the Faithfulness component of UG. This leads to a request for a more informed theory of Faithfulness, in the hopes that a more sophisticated understanding will yield a better sense of how much computational effort the learner ought to exert in making these ranking decisions during learning.

Appendix 1: Problems with ranking conservatism

In the algorithms we propose in the main body of the chapter, learning proceeds through accumulation of mark-data pairs, and the current grammar is whatever emerges from applying BCD to the total accumulated mark-data pair list. It is perhaps more usual to assume that the learner retains only a grammar, and that learning proceeds by modifying the current grammar-hypothesis directly in the light of incoming pieces of data, which are then forgotten once their effects are felt. How, on this grammar-centred view, is the M»F bias to be sustained throughout the process of learning? Itô and Mester (1999a) pursue an attractive approach: assume M»F only as an initial state, and in response to data, change the current hierarchy *conservatively*, so as to preserve as much as possible of the already determined ranking relations. The hope is that ranking conservatism, although insensitive to the M/F distinction, will appropriately carry forward the properties of the initial state to produce successor grammars that accord with the M»F bias to the degree allowed by the data.

Here we examine two problems with this general approach, which appear to exclude it, given current understanding. First, we show that conservative re-ranking quickly loses track of the distinction between motivated and unmotivated rankings and the M/F distinction along with it. Second, we relate an argument due to Broihier (1995) which establishes the catastrophic result that conservative re-ranking (quite independent of M/F considerations) can fail to find any solution at all for perfectly consistent data.

7.1   Problem 1: losing track of initial M»F structure

Itô and Mester (1999a) define conservatism in this way: if C_1 and C_2 belong to the same stratum, imposing C_1»C_2 is low-cost, because it does not contradict anything already established; but if C_1»C_2 is in the current state, it is especially undesirable to reverse it to C_2»C_1. Let us call the number of such complete reversals the *Permutation Index* (PI) of a re-ranking. This idea suggests a direction for development, but does not fully specify an algorithm: the immediate problem is what to do in situations where more than one alternative has the same, minimal PI. Consider a hierarchy with a stratum {A,B,C}. If we need A»C, do we go to {A,B}»C or to A»{B,C}? Or consider a ranking sequence A»B»C»D; if data demanding D»A arrives, do we go to B»C»D»A or D»A»B»C? In each case, PI = 3. For concreteness here, we shall assume the first, 'demoting' type of solution.

Given a hierarchy M»F for sets of constraints M, F, the strategy of minimising the PI will favour solutions *within* the unranked M and F blocs. However, once strict orderings are imposed, the algorithm loses track of which ranking relations are data-required and which are mere artifacts of the order of data presentation. Preserving artifactual relations leads to an inability to distinguish M from F solutions. This effect can show up quite rapidly, even with small sets of constraints. Consider the following collection of 3 mark-data pairs and 4 constraints:

(19)

	M_1	M_2	F_1	F_2
I		L		W
II	L		W	
III		L	W	

The rankings required by {I, II, III} are these: F_1 » {M_1 M_2} and F_2 » M_2. While RCD will simply put F_1 and F_2 together at the top of a two-stratum hierarchy, BCD gives the following:

$$\{F_1\} » \{M_1\} » \{F_2\} » \{M_2\} \quad r = 1$$

Let us examine the results of confronting the data in the order I, II, III, using ranking conservatism to guide the process. We start out with the initial state:

(20) $\{M_1 M_2\} » \{F_1 F_2\}$

For conciseness and visibility, we shall write this with bars separating the strata:

(21) $M_1 M_2 \mid F_1 F_2$

Now, mark-data pair I requires F_2 » M_2.

(22) $M_1 M_2 \mid F_1 F_2 \rightarrow M_1 \mid F_2 \mid M_2 \mid F_1 \quad PI = 1$

This is the minimal perturbation, inverting only the relation between M_2 and F_2. But it has induced an apparent total ranking on the constraint set, of which only the one ranking is actually motivated. Note in particular F_2 » F_1, the opposite of what the M-high solution requires.

Now consider the effect of mdp II, which requires F_1 » M_1.

(23) $M_1 \mid F_2 \mid M_2 \mid F_1 \rightarrow F_2 \mid M_2 \mid F_1 \mid M_1 \quad PI = 3$

The arrival of mark-data pair III, F_1 » M_2, seals the case:

(24) $F_2 \mid M_2 \mid F_1 \mid M_1 \rightarrow F_2 \mid F_1 \mid M_2 \mid M_1$ PI $= 1$

The desired outcome, $F_1 \mid M_1 \mid F_2 \mid M_2$, has a PI of 4 with respect to the input ranking of (24), $F_2 \mid M_2 \mid F_1 \mid M_1$. Ranking conservatism has led us far away from the best M » F solution.

Problem 2: Broihier's Cycle

This problem is more severe. The background idea is to take a constraint de-motion algorithm of provable success, 'online CD', and impose conservatism on it. Online CD works by modifying an old ranking into a new one, working one mark-data pair at a time. (RCD constructs an entire ranking from a set of mark-data pairs.) Broihier (1995: 52–54) considers a variant of online CD that places each demoted constraint in its own stratum: this will have the effect of preserving as many ranking relations as possible, in the manner of ranking conservatism. Thus, starting from AB|C, and given data entailing A » B, we go to A|B|C, preserving the relation B » C. By contrast, standard online CD would go to A|BC, keeping both B and C as high as possible. The problem is that B » C is not secure as a relation worth preserving. In a stratified hierarchy, AB|C as an intermediate state means that *either* A or B dominates C in the final grammar. Under Broihier's version of conservatism, the implicit interpretation is rather that *both* A and B dominate C, which cannot be sustained and leads to disaster.

The result of this method of demotion is that the order in which forms are encountered can impose phony domination relations. Preserving these can run afoul of the treatment of disjunctions in ranking arguments, leading to the interpretation of consistent data as contradictory. The problem is with a disjunctive choice in a mark-data pair, and with the fact that one of the disjuncts is made to appear unavailable through artifactual lowering of a constraint that could just as well be high-ranked. The clever move in the construction of the example is that one of the disjuncts *contradicts* other data, but the non-contradictory disjunct is discarded by the algorithm on the grounds of conservatism.

Here we present Broihier's example.

Imagine that we are targeting A|B|C|D, but we preserve ranking relations maximally. Suppose we see data motivating the rankings I:A » B, II:A » C, and III:A » D, in that order. The following sequence of hierarchies emerges:

(25)   ABCD $\rightarrow_I$ ACD|B $\rightarrow_{II}$ AD|C|B $\rightarrow_{III}$ A|D|C|B

Observe that standard CD would come up with A|BCD, regardless of order of data presentation.

Now we encounter data entailing IV:C » D:

(26)   A|D|C|B →$_{IV}$ A|C|D|B

Suppose now we are faced with data (Vab) leading to the disjunctive choice '*either* (D»C) *or* (B»C)'. This is perfectly consistent with everything seen so far, because even though the first disjunct contradicts IV and therefore must be false, the second disjunct can be true. The analyst can see this, but the algorithm, working one datum at a time, cannot: all the algorithm knows is that both disjuncts contradict the current ranking. We have therefore two choices:

(27)   A|C|D|B ?→$_{Vb}$ A|D|**B**|C   PI = 2, enforcing B»C, so that C drops
                                                              2 in the ranking.

(28)   A|C|D|B ?→$_{Va}$ A|**D**|C|B   PI = 1, enforcing D»C.

The desideratum of keeping C as high as possible and putting it in its own stratum (maximally preserving its previous ranking relations) forces us to act on the D»C disjunct – the one that contradicts previous data! So the following is the outcome of the encounter with mark-data pair V:

(29)   A|C|D|B →$_V$ A|D|C|B

But this is exactly the ranking we arrived at *before* the presentation of IV. We are in a cycle, and we must persist in it interminably, bouncing between the last two pieces of data considered.

Appendix 2: Getting greediness to fail

Here we show a contrived situation in which ranking a smaller set of faithfulness constraints at a given stage ultimately results in a lower r-measure than does the ranking of a larger set of faithfulness constraints at the same stage. We believe that this is the smallest case that can be constructed.

	M1	M2	M3	M4	F1	F2	F3	F4
P1	L				W	W		
P2	L				W		W	
P3	L				W			W
P4		L	L	L		W	W	
P5		L	L	L		W		W
P6		L	L	L			W	W

The example has 8 constraints, 4 markedness constraints **M1–M4**, and 4 faithfulness constraints **F1–F4**. It has six mark-data pairs, **P1–P6**. Initially, each of the markedness constraints prefers a loser in at least one of the pairs, so none of them may be ranked at the top of the hierarchy. Thus, at least one faithfulness constraint must be ranked first.

The set {F1}, consisting of only a single faithfulness constraint, is adequate to free up a markedness constraint, specifically, M1. Once those two constraints have been ranked, all of the other faithfulness constraints must be ranked before any more markedness constraints are freed up. The result is the following hierarchy, with an r-measure of 3.

(30)   {F1} » {M1} » {F2 F3 F4} » {M2 M3 M4}   r = 3

If, instead, the learner were to rank the other three faithfulness constraints first, then all four markedness constraints would be freed up, permitting F1 to be dropped all the way to the bottom of the hierarchy. Perhaps surprisingly, the result is a hierarchy with a larger r-measure, 4.

(31)   {F2 F3 F4} » {M1 M2 M3 M4} » {F1}   r = 4

Finally, an even higher r-measure results from initially ranking any two of F2–F4.

(32)   {F2 F3} » {M2 M3 M4} » {F1} » {M1} » {F4}   r = 7

This third hierarchy also illustrates that the strategy of selecting that subset of the faithfulness constraints that frees up the most markedness constraints also can fail to produce the highest r-measure: initially, {F2 F3 F4} frees up 4 markedness constraints, while {F2 F3} only frees up 3 markedness constraints, yet it is the latter that leads to the higher r-measure.

Observe that the pattern of relative violation of the constraints in this example is quite odd, from a linguistic point of view. First of all, markedness constraints M2–M4 are entirely redundant. For these mark-data pairs, at least, one would do just as much work as the three. This is not by accident; if one of M2–M4 did not prefer the loser in one of P4–P6, then it would be possible to free that markedness constraint with only one faithfulness constraint, and the contrary result would not occur. Pairs P4–P6 cannot be resolved by the ranking of any single faithfulness constraint, but neither is any single faithfulness constraint required: any subset of size 2 or greater of F2–F4 will do the job.

Observe also that the pairs suggest that faithfulness constraint F1 is 'equivalent' to the combination of {F2 F3 F4} with respect to justifying violation of M1. However, it must be so without any of F2–F4 constituting special cases of F1, or else the relevant facts about pairs P4–P6 would change, with F1 single-handedly freeing all markedness constraints.

Of particular interest is the extent to which the cases where the algorithm fails to optimise the r-measure are also cases where the r-measure fails to correlate with actual restrictiveness. If the differences in r-measure are among hierarchies generating identical grammars, then failure to find the hierarchy with the best r-measure is not a problem, so long as the hierarchy actually learned is one generating the restrictive language.

Appendix 3: Unexpected special/general relations

More details of the p/b/s example. The grammars given are constructed by BCD, with different choices of F for the second stratum.

Grammar 1. General F:STOP-VOI high. r = 10

{M:AGREE} » {**F:STOP-VOI**} » {M:*b, M:*z} » {F:STOP-VOI/O, F:FR-VOI/O, F:FR-VOI}

In the rows below the heavy line, inputs are tracked that do not come from observation of positive evidence, but that give information about the further predictions of the induced grammar. The key result is /absa, abza/ → abza, introducing *z* in a nonobserved context. Stop-voicing is always preserved and therefore 'dominant' in clusters.

	M	F	M		F		
	M:Agr	**F: stp-voi**	M:*b	M:*z	F: stp-voi/O	F: fr-voi	F: fr-voi/O
ba ~ pa		W	L		W		
ab ~ ap		W	L				
azba ~ aspa		W	L	L	W	W	
⋆/abza/→ **abza** ~ apsa		W	L	L		W	W
⋆/absa/→ **abza** ~ apsa		W	L	L		L	L
/za/ → sa ~ za				W		L	L
/az/ → as ~ az				W		L	

Grammar 2. Special F:STOP-VOI/ONS high. r = 9

{M:AGREE} » {**F:STOP-VOI/O**} » {M:*z} » {F:STOP-VOI} » {M:*b} » {F:FR-VOI/O, F:FR-VOI}

This is the most restrictive grammar and introduces no further *z* than are observed. Stop-voicing spreads regressively in clusters, which are otherwise voiceless: /abza, absa/ → apsa.

	M	F	M	F	M	F	
	M:Agr	**F:** **stp-voi/O**	M:*z	**F:** stp-voi	M:*b	**F:** fr-voi	**F:** fr-voi/O
ba ~ pa		W		W	L		
ab ~ ap				W	L		
azba ~ aspa		W	L	W	L	W	
✻/abza/→ apsa ~ abza			W	L	W	L	L
✻/absa/→ apsa ~ abza			W	L	W	W	W
/za/ → sa ~ za			W			L	L
/az/ → as ~ az			W			L	

Grammar 3. F:FR-VOI high. r = 9.

{M:AGREE} » {**F:FR-VOI**} » {M:*z} » {F:STOP-VOI} » {M:*b} » {F:FR-VOI/O, F:STOP-VOI/O}

This grammar preserves all /z/, and therefore predicts the widest range of non-observed forms through new identity maps: /abza/ → abza, /za/ → za, /az/ → az. Fricatives retain voicing everywhere and therefore fricative voicing is dominant in clusters.

	M	F	M	F	M	F	
	M:Agr	**F:** **fr-voi**	M:*z	**F:** stp-voi	M:*b	**F:** fr-voi/O	**F:** stp-voi/O
ba ~ pa				W	L		W
ab ~ ap				W	L		
azba ~ aspa		W	L	W	L		W
✻/abza/→ **abza** ~ apsa		W	L	W	L	W	
✻/apza/→ **abza** ~ apsa		W	L	L	L	W	
/absa/→ apsa ~ abza		W	W	L	W	W	
/za/ → **za** ~ sa		W	L			W	
/az/ → **az** ~ as		W	L				

NOTES

* The authors' names are given alphabetically. Prince would like to thank the John Simon Guggenheim Memorial Foundation for support. Thanks to Jane Grimshaw, John McCarthy, Paul Smolensky, and the Rutgers Optimality Research Group for helpful discussion.

    Hayes (this volume) independently arrives at the same strategy for approaching the learning problems dealt with here, and he offers similar arguments for the utility and interest of the approach. We have tried to indicate by references in the text where the identities and similarities lie. Along with the overlap in basics, there are significant divergences in emphasis, analytical procedure, and development of the shared ideas; we suggest that readers interested in the issues discussed below should consult both papers.

1. The non-existence of long high vowels on the surface in Yawelmani Yokuts, coupled with their underlying necessity, is the centrepiece of generations of commentary. Bruce Hayes reminds us, however, that the allomorphs of the reflexive/reciprocal suffix contain the otherwise unobserved high long vowels, indicating the need for a more nuanced view of their still highly restricted distribution in the language.

2. Different kinds of interactions have led Dresher and Kaye (1990) and Dresher (1999) to hypothesise elaborate paralinguistic strategies such as pre-establishing, for each subsystem, the order in which its parameters must be set. This is meant to replace learning from error. Ambiguity of analysis, rather than the subset relation, provides the central difficulty they focus on.

3. Swimming against the tide, Hale and Reiss (1997) insist on F»M as the default. For them, then, word learning yields no learning of phonology. To replace M»F learning, they offer an 'algorithm' that regrettably sets out to generate and sort the entirety of an infinite set in its preliminary stages.

4. For ease of exposition, we write as if there were only one constraint with the effect *š and one with the effect *si. In a fuller treatment of the example, we would see that *all* such constraints would be subordinated in (a) and that *some* M(*si) would have to dominate all M(*š) in (b). The thrust of the argument – distinguishing between Markedness and Faithfulness solutions to ambiguous data – is preserved amidst any such refinements.

5. Hayes (this volume) operates under the same I = O assumption, which he attributes to a suggestion from Daniel Albro.

6. The two diverge when a language admits forms which are not fixed points. Such forms do not add to the number of fixed points, but do increase the number of forms overall. A simple illustration is a language with a chain shift. Consider the following two mappings: $[x \rightarrow y, y \rightarrow z, z \rightarrow z]$ and $[x \rightarrow z, y \rightarrow z, z \rightarrow z]$. The two mappings have the same number of fixed points (one), but differ in the languages produced: the first, with the chain shift, produces $\{y,z\}$ while the second produces the more restrictive $\{z\}$. We are assuming that the learning of all non-identity mapping relations, including chain shifts, is done at the stage of morphophonemic learning.

7. This correlates with the fact that there is typically going to be a number of different grammars, with different patterns of Faithfulness violation, that produce the same repertory of output forms. For example, whether syllable canons are enforced by deletion or epenthesis cannot be determined by distributional evidence. Similarly, in

the complementary distribution case, we simply assumed a set of mappings among the allophones – but the same pattern could be got by deleting the restricted allophone from environments where it does not appear. The expectation is that improved theories of constraints will restrict such options, and that even when no improvement is possible, morphophonemic learning will be able to profit from the partial success obtained by identifying the high-ranked markedness constraints.

8. In order to deal with such intermediate grammars, a definition of 'optimum' must be offered for cases where the (mutually unranked) constraints within a stratum turn out to conflict. Tesar (1997) proposes the computationally efficient heuristic of merely lumping together the violations. Errors produced under this definition will always be informative, but some useful suboptima will be missed. Tesar (2000) offers further discussion of this point, along with a proposal for reducing the number of missed suboptima.

9. In this regard, our proposal is identical to Hayes's (1999: section 7.6.3, this volume). Beyond this, the proposals diverge in their handling of cases where more than one F constraint prefers some winner.

10. See Appendix 2 for the details of such an example.

11. See Appendix 2 for the details of such a case.

12. We gloss over the distinction noted by Prince (1997 *et seq.*) between stringency on the elements of structure and stringency on whole candidate forms. The constraints we discuss guarantee only the former, but only the latter leads to true special-case/general-case behaviour. The two converge when competing forms contain the same number of instances of the focal configuration, as in all the cases considered here.

13. A tension has developed here between the r-measure, which will in general favour those F constraints that set out the most Ws, giving them the greatest chance at freeing up M constraints, and considerations of specificity, which will have the opposite effect.

14. The key issue is the (un)availability of competitors that will 'turn on' the F constraint in every region of candidate space. For example, the true generality of F:FR-VOI will only be seen when competitions like *sa~za* and *as~az* are evaluated, leading to Ws that encode the implicit declaration 'relevant to onsets', 'relevant to codas', etc. But in such cases the required competitors are *more marked* than the desired optimum, and they will never present themselves as false optima from an earlier grammar hypothesis. Hence, they simply will not be found by the error-driven method of competitor-generation. Additional, more inclusive methods of competitor generation might also be considered, which could increase the informativeness of the distribution of Ws. But it bears emphasising that exhaustive inspection of all competitors is computationally intractable.

References

Angluin, D. (1980). Inductive inference of formal languages from positive data. *Information and Control* **45**. 117–135.

Baker, C. L. (1979). Syntactic theory and the projection problem. *LI* **10: 4**. 533–581.

Beckman, J. (1998). *Positional Faithfulness*. Ph.D. dissertation, University of Massachusetts, Amherst. [ROA 234, http://roa.rutgers.edu]

Bernhardt, B. and J. Stemberger (1997). *Handbook of Phonological Development: from the Perspective of Constraint-Based Nonlinear Phonology*. San Diego: Academic Press.

Berwick, R. (1982). *Locality Principles and the Acquisition of Syntactic Knowledge*. Ph.D. dissertation, MIT.

Broihier, K. (1995). Optimality theoretic rankings with tied constraints: Slavic relatives, resumptive pronouns and learnability. MS., MIT. [ROA 46, http://roa.rutgers.edu]

Chafe, W. (1977). Accent and related phenomena in the Five Nations Iroquoian languages. In C. N. Li and L. M. Hyman (eds.) *Studies in Stress and Accent. Southern California Occasional Papers in Linguistics*, **4**. 169–181.

Clark, R. (1992). The selection of syntactic knowledge. *Language Acquisition* **2: 2**. 83–149.

Demuth, K. (1995). Markedness and the development of prosodic structure. *NELS* **25**. 13–25. [ROA 50, http://roa.rutgers.edu]

Dresher, B. E. (1999). Charting the learning path: cues to parameter setting. *LI* **30: 1**. 27–67.

Dresher, B. E. and J. Kaye (1990). A computational learning model for metrical phonology. *Cognition* **34**. 137–195.

Gnanadesikan, A. (this volume). Markedness and faithfulness constraints in child phonology.

(1997). *Phonology with Ternary Scales*. Ph.D. dissertation, University of Massachusetts, Amherst. [ROA 195, http://roa.rutgers.edu]

Goldsmith, J. (1993). Phonology as an intelligent system. In D. J. Napoli and J. Kegl (eds.) *Bridges between Psychology and Linguistics: a Swarthmore Festschrift for Lila Gleitman*. Hillsdale, N.J.: Lawrence Erlbaum Associates. 247–267.

Hale, M. and C. Reiss (1997). Grammar optimization: the simultaneous acquisition of constraint ranking and a lexicon. MS., Concordia University. [ROA 231, http://roa.rutgers.edu]

Halle, M. (1959). Questions of linguistics. *Supplemento a Il Nuovo Cimento* **13**, ser. **10**. 494–517.

Hayes, B. (this volume). Phonological acquisition in Optimality Theory: the early stages.

Itô, J. and A. Mester (1997). Sympathy theory and German truncations. In V. Miglio and B. Morén (eds.) *University of Maryland Working Papers in Linguistics 5: Selected Phonology Papers from Hopkins Optimality Theory Workshop 1997/University of Maryland Mayfest 1997*. 117–139. [ROA 211, http://roa.rutgers.edu]

(1999a). The structure of the phonological lexicon. In Tsujimura, Natsuko (ed.) *The Handbook of Japanese Linguistics*. Malden, Mass., and Oxford: Blackwell Publishers. 62–100.

(1999b). On the sources of opacity in OT: coda processes in German. To appear in C. Féry and R. van de Vijver (eds.) *The Optimal Syllable*. Cambridge: Cambridge University Press. [ROA 347, http://roa.rutgers.edu]

Jacubowitz, C. (1984). On markedness and binding principles. *NELS* **14**.

Keer, E. (1999). *Geminates, the OCP, and the Nature of* CON. Ph.D. dissertation, Rutgers University, New Brunswick. ROA-350.

Kiparsky, P. (1980). Vowel harmony. MS., MIT.

(1982). Lexical phonology and morphology. In I. S. Yang (ed.) *Linguistics in the Morning Calm*. Seoul: Hanshin. 3–91.

Kisseberth, C. (1970). On the functional unity of phonological rules. *LI* **1**. 291–306.

Koutsoudas, A., G. Sanders, and C. Noll (1974). The application of phonological rules. *Lg* **50**. 1–28. (Drafted September 1971: fn. 2)

Levelt, C. (1995). Unfaithful kids: place of articulation patterns in early child language. Paper presented at the Department of Cognitive Science, The Johns Hopkins University, Baltimore, Md.

Lombardi, L. (1999). Positional faithfulness and voicing assimilation in Optimality Theory. *NLLT* **17**. 267–302.

McCarthy, J. (1998). Morpheme structure constraints and paradigm occultation. MS., University of Massachusetts. To appear in C. Gruber, D. Higgins, K. Olson, and T. Wysocki (eds.) *CLS 32, vol. II: The Panels*. Chicago: Chicago Linguistic Society.

Michelson, K. (1988). *A Comparative Study of Lake-Iroquoian accent*. Dordrecht: Kluwer Academic Publishers.

Oostendorp, M. van (1995). *Vowel Quality and Phonological Projection*. Ph.D. dissertation, Tilburg University. [ROA 84, http://roa.rutgers.edu]

Prince, A. (1997). Paninian relations. Lecture given at LSA Summer Institute, Cornell University.

(2000). Comparative tableaux. MS., Rutgers University, New Brunswick. [ROA 376, http://roa.rutgers.edu]

(2001a). Entailed ranking arguments. *RuLing Papers* **2**. 117–140. Rutgers University, New Brunswick.

(2001b). Entailed ranking arguments (extended version). MS., Rutgers University, New Brunswick. [ROA-500].

Prince, A. and P. Smolensky (1993). Optimality Theory. Technical Report RuCCS-TR-2, Rutgers Center for Cognitive Science. To appear, Blackwell [ROA-537].

Samek-Lodovici, V. and A. Prince (1999). Optima. MS., University of London and Rutgers University, New Brunswick. [ROA-363]

Sherer, T. (1994). *Prosodic Phonotactics*. Ph.D. dissertation, University of Massachusetts, Amherst. [ROA 54, http://roa.rutgers.edu]

Sommerstein, A. H. (1974). On phonotactically motivated rules. *JL* **19**. 71–94.

Smith, J. (1999). Special-general relations among faithfulness constraints and learning. Paper presented at the Rutgers-UMass Joint Class Meeting.

Smolensky, P. (1996a). On the comprehension/production dilemma in child language. *LI* **27**. 720–731. [ROA 118, http://roa.rutgers.edu]

(1996b). The initial state and 'Richness of the Base'. Technical Report JHU-CogSci-96-4. [ROA 154, http://roa.rutgers.edu]

Tesar, B. (1995). *Computational Optimality Theory*. Ph.D. dissertation, University of Colorado, Boulder. [ROA 90, http://roa.rutgers.edu]

(1997). Multi-Recursive Constraint Demotion. MS., Rutgers University. [ROA 197, http://roa.rutgers.edu]

(1998). Using the mutual inconsistency of structural descriptions to overcome ambiguity in language learning. *NELS* **28**. 469–483.

(2000). Using inconsistency detection to overcome structural ambiguity in language learning. MS., Rutgers University, New Brunswick. [ROA 426, http://roa.rutgers.edu]

Tesar, B. and P. Smolensky (1998). The learnability of Optimality Theory. *LI* **29: 2**. 229–268.

(2000). *Learnability in Optimality Theory*. Cambridge, Mass.: MIT Press.

Vapnik, V. N. and A. Y. Chervonenkis (1971). On the uniform convergence of relative frequencies of events to their probabilities. *Theory of Probability and its Applications* **16**. 264–280.

Wexler, K. and R. Manzini (1987). Parameters and learnability in binding theory. In T. Roeper and E. Williams (eds.) *Parameter Setting*. Dordrecht: Reidel. 41–76.

Zoll, C. (1998). Positional asymmetries and licensing. MS., MIT.
[ROA 282, http://roa.rutgers.edu]

9   Emergence of Universal Grammar in foreign word adaptations*

Shigeko Shinohara

1.   Introduction

There has been a renewal of interest in the study of loanword phonology since the recent development of constraint-based theories. Such theories readily express target structures and modifications that foreign inputs are subject to (e.g., Paradis and Lebel 1994, Itô and Mester 1995a,b). Depending on how the foreign sounds are modified, we may be able to make inferences about aspects of the speaker's grammar for which the study of the native vocabulary is either inconclusive or uninformative. At the very least we expect foreign words to be modified in accordance with productive phonological processes and constraints (Silverman 1992, Paradis and Lebel 1994). It therefore comes as some surprise when patterns of systematic modification arise for which the rules and constraints of the native system have nothing to say or even worse contradict. I report a number of such 'emergent' patterns that appear in our study of the adaptations of French words by speakers of Japanese (Shinohara 1997a,b, 2000). I claim that they pose a learnability problem. My working hypothesis is that these emergent patterns are reflections of Universal Grammar (UG). This is suggested by the fact that the emergent patterns typically correspond to well-established cross-linguistic markedness preferences that are overtly and robustly attested in the synchronic phonologies of numerous other languages. It is therefore natural to suppose that these emergent patterns follow from the default parameter settings or constraint rankings inherited from the initial stages of language acquisition that remain latent in the mature grammar. Thus, the study of foreign word adaptations can not only probe the final-state grammar but may also shed light on the initial state. The implication for L2 acquisition is that UG latent in L1 is accessible in a later stage in life (cf. Epstein, Flynn, and Martohardjono 1996, see Broselow and Park 1995, Broselow, Chen, and Wang 1998 reporting similar UG emergent patterns in their studies of inter-language phenomena). Of course, this hypothesis awaits confirmation from acquisition studies.

Under the assumption made above about the Emergence of the Unmarked in foreign word adaptation, it is possible to derive evidence bearing on the default

UG pattern(s) through the study of adapted forms. We shall discuss default patterns as we analyse the data in the Optimality framework. In Optimality Theory (OT) (Prince and Smolensky 1993) the learning process of a particular language consists in determining the ranking of the universal constraints. In recent proposals on learning theory in OT (Smolensky 1996, Gnanadesikan this volume, Davidson, Jusczyk, and Smolensky this volume, Prince and Tesar this volume, Hayes this volume), the ranking of Markedness (M) over Faithfulness (F) constraints (or an equivalent in the learning process, see Hayes this volume) is presumed to be the default, initial state of the language faculty because such ranking leads to a more restrictive grammar. In the course of acquisition, the child will re-rank F over M when provided with positive evidence of violation of Markedness constraints. In this study we shall examine several emergent patterns in adaptation data and characterise the constraint rankings they imply in terms of possible ranking schema: $M \gg F$, $M \gg M$, $F \gg F$ and $F \gg M$.

In the next section, I shall provide more explanation about the data and adaptation process in Japanese. In section 3 I shall explain the theoretical framework. Then, in the following sections, I shall present examples of the 'Emergence of UG' patterns. The analyses of the data consist of three parts: in section 4 we shall study the segmental level of adaptation, particularly assibilation of alveolar plosives; sections 5 and 6 treat pitch accent assignment and an aspect of syllabification, respectively. The chapter closes with a summary and issues for future study.

2.   Data and adaptation process

In this section, I shall give some information about the data and sketch the general process of adaptation.

My study is based mainly on Japanese adaptations of French words (Shinohara 1997b) (English words are used for comparison in the study of accentuation). By 'adaptation' I mean the process whereby native speakers of L1 adjust foreign words (L2) in such a way that the resulting forms are acceptable as L1 sound sequences. The following are Japanese adaptations of French and English (British 'Received Pronunciation') words:

(1)   Japanese adaptations
       French word   *université* |ynivɛʀsite| /junibeʹrusite/[1]
       English word   *university* |jʊnɪvɜːsɪtɪ| /junibaʹasitii/

Data were collected from three speakers of Tokyo Japanese of the same generation (30–40 years old) residing in Paris. The informants are proficient in L2. They spent several years in the L2 environment (Northern Standard French) after high school education in Japan. They were asked to convert the sounds of French words in a written word list to Japanese ones employing the type of adaptation used in code-switching or by interpreters when a Japanese equivalent is not available (e.g., in the case of proper nouns). They produced the adapted forms for the author and the author transcribed them. The procedure was repeated after a few weeks so that any variation could be observed. I employed this method rather than collecting loanwords from a dictionary. Loanwords often reflect peculiarities of spelling as well as features of the dialect of the particular adapter that are difficult to control. Therefore, we shall mainly study the adaptation process actively employed by our informants; however, loanwords will also be considered when they are comparable to the adapted forms.

The general process of adaptation is shown in (2). I suppose that the foreign input forms consist of phonemic strings of L2 (with certain prosodic features), rather than uncategorised sound sequences. The reason for this hypothesis is that there is a correspondence between the phonemes of L2 and L1, but not between their allophones. A phonemic categorisation of L2 sounds by L2 learners can be defective compared to that of L2 native speakers. For example, French phonemes |e| and |ɛ| can be grouped as a single /e/ sound in the French sound system of Japanese or Spanish learners who have not yet acquired the distinction. Even if defective, without such an initial sound categorisation by L2 learners, it would be difficult to explain a systematic correspondence between the phonemes of L1 and L2. Concerning my informants, they are learners who have reached a good level of perception and production in L2. In the data obtained from my informants, the correspondence between phonemes is consistent (for a fuller discussion of input forms, see Shinohara (1997b) and Paradis and LaCharité (1997), and for an opposing view, see Silverman (1992)).

I recognise three levels in the process of Japanese adaptation, but they do not have to be ordered procedurally.

(2)   Process of adaptation

Inputs:	French forms	Ex: *calmer, bac* |kalme|, |bak|
Segmental level	Segmental correspondence	karme, bak
Syllabic level	Vowel epenthesis, Prefinal syllable lengthening	karume, bakku
Accentual level	Pitch accent assignment	ka'rume, ba'kku
Outputs:	Adapted forms	/ka'rume/, /ba'kku/

On the segmental level, Japanese segments are substituted for French ones. Japanese syllable structure is relatively restricted; (3) below provides a list of the licit syllable types. When the input loanword contains a consonantal sequence that cannot be parsed into one of these syllable types, vowel epenthesis applies to allow the consonants to be syllabified.

(3)   *Syllable structure of Japanese*
        Light syllable: (C)(j)V   (ex. /ha/ 'tooth', /tja/ 'tea')
        Heavy syllables: (C)(j)VV   (ex. /too/ 'tower', /dai/ 'title')
                          (C)(j)VN   (ex. /teN/ [teŋ] 'point')
                          (C)(j)VQ   (ex. /haQ.pa/ [hapːa] 'leaf')
        (N: moraic nasal)
        (Q: moraic obstruent; the first half of a geminate obstruent)

On the syllabic level, the phenomenon I shall call 'pre-final lengthening' is also observed. When a foreign word ends in a syllable closed by a single consonant, as in |bak| *bac*, the prefinal syllable of the adapted form is lengthened by a gemination, as in /bakku/. On the accentual level, pitch accent is assigned. I shall present some of the adaptation phenomena that appeared in each level in later sections.

3.   Constraint interaction

In this section, I shall explain briefly the theoretical framework that I shall use and its significant consequences. The data are analysed in the Optimality framework (Prince and Smolensky 1993, McCarthy and Prince 1995). OT defines the grammar of a language as a hierarchy of universal constraints. The constraints are divided into two broad categories: Structural (or markedness) constraints reflecting unmarked forms as defined by UG; faithfulness constraints for preservation of input properties.

I shall illustrate the interaction between the two types of constraints by taking the example of plosive assibilation. Assibilation is a process whereby a plosive becomes an affricate in certain phonological environments (cf. Walter 1988). For example, [t] alternates with [ts] before high front vowels in Quebec French. The feature change in these segments is expressed by using aperture features (Steriade 1993):

(4)   Closure $[A_0]$: total absence of oral air flow.
        Fricative $[A_f]$: degree of oral aperture sufficient to produce a turbulent air stream.
        Approximant $[A_{max}]$: degree of oral aperture insufficient to produce a turbulent airflow.

According to Steriade (1993), a released plosive has a complex feature structure $[A_0 A_{max}]$. The first part $[A_0]$ corresponds to the closure stage and the second part [A_{max}] to the release stage. An affricate has the closure in common with a plosive, but the release is with friction, hence, its feature specification is [$A_0 A_f$].

Turning to Japanese, let us formulate two constraints in conflict regarding the assibilation of alveolar plosives:

(5)　　**ASSIBILATION** (*TU): No coronal plosive is followed by a high nonback vowel.[2]

　　　　IDENT-[A_{max}]: the release feature [A_{max}] of a plosive must be identical in the input and the output.

Assibilation above is a Markedness constraint. IDENT-[A_{max}] belongs to the Faithfulness constraint family. In tableau 1, the input /mat-u/ 'wait, non past' from a Japanese /t/-ending verb stem followed by the suffix /-u/ contains a /tu/ sequence. Suppose that this input /t/ has the plosive release feature [A_{max}]. When the Markedness constraint dominates Faithfulness, the grammar neutralises the release feature of /t/, and gives the output [matsu], with assibilation:

Tableau 1
Markedness ≫ Faithfulness

mat-u	*TU	IDENT-[A_{max}]
matu	*!	
→matsu		*

If the constraints are ranked in the reversed order IDENT-[A_{max}] ≫ *TU, the consonant [t] will preserve its release feature, and the output is without assibilation [matu], as shown below.

Tableau 2
Faithfulness ≫ Markedness

mat-u	IDENT-[A_{max}]	*TU
→matu		*
matsu	*!	

Assibilation is regularly present in Japanese native Yamato and Sino-Japanese lexicon, while recent borrowings violate this constraint. The loanword /tii/ < *tea* is realised as [ti:] without assibilation. In my adaptation data, assibilation is also violated. For this discrepancy across strata I adopt the idea that the different behaviour of loanwords reflects a distinct grammar, where a minimal re-ranking from the native one has taken place (cf. Itô and Mester 1995b; for other approaches to sub-lexica, see Inkelas 1994, Fukazawa 1997). Minimal re-ranking across strata in Itô and Mester's approach is to a large extent comparable to the acquisition process: once F ranks over M within a stratum with a positive evidence, in the next (newer) stratum this ranking remains as an established one instead of being reset to the initial state $M \gg F$ (relevant discussion is found in section 6.2.2).

With these analytic preliminaries completed, we now turn to some of the emergent patterns found in our study of Japanese adaptations.

4.   Emergent pattern 1: subdivision of the constraint *AFFRICATE

The first example of the emergence of UG in my data concerns the relative ranking of two markedness constraints on affricates. We shall compare the assibilation of the alveolar plosives in two lexical strata, the native stratum and the stratum of relatively old loanwords. A difference in the treatment of voiced and voiceless alveolar plosives followed by a high vowel is observed in these strata. I shall discuss three phenomena that are, in one way or another, influenced by the constraint of assibilation.

Let us first describe the facts in the native lexicon. In the native lexicon of Japanese, as we have seen in the preceding section, the alveolar plosives /t/ and /d/ surface as affricates before the high vowels /i/ and /u/. As shown in examples (6a,b,c) input sequences /tu/ and /du/ give [tsu] and [dzu] in the output, respectively. In addition to the assibilation, for the voiced alveolar plosive, there is another phenomenon taking place. The input sequences /du/ (and /di/) neutralise with /zu/ (and /zi/). Examples (6c,f,i) show the case of affrication of the input sequences /du/ and /zu/ in post-nasal and word-initial position, while (6d,g) provide examples of frication in intervocalic position. Thus, we see that the closure feature [A_f] (friction) of the input consonant /z/ and the [A_0] (occlusion) of the /d/ change on the surface depending on the environment. I shall call this phenomenon 'mutation'. Mutation is a cover-term for the weakning/ hardening process affecting voiced obstruents. The important point here is that mutation occurs only with the voiced alveolar plosive; the voiceless plosive does not mutate (cf. 6a,b,e,h).

(6)   *Assibilation and mutation in the native lexicon*
       (a) /tuki/ [tsuki] 'moon'
       (b) /natu/ [natsu] 'summer'
       (c) /kaNduki/ [kandzuki] 'cold month'
       (d) /mikaduki/ [mikazuki] 'increasing moon'
       (e) /su/ [su] 'vinegar'
       (f) /poNzu/ [pondzu] 'vinegar with lemon'
       (g) /gomazu/ [gomazu] 'vinegar with sesames'
       (h) /nasu/ [nasu] 'aubergine'
       (i) /zubora/ [dzubora] 'laziness'

Let us first turn to the analysis of assibilation and mutation in the native lexicon. I assume the universal constraint *AFFRICATE, reflecting the markedness of affricates as opposed to plosives. To explain the fact that the mutation is observed for /d/ but not for /t/, I shall split *AFFRICATE into two subcategories:

(7)   ***DZ**: Do not have voiced affricates
        *TS: Do not have voiceless affricates

By using these two constraints, the mutation for /d/ and the absence of the mutation for /t/ is explained as follows. On the one hand the faithfulness constraint for the closure feature, IDENT-[A_0] (see (8)) dominates *TS, as illustrated in tableau 3 below.

(8)   **IDENT-[A_0]**: the feature [A_0] of corresponding segments in the input and in the output must be identical.

Tableau 3
/ . . . tu/

	. . . tu	*TU	IDENT-[A_0]	*TS
1.	. . . tu	*!		
2.	. . . su		*!	
3. →	. . . tsu			*

On the other hand, IDENT-[A_0] is dominated by *DZ. Consequently, *DZ prevents the closure feature (A_0) of the voiced affricates from appearing in the output as shown in tableau 4.

Tableau 4
/ . . . du/

	. . . du	*TU	*DZ	IDENT-[A_0]	*TS
1.	. . . du	*!			
2. →	. . . zu			*	
3.	. . . dzu		*!		

Finally, the distribution of [dz] in non-intervocalic positions is accounted for by an undominated constraint *#Z (see (9)). Tableau 5 illustrates the effect of this ranking.

(9)   *#**Z**: no voiced fricative in non-intervocalic positions (i.e., the beginning of an utterance and postnasal position).

Tableau 5
/# du/

		#du	*#Z	*TU	*DZ	IDENT-[A$_0$]	*TS
1.	du			*!			
2.	zu		*!			*	
3. →	dzu				*!		

The summary of the constraint ranking is shown in (10).

(10)   *#Z, *TU ≫ *DZ ≫ IDENT-[A$_0$] ≫ *TS

We have established the following hierarchy between the markedness constraints against affricates: *DZ ≫ *TS. The ranking *DZ ≫ *TS reflects the Markedness of voiced affricates in the native lexicon of Japanese. The preference for voiceless affricates over voiced ones is observed in languages such as German and Russian, which possess voiceless affricates [ts] but lack the voiced counterpart. It is a plausible universal and perhaps an instance of the more general preference for voiceless obstruents over voiced ones, motivated by well-known phonetic considerations (i.e., the difficulty of maintaining vocal fold vibration in the face of oral closure). Such Markedness preferences are formalised in OT by assuming that the relevant constraint rankings are fixed. See Prince and Smolensky (1993) for discussion of Markedness scales in these terms.

The same M ≫ M ranking, *DZ ≫ *TS, has a striking effect in the adaptation process. Japanese has a five vowel system /a, i, u, e, o/. The high round back vowel |u| and the round schwa |ə| of French are generally adapted as /u/ both in loanwords and in my adaptation data. In the category of relatively old loanwords, such as the ones shown in (11), the input sequence |tu| of the French word *Toulouse* is adapted with the affricate [ts]: /tsuuruuzu/, while |du| of *Pompidou* is adapted as [do]: /poNpidoo/. The latter preserves the release feature [A$_{max}$] of the plosive /d/ by lowering the vowel from /u/ to /o/.

(11)   *Relatively old loans*
        (a) /tsuuruuzu/ < |tuluz| *Toulouse* 'place name', loan from French
        (b) /tsuupiisu/ < |tu:pi:s| *two-piece(s)*, loan from English
        (c) /poNpidoo/ < |pɔ̃pidu| *Pompidou* 'personal name', loan from French
        (d) /kaɸe do ɸurooru/ < |kafe də flɔʀ| *Café de Flore* 'name of a coffee shop', loan from French

The choice of vowels in each case is explained as follows. The [high] feature of the vowel |u| is more important than the appearance of the voiceless affricate [ts], thus the adapted form /tsuuruuzu/ preserves the high vowel /u/, as shown in tableau 6.

Tableau 6
Toulouse /tsuuruuzu/

	. . . tu	*TU	*DZ	IDENT-[high]	*TS
1.	. . . tu	*!			
2.	. . . to			*!	
3. →	. . . tsu				*

Whereas in /poNpidoo/ the more marked voiced affricate is avoided at the cost of sacrificing the vowel identity. This is easily described in the OT model as the insertion of the Faithfulness constraint IDENT-[high] within the Markedness preference ranking for voiceless over voiced affricates: *DZ ≫ IDENT-[high] ≫ *TS. Tableau 7 illustrates the effect of this ranking.

Tableau 7
Pompidou /poNpidoo/

	. . . du	*TU	*DZ	IDENT-[high]	*TS
1.	. . . du	*!			
2. →	. . . do			*	
3.	. . . dzu		*!		

We obtain the ranking shown in (12).[3]

(12)   *TU, *DZ ≫ IDENT-[high] ≫ *TS

The effect of the ranking *DZ ≫ *TS thus emerges here again. I consider this as an aspect of UG appearing in the adaptation process. The ranking *DZ ≫ IDENT-[high] differs from the native one, since the native sequence /du/ allows the output [dzu] without lowering the vowel height. Thus, this loanword category constitutes its own stratum (or at least it did so at the time of adaptation of these items). Of course, once the items are integrated in L1 as loanwords, speakers do not necessarily have access to the source words. The items may then be stored with the output sequences. Without other evidence it is impossible to decide between these alternative analyses.

In sum, we have reviewed two quite distinct places in the grammar of Japanese where the preference for voiceless affricates over voiced ones asserts itself. First, in the native vocabulary intervocalic /t/ before an /u/ is realised as an affricate (/natu/ → [natsu] 'summer') while /d/ is spirantised (/mikaduki/ → [mikazuki] 'increasing moon'). Second, in loanword adaptation /tu/ is realised with an affricate (*Toulouse* → [tsuuruuzu]) while /du/ changes the vowel (*Pompidou* → [poNpidoo]). While it could be argued that the former process establishes the *DZ ≫ *TS ranking, it is implausible that the change of vowel that we see in *Pompidou* → Pompi[doo] is a direct consequence of the avoidance of [dz] seen in /mikaduki/ → [mikazuki]. After all, spirantisation and lowering of a high vowel are quite different phonological substitutions. But viewed in the OT constraint-based approach, both phenomena reflect the marked status of voiced affricates relative to voiceless ones that is encoded in the fixed ranking *DZ ≫ *TS that by hypothesis forms part of the initial stage of acquisition. If this reasoning is correct, then we see an aspect of UG emerging in the adaptation process and the latter provides a window on the former.

5.   Emergent pattern 2: accentuation

I shall present other cases of the emergence of UG encountered in the study of accent assignment in the adaptation process (see Shinohara 1997b, 2000 for more extensive discussion). Japanese is a pitch accent language. For many Japanese lexical items, the accent is lexical (unpredictable), while for certain others, the accent is assigned by default (predictable). Foreign word adaptation is a good vantage point to observe default accent patterns, because input words do not always contain an accent specification. According to my study of Japanese adaptation, the accentuation of adapted forms falls into two categories: (1) the accent is carried over from the accent of the source word, which is the case for the adaptations of English words; (2) no accent is recognised in the source words and the accent is assigned by default, which is the case observed in adaptations of French words. Differing from the previous case of affricates, the accent assignment analysis does not involve lexical stratification. Since default accentuation identified in foreign word adaptations is also found in certain restricted parts of the Japanese lexicon such as proper names, certain derived words, etc., I assume that a single grammar is responsible for default accent for the entire lexicon. However, the patterns appearing in French adaptation are richer than the ones found in those restricted classes. In the analysis of the default accent patterns, I have encountered several instances of the emergence of UG. Before we look at the data from adaptations, let us briefly explicate the pitch accent system of Tokyo Japanese.

5.1   *Pitch accent system in Tokyo Japanese*

In a Japanese word, the accent is marked by a falling pitch. The accented syllable is the one just before the drop in pitch. In the word /tama'go/ 'egg', the pitch drops after the second syllable /ma/, which is the accented syllable. In an accented heavy syllable, the pitch falls after the first mora. In /ko'omori/ 'bat', the first syllable is a heavy one consisting of a long vowel. In the heavy syllable, only the first mora can bear the accent. Following the traditional convention I shall mark the accent with an apostrophe after the accented mora.

Let us turn to the specification of the place of accent. A Japanese word is specified as either 'unaccented' or 'accented'. In accented nouns, the position of the accent is in most cases unpredictable. In (13), three-syllable words are followed by an accentually neutral subject marker, /-ga/. Since any syllable can bear the accent, and a word can be also unaccented, there exist four possible accent patterns.

(13)   Accentuation in nouns

Three syllable nouns followed by the subject marker ga	me'gane-ga 'glasses'	koko'ro-ga 'heart'	otooto'-ga 'brother'	usagi-ga 'rabbit'

The accentuation of underived verbs and underived adjectives is limited to two types: accented or unaccented. In the infinitive form of the class of accented verbs, the accent falls on the syllable containing the penultimate mora (cf. (14)).

(14)   *Accentuation of verbs and adjectives*

	accented		unaccented	
verbs	tabe'ru	'eat'	nemuru	'sleep'
	ha'iru	'enter'	akeru	'open'
	omo'o	'ponder'		
adjectives	haja'i	'fast'	akai	'red'
	naga'i	'long'	marui	'round'

5.2   *Tracking of accent in English and French words*

In relation to accent specification, I shall now present adaptations of English words (Shinohara 1997b). For the English data, three informants studying in London sent the author their adapted forms written in 'kana' syllabary supplemented with pitch accent marks.[4] As shown in (15), the place of accent in an adapted form of an English word always corresponds to the primary stress position in the English word.[5]

(15)   *English stress and pitch accent placement of the adapted forms of English words*

Nouns	Adapted forms	Verbs	Adapted forms
pícnic	/pi'kunikku/	mátter	/ma'taa/
ínfluence	/i'NhurueNsu/	órganize	/o'oganaizu/
beháviour	/bihe'ibijaa/	invéstigate	/iNbe'sutigeito/
techníque	/tekuni'iku/	implý	/iNpura'i/
dífficulty	/di'fikarutii/	contríbute	/koNtori'bjuuto/

The primary accent (or stress) of an English word is marked by a relative prominence manifested by an increase in amplitude and duration. The accented syllable is also the anchoring site of phrasal tones (i.e., intonation) (cf. Liberman 1975). The only acoustic correlate common between English and Japanese accents is the falling pitch, which is used as the declarative nuclear accent in English. In spite of the distinct realisations of the accent of both languages, the accented syllables in English words seem to be interpreted as carriers of a lexical accent in the Japanese adaptation process.

In contrast with the English case, in French words no accent is recognised by Japanese speakers. Nevertheless, an accent is assigned to certain positions in the adapted forms. In French, phrase-final syllables are lengthened. We might think of several reasons why French phrase-final lengthening is not recognised as accent by Japanese speakers: (1) because it is fixed and predictable, it is not interpreted as lexical; (2) the phonetic correlates (duration in the French accent vs. pitch drop in Japanese) do not allow a correspondence between them; (3) phenomena at the phrasal level are excluded from the lexical representation. Without sufficient evidence from the adaptation of other languages, I cannot determine the reason. I shall, thus, simply assume no accent specification in the French input.

5.3   Default accentuation

Adapted forms of French words have been accented by the informants in the following ways:

I   If the final syllable of the adapted form is light, the accent falls on the syllable containing the antepenultimate mora (see (16)).

(16)   Accent on the syllable containing the antepenultimate mora

mâchicoulis	|maʃikuli|	'machicolation'	/masi'kuri/
travesti	|tʀavɛsti|	'travesty'	/torabe'suti/
crudité	|kʀydite|	'raw vegetables'	/kurju'dite/
alerte	|alɛʀt|	'alert'	/are'ruto/

philatélie	|filateli|	'philately'	/ɸiraˈteri/
automatique	|ɔtɔmatik|	'automatic'	/ootomatiˈkku/
boulangerie	|bulɑ̃ʒʀi|	'bakery'	/buraˈNzjuri/
pointe	|pwɛ̃t|	'point'	/powaˈNto/

II If the final syllable is heavy, the accent falls on the syllable containing the pre-antepenultimate mora (see (17)).

(17)   Accent on the syllable containing the pre-antepenultimate mora

potiron	|potiʀɔ̃|	'pumpkin'	/poˈtiroN/
sarrasin	|saʀazɛ̃|	'a type of wheat'	/saˈrazaN/
poinçon	|pwɛ̃sɔ̃|	'punch'	/powaˈNsoN/

It follows from (16) and (17) that if we exclude the final syllable and construct a bimoraic foot from the end of these forms, the accent falls on the first mora of the foot. Hence, the basic accent position is defined as being the head of the rightmost non-final bimoraic foot:

(18)   -(μ'μ)σ#   (the final syllable σ can be light or heavy)

This bimoraic metrical structure is the one that previous research has shown to play a role in the formation of 'prosodically derived' words in Japanese, including: (a) hypocoristics (Tateishi 1991, Poser 1990); (b) truncation (Itô 1990, Itô and Mester 1992, Suzuki 1995); and (c) reversed language of jazz musicians (Tateishi 1991, Poser 1990, Itô, Kitagawa, and Mester 1996):

(19)   (a) Hypocoristics:
            (aˈki)-tjan<akiˈtaka,
            (maˈa)-tjan<manami,
            (aˈt)-tjan<aˈtuko

        (b) Truncation of loanwords:
            (aˈni)me<animeˈesjoN 'animation',
            (deˈmo)<demoNsutoreˈesjoN 'demonstration'

        (c) Japanese musicians' argot (ZG):
            (jano)pi<pijano 'piano',
            (zuu)zja<zjaˈzu 'Jazz'

We learn from the analysis of default accentuation that the use of the bimoraic feet extends to the accent assignment in Japanese, as in many other languages. The constraints we shall use for the analysis of the default accent are essentially the following (see Shinohara 1997b, 2000 for more detailed discussion):

(20)   Main constraints:
        HEAD-LEFT (HEAD-L): trochaic feet.
        ALIGN (F, R, PrWD, R) (ALIGNR): align right edge of every foot with the right edge of a prosodic word.

NON-FINALITY (NONFIN): no prosodic head (accented foot (F) or syllable (σ)) of PrWd is final in PrWd.
MAX/MIN FOOT-BINARITY (MAX/MINBIN): feet are maximally/minimally binary at some level of analysis (μ,σ).
PARSE-SYLLABLE (PARSE-σ): parse every syllable into a foot.

The constraints are ranked as follows:

(21)   Main ranking for the basic patterns:
        NONFIN ≫ ALIGNR ≫ PARSE-σ
        MAX/MINBINARITY, HEAD-LEFT: one or the other is undominated in the ranking above.

The effects of this ranking are shown in tableau 8.

Tableau 8
mâchicoulis /masiˈkuri/

	maSikuli	NONFIN	ALIGNR	PARSE-σ	ALIGN L
1. →	ma(siˈku)ri		*	**	*
2.	(maˈsi)kuri		**!	**	
3.	masi(kuˈri)	F!		**	**
4.	(masi)(kuˈri)	F!	**		**

In tableau 8, candidate 1 is better aligned to the right than candidate 2 is. Candidate 3, though better aligned to the right than candidate 1, loses: this shows the NON-FINALITY constraint in force. Since Japanese words have at most one accent, I shall assume there is only one foot in a Japanese prosodic word.[6] In order to obtain non-iterative foot-parsing, PARSE-SYLLABLE is ranked under ALIGNR. Candidate 3 wins over candidate 4 by virtue of having a single aligned foot: the final feet of candidates 3 and 4 are aligned, but the first foot of candidate 4 is misaligned by two syllables.

We have seen the basic default accentuation patterns and the mechanism yielding these patterns. We shall turn to the case involving accent shift effect due to the presence of epenthetic vowels in the next section.

5.4   Vowel epenthesis and accent

An instance of the emergence of UG appearing in the accentuation concerns the avoidance of placing accent on epenthetic vowels, a phenomenon not found in L1 Japanese grammar (due to lack of epenthesis in monomorphemic words[7]). In the adapted forms of French words, syllables containing epenthetic vowels count as prosodic constituents relevant for accent placement; however, the accent seems to shift when the predicted position is filled by an epenthetic vowel.[8] In (22) and (23), adapted forms end in a light syllable, thus we expect that the accent falls on the antepenultimate mora. As shown in (22), when an input contains a non-epenthetic vowel in this position, the accent is placed on the antepenultimate mora as predicted. Epenthetic vowels are marked by italics.

(22)   (a) *otarie* |otaʀi| 'sea-lion'   /o'tari/
        (b) *mâchicoulis* |maʃikuli| 'machicolation'   /masi'kuri/
        (c) *alerte* |alɛʀt| 'alert'   /are'rɯto/
        (d) *travesti* |tʀavɛsti| 'travesty'   /torabe'sɯti/

Notice in examples (c) and (d) above that the epenthetic vowels after the antepenultimate mora are counted for foot construction, otherwise the accent would fall on a syllable closer to the beginning of the forms as in */a'rerɯto/ and */tora'besɯti/.

Now we observe the case where the accent would fall on an epenthetic vowel. When the antepenultimate mora of an adapted form does not correspond to a French vowel in the input, the accent shifts, as shown in (23).

(23)   (a) *stylo* |stilo| 'pen'   /sɯti'ro/
        (b) *patronat* |patʀona| 'patronate'   /patoro'na/
        (c) *abricot* |abʀiko| 'apricot'   /abɯri'ko/
        (d) *cercle* |sɛʀkl| 'circle'   /se'rɯkɯrɯ/

Across languages epenthetic or 'weak' vowels tend to avoid the accent. Here are a few examples from the literature:

> Epenthetic vowels: schwa in Hebrew (Prince 1975) and in Mohawk (Michelson 1988, Hagstrom 1997), /i/ in Palestinian Arabic (Brame 1973 cited in Kenstowicz 1981).
> Weak vowels: schwa in Chukchee (Kenstowicz 1993b), high vowels in Moksan (Kenstowicz 1993b), etc.

The tendency to avoid accent on weak vowels clearly looks like the effect of a markedness constraint. But in order to distinguish an epenthetic vowel from a phonetically identical vowel that has an input correspondent, the constraint must evidently refer to the input. I shall not discuss this point here and simply adopt the constraint in (24) from Alderete (1995) that expresses this type of input–output faithfulness relationship.

(24)   **HEAD(PCAT)-DEP**: Every segment contained in prosodic head PCat in S2 has correspondent in S1. If PCat is a prosodic head in S2, and PCat contains β then, β ∈ Range.

In our case HEAD(FOOT)-DEP is high ranking and it will force the accent to avoid an epenthetic vowel as illustrated in tableau 9.

Tableau 9
abricot /aburi'ko/

	abʀiko	HEAD(F)-DEP	DEFAULT ACCENT
1. →	aburi'ko		*
2.	abu'riko	*!	

With HEAD(FOOT)-DEP in the undominated position, the foot in the winning candidate must not contain an epenthetic vowel, thus, its foot parsing is /abu(ri'ko)/. Forms such as /(a')buriko/ and /abu(riko')/ are ruled out by FOOT-BINARITY and NON-FINALITY(σ) respectively. See Shinohara (1997a,b, 2000) for other possible analyses.

We have seen that accented epenthetic vowels are avoided in French word adaptation. Since the Japanese lexicon lacks epenthesis, this is an effect of UG asserting itself in the context of adaptation.

5.5   UG preference for the bimoraic foot

Another instance of emergence of UG appears when we compare stable accent patterns with a variable pattern in the adaptation data. When the penultimate and antepenultimate syllables are light then accent systematically appears on the antepenult (as long as it is not epenthetic). But when the antepenult is heavy, then there is variation between penultimate and antepenultimate accent. In (25), H denotes a heavy syllable, and L denotes a light syllable:

(25)   Variation in HLσ
        1. H'LL/HL'L: a'Ntere/aNte're <*intérêt* 'interest'
        2. H'LH/HL'H: mo'NtoroN/moNto'roN < *Montholon* 'place name',
                         pa'NteoN/paNte'oN/ < *Panthéon* 'Pantheon'

These words contain syllable sequences which cannot be easily parsed as a bimoraic foot. In moraic languages, there are different strategies for parsing such problematic HL syllable sequences. In classical Latin, bimoraic contiguous footing is assured by syllable shortening: /HLH/ → [HLL] (Mester 1994). In Tongan, where penultimate accent is imposed, an /HL/ input appears as [LL'L]; thus a final bimoraic foot is assured by breaking up H into LL (Prince and Smolensky 1993). In my data, however, there is not any syllable quantity change. What we find instead is a variation in accent location.[9] According to the analysis in Shinohara (1997a,b, 2000), we obtain the following foot grouping in the winning candidates: (H')Lσ and H(L')σ (or (H'L)σ and H(L')σ depending on the particular analysis).

The sequence HL is difficult for a bimoraic foot parsing. If the bimoraic structure is the one preferred by UG for trochaic accent, this difficulty should be reflected in some way or another. In the default accentuation of Japanese (identified in French word adaptations), it is reflected by variability in grouping.

5.6   Summary of the section

The accentual data reviewed in this section have a number of implications for acquisition and UG. First, the default accent pattern is found in restricted and relatively sparsely populated sections of the Japanese lexicon: compounds and proper names. (See Shinohara (2002) for an analysis of compound accent.) Therefore a theory which would assign accent to an adapted form according to the statistically most frequent pattern in the lexicon will not work. Rather, the adaptation data (cf. English vs. French adaptations) reconfirm the traditional generative assumption that inputs record unpredictable, contrastive information only. The default accent assigned by the constraint rankings in (21) steps in whenever the input lacks an accent. Given that French words are perceived as lacking an accent while English words are perceived as having an accent, only the former will be assigned an accent via the default accent schema.[10]

Second, the constraint barring accent on an epenthetic vowel is a truly emergent pattern because epenthesis does not operate in the native lexicon. The systematic avoidance of accent on an epenthetic vowel must arise from a constraint that is latent in the mature grammar and inherited from the initial state. The fact that epenthetic vowels are skipped by stress processes in a number of other languages provides support for the idea that this effect is due to a constraint belonging to UG (however it is eventually formulated).

Third, the vacillation between penultimate and antepenultimate accent for HLσ# sequences in the face of the stable antepenultimate accent for LLσ# sequences suggests that the constraints enforcing foot binarity are ranked high in the default UG constraint ranking. Both HEAD(F)-DEP and FOOT BINARITY are constraints on the internal structure of a metrical foot while NONFINALITY and ALIGNMENT position the foot with respect to the edges of the word. Perhaps in the default ranking of the initial state constraints on metrical form dominate constraints on alignment. This speculation obviously awaits confirmation from first language acquisition studies.

6.   Emergent pattern 3: syllabification and prefinal lengthening

This section presents two cases of emergence of UG in the analysis of 'prefinal lengthening' in adaptations of French words. Stem-syllable alignment is a constraint that appears to be active only in the adaptation process. It might be thus a case of emergence of UG. The other case concerns a markedness scale for geminates. Let us first review 'prefinal lengthening'. When a French word ends in a single consonant, in the adapted form, the rhyme corresponding to this syllable is lengthened.[11] It can be heavy in the following ways (lengthened rhymes are italicised):

(26)   1. It ends in the first half of a geminate consonant: /arusjub*ekk*u/
           <*archevêque* |aʀʃəvɛk| 'archbishop'.
        2. It contains a long vowel: /madur*eenu*/<*madeleine* |madlɛn|
           'a type of cake'.

Following Tsuchida (to appear), I interpret the prefinal lengthening as the result of alignment between the stem edge and a syllable edge. The choice between the types of lengthening is explained by a conflict among certain constraints including markedness constraints for gemination for certain types of consonants. Let us first observe some important facts.

6.1   Facts about the prefinal lengthening

The type of lengthening obtained depends on two factors:
1. Nature of the consonant;
2. Whether the vowel is 'lengthening' or not (see below).
   Here are some examples.

6.1.1   Voiceless obstruent

When a French word ends in a voiceless obstruent, this obstruent is consistently geminated in the adapted output.

nappe	|nap|	'table cloth'	/nappu/
patte	|pat|	'paw'	/patto/
lac	|lak|	'lake'	/rakku/
mèche	|mɛʃ|	'lock'	/messju/

6.1.1.1   Voiceless obstruent preceded by a lengthening vowel

There are special cases to add to the preceding one: when the vowel in the final closed syllable is spelled with more than one letter (*au, ou,* etc.) or with a circumflex accent (*ê, â,* etc.) the vowel can optionally lengthen instead of the consonant. I shall call these vowels 'lengthening vowels'.

| *haute* | |ot| | 'high' | /ooto/ or /otto/ |
| *fête* | |fɛt| | 'party' | /ɸeeto/ or /ɸetto/ |

The variation in this particular case is explained as follows. The choice depends on whether the vowel is recognised by the speaker as a lengthening vowel or not. If it is, then the vowel is lengthened; otherwise, the regular consonant gemination in (a) applies.

6.1.2   Voiced fricative   In case the final consonant is a voiced fricative, it is always the vowel that is lengthened.

| *rose* | |roz| | 'rose' | /roozu/ |

6.1.3   Voiced plosive or nasal stop; variation

robe		ʀɔb		'dress'	/robbu/ or /roobu/
aide		ɛd		'help'	/eddo/ or /eedo/
pomme		pɔm		'apple'	/pommu/ or /poomu/
reine		ʀɛn		'queen'	/rennu/ or /reenu/

We now turn to analyses of these facts.

6.2   Alignment between stem and syllable edges

6.2.1   Emergence of stem–syllable alignment   'Prefinal lengthening' is commonly observed in recent loanwords in Japanese (Hirozane 1992, Kawakami 1995, among others). In a previous study of English loanwords, Tsuchida (to appear) analyses it in terms of alignment between morphological and prosodic categories (cf. McCarthy and Prince 1993b) with the following constraint:

(27)   **ALIGN-R (Stem, R, Syllable, R)**: The right edge of the stem in the input must be aligned with the right edge of the syllable in the output. (Tsuchida to appear: 17 (34))[12]

The lengthening of consonants observed in (a) and (c) in section 6.1 above is explained by this alignment: by geminating the final consonant of the input |nap| it becomes a coda, thus it satisfies constraint (27). The second half of the geminate occupies the onset of the epenthetic syllable to satisfy the ONSET constraint. This analysis explains nicely why the gemination does not appear for the vowel-ending words (cf. (28a) below)[13] nor for word-medial consonants (cf. 28b and 28c).

(28)   (a) *pâté* |pate| 'paste'   /pate/, */patee/
       (b) *magma* |magma| 'magma'   /maguma/, */magguma/
       (c) *pique-nique* |piknik| 'picnic' /pikunikku/, */pikkunikku/

As shown in tableau 10, the ALIGN-R constraint forces the insertion of a mora on the consonant. The consonant gemination is, thus, explained by this mechanism.

Tableau 10
ALIGN-R ≫ DEP-μ

	lak#	ALIGN-R	DEP-μ
1. →	rak.ku		*
2.	ra.ku	*!	

ALIGN-R is a constraint observed in the adaptation process, but not in the other parts of Japanese lexicon. It is arguably another case of emergence of UG. Stem–syllable alignment is in fact found in many other languages such as: Axininca Campa, Bedouin Arabic, Biblical Hebrew, Kamaira (McCarthy and Prince 1993b), Tiberian Hebrew (McCarthy 1997), and Malay (Teoh 1987).

6.2.2   Absence of stem–syllable alignment in Sino-Japanese morphemes   In this subsection, we shall discuss a question about learning algorithms and re-ranking across strata. Having said that stem–syllable alignment does not appear in the other parts of the lexicon, there is thus a discrepancy between the Sino-Japanese sub-grammar and the adaptation sub-grammar.[14] Sino-Japanese morphemes can end in a consonant in input forms (Itô 1986); however, this consonant does not geminate at the right stem edge. Here are examples of Sino-Japanese (compound) words.

(29)   (a) /bet/ 'separate' + /sit/ 'room' → [bes.si.t*u*] 'separate room'
       (b) /kat/ 'lively' + /doo/ 'movement' → [ka.t*u*.doo] 'activity'
       (c) /bet/ → [bet*u*] 'separation'

In (29a), the first consonant of the second morpheme is geminated. This type of gemination occurs when a voiceless consonant is preceded by a morpheme-final /t/ (under certain circumstances morpheme-final /k/ triggers gemination as well). The absence of this gemination in (29b) is explained by the anti-gemination constraint for voiced consonants (cf. the gemination scale in the following section). The point of interest in (29) is the absence of gemination of the final /t/ of the second morpheme in (a) and (c) which violates the stem-alignment constraint. To allow the form without gemination, DEP-μ must dominate ALIGN-R. This is illustrated in tableau 11.

Tableau 11
DEP-μ ≫ ALIGN-R (Sino-Japanese)

	bet#	DEP-μ	ALIGN-R
1. →	betu		*
2.	bet.tu	*!	

   The native stratum, on the other hand, does not provide any evidence for ranking these two constraints given that input noun stems do not end in a consonant.
According to standard assumptions, in the initial state of UG Markedness is
ranked over Faithfulness. In the Sino-Japanese grammar we observe Faithfulness (DEP-μ) over Markedness (ALIGN-R). Therefore, a re-ranking from the
initial state must have taken place in the Japanese grammar through positive
evidence provided by the Sino-Japanese lexicon. However, in adaptation of
loanwords M ranks over F, as in the initial state. The question thus arises as
to why the adaptation grammar (M ≫ F) involves a different ranking from the
Sino-Japanese grammar (F ≫ M) and furthermore one that goes in the opposite
direction from the learning algorithm. Let us consider this problem together
with the grammar structure of lexical strata. One possible interpretation is that
F ≫ M is specific to the Sino-Japanese stratum while in other strata lacking
positive evidence for re-ranking M ≫ F remains. There are other features such
as size restrictions that identify morphemes as belonging to the Sino-Japanese
sector. Adaptations from French and English typically lack these features and
hence are not assigned to the Sino-Japanese class. If we make this assumption
then we can say that the M ≫ F ranking of ALIGN-R ≫ DEP-μ inherited
from the initial state remains latent in the mature grammar and emerges when
given the appropriate inputs. However, under the core–periphery view of lexical strata proposed by Itô and Mester (1995a,b) the Sino-Japanese grammar
stands between the native Yamato and the adaptation grammar. Furthermore,
Itô and Mester (1995b) claim that strata differ simply by the relative ranking of
Faithfulness and Markedness with more F ≫ Ms in peripheral sectors. On this
view then the passage from Sino-Japanese grammar to the adaptation grammar
would involve contradictory re-rankings: initial/native M ≫ F → Sino-Japanese
F ≫ M → adaptation M ≫ F. We must leave this problem for a future investigation. It will be interesting to see if such stem-final gemination that we see in
adaptation arises in primary language acquisition.

6.3   Markedness ranking for gemination

6.3.1   Compensatory lengthening in OT   Let us move on now to the case
where a vowel lengthens. It will provide evidence for another emergent pattern.

Input /ʀoz/ 'rose' is realised as /roo.zu/ instead of /roz.zu/. From a derivational perspective we can think of this input–output mapping as follows. First, there is gemination to satisfy ALIGN-R /roz.zu/; this is followed by degemination of /zz/ but preservation of the inserted mora which is then reassigned to the preceding vowel to give /roo.zu/ – a classic case of compensatory lengthening. This analysis can be translated into the OT framework by appealing to McCarthy's (1997) notion of 'Sympathy'. The constraint *ZZ, (30) below, is one of the markedness constraints against gemination of voiced fricatives:

(30)   Gemination constraint:
        *ZZ: Do not geminate voiced fricatives.

There are several constraints against different kinds of geminates which indicates that some consonants are easier to geminate than others. Given the constraint ranking established (*ZZ ≫ ALIGN-R ≫ DEP-μ) in tableau 12 below, candidate 3 should be the winner.

Tableau 12

	ʀoz#	*ZZ	ALIGN-R	DEP-μ
1.	roz.zu	*!		*
2.	roo.zu		*	*!
3. ? →	ro.zu		*	

We can block the incorrect /ro.zu/ and allow the correct /roo.zu/ to win by invoking a special Faithfulness constraint for moraic weight to the sympathetic (indicated by ✿ in tableau 13) but failed candidate (see (31)).

(31)   **✿-FAITH-μ**: Every mora of the flowered candidate must have a correspondent in the output.

If this constraint ranks above DEP-μ, it will block /ro.zu/ because the latter lacks the crucial extra mora which /roz.zu/ has.

Tableau 13

	ʀoz#	✿-FAITH-μ	DEP-μ
1. ✿	roz.zu		*
2. →	roo.zu		*
3.	ro.zu	*!	

We obtain the following ranking:

(32)   *ZZ ≫ ALIGN-R ≫ DEP-μ
       ⊕-FAITH-μ≫ DEP-μ

We shall now compare this result with the other cases of gemination in the next section.

6.3.2   Variation   We can now ask what are the degeminating consonants that give rise to compensatory lengthening. The voiced fricative /z/ always does (/roo.zu/ < |ROZ| *rose* 'rose'), while a voiceless obstruent (T) never does (/nap.pu/ < |nap| *nappe* 'table cloth'). For voiced stops (D) and nasals (N) there is variation between degemination and alignment: (/robbu/ or /roobu/ < ROB *robe* 'dress') and (/rennu/ or /reenu/ < REN *reine* 'Queen'). To account for the variation, I shall follow the free ranking approach taken by Reynolds (1994), Itô and Mester (1997), Anttila (1997), among others. In this approach, within a grammar constraints A and B may be unranked. That means, the constraints A and B are ranked A ≫ B in one sub-grammar, and B ≫ A in the other. Each sub-grammar will allow a single candidate to win. I assume that ranking between two constraints *DD/*NN (anti-gemination constraints of D and N respectively) and ALIGN-R is free. In tableau 14 *DD dominates ALIGN-R which gives /roobu/ as the optimal output; in tableau 15 ALIGN-R dominates *DD; this grammar allows /robbu/ to win.

Tableau 14
Sub-grammar A: *DD ≫ ALIGN-R

	ROB#	⊕FAITH-μ	*DD	ALIGN-R
1. ⊕	rob.bu		*!	
2. →	roo.bu			*
3.	ro.bu	*!		*

Tableau 15
Sub-grammar B: ALIGN-R ≫ *DD

	ROB#	⊕FAITH-μ	ALIGN-R	*DD
1.→ ⊕	rob.bu			*
2.	roo.bu		*!	
3.	ro.bu	*!	*	

(33)   Sub-grammar A: *DD/*NN ≫ ALIGN-R
         Sub-grammar B: ALIGN-R ≫ *DD/*NN

Comparing the ranking in (32) with sub-grammar B in (33), the following
Markedness ranking for gemination obtains:

(34)   *ZZ ≫ *DD/*NN

In sum, the crucial constraint rankings for the degemination phenomenon are
reviewed in (35):

(35)   *ZZ ≫ {*DD/*NN, ALIGN-R} ≫ *TT

The relative dispreference for a voiced geminate compared to a voiceless one can
be related to the well-known phonetic difficulty of maintaining voicing during
an oral constriction – a plausible Markedness scale inherited from the initial
state grammar. The degemination of voiced fricatives is thus another emergent
phenomenon. In the native vocabulary geminate /zz/ as well as geminate voiced
stops and nasals are not subject to degemination. This effect arises only in the
adaptation process.

7.   Summary and implications

In this chapter, we have observed several instances of the emergence of UG
in the Japanese adaptation of French words. First, in the segmental adaptation
process (section 4), the UG ranking *DZ ≫ *TS, which is already separated by
IDENT-[Ao] in the native grammar of Japanese, is further corroborated in the
adaptation data. The fact that there is affrication of |tu| in /tsuuruuzu/ < *Toulouse*
but lowering of the vowel in /poNpidoo/ < *Pompidou* is accounted for by the
insertion of IDENT-[high] between *DZ and *TS. Second, the accentuation
in French word adaptation data (section 5) confirms the default accentuation
pattern observed in restricted areas of the Japanese lexicon. There are also two
aspects of the accent patterns that may reflect UG. First, avoidance of accent
on epenthetic vowels is uniquely observed in adaptation data. Second, HLσ#
sequences are accented as either H'Lσ or HL'σ. This instability indicates the UG
preference for a bimoraic foot. Finally, in the syllabification data (section 6), a
stem–syllable edge alignment and UG preference scale for geminate consonants
emerge.

The unmarked patterns that appear in the adaptation process can be interpreted as the emergence of M ≫ F from the initial state of the grammar as
defined by the leaning theory. Markedness orders are observed in two places:
*DZ ≫ *TS and *ZZ ≫ *DD/*NN ≫ *TT. They may be phonetically driven
universal scales. One question arose when M ≫ F (stem–syllable alignment)

emerged in the adaptation process in spite of the fact that the reversed order (F ≫ M) is active in the Sino-Japanese stratum. A relevant issue worthy of further study is the 'core and periphery' structure of stratified lexicon (Itô and Mester 1995a,b).

Two general issues for further research arise from our consideration of these UG-emergent patterns. One issue is whether similar adaptations emerge in other languages. This is predicted to be the case if they reflect constraint rankings/parameter settings that are inherited from the initial state of UG and remain latent in the mature grammar. Another issue is the extent to which these UG reflecting patterns also emerge in second language acquisition, which is also predicted to occur on the grounds that aspects of the initial state remain in the mature L1 grammar.

NOTES

* I wish to thank René Kager, Wim Zonneveld, the audience at the Utrecht Workshop June 1998 and participants in the Phonology Circle in November 1998 at MIT for useful comments. Special thanks are due to Michael Kenstowicz for helpful discussions on the topics discussed in this chapter during my visit to MIT. I thank Ruben van de Vijver and Joe Pater for carefully reading the manuscript and making valuable comments and suggestions. But I am solely responsible for any errors. My son was born during the revision of this chapter, which encouraged me to continue my studies of phonological acquisition.

1. Hereafter, the input phonemic sequences are presented in vertical lines | |; the adapted forms in Japanese phonemic sequences are indicated by / /; [] indicates any phonetic output. Pitch accents are marked by an apostrophe after the accented mora.

2. Note that the Japanese /u/ phoneme is realised as a relatively centralised high vowel. One may suspect that assibilation represents a process of assimilation between [t/d] and high/frontness of the following vowel. I must, however, leave the nature of this phenomenon for a topic of future investigation.

3. Assibilation is violated in relatively new loanwords as well as in my data from adaptation: input sequences |t/d| followed by a high vowel are adapted without assibilation: /tudei/ < *Today* (part of the title of a column in a newspaper), /dubai/ < *Dubai* (loanword); /tuzjuuru/ < |tuʒuR| *toujours* 'always', /duuzu/ < |duz| *douze* 'twelve' (French word adaptations). Here IDENT-[A_0] is promoted above *TU. When the vowel is epenthetic, in both the relatively old and the recent loan classes the vowel is lowered to /o/ from the regular epenthetic vowel /u/ found in the other environments (in adaptation, it fluctuates between /o/ and /u/), but this time lowering occurs after both /t/ and /d/ (in the examples below, epenthetic vowels are marked by italics).

   (a) /katoriinu donuubu/ < |katRin dənœv| *Catherine Deneuve* 'personal name', loanword from French

   (b) /batto/ < |bat| *bat*, loanword from English

   (c) /esutoraddo/ < |estRad| *estrade*, 'stage', adaptation (with variation /esuturaddu/). In epenthetic vowels, vowel features are absent in the input; consequently IDENT-[high] does not determine the winner. Between candidates 2 and 3 in the tableau

below, candidate 2 is the winner with respect to *TS, unlike the case of /tsuuruuzu/
< *Toulouse* with a lexical /u/ that violates *TS and respects higher ranked IDENT-
[high].

bat/batto/

	bat	ASSIB	*DZ	IDENT-[high]	*TS
1.	battu	*!			
2. →	batto				
3.	battsu				*!

4. The Japanese writing system itself does not indicate the pitch accent. My informants for the English data were able to identify accent locations and also knew the notation.
5. Established loanwords from English do not always carry accent on the syllable corresponding to the original accent position. Such words are often accented according to the default accentuation that we shall discuss shortly: /hariu'ddo/ < *Hóllywood* (McCawley 1968, Haraguchi 1991, Suzuki 1995, Katayama 1995, 1997). Some others are unaccented: /kariforunia/ < *Califórnia*. Non-uniformity of accent patterns in loanwords may be due to dialectal variability of adapters and to the fact that they can be accented on the basis of written forms by a speaker who has no access to the source language.
6. Some of the four-mora forms of prosodically derived words, namely the abbreviated compounds and words in the reverse language, can be analysed as comprising two feet: (waa)(puro) 'word processor', (hi:)(ko:) 'coffee'. These four-mora forms are systematically unaccented. I therefore suspect a relationship between the two-foot structure and the lack of accent. The presence of only one foot might be a condition for the accent, but I leave this as a topic for future investigation.
7. In compound words the accent can be aligned with a morpheme boundary: kami' kaze < ka'mi 'divine' + kaze 'wind'. Consequently, in Sino-Japanese compounds where a morpheme can end in a consonant (Itô 1986) an epenthetic vowel can receive the boundary accent: gaku'moN < gak+moN 'study'. I think in this case the alignment constraint overrides the constraint barring the accent on an epenthetic vowel, which will be discussed shortly. This is consistent with multi-morphemic adapted forms: /suburenu'te/ < *souveraine-té* |suvRente| 'sovereignty'.
8. There are loanwords accented on an epenthetic vowel: kurisu'masu < *Christmas*. When loanwords are written in Japanese, there is no indication of epenthetic status of vowels. Loanwords can be accented on the basis of the written form by a speaker who has no access to the source sounds.
9. In Japanese native proper names where the default accentuation is detectable, an HLH sequence mostly receives initial accent (e.g., /ka'Nziroo/, /ka'NemoN/), whereas HLL seems to be uniformly unaccented. However, the data are too scanty to conclude that L1 default patterns on the HLH shape are distinct from the result in the adaptation data.
10. This implies that the unaccented class in Japanese must be considered 'marked': given the choice, it is more optimal for a word to have an accent than to lack one.

11. A somewhat parallel case is observed for word-final obstruent-liquid clusters, while other word-final clusters do not trigger any lengthening. We shall not discuss cases with word-final clusters in this chapter; see Tsuchida (to appear) among others for similar phenomena in loanwords from English, and Shinohara (1996, 1997b) for French adaptations.

12. As is stated, this constraint forces an alignment between a stem in the input and a syllable edge in the output, which is at odds with the standard OT assumption that the output does not refer to the input properties. However, we shall not be concerned with this problem here and we shall use ALIGN-R to mean the alignment between the stem and the syllable on the output level.

13. Exception: when the vowel is a 'lengthening' one as mentioned in section 6.1, a vowel can optionally be long in any position.

14. Sino-Japanese morphemes constitute their own stratum: compared to the native lexicon, Sino-Japanese morphemes allow freer distribution of segments but their size is limited to two moras.

References

Alderete, J. (1995). Faithfulness to prosodic heads. MS., University of Massachusetts, Amherst.

Anttila, A. (1997). Deriving variation from grammar. In F. Hinskens, R. van Hout, and L. Wetzels (eds.) *Variation, Change and Phonological Theory*. Amsterdam: John Benjamins. 35–68.

Brame, M. (1973). On stress assignment in two Arabic dialects. In S. Anderson and P. Kiparsky (eds.) *A Festschrift for Morris Halle*. New York: Holt. 14–25.

Broselow, E. and H.-B. Park (1995). Mora conservation in second language prosody. In J. Archibald (ed.) *Phonological Acquisition and Phonological Theory*. Hillsdale: Erlbaum. 151–168.

Broselow, E., S.-I. Chen, and C. Wang (1998). The Emergence of the Unmarked in second language phonology. *Studies in Second Language Acquisition* 20. 261–280.

Davidson, L., P. Jusczyk, and P. Smolensky (this volume). The initial and final states: theoretical implications and experimental explorations of Richness of the Base.

Epstein, S. D., S. Flynn, and G. Martohardjono (1996). Second language acquisition: theoretical and experimental issues in contemporary research. *Behavioral and Brain Science* 19. 677–758.

Fukazawa, H. (1997). Multiple Input-Output Faithfulness relations in Japanese. [ROA 260, http://roa.rutgers.edu].

Gnanadesikan, A. (this volume). Markedness and faithfulness constraints in child phonology.

Hagstrom, P. (1997). Contextual metrical invisibility in Mohawk and Passamaquoddy. In B. Bruening, Y. Kang, and M. McGinnis (eds.) *PF: Papers at the Interface, MIT Working Papers in Linguistics* 30. 113–182.

Haraguchi, S. (1991). *A Theory of Stress and Accent*. Dordrecht: Foris Publication.

Hayes, B. (this volume). Phonological acquisition in Optimality Theory: the early stages.

Hirozane, Y. (1992). Perception by Japanese speakers of some English sounds as the Japanese choked sound /Q/. *The Bulletin of the Phonetic Society of Japan* 201. 15–19.

Inkelas, S. (1994). The consequences of optimisation for underspecification. MS., University of California, Berkeley.

Itô, J. (1986). *Syllable Theory in Prosodic Phonology*. Ph.D. dissertation, University of Massachusetts, Amherst.

(1990). Prosodic minimality in Japanese. In K. Deaton *et al.* (eds.) *CLS* **26**, *Part II: Papers from the Parasession on the Syllable in Phonetics and Phonology*. 213–239. Chicago: CLS, University of Chicago.

Itô, J., Y. Kitagawa, and A. Mester (1995). Prosodic faithfulness and correspondence: evidence from a Japanese argot. *Journal of East Asian Linguistics* **5**. 217–294.

Itô, J. and A. Mester (1992). Weak layering and word binarity, LRC-92-09. Santa Cruz: University of California, Linguistic Research Center.

(1995a). Japanese phonology. In J. Goldsmith (ed.) *The Handbook of Phonological Theory*. Oxford: Blackwell. 817–838.

(1995b). The core-periphery structure of the lexicon and constraints on reranking. In J. Beckman, L. Dickey, and S. Urbanczyk (eds.) *UMOP Papers in Optimality Theory* **18**. 181–209. Cambridge, Mass.: University of Massachusetts, Amherst.

(1997). Correspondence and compositionality: the *ga-gyo* variation in Japanese phonology. In I. Roca (ed.) *Derivations and Constraints in Phonology*. Oxford: Clarendon Press. [ROA 146, http://ruccs.roa.rutgers.edu/roa/html]

Katayama, M. (1995). Loanword accent and minimal reranking in Japanese. *Phonology at Santa Cruz* **4**. 1–12.

(1997). *Optimality Theory and Japanese Loanword Phonology*. Ph.D. dissertation, University of California at Santa Cruz.

Kawakami, I. (1995). Shakuyougo ni miru sokuonka to rizumushoutotsu (Consonant gemination in loanword phonology and rhythm clash). *Gengokenkyuu* **108**. 46–73.

Kenstowicz, M. (1981). Vowel harmony in Palestinian Arabic: a suprasegmental analysis. *Linguistics* **19**. 449–465.

(1993). Peak prominence stress systems and Optimality Theory. *Proceedings of the 1st International Conference on Linguistics at Chosun University*. 7–22. Kwangiu, Korea: Foreign Culture Research Institute Chosun University.

Liberman, M. (1975). *The Intonational System of English*. Ph.D. dissertation, Cambridge, Mass.: MIT.

McCarthy, J. (1997). Sympathy and phonological opacity. Handout Hopkins Optimality Theory Workshop/Maryland Mayfest.

McCarthy, J. and A. Prince (1993). Generalised alignment. *Yearbook of Morphology*. 79–153.

(1995). Faithfulness and reduplicative identity. In J. Beckman, L. Dickey, and S. Urbanczyk (eds.) *UMOP Papers in Optimality Theory* **18**. 249–384. Cambridge, Mass.: University of Massachusetts, Amherst.

McCawley, J. D. (1968). *The Phonological Component of a Grammar of Japanese*. The Hague: Mouton.

Mester, A. (1994). The quantative trochee in Latin. *NLLT* **12**. 1–62.

Michelson, K. (1988). *A Comparative Study of Lake-Iroquoian Accent*. Dordrecht: Kluwer.

Paradis, C. and D. LaCharité (1997). Preservation and minimality in loanword adaptation. *JL* **33: 1**. 379–430.

Paradis, C. and C. Lebel, (1994). Constraints from segmental parameter settings in loanwords: core and periphery in Quebec French. *Toronto Working Papers in Linguistics* **13: 1**. 75–94.

Poser, W. (1990). Evidence for foot structure in Japanese. *Lg* **66**. 78–105.

Prince, A. (1975). *The Phonology and Morphology of Tiberian Hebrew.* Ph.D. dissertation, Cambridge, Mass.: MIT.

Prince, A. and P. Smolensky (1993). Optimality Theory: constraint interaction in generative grammar. MS., Rutgers University.

Prince, A. and B. Tesar (this volume). Learning phonotactic distributions.

Reynolds, B. (1994). *Variation and Phonological Theory.* Ph.D. dissertation, Philadelphia, Penn.: University of Pennsylvania.

Shinohara, S. (1996). The roles of the syllable and the mora in Japanese adaptations of French words. *Cahiers de Linguistique – Asie Orientale* **25: 1**. 87–112.

　(1997a). Default accentuation and foot structure in Japanese: analysis of Japanese adaptation of French words. In B. Bruening, Y. Kang, and M. McGinnis (eds.) *PF: Papers at the Interface MIT Working Papers in Linguistics* **30**. 263–290.

　(1997b). *Analyse phonologique de l'adaptation japonaise de mots étrangers.* Ph.D. dissertation, Université Paris III. [ROA 243, http://roa.rutgers.edu]

　(2000). Default accentuation and foot structure in Japanese: evidence from Japanese adaptations of French words. *Journal of East Asian Linguistics* **9: 1**. 55–96.

　(2002). Metrical constraint and word identity in Japanese compound words. In A. Csirmaz, Z. Li, A. Nevius, D. Vaysmann and M. Wagner (eds.). *Phonological Answers (and their Corresponding Questions). MIT Working Papers in Linguistics.* **42**. 311–325.

Silverman, D. (1992). Multiple scansions in loanword phonology: evidence from Cantonese. *Phonology* **9**. 289–328.

Steriade, D. (1993). Closure, release and nasal contours. In M. Hoffman and R. Krakow (eds.) *Nasals, Nasalization and the Velum.* San Diego: Academic Press. 401–470.

Suzuki, H. (1995). Minimal words in Japanese. *Proceedings of CLS* **31**. 448–463.

Tateishi, K. (1991). Les implications théoriques du langage des musiciens japonais. *Langages* **101**. 51–72.

Teoh, B. S. (1987). Geminates and inalterability in Malay. *Studies in the Linguistics Science* **17: 2**. 125–136.

Tsuchida, A. (to appear). English loans in Japanese: constraints in loanword phonology. MS., Cornell University, Ithaca.

Walter, H. (1988). *Le Français dans tous les sens.* Paris: Robert Lafont.

10   The initial and final states: theoretical implications and experimental explorations of Richness of the Base

Lisa Davidson, Peter Jusczyk, and Paul Smolensky

In this chapter we present the initial stages of work that attempts to assess the 'psychological reality' of one of the more subtle grammatical principles of Optimality Theory (OT; Prince and Smolensky 1993), *Richness of the Base*. Within the OT competence theory, we develop several of this principle's empirical predictions concerning the grammar's final state (section 1) and initial state (section 2). We also formulate linking hypotheses which allow these predictions concerning competence to yield predictions addressing performance. We then report and discuss the results of experimental work testing these performance predictions with respect to linguistic processing in infants (section 3) and adults (section 4).

1.   Introduction

Optimality Theory (henceforth OT) is a highly output-oriented grammatical theory. The strongest hypothesis is that *all* systematic, language-particular patterns are the result of output constraints – that there is no other locus from which such patterns can derive. In particular, the *input* is not such a locus. Thus, for example, the fact that English words never begin with the velar nasal ŋ cannot derive from a restriction on the English lexicon barring ŋ-initial morphemes. Rather, it must be the case that the English grammar *forces* all its outputs to obey the prohibition on initial ŋ. This requirement amounts to a counterfactual: *even if there were* an ŋ-initial lexical entry in English, providing an ŋ-initial *input*, the corresponding *output* of the English grammar would *not* be ŋ-initial. Thus, the absence of ŋ-initial words in English must be explained within OT by a grammar – a ranking of constraints – with the property that *no matter what the input*, the *output* of the grammar will not be ŋ-initial. That is, the OT analysis of English must consider a set of inputs to the grammar – the *base* – that is as *rich* as possible: the base includes all universally possible inputs, including those that are ŋ-initial, those that contain clicks, those that consist of seventeen consecutive consonants, etc.

    This principle – *Richness of the Base* – means that it is not sufficient that the ranking constituting the English grammar derive the correct outputs from inputs drawn from a putative English lexicon of underlying forms. In addition, the grammar must also ensure that any hypothetical input at all, even one that violates the systematic patterns of English, produces an output that obeys these patterns.

This constitutes the first 'prediction' of Richness of the Base relevant here: the final ranking of an English learner must filter out initial ŋs as well as, say, consonant clusters that are not legal in English. Thus, for example, when subject to the English constraint ranking, the input /ktobi/ must be mapped to an output such as [kətobi] which lacks the English-illegal onset [kt].

This prediction resides in the OT competence theory: it is a claim about an abstract input–output mapping. In order to use this prediction to assess the 'psychological reality' of Richness of the Base, we need a working hypothesis linking competence to performance. For example: if auditorily presented with [ktobi] – produced fluently by a Polish speaker, for example – and asked to employ this 'place name' fluently in a sentence, adult native monolingual English speakers will produce [kətobi] or some other form respecting English phonotactic patterns. We seek experimental confirmation of this prediction in section 4 below. Clearly, a naturalistic approximation to this situation occurs in loanwords, and the broad empirical generalisation is that indeed foreign words are adapted to conform to native patterns. However, this adaptation is often only partial: loanwords frequently contain structures illegal in the borrowing language. The experimental results we report below also display this incomplete nativisation as well, with outputs exhibiting deviations from English with interesting regularities. In section 4 we shall attempt an extension of Richness of the Base that recognises particular propensities for partial nativisation as an integral part of the final state of a native grammar.

The second prediction we exploit from Richness of the Base is more subtle, and concerns not the final but the *initial* state of the grammar. Section 2 develops a learnability argument leading to this prediction, which is simply stated: in the initial state, markedness constraints must dominate faithfulness constraints – otherwise the final state demanded by Richness of the Base could not be achieved in certain problematic cases. The assumption here is that OT grammars comprise only two types of constraints: faithfulness constraints, which compare the input and output and demand that they be equal; and markedness constraints, which examine only the output and penalise universally dispreferred or *marked* structures. We operate within this core structure of OT, with an eye to future research addressing richer versions of OT.

Like the derivation of the prediction Markedness » Faithfulness concerning the initial state, the linking hypothesis connecting this prediction to performance is somewhat complex: we take it up in section 3. The result is an experimental paradigm designed to test whether infants behave in accordance with the

'Markedness dominates Faithfulness' prediction. The outcomes of such experiments are also presented in section 3.

2.   Learnability and the initial state

How does the adult language-specific grammar – constraint ranking – come about? There are two aspects of this grammar to consider: the origin of the constraints themselves, and the determination of their relative ranking. Since the ranking is language-particular, it must be learned; we turn to this matter shortly. But since the constraints themselves are universal, it is not necessarily the case that they are learned from experience: it is logically possible that they are somehow innately specified, and OT makes no commitment on this issue. The research summarised in this section extracts a theoretical prediction from the hypothesis that knowledge of universal constraints in OT is innate; the research summarised in the next section attempts to put this prediction to an experimental test.

According to the learning theory for OT proposed in Tesar and Smolensky (1993, 1998a,b, 2000), the language learner re-ranks constraints in the face of learning data. When the learner's current grammar declares that the optimal output for a word is an erroneous pronunciation, constraints are minimally demoted so that the correct pronunciation is declared optimal by the revised grammar. The learning algorithm for a stochastic version of OT proposed in Boersma (1998) performs more gradual re-ranking, but it is also driven by the errors made by the learner's current grammar.

2.1   The initial state

What is the initial ranking of constraints, prior to the re-ranking induced by the data of the language to be learned? Adopting the working hypothesis that the universal OT constraints are innate and thus present in the initial state, and elaborating an argument originally from Prince (1993), Smolensky (1996a) developed a learnability argument showing that as a class, *markedness constraints must outrank faithfulness constraints in the initial state*, or certain languages would not be learnable. This characterisation of the initial ranking is consistent with a body of work analysing data from child phonology within the OT framework (Demuth 1995, Gnanadesikan this volume, Levelt 1995, Levelt and Van de Vijver this volume, Pater and Paradis 1996). Broadly speaking, with Markedness dominating Faithfulness in the initial ranking, the child's productions will contain only unmarked forms: violations of markedness constraints can only be optimal if higher ranked faithfulness constraints require them, and in this initial state there *are no* higher ranked faithfulness constraints.

Smolensky (1996b) exhibited a perhaps surprising consequence of the assumption that in the initial state markedness constraints are present and dominate faithfulness constraints: this assumption can broadly explain the discrepancy observed in language learners' early production and comprehension abilities. In particular, perceptual capacities that infants display in speech processing contrast with the inaccuracies that are apparent in their speech production. On the surface, the skill that infants show in comprehension appears to demand that faithfulness constraints be highly ranked, whereas their difficulties in producing speech seem to require that faithfulness constraints be low ranked. However, Smolensky (1996b) argued that what distinguishes production from comprehension is only which structures compete: in production, it is structures sharing the same underlying form; whereas in comprehension, it is structures sharing the same surface form. Once this difference in competition is taken into account, a single ranking – with Markedness dominating Faithfulness – accounts both for highly unfaithful child production and relatively faithful child comprehension.

We now quickly sketch the learnability argument showing that Markedness must outrank Faithfulness initially, illustrating with the example of word-initial ŋ. The question facing the learner here is, what is the correct ranking of the relevant markedness and faithfulness constraints? The markedness constraint is violated by ŋ-initial words; for expository purposes we shall take it to be a constraint against syllable-initial ŋ, and simply call it M_η. The relevant faithfulness constraints, which we shall call F_η, require that an underlying initial ŋ be faithfully mapped to an initial ŋ in the output. Again, the learner's problem is to determine the relative ranking of M_η and F_η.

There are three cases to consider. The first is the easiest, the case illustrated by Vietnamese. Here, some words of the language are pronounced with an initial ŋ in violation of M_η. This violation must be forced by a higher ranking constraint $\mathbb{C}$: $\mathbb{C} \gg M_\eta$. $\mathbb{C}$ cannot be a markedness constraint: there is no evidence for a universal constraint *favouring* initial ŋ. So $\mathbb{C}$ must be a faithfulness constraint, F_η. Thus the presence of ŋ-initial words in this type of language immediately informs the learner that the ranking must be $F_\eta \gg M_\eta$. Only under this ranking can an ŋ-initial underlying lexical form actually be pronounced with an initial ŋ. This first case will be called that of *a marked inventory*: the language's inventory of allowed sound structures includes the marked element in question – initial ŋ.

In the remaining two cases, the target ranking is the reverse: $M_\eta \gg F_\eta$. these are the cases of *unmarked inventories*. One such case is English, but first we take up the easier case, a hypothetical language we shall call English′. English′ contains words like *sing* taking a suffix *-er* to form *singer*. The pronunciations of these two forms in English′ are [sɪŋ] and [sɪ.nɚ] (the period marking a syllable boundary): *sing* is pronounced as in real English, with a ŋ in the syllable coda, but in the pronunciation of *singer*, the nasal is pronounced *n* (as in *sinner*) – because it is now in syllable-initial (onset) position. The English' pronunciation of *singer* violates the faithfulness constraint F_η: the underlying form has a velar nasal while the pronounced form has a coronal nasal. This alternation of a sound between ŋ and *n* tells the child learning English' that in this language, F_η is lower ranked than the markedness constraint M_η that prohibits ŋ in onset position. Thus, when a language exhibits alternations of this sort, there is explicit evidence available to the child for the language-particular ranking M » F; this case will be called *an unmarked inventory with alternation*.

But such evidence is not always present. The third case – *an unmarked inventory without alternation* – is illustrated by real English: there is no alternation between ŋ and *n* like that found in English'. None the less, the adult speaker of English must, according to Richness of the Base, rank M_η » F_η. Since the lexicon of English only places ŋ where it can be syllabified faithfully into the coda, the pronunciation of English words never forces the child to choose between satisfying M_η and satisfying F_η: by faithfully pronouncing each underlying ŋ in coda position, *both* M_η and F_η are always satisfied. Regardless of how M_η and F_η may be ranked, the learner will make no errors in pronunciation. Therefore, there will be no evidence of the sort used in the learning algorithm to drive constraint re-ranking. Thus if the learner's constraints are to end up – as Richness of the Base requires – with M_η » F_η, then these constraints *must start off with this ranking*.

Because this same argument can apply to any pair of potentially conflicting markedness and faithfulness constraints, the conclusion is quite general: in the initial state, markedness constraints must outrank faithfulness constraints. Only if the language provides overt evidence contradicting this ranking – the case of a marked inventory – will the reverse ranking come to be posited by the learner.

It is worth noting that what is crucial to the learnability argument is that the M constraint is *contrast neutralising* and the F constraint is *contrast inducing*. The force of M is to restrict the output to the unmarked pole of a dimension of possible variation (e.g., to prevent ŋ-initial words rather than to allow words to be either ŋ-initial or not). The force of F is to require that input differences along this dimension be maintained in the output. So the argument's conclusion might be generally stated that neutralisation-inducing constraints must dominate contrast-inducing constraints. Thus it is not actually critical to any of the analyses in this chapter whether the phonological phenomenon in question is literally a contest between Markedness and Faithfulness; 'M' and 'F' should be taken to refer to the relevant contrast-suppressing and contrast-inducing constraints, whatever their formal character. Thus the conclusion of the learnability argument can in fact be stated in rather theory-neutral terms: in the initial state, the grammar favours neutralisations to the unmarked, and only under pressure of observed marked forms does the grammar change to allow marked structures to surface.

As pointed out in Hayes (this volume) and Prince and Tesar (this volume), the pressure that Richness of the Base imposes for Markedness » Faithfulness is not limited to the initial state. Through interaction with other constraints, re-ranking that occurs during learning can disturb the initial ranking M » F even in a language lacking marked structures, where this ranking must prevail in the end. These authors propose various mechanisms by which the pressure towards Markedness » Faithfulness can be continually imposed by a learning algorithm, reinstating this aspect of the initial state, except where this pressure is overcome by positive evidence that F » M – evidence provided by the presence of marked structures in the target language.

Opposing the line of argument we have just summarised is another view. From the perspective of a developmental psychologist, one might have had an entirely different expectation: that, at the outset, faithfulness constraints should dominate markedness constraints (see also Hale and Reiss 1997). According to this alternative point of view, the simplest assumption that an infant might make is that surface forms faithfully mirror their underlying structure. Only in the face of evidence to the contrary would the learner assume that there is a more complicated relationship between surface forms and their underlying representations. The assumption that surface forms faithfully mirror underlying forms amounts to the assumption that faithfulness constraints outrank marked-ness constraints; this would then be the initial state as infants begin to acquire a native language. In this alternative theory, inaccuracies in the earliest produc-tions of words would be ascribed not to grammar, but to difficulties that infants have in co-ordinating the actions of the articulators.

As a new source of evidence complementing these theoretical arguments concerning the character of the initial state, we have conducted experimental studies to evaluate the relative ranking of Markedness and Faithfulness in the earliest grammars.

2.2   Nasal place assimilation

To date our experiments addressing the relative rankings of Markedness and Faithfulness in the initial state have addressed a single phonological phe-nomenon, nasal place assimilation. For now, we shall assume that nasal place assimilation is driven by a markedness constraint requiring that every nasal that is followed by a consonant must have the same place of articulation as that consonant; we shall call this constraint '$M_{NASALPL}$' or simply 'M_{NP}'. This markedness constraint potentially conflicts with the faithfulness constraints F_{NP} requiring that the place of articulation of a consonant in the input be preserved in the output. At issue will be the relative ranking of M_{NP} and F_{NP}.

Since the experiments we report here involve English-learning infants, it is relevant to consider the status of nasal place assimilation in English, which is somewhat complex. Within a single morpheme, it is almost always respected; for example, we have words like *bend*, *bump*, and *bank* [bæŋk], but no words like hypothetical *bemd*, *bunp*, or *bamk*. However, when a nasal at the end of one morpheme contacts a consonant at the beginning of a following morpheme, two outcomes are possible, depending on whether the morpheme boundary is the 'inner' type characteristic of Level 1 affixation, or the 'outer' type of Level 2. For the inner type, the nasal behaves as if it were in the same morpheme as the following consonant: it assimilates. An example of this type is the prefix *in-*, meaning 'not', as in *inaudible* and *inexpensive*. The nasal consonant of this prefix is pronounced [n] before coronal stops such as [t, d] (*intolerable, indefinite*), but the same input is pronounced [m] in cases where the consonant immediately following the prefix is a labial stop, /p, b/: *imperfect, imbalance*.[1] While an affix of the first, inner type will alternate, exhibiting assimilation, an affix of the second type will not; for example we get *input* and *incoming* with a different morpheme *in-* (meaning 'directed inward' rather than 'not').

Thus the situation confronting the learner of nasal place assimilation in English is in fact a composite of the three cases illustrated above for word-initial ŋ. Considering only simple, mono-morphemic words, English clusters are assimilated, that is, unmarked with respect to M_{NP}: English has an unmarked inventory without alternations. This is the hard case for learning, where the initial ranking must rank M_{NP} above F_{NP} in order for the language to be learnable. For morphologically complex words with inner, Level 1, affixation, clusters are still unmarked: here, English has an unmarked inventory *with* alternations, as exhibited by *in-*, 'not'. Finally, for morphologically complex words with Level 2 affixation, English does allow unassimilated clusters violating M_{NP}, so now the inventory appears to be marked.

This heterogeneous pattern is, of course, quite familiar in morphophonology, where, to oversimplify grossly, morpheme junctions at an inner level look like morpheme-internal environments, whereas junctions at an outer level look like the simple concatenation of separate words with little or no influence on one another. Although there are several theoretical proposals for handling this general pattern within OT and other phonological frameworks, we shall adopt here a highly simplified approach adequate to our limited needs. We shall assume that the markedness constraint M_{NP} requires that a nasal consonant have the same place of articulation as a following consonant if these two consonants are in the same *stem*. On this simplified view, inner, Level 1 morpheme junctions lie within the stem, while more superficial, Level 2 junctions lie outside the stem. Thus in *imperfect* the (Level 1) prefix *in-* 'not' falls within the same stem as the root *perfect*, so M_{NP} applies, requiring assimilation. In *input*, however, the (Level 2) prefix *in-* 'directed inward' falls outside the stem containing the root *put*, so M_{NP} does not apply, just as it fails to apply between the two words in the compound *pinpoint* or the two words in the phrase *in petroleum*.

On this analysis, the adult English ranking is $M_{NP} \gg F_{NP}$. There is evidence in the language for this ranking from alternations, but these are highly limited, applying to *in-* 'not' (before labial stops only) and perhaps also to *con-* 'together' (*contemporary, compatriot, congruence*). It seems reasonable to assume that children cannot exploit this evidence during their first two years, the period of time we examine in the experiments discussed below. So for all intents and purposes, for infants, English nasal assimilation presents the difficult case of an unmarked inventory without alternations – the case for which learnability requires that the initial ranking be Markedness » Faithfulness. Furthermore, at the age of the youngest children we tested (4.5 months), the literature shows no evidence of the acquisition of language-particular phonotactics (Jusczyk *et al.* 1993, Jusczyk *et al.* 1994, Mattys and Jusczyk in press). Thus it is unlikely that any behaviour we see in these infants is the result of statistical analysis of English consonant clusters. Any evidence we find that these youngest infants rank Markedness above Faithfulness would seem to support the nativist learnability argument that this is knowledge encoded in the initial state.

Thus we ask the experimental question: do infants show evidence of the ranking Markedness » Faithfulness? Focusing on nasal place assimilation, our goal then is to determine whether the youngest English learners give evidence of observing each type of constraint, and if so, to determine how they rank these two types of constraints with respect to one another.

3.   Experimental explorations of the initial state

Section 2 argued that under the nativist hypothesis, a principle fundamental to Optimality Theory, Richness of the Base, entails that in order for languages with unmarked inventories to be learnable, the initial state must be characterised by the schematic ranking Markedness » Faithfulness. In this section we undertake experimental assessment of this conclusion.

3.1   *Experimental methods, hypotheses, and predictions*

The work discussed here attempts to assess the hypotheses stated in (1).

(1)   **The central grammatical hypotheses (initial state)**
        Insight into infants' processing of linguistic input can be gained from the assumptions that, in the infants' grammars:
        (a) Markedness constraints are present;
        (b) Faithfulness constraints are present;
        (c) Markedness » Faithfulness.

The technique we employ for observing the linguistic processing of infants is the Headturn Preference Procedure, a computer-automated method used extensively in infant speech research (Jusczyk, 1998, Kemler Nelson *et al.* 1995). The dependent variable is the listening time to two types of spoken stimuli designed to differ significantly only along the linguistic dimension of interest – the independent variable. In this procedure, each infant sits on a caregiver's lap in a chair in the centre of a three-sided enclosure. A test trial begins with the flashing of a light on the centre panel. When the infant fixates the centre light, it is extinguished, and a light on one of the side panels begins to flash. When the infant makes a head turn of at least 30 degrees in the direction of the flashing light, the experimenter initiates a speech sample from the loudspeaker on the same side as the light and begins recording the infant's looking time by pressing a button on the response box. If the infant turns away from the loudspeaker by 30 degrees for less than 2 consecutive seconds, and then reorients in the appropriate direction, the trial continues, but the time spent looking away from the loudspeaker is eliminated from the total orientation time on that particular trial (the experimenter presses another button on the response box to stop the timer). If the infant looks away for more than 2 consecutive seconds, the trial is terminated. Both the experimenter and the caregiver wear sound-insulated headphones and listen to loud masking music to prevent them from hearing the stimulus materials throughout the duration of the experiment.

To link OT principles concerning the competence grammar to the performance of infants, we adopt the working hypothesis given in (2).

(2)   **Linking hypothesis, initial state: Higher Harmony $\Rightarrow$ longer listening time**
   (a) Infants will attend longer to stimuli that conform better to their current grammar, all else equal.
   (b) Phonologically unrelated stimuli presented as isolated words 'conform to a grammar' if they are each a possible output of the grammar.
   Relative version: Given two such stimuli A and B, A 'conforms better' to a grammar if, treated as isolated outputs and evaluated by the grammar, A has higher Harmony than B. Underlying forms for these outputs are assumed to be chosen to maximize Harmony (as in the lexicon optimization of Prince and Smolensky 1993: ch. 9 or the robust interpretive parsing of Smolensky 1996b and Tesar and Smolensky 1996, 1998b, 2000).
   (c) Phonologically related stimuli presented in a potentially grammatically related configuration 'conform to a grammar' if they are in fact so related by the grammar. In particular, consider a set of spoken items presented as a list of triads consisting of three prosodic words of the form

X ... Y ... XY′

where XY′ is a concatenation of X and Y in which some sound changes may have possibly occurred (e.g., *on ... pa ... ompa*). Such a triad 'conforms to a grammar' if there is a choice of inputs /x/ and /y/ such that X, Y, and XY′ are respectively the output of the grammar for the three inputs /x/, /y/, and /xy/, in which /xy/ is literally the concatenation of x and y (possibly separated by a morphological boundary). (Thus, depending on the ranking of Faithfulness in the grammar, the conforming XY′ may be a faithful concatenation of X and Y, or an unfaithful concatenation reflecting phonology.)

Relative version: One set of such stimuli A 'conforms better' to a grammar than another set B if A has higher Harmony according to the grammar. The inputs /x/ and /y/ are presumed chosen to maximize Harmony. (Thus *on ... pa ... ompa* conforms better to a grammar than does *on ... pa ... onpa* if the grammar assigns higher Harmony to the mapping /onpa/ $\rightarrow$ *ompa* than it does to the input–output mapping /onpa/ $\rightarrow$ *onpa*.)

Hypothesis (2b) suffices for evaluation of the hypothesis (1a) that markedness constraints are evidenced in the initial state, because markedness constraints involve only outputs. The more complex hypothesis (2c) is necessary, however, for assessing Faithfulness and its ranking relative to Markedness, since inputs as well as outputs of the grammar must be involved. Use of triad stimuli of the form described in (2c) will be referred to as the *X/Y/XY paradigm*.

The work reported in this section shows the initial results of a general research programme with a wide range of potential applications within grammatical theory. If the proposed Linking Hypotheses (2) – including the X/Y/XY paradigm – bears up under experimental investigation, listening times can be used to investigate many aspects of the grammars of infants. The initial work reported here involves two dimensions of phonological markedness: syllable structure and nasal place assimilation. The corresponding markedness constraints are respectively ONSET/NOCODA and $M_{NASALPL}$, a constraint (introduced in section 2.2) requiring that the place of articulation of a nasal consonant agree with that of a following consonant.

With respect to syllable structure, we examine a prediction of the Basic C/V Syllable Theory (Prince and Smolensky 1993: ch. 6): a single intervocalic consonant will universally be parsed into the onset of the following syllable rather than the coda of the preceding syllable. That is, ... VCV ... will always be parsed ... V.CV ... rather than ... VC.V ..., where the period marks the syllable boundary. Thus, all else equal, stimuli with the syllable structure ... V.CV ... (such as *ba.di to.ma ...*) will conform better to any grammar than those with the structure ... VC.V ... (*bad.i tom.a ...*). The reason is as follows. These forms may well violate many markedness constraints – e.g., *toma* violates a constraint prohibiting nasals – but the two matched lists will fare equally well with respect to all constraints except those sensitive to the only difference between the lists, the location of the syllable boundary. And here, both the constraints ONSET ('syllables have onsets') and NOCODA ('syllables do not have codas') are violated by all the forms in the second list and satisfied by all those in the first. Regardless of where these markedness constraints may be ranked in the infant's current grammar, this entails that the first list is more harmonic than the second, and by hypothesis (2b), infants are thus predicted to attend longer to the first list – if ONSET or NOCODA is indeed present in their grammars.

The case of syllable structure was chosen for the initial study in part because the competing alternatives – different syllabifications (e.g., *to.ma* vs *tom.a*) – are equally faithful to any underlying form.[2] There can therefore be no question of conflict between the markedness constraints ONSET/NOCODA and faithfulness constraints. This allows for a relatively simple experiment, but does not allow us to test the hypothesis concerning the relative ranking in the initial state of Markedness and Faithfulness. For this purpose, we turned to a different markedness constraint, $M_{NASALPL}$: satisfying this constraint can require changing the place of articulation of a consonant, violating Faithfulness and thereby setting up a conflict of the desired type.

The experimental study of $M_{NASALPL}$ tests all three hypotheses in (1). First, to test the hypothesis that Faithfulness is present in the infants' grammars and relevant to their behaviour in the way hypothesised in (2c), we compare a list of items of the form *om ... pa ... ompa in ... du ... indu ...* with a matched list of items of the form *om ... pa ... indu in ... du ... ompa. ...*[3] The lists are designed to fare equally well on all constraints except Faithfulness, which is satisfied in the first list and violated in the second. In particular, note that the lists are constructed so that the XY forms do not violate $M_{NASALPL}$: the final nasal in X always agrees in place with the initial stop in Y. Thus if Faithfulness is present in the infants' grammars and relevant to their behaviour in the way hypothesised in (2c), infants should attend longer to lists of the first – faithful – type.

Next, to test whether M_{NP} is in fact present in infants' grammars, we compare lists such as *ompa ... indu ...* with matched lists *omdu ... inpa. ...* The first list satisfies M_{NP} while the second list violates it, and the matching of syllables employed in the two lists means that the two lists fare equally with respect to other constraints. Thus if M_{NP} is present in the initial state then, according to (2b), we predict infants will attend longer to the first type of list.

For direct comparison with the Faithfulness experiment, it is actually preferable to design the Markedness experiment using lists of triads comparable to those used for studying Faithfulness. The first type of list includes triads of the form *om . . . pa . . . ompa in . . . du . . . indu . . .* while the second type of list is a matched list of items of the form *in . . . pa . . . **inpa** om . . . du . . . **omdu**. . . .* Both lists satisfy Faithfulness because each 'XY' bisyllable is a faithful concatenation of the 'X' and 'Y' monosyllables. But the consonants coming into contact in XY were selected so that nasal place assimilation was satisfied in the first list and violated in the second. Again, we predict from (2c) that infants will attend longer to the first type of list. This is the paradigm actually employed in the experiments described below.

Finally, to test whether Markedness » Faithfulness, we must pit F_{NP} against M_{NP}. Now the first list consists of triads of the form *on . . . pa . . . ompa* while the second list contains matched items *on . . . pa . . . onpa*. The first list violates F_{NP} but satisfies M_{NP}, and the reverse is true of the second list. The prediction from the Richness of the Base argument in section 2 is that infants will attend longer to lists of the first type.

Clearly, if the overall research programme enabled by the linking hypothesis (2) is viable, experiments of this general sort can be used to address virtually any putative markedness constraint. The approach may even extend to syntax in older children.

3.2   Experimental results: youngest infants

In determining the age groups to test, we took into consideration experimental results showing that although 9-month-old infants show significant listening preferences for sound patterns that observe the phonetics and phonotactics of English, 6-month-olds do not (Jusczyk *et al.* 1999, Jusczyk *et al.* 1993, 1994, Mattys and Jusczyk in press). We thus felt it important to test infants no older than 6 months in order better to access initial state, prior to acquisition of significant language-particular knowledge of phonology. The youngest age at which infants have sufficient head and neck control to be tested in the Headturn Preference Procedure is about 4.5 months.

The experimental results are summarised in table (3). Each row corresponds to a single experiment. The column labelled 'Markedness' indicates whether a given experiment addressed markedness of syllable structure or nasal place of articulation. The ages of infants participating in these experiments are indicated as well: 6 and 4.5 months, respectively. In each experiment, we tested the prediction that infants will attend longer to stimuli with greater Harmony, according to the hypothesised initial grammar. In the experiments labeled 'Markedness' in the 'Constraints' column, the stimuli presented differed only in that the forms with lower Harmony violated the markedness constraint(s) in question ('*M'), while the forms with higher Harmony satisfied the markedness constraint(s) ('TM'). In the 'Faithfulness' experiment, the higher Harmony stimuli satisfied Faithfulness ('TF') while the lower Harmony stimuli did not ('*F'). In the 'Markedness vs. Faithfulness' experiment, the higher Harmony triads respected Markedness but violated Faithfulness, while the reverse was true of the lower Harmony triads. In all other respects, the two types of stimuli were matched in each experiment.

The infants' listening times to the two types of stimuli presented in each experiment are shown in the columns headed 'Higher Harmony' and 'Lower Harmony'. The mean times are shown in boldface, with the standard deviation (SD) and standard error (SE) shown beneath. The difference in listening times for each experiment is assessed by several measures in the final column. The proportion of infants preferring the higher Harmony stimuli are shown as a fraction with denominator 20 or 16, depending upon whether the data from 20 or 16 infants were used in the experiment. In boldface, the P-value of the significance of the difference in mean listening times is shown, according to a paired t-test; t values are shown beneath the P value.

(3)

Results of experiments addressing the initial state

	Markedness	Age (mo)	Constraints	Higher Harmony Example **Mean Time** SD / SE (sec)	Lower Harmony Example **Mean Time** SD / SE (sec)	Difference Proportion ***p*** *t*
1	Onset/ NoCoda	6	Markedness	V. CV **10.99** 2.77/0.62	VC. V **9.35** 2.98/0.67	14/20 **.007** 2.996
2	Onset/ NoCoda	6	Markedness	CV **10.63** 1.64 / 0.37	VC **9.50** 1.94 / 0.43	14/20 **.017** 2.63
3	M$_{NasalPl}$	4.5[4]	Faithfulness	*ɪm…po…ɪmpo* TM TF **15.36** 3.89 / 0.97	*ɪm…po… uŋkɚ* TM *F **12.31** 4.55 / 1.14	11/16 **.006** 3.22
4	M$_{NasalPl}$	4.5	Markedness	*ɪm…po…ɪmpo* TM TF **15.23** 4.49 / 1.12	*ɪm…po…ɪmp o* *M TF **12.73** 4.80 / 1.20	11/16 **.044** 2.21
5	M$_{NasalPl}$	4.5	Markedness vs. Faithfulness	*ɪm …po…ɪmpo* TM *F **16.75** 4.58 / 1.14	*ɪm…po…ɪmpo* *M TF **14.01** 4.01 / 1.00	12/16 **.001** 4.21

As shown in (3), the results of experiment 1 provide evidence that at 6 months infants' grammars include a markedness constraint on syllable structure (either Onset or NoCoda). Since natural production of the marked syllable structure VC.V is problematic, these stimuli were created by splicing together two separately recorded syllables. The forms V.CV were also produced by splicing, in order to minimise differences other than syllable structure between the two types of stimuli. As a check on the results of experiment 1, in experiment 2 we tested infants' preference between lists of simple CV or of VC forms; these stimuli involved no splicing, although it is no longer as obvious that they equally well satisfy Faithfulness. None the less, hypothesis (2b) implies that infants should attend longer to the CV forms than the matched VC forms, since the latter but not the former violate ONSET/NoCODA, while the lists fare equally well with respect to markedness constraints evaluating individual segments. The results shown in (3) confirm the presence of syllable markedness constraints in the grammar of 6-month-old infants.

The table further displays the results of experiments 3 and 4, which provide evidence for the presence of Faithfulness and Markedness with respect to nasal place, respectively. The relative ranking of these constraints was examined in experiment 5, which provides evidence confirming the nativist learnability argument's prediction that Markedness » Faithfulness in the grammars of 4.5-month-old infants, the youngest age at which this method can be employed.

3.3   Markedness and Faithfulness in older infants

A complete presentation of experiments 3−5 is provided in Jusczyk, Smolensky and Allocco (2000), which also presents seven other experiments. These additional experiments examine nasal place markedness in infants at ages 10, 15, and 20 months. Faithfulness experiments at 10 months confirm the presence of Faithfulness as assessed in the X/Y/XY paradigm, as experiment 3 above did at 4.5 months. Markedness experiments at 10 and 15 months confirm the presence of $M_{NASALPL}$, as experiment 4 above did at 4.5 months. The results of the Markedness vs. Faithfulness experiments are more complex. At 10 months, infants show the same result as the 4.5-month olds did in experiment 5 above: they favour Markedness over Faithfulness. At 15 months, however, infants show no preference: there is no significant difference between listening times for the two types of stimuli. This experiment was repeated with a different set of 16 children at age 15 months, with precisely the same results. But this state of indeterminate ranking is short lived. By 20 months, infants return to a clear preference for forms obeying Markedness at the expense of Faithfulness.

What factors are responsible for the absence of any clear ranking of these markedness and faithfulness constraints in 15-month-olds? The fact that two separate groups of infants at this age displayed exactly the same pattern of results indicates that the absence of any consistent ranking of these constraints should be taken seriously. D. A. Dinnsen (personal communication, November 1998) has suggested a possible explanation for the uncertainty in the ranking at

15 months. In particular, it is at this age that infants show the first signs of learning about morphology in their comprehension of language. For example, Shady (1996) found that neither 12- nor 14-month-old English-learning infants showed significant listening preferences for passages with function words (functor morphemes) in the proper position (natural passages) over passages with function words in improper positions (unnatural passages). However, by 16 months, English learners are sensitive to the phonetic and distributional properties of function words and listen longer to the natural passages. Similarly, Santelmann and Jusczyk (1998) explored English learners' sensitivity to the relationship between the auxiliary verb *is* and the verb ending *-ing*. The *-ing* morpheme is one of the earliest acquired morphemes in children's productions of English (Brown 1973, De Villiers and De Villiers 1973). Santelmann and Jusczyk found that sensitivity to the basic dependency between the function morpheme *is* and the morpheme *-ing* develops between 15 and 18 months of age. Together, these two studies provide evidence that, beginning at approximately 15 months of age, infants are becoming sensitive to the presence of morphemes in the speech around them.

As L. Benua (personal communication, September 2000) has pointed out to us, the beginnings of morphology pose difficulties for the child's analysis of nasal assimilation in English. Presented with a single-syllable item like *im* in a stimulus triad of the experiment, 15-month-old infants may now explore the new possibility that this is a prefix, combining with the following root *po* to form a morphologically complex word *impo*. Now under this analysis, it is unclear whether a prefix-final nasal should assimilate to a following consonant: the evidence available from English is mixed. As we have seen, an 'inner', Level 1, affix like *in-* 'not' will assimilate; an 'outer,' Level 2, affix like *in-* 'directed inward' will not. Until the child's morphology becomes sophisticated enough to sort out such subtleties, the evidence will provide conflicting information about whether it is Markedness or Faithfulness that should dominate here. The result might well be indefiniteness of ranking of the sort exhibited by the 15-month-olds in our study.

By 20 months it may be that children are no longer treating the hypothetical forms in the experiment as novel affixes. Perhaps their receptive lexicons are now substantial enough that the complete absence of recognisable lexical items suggests to them that, while the sound patterns they are hearing are highly English-like, these are not actually English lexical items. Thus perhaps the 20-month-olds are not attempting lexical and morphological analysis, just as an adult presumably would not. The forms are being treated as morphologically simple items, subject to the basic patterns of English phonology, which, as we have seen, demand that nasals assimilate. The constraints that are being applied to the experimental stimuli are the most basic ones, where nasal place Markedness dominates Faithfulness.

3.4   Extensions

We have discussed initial work in an experimental research programme that attempts rather directly to observe the presence and ranking of grammatical constraints in infants too young to be producing any linguistic utterances. If this research programme proves successful, it may become possible for such experimental observation directly to inform theory development, even with respect to some of the most theoretically intricate issues in linguistic theory.

Take nasal place assimilation, for example. It can be exploited to examine a deep theoretical question concerning OT: must the type of optimisation used in OT to date be modified to allow constraints to be highly selective in the forms that they compare? In recent work, Wilson (2000) proposes such a fundamental modification of the theory in order to address what he argues to be a fundamental problem in standard OT. While the problem is much more general, it is nicely illustrated by nasal place assimilation. (Here we apply Wilson's general approach to the particular case of nasal assimilation; this is not a case Wilson treats explicitly.) It appears to be a strong empirical generalisation that when a nasal comes in contact with a following consonant with a different place of articulation, if place assimilation occurs, *it must be the nasal that assimilates.* Within standard OT, an output constraint like $M_{NASALPL}$ that requires a nasal consonant N to agree in place with a following consonant C *can* be satisfied by changing the place of C, and, as shown in a number of such cases in Wilson (2000), this entails that in the typology predicted by standard OT, there are languages in which it is C not N that assimilates under certain general conditions. In Wilson's proposed modification of OT, the markedness constraint $M_{NASALPL}$ is replaced with a different type of constraint which we shall call $^{\rightarrow}M_{NASALPL}$. Now $M_{NASALPL}$ asserts that a form in which a nasal fails to agree in place with a following consonant is less harmonic than *any* form lacking such an agreement failure. But $^{\rightarrow}M_{NASALPL}$ is a *targeted constraint*: it asserts *only* that a form S in which a nasal fails to agree in place with a following consonant is less harmonic than the single form S' which is exactly like S except that the nasal's place has changed to agree with that of the following consonant.

Targeted constraints solve this and many other important problems for standard OT. But the formal definition of optimisation required in the new theory – called TCOT ('TC' for 'targeted constraints') – must be made significantly more complex in order to deal with the new possibility that constraints can be targeted, because such constraints refuse to assert a Harmony relationship between all but a small set of closely related pairs of forms (like S and S').

A new source of evidence that a move from OT to the more formally complex TCOT is empirically warranted might be provided by experiments of the sort discussed above. According to standard OT, triads like *on . . . pa . . . onda* should satisfy $M_{NASALPL}$ and thus be preferred to their faithful counterparts *on* ... *pa* ... *onpa*. But according to TCOT, the opposite is the case. In TCOT, being unfaithful to the place of a nasal N in order to achieve agreement with a following consonant C will raise Harmony when Markedness outranks Faithfulness. But unfaithfulness to the place of C cannot raise Harmony: the agreeing form is *not* declared more Harmonic by the *targeted* constraint $^{\rightarrow}M_{\text{NASALPL}}$ – it is merely unfaithful. The studies reported here are neutral concerning the difference between OT and TCOT: since the triads used in the experiment always altered the place of the nasal, both OT and TCOT agree that the resulting unfaithfulness will increase Harmony when Markedness outranks Faithfulness. Thus empirical light of a new sort might be directed towards fundamental theoretical questions in phonology by further experiments examining unfaithfulness in the postnasal consonant, and potentially many other theoretically important contexts as well.

4.   Experimental explorations of the final state

In section 3, we discussed experimental evidence suggesting that, at the earliest time we can test them (4.5 months), infants possess markedness and faithfulness constraints, and rank them Markedness » Faithfulness, as predicted for the initial state by Richness of the Base in a nativist interpretation of OT. We now turn to experimental exploration of the final state. In section 4.1 we consider theoretical implications for Richness of the Base of partial nativisation of loanwords; this leads to the concept of *hidden rankings* and an extended formulation of Richness of the Base itself. In section 4.2 we formulate a hypothesis linking Extended Richness of the Base to phonological performance, and present the design of our primary experimental condition. The experimental results are presented in section 4.3; they reveal *hidden strata* among the onset clusters illegal in English. In section 4.4 we undertake an analysis of the experimental results, introducing the crucial notion of local conjunction of constraints. In section 4.5 we discuss the other experimental conditions we examined, and their implications for our proposed analysis. Finally, we briefly consider alternative possible types of explanations of the experimental findings in section 4.6, and, in section 4.7, possible explanations for the origin of hidden rankings.

As explained in section 1, a prediction concerning the final state of the grammar follows immediately from Richness of the Base, and might even be taken as definitive of it: the constraint ranking of an adult who has mastered English always outputs a form consistent with the general patterns of English, regardless of the input given to the grammar. To probe this aspect of the final state, we wish to induce adult English speakers to give as inputs to their phonological grammars underlying forms that, if faithfully parsed, would be illegal in English. Under such conditions, if Richness of the Base is correct, the grammar must 'repair' these 'defects', producing an English-legal output.

4.1   Covert grammars

The actual situation must, however, be more complex. We know that when foreign words are borrowed into a language in which they would be illegal, many types of defects are repaired, but often some types of defects are systematically left untouched (e.g., Kiparsky 1968, Saciuk 1969, Holden 1976, Yip 1993, Itô and Mester 1995b). It is as though the final grammar does not treat all illegal structures equally: some it simply will not tolerate; others it will let slide. As a case in point, consider the well-studied case of Japanese, where, roughly speaking, the established lexicon provides a kind of archaeological slice through time, in which forms that were borrowed at different points in time display different regularities. Itô and Mester 1995a, 1995b, 1999 present an extensive OT analysis which allows us to state this precisely; this has been the point of departure for further work in OT (e.g., Davidson and Noyer 1996, Fukazawa 1998, Fukazawa, Kitahara and Ota 1998, Katayama 1998).

The truly native or Yamato vocabulary of Japanese can be characterised by a certain constraint ranking which sharply divides all forms into the legal and the illegal. But among forms borrowed from Chinese, some of the constraints observed by all Yamato forms are seen to be imposed on the foreign forms, while others are not. Itô and Mester exploit the Markedness/Faithfulness structure of OT to provide an elegant formal analysis of this mixed situation. According to their analysis, among all the constraints obeyed by Yamato forms, some have stronger force than others: they are higher ranked. Schematically:

(4) $M_1 \gg M_2 \gg F \gg M_3$

where

(5)   Constraints relevant to Japanese lexical stratification
    (a) M_1 No voiced geminates
    (b) M_2 No unvoiced obstruents following a nasal
    (c) F Voicing of input segments must be preserved in the output – IDENT([voice])
    (d) M_3 NoCoda

According to this ranking, in native words, the markedness constraint M_3 can be violated, but both M_1 and M_2 must be respected because they dominate a relevant faithfulness constraint F. In the Yamato lexicon, there is no evidence for the relative ranking of M_1 and M_2; their relative ranking might just as well be reversed:

(6) $M_2 \gg M_1 \gg F \gg M_3$

Alternatively, we could say that the Yamato lexicon provides evidence only for the partial ranking:

(7) $\{M_1, M_2\} \gg F \gg M_3$ – base form of grammar

But in processing a Chinese loan input, suppose some faithfulness constraints are allowed to move up in rank:

(8) $M_1 \gg M_2 \gg F \gg M_3$

This means that the Chinese borrowings will be 'repaired' to satisfy M_1, but violations of M_2 will now be tolerated. Such is actually the case in Sino-Japanese forms with the constraints in (5).

We propose to explore what we believe to be a new interpretation of this state of affairs: at the time when the Chinese forms were being borrowed, the base adult Japanese grammar actually was (4). The ranking $M_1 \gg M_2$ was a *hidden ranking*: there was no evidence for it in the Japanese lexicon at that time. The forms violating M_1 and those violating M_2 define two *hidden strata* of Japanese, a covert distinction among Japanese-illegal forms.

Suppose furthermore that at the time of borrowing, the ranking of F was somewhat variable: it was a *floating constraint* (Reynolds 1994, Zubritskaya 1994, 1997, Nagy and Reynolds 1997, Anttila 1998, Boersma 1998, Boersma and Hayes 1999, Legendre *et al.* 2000):

(9) $M_1 \gg M_2 \gg M_3$ – covert form of grammar

$$\overline{\quad F \quad}$$

Each time a form is pronounced, the position of a floating constraint is fixed somewhere in its range. Thus, rather than the ranking (4), sometimes the following ranking will apply:

(10) $M_1 \gg F \gg M_2 \gg M_3$

When F occupies the lowest ranking in its range, we shall say it is in its *base position*, and the resulting grammar we shall call the *base ranking* (4). In both of the total rankings generated by the floating constraint – (4) and (9) – M_1 will be respected in all outputs; but M_2 will be respected only by the outputs of the base grammar. Suppose we assume, as a mutual constraint between the lexicon and the grammar, that a native vocabulary item must be assigned a consistent pronunciation by the grammar: that is, the output must be the same for both rankings (4) and (9). The native forms, then, must all obey M_2. The result is that, considering only these native lexical forms, there is now no evidence for the true full ranking (9) – only for the partial ranking (7).

But the non-native inputs provided by Chinese allow us to see the hidden rankings in the final state. Suppose that, perhaps with the commitment of additional cognitive resources, the ranking of F can sometimes be pushed by the speaker up to its elevated position. This allows for a more faithful pronunciation of the foreign input, although not generally a fully faithful pronunciation, as there remain markedness constraints like M_1 which are still higher ranked than elevated F. The result is that the foreign input will be partially nativised. And the character of the partial nativisation in the output provides information about the adult Japanese grammar that could not be extracted by considering native forms alone: it shows that the grammar possesses the hidden rankings in (9), and that the description in (7) is inaccurate.

Over time, the incorporation of a large number of borrowed Chinese forms into the Japanese lexicon presumably led to the establishment of a standardised elevated 'docking' position for F, with the now-partially nativised Sino-Japanese lexical items marked in the lexicon as forming a distinct 'stratum' corresponding to this elevated Faithfulness position. At this point, learning Japanese includes learning the different positions for F, so no special cognitive effort is involved in employing the Sino-Japanese vocabulary.

The ultimate fate of loanwords in a language is not our direct concern here. What is relevant to our discussion is only the initial point in the borrowing process, a point at which a foreign input is being processed by a grammar that was learned in a linguistic environment in which such forms were absent. Our interest in this arises because of its potential to reveal the structure of the final state of a native grammar.

The above considerations lead to the following extension of Richness of the Base to grammars with floating Faithfulness.

(11)   **Extended Richness of the Base**
(a) The final state of the grammar is in general a partial ranking containing floating faithfulness constraints.
(b) The location of a faithfulness constraint within its range is probabilistic. For any given input, this range of total rankings yields a set of outputs (possibly a singleton); the probability of each output in this set equals the probability of the collection of all total rankings yielding that output.
(c) Marginally, this may lead to variation in the surface forms of the language.
(d) Abstracting away from surface variation, the core generalisations exhibited in the (non-varying) surface forms of a language arise because its lexical items are subject to the meta-constraint that their outputs must be constant over the grammar, that is, constant over the floating range of faithfulness constraints. Underlying forms are otherwise unconstrained.

(e) Thus for a native input, the output of the grammar is non-variable, and therefore equal to the single output of the base grammar (with faithfulness constraints at the bottom of their floating range). For native inputs, only the base grammar need be considered; floating can be ignored.

(f) Inputs that are *not* drawn from the native lexicon will in general yield variable outputs; with Faithfulness elevated from the base grammar, outputs of non-native inputs will in general violate the surface generalisations of the language.

(g) It follows that the base grammar satisfies standard Richness of the Base: it generates only outputs respecting the surface generalisations of the language, given any input whatsoever.

An argument for the crucial final point (11g) goes as follows. Suppose there were some possible input I which the base grammar mapped to an output O that violated a surface generalisation. This would arise because the relevant markedness constraints were outranked by relevant faithfulness constraints in their base position. But then I would also yield O with Faithfulness elevated from its base position. Thus I would yield O consistently across the full grammar with floating constraints, so I would be a potential underlying form. Since there are no other constraints on underlying forms, there is nothing to bar such an I from the lexicon, thereby destroying the observed surface generalisation.[5] Therefore such an I cannot exist.

An important feature of Extended Richness of the Base (11) is that it subsumes previous work in OT under standard Richness of the Base: this work is now taken to be the study of base grammars, which are determined by the inventory of native forms. The consequences of floating Faithfulness only arise when analysing the partial nativisation evident in actual outputs from non-native inputs, or the residue of such partial nativisation in borrowing-induced lexical strata. It is precisely for such analysis that floating Faithfulness has been previously invoked.

Knowing the articulated depiction of the final ranking provided in the covert form displayed in (10) – rather than the less-informative base form illustrated in (7) – is important not just for precisely accounting for the partial nativisation of foreign words, but also for second language acquisition. It is commonly assumed in the L2 literature that for adults learning a second language, the initial state for L2 acquisition is the final state of L1 (Broselow and Finer 1991, Archibald 1993, Broselow and Park 1995, Pater 1997, Broselow, Chen, and Wang 1998, Hancin-Bhatt and Bhatt 1998). But the unarticulated base form of the grammar of L1 is generally silent on distinctions that are important in

L2. For inputs from the L1 vocabulary, the base form suffices to determine the optimal output, but for the foreign inputs of L2, other rankings can be crucial. And in order to account for early L2 productions and the influence of L1 on the initial course of L2 acquisition, the ability of L1 speakers to elevate faithfulness constraints in the face of foreign inputs needs to be precisely specified, as it is in the covert form of the ranking.

Because ultimate application to L2 was a primary motivation for the work reported below, the phonological domain we chose to explore in our experimental work was one that has received considerable prior attention in the L2 literature: consonant clusters. Previous work has focused on cases in which L2 is English, and L1 is a language with an inventory of clusters that is impoverished relative to English (Broselow 1983, Anderson 1987, Tropf 1987, Broselow and Finer 1991, Eckman and Iverson 1993, Archibald 1998, Carlisle 1998, Hancin-Bhatt and Bhatt 1998). Due to constraints on the availability of experimental participants, we chose English for L1, and tested the production of clusters that are illegal in English. As a convenient way to get a large number of fluently produced English-illegal clusters, we used a Polish speaker to generate the experimental stimuli. While our results have implications for English-speaking learners of Polish, that is not the topic of this research. Rather, our goal is to examine the consonant-cluster component of the final state of the English grammar.

4.2   Experimental design

In the experimental work we now summarise, our goal is to determine the degree to which phonological theory in OT can contribute an understanding of performance. To this end we adopt the following strong working hypothesis linking competence and performance, with the intention of backing off from this hypothesis only as compelled by the performance data.

(12)   **Linking hypothesis, final state: probability of production = probability of grammar output**

(a) In the face of non-native inputs, speakers can, when sufficient cognitive resources are allocated, elevate a faithfulness constraint from its base position to a higher position within its floating range. Increasing the probability of greater deviation from the base position requires allocating greater cognitive resources at the time of production.

(b) Given a non-native form to pronounce, the probability that a speaker will actually produce a given output is the probability assigned to that output by the grammar, where the input to the

grammar is the underlying form faithful to the given form. This
assumes the speaker has sufficient cognitive resources to enable
the form to be correctly perceived and retained in memory until
the time of production.

In section 4.6, we return to examine this hypothesis in light of our experimental
results; for now we simply adopt it in order to see how much insight into
performance can be directly provided by grammatical theory.

A task that makes available ample cognitive resources is simple repetition
of a foreign form. This is the condition under which Faithfulness can best be
elevated, sometimes resulting in quite faithful rendering of forms that violate
multiple surface generalisations of the native language. We shall discuss experimental results concerning the repetition task in section 4.5. Our primary
concern, however, is to design an experimental condition that best reveals the
base grammar of the language, which, according to Richness of the Base, forces
any input to meet the surface generalisations of English.

In our experimental design, 16 monolingual adult native English speakers were asked to produce forms with initial clusters illegal in English. The
procedure is schematically shown in (13). (For full details, see Davidson
2001.)

(13)   Experimental procedure

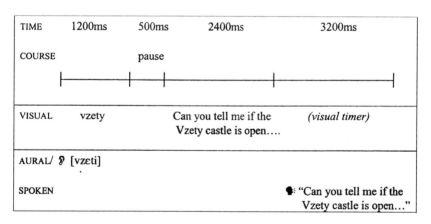

The target item – *vzety* in the diagram (13) – was presented in both aural
and written form; the orthography was English-like (not IPA or Polish). The
written forms were intended to decrease the probability of misperception of
the consonants in the cluster; it is likely that the combined aural and visual

presentation also produced a stronger representation in memory, decreasing the probability of memory errors. Speakers were asked to produce the target item in the middle of a carrier sentence that was presented visually; this was intended to increase the probability that the 'normal' English grammar was employed during production of the target item. Two further aspects of the design were also intended to minimise deviations from English. During production, the written form of the sentence was not available, so speakers could not simply read the target item; they had to generate it, along with the rest of the sentence, from a memorial representation. Further, a visual timer provided pressure for a slightly speeded response, again with the intention of minimising opportunities for shifting out of the English grammar. Finally, to discourage speakers further – at a conscious level – from deviating from 'normal' English in order to produce the foreign item, speakers were told to imagine themselves as American spies in a foreign country. They were told that in order to avoid raising suspicion, they were to act as a 'typical American tourist': if they were too accurate with their pronunciations of the foreign words, they would be uncovered as an American spy.

In the terms of the linking hypothesis (12) above, the experiment was designed to strike a delicate balance with respect to the cognitive resources available to the speakers at the time they produced the target item. Combined visual and aural presentation of the target item was intended to provide a representation of the target that was accurate and robust, so the demands of the task would not be so great as to induce errors in what we analyse as the *input* to the grammar. The other factors were intended to make the task sufficiently demanding at production time that there would not be ample resources available to elevate faithfulness constraints. Below we shall compare the performance in this experimental condition with other conditions that presumably lead to a greater allocation of cognitive resources to elevating Faithfulness; we shall see that the propensity to nativise the input then reduces substantially.

The particular initial consonant clusters employed in the experimental materials were chosen to meet several criteria: they must be present in Polish; they must be absent in English but involve no non-English segments; they must be sufficiently few to enable all trials of the experiment to be completed in a sufficiently short time; they should vary along multiple phonetic dimensions and sample clusters with varying sonority distances. The last criterion reflects a hypothesis discussed below that a substantial factor in performance on a target cluster is whether English permits the sonority distance between its segments. The experimental materials had 15 clusters, each used as the onset of four different bisyllabic pseudo-Polish words; there were 30 carrier sentences, each used twice.

4.3   Experimental results

The results of the experiment are displayed in (14), which also shows the particular target clusters employed. Plotted is the mean proportion correct over all speakers and all tokens of a given cluster.

(14)   Experimental results

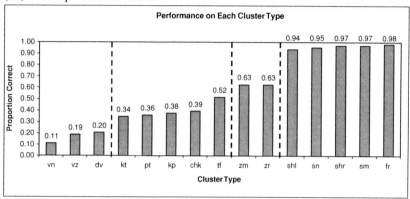

The clusters fall into four rather distinct groups. Performance is above 90 percent on all English-legal clusters, assuming *šl* to be legal at least in the East Coast American dialect predominating in our experimental participants. Performance drops to 63 percent for what we will call the 'Easy' non-English clusters, *zm* and *zr*. Performance drops again to 34−39 percent for the 'Intermediate' clusters *kt*, *pt*, *kp*, *čk*. The cluster *tf* falls halfway between the Intermediate and Easy clusters; it is convenient for analysis to group it with the Intermediate clusters, which can then be characterised as the voiceless-stop-initial clusters. (Obviously, more extensive and systematic follow-up experiments will be needed for a more definitive classification of clusters of this type.) Finally, dropping to 11−19 percent correct, we find the 'Difficult' clusters *vn*, *vz*, and *dv*.

While the labels 'Easy/Intermediate/Difficult' are transparent, it should be emphasised that the dependent measure in the experiment is *accuracy*, not *difficulty per se*.

Pairwise comparison of performance on individual clusters shows statistical justification for the post-hoc three-way grouping of the English-illegal clusters. In (15) we summarise the significance levels of performance differences, taking $p < 0.1$ as our criterion. The greyed cells correspond to comparisons of clusters in the same class; these should not be significantly different, and they are not. The white cells correspond to comparisons of clusters in different classes;

these should show significant differences, and they do. The only exceptions are indicated by the numbers in (15), which give *p* levels too high to satisfy the criterion. We have only listed one cluster in the English-legal class, since all these clusters behave alike statistically.

(15)   Pairwise cluster differences (where not indicated otherwise, white: $p < 0.1$; grey: $p = 0.1$)

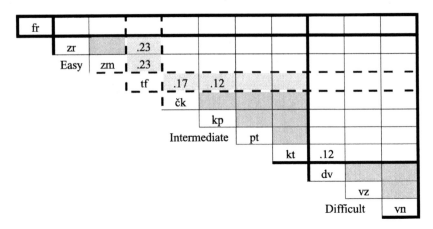

At the boundary between the Intermediate and Difficult classes, the comparison *kt* vs. *dv* barely fails the criterion of significance, with $p < 0.12$. The other exceptions all involve *tf*; it fails to be significantly different from both members of the Easy class (*zr*, *zm*); while significantly different from the two members of the Intermediate class on which performance was worst (*pt* and *kt*), it fails to be significantly different from the other two (although with *kp* it is close). (While there may be some indication here that *tf* is better classified as Easy, we shall await more significant results before complicating the analysis proposed below in order to account for such a classification.[6])

As a final, within-speaker means for confirming our grouping of clusters, we test the following prediction implicit in the grouping: each subject should produce more correct forms for clusters of the Easy class than for clusters of the Intermediate class, and similarly more for the Intermediate than for the Difficult class. In the scatter plots shown in (16), each point represents the performance of a single speaker. In the first plot, proportion correct on Easy clusters is plotted on the *y*-axis, while Intermediate cluster performance is plotted on the *x*-axis. All points are predicted to lie above the principal diagonal ($y = x$), that is, in the upper left triangle. This prediction is confirmed, with only two speakers failing to meet it. The significance of this result is $p < .002$. Exactly the same result holds in the Intermediate/Difficult comparison shown in the second scatter plot.

(16)   Performance comparisons between accuracy classes

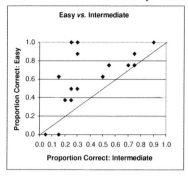
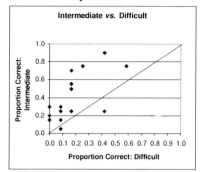

The experimental results seem to suggest that the grammar of English initial clusters contains 'hidden strata' among the illegal forms, each group of clusters defining a stratum. Inputs with clusters of the Easy stratum are most likely to produce faithful, English-illegal outputs, with no nativisation. Inputs with clusters in the Intermediate and Difficult strata are successively less likely to surface faithfully, that is, more likely to undergo nativisation.

The 'repairs' performed when English-illegal inputs failed to surface faithfully were overwhelmingly epenthesis, as shown in (17).

(17)   Error types

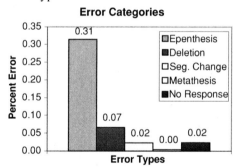

4.4   Analysis

We now examine whether phonological theory can shed light on the hidden strata revealed by the experiment. One hypothesis already proposed in the literature, which in fact guided the selection of the clusters used, is that sonority distance should play a primary role. English allows some clusters with a sonority distance of 1 (e.g., *sn*) but none with sonority distance 0 (e.g, **pk*). This hypothesis predicts then that the class of English-illegal clusters with a legal sonority distance (1 or more) should be produced more accurately than the class of clusters with the illegal sonority distance 0. As shown in (18), however, this is not the case.

(18)   Sonority distance vs. cluster accuracy

sonority distance	Difficult			Intermediate					Easy	
	vn	*vz*	*dv*	*kt*	*kp*	*pt*	*čk*	*tf*	*zm*	*zr*
0		.		.	.	.	.			
≥ 1	.		.					.	.	.

In (18) the clusters are listed in order of increasing proportion correct; there is little correlation between this and the distinction between sonority distances. The lack of performance difference between the two sonority-distance categories was evident in a one-way repeated measures Analysis of Variance (ANOVA) across the mean proportion correct for each category; among English-illegal clusters, there was no significant effect either by subjects [$F_1(1,15) = 2.65$, $p > .12$] or by items [$F_2(1,38) = 1.75$, $p > .19$]. (There was, of course, a very significant effect of the English-legal vs English-illegal factor among the clusters with non-zero sonority distance; $p < .0001$ by both subjects and items.)

Given that sonority distance appears to distinguish clusters too coarsely, we turn to a more fine-grained analysis in terms of phonological features, many of which provide the substrate for sonority conditions on onset well-formedness. Can the markedness of different feature combinations, suitably formalised, account for the hidden strata? The table in (19) is suggestive.

(19)   Featural analysis of clusters (S=stop; F=fricative; A=approximant;
          Ā=non-approximant)

English Legal Clusters	(voiceless S)A — *pl, pr, tr, kl, kr*	
	(voiceless **F**)A — *fl, fr, sl, šl, šr*	
	(voiceless, coronal **F**)Ā — *sm, sn, šn, šm, sv, sf*	
	(**voiced** S)A — *bl, br, dr, gl, gr*	
English Illegal	(**voiced**, coronal **F**)A — *zr*	Easy
	(**voiced**, coronal **F**)Ā — *zm*	
Clusters (from experiment)	(voiceless, coronal $S^{\daleth}$)Ā — *tf, čk*	Intermediate
	(voiceless, ***non-coronal*** $S^{\daleth}$)Ā — *kt, kp, pt*	
	(**voiced**, coronal $S^{\daleth}$)Ā — *dv*	
	(**voiced**, ***non-coronal* F**)Ā — *vn, vz*	Difficult

What the table shows is that as the clusters get worse, as measured by performance in the experiment, they also get more and more *marked*. In (19), marked feature values along various dimensions have been highlighted; the basic markedness constraints involved are given in (20). The markedness of [+voice] for obstruents is indicated by highlighting this feature in boldface; the markedness of non-coronal place, by bold italics. The markedness of [+continuant] for obstruents (or perhaps for onsets) is indicated by boldface on F = fricative. And underlining highlights the markedness of a stop followed by a non-approximant ($\bar{A}$): in this environment, the stop is marked because it is unreleased, as indicated in (19) by $S^{\urcorner}$. We return to this dimension of markedness in a moment.

(20) Segmental markedness constraints
  (a) *F   *[+continuant, −sonorant]   No fricatives
  (b) *Voi$_{-son}$ *[+voice, −sonorant]   No voiced obstruents
  (c) *Cor   *Pl/{[labial], [dorsal]}   No non-coronal place

What (19) suggests is that, if the compounding of markedness with decreasing accuracy can be properly formalised, it should allow an explanation of the hidden strata. But the strong interaction of markedness dimensions evidenced here requires a new technical device that allows a special type of inventory: one that excludes only the 'worst of the worst' (Prince and Smolensky 1993: 180). As a simple example, consider the interaction of voicing and continuancy, both of which are marked in obstruents. As the initial member of a cluster, a voiced obstruent is marked – but it is none the less included in the inventory of English clusters (e.g., *bl*). Similarly, a continuant obstruent (fricative) is marked – but as an initial consonant it is allowed in the English cluster inventory (e.g., *fl*). But an initial obstruent that is *both* voiced *and* continuant – the worst of the worst – is excluded from the inventory (e.g., *vl*). Such an inventory – one that excludes only the worst of the worst – cannot be achieved by simply ranking the relevant faithfulness constraints with the relevant markedness constraints *F and *Voi$_{-son}$. For allowing any fricatives at all requires that *F be outranked by all relevant faithfulness constraints (e.g., Max); otherwise, optimal outputs would be unfaithful to avoid violating *F. The same must be true of *Voi$_{-son}$ since voiced obstruents are allowed in the inventory. But now it must follow that the inventory also contains obstruents that are *both* continuant and voiced – voiced fricatives – because all relevant faithfulness constraints must outrank both *F and *Voi$_{-son}$.

Not only are inventories that bar only the worst of the worst common, they are, it would seem, a type of inventory for which OT ought to provide a natural account, since they are readily understood in terms of barring sufficiently marked elements. (More formally, these inventories have the central OT property of *harmonic completeness* – they are, in fact, necessary in general to fill out OT

typologies sufficiently to achieve *Strong Harmonic Completeness*; Prince and
Smolensky 1993: 187.) A simple, general means for admitting worst-of-the-
worst inventories in OT was first proposed in Smolensky (1993), developed in
Smolensky (1995), and applied in Smolensky (1997) to a complex problem in
tongue-root vowel harmony which displays considerable formal similarity to
the problem posed here by cluster inventories. The proposal is that, in addition
to domination, constraints in OT interact via *the local conjunction operator*,
&. We illustrate with the current example in tableau (21). *F & *Vo$\text{I}_{-\text{son}}$ is
a constraint violated by a segment that is *both* a fricative *and* a voiced obstruent. This constraint makes it possible to strengthen the interaction between *F
and *Vo$\text{I}_{-\text{son}}$ beyond that which arises by mere domination; it now becomes
possible for OT to yield the desired inventory banning only the worst of the
worst. In addition to the rankings discussed above, which admit into the inventories obstruents that are either continuant or voiced but not both, we add the
local conjunction *F & *Vo$\text{I}_{-\text{son}}$ to the grammar, ranking it above all relevant faithfulness constraints. Now, while the markedness incurred by either *F
or *Vo$\text{I}_{-\text{son}}$ alone is *not* sufficient to render an unfaithful output optimal, the
Markedness incurred by both together *is*. (The individual violations of the basic
constraints *F and *Vo$\text{I}_{-\text{son}}$ are marked by '❂' when they combine to trigger a
violation of their conjunction *F & *Vo$\text{I}_{-\text{son}}$. We consider here only the special
case of a cluster-initial consonant; how this restriction is achieved in the actual
proposed analysis – via further local conjunction – will be evident shortly.)

(21)   Local conjunction enables inventories that ban only the worst of the
        worst

	*F & *Vo$\text{I}_{-\text{son}}$	M A X	*F	*Vo$\text{I}_{-\text{son}}$
/blik/				
☞ **blik**				*
lik		*!		
/flik/				
☞ **flik**			*	
lik		*!		
/vlik/				
vlik	*!		❂	❂
☞ lik		*		

In general, the conjunction of a constraint C_1 with another constraint C_2 local to a domain type D, written $C_1 \&_D C_2$, is a new constraint that is violated iff there is both a violation of C_1 and a violation of C_2 within a single domain of type D. The relevant domain is frequently the segment, as it is in the analysis we propose here.[7]

Before showing how local conjunction provides the necessary means of combining markedness dimensions to account for the hidden strata in the English cluster grammar, we return to a dimension of markedness particular to the cluster environment, one involving consonant release.

According to Steriade (1993), a plain, released stop is a plosive (total absence of oral airflow) followed by an approximant (maximum degree of oral aperture): a liquid, glide, or vowel. In English onsets, stops can only appear before approximants: unreleased stops are prohibited. In medial and final positions, on the other hand, this prohibition does not hold (*apt, aptitude*). The following constraint expresses the markedness of a stop that is followed by a non-approximant:

(22) $*S_{\bar{A}}$ A stop must release into an approximant in onsets (no S before $\bar{A}$)

    $*S_{\bar{A}}$ is related to the following constraint, which prefers CV syllables.

(23) $*C_C$ A consonant must release into a vowel in onsets (no C before C).

Any violation of $*S_{\bar{A}}$ – a stop followed by a non-approximant, hence non-vowel – will entail a violation of $*C_C$. Hence $*S_{\bar{A}}$ is in a Pāṇinian relation with the more general constraint $*C_C$. And so, by Pāṇini's Theorem, in order for $*S_{\bar{A}}$ to be active, it must be ranked above $*C_C$ (Prince and Smolensky 1993: 82). That SĀ clusters are banned in English, but not all clusters are, is due to the existence of a relevant faithfulness constraint ranked between the two constraints $*S_{\bar{A}}$ and $*C_C$: this admits into the inventory FĀ and SA clusters (which both satisfy $*S_{\bar{A}}$), but bars SĀ clusters. For concreteness of exposition, we shall assume that the specific faithfulness constraint relevant here is DEP, since epenthesis was the most common simplification strategy employed in the experiment. Since there were few errors of deletion or segment change, MAX and IDENT evidently outrank DEP.

With these tools in place, a ranking can be posited to account for the hidden strata in the English grammar. In (24), the table (19) has been expanded to show the constraint violations of legal English clusters and the illegal clusters used in the experiment. Going down the table, the final column shows the local conjunctions which render each class of clusters more marked than those appearing higher in the table; the violations of the individual constraints in these conjunctions are marked with '❂', as in (21).

The interpretation of this table (24) may be illustrated as follows. The clusters *zr, zm* are more marked than legal English clusters because the initial segment is the locus of *three* simultaneous constraint violations: $*VOI_{-SON}$, $*F$, and $*C_C$; the three marks '☉' incurred by the initial *z* in these clusters entail violation of the local conjunction $*VOI_{-SON}$ & $*F$ & $*C_C$. Note that violating any *two* of these constraints in the same segment does *not* generate sufficient Markedness to result in exclusion from English. Violating $*F$ and $*C_C$ in the same segment is permitted, as in the cluster *fl*; violating $*VOI_{-SON}$ and $*C_C$ is likewise acceptable (*bl*). And violation of both $*VOI_{-SON}$ and $*F$ occurs in every single voiced fricative (*z*).

Note that all clusters violate $*C_C$, which functions like the *COMPLEX of Prince and Smolensky (1993), except that it explicitly localises its violation to the initial C of a CC cluster. Thus, to violate a *local* conjunction $\mathbb{C}$ & $*C_C$, the violation of $\mathbb{C}$ must occur in the *initial* segment of a CC cluster (or, more generally, in a C that is not the final segment of a cluster).

(24)   Decreasing accuracy with increasing markedness (constraints unranked)

			$*S_{\bar{A}}$	$*C_C$	$*VOL_{-SON}$	$*F$	$*\overline{COR}$	Crucial violated constraints
English	(–voi S)A	*tr, pl, pr, kl, kr*	*				(*)	
	(–voi F)A	*sl, šl, šr, fl, fr*	*			*	(*)	
	(–voi, cor F)Ā	*sm, sn, šn, šm, sv, sf*	*			*		
	(+voi S)A	*dr, bl, br, gl, gr*	*		*		(*)	
Easy	(+voi, cor F)C	*zr, zm*		☉	☉	☉		$*VOL_{-SON}$ & $*F$ & $*C_C$
Inter.	(–voi, cor S̲)Ā	*tf, čk*	☉	*				$*S_{\bar{A}}$
	(–voi, ¬*cor* S̲)Ā	*kt, kp, pt*	☉	*			*	$*S_{\bar{A}}$
Diff.	(+voi, cor S̲)Ā	*dv*	☉	*	☉			$*VOL_{-SON}$ & $*S_{\bar{A}}$
	(+voi, ¬*cor* F)Ā	*vn, vz*		☉	☉	☉	☉	$*\overline{COR}$ & $*VOL_{-SON}$ & $*F$ & $*C_C$

To take one more example from table (24): like the Easy clusters, the Difficult clusters *vn, vz* also violate the third-order conjunction [$*VOI_{-SON}$ & $*F$ & $*C_C$]. In addition, however, the initial consonant *v* has marked place, that is, it violates $*\overline{Cor}$. Thus the increased markedness of these Difficult clusters is registered by their violation of the fourth-order conjunction $*\overline{Cor}$ and [$*VOI_{-SON}$ & $*F$ & $*C_C$].

It is clear in (24) that constraint ranking plays an important role in distinguishing the hidden strata. The cluster *tf*, like many English legal clusters, violates only two of the listed constraints, yet it is in the Intermediate stratum, while the cluster *zr*, violating three constraints, falls in the Easy stratum. Unlike *zr*, the cluster *tf* violates $*S_{\bar{A}}$, a constraint that is unviolated among the

English-legal clusters. The high rank of $*S_{\bar{A}}$ is responsible for its strong impact, single-handedly separating the Easy clusters (which satisfy it) from the Intermediate clusters, which do not.

The formal definition of each conjunctive constraint in (24) follows automatically from the general definition of constraint conjunction, together with the substantive definitions of the basic constraints that are conjoined, given above in (20), (22), and (23). It is useful, however, to provide an English paraphrase of the *effect* of these conjunctions; this is given in (25).

(25)   Exegesis of local conjunctions (within onset clusters)

    (a) $*\text{VOI}_{-\text{SON}}$ & *F & $*C_C$ Violated by a voiced fricative before any C.

    (b) $*\text{COR}$ & $*\text{VOI}_{-\text{SON}}$ & *F & $*C_C$ Violated by a non-coronal voiced fricative before any C.

    (c) $*\text{VOI}_{-\text{SON}}$ & $*S_{\bar{A}}$ Violated by a voiced stop before an obstruent or nasal.

The ranking implicit in the table (24) is made explicit in (26). The floating range of DEP is indicated, with four positions indicated by the circled digits. The base position **❶** defines the base grammar of English, which admits only those clusters appearing in English lexical items. Elevating DEP to the next-higher position ② now adds to the inventory the group of Easy clusters. Elevating DEP still further, to position ③ and then to ④, incrementally adds the Intermediate and then the Difficult clusters.

(26)   English grammar, showing hidden constraint rankings and hidden cluster strata

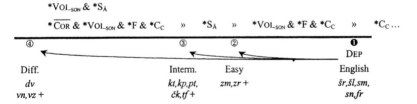

To relate this grammar explicitly to the dependent variable observed in the experiment, proportion correct, first consider the simplest assumption, 'uniform floating' (Anttila 1998). On this assumption, all positions **❶** – ④ are visited with equal probability under the conditions of the experiment. The predicted values for percent correct production in the four strata are given in (27). For a cluster in the Difficult stratum (last row) to be correctly produced, DEP must float to its highest position (④), which, under the uniform floating hypothesis, occurs on 25 percent of productions. For the Intermediate stratum, floating to ④ entails correct production, but so does floating to ③. Thus the predicted percent correct production is now 50 percent. And so forth up to the English-legal stratum, where correct production is predicted to occur 100 percent of the time.

(27)   Proportion correct across hidden strata

	EXPERIMENT	THEORY	Uniform Floating		Empirically Fit Floating	
Cluster Stratum	Observed Correct	FAITH Position	Visitation Probability	Predicted Correct	Visitation Probability	Predicted Correct
šr, šl, sm, sn, fr	96%	❶	25%	100%	33%	96%
zm, zr	63%	②	25%	75%	23%	63%
kt, kp, pt,čk, tf	40%	③	25%	50%	24%	40%
dv, vn, vz	16%	④	25%	25%	16%	16%

It is important that the theory correctly accounts for the qualitative ordering of the strata, regardless of the quantitative assumptions concerning the probability of DEP floating to each of the four positions. Each position that yields correct production in one stratum *s* also yields correct production in the strata listed above *s* in (27). Thus, whatever the quantitative value of the probabilities of visiting different positions, the predicted percent correct will increase up the table. (This would even be true if the probability were greatest for ④ and least for ❶.)

Using the observed percent correct values, it is easy to fit the data with assumed values for the visitation probabilities, as shown in the portion of the table in (27) headed 'Empirically Fit Floating'. Thus the experimental results suggest that the probability of elevating DEP to different positions decreases as the degree of elevation increases; most probable is the base position ❶ (33 percent), least probable the highest position ④ (16 percent).

The values for visitation probabilities in (27) are fit to average accuracy values over all subjects. The scatter plots in (16) – with a separate point for each speaker – show considerable variance across speakers. On the analysis we are proposing, this variance may be attributed to differences across speakers and trials of the effectiveness of cognitive resources allocated to the elevation of Faithfulness. The relative rankings of markedness constraints, however, are what define the hidden strata, and the evidence is consistent with a common underlying hidden ranking of Markedness across speakers. While one speaker might be unusually successful at elevating Faithfulness, a shared hidden Markedness ranking entails that, no matter how good that speaker's performance may be on Difficult clusters, that same speaker's performance on Intermediate clusters must be better, and on Easy clusters, better still. Averaging within speakers over the clusters defining each hidden stratum, (16) shows that this prediction is borne out to a striking degree, holding for all but two of sixteen speakers.

4.5   Other experimental conditions

As explained in section 4.2, the experimental condition we have discussed so far was designed to minimise the cognitive resources allocated to elevating Faithfulness in response to a clearly foreign input, without overly taxing the resources required to accurately perceive and recall that input. According to the Linking Hypothesis (12), if greater resources are made available, the probability of elevating FAITH should increase, predicting higher proportions of faithful pronunciations.

The same speakers who participated in the experimental condition reported above also participated in two other conditions. The first of these – the 'Foreign Condition' – is just like the one reported above, except that the instructions were different (the stimuli were identical). Now speakers were asked to imagine themselves as tourists travelling in a foreign country. While they did not know the language of this country, they would find themselves having to ask natives for directions to different places, or how to buy different products. They could assume that the natives spoke some English, but they were warned to pronounce the foreign word as carefully as possible, since if they did not, the natives might misunderstand them.

The intention in this manipulation was to probe the conscious, meta-linguistic component of the task. In the condition reported above – the 'English Condition' – speakers were discouraged at a conscious level from making special efforts faithfully to pronounce the foreign words; in the Foreign Condition, speakers were explicitly encouraged to make such efforts.

In the third, 'Repetition', condition, subjects heard two repetitions of one token of a word and were then asked to repeat it. The English-like orthographic representation of the word was available throughout the trial, during both perception and production of the word. The same pseudo-Polish words were used as in the other two conditions.

We assume that, in the terms of the Linking Hypothesis (12), the cognitive resources available for elevating FAITH are greatest in the Repetition Condition, least in the English Condition, and intermediate in the Foreign Condition. Accordingly, this hypothesis predicts that the proportion of faithful productions should increase from the English to the Foreign and again to the Repetition Condition. More specifically, the prediction is that the same hidden strata should be evident in all three conditions: these strata are defined by the relative rankings of markedness constraints, which are unaffected by the across-condition manipulations.

The experimental results are shown in the graph (28). As the graph shows, there is a very strong correlation between the performance ordering of clusters across the three conditions. In fact, the rank correlations between the English and Repetition conditions is 0.97, that between the English and Foreign conditions is 0.91, and between the Foreign and Repetition is 0.89 (all $p < .001$).

There is some evidence for discrete strata in the Foreign Condition, and while these correlate with those of the English Condition, the boundaries of the Intermediate stratum seem to shift: *čk* approaches the Difficult group while the others approach the Easy group. Evidence for strata in the Repetition Condition is even murkier, perhaps because a ceiling effect is starting to set in: as performance starts to approach 100 percent, there is less variation across the majority of clusters and so achieving statistically significant differences requires more experimental power. We leave detailed investigation of such questions to future experiments which will aim to provide that power.

As far as the manipulation concerning instructions are concerned, there is little evidence that conscious attempts to 'sound American' vs. 'sound foreign' affect the relative accuracy of the clusters, although the proportion of faithful utterances increases for nearly all clusters. The only exceptions are *sn*, *sm*, where speakers displayed a tendency to produce *šn*, *šm*.

(28)   Experimental results: English, Foreign, and Repetition Conditions

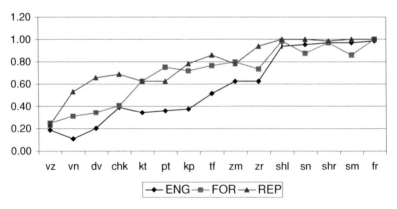

4.6   Alternative hypotheses

In this section we briefly consider several alternative approaches to explaining the experimental findings.

4.6.1   Final grammar = base grammar   In our basic hypothesis (11), we have assumed that the final state of the grammar includes floating Faithfulness, with the lowest positions of faithfulness constraints defining the base grammar. The native lexicon is constrained to yield consistent outputs from the full grammar, and as a consequence floating Faithfulness has no effect on the outputs from native inputs. With non-native inputs, however, we can see the effects of floating Faithfulness, thus revealing the full final grammar, including covert rankings.

An obvious alternative is simply to assume that the final state of the grammar is the base grammar, with no floating Faithfulness (leaving aside the flotation responsible for variation in native outputs, which we have been neglecting in our general discussion). Faced with a non-native input, the speakers in our experiment simply depart from their final English grammar, 'artificially' elevating Faithfulness in a way that is driven by the particular demands of the arguably artificial tasks we ask them to perform.

The differences between this interpretation and the one presented in (11) are subtle, and we take no strong stance. We presented (11) as our initial hypothesis because it is the grammatically strongest one, in the sense of making the grammar responsible for explaining the greatest range of data. It appears necessary for OT grammars to admit floating constraints in order to deal with multiple types of variation: synchronic adult variation in phonology (Nagy and Reynolds 1997, Anttila 1998) and syntax/semantics (Anttila and Fong 2000), diachronic variation (Zubritskaya 1997, Anttila and Young-mee to appear), variation in child language (Legendre *et al.* 2000), and (under our interpretation here) variation across lexical strata (Itô and Mester 1995b, etc.). With this mechanism already introduced within grammatical theory, the grammatically strongest hypothesis would appear to be that it accounts for any other type of variation. The type of variation observed in our speakers' productions appears to be one for which the floating constraint mechanism provides insight. If the adult speakers' grammar encodes their knowledge of phonology, part of that knowledge – according to Richness of the Base – concerns the pronunciations of non-native inputs, and, as far as we have been able to determine experimentally, that part of their knowledge of phonology can be usefully formalised with floating constraints.

4.6.2   Statistics   In the previous subsection we considered backing off – very slightly – from the point of view we have pushed, that the grammar should encode the knowledge speakers display in these experiments. On the slightly grammatically weakened view of section 4.6.1, as on the view we have favoured, covert rankings of markedness constraints are responsible for the relative accuracy of non-native clusters; but the Faithfulness elevation necessary to account for non-English outputs is not seen as part of the final state *per se*. A much more severe weakening of the grammatical perspective would in addition deny that covert Markedness rankings are responsible for relative accuracy – that relative accuracy is not a consequence of the grammar which, say, treats all non-native forms equally. Instead, explanation of relative accuracy might be sought in the statistics of English, with greater frequency predicting greater accuracy. Of course, in onset position, the frequency of the non-English clusters is nominally zero, by definition. But one might look to the relative frequency of hetero-syllabic and coda clusters for explanation.

A frequency count from the CELEX 2 Lexical Database is not encouraging for the statistical perspective, however.[8] As shown in (29), whereas a statistical explanation would require that accuracy is a monotonically increasing function of frequency, there is in fact essentially no correlation between the orders of relative accuracy and relative frequency, whether of tokens or types. The rank correlation coefficients between frequency and accuracy in the experiment is only 0.14 ($p > 0.3$) for tokens, and 0.06 ($p > 0.4$) for types. The poor rank correlation between frequency and accuracy is also shown in (30). In (30a), the clusters are listed from lowest to highest accuracy in the experiment, with boldface marking the Difficult stratum, bold italics marking the Intermediate stratum, italics marking the Easy stratum, and regular typeface indicating English-legal clusters. In (30b–c), the clusters are listed in order of increasing token and type frequencies.

(29)   Statistical status of relative cluster accuracy

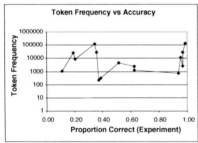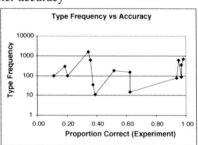

(30)   Orderings of clusters by frequency and accuracy
     (a) Accuracy ordering (experiment): **vn vz dv** *kt pt kp čk tf* zm zr šl sn šr sm fr
     (b) Token frequency ordering: *kp čk* šl **vn** zr zm šr *tf* dv sn **vz** sm *pt kt* fr
     (c) Type frequency ordering: *čk* zr *kp* šl šr **vn dv** zm *tf* **vz** sm sn *pt* fr *kt*

Of course, it is impossible to prove the impossibility of a statistical account, given the potential infinity of statistics that might be computed. For example, it is possible that an extremely careful analysis of casual and fast speech would reveal that vowel deletion yields onset clusters that are nominally illegal in English, with statistical distributions that might mirror the accuracy data. We return to this avenue shortly.

4.6.3   Phonetic unfaithfulness   In order to maximise the explanatory burden on phonology, we have hypothesised that when a speaker utters *kətobi* for /ktobi/, the schwa results from epenthesis in the phonology. Alternatively, one might hypothesise that phonology proper outputs a faithful *ktobi*, but that our speakers' phonetic systems, unpractised with *kt* clusters, often fail to provide a faithful rendering of that cluster, with mistiming of gestures leading to the intrusion of a reduced vowel.

Such an alternative is not readily distinguished from our phonological hypothesis, but in future work we hope to investigate one potential avenue. If a fundamental distinction between phonology and phonetics concerns the discreteness of the former relative to the latter, then phonological epenthesis might be distinguished from phonetic 'epenthesis' by the distribution of phonetic characteristics of the schwa: perhaps a fleshed-out version of the phonetic vs. phonological epenthesis hypotheses would predict that, say, the duration of the schwa should be distributed with a mode at 0 msec if the epenthesis results from articulatory mistiming, but with a non-zero mode if the epenthesis is phonological. Detailed phonetic analysis of this issue must await future research. Such analysis is also needed to examine the related hypothesis that the higher error rate induced by voicing (e.g., Difficult *dv* vs. Intermediate *tf*) reflects voicing during articulatory mistiming, acoustically detectable as a vowel, even though the degree of mistiming is identical to that in the corresponding unvoiced cluster. This phonetic hypothesis needs to be contrasted with the hypothesis that the environment of two voiced obstruents leads to phonological epenthesis while the corresponding unvoiced environment does not.

4.7   Origin of hidden rankings

We have attempted to contrast explanations of relative cluster accuracy based on phonological, statistical, and phonetic distinctions. A fundamental challenge in this regard is the intrinsic connectedness of these factors. Phonological markedness constraints can often be seen as the grammaticisation of articulatory difficulty (e.g., Archangeli and Pulleyblank 1994, Jun 1995, Steriade 1997, Boersma 1998, Kirchner 1998, Hayes 1999a), so distinctions based on articulatory difficulty in a phonetic explanation will necessarily correlate with distinctions based on markedness in a phonological explanation. If the speakers' grammars contain constraints militating against marked structures, all else equal, the frequency with which structures surface should be inversely correlated with their markedness. Further, if grammars include floating constraints with probabilistic positions, grammatical structure manifests itself in the statistics of output distributions, as we saw in (27).

This tight coupling of phonology, phonetics, and surface statistics is at play not only in the final, adult state, but also in the learning process. As a final issue, we briefly consider how the covert rankings could be learned. The case of interest is when there are few non-native forms in the learner's environment, so sufficient direct evidence of the sort elicited in the experiment is not available.

Future research will assess the degree to which the covert rankings uncovered in the experiment reflect universal markedness tendencies. Such tendencies would raise the possibility of nativist grammatical explanations of covert rankings, encoded perhaps in the initial state. And these tendencies might well reflect factors of articulatory difficulty.

How might language-particular covert rankings be learned? One possibility, first suggested to us by Rochelle Newman (personal communication, 1999), is that the frequency with which an 'illegal' onset cluster arises in rapid speech might reflect its hidden stratum. As mentioned above, if empirically substantiated, this might suggest a statistical mode of explanation, or perhaps a phonetic one (Kohler 1990).

But a grammatical line of explanation might also be developed by extending our Linking Hypothesis (12). In this extension, the degree of elevation of a constraint $\mathbb{C}$ from its base position determines the extent of reduction for rapid speech. The constraint $\mathbb{C}$ is, however, not the faithfulness constraint DEP-V, but a conceptually related markedness constraint in the family *STRUC banning structure (Prince and Smolensky 1993). Epenthesis of schwa into a cluster creates additional structure, in particular, a weak syllable (an open syllable headed by a reduced vowel, perhaps one problematic for metrical foot parsing). Let us call the *STRUC constraint violated by such syllables *ŏ.

(31)   *ŏ   No weak syllables (*STRUC family)

Replacing DEP-V by ŏ above does not affect the analysis, since for the inputs of interest, which possess an initial CC cluster, the two constraints are violated by the same candidates. But if we turn to reduction of native forms in rapid speech, what is at issue is not whether to epenthesise a reduced vowel, but whether to delete one, and here *ŏ is no longer equivalent to DEP-V.

In its base position, *ŏ must be dominated by MAX-V so that the base English grammar retains weak syllables; this is illustrated in tableau (32), which shows a range of relevant hypothetical inputs. The base grammar allows the initial, weak vowel in inputs like /$C_1$$C_2$ant/ to surface faithfully, for any pair of consonants

C_1 and C_2. This grammar also allows the initial cluster *pl* to surface faithfully, but not the illegal clusters *pt* (Intermediate stratum) and *dv* (Difficult stratum); as in the analysis above, these clusters are broken up by epenthesis. In this tableau the unfaithful candidates are in italics, and a preceding '*' marks faithful candidates that are non-optimal; these flag the clusters banned by this ranking. Weak vowels in candidates are marked V̆ to distinguish them from other vowels, marked V́. The sub-hierarchy of markedness constraints *VOI$_{-SON}$ & *S$_Ã$» *S$_Ã$» *C$_C$ constitute the hidden rankings proposed above which separate the hidden strata occupied by the clusters *dv*, *pt*, and *pl*.

(32)   Exposing covert rankings 1: English Base Grammar

	*VOI$_{-SON}$ & *S$_Ã$	*S$_Ã$	MAX-V	*ŏ	DEP-V	*C$_C$
/pɪlant/						
☞ pɪ́lánt				*		
plánt			*!			*
/plant/						
☞ plant						*
pŏlánt				*!	*	
/pɪtant/						
☞ pɪ́tánt				*		
ptánt		*!	*			
/ptant/						
* ptánt		*!				
☞ *pŏtánt*				*	*	
/dɪvant/						
☞ dɪ́vánt				*		
dvánt	*!		*			
/dvant/						
* dvánt	*!					
☞ *dŏvánt*				*	*	

Now elevating *ŏ just above MAX-V enables some weak vowels to be deleted for rapid speech. Such deletion typically creates clusters, and these are subject to the hierarchy of constraints with the covert rankings in question. With minimal elevation of *ŏ, deletion of weak vowels occurs if this creates an English-legal cluster, but is blocked if an illegal cluster would result. This is illustrated in tableau (33).

When the ranks of the constraints violated by illegal clusters are infiltrated by floating *ŏ, their relative rankings are exposed. Tableau (34) illustrates a degree of elevation in which *ŏ is still ranked below the constraints violated by clusters in the Difficult stratum, but above those violated by clusters of the Intermediate stratum. Now weak vowels delete when this creates a cluster that is either English-legal (*pl*), or within the first two (Easy; Intermediate: *pt*) hidden strata of the illegal clusters. Weak vowel deletion is however blocked when an illegal cluster in the third (Difficult, *dv*) hidden stratum would result.

(33)   Exposing covert rankings 2: Rapid Speech Grammar, English-legal clusters only

	*VOI₋ₛₒₙ & *S$_Ä$	*S$_Ä$	*ŏ	MAX-V	DEP-V	*C$_C$
/pɪlant/						
* pɪlánt			*!			
☞ *plánt*				*		*
/plant/						
☞ plant						*
pŏlánt			*!	*		
/pɪtant/						
☞ pɪtánt			*			
ptánt		*!		*		
/ptant/						
* ptánt		*!				
☞ *pŏtánt*			*	*		

(34)   Exposing covert rankings 3: Rapid Speech Grammar, English+ Easy+Intermediate Clusters

	*VOI₋ₛₒₙ & *S$_Ä$	*ŏ	*S$_Ä$	MAX-V	DEP-V	*C$_C$
/pɪlant/						
* pɪlánt		*!				
☞ *plánt*			*!			*
/plant/						
☞ plant						*
pŏlánt		*!		*		
/pɪtant/						
* pɪtánt		*!				
☞ *ptánt*			*	*		
/ptant/						
☞ ptánt		*				
pŏtánt		*!		*		
/dɪvant/						
☞ dɪvánt		*				
dvánt	*!			*		
/dvant/						
* dvánt	*!					
☞ *dŏvánt*		*		*		

Just as in the analysis of the experimental results developed above, floating *ŏ exposes the hidden strata by rendering reduction increasingly less probable as the resulting clusters enter hidden strata increasingly more distant from base English.

We hasten to reiterate that it remains for future research to evaluate the empirical soundness of any line of explanation based in rapid speech. Our intent here is only to suggest that, while such an explanation might invite an agrammatic, simply-statistical interpretation, it appears that there is in fact at least one grammatical approach that may offer a unified explanation of the patterns exhibited in rapid speech and in the pronunciation of non-native inputs.

5.   A final word from our sponsor

In this work we have attempted to formulate working hypotheses that place the greatest demands on phonological theory to explain phonological performance. The theory is asked to produce a prediction about the phonological knowledge initially present in infants, and it does so with the help of a nativist hypothesis: universal constraints are present and ranked broadly as Markedness » Faithfulness. The theory is next asked to predict the phonologically relevant behaviour of infants, and it does so, with the help of a linking hypothesis that one of the few reliably measurable behaviours of infants, orientation time, will positively correlate with the degree to which phonological stimuli conform to their knowledge – their phonological grammars. The theory is finally asked to characterise the expected behaviour of adults producing forms that violate their phonological knowledge, and it does so with the help of the previously developed notion of probabilistically floating constraints. When experiments are conducted to test all these theoretical predictions, we find that the theory does indeed allow the experimental data to be put into sharp focus. We have identified several respects in which the current state of the experimental programme needs strengthening in future work. The experiments reported here are literally the first we have conducted. Our hope is only to have made the case that such a programme of research – directly confronting OT phonological theory with performance data – is one worth pursuing further. We hope also to have shown how Richness of the Base – a subtle, inherently counterfactual principle of OT which might have been thought to have only abstruse theoretical import – may in fact have a surprisingly important role to play in the explanation of human linguistic performance.

NOTES

1. This morpheme *in-* 'not' fails to assimilate to other following consonants, however, as in *incompetent*, *ingratitude*, *informal*, and *involuntary*.
2. We are assuming here that syllabification is not present in underlying forms. This is commonly assumed to account for the strong cross-linguistic generalisation that syllable structure is not lexically contrastive. If syllable structure were present in underlying forms, the predictions stated in the text would still follow, but now because of the ranking structure of the initial state: Faithfulness to underlying syllable structure would be dominated by Markedness. See the discussion of nasal assimilation below for an experimental approach to testing such a ranking.

3. There were six lists of each of the two types in each experiment. The X items had the form VC or CVC, with the initial C an obstruent and the final C one of the nasals *n*, *m*, or *ŋ*; in each list of eight triads, all X forms had the same nasal. The Y items had the form CV with C a voiced or unvoiced obstruent and V a vowel occurring word-finally in English. X, Y, and XY' were each naturally produced (by a female native speaker of English) as a single prosodic word; XY' was produced with initial stress and was not an English word. Triads were separated by 1 sec. and items within each triad were separated by 0.5 sec. The total duration of each list was approximately 25 sec.

4. In each of experiments 3–5, 16 infants (7 males, 9 females), from monolingual English-speaking homes, were tested. The average age of the infants for each experiment fell between 4 months, 16 days and 4 months, 20 days, with ages of individual infants ranging from 4 months, 2 days to 5 months, 8 days. Additional infants (6 for experiments 3 and 4, 14 for experiment 5) were tested but not included for reasons of excessive fussiness or crying, failing to orient properly to the test apparatus, experimenter error, or parental interference.

5. This abbreviated argument assumes a simplified situation like that discussed above, in which a single faithfulness constraint is floating. An argument considering the fully general case, with multiple faithfulness constraints that may change their relative ranking by floating, is beyond the scope of the present discussion.

6. A natural direction for refining the analysis would be to consider *tf* to occupy its own stratum between Easy and Intermediate, and analyse it by extending the hierarchy proposed below for consonant release: $*S_{\bar{A}} \gg *C_C$ (22)–(23). Introducing a new constraint in this family, ranked above the other two, $*S_{[-con]}$: A stop must not release into a non-continuant, would distinguish *tf*, which satisfies the new constraint, from the Intermediate clusters, which violate it. (Although the status of the affricate in *čk* is a complexity we systematically ignore here, simply treating it like a stop.)

7. Local conjunction has been employed for a variety of purposes in OT phonology and syntax, see Smolensky (1993, 1997); also, e.g., Kirchner (1996), Aissen (1999), Legendre (2000), and Lubowicz (2002).

8. We are extremely grateful to Matt Goldrick for his assistance with these counts.

References

Aissen, J. (1999). Markedness and subject choice in Optimality Theory. *NLLT* **17**: 4. 673–771.

Anderson, J. (1987). The Markedness Differential Hypothesis and syllable structure difficulty. In G. Ioupo and S. Weinberger (eds.) *Interlanguage Phonology: the Acquisition of a Second Language Sound System*. Cambridge: Newbury House.

Anttila, A. (1998). Deriving variation from grammar. In F. Hinskens, R. van Hout, and W. L. Wetzel (eds.) *Variation, Change, and Phonological Theory*. Amsterdam: John Benjamins. 35–68.

Anttila, A. and V. Fong (2000). The partitive constraint in Optimality Theory. [ROA 416, http://roa.rutgers.edu]

Anttila, A. and Y. C. Young-mee (to appear). Variation and change in Optimality Theory. *Lingua*.

Archangeli, D. and D. Pulleyblank (1994). *Grounded Phonology*. Cambridge, Mass.: MIT Press.

Archibald, J. (1993). *Language Learnability and L2 Phonology*. Dordrecht: Kluwer Academic Publishers.

———— (1998). *Second Language Phonology*. Philadelphia: John Benjamins.

Boersma, P. (1998). *Functional Phonology: Formalizing the Interactions between Articulatory and Perceptual Drives*. The Hague: Holland Academic Graphics.

Boersma, P. and B. Hayes (1999). Empirical tests of the Gradual Learning Algorithm. [ROA 348, http://roa.rutgers.edu]

Broselow, E. (1983). Nonobvious transfer: on predicting epenthesis errors. In S. Gass and L. Selinker (eds.) *Language Transfer in Language Learning*. Rowley, Mass.: Newbury House.

Broselow, E., S. Chen, and C. Wang (1998). The Emergence of the Unmarked in second language phonology. *Studies in Second Language Acquisition* **20**. 261–280.

Broselow, E. and D. Finer (1991). Parameter setting in second language phonology and syntax. *Second Language Research* **7**: **1**. 35–59.

Broselow, E. and H. B. Park (1995). Mora conservation in second language prosody. In J. Archibald (ed.) *Phonological Aquisition and Phonological Theory*. Hillsdale: Lawrence Erlbaum. 151–168.

Brown, R. (1973). *A First Language*. Cambridge, Mass.: Harvard University Press.

Carlisle, R. (1998). The acquisition on onsets in a markedness relationship: a longitudinal study. *Studies in Second Language Acquisition* **20**. 245–260.

Davidson, L. (2001). Hidden rankings in the final state of the English grammar. In G. Harwood and S. Kim (eds.) *Ruling Papers II*. New Brunswick, N.J.: Rutgers University.

Davidson, L. and R. Noyer (1996). Loan phonology in Huave: nativization and the ranking of faithfulness constraints. *WCCFL* **15**.

Demuth, K. (1995). Markedness and the development of prosodic structure. *NELS*. 13–25. Amherst, Mass.: Graduate Linguistic Student Association (GLSA), University of Massachusetts.

De Villiers, J. G. and P. A. de Villiers (1973). A cross-sectional study of the acquisition of grammatical morphemes in child speech. *Journal of Psycholinguistic Research* **2**. 267–273.

Eckman, F. and G. Iverson (1993). Sonority and markedness among onset clusters in the interlanguage of ESL learners. *Second Language Research* **9**. 234–252.

Fukazawa, H. (1998). Multiple input-output faithfulness relations in Japanese. MS., University of College Park. [ROA 260, http://roa.rutgers.edu]

Fukazawa, H., M. Kitahara, and M. Ota (1998). Lexical stratification and ranking invariance in constraint-based grammars. MS., University of Maryland, College Park, Indiana University, and Georgetown University. [ROA 267, http://roa.rutgers.edu].

Gnanadesikan, A. (this volume). Markedness and faithfulness constraints in child phonology.

Hale, M. and C. Reiss (1997). Grammar Optimisation: the simultaneous acquisition of constraint ranking and a lexicon. MS., Concordia University. [ROA 231, http://roa.rutgers.edu]

Hancin-Bhatt, B. and R. Bhatt (1998). Optimal L2 syllables: interactions of transfer and developmental effects. *Studies in Second Language Acquisition* **19**. 331–378.

Hayes, B. (1999). Phonetically-driven phonology: the role of Optimality Theory and inductive grounding. In M. Darnell, E. Moravscik, M. Noonan, F. Newmeyer, and

K. Wheatly (eds.) *Functionalism and Formalism in Linguistics, Vol. I: General Papers*. Amsterdam: John Benjamins. 243–285.

(this volume). Phonological acquisition in Optimality Theory: the early stages.

Holden, K. (1976). Assimilation rates of borrowings and phonological productivity. *Lg* **52**. 131–147.

Itô, J. and R. A. Mester (1995a). The core-periphery structure of the lexicon and constraints on reranking. In J. Beckman, L. Walsh Dickey, and S. Urbanczyk (eds.) *UMOP 18: Papers in Optimality Theory*. Amherst, Mass.: UMass GLSA. 181–210.

(1995b). Japanese phonology. In J. Goldsmith (ed.) *Handbook of Phonological Theory*. Oxford: Blackwell. 817–838.

(1999). The phonological lexicon. In N. Tsujimura (ed.) *Handbook of Japanese Linguistics*, Oxford: Blackwell. Ch. 3.

Jun, J. (1995). *Perceptual and Articulatory Factors in Place Assimilation: an Optimality Theoretic Approach*. Ph.D dissertation, UCLA.

Jusczyk, P. W. (1998). Using the Headturn Preference Procedure to study language acquisition. In C. Rovee-Collier, L. P. Lipsitt, and H. Hayne (eds.) *Advances in Infancy Research*, Vol. 2. Stamford, Conn.: Ablex. 88–204.

Jusczyk, P. W., A. D. Friederici, J. M. I. Wessels, V. Y. Svenkerud, and A. Jusczyk (1993). Infants' sensitivity to the sound patterns of native language words. *Journal of Memory and Language* **32**. 402–420.

Jusczyk, P. W., D. Houston, and M. Newsome (1999). The beginnings of word segmentation in English-learning infants. *Cognitive Psychology* **39**. 159–207.

Jusczyk, P. W., P. A. Luce, and J. Charles-Luce (1994). Infants' sensitivity to phonotactic patterns in the native language. *Journal of Memory and Language* **33**. 630–645.

Jusczyk, P., P. Smolensky, and T. Allocco (2000). How English-Learning Infants Respond to Markedness and Faithfulness Constraints. MS., Dept of Cognitive Science, Johns Hopkins University. Baltimore, Md.

Katayama, M. (1998). *Optimality Theory and Japanese Loanword Phonology*. Ph.D. dissertation, University of California, Santa Cruz.

Kemler Nelson, D. G., P. W. Jusczyk, D. R. Mandel, J. Myers, A. Turk, and L. A. Gerken (1995). The Headturn Preference Procedure for testing auditory perception. *Infant Behavior and Development* **18**. 111–116.

Kiparsky, P. (1968). How abstract is phonology? In O. Fujimura (ed.) *Three Dimensions of Linguistic Theory*. Tokyo: TEC. 5–56.

Kirchner, R. (1996). Synchronic chain shifts in Optimality Theory. *LI* **27**. 341–350.

(1998). *An Effort-based Approach to Consonant Lenition*. Ph.D. dissertation, UCLA. [ROA 276, http://roa.rutgers.edu]

Kohler, K. J. (1990). Segmental reduction in connected speech in German: phonological facts and phonetic explanations. In W. J. Hardcastle and A. Marchal (eds.) *Speech Production and Speech Modelling*. Dordrecht: Kluwer. 69–92.

Legendre, G., P. Hagstrom, M. Todorova, and A. Vainikka (2000). An Optimality-theoretic model of acquisition of tense and agreement in French. In L. Gleitman and A. Joshi (eds.) *Proceedings of the Twenty-Second Annual Conference of the Cognitive Science Society*. Mahwah, N.J.: Lawrence Erlbaum. 292–297.

Levelt, C. (1995). Unfaithful kids: place of articulation patterns in early child language. Paper presented at the Department of Cognitive Science, Johns Hopkins University. Baltimore, Md.

Levelt, C. and R. van de Vijver (this volume). Syllable types in cross-linguistic and developmental grammars.

Lubowicz, A. (2002). Derived environment effects in Optimality Theory. *Lingua* **112**. 243–280.

Mattys, S. and P. W. Jusczyk (in press). Phonotactic cues for segmentation of fluent speech by infants. *Cognition* **78**. 91–121.

Nagy, N. and B. Reynolds (1997). Optimality Theory and variable word-final deletion in Faeter. *Language Variation and Change* **9**. 37–55.

Pater, J. 1997. Metrical parameter missetting in second language aquisition. In S. J. Hannahs and M. Young-Scholten (eds.) *Focus on Phonological Acquisition*. Amsterdam: John Benjamins. 235–261.

Pater, J. and J. Paradis (1996). Truncation without templates in child phonology. *Proceedings of the Boston University Conference on Language Development*. Somerville, Mass.: Cascadilla Press.

Prince, A. and P. Smolensky (1993). Optimality Theory: constraint interaction in generative grammar. Technical Report CU-CS-696-93, Department of Computer Science, University of Colorado at Boulder, and Technical Report TR-2, Rutgers Center for Cognitive Science, Rutgers University, New Brunswick, N.J. To appear, Blackwell.

Prince, A. and B. Tesar (this volume). Learning phonotactic distributions. [ROA 353, http://roa.rutgers.edu]

Reynolds, W. (1994). *Variation and Phonological Theory*. Ph.D dissertation, University of Pennsylvania.

Saciuk, B. (1969). The stratal division of the lexicon. *Papers in Linguistics* **1**. 464–532.

Santelmann, L. M. and P. W. Jusczyk (1998). Sensitivity to discontinuous dependencies in language learners: evidence for limitations in processing space. *Cognition* **69**. 105–134.

Shady, M. E. (1996). *Infants' Sensitivity to Function Morphemes*. Ph.D. dissertation, State University of New York at Buffalo.

Smolensky, P. (1993). Harmony, markedness, and phonological activity. Handout of keynote address, Rutgers Optimality Workshop-1. [ROA 87, http://roa.rutgers.edu] Paper presented at the Rutgers Optimality Workshop-1, Rutgers University, New Brunswick, N.J.

(1995). On the internal structure of *Con*, the constraint component of UG. Paper presented at UCLA, Los Angeles, CA. [ROA 86, http://roa.rutgers.edu]

(1996a). The initial state and 'Richness of the Base' in Optimality Theory. Technical Report JHU-CogSci-96-4, Cognitive Science Department, Johns Hopkins University, Baltimore, Md. [ROA 154, http://roa.rutgers.edu]

(1996b). On the comprehension/production dilemma in child language. *LI* **27**. 720–731. [ROA 118, http://roa.rutgers.edu]

(1997). Constraint interaction in generative grammar II: Local Conjunction (or, Random rules in Universal Grammar). Paper presented at the Hopkins Optimality Theory Conference/University of Maryland Mayfest, Baltimore, Md.

Steriade, D. (1993). Closure, release, and nasal contours. In M. Huffman and R. Krakow (eds.) *Nasals, Nasalization, and the Velum*. San Diego: Academic Press. 401–470.

(1997). Phonetics in phonology: the case of laryngeal neutralisation. MS., Linguistics Department, UCLA, Los Angeles.

Tesar, B. and P. Smolensky (1993). The learnability of Optimality Theory: an algorithm and some basic complexity results. Technical Report CU-CS-678-93, University of Colorado at Boulder. [ROA 2, http://roa.rutgers.edu]

 (1996). Learnability in Optimality Theory (long version). Technical Report JHU-CogSci-96-3, Cognitive Science Department, Johns Hopkins University, Baltimore, Md. [ROA 156, http://roa.rutgers.edu]

 (1998a). Learnability in Optimality Theory. *LI* **29**. 229–268.

 (1998b). Learning Optimality-Theoretic grammars. *Lingua* **106**. 161–196. Reprinted in A. Sorace, C. Heycock, and R. Shillcock (eds.) (1998). *Language Acquisition: Knowledge Representation and Processing*. Amsterdam: Elsevier.

 (2000). *Learnability in Optimality Theory*. Cambridge, Mass.: MIT Press.

Tropf, H. (1987). Sonority as a variability factor in second language phonology. In A. James and J. Leather (eds.) *Sound Patterns in Second Language Acquisition*. Dordrecht: Foris. 173–192.

Wilson, C. (2000). *Targeted Constraints: an Approach to Contextual Neutralisation in Optimality Theory*. Ph.D. dissertation, Johns Hopkins University, Baltimore, Md.

Yip, M. (1993). Cantonese loan word phonology and optimality theory. *Journal of East Asian Linguistics* **2**. 261–292.

Zubritskaya, K. (1994). Markedness and sound change in OT. *NELS* **25**. 249–264.

 (1997). Mechanism of sound change in Optimality Theory. *Language Variation and Change* **9**. 121–148.

11 Child word stress competence: an experimental approach*

Wim Zonneveld and Dominique Nouveau

1. Introduction

Children at the age of 3 are usually credited with almost full mastery of the sound system of their mother tongue, and they spend the 'stage of mastery' between 3 and 7 becoming perfect speakers.[1] This chapter reports on the results of a range of experiments that aimed to establish whether at the beginning of the latter stage, at the ages of 3 and 4, Dutch children have full competence (or not) in the word stress system of their mother tongue. This research question is all the more interesting because the Dutch word stress system is lexical, in the sense that, just as in English, the major regularities are disturbed by morphological factors (i.e., the stress-sensitive vs. stress-neutral affixation distinction) as well as by lexical exceptions. The first aim of the discussion is to show that the outcome of the experiments indicates that children of this age indeed appear 'to know' this complex system to a considerable degree, and the 4-year-olds 'know it better' than the 3-year-olds. Second, the interpretation of the experimental results motivates a new look at the adult system: a significant new subpattern emerges, surprisingly so in a research area that has been more or less empirically stable for approximately two decades. This seems an interesting result in its own right, both from the point of view of general methodology and the study of the language-specific grammar. Third, it is shown that the 're-vised' Dutch word stress system which follows from these new findings, when put into an Optimality constraint-based account, has an interesting property: the account of the new subpatterns requires the active presence in the grammar of a NO-CLASH constraint, whose services are not immediately apparent from the traditional data, whether regular or irregular. It is proposed that this section of the chapter can be viewed as an example of Inkelas's (1999: 178) proposal 'that exceptions play a more central role in, rather than function as a footnote to, theoretical analysis'. Finally, recognising that currently there are broadly two ways of dealing with exceptionality, to wit reversed constraint ranking (McCarthy and Prince 1993) and prespecified underlying forms inputted to a single fixed ranking (Pater 1995, Inkelas, Orgun and Zoll 1997, Inkelas 1999), it will be shown that the active role of NO-CLASH holds under both approaches. In this discussion, we shall also indicate how, by reformulating the reversed ranking analysis of Nouveau (1994), such an approach to exceptionality might be constrained; and that the only 'prespecified underlying form' analysis of Dutch currently around, that of Van Oostendorp (1997), has a number of flaws that, until further notice, make it hard to accept as a contender.

The remainder of this chapter is structured as follows. Section 2 discusses the properties of the Dutch word stress system, captured in a more or less standard parametric framework. Section 3 discusses the general aims of the experiments, and the way pretests were carried out. Section 4 discusses the first aim of the enterprise, as described above. Section 5 takes combined care of the second and third aims, and section 6 comments on an existing underlying form analysis. Section 7 reiterates the major conclusions.

2.   The Dutch word stress system

The Dutch word stress system resembles that of English to a considerable degree, yet differs from it in a number of details. Thus, cognates may have the same stress pattern, as in E(nglish)/D(utch) *márathon, agénda, cemént*, but may also differ precisely in stress: E. *Mónaco, horízon, président* vs D. *Monáco, hórizon, presidént*. Among the major generalisations true for both languages is the fact that main stress is typically on one of the rightmost three syllables of the word (the right edge trisyllabic window: *abracadábra, Jerúsalem*), and the violation of this generalisation by the possible addition of stress-neutral affixes (E. *cháracterise, sériousness*, D. *hórizonloos* 'horizon-less', *álmanakje* 'little almanac'). Granting but not discussing the latter phenomenon here, the observations and analysis of this chapter will pertain to the 'Level 1' lexicon, that is: to underived words and words containing 'stress-sensitive' affixes.[2]

Given these preliminaries, the properties of the Dutch word stress system can be presented most profitably by observing the crucial role of the contents of the final syllable of the word. For the regular cases, the following three generalisations hold (see Kager, Visch, and Zonneveld 1987, Kager 1989, Trommelen and Zonneveld 1989, 1999):

• if the final syllable is open (-V), main word stress is on the penultimate syllable;
• if the final syllable is closed (-VC), main word stress is penultimate or antepenultimate (depending on the nature of the penultimate syllable: if it is closed, stress is penultimate, otherwise antepenultimate);
• if the final syllable is superheavy (-VVC or -VCC), main word stress is final.

Let us consider some examples of each of these generalisations and, at the same time, some irregular cases per generalisation.

Words ending in an open syllable have penultimate main stress. The nature of that penultimate syllable is immaterial: it can be open or closed. Two classes of exceptions occur: some words have antepenultimate stress, others have final stress; the former outnumber the latter.

(1)   (a) Chína   pásta   (b) Cánada   (c)[3] menú

	(a)		(b)	(c)[3]
	Chína	pásta	Cánada	menú
	casíno	agénda	bróccoli	buréau
	aréna	placénta	líbido	chocolá
	macaróni	influénza	harmónica	cavalaríe
	abracadábra	Esperánto	Cleópatra	onomatopée

Words ending in a superheavy syllable have final main stress. These syllables virtually always occur at the right edge of a word (for discussion see Trommelen 1983, Kager 1989, Zonneveld 1993). For this type of word exceptional stress patterns exhibit penultimate or antepenultimate main stress.

	(a)		(b)	(c)
	sopráan	studént	Nícolaas	líchaam
	gambíet	apárt	úniform	árbeid
	telefóon	presidént	ólifant	ásbest
	karikatúur	deodoránt	Sebástiaan	Prométheus

These word-final superheavies aside, Dutch rhymes usually have just two positions: VX, where X can be the second half of a long vowel (the second element of a diphthong), or a consonant. It has been argued, therefore, that the superheavies are surface manifestations of configurations comprising a regular bipositional VX syllable, followed by an onset introducing a defective syllable whose nucleus/rhyme is empty (Zonneveld 1993). Under the assumption that the interpretation of the empty rhyme is 'minimal' (i.e., 'open syllable'), the stress behaviour of superheavies reduces to the regular penultimate stress pattern of words with final open syllables (*stu-dén-tV*, for instance). This analysis will be adopted here. (The exceptions in (2b/c) clearly must have a different explanation).

Finally, words ending in closed syllables have two regular main stress patterns: third from the right if the penultimate syllable is open; second from the right if the penultimate one is closed (or, naturally, if the word is bisyllabic). Again, two classes of exceptions occur.

	(a)		(b)	(c)
	álmanak	hárnas	messías	kolóm
	báriton	róbot	Celébes	balkón
	rinóceros	Gibráltar	Melchizédek	klarinét
	Jerúzalem	rododéndron	Torremolínos	cholesteról

Still pretheoretically, these data can be rearranged so as to bring out, per word class, a subdivision into regular cases (let us call them A), exceptional ones (B) and very irregular – but existing – cases (C).

(4)   final syllable   A   B   C
        open (-V)   aréna   Cánada   chocolá
        superheavy (-VVC/VCC)   telefóon   ólifant   Prométheus[4]
        closed (-VC)   álmanak   klarinét   Celébes
                                Gibráltar

Support for this subdivision comes from a number of areas. A purely statistical underpinning can be found in Trommelen (1991). Non-standard shifts (e.g., *vágina* → *vagína, mónstrans* → *monstráns*) virtually consistently favour the A-pattern. Fully accepted or common Dutch pronunciations favour an A-pattern over the pattern of the language of origin: *mérci* (Fr. mercí), *Bríndísi* (It. Bríndisi), *Alcála* (Sp. Alcalá), *Niagára* (E. Niágara), *Marlbóro* (E. Márlboro), *Navratilóva* (Cz. Návratilova), *Crístobal* (Sp. Cristóbal), *Bólivar* (Sp. Bolívar), *Pótomac* (E. Potómac), *McÉnroe* (E. M[á]cenroe), *Manchéster* (E. Mánchester), as do pronunciations of semi-familiar foreign words: *babúshka* (Russ. bábushka), mispronunciations when speaking a foreign language: *to commént* (E. to cómment), and children's pronunciations of oddly spelled words: [maˈrɑthɔn] (D. márathon [ˈmaratɔn]).[5]

In a parametric framework (Kager 1989, Trommelen and Zonneveld 1989, 1999) Dutch is described as the following type of language:

parameter	*setting*	
(un)bounded:	bounded	(= binary feet)
foot type:	trochee	(as opposed to iamb)
direction:	right-to-left	(for foot formation and the word rule)
quantity:	quantity sensitive	(closed syllables heavy)
extrametricality:	yes	(heavy syllables)[6]

The grids of the regular A-cases follow from these settings:

(5)   x   x   x   x
        . (x .)   (x .) (x .)   (x .) <x>   .   (x) <x>
        a-re-na   te-le-foo-n   al-ma-nak   Gi-bral-tar

Trochaic feet are assigned from right-to-left. Feet are assumed to be binary, so stray syllables may occur at the left edge. Closed syllables are always heavy; they are not allowed to be right branches of feet, and they (exclusively) are extrametrical at the right edge of the word. Underlyingly superheavies are a full binary foot, as indicated above.

The irregular B- and C-cases are subject to their own respective exceptionality devices. First consider the B-cases:

(6)   x   x   x
         (x .)<x>   (x .) <x>   (x .) (x)
         Ca-na-da   o-li-fant   kla-ri-net

The *Cánada* pattern is obtained by providing the final (open) syllable with a gridmark, which – being absent from regular forms – counts against it; then antepenultimate stress is derived by regular extrametricality of that final syllable. If *ólifant* is marked as exceptional with regard to its final syllable (which irregularly remains closed and superheavy), again antepenultimate stress automatically follows by extrametricality. A main-stressed final -VC syllable (*klarinét*) can be obtained by marking it irregularly as non-extrametrical.

Finally, consider the C-cases:

(7)   x   x   x
         (x .) (x)   . (x) <x>   (x) (x) <x>
         cho-co-*la*   Pro-*me*-theus   mes-*si*-as

Each of these cases involves an exceptional lexically specified gridmark on an open syllable, either in final or penultimate position (underscored); this therefore turns out to be a common denominator of this class. In addition, *chocolá* must be an exception to extrametricality (by which it therefore becomes more heavily marked than *Cánada* among the words with final open syllables); *Prométheus* has a final syllable which exceptionally remains closed and superheavy (and therefore extrametrical).

The representations in (5)–(7), together with the overview in (4), are the foundation for the experiments in Dutch child word stress competence reported on below.

3.   The experiment: preliminaries

The research strategy underlying the word stress experiments conducted on Dutch 3- and 4-year-olds was the following:

> Dutch 3- and 4-year-olds have full competence in the Dutch word stress system if the picture of (4) emerges from word stress experiments conducted on them.

This strategy was modelled on that first expressed in Hochberg's (1986, 1988) investigation into Spanish, which has a word stress system not dissimilar from

Dutch. Aiming to show that 'the hypothesis that children learning Spanish as a first language learn rules for assigning stress, as opposed to simply memorizing stress on a word-by-word basis' (1988: 683), she found that:

> From a developmental perspective, the most striking conclusion is that children did learn stress rules, although [. . .] doing so was neither necessary nor straightforward. It seems that children's propensity to hypothesize linguistic rules is so strong as to tolerate a high degree of exceptionality. [Moreover], this study has highlighted a fact of Spanish stress [. . .] that remains to be accounted for under any current theory. [. . .] The fact that this disfavoring is relative, not absolute (since some Spanish words of this type do exist) shows that the notion of degrees of irregularity should be encompassed in future accounts. (1988: 704–705)

In the study reported on here a very rich system has to be coped with, with respect to syllable structure and stress types. It is therefore necessary to gather data which reliably represent the wide range of strings present in that system in order to get a thorough picture of the child's knowledge. Two main approaches usually compete in studies of language acquisition, naturalistic sampling and experimental settings, and the latter was judged more suitable to the present aims, the former (patient longitudinal collecting by a caregiver in familiar situations) giving no guarantee at all that all data of interest would occur. For instance, words of the same category with different stress types might be either absent from the data or disseminated over the whole period of study. The experiment of this contribution focuses on the elicited production of Dutch meaningful and nonsense words.[7] A group of meaningful bi-, tri-, and quadrisyllabic words was assembled of the types described in the previous section, which could be assumed to be known by subjects of the pertinent age (words denoting animals, toys, and sweets, mainly). Testing out these existing words served as a pilot study to a further test which used nonsense words (again, of the shapes and sizes described in the previous section) because the most reliable way to conduct our investigation implied a direct comparison between adult results, based on adult ('rule-based') intuitions, and child results, similarly based on child intuitions about exactly the same language material. In such a situation nonsense words are preferable to existing ones because we do not want to run the risk of the adult (and the child, for that matter) simply retrieving a fully specified memorised item from his or her lexicon, bypassing *the rule system* to be probed.

Thus, the experiment proceeded in two steps. First, 36 children (18 3-year-olds and 18 4-year-olds) produced the set of *meaningful words* with the help of a picture book. The aim was to diagnose whether the degree of regularity of stress in known items (A > B > C in (4)) had some impact on the children's realisations. More precisely, the following hypothesis was assumed:

The more irregular the test words, the more likely children are to make errors in producing them. Independently, these errors are expected to lead to more regular forms.

Second, 20 3-year-olds and 20 4-year-olds imitated the *nonsense words* contrasting in stress positions. The assumption underlying this second test was the same: the ease of production would depend on stress type, and errors would lead to more regular forms. The fact that this study involved three age groups allowed for a developmental analysis, expecting 4-year-olds to have a stress system more similar to the adult model.

Particular attention was paid to the preparation of the set of novel words. A list of preliminary stimuli was presented to 8 native speaker experts in Dutch phonology, phonetics, and morphology, and they were asked to judge whether these words (i) were close enough to existing words to act as equivalent to them; (ii) were not actually too similar to existing words; and (iii) could genuinely count as underived (as opposed to derived or compounded). These judgements converged on the following list (the adult test preceded the child test; the bracketed items were present in the adult test, but absent from the child test: a smaller number of items gave the children more time to cope with the test):

(8)   -V: bola   fenimo   kanakta   karabilo
                  [pato   fagurie   marotko]
         -VC: jakot   dapiton   talaktan   monitaron
                  [bizak   merotak   baralton]
         -VVC: bokaat   karimoon
                  karei   dolimei[8]
         -VCC: kadont   falimont

Notice that all syllables in these words begin with an onset, this both to accomplish structural unity among the word categories and to avoid perceptual confusion. The meaningful words act as fillers in the adult (reading) test, in the expectation that errors will be completely absent from them. In the children's naming test (pictures of familiar objects which the children have to name) the goal, on the other hand, was to establish the extent to which the children's productions conform to the adult model.

Twenty students (11 females, 9 males) of Utrecht University took part in the adult reading test, which they performed individually in a quiet room. They received no information about the goal of the test. Randomised test words (including a number of meaningful filler words) were presented on separate cards, and the testees were invited to read these words aloud. These utterances were recorded; all recordings turned out to be of good quality and all test patterns perfectly intelligible. The test's results are depicted in table 1.

(9)

Table 1. *Nonsense words test, adults*

		ANT	PEN	FIN	
-VV:	bola		20 (A)	– (C)	
	pato		15	5	
	fenimo	15 (B)	1	4	
	fagurie	1	9	10	
	kanakta	–	20	–	
	marotko	–	20	–	
	karabilo	1	18	1	
-VC:	jakot		9 (A)	9 (B)	(2 uninterpretable[9])
	bizak		14	6	
	talaktan	2 (P)	11	7	
	baralton	6	7	7	
	merotak	13 (A)	2 (C)	5 (B)	
	dapiton	11	1	8	
	monitaron	6	8	6	
-VVC:	bokaat		–	20 (A)	
	karimoon	2 (B)	–	18	
	karei		–	20	
	dolimei	3	–	17	
-VCC:	kadont		–	20	
	falimont	4	–	16	

Importantly, the right edge 'three syllable window' restriction is never violated in those two cases in which the subjects had the opportunity (*karabilo*,
monitaron). The results for the words ending in open syllables can be taken to
confirm this syllable's weak metrical status. The glaring exception is the preferred antepenultimate stress pattern of *fénimo*. This is probably the result of
a subpattern to the effect that comparatively many words, especially frequent
ones, with the vowel *-i-* in the penultimate syllable, have antepenultimate main
stress, according to the B-pattern (cf. *ánimo* 'zest', *dóminee* 'vicar', *África*; see
also Trommelen and Zonneveld 1989: 65–66). The predominant final pattern
for superheavies is confirmed, too. But clearly the most interesting mixture is
constituted by the group of words with final *-VC* syllables, in which in two
cases even the notion of *P*(rohibited) appears, i.e., a stress situation impossible
within the system (in these cases because these results violate Quantity Sensitivity). A rearrangement of the data for this particular class is presented in
table 2.

(10)   Table 2. *Nonsense words test, adults, -VC final words only*

		A	B	C	P
-VC:	jakot	9	9		
	bizak	14	6		
	talaktan	11	7		2
	baralton	7	7		6
	merotak	13	5	2	
	dapiton	11	8	1	
	monitaron	6	6	8	

For all words involved the B-pattern is popular, although significantly never more so than the A-pattern. For some individual endings it is notoriously difficult to state which of them is regular (cf. *róbot* vs. *schavót* 'scaffold', *kájak* 'kayak' vs. *tabák* 'tobacco', *rótan* 'rattan cane' vs. *Japán*, *márathon* vs. *pelotón* 'pack (of athletes)'), and this shines through in the results. The greatest surprises are in two separate situations: two trisyllabic words allow P-patterns, and the (single) quadrisyllabic word has the C-pattern as its most popular. There are two aspects to the former observation. First, it is odd that violations of Quantity Sensitivity (QS) (*tálaktan*, *báralton*)[10] are possible at all (and apparently function as C-patterns). Models for this pattern are virtually completely lacking. On the one hand, a geographical name like *Kázakstan* probably ends in a (stress-neutral) affix, and *bíatlon* and *tríatlon* presumably are cases of contrastive stress in a semantically related pair (just as *ímport* and *éxport*, which ought to have final syllable stress). On the other hand, the stress pattern of foreign placenames such as *Dúbrovnik* (Serbo-Croatian) and *Gibraltár* (Spanish) converges in Dutch on prefinal syllable main stress: *Dubróvnik*, *Gibráltar*.[11] Second, skipping a penultimate closed syllable (violating QS) seems to be possible (cf. table 1) just when the final syllable is closed, too, not when it is open. In fact, penultimate stress on a 'closed-open' final sequence is completely exceptionless in the test, a remarkable fact given the possibility of irregular main stress on final open syllables. The case of quadrisyllabic *monitáron* is strange in view of the overall system, but may, generally speaking, be due to a preference for rhythmically balanced structures (two times two syllables, rather than one followed by three). So far this pattern as such is a C-pattern in terms of (4), and exists in the language, albeit characteristically in highly unfamiliar words: *Melchizédek*, *Archimédes*, *oxymóron*.

Thus, the net result of the nonsense words test with adult native speakers is twofold. First, the picture in (4) as a summary of Dutch word stress patterns is broadly speaking correct, but some of the details of (10) must be kept in mind, too. In this sense, this corpus of adult test results will serve as a frame of reference for the analysis of the children's imitations. Second, the hypothesis about the state of full competence in the Dutch word stress system for 3- and 4-year-olds will have to be modified accordingly, from this stage onwards pertaining to (4) and (10) combined.

4.   Child word stress competence: the experimental approach

The goal of the first child experiment was to examine the realisations of meaningful words by 3- and 4-year-olds (henceforth: 3yos and 4yos), with respect to all relevant factors: the proximity of these realisations to those of adults, the developmental difference between the two age groups, the distribution of errors among stress types, and so forth. This test was conducted at a daycare centre in Nijmegen, and 18 3yos (10 boys and 8 girls) and 18 4yos (9 boys and 9 girls) took part. Data collection took place in a quiet room, with 2 adults present: the investigator technically supervised the recordings, and the actual interviews were conducted by a carefully instructed MA level student of linguistics. Data were elicited by means of a picture book, sometimes the elicitor had to assist some children by mildly helpful remarks. Most children seemed very willing to participate. The taped data were independently transcribed by three linguistically trained persons. The 21 words of the test were these:

(11)	final syllable	*A*	*B*	*C*
	open (-V)	zébra	páprika	café
		fóto	éskimo	kadó
		pyjáma		chocolá
		piáno		paraplú
	closed (-VC)	róbot	ballón	
		lúcifer	sigarét	
		ánanas	krokodíl	
	superheavy (-VVC)	kaméel	óoievaar	
		telefóon		
		papegáai		
	superheavy (-VCC)		ólifant	

Analysis of the results of this test soon revealed that the children had been quite good at it,[12] sufficiently so to wonder about the significance of an attempted analysis of the details. A discussion of these details can be found in Nouveau (1994: 108–119), and will not be repeated here. Some of the overall results were the following.

As was anticipated, not all test words were known to (or producible in the test situation by) all children. The 3yos had an average of 15 output words (out of 21), the 4yos of 17. This suggests a small-scale developmental pattern. A developmental pattern is clearer, though, when the results are considered per word type. In table 3 the respective columns have the following interpretation:

no. is the sheer amount of expected output words, *O* is the output actually found, *C* the number of fully correct words, *E* the ones with one or more mistakes in them (simply *O*-minus-*C*).

(12)   Table 3. *Existing words test, children (age 3–4)*

	no.	\multicolumn{4}{c}{3yo}	\multicolumn{4}{c}{4yo}
		O	C	%	E	O	C	%	E
-VV	180	116	105	90	11	137	128	94	9
-VC	108	64	58	91	6	90	87	97	3
-VVC	72	52	48	92	4	55	54	98	1
-VCC	18	18	18	100	–	18	18	100	–
Total	378	250	229	91.6	21	300	287	95.6	13

Clearly 4yos are better as performers of the test than 3yos are, for each pair of equivalent cells, but this is something different from claiming that they have better word stress competence. If there is a meaningful component in this table, it is that the corresponding figures of the O-columns become higher, while at the same time those of the E-columns become lower. These two tendencies combined are expressed in the two columns of percentages, of C/O. It must be admitted, however, that the differences between these two latter columns, although clearly present, are connected to extremely low figures of E.

Table 3 indicates that the children made 34 errors: 21 plus 13. Output was counted as 'erroneous' when it contained a deviation from the adult model in a manner potentially affecting the stress type of the word: this could be a pure stress shift, a change in the weight of a syllable (open vs. closed), or a change in the number of syllables in the word (more or less). Among the actual 34 errors two types were found: rhyme adaptations (changes of weight), and truncations of non-primary stressed syllables. No stress shifts were found. Most of the errors turned out not to affect the stress type of the word. Thus, child output [róbo], a rhyme adaptation, is of the same type (A) as the target word *róbot*. And [páma] and [plaplý], both truncations, are of the same types (A and C, resp.) as the target words *pyjáma* and *paraplú*. Just 4 errors, a very small number indeed, implied a change of type, all of them from either B or C to A, as hoped for:

(13)   3yo   óoievaar (B)   →   [ója] (A)
              kadó (C)   [kadót] (A)   (twice)
        4yo   páprika (B)   [páka] (A)[13]

The remainder of this section will be occupied with a summary of the second child experiment, that using nonsense rather than meaningful words, in an attempt at fully involving knowledge of 'the system' rather than that of stored lexical items. The aims of the experiment were these. From a developmental perspective it investigated the extent to which these children's output is identical to that of adults (presented in (9)), and the extent to which the children differ among themselves in age groups. The distribution of errors among stress types was to be explored, just as the hypotheses that children will make more errors in irregular words than in regular ones, and that their errors tend towards regularisation of stress.

Forty children took part in this second test, from two daycare centres and two nursery schools in Nijmegen and Utrecht. There were 20 3yos (6 boys and 14 girls) and 20 4yos (8 boys and 12 girls).[14] The tests were conducted under circumstances equivalent to those of the 'meaningful word test'. Since the children's attention had to be held during the whole experiment, they were invited to join in simple games. For each game different materials were used (objects, pictures of imaginary animals, puppets), but the elicitation procedure was always the same. Children were instructed that they: (i) would be presented with unknown objects; (ii) had to listen carefully to the names of these objects; and (iii) would have to give the names when asked for by the investigator. The session started with a short practice phase with familiar objects to ensure that the child understood the imitation task and was aware of the importance of waiting for the investigator's request before realising the imitation. In the first step of a game, the interviewer mentioned the name of an object twice, using a word out of the list of nonsense words. She was trained to pronounce the stimuli clearly without exaggerations with regard to stress. Then, a mechanical direct imitation of the stimulus by a child was avoided by means of a stereotyped question: 'X, do you know what the name of this object is?' The child was expected to answer yes, the interviewer would ask: 'What is its name, then?', and the child would say the name. When for some reason deviations from this procedure occurred, new imitations of the relevant items were elicited at the end of the session. The taped data were analysed independently by three transcribers (one of whom was Nouveau), using broad IPA notation. Transcriptions were compared, and only those on which the transcribers agreed obtained a pass. Disagreement in the interpretation of the data seldom occurred, however, and could almost always be solved by reconsidering the recordings.

The basic material of the test was that of (8), minus the bracketed items. There were many more than just 14 test items, however, because the full list contained per item as many variants as there were syllables. This gave the 39 items below in (14):

(14)

	A	B	C	P
-	bóla		bolá	
	fenímo	fénimo	fenimó	
	kanákta		kanaktá	kánakta
	karabílo	karábilo	karabiló	kárabilo

-	jákot	jakót		
	dápiton	dapitón	dapíton	
	taláktan	talaktán		tálaktan
	monítaron	monitarón	monitáron	mónitaron
-	bokáat	bókaat		
	karimóon	kárimoon	karímoon	
	karéi	kárei		
	doliméi	dólimei	dolímei	
	kadónt	kádont		
	falimónt	fálimont	falímont	

Each age group consists of 20 subjects who each imitated the same 39 stimuli. For either corpus there are a total of 780 imitations, involving 700 words with authorised stress patterns, and 80 with prohibited stress. We shall conclude that the children of the test have mastered the Dutch word stress system when (i) their error rates conform to the markedness rating in (14) (A < B < C < P); and (ii) the errors they make generally go from 'bad' to 'less bad'. We shall use information on the quality of imitations (identical vs. in some way erroneous) to measure error rates in all data representing a certain stress type, and then in each item. We shall also measure whether errors in individual items lead more frequently to a regularisation (or not). First, these measurements will be done for each age group separately; subsequently we shall proceed to a comparison of the results, which will help us detect developmental tendencies in the acquisition of stress.

Table 4 gives a summary of the test results per stress type and per age group, where the percentages are based on the number of errors. (Notice that this time output was always obtained for any item for any child.)

(15)   Table 4. *Broad results nonsense words test for 2 age groups: 3yos and 4yos*

Age group	Stress types				
	A (280)	B (240)	C (180)	P (80)	
3yo	22% (61)	40% (97)	50% (91)	64% (51)	38.5 (300)
4yo	16% (45)	31% (76)	55% (99)	60% (48)	34.3 (268)

The sum total of errors for the 4yos is not much lower than that for the 3yos. Yet the percentages express a virtually perfect relationship between the degree of stress regularity of nonsense words and the rate of errors made during the imitation task. The results reflect the markedness hierarchy (A < B < C < P). Regular nonsense words (type A) were easier to imitate than their irregular counterparts (B and C), while prohibited patterns (P) were more difficult than all other types.

These scores may be taken as a first indication that children by the age of 3 already have internalised much of the stress system of their mother tongue, since they appear to be sensitive to various degrees of regularity in the system. As a general tendency, 4yos made fewer errors in imitations within each stress type than the 3yos, with the exception of type C. Moreover, these scores provide strong independent support for the subdivision of Dutch stress patterns in the categories A, B, C, and P, as employed in this chapter.

Since these general scores support the prediction that the error rate depends on the regularity of the stress patterns, table 4 will now be set off against the whole range of data, separated out into the two age groups. After that, the results will be combined and an attempt will be made to detect developmental patterns.

(16)   Table 5. *Results (errors) nonsense words for 3yos, per individual word*

Stimulus	Pre-ant.	Antep.	Penult	Final
bola			– (A)	35% (C)
jakot			15% (A)	30% (B)
bokaat			70% (B)	15% (A)
karei			40% (B)	10% (A)
kadont			30% (B)	10% (A)
fenimo		30% (B)	10% (A)	40% (C)
kanakta		75% (P)	10% (A)	65% (C)
dapiton		**20% (A)**	40% (C)	**15% (B)**
talaktan		**65% (P)**	30% (A)	**70% (B)**
karimoon		60% (B)	90% (C)	50% (A)
dolimei		**15% (B)**	45% (C)	**45% (A)**
falimont		40% (B)	**30% (C)**	35% (A)
karabilo	65% (P)	30% (B)	20% (A)	65% (C)
monitaron	**50% (P)**	35% (A)	45% (C)	**55% (B)**

(Stress Location spans Pre-ant., Antep., Penult, Final)

As indicated in bold, there are 5 cases of deviation from the expected patterning. Before we go into them, let us have a look at some general tendencies that stand out in this table.

All results of the top half conform to the expectations; more generally, two types of data do so: bisyllabic words, and words (of all sizes) ending in open syllables. Interestingly, the latter type includes the case of *fenimo*, for which these 3yos 'prefer' penultimate stress, where adults had antepenultimate stress (cf. table 1 in (9)); apparently, the interfering role of -*i*- is not (yet) part of these children's grammar. In the bottom half, *karimóon* is a comparatively unproblematic pattern. Among the 5 more problematic cases, A is still the best pattern in 2 words: *taláktan* and *monítaron*. The deviation in the case of *dapiton* is only slight, since type B scores 3 errors out of 20 imitations, whereas type A scores 4. With respect to *falimont*, some uncertainty seems to reign as to the best stress pattern: range 30 to 40 percent. Furthermore, it seems that by favouring antepenultimate stress in *dolimei* (actually type B), children overgeneralise the regular pattern of trisyllabic words with final closed syllables to those with a final diphthong. The results for these latter two items could indicate that 3yos do not yet master complex rhymes very well, such as superheavies ending in clusters, and diphthongs.

It can also be observed, however, that even though P(rohibited) patterns scored a very high error rate across-the-board (range 50 to 75 percent), which is just as expected, this is not always the highest error rate for each individual word. The dissenting examples are **mónitaron* and **tálaktan*, which were both easier to imitate than their final-stressed counterparts (which are type B). Similarly, both in non-conformist and completely conformist examples, these children often have difficulty in imitating final stress: one way to look upon the *monitaron* results is to say that the B-pattern is difficult, and *kanakta* and *karabilo* have an error rate of 65 percent for their C-pattern.

Table 6 gives the results of the same test, administered to the 4yos.

(17)   Table 6. *Results (errors) nonsense words for 4yos, per individual word*

Stimulus	Pre-ant.	Antep.	Penult	Final
			Stress Location	
bola			- (A)	45% (C)
jakot			- (A)	5% (B)
bokaat			40% (B)	25% (A)
karei			50% (B)	15% (A)
kadont			30% (B)	25% (A)
fenimo		**10% (B)**	**25% (A)**	30% (C)
kanakta		**65% (P)**	5% (A)	**80% (C)**
dapiton		5% (A)	45% (C)	10% (B)
talaktan		45% (P)	25% (A)	40% (B)
karimoon		40% (B)	80% (C)	30% (A)
dolimei		25% (B)	55% (C)	10% (A)
falimont		45% (B)	45% (C)	20% (A)
karabilo	70% (P)	30% (B)	5% (A)	50% (C)
monitaron	**60% (P)**	35% (A)	**65% (C)**	55% (B)

An obvious interpretation of these results observes an increase in awareness of the intricacies of the word stress system. Out of the earlier 5 cases of deviation,

4 have disappeared, i.e., have become regularised. The remaining example is that of *monitaron*, for which all stress patterns except the fully regular one have high error percentages, with those for C and P reversed (but notice that even its A-pattern has the highest error percentage for As in the entire table). It turns out that a developmental distinction between patterns also exists in the following way. Comparing cell by cell, not each individual error percentage in table 6 (4yos) is lower than that of its direct counterpart in table 5 (3yos). This is the result of a full comparison:

(18)   Table 7. *Cell-by-cell comparison of error percentage*

| | | At age 4 (as compared to age 3) | | |
Pattern type	Occurs x times	Lower	Same	Higher
A	14	9	1	4
B	12	6	3	3
C	9	3		6
P	4	2		2

This picture indicates that, although the categorisation of stress according to markedness and prosodic restrictions can be said to be approximated by children by the age of 3, the children's stress systems keep expanding gradually and in a systematic way.

Two unexpected patterns newly occur in the top half of table 6. The first of these, antepenultimate stress in *fenimo*, has a cause discussed above. The second, for *kanakta*, can be formulated in two ways: final stress has an extremely high error percentage here (absolutely the highest in the table, and relatively the highest when compared to the other test items ending in open syllables); and for this word the P-pattern scores better than the C-pattern, although the former is a violation of Quantity Sensitivity. Possibly in connection with this, also observe that *talaktan* has the lowest error rate of the table for its own P-pattern. When we compile earlier findings for these data as in (19), using subparts of (9) and (10), we get a better view on what seems to be happening.

(19)   Table 8. *A developmental picture of Quantity Sensitivity*

| | 3yos | | | 4yos | | | adults | | |
	antep.	pen.	fin.						
ka-nak-ta	75(P)	10(A)	65(C)	65	5	80	–	20	–
ma-rot-ko							–	20	–
ta-lak-tan	65(P)	30(A)	70(B)	45	25	40	2	11	7
ba-ral-ton							6	7	7

The figures indicate percentages of error rates for the children; for the adults they provide the absolute number of times a given stress pattern was used in the 20 subject adults pre-test (indicating the relative popularity of that pattern among adults). For *talaktan*, the expected correlation between the two sets of data (children vs. adults) is introduced at the age of 4, although *tálaktan* and adult *báralton* (both P) remain unexpectedly popular. For *kanakta* the expected correlation exists at all ages, with a strong dislike for anything other than penultimate stress at all stages. These results will be readdressed in the next section.

The overall finding that children's errors were more frequent in irregular and prohibited patterns than in regular ones cannot, of course, be confirmed without an investigation of *error directionality*. The question is: when children make imitation errors, do these lead to a regularisation or an irregularisation of stress? All arguments in favour of the markedness categorisation presented above would be undermined if it were discovered that changes in the imitations tend to result in a deterioration of stress status. Conversely, our results so far will receive strong support if errors improve irregular and prohibited words, and leave already regular words – more or less – intact. In (20) are examples of the types of errors that were exhibited in our data:

(20)   (L is an open syllable, H is closed, S is superheavy, D is diph-
        thongal)
        (a) stress shift
             LL → LL   bolá (C)   →   [bóla] (A)
             LLL → LD   fenimó (C)   [femáo] (A)
             LHL → LHL   kanaktá (C)   [kanákti] (A)
             LLLL → LLLL   karabiló (C)   [karabílo] (A)
             LLL → LLL   fenimó (C)   [fénimo] (B)
             LHH → LHH   taláktan (A)   [dólaktɔn] (P)
             LHH → LHH   talaktán (B)   [tálaktan] (P)

        (b) rhyme shape adaptation
             LLL → LLH   fénimo (B)   [fénimɔn] (A)
             LLL → LLS   fenimó (C)   [fenimón] (A)
             LLH → LLL   dapíton (C)   [dapíto] (A)
             LHL → LLL   kánakta (P)   [kánata] (B)
             LLS → LLH   karímoon (C)   [karímɔn] (C)
             LHL → LLL   kanaktá (C)   [kanatá] (C)
             LLLH → LLLL   monítaron (A)   [monítaro] (B)
             LS → LH   kadónt (A)   [kadɔ́n] (B)

        (c) word length affected
        c(i) - truncation
             LH → H   jakót (B)   [kɔt] (A)
             LLH → LH   dapíton (C)   [píton] (A)

LLLH → LLH	mónitaron (P)	[módirɔn] (A)
LLLH → LLL	mónitaron (P)	[mólila] (B)
LLS → LS	karímoon (C)	[kíron] (B)
LLLL → LLL	kárabilo (P)	[kábilo] (B)
LLL → LL	feními (A)	[nío] (A)
LLLL → LLL	karabílo (A)	[kabílo] (A)
LHL → HL	kanákta (A)	[kákta] (A)
LLH → LH	dápiton (A)	[dátɔn] (A)
LLLH → LLH	monítaron (A)	[mítarɔn] (A)
LS → S	bokáat (A)	[kát] (A)
LLS → LS	falimónt (A)	[famɔ́nt] (A)
LLLL → LLL	karábilo (B)	[klábilo] (B)
LLL → LL	fenimó (C)	[femó] (C)
LLLL → LLL	karabiló (C)	[kalimó] (C)

c(ii) - syllable addition

LLH → LLLH	karímon (C)	[karínomon] (B)
LH → LLH	jakót (B)	[jakakɔ́t] (B)

(d) mixed cases
   - stress shift and rhyme shape adaptation

LLD → LLL	doliméi (A)	[dólina] (B)

   - stress shift and truncation

LLLL → LLL	karabiló (C)	[kabílo] (A)
LLLL → LLL	kárabilo (P)	[kalíbo] (A)

An obvious way for the child to deal with an irregular stress pattern is by stress shift: this will always lead to a change in stress status. Rhyme shape adaptation affects syllable weight, and may or may not have repercussions for stress type. In our data, most changes modifying word length are truncations, although cases of syllable addition are found too. Both kinds of latter error may affect the stress status of imitations. Truncated forms concern items with pre-antepenultimate stress (e.g., *kábilo* for **kárabilo*), antepenultimate stress (*dáton* for *dápiton*), penultimate stress (*níno* for *fénimo*), and final stress (*káat* for *bokáat*). This process affects *non-final unstressed open syllables*. That is: it typically occurs under the same circumstances as truncation in early child speech (Echols and Newport 1992, Lohuis-Weber and Zonneveld 1996, Kehoe and Stoel-Gammon 1997, Pater 1997), and under conditions very similar to vowel reduction in the adult language (Kager 1989, Trommelen and Zonneveld 1989, 1999).

However, occasionally truncation may also affect final syllables, which are usually immune to it. Such a modification could be observed in the four forms in (21):

(21)   Stress   Stimulus (type)   Truncation (type)
         ANT   kánakta (P)   [kánɑk] (A)
                      kánakta (P)   [kánɑkt] (B)
                      tálaktan (P)   [tálɑk] (A)
         PRE-ANT   mónitaron (P)   [mólila] (B)

The different character of this process is illustrated by the fact that it affects both open and closed syllables. It always occurs under extreme circumstances, when (P)rohibited stimuli (violations of the three-syllable-window restriction, or of Quantity Sensitivity) yield an authorised (A or B) stress pattern.

Errors in imitations can be classified into 3 classes (better – same – worse) using the P > C > B > A scale of stress types. Obviously, 'better' then stands for an error which makes a test item more regular, 'same' refers to one that does not affect the classification, and 'worse' characterises errors which make an item more irregular. Below, both for the 3yos and the 4yos, tables are presented which contain the percentages for effects of errors calculated out of the total number of errors found in either corpus. In the majority of cases irregular patterns are expected to become regular, and prohibited patterns to be changed into authorised ones, and not vice versa.

(22)   Table 9: Error directionality

(a) 3yos

Stimulus Type	Result of error			Total no. N
	Better	Same	Worse	
A	n.a.	70.5% (43)	29.5% (18)	61
B	63.9% (62)	30.9% (30)	5.2% (5)	97
C	75.8% (69)	24.2% (22)	0.0% (0)	91
P	94.1% (48)	5.9% (3)	n.a.	51
overall	59.7% (179)	32.6% (98)	7.7% (23)	300

(b) 4yos

Stimulus Type	Result of error			Total no. N
	Better	Same	Worse	
A	n.a.	60.0% (27)	40.0% (18)	45
B	57.9% (44)	38.2% (29)	3.9% (3)	76
C	80.8% (80)	19.2% (19)	0.0% (0)	99
P	89.6% (43)	10.4% (5)	n.a.	48
overall	62.4% (167)	29.8% (80)	7.8% (21)	268

Very clearly the general tendency of errors in imitations is towards regularisation: regular words (type A) more often simply stay regular; for words of types B and C (in which in principle errors can result either in a regularisation or a deterioration) regularisation is also preferred in the large majority of cases. Moreover, whereas *a priori* type A is as likely to get worse as type P is to improve, a high percentage of P-items gets better, and a comparatively low percentage of A-items gets worse. Finally, the developmental picture of table 7 (4yos do better than 3yos specifically on A and B patterns for the large majority of individual words) is reconfirmed in a distinction between a reduction of errors for types A and B on the one hand, and types C and P on the other.

Summarising, with respect to the first aim of this contribution, it has been shown in this section that the ease of imitation of test stimuli follows the hierarchy of regularity predicted by the metrical theory of Dutch word stress. Both research predictions have been found corroborated. First, children find words with irregular and prohibited stress more difficult to imitate than words with regular stress. Second, the analysis of the nature of structural errors shows that children tend to regularise irregular and prohibited patterns, and to preserve regular stress. The fact that, as observed, 3-year-old children have already mastered most of the stress system suggests that the acquisition of the Dutch stress patterns is precocious. The system improves with age, and does so in a systematic way: development corresponds to a refinement in the discrimination of stress types. The 4-year-olds have a stress system which is more similar to the adult model. They have mastered the markedness hierarchy in more words than younger subjects, and they make fewer errors in imitating most authorised stress types. Finally, among the experimental results are data concerning Quantity Sensitivity (cf. (19)) that cannot be easily reconciled with a parametric approach, which takes a relatively rigid (yes/no) attitude towards such situations.[15] It is here that the link exists with the next sections of the chapter, the aim of which is to develop and show the interest of a detailed Optimality account of the 'revised' Dutch word stress system that takes the experimental results into account. Towards this, consider the following.

5.   An Optimality interpretation of the test results

This section analyses the test results presented above in an Optimality framework. Basically, we present a modified version of the Optimality analysis of Dutch of Nouveau (1994), which succeeds the parametric account of section 2 of this chapter. An issue not raised by Nouveau, however, was that of the two possible ways of dealing with exceptional patterns (McCarthy and Prince 1993, Inkelas 1999): by dint of different constraint rankings for (regular vs. irregular) groups of lexical items, or by idiosyncratically prespecified underlying forms, just as in the parametric account of section 2 (although, of course, the prespecifications need not be the same). Nouveau provides the former type of analysis, but Van Oostendorp (1997), in a review of her work, gives the latter. The aim of this section will be twofold: first, as pointed out in the introduction, to present a case in which a well-known substantial metrical constraint (NO-CLASH) turns out to be active in the grammar, its active status motivated specifically by exceptional forms whose relevance only transpired through our experiments; and second, to propose restrictions on the extent to which different constraint rankings may potentially coexist in a single grammar. Similarly, the next section will have a twofold aim: first, to show that the choice of exceptionality theory does not appear to affect the argument concerning the unexpected role of NO-CLASH; and second, that the single published 'prespecified underlying form' analysis of Dutch has a number of drawbacks that make it difficult to accept it as a contender, at this stage of development.

5.1   A-, B-, and C-patterns

With reference to the summary of the Dutch stress system in section 2, an Optimality account (basically the one proposed by McCarthy and Prince (1993: 90–100) for 'Garawa-type languages of the English variety') will contain constraints for the proper distribution of feet, and for the selection of main stress. They are: BIN (feet are binary), TROCHEE (feet are left-headed), ALL-FT-R (align (all) feet with the right wordedge), ALIGN-EDGE-L (the left edge must start with a foot), NON-FIN ('extrametricality', i.e., the syllable with main stress cannot be word-final), and HEAD-R (main stress at the right wordedge, also known as EDGEMOST-R). Clearly among the final two constraints, NON-FIN and HEAD-R, the former constraint dominates the latter; this will ensure output such as those below for the simplest cases, namely those ending in open syllables:

(23)[16]   (i) (Chí - na)   (ii) ca (sí - no)
         (iii) (mà - ca) (ró - ni)   (iv) (à - bra) ca (dá - bra)
          (v) (Àn - ti) (nà - na) (rí - vo)
          (vi) (Jè - ro) so (lì- mi) (tá - ni)
                         'friars of the order of Jerusalem'

Case (iv), with initial stress followed by a lapse, shows that ALIGN-EDGE-L dominates ALL-FT-R. Case (vi), a precious example from the fringes of the Dutch lexicon, shows that ALL-FT-R is the proper generalisation for foot distribution rather than its mirror image twin.[17] Finally, HEAD-R dominates ALIGN-EDGE-L in order to ensure prefinal stress in case (ii). (Thus, combined: NON-FIN » HEAD-R » ALIGN-EDGE-L » ALL-FT-R.)

The occurrence of stray syllables in these representations implies that here 'exhaustive footing' (Halle and Vergnaud 1987) is not seen as a necessary characteristic of metrical representations. This is relevant for the positioning of the well-known PARSE-SYL constraint of McCarthy and Prince (1993: 90–93), requiring that all syllables must be footed. If capturing both main and secondary stresses implies more than a single foot in a representation, then PARSE-SYL dominates ALL-FT-R: any non-right edge foot violates the latter. On the other hand, McCarthy and Prince also propose that 'exhaustive footing cannot be achieved through the use of unit feet', formalising this as BIN » PARSE which is assumed to be 'normal', perhaps 'universal'. (Thus, combined: BIN » PARSE-SYL » ALL-FT-R; so far two strands of ranked constraints meet at ALL-FT-R.)

Following Zonneveld (1993) and Nouveau (1994), we assume that the behaviour of superheavy syllables can be reduced to that of final open ones (see section 2). Thus, the analysis so far is simply extended to the cases in (24):

(24)   (i) -   (ii) so - (prá - nV)
        (iii) (tè - le) (fó - nV) (iv) (kà - ri) ka (tú - rV)

Finally, the words ending in -VC syllables must be accounted for. Recall that two regular patterns here are differentiated by the nature of the penultimate syllable: main stress is on the penult when it is closed (*Gibráltar*), and on the antepenult when the penult is open (*álmanak*). The first pattern is a direct consequence of the current analysis:

(25)   (a) * gi (bral) (tár)   worse than all others by
                                         NON-FIN » HEAD-R

        (b) ☺ gi (brál) (tar)

        (c) ☺ gi (brál - tar)

        (d) * (gí - bral) (tar)   worse than (b) and (c) by
                                         HEAD-R

        (e) * (gí) (bral) (tar)   BIN-violation, and worse than
                                         (b) and (c) by HEAD-R

Following Prince (1980), Kager (1989), and Nouveau (1994), BIN(arity) is proposed to cover two types of feet: (i) bisyllabic ones, independently of whether these are open (light) or closed (heavy); and (ii) single specimens of closed (heavy) syllables. Interestingly *(d) is a near-perfect representation that violates neither BIN nor PARSE-SYL: rejecting it can be ensured by a constraint hierarchy assumption: HEAD » PARSE-SYL. This is a first point where the two constraint strands interlock. Notice that two different structures with penultimate stress survive; for the time being (we shall reconsider this point immediately below), low-ranked ALL-FT-R prefers (c) to (b).

The *álmanak* pattern requires the addition of some notion of weight sensitivity: WSP (the Weight-to-Stress Principle) bans any candidate that has a closed (H) syllable in a non-head position (i.e., it bans L-H and H-H feet, and unparsed H), cf. (26):

(26)

(a) * (al - ma) (nák)   NON-FIN (» HEAD-R) violated, WSP not violated
(b) * (al) (má - nak)   WSP violated (assuming WSP » HEAD-R)
(c) * (al) (má) (nak)   BIN violated (assuming BIN » HEAD-R)
(d) ☺ (ál - ma) (nak)   NON-FIN, BIN, WSP not violated

Comparison of candidates (b) and (d) establishes WSP » HEAD-R, and comparison of (c) and (d) establishes BIN » HEAD-R (both in order not to derive penultimate stress, simply by NON-FIN » HEAD-R). The former of these new rankings (WSP » HEAD-R) affects (25). In (25), candidates (c) and (d) will now be eliminated at a relatively early stage by WSP, and (b) will be optimal. When *(d) is eliminated by early-ranked WSP, the ranking of HEAD-R » PARSE-SYL is no longer motivated by this candidate. But (25) clearly shows that PARSE-SYL should still be kept in check by WSP » PARSE-SYL (in order for WSP to eliminate *(d)).

This concludes the account of the A-patterns of Dutch word stress. The grammar that takes care of them has the following form:

(27)   Optimality grammar of Dutch word stress (based on A-patterns)

TROCHEE
NON-FIN » HEAD-R » ALIGN-EDGE-L » ALL-FT-R (23)
        ↗ (26) (↘)
        BIN   » PARSE-SYL   » ALL-FT-R (exh. binary footing)
        WSP   » PARSE-SYL
                (25/26)

As indicated, HEAD-R » PARSE-SYL could still be true: this will indeed turn out to be the case below, for a novel reason.

TROCHEE can be assumed to be undominated. Moreover, at the top of the list HEAD-R is preceded by all of NON-FIN, BIN, and WSP, but in fact a more intricate relation holds between these latter three constraints. This is shown by the case of *róbot*, a bisyllabic word with L-H structure (the final syllable is extrametrical in the parametric analysis, and the word would have antepenultimate stress if longer, in a manner of speaking). A word of this type has three reasonable candidates, each violating its own constraint, of which one is blatantly ungrammatical:

(28)   (a) (ró) (bot)   violation of BIN
        (b) (ró bot)   violation of WSP
        (c) ro (*bót)   violation of NON-FIN

Any ranking in which NON-FIN is last of three must be avoided, because it leads to the selection of incorrect final stress. Rankings in which BIN is last select [(*ró*)(*bot*)]; and rankings in which WSP is last select [(*róbot*)]. So these three constraints have four possible rankings, each leading to penultimate stress, albeit by different foot structures (this issue will be returned to below).

As pointed out earlier, two types of analysis exist in the literature for irregular patterns. The first employs non-canonical constraint rankings. The first reference to this possibility seems to be the 'lexically determined ranking reversal' for Ulwa infixation vs. suffixation in McCarthy and Prince (1993: 109–112). Slightly later cases are the 'ranking reversal' proposed as a solution to the phenomenon of *h aspiré* in French in Tranel (1994), and the 'lexically determined non-rigid ranking' contemplated by Cabré and Kenstowicz (1995: 699–700) in their analysis of the variation found in Catalan hypocoristic formation. Inkelas *et al.* (1997) and Inkelas (1999) call such different rankings 'co-phonologies'. The second type of analysis uses prespecified underlying forms, essentially as in the parametric analysis of section 2, and Inkelas (1999) argues that this device is superior to the former for Turkish word stress.[18] An Optimality account of Dutch word stress of the former type was proposed in Nouveau (1994), one of the latter type in elaborate comments on Nouveau's work, by Van Oostendorp (1997). We will now show how a revision of Nouveau's analysis deals with the exceptional Dutch cases; we shall return to the latter type of analysis in section 6.

First, consider the B-pattern for words ending in open syllables: *(Cána)da*, *A(méri)ca*, *(har)(móni)ca*. Nouveau (1994: 198–199) proposes that this situation be taken care of by a constraint of the NON-FIN variety, one saying that the foot containing the main stressed syllable cannot be word-final. This constraint (let us call it NON-FIN-FT) was not crucially involved in the core analysis above, although clearly HEAD-R » NON-FIN-FT must hold in it. For these irregular cases, this latter ranking would have to be reversed to NON-FIN-FT » HEAD-R.[19]

Second, under the proposed account of superheavy syllables Dutch is a language completely lacking main stress on final syllables, in much the same way core English is. This implies that any example of final stress, whether of the B-type (ending in a closed syllable) or the C-type (ending in an open syllable), will be irregular. Following Nouveau (1994), the ranking reversal effectuating final stress is the irregular demotion of NON-FIN to a position below HEAD-R: the VC-final example *klari-nét* from (6) is a case in point. The example *choco-lá* from (7) needs a more complex demotion: both NON-FIN *and* BIN to a position below HEAD-R. The differences between these two types of ranking reversal seem to correspond well to their respective characterisations as B- and C-type irregular forms.[20]

Third, the C-pattern for VC-final words, of which *Celébes* from (3) is an example, receives the following analysis: the regular WSP » HEAD-R ranking is reversed to HEAD-R » WSP.[21]

Finally, we follow Nouveau (1994) in dealing with *Nícolaas* and other exceptional words among those ending in superheavy syllables (cf. (2b)) in the following two-step way. First, the irregular promotion of NON-FIN-FT implies the selection of [*(Níco)(la-sV)*] over the candidate with main stress in the final foot. Second, [*Ni-(cóla)-sV)*] is eliminated by requiring that defective syllables must always be footed, but cannot be heads of feet. These proposals imply that the C-pattern example *Prométheus* cannot be generated: it will be a P-pattern word; this is not necessarily a bad result in view of its unique status (cf. (4) and n. 4).[22]

The different ranking reversals that together constitute the Optimality analysis of irregular Dutch word stress patterns in that framework are the following (leftward arrow means 'promoted', rightward arrow means 'demoted'):

(29)   Regular Ranking reversals

	A	B	C
-VV:	= (27)	NON-FIN-FT $\Leftarrow$	NON-FIN, BIN $\Rightarrow$
-VC	= (27)	NON-FIN $\Rightarrow$	WSP $\Rightarrow$
-VXC:	= (27)	NON-FIN-FT $\Leftarrow$	n.a.

all pro- and demotions relative to HEAD-R

This display clearly contains a far from arbitrary collection of ranking reversals. Rather, a number of potentially interesting (and, we submit, possibly universal) restrictions on this otherwise powerful mechanism appear to apply. Two notions are central to these restrictions: that of a 'pivot' in the system, and that of the 'minimal number of constraints' allowed to create a distance between the regular system and irregular forms. First, the 'designated pivot' of *all* ranking reversals is the HEAD-R constraint: all demotions occur relative to it to the ranking position immediately after it, and likewise all promotions occur relative to it to the ranking position immediately before it. No other reversals are required. This function of HEAD-R should not surprise us, because in a sense this constraint may be called the 'functionally central' one of the system, word stress being known to be an edge phenomenon since Trubetzkoy (1929: ch. II: ii). Second, in all cases (but one) just a *single* constraint is pro- or demoted to capture the irregular class. All B-irregularities involve a single constraint of the NON-FIN family, all C-irregularities either involve the single WSP constraint, or NON-FIN and BIN demoted as a pair. This latter case is therefore emblematic of the high degree of markedness involved in main stressed final light syllables. Irregularities involving the position of main stress but preserving most of the system ([*(har)(móni)ca*], [*(klari)(nét)*], [*(óli)(fantV)*]) are preferred to light syllables receiving main stress by brute force, that is: when not immediately in front of another light syllable ([*(choco)(lá)*], [*(Ce-(lébes)*]). Some constraints do not appear to be involved in the co-phonologies system at all: neither of the (low-ranked) ALIGN constraints, for instance, seem to participate, nor does PARSE-SYL. In the next section, where we confront the Dutch stress system with our experimental findings, we shall continue to assume that these restrictions on possible co-phonologies (HEAD-R is the pivot, modifications are minimal) act as if governing the range of possible analyses.

5.2   *Incorporating the test results*

This much observed about the system, let us turn to the central point of this section. An important property of the Optimality system of Dutch word stress in (27)-cum-(29) is that its design, just as that of the parametric system of section 2, completely excludes leftward violations of the Weight-to-Stress Principle, within the three syllable window: a candidate output 'σ-*cvc-cv(c)* (='X-H-X) will always be overruled by one with penultimate stress, by WSP and HEAD-R (main stress as far to the right as possible). However, some of the experimentally obtained results of the previous section, repeated here for convenience in (30a), have shown that this claim cannot be maintained in that absolute fashion. These results can now be interpreted as indicated in (30b) (existing words are simply in Roman type, test nonsense words are bracketed):

(30)

(a) Experimentally obtained X-H-X data.

	3yos			4yos			adults		
	antep.	pen.	fin.						
ka-nak-ta	75(P)	10(A)	65(C)	65	5	80	-	20	-
ma-rot-ko							-	20	-
ta-lak-tan	65(P)	30(A)	70(B)	45	25	40	2	11	7

(b)

A	B	C	P
a-gén-da	-		-	[ká-nak-ta]
			fri-kan-dó (so far C)[23]
gi-brál-tar	bom-bar-dón	[tá-lak-tan]	(so far P)

Thus, we face a twofold challenge: first, to allow a Quantity Sensitivity violation when the final syllable is *closed* (*tálaktan* apparently is better-than-P); and second, completely to limit freedom to a single output type (*agénda*) when the final syllable is *open* (*ágenda* = *kánakta* must be blocked by Quantity Sensitivity, *fricandéau* = *kanaktá* apparently is a P- rather than a C-type).[24] An independent reason to strive towards the second modification is that it will improve our insight into cases of rhyme shape adaptations such as those below, presented earlier in (20b):

(31)   LHL → LLL   kánakta (P) → kánata (B)   better
             kanaktá (C) → kanatá (C)   same (but rather: P → C?)

So far, the fact that the penult is subject to a change of weight in both imitations leads to a change in status in the former case, but not in the latter. Obviously, there is something odd in this distinction, because in both cases the change of weight eliminates essentially the same, apparently disfavoured, configuration of adjacent 'L-H or H-'L syllables. It seems that the second case should therefore be interpretable as a case of regularisation as well. The reinterpretation proposed in (30b) and (31) effectuates this.

The two reclassifications implied by (30b) can be attacked as follows. Below, first consider the full analysis of the regular case *taláktan=gibráltar*. This tableau spells out the preliminary analysis in (25), and it allows assessing the possibilities of 'ranking reversal'.

(32)   Tableau of regular *gibráltar=taláktan*[25]

		Bɪɴ	N-F	WSP	Hᴅ-R	[see (25)]
-	(tálak)(tan)			*	**	(gíbral)(tar)
	(tá)(lak)(tan)	*			**	(gí)(bral)(tar)
	(tá)(laktan)	*		*	**	(gí)(braltar)
-	ta-(láktan)			*	*	gi-(bráltar)
☺	ta-(lák)(tan)				*	gi-(brál)(tar)
-	ta-(lak)(tán)		*			gi-(bral)(tár)
	(talak)(tán)		*	*		(gibral)(tár)

As shown, it is WSP that makes the crucial decision, although Hᴇᴀᴅ-R could have made it too (recall that WSP » Hᴇᴀᴅ-R is demanded by the *álmanak* case in (26)). Exceptional final stress (*talak-tán*) can be produced by demoting

NON-FIN to immediately below HEAD-R (as in the case of *klari-nét*). Exceptional antepenultimate stress is not so easily produced, however. First, there is no way of promoting or demoting any of the tableau's constraints such that *tálaktan* is produced as a possible (C-)pattern. Second, irregularly introducing NON-FIN-FT into it as a possible way of generating antepenultimate stress (recall *Cána-da*) is of no avail since the optimal candidate does not violate this constraint.

Accepting this as a preliminary result, let us reinvestigate the *agenda= kanakta* case (i.e., with final *open* syllables), trying to ensure that there is no possible pattern other than penultimate stress. Consider the tableau of the completely regular case:

(33)   Tableau of regular *agénda=kanákta*

		BIN	N-F	WSP	H-R	
-	(kának)(ta)	*		*	**	(ágen)(da)
	(kának)-ta			*	**	(ágen)-da
	(ká)(nak)(ta)	**			**	(á)(gen)(da)
	(ká)(nak)-ta	*			**	(á)(gen)-da
	(ká)(nakta)	*			**	(á)(genda)
-	(ka)(nákta)	*			*	(a)(génda)
☺	ka-(nákta)				*	a-(génda)
☺	ka-(nák)-ta				*	a-(gén)-da
	(ka)(nák)-ta	*			*	(a)(gén)-da
	(ka)(nák)(ta)	**			*	(a)(gén)(da)
-	(kanak)(tá)	*	*	*		(agen)(dá)
	ka-(nak)(tá)	*	*			a-(gen)(dá)
	(ka)(nak)(tá)	**	*			(a)(gen)(da)

Again WSP makes the crucial decision, although HEAD-R could have made it too. Interestingly, even if NON-FIN-FT is introduced into this tableau assuming ranking reversal, penultimate stress will prevail:

(34)   Tableau: no *ágenda by promoting NON-FIN-FT

	BIN	N-F	WSP	[N-F-F]	HD-R
(ágen)-da			*		**
a-(génda)				*	*
☺ a-(gén)-da					*

If antepenultimate stress is excluded for this case, the next question is: can final-stressed *kanaktá* (=*fricandéau*=*agendá*) be blocked too? Unfortunately, the answer is: not really. Irregular final main stress on an L-syllable is accounted for by simultaneous demotion of BIN and NON-FIN, and (33) makes clear that under these circumstances there is a form (the bottom one) that violates none of the constraints WSP, PARSE-SYL and HEAD-R. This form will be the winner. This threatens to be a second unsatisfactory result, but before we accept this, consider the following.

In itself, final main stress on an L-syllable is available as a C-pattern for cases such as *chocolá*; it is just *tanaktá* (= *agendá*) that we are trying to block. Is there a constraint that we can invoke that has the following two properties: it distinguishes between these two cases, and it trivialises evaluations by WSP, PARSE-SYL and HEAD-R? In fact, the difference in syllable shape between the two cases suggests what is going on. A constraint will be invoked which so far has played no role whatsoever in the analysis, and which interestingly will be rankable in absolute topmost position: it will be unviolated. The constraint is that in (35):

(35)   NO-CLASH: No adjacent heads.

NO-CLASH is one of the OAP constraints of Metrical Phonology, dating from more than a decade prior to fully constraint-based approaches: it was invoked by Liberman and Prince (1977) to serve as a trigger for Iambic Reversal, by which, for instance, *thirtèen mén*, with immediately adjacent stresses, becomes *thìrteen mén*.

We shall assume that this constraint, which was not mentioned in the pro- and demotion survey in (29), being newly introduced here, is among the constraints that do not take part in the co-phonologies system: there is no reason not to assume that it will *always* be top-ranked. Given this, its impact on the analysis will be this. In both (33) (*agénda* tableau) and (34) (*ágenda* tableau), the regular and optimal form has no clash(es), so it happily remains optimal. With BIN and NON-FIN irregularly demoted (absent, as it were, from tableau (33)),

No-Clash will eliminate the bottom two final-stressed forms of (33), while WSP will continue to eliminate *(agen)(dá)*, leaving Head-R the task of selecting *a-(génda)*, exactly as required: hence *agénda* is the only pattern made available by the grammar. In the *casíno-cánada-chocolá* triad (in which the prefinal syllable is open) none of the optimal candidates contains a clash, so none will be affected: *agendá* is excluded but *chocolá* is allowed.

Next, consider the new No-Clash tableau for *talaktan/gibraltar* in their regular mode, shown in (36) (it replaces (32)).

(36)   New tableau for *taláktan*, given No-Clash

		NC	Bin	N-F	WSP	H-R	Prs	
-	(tálak)(tan)				*	**		(gíbral)(tar)
	(tá)(lak)(tan)	*	*			**		(gí)(bral)(tar)
	(tá)(laktan)	*	*		*	**		(gí)(braltar)
☺ -	ta-(láktan)				*	*	*	gi-(bráltar)
	ta-(lák)(tan)	*				*	*	gi-(brál)(tar)
-	ta-(lak)(tán)	*		*			*	gi-(bral)(tár)
	(talak)(tán)			*	*			(gibral)(tár)

The optimal candidate now is *ta-(láktan)*, with penultimate stress as the result of a final trochaic foot: *ta-(lák)(tan)* contains a clash, and is eliminated. This new set-up reimplies that Parse-Syl must be deactivated by Head-R » Parse-Syl, as hinted at earlier.

The two irregular patterns are derived as follows. First, when Non-Fin is demoted to immediately below Head-R, final stress follows (bottom candidate of (36)). Second, precisely because *ta-(lák)(tan)* is eliminated by No-Clash, irregular antepenultimate stress in *tálaktan* can be accounted for by promoting Non-Fin-Ft, to immediately above Head-R (just as in the case of *Cána-da*). This can be seen by considering the three candidates that survive No-Clash in (36): introducing Non-Fin-Ft » Head-R into that tableau makes [*(tálak)(tan)*] the optimal output. This suggests that a reasonable new version of the Dutch pro- and demotion schema of (29) is that below:

(37)

	A	B1	B2	C
-VV:	= (27)		NON-FIN-FT ⇐NON-FIN, BIN ⇒	
-VC	= (27)	NON-FIN ⇒	NON-FIN-FT ⇐WSP ⇒	
-VXC:	= (27)		NON-FIN-FT ⇐n.a.	

all pro- and demotions relative to HEAD-R

Demotion of NON-FIN is vacuous in the remaining two B1 cases, given foot binarity (which excludes main stress on a final open syllable). NON-FIN-FT consistently takes care of all cases of irregular antepenultimate stress. Demotion of constraints other than NON-FIN or NON-FIN-FT is involved in irregularity at the fringes of the system.

The introduction of NO-CLASH has an interesting and welcome consequence for at least one further aspect of Dutch word stress. In the area of secondary stress, Dutch much more so than English (Kager 1989) allows initial trochees of the L-H foot type, preferring [(à-lek)(sán-dra)] to *[a-(lèk)(sán-dra)] (similarly: ànecdóte, Yàwelmáni, Ràwalpíndi). Without NO-CLASH, the ungrammatical form would be the winner, because its rival contains a WSP violation (both obey BIN and NON-FIN); with NO-CLASH the correct candidate is selected, assuming NO-CLASH » WSP (which was assumed all along). One can think of two other ways of getting this result: by PARSE-SYL (as in Pater 1997: 212) or by ALIGN-EDGE-L. But these attempts fail, because both constraints are known to be ranked below WSP.

In dominating WSP, NO-CLASH also enforces a stresswise less crucial choice between the two representations (róbot) and (ró)(bot), in favour of the former. The L-H foot type implied in these examples is neither frequent nor uncontroversial. It has been argued to exist, however, as part of the 'Germanic foot' inventory of Old English by Dresher and Lahiri (1991), of the 'secondary stress foot inventory' of modern English by Pater (1997), and of the foot inventory of Finnish by Hanson and Kiparsky (1996). It was employed by Prince and Smolensky (1993: 50–53) in their analysis of Latin word stress to which the current analysis of Dutch is partly similar.[26]

This concludes the analysis of the incorporation of the test results of this chapter into an Optimality account of Dutch word stress.

6.   Some remarks on the prespecified underlying representation analysis

In our juxtaposition of two types of analysis for metrical exceptionality, reversed ranking and prespecified underlying forms, we shall use Van Oostendorp (1997), a review article of Nouveau (1994), as a representative of the latter approach. At the end of this section we shall point out that it appears to be flawed, but let us summarise its main characteristics first.

Taking as his point of departure the A-pattern grammar of (27) (or one equivalent to it for present purposes), Van Oostendorp's alternative proposal for B-pattern exceptionality in words ending in open syllables (*cánada*) takes the following form: assume that the irregular foot structure of this type of example (*((cána)da*) is contained in the underlying form; then add to the grammar a constraint demanding no deviations between underlying and surface foot structure: FAITH-FOOT.[27] As shown by Pater (1995) and Inkelas (1999), such faithfulness constraints are an integral part of this approach. C-pattern exceptions (*chocolá*) are treated differently. BIN is circumvented by a segmental modification of the input, to the effect that these words underlyingly end in an abstract consonant, which acts as a trigger for the analysis 'normally' reserved for superheavy syllables: *(choco)(lá*-CV*)*.

No exceptional VC-final patterns are discussed in the Van Oostendorp paper, but, given what it does say, their properties may be presumed to run like this. The analysis of B-type *klarinét* follows from underlying *(klari)(nét*-CV*)*, just as *chocolá*. For C-type *Celébes* we want to prespecify the apparent surface foot structure in the input (*/(Ce-(lébes)/)*, and then demand input output foot faithfulness. The irregular patterns for the class of words ending in final superheavy syllables are also not discussed by Van Oostendorp, and it will be deemed unfruitful to speculate on these cases here.

Nouveau's (two) experimental results are incorporated as follows. First, the penultimate-stressed form *a-(génda)* will always be the winner (as it should) as long as the A-type analysis (i.e., tableau (33)) is allowed to run its full course. This means that FAITH-FOOT (underlying /(agen)da/ implies the incorrect possibility of antepenultimate stress) will have to be ranked below WSP, which makes the crucial choice. Second, the B-output *(talak)(tán)* follows, presumably, from an abstract final -C. Crucially, for *(tálak)(tan)* even here NO-CLASH will have to be posited: if FAITH-FOOT is ranked below WSP (suppose this to be the case in (36a)), *(tálak)(tan)* will follow as (irregularly) optimal from an underlyingly specified foot only if *ta-(lák)(tan)* is eliminated as a candidate by NO-CLASH. It was exactly this point that was anticipated in the introduction to this chapter when we said that 'the active role of NO-CLASH holds under both approaches'.

Accepting this result, we cannot at the same time avoid pointing out what we perceive to be drawbacks of this analysis, precisely involving those two points that serve as the analytical execution of the alternative: the FAITH-FOOT constraint, and the abstract consonants.

Foot faithfulness poses the following problem. It has been pointed out in the second half of the previous section that words of the type *agenda* completely lack either possibility of irregular stress: NO-CLASH and/or WSP eliminate them, and just *agénda* survives. In order to eliminate the possibility of **ágenda* in the prespecified underlying form framework, the following constraint ranking obtains: WSP » FAITH-FOOT (preempting /(agen)-da/). But there is conflicting evidence that this cannot be so. The irregular C-pattern *Celébes* derives from the prespecified foot /ce-(lebes)/, but will be beaten by the regular form (cf. (26a)) unless FAITH-FOOT » WSP. FAITH-FOOT is the central constraint of the analysis. These remarks show either that the analysis has to adopt reversed ranking too, obviating the exercise, or that it simply does not work, at least in its present form.

Although far from Pavlovian anti-abstractionists ourselves, we cannot escape pointing out that abstract word-final consonants (or vowels, for that matter) that trigger word-final stress have been under attack since Kiparsky's (1968) partial review of Chomsky and Halle (1968), and have remained suspect ever since.[28] Van Oostendorp revives them for Dutch stress-final forms (with no independent motivation provided). The abstractness issue aside, an empirical criticism of this approach is that in cases of variation, such as in pairs like *cárnaval-carnavál* and *rócoco-rococó*, the analysis forces one to assume segmentally different underlying forms. This seems qualitatively inferior both to the non-segmental lexical markings of the parametric analysis, and to the co-phonology markings of the reversed ranking framework. In defence, it might be pointed out that pairs of this nature independently exist with *visible* segmental material. A case in point would be the pair *chocolá(de)*, whose two different forms belong to different stress classes (a regular long form and a completely irregular short form); another example is *plafón(d)* (also a regular long form and an irregular short form). However, these latter cases are different in that typically, in spite of the segmental difference, stress does *not* shift, suggesting a form of output–output correspondence in the sense of Benua (1995) and McCarthy and Prince (1999).[29] Our assessment is that a fully satisfactory prespecified underlying form analysis of Dutch stress irregularity has so far not been put forward in the literature.

7.   Conclusions

With regard to the goals of this chapter, it has been shown, first, that the ease with which Dutch children of 3 and 4 years of age imitate carefully selected test stimuli follows the hierarchy of regularity for word stress patterns predicted by the metrical theory of Dutch word stress. Children find words with irregular and prohibited stress more difficult to imitate than words with regular stress; and children tend to regularise irregular and prohibited patterns, and to preserve regular stress. The fact that, as observed, 3-year-old children have already mastered most of the stress system suggests that the acquisition of the Dutch stress patterns is precocious. But the system also improves with age, and does so in a systematic way: the 4-year-olds have a stress system which is more similar to the adult model. They have mastered the markedness hierarchy in more words than younger subjects, and they make fewer errors in imitating most authorised stress types. Second, given subtle new data obtained both for children and adults in our tests regarding the Quantity Sensitivity of the stress system, it was shown that Optimality Theory has the flexibility that the parametric approach lacks in dealing with these data, in both current frameworks of exceptionality: the ranking reversal analysis and the prespecified underlying representation analysis. It was pointed out that in both views the new, experimentally obtained, Quantity Sensitivity data argue for the active presence in the grammar of the No-Clash constraint, undominatedly. This constraint turned out to have been part of the analysis all along, although it made its presence felt only in deep probes of the Dutch word stress system. On the one hand, a number of restrictions were proposed in order to limit the possibilities of the ranking reversal approach. On the other, it was also pointed out that the only existing attempt at a 'prespecified underlying representation' analysis for the data of this chapter fails to be a contender because it appears to be flawed in a number of ways.

Finally, observe that the empirically supported relevance of undominated No-Clash, both to the child data as well as to the adult data, is interesting from another acquisitional point of view. Given the current general assumption that phonological acquisition is essentially the empirically driven modification of a starting-point at which all substantive constraints precede all faithfulness constraints (Gnanadesikan 1995/this volume, Tesar and Smolensky 1998), there is nothing odd in the view essentially proposed here that No-Clash serves as an unviolated constraint supervising all acquisitional stages up until adulthood. This chapter therefore can be said to illustrate well the point made by Inkelas (1999) cited at the end of the introduction.

NOTES

* This contribution is a revised version of chapters 4 and 5 of Nouveau (1994). We are grateful to Jan Don, René Kager, and Joe Pater for comments on an earlier version of this chapter, and to Marc van Oostendorp (1997) for his elaborate comments on Nouveau (1994).

1. See, for instance, Berko Gleason (1997: 106–7): 'By three, most children can produce all the vowel sounds and nearly all the consonant sounds. This does not mean that their productions are 100 percent accurate, but rather that the sounds are produced correctly in at least a few words. Consonants that are likely to be in error [in English], even at the age of four or five, are the liquids [and both *th*'s]. In most cases, correct production of all sounds is achieved by around seven years of age.' It has to be taken into account, of course, that for any given child perception will be ahead of production.

2. At Level 1, the right edge trisyllabic window is violated only under very special circumstances. The suffix *-ief*, for instance, usually carries main stress (*normatíef* 'normative', *sensitíef* 'sensitive'), but names of grammatical cases, which typically

contain this suffix, have initial stress in disregard of the right edge window: *génitief*, *nóminatief*, *áccusatief*, etc. There are a number of further classes of this type.

3. Occasional subregularities interfere, not surprisingly, with the broad picture. Final main stress is, for instance, the dominant pattern among words ending in front round vowels, which are mostly loans from French: *menú*, *continú*, *parvenú*, *individú*, *miliéu*, *gonorróea* [-'rø] (vs. *jiujítsu*, *Málmö*).

4. Curiously in Dutch originally Greek names ending in *-eus* are pronounced with (unstressed) [-œys]: *Zeus* [zœys], *Néreus* ['nerœys]. *Prométheus* [pro'metœys] is exactly the only case of its type: prefinal stress when the final syllable is superheavy, in a word of three or more syllables.

5. For further examples, see Van Marle (1980) and Kager (1989).

6. Thus, Dutch differs from English in two respects: (i) just heavy syllables are extra-metrical rather than all syllables; (ii) the light/heavy distinction is defined as open vs. closed, Dutch lacking the distinction between long and short vowels in open syllables; for further discussion, see Kager (1989), Zonneveld (1993).

7. See Hochberg (1988: 690–693) for a description of the similar design of her study of Spanish stress.

8. So far, words ending in a diphthong ([ɛi] in these two cases) were not discussed here. Their stress behaviour closely resembles that of superheavy syllables (*averíj*, *karwéi* 'job'), so they are added in this subsection of the test items.

9. Since these items were read out, they invited irregular but existing spelling↔pronunciation correspondences. In this case [ja'ko] was found twice, presumably modelled on *depot* [de'po] and *Peugeot* [pø'zjo].

10. Nouveau (1994: 102–103) attaches significance to the observation that the violation is more frequent when the medial syllable ends in a sonorant. It may well be the case, however, that the latter's higher number is caused by the influence of the similar (and regular) existing word *báriton* 'baritone', implying that the P-figure for the sonorant example is excessively high (rather than that of the internal obstruent case surprisingly low).

11. Curiously, the loan *Colargol*, the name of a popular (originally French) cartoon bear à la Pooh, has either final (as in French) or initial main stress; there is no doubt, on the other hand, that *Bibendum*, the original French name of the 'Michelin man', is pronounced with prefinal stress.

Data are slightly more numerous when the initial syllable is closed. *Hermandad* 'the Police' (prefinal stress in Spanish) can have main stress on each of its syllables. Spanish family names such as *Fernandez* have either prefinal (as in Spanish) or final stress. Foreign geographical names such as *Léxington*, *Dárlington*, and *Hélsingfors* may be assumed to have a morphological structure that blocks the application of the (Level 1) stress rules to the full word. The word *badminton* (the game, few speakers of Dutch are aware that it is the name of a town, too) can have main stress on the initial syllable (as in English), but also has a regularised variant with prefinal stress.

Such VC-final examples are just about as (in)frequent as ones ending in open syllables, such as *Hélsinki*/*Helsínki* and *chímpansee*/*chimpansée* (*Timbouktu* has prefinal stress, *Katmandu* has prefinal or final stress); or ones ending in superheavies, such as *Ístanboel* (main stress on the other syllables occurs too).

12. A detailed account of the growth of prosodic competence in Dutch children between the ages of 1;6 and 2;6 can be found in Fikkert (1994, 1998).

13. Chances are that [kadót] is a regular item in the speech of the children involved, since it is also known as a relatively common child speech misanalysis of the 'stem' of the frequent diminutive *kadóo-tje* '(little) present' (as *kadóot-je*, which is a formal possibility, cf. *bóot-je* 'little boat'). Given what was said above, *páprika* may be an A-type example of a subpattern for words with prefinal *-i-*, and therefore not a genuine case of improvement.

14. Although investigating further age groups (2- and 5- or 6-year-olds, for instance) might have provided additional insights, there were two reasons for not executing such experiments: the limited timespan available to the Ph.D. trainee (Nouveau), and the outcome of an informal pilot test that the required task was completely unsuitable for 2-year-olds.

15. For a similar way of viewing the difference between Parameter Theory and OT, see Itô and Mester (1996: 185); for a criticism of their approach to 'lexical strata', see Inkelas *et al.* (1997: 403–404).

16. In order to save space we use in this discussion representations that linearly indicate syllable structure, footing, and accentuation; grid configurations of the kind used in section 2 are implied throughout, however.

17. In the vocabularies of many (non-Germanic) languages words occur that are completely meaningless to the Dutch ear and eye, which can serve as nonsense test items in order to confirm or disconfirm the intuition leading to this foot organisation. Words such as *Shravanabelagola* (town in India) and *Catapathabramana* (Old Indic manuscript) appear to share the structure indicated.

18. Her model does allow co-phonologies, but just when systematically associated with (consecutive) 'levels' of the lexicon, not within a single level. Pater (1995), in an unpublished study of secondary stress in English, has (i) prespecified underlying forms for truly exceptional forms, and (ii) a device he calls 'lexically specific ranking' for 'lexically based variation'. In the latter case, the following situation obtains: C1sp » C2 » C1gen, where the two versions of C1 apply in lexically specified cases and in the general case, respectively. This looks like 'reversed constraint ranking', but an investigation into the similarities and differences beween the two approaches has not been carried out in the context of our research on Dutch stress.

19. There still is a task for BIN, because *Ca(ná)da*, i.e., simply a variant of the regular form satisfying NON-FIN-F, must be excluded (henceforth bracketing in a tableau indicates the exceptionality of the constraint's hierarchical position).

		BIN	NON-FIN	[N-FIN-F]	HEAD-R
☺	(cána)-da				**
	ca-(náda)			*	*
	ca-(ná)-da	*			*

20. An alternative would be to reverse the TROCHEE » IAMB hierarchy implicit in the analysis, leading to a violation of the standard foot type of the language for at least some irregular forms: *cho-(colá)*. To have more than one foot type in a language is usually considered highly undesirable (Inkelas 1999: 144, 150), but cases are

known to exist, Yidin[y] being the standard reference (Hayes 1985: 442, 1995: 260–262). Even in this latter case, however, individual words must show LABELING HARMONY: 'if at least one foot of a word constitutes a canonical iamb, then all the feet of the word are made iambic; otherwise all feet are made trochaic' (Hayes 1995: 260). Dutch is not like that, as shown by four-syllabic examples such as *càvalaríe* (in (1)), *individú*, and so on. Below we shall formulate another reason why the iambic analysis of these cases goes against the grain of the language.

21. Irregular *Celébes*, cf. regular *álmanak* in (26), esp. (26b).

		NON-FIN	HEAD-R	[WSP]
	(Céle)(bes)		**	
☺	Ce-(lébes)		*	*

22. It also implies that bisyllabic exceptional words such as *líchaam* 'body' and *árbeid* 'work' from (2c) cannot be generated. The proposed solution for these cases lies in the distinction between the 'native' and 'non-native' Dutch vocabulary, which can be shown to exist on synchronic phonological and morphological grounds (Zonneveld 1993, Trommelen and Zonneveld 1992). The words in question belong to the 'native' lexicon, to which the defective syllable analysis fails to apply. If these words are bisyllabic, non-final stress follows.

23. With hindsight, this move is statistically motivated, too: *fricandéau* is one of the very few examples of X-H-'L words. Two others are *Katmandú* and *chimpansée*, the latter of which has an alternative pronunciation *chímpansee*, which is one of the very few violations of Quantity Sensitivity in the language (see n. 11). The frequency of the stressed nominalising suffix *-íe* after stems ending in consonant clusters (next to *strateg-íe* one finds *isomorf-íe*, *monarch-íe*, *industr-íe*) invites a careful analysis of this suffix in terms of the Level 1/Level 2 distinction. (This suffix also has an irregular plural, violating the generalisation that Dutch nouns ending in vowels take *-s* rather than *-en*: *strategíe-en*, *monarchíe-en*, and so on; Zonneveld 1999, ch. 9, points out that historically this suffix was *-íë* [-íjə].)

24. The weight of the penultimate syllable is indeed to blame for this test result, and not the popularity of final vowel main stress as such; recall the following additional test results, which show that children make far fewer mistakes when the penultimate syllable is open, and adults consider final main stress an option:

	3YOs			4YOs			adults		
	antep.	pen.	fin.						
fe-ni-mo	30(B)	10(A)	40(C)	10	25	30	15	1	4
fa-gu-rie							1	9	10

25. In an unhappy lapse of accuracy, Van Oostendorp (1997: 140, tableau 5) crucially misrepresents this case by failing to mention *(tálak)(tan)*, giving – instead – *(tálak)-tan*, as a candidate violating WSP, but also, completely trivially, PARSE.

26. One might think head-ship (or not) of the final syllable to matter, for instance, for vowel reduction. Among the intricacies of Dutch vowel reduction, however, is the

immunity of word-final syllables (of any type) to it. For discussion see Kager (1989) and Trommelen and Zonneveld (1999).
27. At this point the purpose of this constraint will be clear; below, its *ranking* will be considered more carefully.
28. An elaborate recent defence of the 'abstract' approach to English stress can be found in Burzio (1994).
29. Zonneveld (1986) came close to this in proposing that these parenthesised elements be considered stress-neutral affixes.

References

Benua, L. (1995). Identity effects in morphological truncation. In J. Beckman, L. W. Dickey, and S. Urbanczyk (eds.) *UMOP 18, Papers in Optimality Theory*. Graduate Linguistic Student Association (GLSA), University of Massachusetts, Amherst. 77–136.

Berko Gleason, J. (1997). *The Development of Language*. Boston: Allyn and Bacon, 4th edn.

Burzio, L. (1994). *Principles of English Stress*. Cambridge: Cambridge University Press.

Cabré, T. and M. Kenstowicz (1995). Prosodic Trapping in Catalan. *LI* **26**. 694–704.

Chomsky, N. and M. Halle (1968). *The Sound Pattern of English*. New York: Holt, Rinehart, and Winston.

Dresher, B. E. and A. Lahiri (1991). The Germanic foot: metrical coherence in English. *LI* **22**. 251–286.

Echols, C. and E. Newport (1992). The role of stress and position in determining first words. *Language Acquisition* **2**. 189–220.

Fikkert, P. (1994). *On the Acquisition of Prosodic Structure*. Ph.D. dissertation, HIL, Leiden University.

(1998). The acquisition of Dutch phonology. In S. Gillis and A. de Houwer (eds.) *The Acquisition of Dutch*. Amsterdam: Benjamins. 163–222.

Gnanadesikan, A. (this volume). Markedness and faithfulness constraints in child phonology.

Hable, M. and J. R. Vergnaud (1987). *An Essay on Stress*. Cambridge, Mass.: MIT Press.

Hanson, K. and P. Kiparsky (1996). A parametric theory of poetic meter. *Lg* **72**. 287–335.

Hayes, B. (1985). Iambic and trochaic rhythm in stress rules. In M. Niepokuj *et al.* (eds.) *BLS* **11**. 429–446.

(1995). *Metrical Stress Theory: Principles and Case Studies*. Chicago, Ill.: The University of Chicago Press.

Hochberg, J. D. (1986). *The Acquisition of Word Stress Rules in Spanish*. Ph.D. dissertation, Stanford University.

(1988). Learning Spanish stress. *Lg* **64**. 683–706.

Inkelas, S. (1999). Exceptional stress-attracting suffixes in Turkish: representations vs. grammar. In R. Kager, H. van der Hulst, and W. Zonneveld (eds.) *The Prosody–Morphology Interface*. Cambridge: Cambridge University Press. 134–187.

Inkelas, S., O. Orgun, and C. Zoll (1997). The implications of lexical exceptions for the nature of grammar. In I. Roca (ed.) *Derivations and Constraints in Phonology*. Oxford: Clarendon Press. 393–418.

Itô, J. and A. Mester (1996). The core-periphery structure of the lexicon and constraints on reranking. In J. N. Beckman, L. Walsh Dickey, and S. Urbanczyk (eds.) *UMOP 18, Papers in Optimality Theory*. GLSA, University of Massachusetts, Amherst. 181–210.

Kager, R. (1989). *A Metrical Theory of Stress and Destressing*. Ph.D. dissertation, Research Institute for Language and Speech, Utrecht University. (Published by Foris, Dordrecht.)

Kager, R., E. Visch, and W. Zonneveld (1987). Nederlandse woordklemtoon (hoofd-klemtoon, bijklemtoon, reductie, voeten). *Glot* **10**. 197–226.

Kehoe, M. and C. Stoel-Gammon (1997). An investigation of current accounts of children's prosodic development. *Lg* **73**. 113–144.

Kiparsky, P. (1968). How abstract is phonology? Distributed by Indiana University Linguistics Club. Also in O. Fujimura (ed.) *Three Dimensions of Linguistic Theory*. Tokyo: Tec 1973. 5–56, and in P. Kiparsky, *Explanation in Phonology*. Dordrecht: Foris 1982. 119–164.

Liberman, M. Y. and A. S. Prince (1977). On stress and linguistic rhythm. *LI* **8**. 249–336.

Lohuis-Weber, H. and W. Zonneveld (1996). Phonological acquisition and Dutch word prosody. *Language Acquisition* **5**. 245–284.

McCarthy, J. J. and A. S. Prince (1993). Generalized alignment. *Yearbook of Morphology 1993*. 79–154.

(1994). The emergence of the unmarked: optimality in prosodic morphology. In M. Gonzalez (ed.) *NELS* **24**. 333–379.

(1999). Faithfulness and identity in prosodic morphology. In R. Kager, H. van der Hulst, and W. Zonneveld (eds.) *The Prosody–Morphology Interface*. Cambridge: Cambridge University Press. 218–309.

Nouveau, D. (1994). *Language Acquisition, Metrical Theory, and Optimality*. Ph.D. dissertation, Research Institute for Language and Speech, Utrecht University.

Oostendorp, M. van (1997). Lexicale variatie in optimaliteitstheorie (Besprekingsartikel van Nouveau 1994). *Nederlandse Taalkunde* **2**. 133–154.2

Pater, J. (1995). On the nonuniformity of weight-to-stress and stress preservation effects in English. MS., McGill University.

(1997). Minimal violation and phonological development. *Language Acquisition* **6**. 201–253.

Prince, A. (1980). A metrical theory for Estonian quantity. *LI* **11**. 511–562.

Prince, A. and P. Smolensky (1993). Optimality Theory, constraint interaction in generative grammar. MS., Dept of Linguistics, Rutgers University, and Dept of Computer Science, University of Colorado at Boulder.

Tesar, B. and P. Smolensky (1998). Learnability in optimality theory. *LI* **29**. 229–268.

Tranel, B. (1994). French liaison and elision revisited: a unified account within optimality theory. Read at the Linguistic Symposium on Romance Languages 24. University of California at Los Angeles and University of Southern California.

Trommelen, M. (1983). *The Syllable in Dutch: with Special Reference to Diminutive Formation*. Ph.D. dissertation, Utrecht University. (Published by Foris, Dordrecht.)

(1991). Dutch word stress assignment: extrametricality and feet. In T. F. Shannon and J. P. Snapper (eds.) *The Berkeley Conference on Dutch Linguistics 1989: Issues and Controversies, Old and New*. Lanham, Md.: University Press of America. 157–172.

Trommelen, M. and W. Zonneveld (1989). *Klemtoon en Metrische Fonologie*. Muiderberg: Coutinho.

(1992). Schappelijke woorden. *De Nieuwe Taalgids* **85**. 112–123.

(1999). Word stress in West-Germanic languages: English and Dutch. In H. van der Hulst (ed.) *Word Prosodic Systems in the Languages of Europe*. Europtype 20–4, Berlin: Mouton de Gruyter. 478–514.

Trubetzkoy, N. S. (1929). *Grundzüge der Phonologie. Travaux du Cercle Linguistique de Prague* **7**.

Van Marle, J. (1980). The stress pattern of Dutch simplex words. In W. Zonneveld, F. van Coetsem, and O. W. Robinson (eds.) *Studies in Dutch Phonology*, Dutch Studies 4. The Hague: Martinus Nijhoff. 79–122.

Zonneveld, W. (1986). C. B. van Haeringen en de moderne taalkundige theorievorming. *De Nieuwe Taalgids* **79**. 207–216.

(1993). Schwa, superheavies, stress and syllables in Dutch. *The Linguistic Review* **10**. 61–110.

(1999). Lutgart's life and Willem's words, 13th century Dutch metre in a European context. MS., Research Institute for Language and Speech, Utrecht University.

Index of subjects

adult speech 59–60, 159
alignment 104, 310–311
allomorphs (see alternations)
allophonic variation 161, 170–173, 187–191, 250
alternations (in acquisition vs. adult speech) 6, 14, 31, 33, 43, 64, 67, 163–168, 188, 192, 196
  acquisition of alternations 186–191, 253–254, 287, 325, 327–328
approximants (see glides)
articulation 46, 61, 171, 196, 359
  articulatory limitations 1, 6, 13, 39, 56, 59, 64–66, 158, 168–191, 359

babbling stage 60, 61, 66, 240

Cancellation/Domination Lemma 255–258, 278
categorical perception 160, 221
chain shifts (counterfeeding) 5, 9, 13, 47, 57, 287
child-directed speech 204–213, 217
closed syllables (see syllable codas)
coalescence (fusion) 11, 88–94, 104, 106, 150
codas (see syllables)
cognitive strategies/resources 11, 68
competence (vs. performance) 322
complementary distribution (see also phoneme inventory) 250
comprehension (see perception)
computational modelling (of Optimality Theory) 61
connectionism 15, 61
consonant clusters (in acquisition) 2, 6, 11, 12, 36–37, 39, 44, 59, 63, 64, 77–78, 104, 127–131, 134, 135, 150, 151, 153, 213, 342, 348–355
  consonant deletion 11, 36–37, 77–78, 89

metathesis 11, 12
/s/-initial clusters 78, 111–115, 123–131
vowel insertion 11, 295, 359
consonant deletion (see also truncation) 12, 36, 64–66
consonant harmony 12, 39, 46, 58, 59, 61, 64, 66, 105, 122
conspiracy 4, 7, 12, 23, 35, 58, 60, 165–166, 186, 192, 196
constraint (general) 1, 4, 12, 14, 18, 38, 45, 55–60
  constraint families 103, 117, 132
  constraint inventory (CON) 19, 28
  constraint ranking 18, 19, 28, 60–62, 73, 116, 139, 323, 390
  constraint ranking algorithm (see learning algorithms)
  constraint ranking conservatism (see markedness >> faithfulness bias)
  fixed ranking 28
  floating constraint 339–341, 353–354, 357
  grounding of (see also phonetic grounding) 29, 39, 196
  targeted constraint 336–337
contiguity 85–87, 105, 140, 153
continuity assumption 115
contrast 2, 21, 60, 63, 66, 73, 161–162, 165–168, 191, 221, 223, 325
contrastive features 21, 172
correspondence 20, 76–77, 85–87, 96, 115, 132
covert strata 337–340, 347, 359–363
'cross-talk' (mutual influence between similar words) 66, 68

default consonant 84, 87, 103
delateralisation 10
depalatalisation 10
derivation 4, 18, 23
developmental stages 191–192, 209
discrimination 196, 221

Index of names